M000218243

EMORY UNIVERSITY STUDIES IN LAW AND RELIGION

John Witte Jr., General Editor

BOOKS IN THE SERIES

Power over the Body, Equality in the Family:
Rights and Domestic Relations in Medieval Canon Law
Charles J. Reid Jr.

Religious Liberty in Western Thought
Noel B. Reynolds and W. Cole Durham Jr., eds.

Hopes for Better Spouses: Protestant Marriage and Church Renewal in Early
Modern Europe, India, and North America
A. G. Roeber

Political Order and the Plural Structure of Society
James W. Skillen and Rockne M. McCarthy, eds.

The Idea of Natural Rights:
Studies on Natural Rights, Natural Law, and Church Law, 1150-1625
Brian Tierney

The Fabric of Hope: An Essay
Glenn Tinder

Liberty: Rethinking an Imperiled Ideal
Glenn Tinder

Religious Human Rights in Global Perspective: Legal Perspectives
Johan D. van der Vyver and John Witte Jr., eds.

Natural Law and the Two Kingdoms: A Study in the Development of
Reformed Social Thought
David VanDrunen

Early New England: A Covenanted Society
David A. Weir

God's Joust, God's Justice
John Witte Jr.

Religious Human Rights in Global Perspective: Religious Perspectives
John Witte Jr. and Johan D. van der Vyver, eds.

Justice in Love
Nicholas Wolterstorff

Political *Agape*

Christian Love and
Liberal Democracy

Timothy P. Jackson

WILLIAM B. EERDMANS PUBLISHING COMPANY
GRAND RAPIDS, MICHIGAN / CAMBRIDGE, U.K.

Published 2015 by
Wm. B. Eerdmans Publishing Co.
2140 Oak Industrial Drive N.E., Grand Rapids, Michigan 49505 /
P.O. Box 163, Cambridge CB3 9PU U.K.

Printed in the United States of America

21 20 19 18 17 16 15   7 6 5 4 3 2 1

Library of Congress Cataloging-in-Publication Data

Jackson, Timothy P. (Timothy Patrick)
    Political agape: Christian love and liberal democracy / Timothy P. Jackson.
        pages   cm. — (Emory University studies in law and religion)
    ISBN 978-0-8028-7246-3 (pbk.: alk. paper)
    1. Christianity and politics. 2. Love — Religious aspects — Christianity.
    3. Liberalism — Religious aspects — Christianity.   I. Title.

BR115.P7J26   2015
261.7 — dc23

                      2014043607

www.eerdmans.com

For
Søren Aabye Kierkegaard
and the Twelve Murder Victims at *Charlie Hebdo* . . .

"When one has once fully entered the realm of love, the world —
no matter how imperfect — becomes rich and beautiful, it consists
solely of opportunities for love."

Kierkegaard, *Works of Love*

"I would rather die standing than live on my knees."

Stéphane Charbonnier, *Le Monde*

Contents

Contents

Preface and Acknowledgments

Political Agape (2015) completes my trilogy on Christian love *(agape),* begun with *Love Disconsoled* (1999) and continued with *The Priority of Love* (2003). The individual volumes stand on their own, I trust, but each has its distinctive tone and foci. *Love Disconsoled,* as the title suggests, is largely deconstructive and sobering. It celebrates Jesus' sacred heart, but it basically seeks to discourage false or destructive hopes. It warms itself with "the fire of love" (Rolle), so to speak, yet it also aims to burn away some theological deadwood. Specifically, it tries to uncouple Christlike love from certainty, invulnerability, and immortality. Epistemic humility grants that foundationalist certitude is a chimera; ethical realism acknowledges that even the good person can be harmed; and eschatological simplicity emphasizes that "eternal life" need not await a postmortem heaven. In this *via negativa,* the challenge is to uphold Christian candor in the face of human finitude without precipitating despair, to defend the reality of radical evil (a.k.a. abomination) without losing sight of radical goodness. My heroes in this enterprise are Abraham overcoming child-sacrifice, F. Scott Fitzgerald going into the dark night of tenderness, and Simone Weil practicing the love of God amid affliction. Behind them all is Christ on the cross, the Messiah full of anxiety and pain yet obedient to the will of God unto death.

The Priority of Love is a more positive and constructive text. Whereas *Love Disconsoled* emphasizes *agape*'s uniqueness, its "supernatural" character in rising above (without neglecting or vilifying) *eros, philia,* and *amor sui, Priority* accents *agape*'s primacy. It explicates Christian love as a metavalue, that good without which we have no substantive access to other valuable things (cf. 1 Cor. 13:1-3). Rather than other loves being demoted, however, now modern justice is relativized. *Agape* is prior but not antithetical to contemporary notions of merit, demerit, and contract. Here I explore forgiveness and reconciliation, violence and nonviolence, and the morality of abortion. Søren Kierkegaard's *Works of Love* is my central inspiration, with significant nods also going to my teachers, Paul Ramsey and Gene Outka. I am indebted as well to feminist critiques of *agape* for making clear that, to be a virtue, self-sacrifice must be charitably motivated, consensual, and constructive.

In *Political* Agape I continue to describe Christian love as affirming but sometimes transcending strict justice, but now the focus is on how prophetic faith engages the nation-state and liberal democracy. Liberal democracy traditionally cherishes liberty and equality, but political *agape* works key changes on these ideas. In part I, I affirm political autonomy, for instance, not as an end in itself but rather for the sake of personal theonomy. Freedom of conscience, freedom of speech, freedom of assembly, the right to vote, the right to keep and bear arms, and the like are crucial checks on tyranny and the human tendency to abuse power, but a Christian exercises (or declines to exercise) these liberties for the sake of service to God and the neighbor. True freedom is to be an instrument of divine grace. We wait on God (Weil), but we don't simply wait on human beings (King).

Equality too is endorsed but baptized by prophetic liberalism. I continue to ground human equality in our sharing the image of God, the need or ability to give or receive agapic love, rather than in rationality or self-conscious volition. For my present purposes, the three most crucial moments for Western egalitarianism are: (1) when Jesus' rigorous Torah piety was rejected by the Jerusalem high priests, and he consequently announced that we all (Jews and Gentiles) are in this thing together; (2) when Abraham Lincoln's proposal for compensated emancipation and African resettlement was rejected by the border states, and he consequently proclaimed that we all (free and slave) are in this thing together; and (3) when Martin Luther King Jr.'s political color blindness was rejected by both Caucasian racists and Negro separatists, yet he nevertheless insisted that we all (whites and blacks) are in this thing together. Saint Paul's Epistle to the Galatians, the Thirteenth and Fourteenth Amendments to the U.S. Constitution, and the civil rights legislation of the 1960s (and 2010s) were the palpable fruits of Jesus, Lincoln, and King. Socrates too glimpsed that we are all children of the Good, but his student Plato could not quite overcome social, psychological, and metaphysical hierarchies, especially of class.

In part II of *Political* Agape, I respond to a host of liberals (Ronald Dworkin, John Rawls, Richard Rorty, Peter Singer, Jeffrey Stout, Nicholas Wolterstorff, et al.), antiliberals (Dietrich Bonhoeffer, Stanley Hauerwas, Robert

Kraynak, Alasdair MacIntyre, John Milbank, Friedrich Nietzsche, et al.), and feminists (Barbara Hilkert Andolsen, Margaret Farley, Ada Maria Isasi-Diaz, Martha Nussbaum, et al.). I then consider in part III how Christian love bears on euthanasia, the death penalty, the Nazi Holocaust, same-sex marriage, and the morality of adoption. This casuistry is the culmination of the entire trilogy.

I am grateful to a number of Emory graduate students, past and present, who have commented on parts of this manuscript. Five in particular — Bradley Burroughs, Zach Eyster, Katie Pimentel Toste, Ted Smith, and Ben Suitt — have assisted me with critical feedback and editing. I wish to thank six former mentors — Margaret Farley, Thomas Nagel, Gene Outka, Paul Ramsey, Richard Rorty, and Rulon Wells — all of whom helped form my moral sense. Seven friends and distant colleagues have also profoundly influenced my views on law, politics, and religion: Eric Gregory, Stanley Hauerwas, Richard Hays, Gilbert Meilaender, Edmund Santurri, Jeffrey Stout, and Cornel West. Five other friends and immediate colleagues have constituted, with me, what I playfully call "the Emory School." Jon Gunnemann, James Gustafson, Michael Perry, Steven Tipton, John Witte, and I disagree on central ethical issues, but we concur that Christianity must keep its own counsels yet critically engage (and be engaged by) the wider society. Engage and serve. This insistence on being in the world, though not of it, resists both the sectarian temptation to withdraw into the church (cf. a certain school in Durham) and a too-easy accommodation of secularity and modernity (cf. a certain school in Boston). Legal, political, and moral matters can and should be brought under the governance of Christian faith, hope, and love without theocratic tyranny or pragmatic relativism. That has been the practice of another Emory colleague, President and Nobel Peace Prize winner Jimmy Carter, and it is the ideal of this book.

This project was supported by a generous grant from the McDonald Agape Foundation to the Center for the Study of Law and Religion at Emory University. The author wishes to thank Ambassador Alonzo L. McDonald and Mr. Peter McDonald, as well as Frank Alexander, Eliza Ellison, Linda King, Anita Mann, Amy Wheeler, and John Witte for their support and encouragement. The opinions in this publication are those of the author and do not necessarily reflect the views of the Foundation or the Center.

I dedicate this book to Søren Kierkegaard and to the ten journalists and two police officers gunned down by perverse jihadists at the Paris offices of *Charlie Hebdo* on January 7, 2015. Kierkegaard is considered by many an apolitical thinker, but his satirical publications in *The Instant* launched a scathing "Attack upon Christendom" not unlike *Charlie*'s lampooning of fundamentalist Islam. SK it was who first faced me with the Christian challenge: to love the individuals I see before me (and God), just as they are, independently of cant and caste. Politics could never be the same for me. For their part, the twelve French murder victims died in defense, not just of freedom of speech, but also of the need for all creeds and communities, religious and secular, to be open to critique. Their deaths are a tragic reminder that some practice a political animus that is anything but liberal or democratic.[1]

"Jihad" originally meant "virtuous (inner) struggle," but the manifest vice of current "jihadism," ethically, is disregard for the sanctity of life. The theological fault is equally troubling: "jihadism" so elevates God's sovereignty over God's goodness as to make God evil. It fails to see that love of God and love of neighbor are of a piece, that God wants steadfast love, not burnt offerings (cf. Hos. 6:6 and Mark 12:33). Without a self-criticism and self-restraint that refuse to elevate some by denigrating others, true piety is impossible. So long as Islamo-fascism neglects "the weightier matters of the law, justice and mercy and faith" (Matt. 23:23), it will be an affront to the Deity and the enemy of prophetic religion, including the best of Islam. The Qur'an enjoins proportionality and moderation in just war, and the Hadith explicitly prohibit the direct killing of noncombatants, especially women and children.

Even terrorists remain our brothers and sisters, of course, recognizable human beings who have succumbed to the temptation to despise what offends or refuses them. Moreover, our own scripture and history are not unproblematic. If you would know the mind of a contemporary jihadist, read the supposedly divine call for mass murder in 1 Samuel 15:3 and the violent revenge fantasies in the book of Revelation. Slaughter of the innocent is wrong when "they" do it (e.g., 9/11), and it is wrong when "we" do it (e.g., Hiroshima and Nagasaki). Islamo-fascists are now trying to do to the rest of the Western world what Christianity once tried to do to Judaism: either convert it or kill it. Hateful intolerance of any stripe — Jewish, Christian, Muslim, Hindu, Buddhist, etc. — must constantly be resisted with all the resources of faith, hope, and love we (with God's help) can muster. That is the heart of political *agape*.

Earlier versions of several of my chapters have appeared elsewhere, and I have not tried to eliminate the overlap between them. Their origination follows: chapter 2, "The Image of God and the Soul of Humanity," in *Religion in the Liberal Polity*, ed. Terence Cuneo (Notre Dame: University of Notre Dame Press, 2005); chapter 3, "The Return of the Prodigal?" in *Religion and Contem-*

---

1. And now (February 14-15, 2015) there have been lethal terrorist attacks in Kierkegaard's hometown, Copenhagen.

porary Liberalism, ed. Paul Weithman (Notre Dame: University of Notre Dame Press, 1997); chapter 4, "To Bedlam and Partway Back," *Faith and Philosophy* 8, no. 4 (October 1991): 423-47; chapter 5, "A House Divided, Again," in *In Defense of Human Dignity,* ed. Robert Kraynak and Glenn Tinder (Notre Dame: University of Notre Dame Press, 2003); chapter 6, "The Theory and Practice of Discomfort," *Thomist* 51, no. 2 (April 1987): 270-98; part of chapter 8, "The Cross and Democratic Politics," *Notre Dame Philosophical Reviews* 3, no. 16 (2012): 1-8; chapter 12, "Suffering the Suffering Children," in *The Morality of Adoption,* ed. Timothy P. Jackson (Grand Rapids: Eerdmans, 2005); and "Prophetic Conclusion," in *The Teachings of Modern Christianity on Law, Politics, and Human Nature,* vol. 1, ed. John Witte and Frank Alexander (New York: Columbia University Press, 2005).

Liberal Introduction: Jesus and Abraham

"I give you a new commandment, that you love one another. Just as I have loved you, you also should love one another."[1]

JOHN 13:34

With malice toward none; with charity for all; with firmness in the right, as God gives us to see the right, let us strive on to finish the work we are in.

ABRAHAM LINCOLN[2]

I. Love *before* Justice, yet Bethlehem *and* Hodgenville[3]

The idea that justice is the central political concern is as ancient as Plato and as contemporary as John Rawls. Socrates attributes the major social ills to injustice, and the major social goods to justice: "For surely, Thrasymachus, it's injustice that produces factions, hatreds, and quarrels . . . and justice that produces

---

1. Unless otherwise noted, all biblical quotations in the book come from the New Revised Standard Version.

2. Abraham Lincoln, "Second Inaugural Address," in *Abraham Lincoln: Speeches and Writings, 1859-1865* (New York: Library of America, 1989), p. 687.

3. Some scholars (e.g. John P. Meier) argue that the frequent biblical references to Jesus as "the Nazarene" suggest that he was born in Nazareth rather than Bethlehem. This is not dispositive. Lincoln was born in Hodgenville, Kentucky, yet Illinois refers to itself as "the Land of Lincoln." In any event, I identify the City of David as Jesus' birthplace for traditional, rather than historical, reasons. See Meier, *A Marginal Jew*, vol. 1 (New York: Doubleday, 1991), p. 407.

1

unanimity and friendship."[4] The early Rawls is particularly emphatic about the "primacy" of justice: "Justice is the first virtue of social institutions, as truth is of systems of thought."[5] For all their differences, both Plato and Rawls agree that social stability and governmental legitimacy depend most fundamentally on giving persons their due (*suum cuique,* in Cicero's Latin). How precisely to define what is due someone has varied across the centuries, but a primary focus on distributive, retributive, and procedural justice has been commonplace among Western philosophers. From Greece to America, rewarding merit, punishing demerit, and honoring contract have been the heart and soul of politics. I argue here, nevertheless, that a justice-centered account of the *civitas* is as mistaken as was the earth-centered account of the cosmos.

For millennia, we have habitually misunderstood, or at least misstated, our relations to one another. Even as Copernicus, Kepler, and Galileo helped us see that the physical world does not revolve around a fixed and static earth, so I hope (with others) to demonstrate that the social world does not revolve around the rationally self-interested agent.[6] Even as the full articulation of heliocentricity awaited Newton's formulation of a new fundamental force — gravity — so the full appreciation of humanity requires a reformulation of an old fundamental force — charity.[7] Neighbor love, not social justice, is the sine qua non that holds us together. For Christians, the cross is the divine instrument, the telescoping of eternity into time, that lets us see this most clearly. But other lenses are available, as I hope to illustrate.

I offer in these pages a vision of *agape* as first political virtue, as primary social value. Love is the foundational norm that ought to structure political principles and policies, from the death penalty to war to marriage to adoption. This book is written by a Christian, but it is an attempt to bring both religious faith and liberal politics under the sovereignty of charity. *Agape,* or love of God and neighbor, is by no means at odds with justice. Rewarding achievement,

4. Plato, *The Republic,* trans. Allan Bloom (New York: Basic Books, 1968), 351d, p. 30.

5. John Rawls, *A Theory of Justice* (Cambridge: Harvard University Press, 1971), p. 3. On page 586, he refers to "the primacy of justice."

6. Amartya Sen also has misgivings about privileging entitlement above needs in political theory. He does not talk much about love, but in *The Idea of Justice* (Cambridge: Harvard University Press, Belknap Press, 2009), he raises the issue of "whether advantage-seeking, in either a direct or an indirect form, provides the only robust basis of reasonable behavior in society" (p. 205). "A related question," he notes, "is whether mutual benefit and reciprocity must be the foundations of all political reasonableness" (p. 205).

7. I could as accurately have said "discovery" and "rediscovery," rather than "formulation" and "reformulation."

punishing guilt, and upholding fair agreements have a key place in a good society. But *agape* is chronologically and axiologically prior. Rational agents capable of benefiting from distributive, retributive, and procedural justice only emerge and endure when human lives are extended unearned care in community. Putting the point another way, the personal dignity that stems from freely pursuing rational interests depends upon our basic needs and potentials being antecedently addressed by others. This necessary condition for dignity, I call sanctity. Dignity is the main concern of justice; sanctity the main concern of love.

Like an empirical scientist standing on the shoulders of giants — like Bruno looking back to Lucretius and Aristarchus — I am deeply indebted to titans writing before me. Most important in my case have been Søren Kierkegaard, Abraham Lincoln, and Martin Luther King Jr. (Jesus, the Messiah, left no written record; moreover, he is eternal, so one looks up to him, rather than back.) Of course, of all the theologians who put love at the core of their political thinking, none is more influential than Saint Augustine. He famously distinguishes the city of God from the city of this world on the basis of the contrasting natures of their loves.[8] Yet, in my judgment, no theologian has caused more error and suffering than the bishop of Hippo. Thus a significant portion of this book is dedicated to rebutting various Augustinian dichotomies, especially "the elect versus the reprobate."

My title, *Political* Agape, will strike some readers as a contradiction in terms, rather akin to "theistic science" or "modern art." The suspicion is that two separate domains or two natural types are being illicitly mixed, as in certain Levitical "abominations." Didn't Reinhold Niebuhr teach us that agapic love is a private excellence, reserved for interpersonal relations, while politics is the world of justly constrained self-interest?[9] Part of my challenge, then, is to explain how love and justice are related but not opposed. What justice assigns to others was generally defined, in the classical period, in terms of status and, in the modern era, in terms of rights. Status may be construed with reference to birth, wealth, power, or character. Rights, in turn, are often a function of the interests and actions of autonomous persons that generate merit (distributive justice), demerit (retributive justice), or contract (procedural justice). When agapic love reigns, on the other hand, human needs and potentials rather

---

8. Saint Augustine, *The City of God,* trans. Henry Bettenson (New York: Penguin Books, 1972), 14.28, p. 593.

9. This paraphrase of Niebuhr is actually far too simple; see my *The Priority of Love* (Princeton: Princeton University Press, 2003), chap. 3.

than personal status or performance are the temporal foci. For Christians, God-in-Christ is the *eternal* focus and the basis of a prophetic witness to the world. My straightforward thesis is that if we rightly understand Christianity as prophetic, then justice-as-respecting-status-or-rights will have its place, but love-as-addressing-needs-and-potentials will be politically foundational. Indeed, when "the prophetic" is given its due, dominant forms of monotheism and democracy are shown to be inadequate, even unethical, but alternate forms emerge as possible.

I do not embrace Christianity in order to make democracy work, but I believe that anyone who is touched by the reality of the God who is love (1 John 4:8) will (or at least ought to) work for democracy of a particularly "liberal" sort. Democracy is not equivalent to Christianity, but neither is it a cultural interloper tempting the faithful to apostasy. Historically, liberal democracy is a prodigal son of biblical faith, in need of reform, rather than an Enlightenment pretender seeking to steal the Christian inheritance. For all its limitations, even the language of "natural rights" is the fruit of Christian reflection and action in the political sphere.[10] Christian theorists drew on Greek and Roman sources, as well as the Bible, but there is no point in denying Western democracy's religious paternity. To deny this paternity is to be false to past history and to obscure the grounds for both critique and support of liberty, equality, and justice. Such a denial can also amount to a self-righteous attempt to escape democratic critique of the church. The Christian church remains a temporal and fallen institution, and it is itself sometimes a prodigal *father* (or *mother*, if you prefer). As in a functional family, critical dialogue can and should run both ways between the generations.

The prophetic Christian will not sell his or her birthright for a "mess of pottage" — much less a "pot of message"[11] — by claiming to speak a neutral political Esperanto or by identifying the faith with a passing political structure. But the alternative to secular gibberish and pagan idolatry is not some lost ecclesial idiom or some pure escapist sect. In particular, a prophetic witness to the primacy of charity will resist various dichotomies that the church has fostered for millennia. Chief among these are "the saved versus the damned," "the elect versus the reprobate," "the Heavenly City versus the earthly city," and "the church versus the world." These invidious contrasts have been profoundly

---

10. See, for instance, Brian Tierney, *The Idea of Natural Rights* (Atlanta: Scholars Press, 1997).

11. The play on Gen. 25:29-34 is Paul Ramsey's; see his *Speak Up for Just War or Pacifism* (University Park and London: Penn State University Press, 1988), p. 36.

influential in the history of Christian thought and practice, but they are the fruit of *hubris* among theological "ins" and the cause of immense suffering among theological "outs." The moment for Christian social teaching to break with these self-congratulatory contrasts is long overdue. Again, this does not mean diluting Christian virtue or assimilating it to alien standards. But it does mean surrendering, at last, the idea that sanctity means departing from time and space or distancing the kingdom of God from "vessels of wrath."[12]

In a pluralistic society, the prophetic voice will be multilingual, translating the logic of Christianity into practical words and deeds that benefit the neighbor and witness to God. In the United States, this role has been fulfilled most conspicuously by Abraham Lincoln and Martin Luther King Jr. Accordingly, I aim herein to be true to the religious identity and teachings of Jesus Christ and the political model and morals of Lincoln and King, with the former measuring and correcting the latter. I see no contradiction in affirming the divinity and unsurpassed authority of Jesus as incarnate Word of God, on the one hand, and the humanity and tragic wisdom of Lincoln and King as prophetic instruments of God, on the other — so long as they are ordered. I dedicate chapter 1 to Lincoln and my conclusion to King, well aware that neither man was perfect; in this "Liberal Introduction," I focus on Jesus and Abraham. For some, for a Christian to praise a president, especially the prosecutor of the bloody American Civil War, is akin to blasphemous emperor worship or a valorization of political violence — Lincoln as the new Tiberius (if Abe is considered pagan) or Constantine (if Abe is considered Christian) or even Bar Kokhba[13] (if Abe is considered messianic). There is no question here of divided loyalty or cultural idolatry, however. Let it be stated emphatically at the outset: no merely historical figure or merely temporal ideology can or should command a Christian's unconditional commitment. No human personality, party, cause, or institution is salvific, and democratic freedom itself can be a siren song, especially in time of war.[14] In referring to "Jesus *and* Abraham," I

12. See Augustine, *The City of God* 15.2, p. 598.

13. Simon Bar Kokhba was the violent figure who led the third Jewish military revolt against Roman rule, in 132 C.E. The revolt initially succeeded in driving the Romans out of Jerusalem, but it brought an imperial backlash that eventually led to the near destruction of Judaism.

14. As C. Day Lewis laments in "Where Are the War Poets?" (1941), the greedy figures who have "enslaved religion, markets, laws" in peace are emboldened in war to "speak up in freedom's cause." Political *agape* endorses a version of "democracy," but motives, means, and consequences matter. The biblical God is the first and transcendent loyalty that keeps liberalism prophetic — theologically, economically, and legally.

don't mean to baptize an American civil religion in which liberty and equality are the highest goods, but rather to bring that national faith under scriptural judgment. If Jesus is Lord of both church and state, then a critical theological politics is indispensable.

Harry Stout has noted that, for many Americans, "through his death, an innocent Lincoln became transformed from the prophet of America's civil religion to its messiah."[15] For my part, I want to highlight the ways in which the mature Lincoln himself *resisted* American civil religion and his own messianic status. He approached Christlike charity exactly to the extent that he recognized the deficiencies of "popular sovereignty" ("We the people") and personal autonomy ("life, liberty, and the pursuit of happiness"). Even American democracy was under divine condemnation, according to Lincoln: "The prayers of both [North and South] could not be answered. That of neither has been answered fully. The Almighty has His own purposes . . . 'the judgments of the Lord are true and righteous altogether.'"[16] There is no need for a second Christ, but there *is* a constant need for additional John the Baptists, preparing the way of the Lord, now in the form of the Holy Spirit. At a crucial moment in its history, Lincoln met that latter need for America: a sinner who helped wash away the national sin of slavery by enacting, however fallibly, a political gospel of love.[17] He did not work for "a Christian America," but he did help in some measure to Christianize the state.

But what, precisely, is "the way of the Lord," politically understood? I defend in this work a vision I call, alternately, "political *agape*" or "prophetic liberalism." I will describe this position in greater detail shortly, but its key feature is that it subordinates all other values and virtues — including liberty, equality, and justice — to charity (agapic love). Such a vision is as old as the Scriptures, yet it is more revolutionary than either the American Constitution or *The Communist Manifesto*. My particular views are indebted to a number of Christian thinkers,[18] but let me close this section by again briefly contrasting

---

15. Harry S. Stout, *Upon the Altar of the Nation: A Moral History of the American Civil War* (New York: Viking, 2006), p. 455.

16. Lincoln, "Second Inaugural Address," p. 687.

17. In my own lifetime, this role was played most conspicuously by Martin Luther King Jr., and I have written on him at length elsewhere, but I dwell in this volume on Lincoln. If Lincoln fought a war for the American nation in part over race, King saved that same nation from a race war. See Jackson, "Martin Luther King, Jr., on Justice, Law, and Human Nature," in *The Teachings of Modern Christianity on Law, Politics, and Human Nature*, vol. 1, ed. John Witte and Frank Alexander (New York: Columbia University Press, 2005).

18. Cornel West, for example, writes movingly of "love and justice" as the chief biblical

prophetic liberalism with various secular forms of democratic theory. I will then, at more length, compare prophetic liberalism with various sectarian forms of ecclesio-centric theology.

As noted, secular defenses of liberal democracy typically emphasize justice as the first political virtue, the virtue that in turn balances or orders the basic goods of liberty and equality. What the defenses disagree on is the means and manner of justice's definition and justification. John Rawls empha-

---

virtues, in service to the poor and vulnerable, and he forcefully insists that "if we are to revitalize the democratic energies of the country, we must reassert the vital legitimacy of . . . prophetic Christianity in our public life." See Cornel West, *Democracy Matters: Winning the Fight against Imperialism* (New York: Penguin, 2004), p. 152. But even the wise and faithful West needs to unpack further the democratic ideals of liberty and equality, subjecting them to the sort of Socratic questioning that he himself extols. West rightly criticizes secular liberals like John Rawls and Richard Rorty for effectively muzzling religion as a threat to civil discourse, and he explicitly acknowledges that prophetic Christians must be "suspicious of all forms of idolatry, including democracy itself as an idol" (p. 163). Nevertheless, West gives the impression at times that prophetic Christianity and Western democracy are, at their best, always symbiotic. It is odd but significant, for instance, that he sees Socrates as a paradigmatic democrat (e.g., pp. 17, 204, and 208) when, in fact, Socrates was deeply critical of democracy as often an untruthful and unstable form of government, bad for both the soul and the polis. *Pace* Rorty, true religion need not be a conversation stopper, but it should be a conversation starter (and startler), even in democratic contexts. West is unsurpassed in courageously exposing American democracy's failure to live up to its values — as evidenced by the enslavement of blacks, the genocidal extermination of Native Americans, the persecution of lesbians and gays, the imperial pursuit of wealth and power, etc. — but he is less instructive on the *limits* of democracy, the ways it needs to be shaken up by faith, even in the optimal case.

Much depends, of course, on how one defines the term "democracy." (Is it rule by the poorest class, by the people in general, even by elites so long as they are sensitive to the common good? See below.) As noted, I too want to defend a form of "liberal democratic politics," but the prophetic voice will be both affirming and critical in this connection. West's use of the phrase "a new democratic Christian identity in America" (p. 163) makes me uneasy, as does his reference in previous works to "Christian Marxism." Moreover, the idioms of a postmodern — not to say Promethean — humanism can sometimes infect his prose, as when he writes that "[democratic armor] only requires that we be true to ourselves by choosing to be certain kinds of human beings and democratic citizens" (p. 218). As with all first-rate thinkers, however, West provides his own best corrective. He writes: "I speak as a Christian — one whose commitment to democracy is very deep but whose Christian convictions are even deeper. Democracy is not my faith. And American democracy is not my idol. . . . To be a Christian — a follower of Jesus Christ — is to love wisdom, love justice, and love freedom. . . . To be a Christian is to live dangerously, honestly, freely — to step in the name of love as if you may land on nothing, yet to keep stepping because the something that sustains you no empire can give you and no empire can take away" (pp. 171-72). These lines put things just right, I believe, and they will be watchwords for my own performance in these pages.

sizes reason and principles arrived at via rational consensus; Michael Walzer emphasizes history and the "complex equality" found in actual Western communities; Richard Rorty emphasizes conversation and liberating practices embedded in pragmatic traditions that don't appeal to truth; Judith Shklar emphasizes cruelty as the worst thing we do and the cooperative means of avoiding injustice; Chantal Mouffe emphasizes emotions and the inescapability of an "agonistic pluralism"; and so on. The common thread in these thinkers is that liberal democracy is most fundamentally concerned with justice, especially distributive justice, and justice is understood as governing the related goods of liberty and equality, usually by adjudicating the interest-based rights of autonomous agents. To repeat, prophetic liberalism, in contrast, puts charity first. Charity has priority because, in the form of Jesus Christ, it is God's first and most indispensable gift to the world (John 3:16): we all live by it and are called to communicate it, and it simultaneously outstrips and supports justice itself. Prophetic liberalism is convinced, that is, that *agape* is *the political virtue,* rather than merely *a private excellence,* and that *agape* must correct as well as uphold liberty, equality, justice, and other social desiderata.

This is not a prescription for the public hegemony of distinctively Christian symbols of charity, nor is it a recipe for vilifying justice or transforming it, in turn, into a merely "inward" or "personal" virtue. A Christian critique of liberalism, on the contrary, will appeal to prophetic moments in the Hebrew Bible, as well as to the redemptive life of Christ, but it will also make use of a wide range of principles of compassion and fairness that characterize some other religious faiths and some forms of humanism. I write as a Christian, but to think that Christian creeds alone carry the truth or that Christian elites alone know the truth is to embody the judgmental tribalism that Jesus himself decisively rejects. I shall be maintaining that social justice is only recognizable and realizable when agapic love is given its due, but prophetic liberalism is far from reducing religious faith to worldly wisdom about how to get along. A Christian is to be in the world but not of it, and the primacy of faith, hope, and love over such traditional "American" values as liberty and equality is unquestionable. Here, then, is no Constantinianism. Yet a Christian must indeed be *in* the world, must love God and the neighbor in and through (and sometimes around) some particular social context. So there is no escaping the burden of articulating and defending those political and economic arrangements deemed most expressive of, or at least compatible with, the holy will of God.

In this protracted era of the "War on Terror," we hear much about democracy, freedom, and the right of self-defense but not enough about faith, hope, and love. The latter three virtues invoked in public inevitably elicit charges of intolerance or paternalism, but I will be arguing that they are essential to honoring individual conscience as well as to cogent social criticism. We should have decried the injustices of the U.S. war in Iraq (2003-2011) and the Israeli bombing of Lebanon (2006) as affronts to Yahweh and his Son, for instance, not just as disastrous diplomatic or military tactics. Similarly, we should be decrying jihadist Islam as an affront to Allah and his prophet, not just as a threat to America or bad for Mideast politics.[19] The point in both cases is that there neither can be nor should be a segregation of theological virtues from "worldly" political judgments.

II. "The World" and "the Church"

No morally sensitive person doubts that "the world is too much with us; late and soon, getting and spending, we lay waste our powers" (Wordsworth). And it is not merely material greed that dissipates us; racial hatred and ethnic violence are commonplaces of the news, nationally and internationally. Nevertheless, I am wary of all sharp distinctions between "the world" and "the church," such that these become two separate communities or cultures governed in turn by entirely contrasting norms or narratives. Such separatism takes on an especially insidious form when coupled with doctrines of divine fatalism in which "the reprobate" are ineluctably damned to hell and "the elect" are equally inevitably going to heaven. Both the church and the world are, or ought to be, governed by the will of God and the theological virtues of faith, hope, and love. Both the church and the world are called to freedom yet caught up in the contingencies of life. Different settings will require different applications of virtue and different expressions of liberty, and I am not recommending a theocracy, in the sense of political rule by the clergy or tests of religious faith for voting rights or candidacy for public office. On the contrary, the refusal of theocracy is itself an *expression* of faith, hope, and love, not a bracketing or muzzling of these virtues. Agapic love recognizes that not everyone will embody religious belief and no one should be compelled to do so. Christian believers will want and need to have fellowship with one another and to share the grace and pedagogy of the sacraments, as well as to deal with unbelievers in ways sensitive

19. As John Kelsay has argued, the Koran (Qur'an) offers some teachings relevant to the justice of war, but these do not readily map onto Western categories such as *jus ad bellum* and *jus in bello*. See Kelsay, *Islam and War* (Louisville: Westminster John Knox, 1993). In the Hadith (the deeds and sayings of the Prophet), however, Muhammad explicitly rules out direct assaults on women and children as contrary to the will of God.

to their unbelief. But, *au fond,* we are all sinners, either struggling to know and do the truth or struggling to flee from this obligation. The world is too much with *us;* sacred faith versus profane politics is ultimately a Manichaean notion.

To be sure, the narrator of John 1:10-11 declares, "He [the true light, Jesus Christ] was in the world, and the world came into being through him; yet the world did not know him. He came to what was his own, and his own people did not accept him." The first sentence may seem to posit a strict opposition between Jesus and the world, even as the second apparently drives a wedge between Jesus and the Jews. Verses 12-13 continue, however, with: "But to all who received him, who believed in his name, he gave power to become children of God, who were born, not of blood or of the will of the flesh or of the will of man, but of God." The main theme of the passages is the new inclusiveness of God's offer of salvation, now open to Jew and Gentile alike, not the inherent differences between people. Jesus calls his disciples "the salt of *the earth*" (Matt. 5:13), not merely of Israel; and John 3:16-17 famously affirms, "For God so loved *the world*" — not merely the church — "that he gave his only Son, so that everyone who believes in him may not perish but may have eternal life. Indeed, God did not send the Son into the world to condemn the world, but in order that the world might be saved through him."[20] By the grace of God, then, charity itself says: "Away with all invidious contrasts between 'us' and 'them'!"

This is not a prescription for a homogeneous universe in which it is perpetual night and all cows are black. Dietrich Bonhoeffer reminds us that Christians are "the light of the world" (Matt. 5:14), and he rightly dismisses as "cheap grace" any vision in which sin, because forgiven, is indistinguishable from faith or in which obedient followers of Jesus, because contrite, are no different from bourgeois philistines.[21] I do not mean to dispense with all metaphysical, moral, or sociological distinctions, then, just the self-serving ones that invite *hubris* and cloud judgment. Christianity is a way of life rather than an abstract doctrine, so its truth must be enacted. But I believe that the Christian message is indeed true and contradicts much that is practiced and preached in Western society — in schools, businesses, hospitals, movies, athletic fields, and country clubs, as well as in churches — so I am far from advocating cultural relativism. There is always a danger of the gospel of Christ being drowned out or appropriated by the materialism and egotism of the day, and this danger must be strenuously resisted by a truly prophetic witness. (If

20. The emphases in these quotes are, of course, my own.
21. Dietrich Bonhoeffer, *The Cost of Discipleship* (New York: Simon and Schuster, 1995), esp. chaps 1 and 7.

one wants to fear for the republic, if not one's own soul, just watch American television for one day — and not just tawdry "entertainment," but also Christian ministers "pimping" the "gospel of prosperity" and the shameful revelations of abuse from Guantanamo and Abu Ghraib.) The point, however, is that "the world" is usually far too abstract and monolithic a notion to stand as the discrete locus of mendacity or violence.

Put another way, there is no palpable joint that permits a clean cut between "the church" and "the world," such that Christians, truth, and goodness are on one side and non-Christians, falsity, and evil are on the other. All such dichotomizing language invites Christians to imagine they have "emigrated to a colony on the Isles of the Blessed," to use Plato's phrase,[22] and attained a unique virtue or destiny as opposed to "the benighted pagan other." In biblical terms, the disciple of Christ is not to judge others but rather to remove the log in his own eye before he worries about the speck in his neighbor's eye (Matt. 7:1-5). Otherwise, one evades both the solidarity of sin and the solidarity of hope that was arguably Jesus' chief proclamation to humanity. Christians have not emigrated to a sublime heaven, nor are they to wait passively for a future eschaton wherein God will exalt them and lower others. Rather, *Christians have been colonized, here and now, by the love of God in Jesus Christ.* In the life and death of the Son, God has already inaugurated his kingdom on earth, and anyone "in Christ" is enjoined to participate in this "new creation" (2 Cor. 5:17). The kingdom is eschatological, but, as Crossan notes, "Eschatology is not, positively not, about the end of this time-space cosmos but rather an end of cosmic time-space evil and impurity, injustice, violence, and oppression. It is not about the evacuation of earth for God's heaven but about the divine transfiguration of God's earth. It is not about the destruction but about the transformation of God's world here below."[23] By all means, we should resist the pretensions of the modern nation-state and the seductions of the unbridled capitalist market, but so too the idolatry of any temporal power or polity — from a self-righteous soul to a self-congratulatory church. As Kierkegaard inclusively observes, "By reason of the infiltration of the State and social groups and the congregation and society, God can no longer get a hold on the individual."[24]

This realization that the congregation too is fallen means a break with

22. Plato, *The Republic* 7.519c, p. 198.

23. John Dominic Crossan, "Bodily-Resurrection Faith," in *The Resurrection of Jesus: John Dominic Crossan and N. T. Wright in Dialogue*, ed. Robert B. Stewart (Minneapolis: Fortress, 2006), p. 174.

24. Søren Kierkegaard, *Concluding Unscientific Postscript*, trans. David F. Swenson and Walter Lowrie (Princeton: Princeton University Press, 1941), p. 484.

the Augustinian distinction between "the city of God" and "the city of this world," interpreted as fixed bodies that can interact physically but are fundamentally discontinuous spiritually. Saint Augustine was never as dualistic as the Donatists, who argued schismatically that they were "the righteous of God," though he too thought of his faith community as the one "true church."[25] In addition, Augustine did not identify the city of God with the visible institutional church; no one, save God, can know for sure who is a member of which city. For the bishop of Hippo, however, you are in either the one or the other from all time and for all time (and eternity).[26] The static character of the two cities' memberships — indeed, the "two cities" terminology itself — grew out of a presumed divide between the elect predestined for beatitude and the reprobate predestined for damnation. This divide has some biblical warrant, and it is informed in Augustine's case by the desire to uphold God's sovereignty and power. (Since God's will for a particular individual cannot be thwarted, whomever God chooses for heaven cannot but have faith, and whomever God leaves to hell cannot but be damned.) Nevertheless, the elect/reprobate dichotomy is finally incompatible with the goodness of God and love for all neighbors as characterized by Scripture itself.[27] To postulate a hard distinction between the irresistibly saved and the immutably damned is to make history a fatalistic futzing around by the Deity for no good purpose, as well as to encourage Christians to write off or vilify those judged to be forever outside God's plans for redemption.[28] To think of the church as a "counterculture" to the world,

25. See Augustine's "Letter 185," to Boniface, chap. 10, para. 46.

26. Augustine, *The City of God*, book 15, esp. chaps. 1–2, pp. 595-98.

27. Augustine is sometimes appealed to by contemporary defenders of liberal democracy, and I do not wish to deny that there are Augustinian resources for such a defense. Most notably, his insistence that earthly institutions are not vehicles of salvation provides warrant for the limited state. I continue to find Augustine's accounts of love and grace problematic, however, both theologically and politically. (See my *Love Disconsoled: Meditations on Christian Charity* [Cambridge: Cambridge University Press, 1999], chap. 3.) For a superb recent effort to reconstruct an "Augustinian liberalism," based not simply on sin and the limits of the political but rather on sin *and love* in dialectical social relation, see Eric Gregory, *Politics and the Order of Love: An Augustinian Ethic of Democratic Citizenship* (Chicago: University of Chicago Press, 2010). For my part, I cannot get past the bishop's social dualism and divine determinism.

28. In *The Enchiridion on Faith, Hope, and Love* (Washington, D.C.: Regnery, 1961), p. 129, Augustine writes: "After the resurrection . . . when the final, universal judgment has been completed, two groups of citizens, one Christ's, the other the devil's, shall have fixed lots; one consisting of the good, the other of the bad." In *The City of God*, Augustine makes it clear that one is a member of either the city of God or the city of this world, depending on what one loves most deeply (God or self). The problem, however, is that, in the aftermath of the Fall at any rate, one's love is itself irresistibly determined by God. Because all humanity was present

even when this is in the name of preserving the "integrity" of the church and of "serving" the world, is, I fear, to remain partially under the spell of the "two

---

"in Adam's loins" and thus participated in his sin, all are now "slaves to sin" and deserve to be punished with perpetual alienation from God. Nevertheless, God has graciously chosen a few (the "vessels of mercy") to be delivered, while all others (the "vessels of wrath") are consigned to just torment (see 15.2). If one seems to have faith but then lapses, this only shows that one was a child of wrath all along, for membership in one city or the other is immutable. Why God chooses to save some but not all is a mystery; moreover, no one can object because it is pure gift that God saves any at all.

Why would Augustine embrace such a dreadfully dualistic vision, with one part of the species effectively fated for heaven and another for hell? One basic reason is his belief that the effects of original sin can be corporately inherited, such that present generations are bound inextricably to false loves. I find this an intriguing (and disturbing) picture of how collective perversions ensnare us all, making group delusion and cruelty all but inescapable for individuals. The modern image of the sublimely autonomous agent is blind to the reality of "principalities and powers" that outstrip individual apprehension and willpower. That said, to tie sin to *biological* generation, as Augustine does, is to risk making sex as such seem dirty — the flesh and its "lust" is, after all, the vehicle or our perdition — and it comes close to identifying embodied finitude itself with sin. Socially, rather than physically, communicated sin is plausible, in other words, though even this is not entirely beyond our control, with God's grace.

I believe that the more fundamental factor in Augustine's dualism is his desire to preserve the awesome sovereignty of God. For Augustine, God's sovereignty requires a foreordained outcome for history, in which all persons willed by God for salvation are ineluctably saved and all left to damnation are ineluctably damned, independent of any effort or even acceptance on their part. Otherwise, creatures could thwart the will of the Creator and the drama of time could turn out rather badly. The infinite power of God, not to mention the peace of mind of believers, must be founded on the certainty that no soul among the elect can be lost and no soul among the reprobate can be retrieved. (This is the certainty that later meant so much to Martin Luther.)

To be sure, Augustine maintains that his account of divine providence does not undermine human freedom and responsibility. He insists, for example, that Christians must affirm both God's foreknowledge and humanity's free will. Augustine's account of freedom is complicated, given that he distinguishes between *liberum arbitrium* (liberty of indifference), which is the neutral power to choose between two or more alternatives, and *libertas* (true liberty), which is the positive power and disposition to know and do the good. Before the Fall, evidently, Adam and Eve had both senses of freedom, though in an unstable or immature form. After the Fall, according to the early Augustine, human beings lost *libertas* but retained some measure of *liberum arbitrium*. Eventually, however, in response to the Pelagians, the later Augustine denied *any* meaningful freedom to postlapsarian creatures, at least with respect to their doing good or achieving salvation. He continued to affirm that human actions are "voluntary," but "voluntary" came simply to mean "proceeding through the will *(voluntas)*," with the will itself moved directly and infallibly by God.

For us Arminians, in contrast, the Augustinian scenario impiously elevates God's power over his goodness.

cities" doctrine.[29] It is to flirt with the self-congratulatory bifurcation of "we-the-elect" and "they-the-reprobate"; worse still, it is to suggest a paternalism of the pure over the impure: "We with the true story and redeemed natures will help you with the false story and unredeemed natures."

Jesus himself sometimes speaks negatively of the Aramaic equivalent of "the world," as when he says to the disciples: "The world cannot hate you, but it hates me because I testify against it that its works are evil" (John 7:7). These lines are followed in the next chapter by Jesus' saying to "the Jews": "You are from below, I am from above; you are of this world, I am not of this world" (John 8:23). Matthew 13:22 offers a third example: "the cares of the world and the lure of wealth choke the word, and it yields nothing." In such cases, however, Jesus refers to a medium in which we all live and move — that is, to whatever and whoever occludes or opposes God's will, including our own hearts and homes, rather than to an external or permanently lost group of persons or institutions.[30] Jesus is using the phrase "the world" as a metaphor for sin or inattentiveness to God, even as Paul uses the phrase "the flesh" in Romans 8:6-9: "To set the mind on the flesh is death, but to set the mind on the Spirit is life and peace. For this reason the mind that is set on the flesh is hostile to God; it does not submit to God's law — indeed it cannot, and those who are in the flesh cannot please God. But you are not in the flesh; you are in the Spirit, since the Spirit of God dwells in you. Anyone who does not have the Spirit of Christ does not belong to him." Paul's rhetoric of "the flesh versus the Spirit" should not be seen as an ontological dualism or a Gnostic rejection of the body, any more than Jesus' contrast between "the world and the kingdom" (cf. John 18:36) should be seen as a prideful flight from earthly existence or a rude dismissal of non-Jews (or non-Christians). Paul is well aware that we are all psychosomatic beings, composed by God of body and soul, even as Jesus

---

29. I have in mind Stanley Hauerwas's *Against the Nations, Resident Aliens, A Community of Character,* and other works. Hauerwas writes: "First and foremost the community [of the church] must know that it has a history and tradition which separate it from the world"; see *A Community of Character* (Notre Dame: University of Notre Dame Press, 1981), p. 68. This too easily papers over the Crusades, the Inquisition, the American churches' complicity in slavery, the *Deutsche Christen,* and other ecclesial sins, and it blinds us to the fact that the world too is called to virtue under God. "The church does not exist to provide an ethos for democracy," he rightly points out (p. 12), reminding us that Christianity is not simply to be equated with any one form of political economy. But Hauerwas ignores the fact that kingdom values are to be applied universally, in both church and state. I discuss Hauerwas's work below and in chapter 8.

30. At John 8:24, Jesus says to "the Jews": "I told you that you would die in your sins, for you will die in your sins unless you believe that I am he." One fears anti-Semitic redaction here, but even this messianic warning is open-ended.

would have his followers live faithfully in the wider world as well as in the society of coreligionists. Jesus prays to the Father, after all,

"Your kingdom come.
Your will be done,
    on earth [not just in the church] as it is in heaven." (Matt. 6:10)

Jesus' fellowship with Jew and Gentile, rich and poor, male and female, publican and sinner, clean and unclean, even a Roman soldier, is iconoclastic in the extreme, designed to resist any "us/them" contrast that would move his disciples to boast about themselves or deny their supposedly derelict neighbors. The hazard of the self-applauding "tale of two cities" — apologies to Dickens — is that it leads us to forget that we all both experience and cause "the best of times and the worst of times." This hazard exists even if the distinctiveness of the church is held to be God's unmerited gift, as in Augustine, since the offensive hierarchy still obtains and tends to blind us to the finite and fallen orders that shape everything that now is. Jesus on the cross has broken the hegemony of those orders, has vanquished "the powers" that pretend to be God, *for anyone and everyone and for all times and places.* To live accordingly is to embrace a costly discipleship, and I suspect that if a Christian never goes to jail for his or her convictions, something is wrong. Yet to submit to jail — or even death — is a witness to God's sublime goodness rather than to any group's or one's own special election.

The incarnation of Christ *in* flesh and history must govern, then, how we understand the "calling *out*" of the church. The *ekklesia* is literally composed of those "called out," but that out of which they are called is sin and a disordered relation to the world, not the world as such. Moreover, those who are called are no fewer than everyone (John 3:16), and the purpose of their being called is reunion, not ostracism. "In Christ God was reconciling the world to himself, not counting their trespasses against them, and entrusting the message of reconciliation to us" (2 Cor. 5:19).[31] The world as a whole has been entered and overcome by Christ, and all creatures, not merely the elect or the churched, are summoned to embody God's own holiness. 1 John depicts "the world" as the domain of "the evil one" and as a source of temptation and opposition for "God's children" (e.g., 5:19), thus seeming to set up a strict dichotomy. As 2:15-17 puts it: "Do not love the world or

---

31. Note that it is the world that needs to be reconciled to God, not God to the world. It is *we* who are the stumbling blocks to redemption, not God's wrath or condemnation. Christ does not convince God to love the world by first making it sinless, as though God's *agape* waits on human merit or even divine retribution. Rather, from all eternity God loves the world and, in the fullness of time, sends his Son so that the world might freely receive that love.

the things in the world. The love of the Father is not in those who love the world; for all that is in the world — the desire of the flesh, the desire of the eyes, the pride in riches — comes not from the Father but from the world. And the world and its desire [or *the desire for it*] are passing away, but those who do the will of God live forever." The author of 1 John even writes, "Do not be astonished, brothers and sisters, that the world hates you" (3:13). But observe that it is "*love* of the world" — that is, an improper orientation toward earthly things — that is condemned. A careful reading of the letter as a whole makes clear that "the world" is typically the fallen context in which we all are enthralled and beset, not a subset of people and places that is uniquely set apart as corrupt or unlovable. The church too is part of the world, so understood, though it is to be in the world in a particular way. As 4:16-17 puts it, "God is love, and those who abide in love abide in God, and God abides in them. Love has been perfected among us in this: that we may have boldness on the day of judgment, because as he is, so are we in this world."

Admittedly, the author of 1 John can at times use the phrase "the world" as shorthand for those who reject God and pridefully covet material goods or social position or both. (Indeed, references to both "the world" and "the Jews" take on an increasingly nasty "us versus them" tenor as the early church feels more and more persecuted.) But this usage is rather like Paul employing "the flesh" as a synecdoche for disordered desire in the person. When Paul writes, for example, "For if you live according to the flesh, you will die; but if by the Spirit you put to death the deeds of the body, you will live" (Rom. 8:13), he is not embracing a metaphysical dualism in which flesh (the body) is evil and only Spirit (the soul) is good. That would be to deny that the human creature is the psychosomatic unity — the animated earth — described in Genesis. It would also be to disavow the incarnation and its eucharistic affirmation of flesh and blood. Paul's target of rebuke is not a part or dimension of the person as such, any more than the author of 1 John is condemning a part of the universe as such; rather, both are aiming at skewed relations to what is otherwise good: "fornication, impurity, passion, evil desire, and greed (which is idolatry)" (Col. 3:5). "Those who belong to Christ Jesus have crucified the flesh with its passions and desires" (Gal. 5:24), but it would be worse than a simple-minded literalism to read this as hatred of the body or refusal of emotion as such. (Alas, this has been the understanding of some Christians.) Such a Gnostic reading of "the flesh" has caused no end of suffering and injustice, even as have Marcionite readings of the Bible that find warrant to despise or betray "the Jews." Properly understood, Christians are in the world, composed of flesh, and from the Jews. These facts are to be not merely acknowledged but celebrated.

Just as it would be a mistake to invite Christians to deny or come out of "the flesh," broadly construed, so it is a mistake to invite them to do the same with "the world." "Conquering" the world (cf. 1 John 5:4-5) involves Christ's redeeming us humans and our responding in faith, not us Christians departing or vilifying the world to accent our righteousness or election. Since Jesus Christ "is the atoning sacrifice for our sins, and not for ours only but also for the sins of the whole world" (1 John 2:2), "the world" cannot be the essentially lost and necessarily vicious other. I take this to imply, moreover, that any critique of the contemporary world must include a critique of the church as well of the state — not simply of "Christendom" as a too close alignment of the two. Putting it another way, even the world might come to know God and even the church may come to forget God.[32] Telling and retelling the stories of the faithful in the language of Scripture are crucial for theological education — and all hail to Karl Barth for his imaginative genius in this regard — but "church dogmatics" should not be the occasion for dogmatic churches.[33]

To summarize as charitably as possible, Christian theologians and even Scriptures equivocate at times on the meaning of "the world." Sometimes the phrase is normatively neutral and connotes the finite, physical universe of sticks and stones, flesh and blood, in which and for which Christ became incarnate (e.g., John 3:16). At other times the phrase is much more loaded and refers to the fallen realm of ungodly principles and sinful practices against which Christ stands (e.g., John 7:7). It is crucial that the two senses not be conflated and that their ambiguities not be exploited to evade the imitation of Christ and love of the neighbor — that is, to belittle others or pump up self or both. More to the point, in neither sense of "the world" is it something that disciples (or anyone else) can simply ignore or avoid. Disciples testify to Christ and resist and condemn evil in themselves and others, but they remain finite and sinful *and a loving presence in the world* even when redeemed. Christlike love affirms just judgments, and divine grace makes it possible to be "not conformed" to the fallen world but rather "transformed" by spiritual renewal (see Rom. 12:2). When Christians are starkly

---

32. I am indebted to Bradley Burroughs for a more nuanced understanding of "the world" in 1 John; see his "Conquering the κόσμος: Understanding the World in 1 John" (unpublished manuscript). As Burroughs observes, "it might be that what passes away [in 2:17] is not the κόσμος [the world] *in se* but rather the perverse way of encountering it which has become so widespread in its present state of oppression under the evil one" (p. 10). This view accords well, he observes, with "the overall non-separatist orientation of 1 John" (p. 10).

33. Barth escapes this temptation, warning us against both the *Deutsche Christen* and a Confessing Church that cares only about governing its own house. See Barth, *The German Church Conflict* (Cambridge: Lutterworth, 1965), esp. chap. 4, "The Confessing Church in National Socialist Germany" (1935).

contrasted with "the Jews," "the flesh," or "the world," however, one rightly suspects that the wagons are being circled by a phobic or haughty church. This is not fidelity to the Lord but a snide redaction of his life and work, a regrettable tactic evident in the church early and late.[34] Jesus explicitly warned his followers against such divisive judgmentalism, typified by the Pharisees (Matt. 7:1).

Many sincere Christians fear that a modern loss of faith and the moral "subjectivism" that often accompanies it will leave them unable to judge right and wrong, but, in fact, faithlessness makes it impossible to *decline* to judge others and to forgive. The turn toward self and away from God does not strip us of the power to draw moral contrasts; it *forces* us to draw maligning contrasts everywhere, to bolster our shaky confidence or to survive "the rat race." Absent the light of the world, we "keep our metaphysics warm" (Eliot) by freezing others out. Yet true unity with God means *not isolation from the world but communion with it,* both because of and in spite of its/our sin. Seeking to elevate self by denying or denigrating others is very close to the core of fallenness, and such a temper spells the end of a prophetic witness that directs attention to God. (The true prophet does not berate or banish people, any more than she capitulates or panders to their evil; instead, she speaks the truth that we are not alone and thereby inspires people with the love of God.) As Dietrich Bonhoeffer perceived, "for man in the state of disunion [with God,] good consists in passing judgement, and the ultimate criterion is man himself."[35] Indeed, judgment is "the irreconcilable opposite of action [in Christ]."[36] The Nazis were paragons of "discriminating" evaluation — their contrasts between Aryans and non-Aryans, the true *Volk* and the false *Volk,* mirror earlier Christian distinctions between the elect and the damned — and even relativists are inevitably dogmatic about their relativism.

Lest I seem too severe here, I grant that sometimes Christian distinctions — for example, Augustine's "two cities" — *become* defamatory over time, perhaps in spite of their authors' conscious intentions. There is no denying, however, that at other times the distinctions in question — for example, "the saved" versus "the reprobate" and "us Christians" versus "them Jews" — are defamatory from the outset. They are *meant* to annul outsiders. The political task of Christians is to say the prophetic word to the world (and the church) in a way that overcomes these vices, voluntary or otherwise. After seventeen hundred years of pogroms, inquisitions, forced conversions, and holocausts, we must be more than wary of any language

---

34. The church must admit that Friedrich Nietzsche's diagnosis of Christian *ressentiment* is troublingly accurate in many cases; see Nietzsche, *The Antichrist.*

35. Dietrich Bonhoeffer, *Ethics* (New York: Simon and Schuster, 1955), p. 34.

36. Bonhoeffer, *Ethics,* p. 47. Bonhoeffer cites here James 4:11.

that metaphysically divides neighbor from neighbor, for this divides everyone from God. It is also — need I say? — an insult to the cross of Christ. Christ could set brother "against" brother, son "against" mother, and so on, but only in the sense of demanding priority for the God who is Love. When God is given that priority, then true reconciliation becomes possible and worldly divisions can cease. To make the name of Jesus Christ itself a tool for writing off or belittling others and for promoting or parading self is more than grotesque, but ecclesial history is full of this. Though modern democracy (at least the American variety) arose out of Protestant Christianity, modern democracy, in turn, may rein in the *hubris* of the Christian churches. National Socialism was partly a return to anti-Christian paganism, but it also traded on and found support in a long tradition of Christian antipluralism and anti-Semitism (see chap. 10). The individualism and materialism of American democracy are the prodigal son of Christianity, but even the prodigal son can help restore the house of the father (see chap. 3).

III. The Ubiquity of Sin and the Priority of God

Christians sometimes speak of "the church" in hushed tones, as a community called to sculpt souls and to be "the body of Christ" in contrast to the nation-state. I share a deep admiration and respect for the ecclesial ideal of embodying faith, hope, and love in a fallen world, but a sober appraisal of church history must temper any inclination to set it apart in some fundamental way. The simple truth I have been emphasizing is that the church itself is beset by sin — including arrogance, lust, and greed. The sectarian language of a "separate city" or "elected polis" smacks of invidious election and limited atonement, and it fails to acknowledge that both the state and the church shape human souls and both the church and the state are in need of redemption. Any political theology that leaves the impression that the Christian church is the repository of positive spiritual value, and the state is the unavoidable but largely dark realm of gross energies, will be false and self-congratulatory.

Christian individuals are members of both church and state simultaneously. Holiness does not reside in a single earthly polis, and the Holy Spirit is not active only in the church. I acknowledge *the axiological priority of God and the neighbor,* over the nation and the fellow citizen, even as I affirm the priority of *agape* over justice and peace. I am reluctant, however, to locate such priority in *the church* as a temporal institution. As far as I can see, the church has been, historically, just as bad as the state at inculcating vicious traits of character and promoting social wrong. (Think of the Inquisition and the churches, Protestant and Catholic, during the Nazi Holocaust.) To be aware of the sins of the Christian church is to grant that the democratic state might teach the church a thing or two, as in the American civil rights movement in the 1950s and 1960s. Ideally, the church is to be a social watchdog, and insofar as it explicitly teaches faith, hope, and love, it has a distinctive moral voice. In reality, however, we learn both virtue and vice from a host of social groups and traditions. The more one privileges "the church," "the city of God," and the like, the more one invites the sort of problematic "us" versus "them" distinctions I documented above.

I myself talk about "the Christian church," but we must finally admit that there are *many Christian "churches,"* with quite varied teachings and practices. Which of these has "axiological priority"? I deem it safer to say that God's holy will has priority, rather than either church or state. The translation of that will into reality must take different forms in different social contexts, but no one temporal institution is the sole or even the main repository of the highest Good. Or, more to the point, all temporal institutions, traditions, and peoples are subordinate to and judged by that Good. This is the heart of a truly prophetic witness. Christ is the Lord, and not the church or the state. Whatever obligation Christians have to the state is subsequent to and filtered through the claim of Christ, but so is whatever obligation Christians have to the church.

In an unguarded moment, Stanley Hauerwas embraces a highly ecclesiocentric vision of the cosmos, relating that "not to sing 'The Star Spangled Banner' is a small thing that reminds me that my first loyalty is not to the United States but to God and God's church."[37] Here God and the church share primacy:

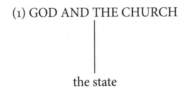

(1) GOD AND THE CHURCH

the state

Hauerwas is actually well aware that the church is a fallen, temporal institution and must not become an idol. In more sober moments, he concedes that "it is never a question of church or world. Rather it is a question of having a people so captured by the worship of God that they can be for the world what the world so desperately needs."[38] This is an improvement over the previous quote,

37. Stanley Hauerwas, *Performing the Faith* (Grand Rapids: Brazos, 2004), p. 203.
38. Stanley Hauerwas and Romand Coles, *Christianity, Democracy, and the Radical Ordinary* (Eugene, Ore.: Cascade Books, 2008), pp. 111-12.

but it still smacks of a "we-the-chosen-people versus they-the-profane-others" dichotomy. At his best, Hauerwas does not mean "to restrict God's care of us to the church,"[39] but he would be even better if he made it clear that the "us" here is everybody, not only Christians. To the extent that he does not, to the extent that he sees "the church" as a unique community of character outside or opposed to "the world" or "the nations,"[40] he affirms a second traditional hierarchy:

(2) GOD IN CHRIST

The church

the state

Such a scheme readily suggests *ressentiment:* "'the kingdom of God' comes as a judgment over his enemies."[41] It is tempting to reject the elevation of the church over the state based on their comparable historical sinfulness — the Inquisition and the Crusades on one side, the two world wars on the other — but the attribution of guilt does not divide so easily along ecclesial and national lines. Think of the complicity of the Christian denominations in the Nazi Holocaust (see chap. 10). A far more positive reason for refusing the hierarchy of church and state is Jesus' having fellowship with tax collectors and centurions, the clean and the unclean, Jews and Gentiles. His more prophetic picture provides a third alternative:

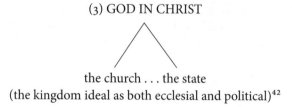

(3) GOD IN CHRIST

the church . . . the state
(the kingdom ideal as both ecclesial and political)[42]

---

39. Hauerwas and Coles, *Christianity,* p. 105.

40. See, for instance, Stanley Hauerwas, *Against the Nations* (Minneapolis: Winston Press, 1985).

41. Friedrich Nietzsche, "The AntiChrist," in *The Portable Nietzsche,* ed. and trans. Walter Kauffman (New York: Viking Penguin, 1982), #40, p. 615.

42. Applying kingdom values to both church and state, to both "religion" and "the world," has strong resonances with what H. Richard Niebuhr calls the paradigm of "Christ

The church and the state have distinctive structures and roles, and the church explicitly preaches faith, hope, and love, but they are not two discontinuous kingdoms. "Even a democratic state is not the kingdom," Hauerwas rightly reminds us,[43] but neither is the church the kingdom come. Indeed, the church is not the only community or institution that anticipates or approximates the kingdom. *Commitment to the theological virtues will have both political and ecclesial implications, and Jesus' "kingdom ideal" ought to permeate every dimension of existence.*[44] *When both church and state are properly subordinate to God, they participate equally in his kingdom.* More negatively, membership in neither the church nor the state as such is salvific, because no temporal institution is salvific. Indeed, no temporal institution is the sole vehicle of grace or the sole judge of all the others. The church must judge (and often resist) the state; the state must also judge (and often resist) the church; and both church and state are subordinate equally to God. Finally, membership in neither temporal body is fixed and the occasion for boasting. Our ultimate allegiance is not to America or even to Christianity, but to God. Or so political agapists believe. God's holy will has axiological priority, with both church and state on a par as finite and fallible servants of that will. The three-tiered model (2) above will inevitably suggest an elite status for the church. Couple that with talk of "election" and "damnation," and we are off to the prideful races.

Nationalism and sectarianism are complementary vices. The love of God (subjective genitive) turns the whole world, including the church and the state. The axiological and chronological priority of the love of God inspires and constrains both national and ecclesial identities. No earthly institution, not even the church, should be given priority over the grace of God. Or, to put it another way, *all* earthly institutions are *equally* subject to the command and judgment of the Father. We must not embrace ecclesio-centrism over Christocentrism, since both state and church are equally under the countenance of God and equally the instruments of God. One should affirm and cooperate with the nation-state if and only if it is in conformity with the will of God, and the same goes for the church. The idea that the church has such authority that it first teaches one virtue, and *then* one enters into the messy

---

the transformer of culture." See Niebuhr, *Christ and Culture* (New York: Harper and Row, 1951), chap. 6.

43. Hauerwas, *Against the Nations*, chap. 7.

44. As I make clear in the balance of this text, this does not mean theocracy or state-imposed religious creeds; it means, rather, citizens and congregations willing to love all their neighbors as Christ loves them.

and secondary world of public life, is both false and dangerous. No temporal institution has such priority. Both the state and the church impact us and check and balance one another from the beginning. Both check evil and promote good, at least ideally.

I am fond of saying, "If one is a Christian and does not go to jail at least once in one's life, something is probably wrong." The flip side of this is, "If one is an American and is not excommunicated at least once in one's life, something is probably wrong." (Just ask Margaret Farley.) The key point, of course, is that "those who follow Christ" are not synonymous with "those in the church." Christians must be constant critics of the secular state. Yet American, English, French, Japanese, Chinese, Spanish, etc., citizens should also insist on remembering the sins of the Christian church — from the betrayal of Jesus to the Inquisition to the dehumanization of Native Americans and blacks to the KKK to the *Deutsche Christen*.

Does this mean that I give equal loyalty to America and to Jesus? Not at all! But it does mean that I give equally conditional loyalty to America and to the institutional Christian church. (Jesus is not the church!) Both of these loyalties are subject to obedience to God and love of neighbor. I simply refuse to order temporal affiliations as though one is inherently more faithful or virtuous than the others. That is idolatry, whether it valorizes the state or it valorizes the church. Thank God, then, when the democratic state steps in and stops the pederasty of Catholic priests and the cover-up by the magisterium! Thank God, then, when the democratic state steps in and stops the genital mutilation of Muslim girls! Thank God, then, when the democratic state steps in and stops the coercion of child brides in the breakaway Mormon sect of Warren Jeffs! I am also very wary of the nation-state — "democratic" or otherwise — but cases like these make it impossible for me to celebrate "the church" in hushed tones.

Concentrated power tends to corrupt, no matter what form it takes — big government, big business, or megachurch. For almost thirty years I have advised men and women in or entering Christian ministry, and the phenomenon they find most ubiquitous and most challenging is *the market church*. The gospel of prosperity, the pressure to swell membership numbers, and the demand by the hierarchy to run the church like a business are all betrayals of the life and teaching of Jesus, I believe, but such tendencies are not isolated to one "sphere" of life or one social institution. The problem is not just the bureaucratic nation-state or the modern capitalist economy; it includes all phases of existence. "There is a crack in everything," as Leonard Cohen says, "that's how the light gets in." Suffice it to say, the church too is cracked — a.k.a.

fallen — and needs the light of Christ. The church does not sit majestically in judgment of all other groups and creeds; the church itself is often the problem.

In sum, Christians must be careful not to fall into the romantic self-congratulation of thinking that only the church — "we believers" — are put into danger when combating evil. *Everyone everywhere is caught in the struggle against sin; everyone everywhere is prone to idolatry; and both the church and the state can be murderous.* Sometimes, it is citizens of a state that are put in danger if they are out of step with the Christian church — think of the Inquisition. Think of the many U.S. civil rights activists in the 1940s through the 1960s who had to resist the racism and segregationism advocated in Christian pulpits across much of the country. Never forget that Chaney, Goodman, and Schwerner were killed in Mississippi in 1964 *by Christians.* (The KKK thought of itself as a pious Christian organization.) Schwerner and Goodman were Jews, Chaney a secular black man, and all three were working for the "Freedom Movement" or the Congress of Racial Equality. They were champions of democratic political values — primarily the right to vote — and they were murdered by "good churchgoing Christians" as a result.

IV. "The Church" Again and Universalism

One might innocently use "the church" to denote those who freely profess Christ and fallibly seek to follow God's commands, and use "the world" for those who at any given moment do not and so need special care or stand in concrete opposition. But then "the world" is no longer an unchanging and alien reality "out there," to be construed as chaff to "the church's" wheat. The church can be a school of virtue, but it is not the only such school. In addition, the church and the world remain dependent on and reconciled in God: "We love because he [God] first loved us" (1 John 4:19). Even as Saint Paul holds that the believing spouse in a mixed marriage ought not to divorce the unbelieving one, as long as the latter consents to live together (1 Cor. 7:12-13), so the Christian ought not to "put away" the world. More positively, even as, for Paul, the believing spouse "makes holy" or "sanctifies" the unbelieving one, thereby ensuring that any children they might have are also "holy" (1 Cor. 7:14), so the Christian citizen may seek to sanctify the wider public and its practices, while yet acknowledging the ubiquity of sin. The household context of marriage and family is more intimate than the political context of nation and citizenry, of course, and the process of sanctification can never be forced or automatic in either setting. The basic principle that faith, hope, and love should be catching applies universally,[45] however. The key is that we prevent a faithful Christocentricity that allows believers to overcome division and resist injustice from lapsing into a prideful ecclesio-centricity that actually causes division and injustice. Ecclesio-centricity can readily give rise to or reflect doctrines of limited atonement, wherein Christ died only for the elect few, thereby contradicting the Messiah's frequent claim to be "the light of the world" (e.g., John 8:12) — which in context clearly means "the *entire* world." Perhaps not everyone will embrace the gospel, but it is addressed to all and all have the capacity to receive it by consenting to God's grace — or else the Deity is not worthy of worship, and, as Kierkegaard says, I cannot be bothered to live.

Kevin J. Madigan and Jon D. Levenson have lately argued that Saint Paul and the early Christian church were not "universalist." They point out that "the only hope for non-Jews, Paul thought, lay in joining the community of the saved, in conversion to Christianity." For Madigan and Levenson, "there is indeed a counterpart in Paul to the duality of Israel and the nations in Judaism: it is the duality of the church and the world." They stress that "the earliest followers of Jesus, including Paul, understood themselves . . . as an *exclusive* community; they did not subscribe to anything remotely like modern religious pluralism."[46] It is crucial to distinguish, however, between "universalism" as the claim that all people *shall in fact* embrace Christian faith and "universalism" as the claim that all people *can in principle* embrace Christian faith. I fully grant that Paul and the early church did not affirm "universalism" in the first sense; they believed that there would be unconverted pagans and that such pagans would be condemned to destruction by God. The question of "universalism" in the second sense is more complicated.

A dozen New Testament texts refer to "the elect," but it is far from clear that membership here is predestined for all time by God, independent of history. Indeed, many texts suggest that membership in God's kingdom is open and mutable, dependent upon divine grace but also upon free human obedience. 2 Peter 1:4-7, for instance, states that, to become "participants of the divine nature," Christians "must make every effort to support your faith with goodness, and goodness with knowledge, and knowledge with self-control, and self-control with endurance, and endurance with godliness, and godliness with mutual affection, and mutual affection with love." God's merciful gift of

---

45. "Universality" is nearly a dirty word in some quarters, associated with the Enlightenment projects of foundationalist epistemology and traditionless politics. As I make clear throughout this book, I reject such an epistemology and politics, while yet finding meaning in Christ's form of universal love of neighbor.

46. See Kevin J. Madigan and Jon D. Levenson, *Resurrection: The Power of God for Jews and Christians* (New Haven and London: Yale University Press, 2008), pp. 32-33.

himself is the sine qua non, so this is not a prescription for works righteousness, but it does imply that God's favor is not fatalistic but rather something to be actively accepted — "confirmed," to use Peter's term. As it is put in 2 Peter 1:10-11: "Therefore, brothers and sisters, be all the more eager to confirm your call and election, for if you do this, you will never stumble. For in this way, entry into the eternal kingdom of our Lord and Savior Jesus Christ will be richly provided for you." Jesus' exasperated cry at Matthew 23:37 straightforwardly acknowledges the need for voluntary responsiveness to grace: "Jerusalem, Jerusalem, the city that kills the prophets and stones those who are sent to it! How often have I desired to gather your children together as a hen gathers her brood under her wings, and you were not willing!" An abundance of additional passages — for example, Matthew 28:19-20, Luke 2:29-32, John 3:16, Romans 3:24-31, 1 Corinthians 13:1-3, and Galatians 3:28 — indicates that the *invitation* to faith is extended to both Jews and Gentiles, that Christ died for *whoever* would hear his message and respond with faith, hope, and love. This amounts to an affirmation of "universalism" in the second sense.

Such an affirmation is critical because it rules out a static and arrogant contrast between those who are forever and by nature beloved by God (inevitably "us") and those who are forever and by nature "unchosen" (inevitably "them"). Madigan and Levenson themselves allow that, for Paul, "only by obeying and believing, and persisting in obedience and faith, does one merit the reward of resurrection and eternal salvation." For this very reason, they note, "the door to salvation within the saved community is always open."[47] Moderns might still be troubled, of course, by the traditional claim that one must explicitly confess Christ to be saved, but this is another matter. My present point is that once one grants the dynamic character of God's salvation — what might be called the growth and permeability of the body of Christ — the division between "the church" and "the world" must become far less dualistic.

V. The Audience of This Book and Prophetic Liberalism

I write explicitly for those committed to Christian faith *and* for anyone, religious or secular, who would evaluate how biblical virtues relate to political values, especially democratic values. I make no pretense of offering a neutral or merely procedural account of the nature or justification of political affiliation, an account that would putatively be persuasive to anyone and everyone worth

---

47. Madigan and Levenson, *Resurrection*, p. 34; see also p. 30.

talking to. In my view, any political vision that aims to be persuasive to all "rational" persons, regardless of their metaphysical beliefs or moral commitments, will be either vacuous or self-deceived (see chap. 4). There is no such "unencumbered" basis of the good polis; there is no escaping controversial truth claims that must be elaborated and defended to all comers. This does not mean that believers and nonbelievers should dogmatically shout at one another — much less that only Christians should be heard in the public square — but it does imply that all who participate in political debate should make explicit their antecedent premises and normative conclusions. Willingness to compromise and make common cause with those who disagree can be a virtue, but compromise and cooperation will themselves be founded on specific and substantive axiological principles — or else they are in want of integrity. In short, in politics, as in most other quarters of life, one must be prepared to explain what is being criticized or defended, and why.

A version of liberal democracy — *prophetic* liberalism — is worthy of Christian defense, just as the mature Abraham Lincoln merits cautious emulation. It is precisely because the Christian ideal of agapic love can find partial translation in liberal democratic principles and because Lincoln helped provide such a translation that I guardedly applaud both the principles and the president. Indeed, Lincoln's signal contribution was to highlight the limits of human aspiration and achievement and the correlative dangers of political self-righteousness and idolatry. Democracy, for him, was ultimately founded not on a universal capacity for autonomy or virtue, delineated by reason, but on our shared fallibility and vulnerability, discerned by charity. In the spirit of the later Lincoln, I hold that trying to ground political liberty and equality in universal rationality or merit is akin to thinking that the only flaw in class-based societies is their failure to see that *everyone* can be an aristocrat of the spirit, that *everyone* can be a domineering master if only of himself or herself. No, the problem for Lincoln, the problem that gave rise to the American Civil War itself, was not just *who* enjoyed liberty and equality but *how* these goods were conceived and defended. With the war, liberty could no longer mean simply popular sovereignty, and equality could no longer mean simply unmolested opportunity for advancement. Lincoln came to see American society, at its best, not as a collection of independent citizens pursuing their enlightened self-interest but rather as dependent creatures aware of their own sinfulness and need for the providential mercy of God.

To defend *prophetic* liberalism is to rebuke other forms of political economy, including other forms of liberal democracy. (As I maintain in chapter 3, contemporary liberalism is Christianity's "prodigal son," in spite of sectarian

attempts to deny paternity.) To accent human dependency and need over personal autonomy and achievement, for instance, is to shift the focus of much
liberal reflection from distributive justice to creative love. As paradoxical as it
may sound to modern ears, dependency and need are prophetic *values;* rather
than being mere obstacles or inconveniences to be lamented, they make human
compassion and *inter*dependence possible and so are to be celebrated. They remind us, most fundamentally, that true power is made perfect in weakness. This
is not to deny the ineliminable sadness that attends a fleshly existence subject to
pain and death, but it is to affirm that, by God's grace, such vulnerabilities can
be addressed courageously and corporately in love. (The cross of Christ is a picture of both human degradation and divine triumph.) The distinctively political
form of Christian love — Jesus' summary of the law echoed in Lincoln's "charity
for all" — is the foundation of and ordering measure for the otherwise quite
fractious social goods of liberty and equality. Without love of God and neighbor, liberty tends to become license and equality envy. The French Revolution
linked liberty and equality to "fraternity," which has resonances with "charity,"
but "fraternity" often connotes a solidarity limited to those like oneself. So an
expansive agapic love — fraternity and sorority with all men and women as
fellow creatures of God — is the needed corrective. Even justice, supposedly the
first political virtue, atrophies without agapic underpinnings, as I hope to show.

VI. The Challenge of Sheldon Wolin

Plato's Paradox

Before turning in the next section to some key definitions and etymologies, I
must face squarely an imposing challenge to the basic aspiration of this book.
That challenge is the life and work of Sheldon Wolin. Wolin is, in my estimation, the most cogent living critic of any effort to tie democratic governance
to eternal truth.[48] In his towering achievement, *Politics and Vision,* he traces
the problem back to the ancient Greeks and what he calls "Plato's paradox."
Let me begin by quoting four key passages from that text:

> [For Plato] political philosophy and ruling had as their objectives the cre-
> ation of the good society; "politics" was evil, and hence the task of philos-

---

48. Wolin has some obvious affinities with John Rawls, discussed in chapter 4, but
Wolin's magnum opus preceded Rawls's by eleven years.

ophy and ruling was to rid the community of politics. Thus the Platonic conception of political philosophy and ruling was founded on a paradox: the science as well as the art of creating order was sworn to an eternal hostility towards politics, towards those phenomena, in other words, that made such an art and science meaningful and necessary.[49]

> [The problem presented by anti-Platonists is] whether the political association has any necessary connection with an eternal truth; or, to say the same thing somewhat differently, whether the sustained pursuit of an ultimate truth does not of necessity destroy the peculiarly political quality of the association. (p. 47)

> The issue is not the existence of an immutable truth, nor whether men can make judgments derived from that source, but whether this kind of truth and judgment has any relevant connection to the special nature of the political association. (p. 55)

> In its political aspect, a community is held together not by truth but by consensus. . . . This gives to political judgments a character different from that of a "true" philosophical or theological proposition. . . . A political judgment, in other words, is "true" when it is public, not public when it accords to some standard external to politics. (p. 58)

In these and related quotes, Wolin emerges as the Einstein (or perhaps the Niels Bohr) of political theory who would relativize all absolute values and judgments.

Even though I am recommending a kind of "Copernican Revolution" in putting love rather than justice at the center of the social system, I am still operating within a Newtonian worldview, so to speak, inasmuch as I assume that there is an actual center and that it can be apprehended as such. I take the sun of God's love for the world and the earth of human needs and potentials to be realities that we discover, however fallibly, rather than invent. Wolin, on the other hand, suggests that there is no objective center to the moral universe and no privileged vantage point on the forever unfixed stars. At least in politics, there is neither transcendental divine Creator nor immanent human good

---

49. Sheldon S. Wolin, *Politics and Vision: Continuity and Innovation in Western Political Thought,* expanded ed. (Princeton and Oxford: Princeton University Press, 2004), p. 39. Page numbers to this work have been placed in the immediately following text.

that is the proper object of action or inquiry. There is no such object prior to the communal practices of negotiation and compromise that generate social consensus and commitment. As light is a wave or a particle, depending on how we measure it, so our political ends are relative to the means we employ to test and express them. Putting the point less cosmologically, politics is pragmatic all the way down, and democracy at its best celebrates this. It is the process that matters, not getting something right.

For Wolin, the effort to ground political decisions in permanent facts is not just irrelevant, it is also dangerous. He suggests at least four major hazards, which I paraphrase:

(1) Because the relevant political truths are supposedly already established, the Platonic account detaches the citizen from meaningful participation in communal decision-making (alienation of the ruled).

(2) Because a unified political vision is supposed to be handed down by those enlightened enough to comprehend it, leaders fail to practice the proper ruler's art, which is dialogue and consensus building (alienation of the ruler).

(3) Because the political vision is supposedly more-or-less complete, departures from it will be seen as heresies or sins and thus will be treated more harshly than honest disagreements ought to be, thus threatening the very unity that is to be preserved (tyranny).

(4) Rather than candidly admitting that the political community is a messy and sometimes violent context in which internal conflicts are resolved adversarially, Platonists view themselves as members of a "virtuous community devoid of conflict and, therefore, devoid of 'politics'" (self-delusion). (see pp. 52-62)

Wolin is admirably aware of Plato's concern over centralized political power, and he acknowledges Plato's "two entirely blameless aims, the good of the whole and the avoidance of tyranny" (p. 51). Wolin sides, nevertheless, with the anti-Platonists. The hazards of the Platonic republic are too great.

Wolin has some interesting things to say about *agape* and Christianity. He allows that "[Platonic] *eros* might bind philosophers together, but not them to the community, or the members of the community to each other. It required the Christian notion of *agape* before there could be an idea of love as a force binding together a community" (p. 52). He even associates the best or most authentic Christian political thinking with the rejection of classical utopianism: "The true Christian counterpart of the absolutely best societies projected by Plato and

Aristotle was to be found in Augustine's City of God. The ideal society existed beyond and not within history; it was a society transcendental, not empirical. The powerful hold that this idea was to gain over the Western imagination had the effect of etherealizing the old classic idea of the best society into the idea of the Kingdom of God" (p. 172). This overstates the extrahistorical nature of Augustine's Heavenly City, I believe: he repeatedly insists that it is *both* here *and* not yet, *both* present in inchoate form on earth *and* awaiting final fulfillment in heaven.[50] The salient point remains, however, that Wolin would surely characterize and reject political *agape* as "an architectonic vision," that is, "one wherein the political imagination attempts to mould the totality of political phenomena to accord with some vision of the Good that lies outside the political order."[51]

How does the political agapist respond to Professor Wolin? My answer requires that we go back and look at Plato's *Republic* and the analogies of the sun, the divided line, and the cave. A proper reading of those analogies, especially the allegory of the cave, provides the clue to seeing just how different Christian *agape* is from classical "Platonic *eros.*" This difference, in turn, gives us the resources to explain how civic agapism escapes what I have called Wolin's "four major hazards."

Socrates' Intimation of Christ, or How to Christianize Plato

Socrates spends much of his energy in *The Republic* convincing his interlocutors to affirm four related hierarchies — one ontological, one epistemological, one psychological, and one political:

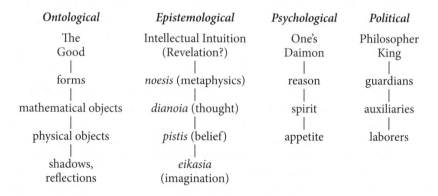

Ontological	*Epistemological*	*Psychological*	*Political*
The Good	Intellectual Intuition (Revelation?)	One's Daimon	Philosopher King
|	|	|	|
forms	*noesis* (metaphysics)	reason	guardians
|	|	|	|
mathematical objects	*dianoia* (thought)	spirit	auxiliaries
|	|	|	|
physical objects	*pistis* (belief)	appetite	laborers
|	|		
shadows, reflections	*eikasia* (imagination)		

50. See, for instance, *The City of God* 14.28, and book 15, passim.
51. Wolin, *Politics and Vision*, p. 19.

The types of beings in the world (ontology) correlate with the modes of their apprehension (epistemology), which correlate with the faculties of the soul (psychology), which correlate with the classes of society (politics). Each of these tiers being in its proper relation to all the others is definitive of justice *(dikaiosynē):* order in the cosmos, wisdom in speech,[52] health in the psyche, and harmony in the polis. Specific individuals are by nature suited to perform specific functions in society, even as specific elements of the soul are suited to specific psychological roles. It is not simply that division of labor tends to lead to political stability and economic efficiency, but rather that static psychic structures and social classes are in harmony with the universe and are therefore normative. Even as reason should rule over the spirited part of the soul and the appetite, so the philosophical guardians should rule over the militaristic auxiliaries and the hungering masses. (The Daimon I associate with the highest capability of reason, even as the philosopher king is selected from the auxiliaries.) When this hierarchical scheme is upset — when appetite controls the soul, say, or the masses govern society — there is incontinence and chaos. That is to say, there is injustice, things are not given their due.

One gets to be a philosopher first and foremost by schooling one's natural *eros. Eros* is defined by Diotima in *The Symposium* as "the desire to have the good forever,"[53] and that definition is applicable to *The Republic* as well. One disciplines *eros* by directing its love away from mutable, temporal things and toward stable, eternal ones. One moves from sensing physical objects, to reflecting on numbers and mathematical equations, to giving accounts in words *(logoi)* of the immaterial forms. Only the forms are incorruptible enough to satisfy the rational quest for permanence. The higher one goes in this ascent, the more one is in touch with reality and the more one realizes oneself, until, ultimately, one has an intellectual intuition of the Good, which is a sort of superform or metavalue. The Good is the creative source of all that is and is beyond *logos,* beyond discursive definition; it can only be apprehended in a kind of revelatory burst of insight.

Socrates' unforgettable elaboration of this process comes in the sun, divided line, and cave analogies. As the sun provides the energy that makes

---

52. More technically, Socrates identifies *noesis* and *dianoia* together as *epistēmē* (knowledge), since their objects are intelligible and stable enough to form justified true propositions about; he identifies *pistis* and *eikasia* together as *doxa* (opinion), since their objects are sensible and "roll around between being and non-being." One can't really know material things, since they are so changeable that no reliable fact about or definition of them is stateable.

53. Plato, *The Symposium,* trans. Christopher Gill (London: Penguin Books, 1999), 206a, p. 43.

earthly things visible and makes them grow, it is a metaphor for the transcendent Good that illuminates the intelligible world. To explain the great chain of being, Socrates offers the divided line analogy, wherein the intelligible is distinguished from the visible. Most central for my purposes, however, is the cave analogy presented to Glaucon:

> "Next, then," I [Socrates] said, "make an image of our nature in its education and want of education, likening it to a condition of the following kind. See human beings as though they were in an underground cave-like dwelling with its entrance, a long one, open to the light across the whole width of the cave. They are in it from childhood with their legs and necks in bonds so that they are fixed, seeing only in front of them, unable because of the bond to turn their heads all the way around. Their light is from a fire burning far above and behind them. Between the fire and the prisoners there is a road above, along which see a wall, built like the partitions puppet-handlers set in front of the human beings and over which they show the puppets."
>
> "I see," he said.
>
> "Then also see along this wall human beings carrying all sorts of artifacts, which project above the wall, and statues of men and other animals wrought from stone, wood, and every kind of material; as is to be expected, some of the carriers utter sounds while others are silent."
>
> "It's a strange image," he said, "and strange prisoners you're telling of."
>
> "They're like us," I said. "For in the first place, do you suppose such men would have seen anything of themselves and one another other than the shadows cast by the fire on the side of the cave facing them?"[54]

As Socrates observes, "such men would hold that the truth is nothing other than the shadows of artificial things."[55]

Socrates then asks Glaucon to imagine what deliverance from this plight would look like: first, a man who is released from his bonds turns around and looks up to the light from the cave-fire; then the same man is dragged out of the cave altogether and into the light of the sun. Initially, in both instances, the man would be blinded and disoriented, but eventually he would become accustomed to his new circumstances and see more and more clearly. Eventually, he would apprehend "what's up above": "things in heaven and heaven

---

54. Plato, *The Republic* 7.514a-515a, p. 193.
55. Plato, *The Republic* 515c, p. 194.

itself," including the sun.[56] After this deliverance, the man would "consider himself happy for the change and pity the others," but Socrates nevertheless demands that he go back down into the cave, to rule as a philosopher king:

> "So you must go down, each in his turn, into the common dwelling of the others and get habituated along with them to seeing the dark things. And, in getting habituated to it, you will see ten thousand times better than the men there, and you'll know what each of the phantoms is, and of what it is a phantom, because you have seen the truth about fair, just, and good things. And thus, the city will be governed by us and by you in a state of waking, not in a dream as the many cities nowadays are governed by men who fight over shadows with one another and form factions for the sake of ruling, as though it were some great good."[57]

In spite of Socrates' heartfelt plea, it has been a puzzlement for almost 2,400 years why the philosopher who has transcended mere opinion, known abstract ideas, and ultimately intuited the Good would go back down into the realm of ignorance and falsity. What could be the motive? To engage in politics is presumably to be mired again in the delusion and strife connected to absorption in changeable matter and contact with the lower classes. Socrates is insistent that the philosopher must be *compelled* to go back down and assist his fellow citizens in chains. But everything he has said previously makes that notion seem unintelligible. Why not kick away the dialectical ladder, why not flee the darkness and forever revel in the sunlight of truth? If you go back down to "the world," you will dirty your hands and likely lose your peace of mind. In fact, the more seriously one takes the correlation of the ontological, epistemological, and psychological hierarchies, the less likely to be realized is the political one. Cosmic reality, philosophical wisdom, and psychic wellness seem to conspire to make political justice impossible. The just man will not, should not, be concerned about the just city. *Indeed, the Platonic philosopher should no more care about empirical contingencies and inferior classes than does the Gnostic who has been enlightened about the evils of time and body, than does the Augustinian who has been elected by God out of "the mass of perdition,"[58] or than does the sectarian Christian who has turned his back on the violent world.*

---

56. Plato, *The Republic* 516a-516b, p. 195.

57. Plato, *The Republic* 520c-520d, p. 199.

58. Augustine, *On the Grace of Christ, and On Original Sin*, in *Nicene and Post-Nicene Fathers*, ed. Philip Schaff, vol. 5 (Grand Rapids: Eerdmans, 1971), 2.36, p. 250.

Wolin emphasizes that philosophy undoes politics, but the fact that politics undoes philosophy is the flip side of "Plato's paradox." There is no solution to this conundrum, I believe, unless we reinterpret the Platonic analogies and finally understand the religious font of Socratic altruism. I take my cue from the fact that *The Republic* is theologically bookended: it begins with Socrates having gone "down to the Piraeus" with Glaucon "to pray to the goddess," and it ends with Socrates hoping with Glaucon that the "tale" just related might "save us" "so that we shall be friends to ourselves and the gods."[59] Allan Bloom reads Socrates as ultimately a skeptic who means to show the limits of political theory, the impossibility of apprehending and applying the Good, "the dangers of what we would call utopianism."[60] According to Bloom's Socrates, who sounds very much like Sheldon Wolin, "striving for the perfectly just city puts unreasonable and despotic demands on ordinary men, and it abuses and misuses the best men."[61] I, in contrast, conclude that Socrates has himself had an intellectual intuition of the Good and has gone down into the agora (a.k.a. the cave) to share his vision with his benighted fellow citizens. He has completed the upward path of dialectic, and he is now embodying the downward. He is trying to found a just city, even as, in his day, Jesus was trying to inaugurate the kingdom of God. Socrates is no naïve idealist, but neither is he a skeptic: "it is hard for it [just lawgiving] to come to be; not, however, impossible."[62] He knows he will probably be killed for his actions,[63] and his motive is as opaque as that of the philosopher king. Why again the self-sacrificial giving?

The answer is induced by Adeimantus's question: "there is something yet greater than justice and the other things we went through?"[64] "*There is . . . something greater,*"[65] Socrates replies, and he proceeds to elaborate the Good in terms of the sun, the divided line, and the cave. Though seemingly obsessed with justice and *eros,* Socrates realizes that they are ultimately dependent on something higher and more divine. The Socratic Good is what the Christian tradition calls God, and it makes possible a new kind of love: what Christianity

---

59. Plato, *The Republic* 1.327a, p. 3; and 10.621c-621d, p. 303.

60. Allan Bloom, "Interpretive Essay," in his translation of *The Republic,* p. 410.

61. Bloom, "Interpretive Essay," p. 410.

62. Plato, *The Republic* 6.502c, p. 182.

63. "If they were somehow able to get their hands on and kill the man who attempts to release and lead up, wouldn't they kill him?" Socrates asks (*The Republic* 7.517a, p. 196). Plato is, of course, writing this after Socrates has been sentenced to death and has drunk the hemlock.

64. Plato, *The Republic* 6.504d, p. 184.

65. Plato, *The Republic* 6.504d, p. 184. I add the emphasis here, noting that these words from Socrates could stand as the watchword of my entire text.

calls *agape*. *Eros* is a child of Resource and Poverty,[66] inventing ways of seizing what it lacks, whereas *agape* is possessed of Plenitude and Power, bestowing worth on others. Plato does not make this as explicit as one would wish, but when the just man or woman cares about others beyond their merit or demerit, he or she ceases to be merely just and becomes universally loving. This reorienting of the self to reality and society is inspired and empowered by the kenotic nature of the Good itself. The Absolute Good makes possible relative goods that can be appreciated for their own sakes.

Consider once more the divided line analogy. To clarify his ontology and the transcendent power of the Good, Socrates invites Glaucon to "take a line cut in two unequal segments, one for the class that is seen, the other for the class that is intellected — and go on and cut each segment in the same ratio." Further instructions are forthcoming, and the fully detailed image that emerges is traditionally depicted as:

The Good

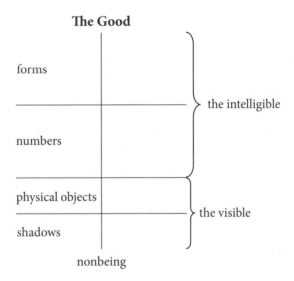

nonbeing

Here the line — more accurately, the line segment — is drawn vertically, with the Good and nonbeing as the end points. This captures nicely Socrates' usual hierarchical accent. Robert Fogelin has pointed out, however, that nothing in Socrates' directions to Glaucon precludes him or us from drawing the line horizontally, with the Good above and off the line, rather than as a limit.[67]

---

66. Plato, *The Symposium* 203b, p. 39.

67. Robert Fogelin, "Three Platonic Analogies," *Philosophical Review* 80, no. 3 (1971): 371-82.

Such a reading actually dovetails better with Socrates' insistence that the Good is "beyond *logos*," and it generates a rather different image of reality:

The Good

forms	numbers	objects	shadows

One might even interpret the line as the edge of a plane extending behind it, with the Good as the infinite source from which the plane radiates. The crucial paradigm shift in this case is that now the Good is equidistant vertically from all forms of being. I believe that this vision becomes increasingly self-conscious in Socrates after he apprehends the Good and descends into the agora. After he has been touched by divine grace and has acted on this revelation publicly, his static ontological hierarchies, his unpoetic denigration of the soul's nonrational faculties, and his obnoxious class distinctions all begin to crumble. Otherwise, to repeat, the enlightened thinker would have no motive to go back down into the cave; politics would undo philosophy. Like the Bodhisattva, the liberated Athenian goes back down to sufferers with a deepening sense of solidarity. We are all one in relation to and dependency on the Good, and we ought to be moved by gratitude to fellowship with each other. On the upward path, compassion and other strong emotions can be a distraction that keeps us awash in worldly concerns, and one is inclined to emphasize the transcendence of the Good and the relative purity of the forms. (After all, one must meet average citizens where they are and wake them from their slumber in the sensual.) On the downward path, however, social emotions are indispensable to political virtue. They are what break down fixed ontologies, false psychologies, and alienating societies.[68]

---

68. Martha Nussbaum is especially helpful in appreciating how much the later Plato, especially in *Phaedrus*, redeems emotion as an epistemic means to important truths. See especially Nussbaum, *The Fragility of Goodness* (Cambridge: Cambridge University Press, 1986); *Love's Knowledge* (Oxford: Oxford University Press, 1990); and *The Therapy of Desire* (Princeton: Princeton University Press, 1994). Nussbaum first brought my attention to the puzzle of the philosopher's decision to rule in *The Republic*. In a Yale graduate philosophy symposium in the late 1970s, she confessed she could not explain it. I took this as a challenge, and it has occupied me for some thirty-five years.

Liberal Introduction

Answer to Wolin

Plato and Wolin both worry about tyranny, but they differ on what is most likely to bring it about. Plato's chief political fear is *factionalism,*[69] *the chaotic breakdown of order* due to competing interest groups that fail to see and act on the common good. Wolin's chief political fear is *coercion,*[70] *the dogmatic imposition of order* due to the concentration of power in one interest group that fails to see and act for the common good. Plato's safeguard against factionalism is a philosophical justice that equates truth with a hierarchy of parts of the soul and of classes of the polis, each doing its own set job. Wolin's safeguard against coercion is a pragmatic justice that rejects large truth claims about self and society, especially inegalitarian ones, in favor of participatory government. "Democracy" is Plato's worst fear realized because it entails rule by the volatile and easily beguiled masses — masses that are inevitably seduced by a tyrannical strongman who cares only for himself or his clan, rather than the body politic. For Wolin, (genuine) "democracy" is the antidote to his worst fear because it entails rule by the widest range of individuals and groups that will check the powers (e.g., money and arms) and debunk the abstractions (e.g., philosophy and bureaucracy) that tend to lead to tyranny.

Wolin's concern over the tyranny of big money/big business, on the one hand, and Big Brother/big government, on the other, leads him increasingly to contrast "liberalism" or "managed democracy" with "egalitarianism" or "pure democracy." Over time, various oppositions become more and more pronounced for him, and I register them below, often in my own terms:

"Liberalism's" Values and Principles
(1) liberty/autonomy
(2) individual dignity
(3) rationality
(4) personal rights based on self-interest/merit
(5) rule by qualified elites
(6) checks and balances among competing powers
(7) periodic elections of public officials or representatives

"Democracy's" Values and Principles
(1) equality/membership
(2) individual sanctity
(3) empathy
(4) human rights based on need/potential
(5) local populist participation by all
(6) shared power
(7) constant direct action by private citizens

69. Plato, *The Republic* 5.464e, p. 144.
70. Wolin, *Politics and Vision*, pp. 279-81.

(8) the common good as double effect   (8) the common good as key motive

(9) free markets   (9) regulated markets

(10) "capitalism"   (10) "socialism"

These contrasts are edifying, yet they carry with them a colossal irony. The very problems that Wolin identifies with managed democracy in *Democracy Incorporated* (2008) — including an "inverted totalitarianism" in which economics subverts politics — are symptomatic of the purely procedural account of politics that he gave in *Politics and Vision* (1960, expanded 2004). Wolin passionately laments: "When the claims and needs of the economy trump the political, and bring in their wake strikingly unequal rewards and huge disparities in wealth and power, inequality trumps democratic egalitarianism."[71] But, having previously denied himself a normative leg to stand on in politics, his indictments collapse into mere name-calling. I share his dislike of American "imperialism," domestic and foreign, but his political vision does not allow this dislike to be anything other than aesthetic.

A thoroughly pragmatic view of politics wherein there is no God, human nature, or common good independent of political processes will itself inevitably collapse into factionalism and power mongering. When we can no longer appeal to an overarching vision of truth, goodness, and beauty that explains and harmonizes our various social roles and responsibilities, market and military mechanisms must overwhelm the political and moral-cultural spheres of life.[72] Profit and utility reign: corporations buy politicians and sell armies, even as politicians buy elections and sell wars. Plato's dread of oligarchy and timarchy is realized.[73] Wolin wants to distinguish between elite democracy and pure democracy, or between "liberalism" and "true democracy," with the former being a perversion of the latter. But how can he talk of the "perversion" of democracy when it has no content or nature beyond convention?

When what Wolin calls "liberal" emphases float free of or overwhelm what he calls "democracy," one gets the valorization of self-interest and possessive individualism. But what holds his "democratic" emphases in check when they float free of "liberal" ones and degenerate into groupthink and the tyranny of the majority? The tensions between liberty and equality have been recognized for millennia. Free markets and meritarian conceptions of justice

71. Sheldon S. Wolin, *Democracy Incorporated* (Princeton: Princeton University Press, 2008), pp. 91-92.

72. Cf. Daniel Bell, *The Cultural Contradictions of Capitalism* (New York: Basic Books, 1976).

73. Plato, *The Republic* 8.544b-549a, pp. 222-26.

typically lead to radical inequality and even disenfranchisement for some, but regulated markets and egalitarian conceptions of justice typically lead to centralization and sameness. I see no hope of reconciling these dual accents, such that they become mutually supportive and corrective, without some truthful account of the limits of human liberty and the grounds of human equality. This is the domain of metaphysics and morality.

Wolin divorces (democratic) politics too completely from metaphysical and moral truth, associating it with process and consensus; through much of *The Republic,* Plato weds (just) politics too completely to a static set of metaphysical and moral hierarchies, largely ignoring process and consensus; but Socrates eventually hints at a (prophetic) *tertium quid* in which both theory and practice matter. Socrates helps us see that action, especially in community, is not merely a way of *expressing* knowledge or of *communicating* belief; it is a way of *acquiring* knowledge and of *testing* belief. Socratic action is a means of philosophizing. Socrates' apprehension of the Good is not simply a cognitive experience that leaves untouched his prior perspective on the world, himself, and other people. As I maintained above, revelation of the Good converts and transforms him, allowing him to see all persons and things as participants in the true, the good, and the beautiful. Thus his "aristocratic" vision is rendered much more egalitarian and respectful of contingency and freedom.[74] The Good, a.k.a. God, is the animating force, a force that stoops to meet us more than we rise to grasp it. At crucial points, we can only wait, pray, and be grateful. So Socrates himself sows the seeds of overcoming the erotic and eudaimonic traditions that he and Plato are credited with helping found.

Insofar as the Good is beyond words, Socrates is a religious mystic trying to eff the ineffable. (Of the cave parable, he sighs: "A god doubtless knows if it happens to be true. At all events, this is the way the phenomena look to me.")[75] But what Socrates intimates of the Good is true of what Søren Kierkegaard says of Christ, and vice versa: "We human beings want to look upward in order to look for the object of perfection (although the direction is continually toward the unseen), but in Christ perfection looked down to earth and loved the person it saw."[76] In the end, Socratic theology harmonizes philosophy, politics,

74. If you doubt the epistemic significance of social action, muse on the fact that the most integrated and least racist group on any given Sunday in America is an NFL football team rather than a Christian church.

75. Plato, *The Republic* 7.517b, p. 196.

76. Søren Kierkegaard, *Works of Love,* trans. Howard V. Hong and Edna H. Hong (Princeton: Princeton University Press, 1995), p. 174.

and economics — or at least it aspires to — by subordinating them all to a divine charity. Such charity provides the motive for reentering the cave, and, "at all events," it is political *agape*'s answer to Sheldon Wolin as well.

VII. Key Definitions and Etymologies

Let me at last define some key terms in my title. *Agape* is the gracious love of God for the world, incarnate in Christ and to be communicated freely to one's neighbors. Understood interpersonally, *agape* has three main features: (1) unconditional willing of the good for the other, (2) equal regard for the well-being of the other, and (3) passionate service open to self-sacrifice for the sake of the other.[77] So defined, *agape* does not represent an algorithmic decision procedure or remove all conflict of values from the world. On the contrary, even Christlike love must be disconsoled away from dogmatism and a too facile view of the nature and attainability of human happiness, either individual or communal.[78] *Agape* does provide a means, however, of living together with uncertainty and tragedy but without injustice or despair.

To elaborate the meaning of "prophetic liberalism" — in contradistinction from other ideas of liberalism, including Wolin's — two etymological digressions are in order. I treat first the English word "liberal," which encrypts many problems and prospects. "Liberal" has its root in the Latin term *liber,* meaning "free," and in modern political contexts "liberal" often connotes a commitment to "unrestrained" or "unrestricted" speech and action. But *liber* also originally meant "worthy of a free man," so "liberal" came at times to mean "pertaining to or suitable to persons of superior social station." (It could even imply such aloofness from public decorum as to equal "licentious.") Hence "liberal" can imply the opposite of civil egalitarianism (not everyone is free). On the other hand, Latin *liber* also meant "bountiful," "generous," and "open-hearted," suggesting a "liberalism" that is "free in bestowing" good.[79] It is this last sense of "liberal" that political *agape* takes as normative and upon which it builds, even as it guards against the invidious tendencies

---

77. For detailed elaboration and defense of this account, see my *Love Disconsoled: Meditations on Christian Charity* (Cambridge: Cambridge University Press, 1999) and *The Priority of Love: Christian Charity and Social Justice* (Princeton: Princeton University Press, 2003).

78. See Jackson, *Love Disconsoled,* chap. 5.

79. *The Compact Edition of the Oxford English Dictionary,* vol. 1 (Oxford: Oxford University Press, 1971), p. 1612. See also Charlton T. Lewis and Charles Short, *A Latin Dictionary* (New York: Oxford University Press, 1987), pp. 1056-57, especially on *liber* as connoting "not a slave."

of unconstrained freedom. Such freedom can indeed become haughty and promiscuous, so at times *prophetic* liberalism must object to other forms of "liberalism" as prodigal. Again, a prodigal liberalism takes liberty for license and construes equality exclusively in terms of achieved dignity rather than shared sanctity.

For my purposes, "liberalism" is short for "liberal democracy," and liberal democracy is standardly committed to two central goods: (1) liberty and (2) equality. Some theorists associate liberalism with additional tenets — such as distributive justice, natural rights, the separation of powers, the protection of minorities[80] — but my assumption is that liberal accounts of justice, rights, etc., are, *au fond,* summaries of how liberty and equality are defined and related. Virtually any political philosophy or theology will offer some perspective on justice and rights, even if this perspective is highly critical, but what is typically *distinctive* about liberalism is its center-staging of liberty and equality as positive values. The precise meaning and content of liberty and equality will become apparent, I trust, as I proceed. But I would emphasize at the outset that to standard pictures of liberalism I add the governing role of an overarching third value: charity, a.k.a. *agape.* Charity, as I conceive it, is a supernatural virtue — inspired by God and directed from God to the neighbor — and thus is lexically prior to democracy and its political agendas. Charity can be strengthened by democratic practices, but it has a deeper root than liberty and equality and is the necessary condition for their full and proper realization.[81] Indeed, placing liberty and equality under the sovereignty of charity transforms these goods and makes for a distinctively *prophetic* brand of liberalism. Putting the main point another way, secular forms of liberalism tend to interpret and interrelate liberty and equality in terms of dignity and interest-based rights (a.k.a. duties of justice), while prophetic liberalism interprets and interrelates liberty and equality in terms of sanctity and need-based rights (a.k.a. duties of love).

It might seem odd to talk about *agape* being or implying a "duty." Doesn't this force as a political requirement what is in fact a gift of the Holy Spirit?[82] Isn't this to limit God and violate conscience? The appearance of oddity disappears, however, when we realize two things: (1) *Agape* is equiv-

---

80. John Kekes, for his part, writes that "the basic liberal values may . . . be identified as pluralism, freedom, rights, equality, and distributive justice." See Kekes, *Against Liberalism* (Ithaca, N.Y., and London: Cornell University Press, 1997), p. 4.

81. As I argue in *The Priority of Love,* agapic love is a metavalue without which other human goods cannot be properly understood or experienced.

82. My Emory colleague, Philip Reynolds, has urged this question on me.

alent to "charity," not in the modern sense of supererogatory philanthropy but in the biblical sense of love of God and neighbor. (2) The grace necessary for embodying love of God and neighbor is freely offered by the Creator to all human creatures, at every moment. The offer does not causally necessitate charity, but it does morally obligate it. Liberty of conscience comes in the decision to accept or reject divine grace, not in the option of being without political responsibility.

Now for the second digression, on the "prophetic." The etymology of the English word "prophecy" is from the Greek prefix *pro* and the root of *phanai*. *Pro* is often translated as "before" and *phanai* as "to speak," thus implying that prophecy is a "speaking before [the fact]" — that is, a fore-telling of the future. This interpretation of the term, then, equates prophecy with prediction — from the Latin *prae* (before) plus *dicere* (to speak). In contrast, as I use the term, a use informed by Hebrew-Christian Scripture, the prophetic may involve an element of prediction, but this is secondary to its deeper meaning. Biblical prophecy focuses on eternity rather than time, or, rather, it seeks to perceive and respond to temporal realities through the eternal perspective and power of God. Biblically understood, the prophetic is that which discerns and conveys the righteous will of God, rather than that which forecasts the future. This discernment and conveyance can entail pronouncements on things to come, to be sure, but the main thrust is present prescription rather than future prediction. Biblical prophecy frequently takes the form of a conditional warning — "If you do not repent and heed the law of God, calamity will befall you" — but the point is to confront listeners with the injunction "You shall be holy, for I the LORD your God am holy" (Lev. 19:2), rather than to "haruspicate or scry."[83] Moreover, there is seldom, if ever, divine determinism involved; there is usually, perhaps always, human responsibility and room to maneuver before God's just judgment. As Jeremiah recounts the word of the Lord, "It may be that they [the cities of Judah] will listen, all of them, and will turn from their evil way, that I may change my mind about the disaster that I intend to bring on them because of their evil doings" (Jer. 26:3).

In effect, biblical texts take the *pro* in the "prophetic" to mean "for" or "in support of" — instead of "before" or "in advance of" — thus implying that prophecy is a "speaking on behalf of [God]." Most characteristically, the Old Testament prophets speak for God by enjoining fair dealings with and compassionate support for those whom God cherishes, especially the weak and vulnerable: the widow and the orphan and the stranger and the downtrodden.

---

83. To borrow a phrase from T. S. Eliot, "The Dry Salvages," in *The Four Quartets*.

> Seek justice,
>> rescue the oppressed,
> defend the orphan,
>> plead for the widow,

says Isaiah 1:17, even as Jeremiah 22:3 commands, "Do no wrong or violence to the alien, the orphan, and the widow, or shed innocent blood in this place." (Compare Lincoln's summoning the nation, in his Second Inaugural, "to care for him who shall have borne the battle, and for his widow, and his orphan" — a clear echo of Hebrew righteousness.) Jeremiah is particularly vehement in calling for divine punishment and in relaying divine threats, suggesting that God has withdrawn his steadfast love and mercy (16:5) and abrogated his original covenant with Israel and Judah (31:32), but even Jeremiah vindicates God's fidelity in the end, promising that God will "make a new covenant" with Israel and write his law "on their hearts" (31:31-34). In the New Testament, Jesus explicitly identifies himself with the hungry, the poor, the vulnerable, and the marginalized: "just as you did it to one of the least of these my brothers, you did it to me" (Matt. 25:40). And he emphatically discounts claims to temporal foreknowledge, both for others and for himself: "Keep awake therefore, for you know neither the day nor the hour," he tells the foolish bridesmaids (Matt. 25:13), and on the end of the world he declares, "about that day and hour no one knows, neither the angels of heaven, nor the Son, but only the Father" (Matt. 24:36).

Even as the biblical prophet is no Delphic oracle, so the prophetic liberal is no worshiper of the Statue of Liberty. A Christian does not love the neighbor because she wants to make democracy work; rather, she wants to make democracy work because she is first loved by God and because she wants to extend the favor to neighbors who need her love both personally and politically (1 John 4:7-12). Rather than being a distraction from or a remote tag-on to politics, then, *agape* must bear on all dimensions of how we live together. Otherwise, it ceases to be the last commandment of Jesus (John 13:34-35) and the first virtue of Paul (1 Cor. 13:13). That said, the critique and defense of liberty and equality is a work of love that sanctifies rather than a gift of faith that justifies. Again, no political creed or social organization justifies — that is, saves — us before God, but those saved by God's grace will tend to work for a prophetic form of liberalism, I believe.

More specifically, strong agapists understand liberty in the light of charity, and so construe it not as autonomy but as theonomy. Rather than accenting self-sufficiency and personal control, as advocates of many secular forms of liberalism do, they make obedience to God and service to the neighbor central to true freedom. Strong agapists also view equality through the lens of love, and so locate its basis not in abstract rational agency (a.k.a. "dignity") but in embodied need and potential (a.k.a. "sanctity"). As I argue at length in chapter 2, the only sense in which human beings really are equal is in their need to receive and potential ability to give agapic love. This feature constitutes the very image of God and is shared by all human beings, including (perhaps especially) "the least of these." Finally, as important as is absence of external coercion (negative liberty), to give and receive *agape* is to be internally empowered (positive liberty).[84] This empowerment is an essential aim of political life, though persons of good faith can disagree on the question of means.

Those who are fearful of big government will object to my phrase "political *agape*," seeing it as a temptation to paternalism. Justice attentive to contract and merit should be the foundational concern of political life, it will be maintained, with love's focus on needs and potentials being left to personal conscience and private associations. There is no doubt a place for *agape* as a *civic* virtue — practiced by synagogues and churches, families and fraternal organizations — but the state and its *political* use of coercive (even violent) force should confine itself to *jus.* Otherwise, we will be concentrating power in dangerous and unwarranted ways: Big Brother as cultural hegemon. Reasonable disagreement over the existence of God and the nature of the good life, together with the responsibility of autonomous individuals to cultivate their own gardens, should preclude liberalism from aspiring to the prophetic, the argument runs. For a host of reasons, nonetheless, I decline to draw such a stark contrast between the political and the civil, especially if this means associating the former exclusively with rational justice and rights and the latter exclusively with prophetic love and service.[85]

I readily grant that "civil society," broadly construed, involves agencies, affiliations, and agendas wider than those associated with local and national government (i.e., the nation-state), even as I appreciate that some define "the political" with narrow reference to governmental power. In my lexicon, however, the ranges of the quoted phrases are not so discontinuous: the political is not synonymous with the governmental, but questions of how to interpret and structure civil society are *political* questions. More to the point, I am a proponent of the principle of subsidiarity — letting the social group or organization closest to a problem handle its solution — and by no means am

84. Compare Isaiah Berlin, *Four Essays on Liberty* (Oxford: Oxford University Press, 1969).

85. Rick Garnett has pressed me on the civil versus political distinction.

I recommending a return to theocracy. The meeting of human needs and the cultivation of human potentials are political mandates, for Christians and non-Christians alike, but the state is not the only (or even the primary) means to these ends. Moreover, religious affiliation or ordination is not a precondition for either citizenship or public office. To set such a precondition would violate the respect for individual conscience and the wariness of institutional dogmatism and elitism at the heart of political *agape*. That said, some political issues cannot be adequately addressed independently of the state, and, in turn, the state's rationale in handling such issues ought not to be divorced from love of neighbor. I discuss in this volume euthanasia, capital punishment, gay marriage, and adoption rights exactly because these are inescapably moral, ecclesial, *and* legal matters that require *agape* for their proper handling. This, at any rate, is the thesis I mean to elaborate and defend.

I defend a version of liberalism as "morally perfectionist," thus contrasting it with morally-empty and morally-basic varieties (see chap. 3). The language of "perfectionism" must not be misunderstood, however. I am not advocating a democratic utopianism that presumes that the human can be transformed in time into the angelic.[86] (Marx's classless society, no longer subject to conflict or in need of authority, is but one of a line of "democratic" delusions.) Prophetic liberalism upholds charity as a political ideal, but it also assumes that sinfulness and finitude are human universals that keep the ideal from being fully realized in this life. Indeed, charity is politically necessary precisely because of the recalcitrance of sin and error and the ubiquity of need and vulnerability. In the twentieth century, Reinhold Niebuhr was one of the most insistent voices reminding us that the worm in human nature goes deeper than any cultural, political, or technological revolution can entirely uproot.[87] In the nineteenth century, a similar role was admirably played by Nathaniel Hawthorne: "How sad a truth, if truth it were, that man's agelong endeavor for perfection had served only to render him the mockery of the evil principle, from the fatal circumstance of an error at the very root of the matter! The heart, the heart, — there was the little yet boundless sphere wherein

---

86. Such utopianism is what Patrick J. Deneen has called "democratic faith," a position he contrasts with a "democratic realism" that affirms insuperable limits to human achievement and indispensable checks on state power. See Deneen, *Democratic Faith* (Princeton: Princeton University Press, 2005). I am a "realist," in Deneen's sense.

87. See, for instance, Reinhold Niebuhr, *Moral Man and Immoral Society* (1932; New York: Scribner, 1960); *Interpretation of Christian Ethics* (1935; New York: Seabury Press, 1979); and *The Children of Light and the Children of Darkness: A Vindication of Democracy and a Critique of Its Traditional Defense* (1944; New York: Scribner, 1960).

existed the original wrong of which the crime and misery of this outward world were merely types."[88] In the twenty-first century, political *agape* may yet champion a positive image of the good life in community, but it is always mindful that the cross is the central (though not the only) symbol of love's way with and in the world.

VIII. Love and Justice

"Self-love, my liege, is not so vile a sin as self-neglecting." So says Shakespeare's Dauphin to the king of England, just prior to the Battle of Agincourt,[89] and a basic political philosophy is suggested by the utterance. A leader's first obligation is to praise and preserve the nation (as himself), according to many theorists, and these actions must be ever guided by rational self-interest. Competing interests, both within and between nations, must be adjudicated by distributive and retributive justice, but such justice is finally hand in glove with political prudence. As noted, however, prophetic liberalism stands athwart this vision and gives priority to love. A central challenge to my alternative picture is to explain how Christian charity may rise above, without subverting, strict justice.[90] The most daunting task here is to defend the ways in which Christian liberalism accepts the qualified need for sacrifice and suffering in political life. Willing, but not uncritical, openness to pain and loss for a greater good is implied by the cross of Christ, and talk of this openness is often hooted off the public stage as morbid or unrealistic. But, in fact, a good society is unthinkable without compassion, service, forgiveness, and other forms of charity; and, taken seriously, the priority of love has major public policy implications.[91]

88. Nathaniel Hawthorne, "Earth's Holocaust," in *Mosses from an Old Manse* (1846; New York: Modern Library, 2003), pp. 319-20. Hawthorne was well aware of the perils of an overactive conscience, leading to a flamboyant (even proud) sense of guilt in oneself or a cruel (if technically truthful) condemnation of others. In "Egotism; or, The Bosom Serpent," in this same collection, Hawthorne even anticipates Niebuhr's famous description of Christlike love as "an impossible possibility" — Hawthorne contending that self-forgetfulness is "a remedy for . . . loathsome evil" yet "an impossible one" (p. 223). But perhaps the most perfect story in *Mosses*, "The Birthmark," is unsurpassed as an allegory of the limits of modern science and the destructiveness of naïve good will.

89. William Shakespeare, *Henry V*, act 2, scene 4, line 74.

90. For more on this dynamic, see my *The Priority of Love*, esp. chap. 1.

91. Glenn Tinder has memorably described acceptance of suffering as part of "the ordeal of liberty" (see his "The Ordeal of Liberty" [unpublished ms.], pp. 323-25). I prefer to call it "a gift of charity," especially since liberty, as such, has no inherent telos and may decline costly

(If "liberalism" is merely about leaving citizens to have fun or be happy, then Christianity can have nothing to do with it.) The prophetic voice in Christian politics will always insist on the priority of faith, hope, and love to any particular party or political economy, and it will make sure that service to others remains consensual and constructive. (Neither masochism nor profligacy is a theological virtue.) But individual integrity and public-spiritedness are mainstays of the democratic tradition itself, at its best, and that tradition is funded as well as checked by Christlike love.

If Jesus, betrayed to the Roman cross, and Lincoln in the midst of an American Civil War could preach love of God and neighbor ahead of all else, then contemporary politics need not and *ought not* be divorced from that virtue. *Both Jesus and Lincoln upheld human justice by highlighting its limits and dependence on divine love.* Jesus' incarnation of God's grace justified sinners in ways that forever transcend politics, yet his refusal of zealotry and tribalism, in favor of forgiveness and the universal fatherhood of God, nevertheless has political implications. Lincoln acted on some of these implications, ultimately preserving the Union by tying both constitutional government and equal liberty to an inclusive charity. Put more technically, *both Jesus and Lincoln replaced an appraisive* eros *with a kenotic* agape *as the first social virtue.* The thrust of prophetic liberalism, in turn, is to supplant an *erotic democracy* that emphasizes justice and human dignity with an *agapic democracy* that accents love and human sanctity. This is not to belittle fairness, autonomy, and reason — the values bequeathed to us by ancient Athens — but it is to appreciate their dependence on Jerusalem's gifts of faith, theonomy, and compassion. Socrates himself saw that rational self-interest is not enough for good character, good government, or good civil society, and character, government, and society are all the concerns of Christian love. Let me be even more specific.

In the post-9/11 world, both religious faith and political democracy in America are in jeopardy, as much from within as from without. The threats of terrorism are real and must be responded to with vigor, but one need only mention the tortures of Abu Ghraib, the curtailing of civil rights by the Patriot Act, the deficit spending of a highly militarized budget, the broad disregard for international law, and the rhetorical arrogance of administrations at war to feel that a prophetic word is needed to return us to some basic truths. The word, need I say, is not mine but Scripture's. The liberal values of equality

---

help to others. Freedom, political and personal, is a great intrinsic good. It is a necessary but not a sufficient condition for civic virtue, however.

and liberty are socially salient, but they are subordinate to a faith, hope, and love that transcends and transforms — that is, judges — them. Without that prophetic transcendence, our country seems poised to become victim to the age-old irony of war: the very goods, material and moral, that we aim to defend are undermined by the means and ends adopted in that defense. Again, *agape* is not embraced because it is a tool of the nation-state; rather, *agape* is and always will be political to the extent that it holds the state, as well as individuals and nongovernmental groups, accountable to something higher.

IX. Christ, Christians, and Charitable Government

In his *Apology* (197 C.E.), Tertullian notes that "[the soul] looks not to the Capitol but to the heavens."[92] He also observes that the Roman government of his time made bearing the name "Christian" a crime: to call oneself a Christian, or to be labeled one by another, was sufficient ground to be punished for treason against the empire, regardless of one's personal character or actual behavior.[93] Some Christian theologians have subsequently returned the favor and made bearing the name "government" a sin: to be identifiable as a civil government is sufficient reason to be dismissed by the faithful as profane and corrupt, regardless of the political ideals or institutional practices involved.[94] There is a grain of truth in each of these extreme views.

A Christian in ancient Rome might be seen as a threat to the empire, not because the Christian actively plotted against the state but because the Christian conception of state authority itself was more than a little tinged with subversion. Jesus Christ was crucified — crucifixion was the Roman punishment for sedition — and radical monotheism will forever put earthly magistrates on their guard and in their place. However, Christ died not because he sought to be Caesar or directly challenge Roman rule but because, in steadfastly loving God and the neighbor, he was more or less blasé about Caesars and their reigns. He broke their pride, and for this they killed him. Christlike faith, hope, and love relativize all worldly powers and principles, thus making any government, not just the imperial government, of secondary import. Again,

92. Tertullian, *Apology* 17, in *The Ante-Nicene Fathers*, vol. 3, ed. Alexander Roberts and James Donaldson (Grand Rapids: Eerdmans, 1978), p. xxx.

93. Tertullian, *Apology* 2, p. 20.

94. John Howard Yoder writes, "There is a very strong strand of Gospel teaching which sees secular government as the province of the sovereignty of Satan." See his *The Politics of Jesus*, 2nd ed. (Grand Rapids and Cambridge: Eerdmans, 1994), p. 194.

Jesus did not seek to foment regime change in the seats of power, but he did aim to sanctify his followers' hearts and minds as they ministered in the streets powerless. Jesus was, in this sense, a political revolutionary who threatened the Roman *dominium;* by his own lights, Pilate was right in having him executed.

Similarly, a government in the post-Roman West might be seen as a temptation to apostasy, not because of any particular misbehavior — though every state has historically misbehaved — but because it cannot escape the vicissitudes of collective power and sin. Political entities of whatever stripe will have to employ coercive force of some kind to sustain a just social order, which force is suspect to all those who would follow Christ in practicing forgiveness and turning the other cheek. However, recall that Christ himself granted a limited legitimacy to Caesar and secular government (Luke 20:25). Christian misgivings about the state are aggravated by the enduring memory of the early church as martyred, but more important to a Christian conscience is the resolve neither *to* martyr *others* nor to abandon those martyred *by others.* Efforts to combine state and church, from Calvin to Hitler, have invariably led to both idolatry and oppression. But any polis — not merely those embodying a palpable tyranny — is ripe for dirty hands even as it carries out its indispensable duties of coordinating social services and sustaining a just peace. It is striking in this regard that, in the temptation scene of Luke 4:5-8, Jesus does not doubt Satan's ability to hand over the governance of "all the kingdoms of the world."[95] Yet it is equally salient that, in the would-be entrapment scene of Luke 20:24-25, Jesus does not tell the disciple to cast away the Roman coin as an abomination but rather tells him to see it for what it is: a small token with a graven image on it. The message of both scenes taken together might be paraphrased as: "Though they both have some power, render nothing unto Satan and precious little unto Caesar, for true power lies with God."

A grain of truth is not the whole beach, then. Particular political creeds will have to be rejected as false, and both nation-states and nongovernmental civic groups will have to be resisted as unjust, but there can be no pious withdrawal from either polemics or politics. Karl Barth sounds separatist when he declares that "in the realm of the State," the church will be "a foreign community"; he immediately adds, however: "but the solidarity of stress and death

---

95. See Yoder, *The Politics of Jesus,* p. 194. Yoder observes that "this position [on the state's satanic tendencies] is offensive to the modern mind because it stands in judgment on modern democratic humanism" (p. 195). Letting Christlike love judge modern democracy is the central purpose of my present writing.

unites Christians with all men, and so also with those who wield political power."[96] The church must refuse "the deification of Caesar," as Barth both wrote and enacted, "yet it still knows that it is responsible for the State and for Caesar."[97] There will always be tension between Christian faith and community and temporal governors and governments; indeed, the calls to civil disobedience for Christians will likely be multiple for those with ears to hear. (I have in mind actions to protest abortion and to support gay marriage, for example.) But a *Christian* acknowledgment of this tension must be based on obedience to God and concern for the neighbor, rather than self-righteousness or *ressentiment*. What distinguishes Barth from contemporary sectarians is precisely that he avoids prideful or peevish exclusions in favor of eschatological optimism *and* solidarity with sinners (i.e., everybody). "If [Christians] are 'strangers and pilgrims' here it is because [the real state, the holy city to come in heaven] constitutes below their faith and their hope — and not because they see the imperfections or even the perversions of the states of this age and this world! It is not resentment, but a positive sentiment."[98]

We must look at political specifics. In addition, we should appreciate that there will also always be tension between Christian faith and *ecclesial* authorities and institutions. If Jesus was executed by Pilate for being a threat to Rome, he was handed over to Pilate by Caiaphas and the Sanhedrin because the latter's priestly power and temple profits were threatened by Jesus as well. The life and message of Christ were originally perceived as both seditious (a hazard to the established state) and blasphemous (a hazard to the established religion). Indeed, Christians contemplating the social order do well to recall that Jesus' most violent and most subversive act, the cleansing of the temple of money changers, was in response to the corruption of *religion* rather than to the hegemony of the *state*. Or, more precisely, it was a response to the corruption of Jewish faith and morals by *both* the Roman Empire *and* the Jerusalem high priests. The cleansing of the temple shortly before Passover was manifestly not a rejection of Judaism as such — Jesus and his disciples were born, lived, and died as devout (if radical) Jews — but rather an indictment of the collusion of Caiaphas and the effete priests with Pilate and the occupying Romans. To be tempted to stake everything on politics and to become an aggressive paramilitary group, like the Zealots, is to forget that neither the

---

96. Karl Barth, *Community, State, and Church: Three Essays* (Eugene, Ore.: Wipf and Stock, 1960/2004), p. 107.

97. Barth, *Community, State, and Church*, p. 107.

98. Barth, *Community, State, and Church*, p. 123.

state nor the church is salvific as such. To be tempted to refuse political life altogether and to withdraw into a pious enclave, like the Essenes, is to forget that neither the state nor the church is demonic as such. As Barth suggests, Christians have *"no* abiding city" in this world,[99] so to talk about the church as a "true polis," "counterpolis," or "superpolis" is to pile confusion on confusion. The shadow of the cross falls on both crown and miter, and *agape* refuses separatism and engages politics as a kenotic act at one with the cross itself. Yet again, everything turns on specifics.

The detailed implications of the cross, political and ecclesial, will become manifest in the balance of this book, I trust, but for now I must continue to unpack my general approach. My focus is on the place of Christian charity *(agape)* in a pluralistic society dedicated to "liberty and justice for all." My title, *Political* Agape: *Christian Love and Liberal Democracy,* aims to be provocative, if not oxymoronic, on two counts. First, liberal theorists often wish to banish theological virtues from the public sphere as either dangerous dogmas or merely private assets. For many, reference to "political *agape*" will seem odd, if not offensive. Richard Rorty and his pragmatic postmodernism are a case in point, but John Rawls's *Political Liberalism* is surely the most influential example of the liberal wariness of religion's political voice. My title is meant to echo, and to counter, Rawls's own. Second, several Christian ethicists have lately rejected liberal democracy as a more or less vicious social philosophy, one that tempts Christians to violence and apostasy. Here Alasdair MacIntyre, Stanley Hauerwas, John Milbank, and Robert Kraynak all come to mind. For them, Christian faith is antithetical to democratic principles and "prophetic liberalism" is a contradiction in terms. My linking "the prophetic" to a version of liberalism distances these traditionalist thinkers.

Rorty and Rawls are articulate exponents of decency and fairness, even as MacIntyre, Hauerwas, et al. are faithful champions of virtuous community. Both the secular defenders and the religious critics sell liberalism short, however. With all due respect to these titans, with friends like Rorty and Rawls, liberalism does not need enemies; and with enemies like MacIntyre and Hauerwas, liberalism needs all the friends it can get. Christians can be friends to liberal democracy precisely because they are first loved by God and subsequently love their neighbors. They practice (or ought to practice) a political

---

99. Barth, *Community, State, and Church,* p. 127. Barth goes on to observe that "the quiet and peaceable life under the rule of the State . . . is no ideal in itself, just as the existence of the Church, in contradistinction to all other men, can be no ideal in itself" (p. 129). As I make clear below, I know of no better rejoinder to the projects of both John Rawls and Stanley Hauerwas.

agape that undergirds, but also outstrips, typical modes of state justice and ecclesial sectarianism.

The dual thrust of the book is: (1) that agapic love of souls is the perilously neglected civic and political virtue of our time, and (2) that such a virtue is indispensable to both support for and restraint of liberal democracy. Political *agape* is, in one basic sense, a "democratic" commitment, in that the common human needs and potentials with which it is occupied are most evident in the *demos,* the poorest and most defenseless class. But *agape* is seen as, with the assistance of grace, a universal human legacy, so the source of governmental legitimacy resides first in the will of God and second in the people in general as bearers of God's image. (In this sense, prophetic liberalism is closer to what Aristotle called *politeia,* which aims at the common good, than to a literal *demokratia,* if this implies rule entirely by or for a limited faction.)[100] Most importantly, political *agape* is not simply identical with or a handmaiden to *any* one social doctrine, institutional arrangement, or factional interest. Christianity has deep affinities, historically and ideologically, with "democratic" governance, as many have pointed out, and I will argue that love of souls bolsters such traditional democratic values as equality and universality. Nevertheless, political *agape* is first and foremost a Judeo-Christian virtue, in that the distinctive worth of human lives is a function of their being made in God's image, and the power to recognize and act on that image is a gift of God's grace.[101] A general love of neighbor is enjoined by the second love command of Matthew 22, yet it is inseparable from "the first and great commandment" to love God without reserve (see Matt. 22:35-40).

For all its democratic resonances, then, political *agape* relativizes such democratic goods as individual freedom and majority opinion. *Indeed, the greatest gift that* agape *can give to any political ideal or institution is to relativize it, to subordinate it to the governance of God and thus strip it of pretension.* One may be tempted to say, courting paradox, that political *agape* is fundamentally "apolitical," but being apolitical has political implications. Less cryptically, *agape* does not disdain or flee from temporal involvements with the neighbor but rather loves the neighbor precisely by assisting him

100. For more on these Greek terms, see John Dunn, *Democracy: A History* (New York: Atlantic Monthly Press, 2005), pp. 47-48.

101. I use the phrases "political *agape,*" "Christlike love," and "love of neighbor" more or less synonymously. I do not mean to imply, however, that Christianity is the only form of love of souls in society. There are analogues in several religions and in some secular philosophies. The best recent secular defense of liberalism is Jeffrey Stout's *Democracy and Tradition* (Princeton: Princeton University Press, 2004), I believe. Yet see my chapter 7 for criticisms.

or her to dethrone temporal goods, including the state and the market and even the church, in deference to God. Worldly goods remain goods, but they are second in priority. Not autonomy but theonomy is the *summum bonum* for Christians, and not polls but piety is the key to both religious virtue and democratic governance. In this connection, *agape* profoundly shapes how we understand and act on freedom, equality, and universality. For many contemporary liberals, the self-conscious capacity for autonomy is the primary (if not sole) basis of equal regard for individuals. Because persons are self-aware beings, capable of rational planning and voluntary choice, they possess a *dignity* that must be recognized politically. Such recognition usually takes the form of interest-based rights for already-existing persons. (*Vide* the work of Ronald Dworkin and Peter Singer, for instance.) The problem with this view is that it places a number of human lives beyond real political consideration: for example, fetuses, infants, the mentally ill or handicapped, and the frail elderly. Such beings lack standard reason and volition, even if they may eventually acquire or reacquire them. Moreover, even normal adults do not make equally rational decisions or achieve equally rational results. Any social vision that grounds human equality on shared powers of intellect and will, including the practice of civil conversation, has put that equality at grave risk.

Dignity has its place, but I shall maintain, in contrast to the liberal norm, that the surest foundation of human equality is *sanctity*. Christianly understood, sanctity is an inviolability that stems from all human lives — young and old, bright and dim — bearing the image of God. If "God is [agapic] love" (1 John 4:8), then, in turn, God's image is plausibly seen to consist in the need and ability to give and receive such love. For this, the highest good, everyone qualifies. Whereas dignity rests on achieved rationality, sanctity resides in needs and potentials that are more basic and indelible: for example, the need for food and companionship and the potential for loving or being loved. It is not rational agency, but charitable patience, that puts humans on a par. Persons only become persons because they are extended a gratuitous care before they reach the age of reason, and persons only remain persons because they benefit from an ongoing solicitude from others, including God. Indeed, in being untouched by compassion for shared human finitude, exclusive concern for achieved dignity must lead to personal and political strife. Too much accent on contingent merit or station leads to envy, elitism, violence, and vendetta, as Shakespeare drove home by opening *Romeo and Juliet* with a description of "two households, both alike in dignity." The pride and self-assertion of the Montagues and Capulets, families equal in rank but nonetheless jealous of and paranoid about one another, make Verona a place "where civil blood makes civil hands unclean."[102]

If true individuality before God, as well as true equality with others, is based on sanctity, then accent on rational self-interest or autonomous choice — as in social contract theory — is misplaced. Prime emphasis should fall, instead, on duties of charity and need-based obligations. As the means of acquiring and expressing a moral identity, liberty must be protected, of course, but it is not the first good. It depends on a solidarity that Christians call *agape,* and that same solidarity provides the main purpose of liberty itself. Perhaps the strongest argument for human equality, and thus for democracy, is not our common rationality but our common mortality. Death is not so much the great equal*izer* as the revelation that we are *already* equal in our finitude. If all human lives did not possess sanctity, then many human deaths (e.g., that of suicides and shut-ins) would not be the sad losses that they are.

The demotion of reason and freedom as fundamental sources of social ethics is not novel, but that this demotion augments rather than threatens the overall case for a form of liberal democracy is not often appreciated. As noted, some Christian traditionalists have begun to turn their backs on democracy in the name of theological virtue. This is unwise, however. Democracy as practiced in the present-day West is, admittedly, Christian faith's prodigal son — leaning toward individualism, materialism, and relativism — but the Christian church ought not to play the resentful older brother and deny consanguinity. One ought, rather, to work for repentance and reform; one ought to celebrate any genuine return to moral responsibility; one ought, in short, to be willing to kill the fatted calf. Visions of liberalism that see it as morally empty or as settling for the lowest common denominator among self-interested agents (cf. Rorty and Rawls) are not the only alternatives. A morally perfectionist — a.k.a. "prophetic" — account of liberalism that rehabilitates robust virtues like mercy and compassion is possible, as I hope first to demonstrate with a little help from the sixteenth U.S. president.

---

102. William Shakespeare, *The Tragedy of Romeo and Juliet,* prologue, lines 1-4.

PART I

Liberalism and *Agape*

CHAPTER 1

Love and Mr. Lincoln

> There is no longer Jew or Greek, there is no longer slave or free, there is no longer male and female; for all of you are one in Christ Jesus.
>
> GALATIANS 3:28

Introduction: Beyond America's Founding Documents

It is often argued that, as the American Civil War unfolded, Abraham Lincoln's stated political priorities moved from national unity and the rule of positive law (as embodied in the U.S. Constitution) to the more distinctively moral goods of "liberty and equality for all" upheld in a version of natural law (as articulated in the Declaration of Independence). Jefferson's Declaration was Lincoln's political "Bible" throughout his life, but even that document could be read with emphasis on patriotic unity rather than human equality. So the struggle to preserve the Union was elevated to a higher plane, the argument runs, when Lincoln issued the Emancipation Proclamation (1863) and made freedom for the slaves an explicit ingredient in and justification for the war effort. Indeed, it was only with his Gettysburg Address (1863) that Lincoln found his full moral voice and enunciated a defense of natural rights and natural law that rejected the historicism and positivism advocated by the likes of Stephen A. Douglas and John C. Calhoun.[1] With this defense, what

---

1. See Harry V. Jaffa, *A New Birth of Freedom: Abraham Lincoln and the Coming of the Civil War* (Lanham, Md.: Rowman and Littlefield, 2000), pp. xii-xiii. In commemorating the cemetery at Gettysburg, Lincoln expressed his belief that the nation, in David Herbert Donald's

Lincoln called "sober reason"[2] carried the day over mob passion.

This common interpretive line has considerable plausibility,[3] and I myself will be celebrating Lincoln's refusal of purely procedural and traditionalist grounds for political association. But the common line tells only a part of the story of Lincoln's evolving political faith. For it fails to appreciate that Lincoln eventually embraced the "charity for all" commanded in Hebrew-Christian Scripture, which charity inspires, governs, and finally transcends both of America's founding documents and both positive law and natural law. The young Lincoln had held, in 1838, that "reason, cold, calculating, unimpassioned reason, must furnish all the materials for our future support and defense."[4] In a very different spirit, Alexander Stephens, the soon-to-be vice president of the Confederacy, declared in 1859 that "African slavery rests upon principles that can never be successfully assailed by reason or argument."[5] Stephens held hierarchy and subordination — the domination of the weak by the strong — to be part of "nature's first law"[6] and evident upon reflection; and, ironically, it was Stephens's opinion that proved, in a sense, to carry the day for the mature Lincoln. It was biblical charity, rather than Enlightenment rationality, that actually triumphed in Lincoln's war-hardened vision. In the brief Gettysburg Address, Lincoln refers to "liberty" and "equal[ity]" in his first sentence and to "God" once in his last, but he nowhere mentions "reason," "rationality," or "natural law." In the Second Inaugural (1865), he again speaks not at all of "reason," "rationality," or "natural law," but he invokes "God," "the Almighty," or "Him/His" ten times.

Stephens too had appealed to "the Almighty" and "Divine law,"[7] but,

---

words, "antedated the 1789 Constitution, with its restrictions on the powers of the national government; it stemmed from 1776. It was with the Declaration of Independence that 'our fathers brought forth, upon this continent, a new nation, conceived in Liberty, and dedicated to the proposition that all men are created equal.'" See David Herbert Donald, *Lincoln* (New York: Simon and Schuster, 1995), p. 462.

2. Abraham Lincoln, "Address to the Young Men's Lyceum of Springfield, Illinois," in *Abraham Lincoln: Speeches and Writings, 1832-1858* (New York: Library of America, 1989), p. 36.

3. In addition to Jaffa and Donald, see Gary Wills, *Lincoln at Gettysburg: The Words That Remade America* (New York: Simon and Schuster, 1993), and Allen Guelzo, *Abraham Lincoln: Redeemer President* (Grand Rapids: Eerdmans, 1999).

4. Lincoln, "Address to the Young Men's Lyceum," p. 36.

5. Stephens, his retirement speech from Congress, cited by Edmund Wilson, *Patriotic Gore: Studies in the Literature of the American Civil War* (New York: Oxford University Press, 1962), p. 410.

6. Stephens, cited by Wilson, *Patriotic Gore*, p. 410.

7. Stephens, cited in Wilson, *Patriotic Gore*, pp. 410-11.

unlike Lincoln, he simply conflated nature and grace — seeing what we today would call Darwinian survival of the fittest as expressive of God's normative will. Lincoln never ceased to value reason and law, but he became increasingly sensitive to the slippage between positive law, natural law, and even divine law (the written "revelations" of the Bible). All these forms of law were mediated by human beings and thus fallible, and all were distinct from eternal law (the mind and heart of God as they are in themselves). Hence, across the war years, Lincoln shifted from analytical jurisprudence to a decidedly more theological (and tragic) idiom to explain himself and his nation. The Second Inaugural's climactic words — "With malice toward none; with charity for all; with firmness in the right, as God gives us to see the right" — live on in history as Lincoln's sublime transcendence of "unimpassioned reason."[8]

Charity emerged as Lincoln's means of holding in proper balance the Constitution's political tenets and the Declaration's ethical ideals, precisely because neither positive law nor natural law alone was enough. Neither the historical legal traditions ensconced in the Constitution, nor the liberty and equality guaranteed in the Declaration, could be relied on for sufficient practical guidance to meet the demands of the times. In fact, without a more fundamental principle, positive law, personal and political liberty, and human equality tended to conflict. (States' rights and popular sovereignty meant slavery for some and inhuman misery for others, for instance.) Charity itself was not a panacea, removing all ambiguity and strife from the embattled American landscape. It did, however, prevent paralysis and allow for compassion in the president as well as many of the American people.

I. The Circling Camps

There is no unanimity, of course, on this reading of "Father Abraham." Opinions on Lincoln's precise motives and convictions, as well as on the meaning and ultimate consequences of his actions, divide roughly into three camps. *Camp 1:* Some maintain that "the Great Emancipator" was at heart no friend of the Negroes, was in fact a white supremacist and profound bigot who had to be compelled to act for the good of all races by a combination of radical abolitionists and military setbacks. Lincoln was incompetent in his running of the government and timid in his conduct of the war, on this view. More

---

8. Interestingly, Stephens was to write after the Civil War: "The secret of my life has been *revenge.*" See Wilson, *Patriotic Gore*, p. 389.

damningly, left to his own devices, he would have been perpetually content to leave slavery alone, so long as it did not expand into new territories, as he had promised in his presidential campaign and as he believed the Constitution required. As Lincoln stated in his famous public letter to Horace Greeley, "My paramount object in this struggle *is* to save the Union, and is *not* either to save or to destroy slavery."[9] Any "evolution" of his views was a matter of political and/or personal expediency. The Emancipation Proclamation, for instance, was defended by Lincoln himself as a military necessity rather than a moral mandate. The proclamation was considered constitutional because, as commander in chief, the president had war powers to confiscate property, including slaves;[10] and Lincoln hinted at times that, once the war was over, the proclamation need no longer be effective. Call this the "Lincoln as forced into glory" school.[11]

Camp 2: Others hold a still more dour view in which not even the semblance of glory was achieved by Mr. Lincoln. Whatever his views on race, neither slavery's abolition nor its limitation was a significant factor in Lincoln's going to war against the Southern Confederacy. According to this second camp, Lincoln's enduring and overriding goal was the centralization of governmental power and the economic and political hegemony this would ensure for the Northern Republican Party and himself as its leader. He could have ended slavery by other means — for example, compensated emancipation, as in Britain — but he chose to conduct "an unnecessary war" to further his agenda of protective tariffs, internal improvements, bureaucratic patronage, and other "mercantilist" and "socialist" measures to which the freedom-loving South objected. Rather than being politically incompetent and militarily timid, that is, Lincoln was a silver-tongued tyrant willing to wage "total war" on civilians to crush Southern resistance to the omnicompetent state and his own political ambitions. In standing against state sovereignty and the right of secession, in particular, Lincoln was an enemy of true democratic governance. He was not "forced into glory"; rather, he was a calculating and quite ignominious foe of

---

9. Abraham Lincoln, "Letter to Horace Greeley" (August 22, 1862), in *Abraham Lincoln: Speeches and Writings, 1859-1865* (New York: Library of America, 1989), p. 358.

10. See Donald, *Lincoln,* p. 456.

11. I take the quoted phrase from Lerone Bennett Jr., *Forced into Glory: Abraham Lincoln's White Dream* (Chicago: Johnson Publishing Co., 1999). Wendell Phillips, Charles Sumner, William Lloyd Garrison, Horace James, Frederick Douglass, and other staunch abolitionists often saw Lincoln as morally obtuse and in need of pressuring, but especially Douglass eventually came to appreciate what Lincoln was up against and thus raised his estimate of the president and what he had achieved.

liberty whose actions helped lead to the imperial presidency. His wartime institution of a draft, suspension of habeas corpus, denial of trial by jury, closing
of opposition newspapers, and confiscation of private property simply confirmed his totalitarian proclivities. Indeed, the young Lincoln was uncannily
(if unwittingly) describing himself when he wrote: "Towering genius disdains a
beaten path. . . . It thirsts and burns for distinction; and, if possible, it will have
it, whether at the expense of emancipating slaves, or enslaving freemen."[12] The
picture, then, is of a Whiggish warmonger, whose inflated image of "Columbia"
and himself left him little or no sensitivity to the suffering of others or to his
own limits. Call this the "Lincoln as gory patriot" school.[13]

Camp 3: Still others maintain that the sweet sixteenth president was
much more consistent ethically and much more liberal politically. On this
account, Lincoln was always convinced of the injustice of slavery and forever inclined to liberate the shackled blacks by any practical means, but he
was also committed to constitutional government and preservation of the
consent of the governed. From early on in his career, Lincoln wanted to put
slavery on the path to "ultimate extinction,"[14] this camp insists, but he was
constrained by politics as the art of the possible. He realized that preserving the Union was the sine qua non of both any legal effort to improve the
lot of blacks nationwide and any practical hope of sustaining a democratic
polity. If a state could nullify laws duly passed by Congress or interpose its
own courts' rulings contrary to the findings of the federal Supreme Court or
ultimately secede at will from the Union itself, then the very idea of representative government would have collapsed into anarchy. Because the Constitution itself had protected slavery in the original colonies, Lincoln could
not simultaneously claim to uphold constitutional order and to seek directly

12. Lincoln, "Address to the Young Men's Lyceum," p. 34.

13. I form this name by playing off of the title of Edmund Wilson's *Patriotic Gore.*
Thomas J. DiLorenzo's *The Real Lincoln: A New Look at Abraham Lincoln, His Agenda, and
an Unnecessary War* (New York: Three Rivers Press, 2002, 2003) is perhaps the purest recent
representative of this view. DiLorenzo is a contemporary Southern nationalist who writes from
the vantage point of von Misean economics, but he largely recapitulates Alexander Stephens's
points in *A Constitutional View of the Late War between the States,* 2 vols. (1867 and 1870).
DiLorenzo treats Lincoln as an evil genius, while Stephens grants him more private virtue and
less public malevolence, but both authors see the president as effectively a despot. This sensibility has led some to criticize the Lincoln Memorial in Washington, D.C., as a bit of "imperialist
propaganda" that strips Lincoln of his imperfections. For a rebuttal, see Andrew Ferguson, "A
Misunderstood Monument," *Wall Street Journal,* May 24, 2008, p. W12.

14. See Abraham Lincoln, "Seventh Lincoln-Douglas Debate," in *Speeches and Writings,
1832-1858,* p. 811. The phrase "ultimate extinction" was borrowed from Henry Clay.

to abolish slavery. Yet, because secession and states' rights threatened the rule of law, Lincoln could justify going to war, as well as suspending various civil liberties, as stemming from his obligation as chief executive to defend the general welfare. To be sure, he had to bide his time — on occasion, even to mix his signals — but eventually he found a way to work his inspired and farseeing will in recognizing the equal dignity of blacks and in restoring domestic tranquility. Though he did not live to see them ratified, the Thirteenth Amendment abolishing slavery and the Fifteenth Amendment guaranteeing black males the right to vote were the final fruits of his martyred life. Call this the "Lincoln as redeemer president" school.[15]

Whether Lincoln's intentions are judged to be base or noble, the key point of convergence of the "forced into glory" and the "redeemer president" camps is in seeing at least a *rhetorical* progression from focus on civic survival and positive law to insistence on moral uprightness and something like natural law, especially a universal sense of justice.[16] That is, camps 1 and 3 see the distinctively moral language of the Declaration of Independence as eventually trumping the legalities of the Constitution for Lincoln, at least publicly. The difference is that the "forced into glory" folks see this development as *merely* rhetorical, not heartfelt, while the "redeemer president" fans see it as an expression of Lincoln's sincere convictions all along. What distinguishes the "gory patriot" school, in turn, is that it sees Lincoln as knowingly violating *both* the Declaration of Independence and the Constitution. Whatever his rhetoric, proponents of camp 2 hold, Lincoln was out to assume dictatorial powers for himself and imperial powers for the central government, and to achieve these ends he had effectively to jettison both of America's founding documents — as well as to slaughter thousands of men, women, and children.

There is some truth in all three perspectives. It is a commonplace to marvel at how protean Lincoln's appearance was, how his much photographed face morphed over time, and how his moral identity was similarly complex and mutable. Still, for my part, I maintain that all three schools offer an incomplete and finally mistaken picture. Camps 1, 2, and 3 all underemphasize the growth of the prophetic Lincoln — his eventual declarations of *dependence* on God (that *other* Founding Father); all three underestimate the limits of "American democracy" — especially when this is equated with the secular values of in-

15. I take the quoted phrase from Guelzo, *Abraham Lincoln.* James M. McPherson, *Abraham Lincoln and the Second American Revolution* (New York: Oxford University Press, 1991), and Jaffa, *A New Birth of Freedom,* are also representative of this view.

16. See Guelzo, *Abraham Lincoln,* pp. 188-89 and 460; and William Lee Miller, *Lincoln's Virtues: An Ethical Biography* (New York: Knopf, 2002), pp. 263-72.

dividual autonomy and majority rule. In his first major political speech, "The Perpetuation of Our Political Institutions" (1838), Lincoln instructed every American to "swear by the blood of the Revolution, never to violate in the least particular, the laws of the country; and never to tolerate their violation by others."[17] Even "bad laws" were to be "religiously observed,"[18] unless and until they could be repealed. "Reverence for the constitution and laws"[19] never left the lawyer Lincoln, but when he spoke in 1862 of the need to "disenthrall ourselves,"[20] he had come to appreciate the limits of such reverence. The Civil War convinced him of the need for a vision of something higher and more authoritative than adherence to positive laws and perpetuation of existing institutions. Natural justice played a key part in this vision, but a charity enjoined by a supernatural God eventually became the dominant virtue. Those who see Lincoln as a prudent but committed reformer, a perhaps overly cautious but sincere enemy of slavery, are much closer to the truth, I believe, than those who see him as a stolid or self-seeking politician, venially indifferent to the fate of enslaved blacks. Similarly, those who see Lincoln as a genuine friend of freedom and equality, though at times overly zealous in their defense, are much closer to the truth than those who see him as an American Caesar swelling party coffers and presidential prerogatives.[21] He was at times conflicted and always crafty, but he was neither forced into glory nor a fascist demagogue. In mid-1864, for instance, even though his reelection was in serious doubt, Lincoln publicly supported the proposed Thirteenth Amendment to the Constitution, a controversial provision to end slavery nationwide.[22] In addition, he favored quickly returning the Southern states to voting membership in Congress so long as representatives swore an oath of loyalty to the federal

17. Lincoln, "Address to the Young Men's Lyceum," p. 32.
18. Lincoln, "Address to the Young Men's Lyceum," p. 33.
19. Lincoln, "Address to the Young Men's Lyceum," p. 36.
20. Abraham Lincoln, "Annual Message to Congress" (December 1, 1862), in *Speeches and Writings, 1859-1865*, p. 415.
21. In this opinion, I side with William Lloyd Garrison over Wendell Phillips and, more recently, with James McPherson over Lerone Bennett. I appreciate the frustrations of the Radical Republicans, like Charles Sumner, in the face of Lincoln's tentativeness, but I do not doubt his fundamental integrity or even his practical wisdom.
22. In 1864, before Lincoln's reelection, the Thirteenth Amendment failed to receive the needed two-thirds majority in the House. In 1865, with the reelected president's strong support, the amendment passed the Thirty-eighth Congress. It was in the process of being ratified by the states when Lincoln was assassinated. Lincoln believed that, being a war powers act, his Emancipation Proclamation would cease to be legally effective once the war was at an end, thus his anxiety to see the Thirteenth Amendment passed before the cessation of armed conflict.

government. Still, Lincoln's character was more morally ambivalent longer than many "redeemer president" commentators allow. He was slow to see the need for full social equality for blacks, for instance, even as he clung too long to constitutional legalism. In the end, however, he did not merely interpret the Declaration and the Constitution, he transformed and transcended them. Hence I defend a view of Abraham Lincoln as a very human figure whose genius nonetheless led his nation through the tragedy of war beyond the turpitude of slavery to "a more perfect Union."[23] Call this (4) the "Lincoln as maturing prophet" school.

II. An Ambivalent Kentucky Prophet

Born in Kentucky, a slave state that did not secede from the Union and the spawning ground of both the fiery abolitionist Cassius Marcellus Clay and the Confederate president Jefferson Davis, Lincoln came by his double-mindedness on race naturally. Harriet Beecher Stowe's protest novel, *Uncle Tom's Cabin,* was set in Kentucky; the derided "Jim Crow" of minstrel shows was named after a slave seen dancing raucously in a Louisville barn;[24] Louisville and Lexington, both visited by Lincoln, were major hubs for the selling of slaves down the Ohio River to the sugarcane plantations of the Deep South, but they were also important stations on the Underground Railroad moving runaway slaves in the opposite direction, across the Ohio River to Cincinnati and as far north as Canada; Lincoln's own family included an abolitionist wife from Lexington and her half sister's husband, a Confederate general who died fighting for states' rights at Chickamauga. It is no wonder that Kentuckian Abe had to labor, both publicly and privately, to integrate his conflicted conscience. As a presidential candidate, he had indeed promised to leave Southern slavery

23. David Brooks has written that "'The historian Allen Guelzo has shown that Lincoln intended to emancipate the slaves from the very first, but he was cautious in the way he proceeded." (See Brooks, "Lincoln's Winning Strategy for 2008," *New York Times,* March 26, 2006.) Much turns, however, on what one means by "intended to emancipate." As I note, Lincoln was always morally against slavery and from the beginning wanted to see it wither away. But leaving slavery alone in the South, in the hope that it would naturally die out over time, was fine by Lincoln at the start of the war. Indeed, he thought it Constitutionally required. The Emancipation Proclamation and support for the Thirteenth Amendment, then, were genuinely new moves inspired by a change of political and moral mind. Guelzo and Brooks downplay this evolution far too much, in my estimation.

24. Ken Emerson, *Do-Dah: Stephen Foster and the Rise of American Popular Culture* (New York: Da Capo Press, 1998), p. xxx.

untouched by the federal government, and he took that promise seriously; the Constitution had indeed protected slavery, however implicitly, and Lincoln felt a duty to uphold the nation's original social contract; finally, Lincoln did indeed have racist sensibilities that made him deny the intellectual and cultural equality of blacks with whites, and he only reluctantly surrendered his plans for compensated emancipation of the slaves and their colonization either back to Africa or on to Central America or the Caribbean. But the point is that he both retained basic allegiances to human liberty and equality and grew in his understanding of what these goods meant and how they were to be sustained *and criticized.*

So what does it mean to call Abraham "prophetic," rather than either "gory" or "redemptive"? Unlike the "gory patriot" school, I do not think that an overweening pride led Lincoln to elevate himself and subvert the Constitution. He was undeniably an ambitious man, as his law partner William Herndon famously observed, but Lincoln sincerely valued democracy and the rule of law. Democratic legality was not, ultimately, Lincoln's *summum bonum,* however. Daniel Farber has argued powerfully that "secession was indeed unconstitutional" and that "military resistance to secession was not only constitutional but also morally justified,"[25] but these remain highly contested claims. It is misleading, in any event, to suggest that constitutionality was the final normative measure for Lincoln. Some of Lincoln's wartime actions were palpably unlawful and could not be defended on constitutional grounds.[26] Unlike both

25. Daniel Farber, *Lincoln's Constitution* (Chicago and London: University of Chicago Press, 2003), p. 3.

26. Daniel Farber grants that "some of what Lincoln and his subordinates did exceed[ed] their constitutional authority," but he immediately adds that "what prevented these unauthorized executive actions from becoming a threat to the entire constitutional order was Lincoln's willingness to seek congressional ratification and face the legal consequences if it was not forthcoming" (*Lincoln's Constitution,* p. 24). Farber concludes that "on careful reading, Lincoln was not arguing for the *legal* power to take emergency actions contrary to statutory or constitutional mandates. Instead, his argument fit well within the classic liberal view of emergency power" (p. 194). Farber appreciates that "it was Lincoln's character — his ability, judgment, courage, and humanity — that brought the Union through the war with the Constitution intact" (p. 200). But even Farber remains too much within a political account of Lincoln's virtue and justification, I believe. Farber accepts "Lincoln's claim that otherwise unlawful actions were justified by necessity," and he construes the "necessity" in question to be national self-preservation (pp. 192-93). To save the Union and the general rule of law, specific laws had to be broken. This analysis holds for the institution of the draft and the suspension of habeas in war zones, as Farber notes, but it makes Abraham Lincoln sound too much like Michael Walzer. Like Walzer on "supreme emergency," Lincoln is interpreted as claiming that, in defense of the nation under conditions of dire "necessity," he "had to choose the lesser of

the "forced into glory" and the "redeemer president" camps, however, I deny that Lincoln found an answer to his moral and legal problems, even rhetorically, in privileging the Declaration and natural law over the Constitution and positive law. Again, it was the *theological* virtue of *agape* that allowed him to rise above his several historical and textual impasses. Lincoln's final judgments on both what to do about secession (affirm and restore the Union) and what to do about racial equality (abolish slavery and secure the right to vote regardless of race) ultimately turned on his deepening sense of what charity required *politically.* Neither saving the Union nor abolishing slavery could be unambiguously, or even consistently, justified without going beyond the limits of both American founding documents and appealing to a virtue higher than liberty, equality, and even legality. Though several of his actions as chief executive were either illegal or extralegal, Lincoln did his best not fundamentally to *violate* the Declaration and the Constitution. Nevertheless, he finally had to look to a third normative document (the Bible) for the means to *uphold and reconcile* the two eighteenth-century texts. It was precisely when the legal compromises of his Kentucky mentor, Henry Clay, proved unworkable that Lincoln stepped into the breach and achieved true greatness.

Nevertheless, Lincoln was prophetic rather than messianic for two main reasons: (1) he had to learn, as opposed to perpetually embodying, charity, and (2) he had to restrain sin with violence rather than expiating it with nonviolence. But Lincoln did learn charity, and he did bring the nation to repentance by the sword; thus he became the American John the Baptist. At the risk of overstatement and knowing that some will accuse me of blasphemy, I will go still further: Jesus' expanding the Hebraic covenant to include the Gentiles found an echo in Lincoln's expanding the American experiment to include the slaves. Jesus is the Christ because his very being was love and his actions were spiritually salvific, while Lincoln is merely the greatest president because he reflected love and his actions were politically liberating. But both Jesus and Abraham relativized the authority of the state — whether an admitted tyranny or a supposed democracy — and both paid for this with their lives.

---

two evils" (p. 195). This may be the core of secular "liberalism," but it is not a plausible explanation of the Emancipation Proclamation and does not do justice to the religious dimension of Lincoln's Second Inaugural Address. Even Farber fails to emphasize that, for Lincoln, the rule of law had to be leavened (and judged) with the rule of love. The preservation of the Union, though a very great good, was not the highest good to be achieved by the Civil War, and the chief force at work during the war was not the president's emergency power but God's righteous providence. This, at least, was Lincoln's considered opinion.

III. "African Americans" and the Subordination of Liberty and Equality

Let me now turn to historical, political, and ethical details. In discussing Lincoln's attitude toward racial equality, we do well not to refer to blacks in his day as "African Americans." In an important sense, there were very few African Americans in the 1850s and early 1860s. The descriptor "African American" denotes a person of color of African descent living in the United States, but it also connotes civic membership in the political, economic, and cultural community of that same nation.[27] "The number of free blacks, which had been tiny before the Revolution, surged during the last quarter of the 18th century,"[28] due to the opportunities for escape from bondage provided by the war itself and to the various acts by Northern states to free their slaves, either immediately or gradually. Even so, free blacks in Lincoln's America were a comparatively small group and remained in most ways disenfranchised. Even free blacks could not vote or hold office in 1860.[29] Harry Jaffa suggests that Lincoln simply did not share the prejudices of most of his fellow countrymen toward both free and enslaved blacks,[30] but this is implausible given Lincoln's words and deeds.

Lincoln was always clear about the wrongness of slavery, regardless of any innate differences between the races, as is evident in both public speeches and private correspondence. In his "Address at Cooper Institute" (1860), he said succinctly: "All they [the Southern people] ask, we could readily grant, if we thought slavery right; all we ask, they could as readily grant, if they thought

---

27. "At first, deaths among slaves . . . exceeded births in the American colonies, but in the 18th century the birth rates rose in those colonies, mortality rates fell, and the slave population became self-reproducing. This transition, which occurred earlier in the upper than in the lower South, meant that even after slave imports were outlawed in 1808, the number of slaves continued to grow rapidly. During the next 50 years, the slave population of the United States *more than tripled,* from about 1.2 million to almost 4 million in 1860. The natural growth of the slave population meant that slavery could survive without new slave imports.

"By the 1770s, only about 20 percent of slaves in the colonies were African-born, although the concentration of Africans remained higher in South Carolina and Georgia. After 1808 the proportion of African-born slaves became tiny." See "Slavery in America," *The American Civil War,* homepage by Ronald W. McGranahan. http://americanrevwar.homestead.com/files/civwar/slavery.html; accessed July 29, 2005.

28. "Slavery in America."

29. Carlton Waterhouse, "The Full Price of Freedom: African Americans' Shared Responsibility to Repair the Harms of Slavery and Segregation" (Ph.D. diss., Emory, 2006).

30. Jaffa, *New Birth of Freedom,* p. 166. Jaffa sees Lincoln as a kind of tragic hero, while I see his tale as that of a pilgrim's progress.

it wrong. Their thinking it right, and our thinking it wrong, is the precise fact upon which depends the whole controversy."[31] Lest this be taken as a narrowly political judgment — with "wrong" meaning, roughly, "imprudent for the state" — one observes that in the sixth Lincoln-Douglas debate (1858) Lincoln had declared: "The Republican Party think it [slavery] wrong — we think it is a moral, a social, and a political wrong."[32] Lest this be dismissed as but a public pose — something said to make a name for himself in the party — one observes that in 1855 Lincoln wrote to his friend Joshua Speed:

> You know I dislike slavery; and you fully admit the abstract wrong of it. . . . In 1841 you and I had together a tedious low-water trip, on a Steam Boat from Louisville to St. Louis. You may remember, as I well do, that from Louisville to the mouth of the Ohio there were, on board, ten or a dozen slaves, shackled together with irons. That sight was a continual torment to me; and I see something like it every time I touch the Ohio, or any other slave-border. It is hardly fair for you to assume, that I have no interest in a thing which has, and continually exercises, the power of making me miserable. You ought rather to appreciate how much the great body of the Northern people do crucify their feelings, in order to maintain their loyalty to the constitution and the Union.[33]

Nonetheless, Lincoln's actions and attitudes were tainted by the racism of his time. He used the "n"-word, told racist jokes, and enjoyed minstrel shows seemingly with little sense of their objectionableness.[34] Most notoriously, he volunteered in the fourth Lincoln-Douglas debate (1858):

> I will say then that I am not, nor ever have been in favor of bringing about in any way the social and political equality of the white and black races, — that I am not nor ever have been in favor of making voters or jurors of negroes, nor of qualifying them to hold office, nor to intermarry with white people; and I will say in addition to this that there is a physical difference between the white and black races which I believe will for ever forbid

31. Abraham Lincoln, "Address at Cooper Institute," in *Speeches and Writings, 1859-1865*, p. 129.

32. Abraham Lincoln, "Sixth Lincoln-Douglas Debate," in *Speeches and Writings, 1832-1858*, p. 740.

33. Abraham Lincoln, "Letter to Joshua F. Speed" (1855), in *Speeches and Writings, 1832-1858*, pp. 360-61.

34. Miller, *Lincoln's Virtues*, p. 356.

the two races living together on terms of social and political equality. And inasmuch as they cannot so live, while they do remain together there must be the position of superior and inferior, and I as much as any other man am in favor of having the superior position assigned to the white race.[35]

It is a truism about prejudice that it seeks to justify denial of basic rights to a despised group on the basis of perceived qualities, real or imagined, that are the direct result of the denial of these rights in the first place. Women or blacks are to be denied education because they lack the intelligence or curiosity to benefit from it, it is claimed, when in fact it is the lack of education itself that withers intelligence and curiosity. The striking thing about Lincoln is that he educated himself to see through this logic, for the most part. His conversations with Frederick Douglass and Sojourner Truth at the White House, together with his looking and seeing how the blacks in the military performed, are a model of democratic experiment and dialogue, and they gave him an ever-increasing appreciation of the aptitude of blacks. If democratic civic society is formed through a deliberative and conversational process, so too is a liberal conscience.

Undeniably, it is sometimes difficult to distinguish, in Mr. Lincoln, between an adroit capacity for balancing ethical norms and crafting political compromises and a deeper ambivalence and more disturbing willingness to trim. (This ambiguity lies at the very heart of democratic freedom and disputation, and is what moves some, like Plato, to see them as anarchy and relativism.) Lincoln's open-mindedness and lack of dogmatism — what might be called his epistemic humility — could seem weak and unprincipled, even to close and congenial associates. Nevertheless, this book is premised on the judgment that Lincoln, for all his limitations, won through to a distinctively American form of political theology. My thesis, more specifically, is twofold: first, and relatively uncontroversially, part of Lincoln's moral genius was his capacity to learn and grow, to embrace new tactics and even to change his mind, without simply surrendering his integrity;[36] second, and more controversially, the basic commitment that moved him, in the end and after much struggle, to abandon various personal promises, the American social contract, and the hope for "ethnic cleansing"[37] was *neither* Union and law *nor* liberty

35. Abraham Lincoln, "Fourth Lincoln-Douglas Debate," in *Speeches and Writings, 1832-1858,* p. 636.

36. Miller's *Lincoln's Virtues* illustrates this characteristic in great detail.

37. This is Lerone Bennett's somewhat loaded way of describing Lincoln's compensated emancipation and resettlement scheme.

and equality. These two sets of paired values were enormously important to him and continued to inform much that he said and did, but they were hopelessly in tension in his mind. His integrity lay elsewhere, in an empathy for suffering that allowed him to transcend and redefine conventional justice in terms of love of neighbor. Once Lincoln's fellow feelings with the slaves could be crucified no longer, he recognized that the only way to enable oppressed Africans to become African Americans was to love them as neighbors.

As many contemporaries pointed out to the president, the rule of law as well as popular sovereignty were arguably on the side of the "rebels." (The Constitution said nothing about human equality, and Jefferson Davis and Alexander Stephens could also quote to their purposes the Declaration of Independence on liberty and self-determination.) Because Lincoln was trained in the law, his thinking was habitually dialectical — pitting antithesis against thesis and waiting for a judge or jury to decide the case — but, in the unprecedented crisis before the country, he struggled for a viable synthesis of the nation's (and his own) fundamental values, without a clear decider in place. The people were belligerently divided, and Lincoln knew that his words and deeds would shape public opinion as well as respond to or administer it. Lincoln slowly realized that he too was "controlled by events" and in need of, as well as subject to, a "higher power" (David Herbert Donald). Indeed, Lincoln was often paralyzed, theoretically and practically, until he trusted in God's prevenient grace and affirmed the "supernatural" virtue of charity (a.k.a. compassion and forgiveness) as heading his political ideals.

At the Cooper Institute, Lincoln noted that "Mr. Jefferson did not mean to say, nor do I, that the power of emancipation [of slaves] is in the Federal Government. . . . The Federal Government, however, as we insist, has the power of restraining the extension of the institution."[38] In his First Inaugural Address (1861), Lincoln reiterated his vow that "I have no purpose, directly or indirectly, to interfere with the institution of slavery in the States where it exists. I believe I have no lawful right to do so, and I have no inclination to do so."[39] I do not doubt the sincerity of this reassurance to the South, and it is manifest that Lincoln's prime prewar concern was to preserve peace and the rule of law rather than to condemn slavery as immoral or unnatural. He explicitly referred to the Constitution twenty-two times in the First Inaugural, and to the Declaration of Independence only once. But the point is that he grew over time.

---

38. Lincoln, "Address at Cooper Institute," pp. 124-25.

39. Abraham Lincoln, "First Inaugural Address," in *Speeches and Writings, 1859-1865,* p. 215.

In his "Proclamation of Thanksgiving" (1864), which set aside the last Thursday in November as "a day of Thanksgiving and Praise to Almighty God the beneficent Creator and Ruler of the Universe," Lincoln refers to the "cause" of the nation at trial in the Civil War as "Freedom *and Humanity*."[40] The reference to "and Humanity" is notable, as is the fact that national gratitude is to be directed to God. It is not possible to have humanity without freedom, but it is possible to affirm freedom without embracing humanity. Both freedom and humanity depended, in Lincoln's view, on divine providence.

Consider what David H. Donald has described as the "three possible plans" for peace and reconstruction being debated in 1863-1864, as Union victories at Gettysburg and Vicksburg initially seemed to be bringing an end to the war only to be eclipsed by the staggering losses of Grant at Cold Harbor and Sherman's defeat at Kennesaw Mountain. The first plan, favored by many Democrats, centered almost exclusively on the restoration of the Union: "it called for the President to withdraw the Emancipation Proclamation and to offer a general amnesty to the rebels. The Southern states, which had never legally been out of the Union, would simply send new congressmen to Washington, and the war would be over."[41] The second plan, proposed by conservative Republicans, added liberty to the good of union but stopped there. "Apart from insisting on the Emancipation Proclamation, [conservative Republicans] favored generous terms for the conquered South. [Secretary of State] Seward[, for instance,] let it be known that he hoped that no conditions, beyond the emancipation of the slaves, would be imposed on the returning rebels."[42] Some of this group, like Postmaster General Montgomery Blair, even recommended "the compulsory deportation and colonization of the freed blacks."[43] The third plan, put forward by the Radical Republicans, affirmed equality, as well as union and liberty, as a third aim of the war. "Most called for a drastic reorganization of Southern social and economic life before the rebellious states could be readmitted." Massachusetts senator Charles Sumner, for example, maintained that "it was the duty of the Congress to ensure that all citizens in the South, regardless of race, were guaranteed the equal protection of the law."[44] Manifestly, Lincoln's thinking underwent considerable change on these questions. For at least the first two years of the war, Lincoln seemed to endorse the stance of the conservative Republi-

---

40. Abraham Lincoln, "Proclamation of Thanksgiving," in *Speeches and Writings, 1859-1865*, p. 637, emphasis added.

41. Donald, *Lincoln*, p. 469.

42. Donald, *Lincoln*, p. 469.

43. Donald, *Lincoln*, p. 469.

44. Donald, *Lincoln*, p. 470.

cans. In short and paradoxically, it was largely Lincoln's religious fatalism that led him to free the slaves and largely his sympathy for the weak and vulnerable, rather than an unwavering commitment to natural liberty and equality, that led him to recognize the shared sanctity of whites and blacks. Lincoln did indeed feel himself "forced into glory," but by a righteous God who inscrutably governs the world, rather than by his own ambitious mind or opposing scheming men who would scurrilously govern others.

This is not to say that Lincoln was an orthodox Christian; he wasn't. And it is not to say that he was not capable of anger or vengefulness; he was. But, like the Abraham of Genesis, Lincoln (1) faced a conflict between fundamental sources of value and authority, and (2) resolved this conflict with reference to a greater good, the righteousness and mercy of God. Both Abrahams had simultaneously to honor and rise above an old order of "justice," based on prior choice and traditional hierarchy, by embracing a new understanding of divine love and human solidarity in the wake of that love. In the biblical Abraham's case, the contradiction was between his affection for and hope in his son Isaac, on one side, and his adoration of and obedience to his God Yahweh, on the other. Isaac was "the child of promise" through whom would be brought forth "many nations," yet God had apparently commanded that a burnt offering be made of that same child.[45] In the American Abraham's case, the contradiction, to repeat, was between positive law and natural law. He evidently could not be true to both the Constitution's pledge of unmolested Southern slavery within the Union and the Declaration's guarantee of liberty and equality for all. The solution for both "fathers of the faith" was "a teleological suspension of the ethical" — that is, a rising above accepted standards to serve some higher end — in which a new dispensation of charity was realized. The Judaic Abraham came to see that God's steadfast love *(hesed)* is incompatible with unbridled paternal power and ritual infanticide, even as the American Abraham at last recognized that God's gratuitous love of the world *(agape)* is at odds with boundless political autonomy and territorially limited slavery. Traditional Christians find unity in Christ Jesus (Gal. 3:28), while Lincoln spoke more often of the divine Father, but both would overcome slavery by appealing to the holiness of God rather than to either the conventions of men or the laws of nature.

What makes Abraham Lincoln such an iconic political figure, to summa-

---

45. I have argued elsewhere that the tension in Gen. 22 is, in reality, between Abraham's *storge* for his son and early Israelite religion's practice of child sacrifice. See Timothy P. Jackson, *Love Disconsoled: Meditations on Christian Charity* (Cambridge: Cambridge University Press, 1999), chap. 6.

rize, is that he struggled to harmonize the values central to liberal democracy at a time when those values were in violent conflict. I would list four major liberal goods with which the president wrestled. These goods are frequently thought today to be complementary, but Lincoln's time showed them to be often competing:

(1) respect for political order and the rule of law
(2) the right to individual self-determination (a.k.a. personal liberty)
(3) the right to political self-determination (a.k.a. popular sovereignty)
(4) the equality of all "men"

In the nineteenth-century American context, (1) primarily meant upholding the Constitution and enforcing its dictates across the entire Union, together with legitimate acts of Congress; (2) primarily meant permitting freedom of speech, movement, assembly, and religion — at least so long as this did not prove injurious to others; (3) primarily meant honoring free and open elections; and (4) primarily meant full recognition of the common dignity of each citizen. Initially, Lincoln gave priority to respect for political order and the rule of law, on the not implausible premise that upholding the Constitution and preserving the Union were indispensable to maintaining or restoring the other liberal desiderata. This was a position that he shared with the so-called War Democrats and conservative Republicans, and it led him initially to deemphasize if not deny personal liberty (e.g., the ending of slavery), popular sovereignty (e.g., accepting that the states could vote secession), and equality (e.g., the full social enfranchisement of the former slaves).

By the end of 1862, Lincoln had become open to a very tentative form of personal liberty for the slaves, yet he still insisted that the Emancipation Proclamation was a war powers act of the president, bearing only on those parts of the country still in revolt, and thus was compatible with the Constitution. He still was not committed to real political liberty for blacks (e.g., the right to vote or to hold public office) or to full civic equality (e.g., the right to serve in the military or to intermarry, etc.). It is crucial to realize that the two senses of liberty I have identified, personal and political, could themselves be subdivided and separated from full equality, at least in the mind of many of Lincoln's fellow Americans. Indeed, Lincoln himself so separated them in 1863 in first promoting union and limited emancipation without the full abolition of slavery nationwide and without the right of blacks to remain in the reconstructed USA as fellow citizens. By the middle of 1864, Lincoln had begun to flirt with both the moral correctness and the political feasibility of affirming at least some version of all four liberal values, simultaneously and indivisibly.

He emphatically made both union and emancipation preconditions of peace with the rebels, and endorsed the prospective Thirteenth Amendment ending slavery throughout the United States.[46] By early 1865, David Herbert Donald observes, Lincoln was meticulously planning for, not just a cessation of armed hostilities with the South, but "a peace that would ensure his war aims of Union, Emancipation, and at least limited Equality."[47] What made Lincoln not merely president but prophet, however, was his effective reversal of the erstwhile order of these values' importance and his locating the justifying ground for this reversal in charity. As difficult as it had been to add black liberty to national unity as a central war aim, Lincoln came to see that even liberty without human solidarity was hollow. It would be quite possible, for instance, to grant the slaves formal freedom and then simply set them adrift in a world of economic poverty, political disenfranchisement, and racial hostility. In fact, this is exactly what happened after Lincoln was shot and Reconstruction failed.

IV. Lincoln's Uniqueness

Michael Walzer has offered a pithy analysis of ethics that can help illuminate Lincoln's uniqueness, though not in ways that Walzer would accept. Walzer notes that there are "three common and important approaches" to morality: "the path of discovery, the path of invention, and the path of interpretation."[48] The path of discovery is exemplified, theologically, by a divine command ethic that sees morality as created by God and revealed to human beings; it is exemplified, philosophically, by a utilitarian ethic that sees values as objective and as apprehended with scientific detachment. The path of invention, in turn,

46. Oddly, at the Hampton Roads peace conference of February 3, 1865, and in subsequent conversations with Democratic representative James W. Singleton, Lincoln seemed to vacillate *once again,* suggesting that the eradication of slavery was *not* a precondition of peace or even an inevitable outcome of the war. David H. Donald declines to see this as a genuine change of mind, however: "It is more likely — though this can only be a speculation — that Lincoln's remarks stemmed from his realization that slavery was already dead. His principal concern now was that the war might drag on for at least another year. His purpose was to undermine the Jefferson Davis administration . . . if necessary through a campaign of misinformation." See Donald, *Lincoln,* pp. 559-60.

47. Donald, *Lincoln,* p. 574.

48. Michael Walzer, *Interpretation and Social Criticism* (Cambridge: Harvard University Press, 1987), p. 3. Walzer does not claim that these three alternatives exhaust the possibilities. See also Michael Walzer, *Thick and Thin: Moral Argument at Home and Abroad* (Notre Dame: University of Notre Dame Press, 1994).

rejects the notion that God's will or natural law is a preexisting reality with a claim on us and goes constructivist, aiming at a concrete decision procedure that produces agreement rather than a timeless insight that captures truth.[49] John Rawls on fair social contract and Jürgen Habermas on ideal speech situations are the foremost exemplars of such proceduralism in contemporary political contexts. For its part, the path of interpretation appreciates the force of the other two approaches, but it tends to see moral discovery as naïve or implausible (God is dead and nature is meaningless), even as it sees moral invention as too minimalist or abstract (like treating a hotel room as though it were a proper home) (pp. 14-15). Interpretation, Walzer's favored meta-ethic, emphasizes historical particularity and begins with texts, principles, and practices already ensconced in a distinctive human society. The interpretive prophet — for example, the Old Testament's Amos — is someone who identifies with his community yet confronts its waywardness and calls it back to its founding narratives and basic ideals. Walzer is aware that his accent on interpretation seems vulnerable to the charge of parochialism or conservatism, but he nonetheless maintains that radical social critique is possible on the basis of this path without appeal to the other two. He does not explicitly reject discovery and invention, but he is "tempted" to think that these are but "disguised interpretations," and he definitely considers them "efforts at escape" that are "unnecessary" (p. 21). Walzer avers, ultimately, that "the experience of moral argument is best understood in the interpretive mode" (p. 21). I have my doubts, however, and Lincoln is a case in point.

Lincoln was indeed what Walzer would call a "connected critic" who is "one of us" (p. 39) — someone who manifests solidarity with, rather than detachment from, his countrymen and countrywomen and their noblest traditions. But the mature Lincoln was not that only. Walzer observes that his three epistemic paths correlate, roughly and respectively, with the three branches of liberal government: the executive discovers, proclaims, and enforces laws; the legislature invents laws; and the judiciary interprets laws (pp. 18-20). But this simply highlights the problem of giving exclusive preeminence to one path/branch. Adequate moral philosophy must appeal to discovery, invention, *and* interpretation, even as adequate democratic politics must combine executive, legislative, *and* judicial functions. No doubt, part of Lincoln's good fortune was that he had legislative and judicial experience that he could put to use as chief executive. Moreover, he drew on many textual and sociological

---

49. Walzer, *Interpretation and Social Criticism*, p. 10. Page references to this work have been placed in the following text.

resources: he respected the U.S. Constitution, positively venerated the Declaration of Independence, and pleaded in his First Inaugural for Southerners to remember their common heritage with the North and to be "not enemies, but friends."[50] Lincoln's prophetic greatness came, however, in his partly rewriting the American story and expanding the ideals of his fellow citizens. In his empathetic feeling for the humanity of slaves and his final resolve to extend the franchise to many (male) blacks, he helped redefine the meaning of liberty and equality and thus to bring about a multiracial democracy that even the Founding Fathers had not imagined or intended. Obviously, Lincoln did not remake his country from scratch, any more than Jesus remade Israel; the "total replacement"[51] of one society by another is neither desirable nor possible. But Jesus and Abraham both embodied an *inspiration* that cannot be captured with the language of "interpretation" alone.

Walzer maintains that moral "argument is about ourselves; the meaning of our way of life is at issue"; and he drives the point home by adding that "there is a tradition, a body of moral knowledge; there is this group of sages arguing. There isn't anything else" (pp. 23 and 32). But this makes it sound like ethics is *all about us.* Walzer writes that "in a secular age God is replaced by other people" (p. 46), but if "standards are [merely] social artifacts" (p. 48), then we must inevitably be forgetful of the Deity in a very un-Lincolnesque way. Overcoming his own antebellum reasoning and rhetoric, Lincoln came to see that equality under God was the cornerstone of the American liberal experiment, with the rule of law and various forms of liberty flowing from this. He also realized, however, that social and political equality depended on not simply an abstract commitment to justice — as in the resettlement to Africa plan — but also a lived sense of fellow feeling. To treasure positive law and even national survival over personal and political liberty was self-defeating, he recognized, but he also saw that liberty without civic equality was hollow and that equality without divinely inspired charity was impossible. Lincoln at no time endorsed what might be called full human equality — political, economic, and cultural parity — for the freedmen. As Donald writes, "unlike the Radicals, he gave no thought to dividing up the estates of the defeated Southern planters and giving each black family forty acres and a mule. He offered no opinions on school integration, interracial marriage, or social equality between blacks and whites."[52] Yet Lin-

50. Lincoln, "First Inaugural Address," p. 224.
51. Walzer, *Interpretation and Social Criticism,* p. 52. Page references to this work have been placed in the following text.
52. Donald, *Lincoln,* p. 583.

coln did fully accept that the two races were now inextricably fellow Americans, and he endorsed suffrage at least for the more intelligent black men and those who had served in the Union army. None of this was legally permitted by the Constitution or morally required by the Declaration of Independence, as he initially construed them. The Declaration's "self-evident" truth "that all men are created equal," for instance, had originally moved Lincoln to condemn slavery and wish to limit its spread, but it did not foster emancipation and the right to vote until backed by the human compassion and understanding generated by the war and a sense of God's judgment upon it.

"Insofar as we can recognize moral progress," Walzer writes, "it has less to do with the discovery or invention of new principles than with the inclusion under the old principles of previously excluded men and women."[53] This may seem to describe what went on in the emancipation and enfranchisement of the American slaves, but moral principles and their human application cannot be so neatly separated. The very humanity of the slaves was at issue in the Civil War, and America's "old principles" themselves had to be changed if black men and women were to be included in civil society. To take more ancient examples, Jesus was not simply applying Hebraic teachings on holiness and neighbor love to publicans and sinners, any more than Saint Paul was simply extending the virtues of Roman manliness — note the etymology of "vir-tue" — to include women and slaves. For the teachings and the virtues were originally defined precisely to exclude publicans and sinners, women and slaves, as at best outsiders and at worst enemies. Sometimes both the extension and the intention, both the range and the meaning, of a value must be revolutionized. And this is exactly what Lincoln at last sought to do with regard to liberty and equality, with incomplete success.[54]

---

53. Walzer, *Interpretation and Social Criticism*, p. 27.

54. Harry Stout has argued that, in spite of Lincoln's charity, he embraced the "total war" represented, most conspicuously, by Sherman's tactics during his "march to the sea." (See Harry S. Stout, *Upon the Altar of the Nation: A Moral History of the American Civil War* [New York: Viking, 2006], passim.) Stout's is a historically learned and morally acute work, documenting in great detail how during the Civil War patriotism and Christianity became "interleaved and virtually inseparable, with patriotism leading and Christian ministers and churches in tow" (p. 124). It impresses upon one, unforgettably, the deeply flawed motives and rhetoric on both sides of the conflict, motives and rhetoric that often elevated nation above God. The book is marred, nevertheless, by two factors: (a) Stout mistakenly asserts that, according to traditional *jus ad bellum* criteria, "the only rationale for a just declaration of war is self-defense" (p. xiii), and (b) the phrase "total war" usually connotes direct, systematic, and lethal attack on civilians (noncombatants), which practice was not endorsed by either Lincoln or Sherman.

With respect to (a), just war theory has typically permitted military intervention either

Lincoln's reordering of the secular priorities listed above — respect for political order and the rule of law, the right to individual self-determination

---

to restore rights wrongly denied or to bring about the conditions necessary for decent human existence. Since World War II and Pope Pius XII, self-defense has been emphasized, but it has never been the only just cause. With respect to (b), various Union blockades, sieges, and confiscations, together with Sherman's and Sheridan's scorched earth policies, certainly did constitute assaults on civilian property and interests, and at times even civilian lives. Moreover, these assaults were incompatible with classical just war teachings, especially on proportionality. But the American Civil War did not involve a wholesale violation of the principle of discrimination, noncombatant immunity, so it is highly misleading to call the war "total." (Stout is aware that some will object to his use of this word; he himself grants that civilians were seldom targeted directly with lethal force, though many lost their lives as the result of foreseeable blockade, siege, and confiscation damage or the ensuing malnutrition and disease.)

Stout is correct to flag the ways in which the Civil War escalated to a fury and scale that few had predicted, and I by no means wish to defend the disproportionate suffering and death caused by Union troops. But Stout is wrong, I believe, to see Union tactics as solely, or even primarily, the result of loss of moral restraint. The story is one of mixed motives, to be sure, but it would be entirely too cynical to suggest (which Stout does not but others have) that the "real" reason the North fought the Civil War was simply hatred or self-interest rather than also genuine concern to uphold the rule of law and, eventually, to end the evil of slavery. In fact, I would maintain that it was partly because of their growing charity for the slaves that Lincoln and Sherman saw the necessity of ideologically and materially crippling a Southern social order based on ownership of human beings, lest that brutal order seek to reestablish itself. Alas, with the collapse of Reconstruction and the rise of Jim Crow, Southern white supremacy indeed reasserted itself, with often deadly effects.

As I make clear below, I consider pacifism to be a legitimate form of Christian conscience, a powerful witness in a violent world, but I also judge just war to be a defensible form of Christian faith. Some pacifist critics seem to assume that just war thinking is inevitably in uncritical service to, or otherwise corrupted by, the nation-state, when in fact it arose historically as a mode of religious criticism of the nation-state and its pretensions. Just war principles can certainly be misused or abandoned, as Stout amply illustrates. (Christians call this "sin," but it taints *all* human endeavors, including peacemaking.) In discussing "supreme emergency," for instance, Michael Walzer does indeed make an idol of the nation and give unqualified license to the use of murderous force in its defense. (See Michael Walzer, *Just and Unjust Wars: A Moral Argument with Historic Illustrations,* 4th ed. [New York: Basic Books, 2006]; see also my critique in *Love Disconsoled.*) But Walzerian "supreme emergency" is another name for "total war" and is not an expression of the just war tradition any more than was Andersonville Prison in Georgia or Abu Ghraib Prison in Iraq. It is, rather, a fundamental denial — dare I say, betrayal — of that tradition. That said, did Lincoln and his generals abuse their powers in the American Civil War? Absolutely, and just war standards highlight this fact. Were Lincoln and his generals justified in taking up the sword to put a stop to secession and slavery? Absolutely, and just war standards highlight this fact too.

For more on the less-than-total bellicosity of the American Civil War, see Mark Neely, *The Civil War and the Limits of Destruction* (Cambridge: Harvard University Press, 2007).

(a.k.a. personal liberty), the right to political self-determination (a.k.a. popular sovereignty), and the equality of all "men" — was not simply an arbitrary or expedient shuffling. It was made possible by appeal to a fifth good, the sacred virtue of charity, that was now seen to outstrip and undergird any and all democratic values. The Second Inaugural's (1865) "with malice toward none; with charity for all; with firmness in the right, as God gives us to see the right"[55] can be read as a triumph of forgiveness, even self-sacrifice, over natural forms of self-interest and self-assertion. Lincoln foreclosed the tendency of a victorious army or nation (or chief executive) to gloat, employing the biblical echo "let us judge not that we be not judged"; and he implicated both sides in guilt for the ongoing conflict, supposing that "He [God] gives to both North and South, this terrible war, as the woe due to those by whom the offence [of slavery] came."[56] This sort of reconciling act was necessary to atone for the Constitution's compromise with slavery — the American original sin — and to bring about a new social righteousness. Lincoln aimed to "achieve and cherish a just, and a lasting peace,"[57] so there is no question that goods other than charity were legitimate and important for him. Moreover, from early on Lincoln judged reason and a sense of duty to be indispensable in checking the passion and self-interest that can threaten a free society. But, as noted, biblical revelation and ecclesial institutions became ever more salient for him.

Walzer holds that, after Moses, "the law is not in heaven; it is a social possession. The prophet need only show the people their own hearts."[58] Lincoln came to see things differently. In his First Inaugural Address, before the bloody years of war, Lincoln sounded like a Walzerian immanent critic. Though he mentioned "the Almighty Ruler of nations," Lincoln did not once use the word "God" and rather blithely lumped together "intelligence, patriotism, Christianity, and a firm reliance on Him, who has never yet forsaken this favored land."[59] He appealed, most poignantly, to "the mystic chords of memory, stretching from every battle-field, and patriot grave, to every living heart and hearthstone," relying finally on "the better angels of our nature."[60] In his Second Inaugural, however, Lincoln was far less sanguine about human

---

55. Abraham Lincoln, "Second Inaugural Address," in *Speeches and Writings, 1859-1865*, p. 687.

56. Lincoln, "Second Inaugural Address," p. 687.

57. Lincoln, "Second Inaugural Address," p. 687.

58. Walzer, *Interpretation and Social Criticism*, p. 74.

59. Lincoln, "First Inaugural Address," p. 223.

60. Lincoln, "First Inaugural Address," p. 224.

hearts, minds, and national history. "The law" was no longer a social possession but a divine judgment. The 1865 Lincoln referred to God, by one name
or another, ten times and made decisively paramount the "true and righteous"
"judgments of the Lord" and the rather inscrutable "providence" of "a living
God."[61] America, North and South, was now not so much favored as it was
tried by the Deity. Even the great good of union was only a relative value, not
something, on the face of it, that was superior to states' rights; union had to be
ennobled by something higher and better: abolition of slavery and contrition
before God for its brutalities. For this purpose, Lincoln, like all true prophets,
had to "stand again at Sinai."[62]

One can admire the dignity and sense of duty embodied in Robert E.
Lee, and one can understand the freedom-loving resistance to centralized authority preached by Alexander Stephens, but, in failing to perceive the larger
issues at stake (including the full evil of slavery), both of these figures fall short
of Mr. Lincoln. Indeed, as Ulysses Grant said of Lee, his "cause was . . . one of
the worst for which a people ever fought"[63] — in spite of his valor and suffering. Such folly is, I believe, the usual result of allowing individual dignity and
popular sovereignty to trump universal sanctity and divine love. Some think
of personal pride and autonomy as the very essence of American liberalism,
and so look elsewhere for social ideals, but this is the defeated Rebels' view
of democracy, not that of the triumphant federals. The equal sanctity of all
human lives, a gift and call of God's love, is Lincoln's moral legacy, however
much this may have been violated in the last 150 years.

Conclusion: "A Sacred Effort"

Frederick Douglass called Lincoln's Second Inaugural "a sacred effort,"[64] and
this helps us see that it was a deeply religious, as opposed to merely political
or historical, achievement. In the end, charity, like other boons, Lincoln appreciated as a grace from God. As he famously said to the black workmen in
liberated Richmond who went to their knees before him and tried to kiss his
feet: "Don't kneel to me. . . . That is not right. You must kneel to God only,

61. Lincoln, "Second Inaugural Address," p. 687.

62. I take the quoted phrase from Judith Plaskow's *Standing Again at Sinai: Judaism
from a Feminist Perspective* (San Francisco: Harper, 1991).

63. Grant, *Memoirs and Selected Letters* (New York: Library of America, 1990), p. 735.

64. Douglass, quoted in *Reminiscences of Abraham Lincoln by Distinguished Men of His
Time,* ed. Allen Thorndike Rice (Kila, Mont.: Kessinger Publishing, 2005), pp. 191-93.

and thank him for the liberty you will hereafter enjoy."[65] Against all separatists, white and black, Lincoln came to see that the races must literally stand or fall together, before something Higher. To this Lincolnesque insight, I will attempt to be true in the balance of this book: prophets from John the Baptist to Martin Luther King Jr. must point ultimately to the Light that precedes any personal merit, state law, national principle, or traditional practice. For Christians, even "liberty and justice for all" must be governed by faith in the God who is agapic love.[66]

65. Donald, *Lincoln,* p. 576.

66. Given his assassination, we will never know how Lincoln would have handled the postwar years of his second administration — whether, for instance, he could have forestalled the emergence of the black codes and Jim Crow laws that effectively reenslaved many blacks. Without the spirit of true solidarity, *Plessy v. Ferguson*'s "separate but equal" principle proved, in Justice Harlan's prophetic words of 1896, "to be quite as pernicious as the decision made by this tribunal [the U.S. Supreme Court] in the *Dred Scott* case." (See John Marshall Harlan, "Dissenting Opinion in Plessy v. Ferguson," in *Civil Rights Since 1787: A Reader on the Black Struggle,* ed. Jonathan Birnbaum and Clarence Taylor [New York and London: New York University Press, 2000], p. 168.) Harlan makes it clear that law is concerned with solidarity and hatred, as well as with justice and injustice: "The destinies of the two races, in this country, are indissolubly linked together, and the interests of both require that the common government of all shall not permit the seeds of race hatred to be planted under the sanction of law" (p. 169). Interestingly, Harlan too was a Kentuckian, who initially supported the Union while opposing emancipation but who eventually came vigorously to oppose slavery. From Kentucky as well was Robert Anderson, the federal officer in charge of Fort Sumter when it fell in April of 1861 and to whom its control was returned in April 1865.

CHAPTER 2

The Image of God and the Soul of Humanity: Reflections on Dignity, Sanctity, and Democracy

If we start with the idea of man as an animal endowed with reason, we are not led by any necessary inference to God, and therefore not to man as a being essentially related to God.

KARL BARTH[1]

"Do not give dogs what is sacred; do not throw your pearls to pigs."

MATTHEW 7:6 NIV

Upon arrival in heaven . . . leave your dog outside. Heaven goes by favor. If it went by merit, you would stay out and the dog would go in.

MARK TWAIN[2]

1. Karl Barth, *Church Dogmatics* III/2, trans. Harold Knight et al. (Edinburgh: T. & T. Clark, 1960), p. 77.
2. *The Autobiography of Mark Twain* (New York: Harper Perennial, 1990).

A version of this chapter appeared in Terence Cuneo, ed., *Religion in the Liberal Polity* (Notre Dame: University of Notre Dame Press, 2005).

Introduction: Cultural Diagnoses

Thomas Jefferson's original draft of the Declaration of Independence held the equality of all men to be a "sacred and undeniable" truth. It was Benjamin Franklin who changed the wording to characterize human (or at least male) equality as simply "self-evident," in order to emphasize that the disgruntled colonists were forming a new nation based on shared reason rather than revealed religion.[3] Neither Franklin nor Jefferson was an atheist, but this shift from sanctity to self-evidence announced (and reinforced) a profound tension between traditional Christianity and the emergent American democracy. For over two and a quarter centuries, the American polity has wrestled with the meaning of this tension. Is the affirmation of human equality — together with rights to life, liberty, and the pursuit of happiness — a matter of secular philosophy alone, or can biblical faith still play a crucial part in our public discourse? Quite generally, are Christianity and democracy fruitfully interrelated, must they be forcefully severed, or is there some third alternative?

I approach these and related questions by examining what Christian political thinkers frequently hold to be the ground of human equality: the image of God. Within the Western Christian tradition, that image has often been identified with humanity's intellect and will — with what Thomas Aquinas, for example, calls "reason" and "rational appetite."[4] Intellect and (free) will, in turn, are frequently held to be the foundation of personal dignity. Our selves, our identities as unique persons, are due respect because of our capacities for independent thought and action; because we can formulate and achieve self-conscious ends, we ourselves are to be treated as ends and not as means only. Just how profound the thought and how ethical the action must be to count as dignified is much debated — must my ideas be brilliant and my deeds heroic, or is it enough to be capable of *any* self-conscious thought and action? — but the key point is that one must *achieve* dignity in time. Minimally, one must reach "the age of reason," or, maximally, one must exercise rational control in some remarkable way. Whatever the specific details, the general commitment to dignity is not to be undervalued. As the engine that drives concern for

3. Walter Isaacson, *Benjamin Franklin: An American Life* (New York: Simon and Schuster, 2003), p. 312; Isaacson is following Becker, Van Doren, and Maier in this observation.

4. According to Saint Thomas, "man is said to be the image of God by reason of his intellectual nature," and, properly speaking, "this image of God is not found even in the rational creature except in the mind" (*Summa Theologiae* I, qu. 93, arts. 4 and 6). Thomas goes on to suggest, however, that other powers of the soul (such as the will) may be called, secondarily, a "trace" of God or in the "likeness" of God (arts. 6, 7, and 9).

individual conscience and defense of democratic freedom, it is one of our chief cultural successes. We in the West have not always practiced respect for dignity, of course — just ask blacks, women, and gays, among others — but the ideal of respect is part of the creed of a faithful church as well as a liberal polity. Too much blood has been lost in this connection, by Christian martyr and American patriot, to belittle the relevant virtue.

Nonetheless, I maintain in this chapter that the praise of dignity has grown myopic and amnesiac. Franklin's "enlightened" editing has effaced too completely Jefferson's intuition about the sacred. In our insistence on dignity, we have become largely blind to and forgetful of its origin in sanctity. We have become increasingly unmindful, that is, that persons with interest-based rights — that is, rights that turn on achieved autonomous agency — only emerge out of impersonal needs and potentials that are communally produced and must be graciously addressed. The self has forgotten the soul, if you will, and the result is an impoverished view of God's image. To counteract this amnesia, I propose, first, to clarify the meaning of "dignity" and "sanctity," "self" and "soul," and the *imago Dei;* second, to argue that neither Christian charity nor liberal democracy can survive when rights are based exclusively on the self and its dignity; then, third, to conclude by gesturing toward some of the practical implications of the views I defend.

To anticipate in more detail, my theological diagnosis, shared by many wanting to rehabilitate Christianity, is that the *imago Dei* has been far too intimately associated with intellect and will. My political diagnosis, shared by many wanting to rehabilitate liberalism, is that the democratic citizen has been far too intimately associated with freedom and dignity. These two excesses are not unrelated, given (especially Protestant) Christianity's historical contributions to democratic culture. The two excesses together suggest a potent prescription: to reconstrue political theology such that both the image of God and the citizen of a democracy are understood with primary reference to sanctity rather than dignity.

I propose that we substantially disassociate the image of God from reason and volition and reconnect it with a particular human need and potential: to give or receive agapic love. If "God is love [*agape*]" (1 John 4:8), then in what else can the divine image consist, what else will lead us, in Barth's words, "to man as a being essentially related to God"? I further propose, more controversially, that bearing the image of God is a sufficient condition for citizenship in a democratic state and thus for the provisions and protections due such a citizen. In many circumstances, the need for agapic love constitutes the right to receive it; even as, in many circumstances, the capacity for agapic love constitutes the duty to give it. To care for the needy and vulnerable — the young, the poor, the disabled, the sick, the senile, the guilty, the alien, et al. — is to acknowledge fully the *demos* from which democracy gets its name. It is also to attend to "the least of these" with whom Christ identifies himself in Matthew 25:37-46.

The right to receive and the duty to give love will differ from the rights and duties associated with contractual or reciprocal justice, but they are no less real. Indeed, the right and the duty are so fundamental to human life that they are almost too important to be called by those terms. The language of "rights" and "duties" usually suggests an adversarial relation in which conscious claims and counterclaims must be adjudicated by principles of fairness. I write, nevertheless, of love's "right" and "duty" in order to avoid the impression that *agape* is merely supererogatory, a matter of private discretion or optional philanthropy. On the contrary, love of neighbor, attentive to the sanctity of life, is the indispensable social good. A "duty of justice" is a matter of rewarding achieved merit, punishing demerit, or keeping promises or contracts, while a "duty of charity" is a matter of responding to God's call or to the claim that another creature has on one simply by virtue of sharing the image of God. Duties of justice turn on reciprocity or retribution, while duties of love are more unconditional and possibly unilateral; duties of justice are founded on personal dignity, while duties of love are based on impersonal sanctity.[5] The straightforward point to grasp, however, is that you cannot even face the former duties without fulfilling the latter.[6]

Love of souls — what I call "political *agape*" — is, then, the perilously neglected civic virtue of our time. It is literally a "democratic" virtue, to reiterate, in that the common needs and potentials with which it is occupied are most evident in the *demos,* the most wretched and most defenseless class. But love of souls is first and foremost a Judeo-Christian virtue, in that (1) the sanctity of human lives is a function of their being made in God's image, and (2) the power to recognize and act on that sanctity in love is considered a gift of God's grace. Such love of neighbor is enjoined by the second love command

5. As I make clear below, I equate the "personal" with the idiosyncratic, the distinctive features of our individual historical lives; I equate the "impersonal" with the universal, the common features of our shared human natures. At times, I refer to this distinction as that between "existence" and "essence" without intending thereby to endorse existential*ism* or essential*ism.*

6. Even as an urban and industrialized society may lose its sense of dependence on nature and foolishly deplete its material resources, thereby visiting ecological and economic disaster on future generations, so an autonomous and dignified culture may lose its sense of dependence on nurture and foolishly devalue its human resources, to similar catastrophic effect.

of Matthew 22, and it is inseparable from "the first and great commandment" to love God without reserve (see Matt. 22:35-40). To acknowledge the primacy of sanctity and grace is to relativize such traditional democratic goods as individual freedom and majority opinion, but it is also to bolster such other democratic values as equality and universality.[7] The basis of human equality — indeed, of true individuality before God — is, for Christians, our universally shared sanctity.

The demotion of rationality and freedom as fundamental sources of social ethics is not novel, but that this demotion augments rather than threatens the overall case for democracy is not often appreciated. Some Christian thinkers — for example, Alasdair MacIntyre, Stanley Hauerwas, John Milbank, and Robert Kraynak — have begun to turn their backs on liberal democracy in the name of virtue. This is unwise, however. Democracy as practiced in the contemporary West is, admittedly, Christian faith's prodigal son — leaning toward individualism, materialism, and relativism — but the Christian church ought not to play the resentful older brother and deny consanguinity. One ought, rather, to work for repentance and reform; one ought to celebrate any genuine return to moral responsibility. Visions of liberalism that see it as morally empty or as settling for the lowest common denominator among self-interested agents are not the only alternatives. A morally perfectionist account of democracy that rehabilitates robust virtues like mercy and compassion is possible.[8]

The prophetic voice in Christian politics will always insist on the priority of charity to any particular party or political economy. Christlike love of God and neighbor will trump both idiosyncratic preference and general utility; it will be attentive to impersonal potency and vulnerability, moreover, as well as to personal liberty and dignity. But this attentiveness is a mainstay of democratic tradition itself, at its best.[9]

---

7. A proper understanding of political *agape* and the equal sanctity of all human lives may help deliver us from the false dichotomy between liberal individualism and communitarian collectivism.

8. See my "To Bedlam and Part Way Back: John Rawls and Christian Justice," *Faith and Philosophy* 8, no. 4 (October 1991): 423-47; later collected in *Moral Issues: Philosophical and Religious Perspectives,* ed. Gabriel Palmer-Fernandez (Englewood Cliffs, N.J.: Prentice-Hall, 1996). See also my "The Return of the Prodigal? Liberal Theory and Religious Pluralism," in *Religion and Contemporary Liberalism,* ed. Paul Weithman (Notre Dame: University of Notre Dame Press, 1997). Revised versions of these two essays are chapters 4 and 3, respectively, of the present work.

9. For a very helpful discussion of these issues, see Jeffrey Stout, *Democracy and Tradition* (Princeton: Princeton University Press, 2004). Stout is committed to the dignity and

I. Dignity and Sanctity

A. Definitions

The Latin term *dignitas* literally means "a being worthy, worth, worthiness, merit, desert," while *sanctitas* means "inviolability, sacredness, sanctity."[10] Though both Latin words and their English cognates have subsequently been used in theological contexts, sometimes interchangeably,[11] *dignitas* seems initially to have been at home in political and economic spheres, referring to the grandeur and authority of a particular office or station,[12] while *sanctitas* originally had ethico-religious overtones, referring to moral purity or holiness, especially when these were seen as divine gifts.[13] The more our English-speaking literature accents rational agency as the *singular* human station, the more the very idea of sanctity may seem quaint or absurd and so the more it will wither in relation to dignity. When this occurs, dignity cannot help but be identified with social elites, those with power and prestige, and those outside of these elites will, in turn, seem worthless or burdensome.

Harkening back to the Latin, I define "dignity" as achieved merit based on personal performance. Dignity is won by individuals in self-consciously embodying the good, freely choosing the right, and effectively maximizing social utility. Whether referring to a virtue of character or a principle of ac-

---

equality of citizens, but his repeated emphasis on "exchanging reasons and requests for reasons" (p. 209) as the fundamental democratic practice makes me worry about those who are *unable* to give and receive such reasons. There is arguably a creeping rationalism, even elitism, at work here: too much emphasis on intellectual virtues of conversation and achieved dignity rather than on human needs and vulnerable sanctity. What about fetuses, infants, the mentally handicapped, and the senile-demented — all those who cannot participate in democratic dialogue and some of whom are not now counted as citizens? Do they not fall under what Whitman calls the "principle of individuality" (p. 282)?

10. See Charlton T. Lewis and Charles Short, *A Latin Dictionary* (New York: Oxford University Press, 1987), pp. 577 and 1626. For similar points, see the entries for "dignity" and "sanctity" in *The Compact Edition of the Oxford English Dictionary* (Oxford: Oxford University Press, 1971), vols. 1 and 2, pp. 726 and 2633, respectively.

11. See, for example, U.S. Catholic Bishops, "Statement on Capital Punishment" (Washington, D.C.: United States Catholic Conference, 1980), p. 7.

12. This sense is still fully manifest in medieval Latin usage, as when Aelred of Rievaulx (1110-1167) writes, in translation, that "great caution must be observed in the conferring of dignities and offices, especially ecclesiastical ones," and that true friendship "is not puffed up by dignities." See Aelred, *Spiritual Friendship*, trans. Mary Eugenia Laker (Kalamazoo, Mich.: Cistercian Publications, 1974), pp. 124 and 115.

13. Lewis and Short, *A Latin Dictionary*, pp. 578 and 1626.

tion, dignity is accomplished in time and inspires or ought to inspire respect and admiration in others. As such, dignity is closely allied with social justice, construed as giving persons what they merit. A dignified party is given her due when she is respected, and she is often respected for being willing and able to give others their due *(suum cuique)*. More broadly, dignity underlies the calculation of rewards and punishments. Insofar as dignity entails the self-conscious exercise of autonomy, it is the necessary and sufficient condition for moral responsibility. For Kant, for instance, to be able to give oneself imperatives and to act on them for the sake of duty, is to be a dignified agent. Such an agent, in turn, is a member of the kingdom of ends and can be held accountable for her personal choices.[14]

I define "sanctity," on the other hand, as gifted inviolability based on impersonal essence. Sanctity inheres in the species by virtue of its typical needs and given potentials: the basic need for food, drink, company, clothing, health, and companionship, for example, together with the passive potential for rational thought, bodily growth, emotional pleasure, and religious faith.[15] Whether understood as a creation of God or a contingency of evolution, sanctity presupposes no particular action in time and induces or ought to induce awe and wonder in others. As such, sanctity is closely allied with agapic love, construed as willing the good for someone independently of merit. A sanctified party is not approached from within economies of exchange, but rather is treated with awe precisely to indicate that he is beyond price. More broadly, sanctity underlies the extension of compassion and self-sacrifice. Insofar as sanctity entails unself-conscious grace, unfulfilled promise, or unmet need, it invites charitable service. For Jesus, for instance, the innocence and fragility of children made them especially sacred.[16] Children are the paradigmatic members of the kingdom of God (Matt. 19:14); together with the hungry, the thirsty, the stranger, the naked, the sick, and

14. Immanuel Kant, *Groundwork of the Metaphysics of Morals,* in *Immanuel Kant: Practical Philosophy,* trans. Mary J. Gregor (Cambridge: Cambridge University Press, 1996), 4:433-36, pp. 83-85.

15. A passive potential (e.g., for language) must be engaged or cultivated by others in order to be realized.

16. The word "innocence" is usually contrasted with "guilt," and young children are standardly judged to be without guilt. But children's innocence/guiltlessness is deeper than that of adults. Calling an adult "innocent" implies that she has not committed some specific wrong, while calling a child "innocent" refers to his being anterior to attributions of praise and blame altogether. Though a human being possesses sanctity, a young child is not yet a morally responsible agent possessing dignity, as I define the term.

those in prison, they are "the least of these" that are intimately identified with Christ himself (Matt. 25:37-46).[17]

The word "sanctification" connotes growth in holiness and thus may seem to imply achieved merit, but this is misleading. The lead definition of "sanctification" in *The Oxford English Dictionary* is: "The action of the Holy Spirit in sanctifying or making holy the believer, by the implanting in him of the Christian graces and the destruction of sinful affections."[18] The key points are: (1) that the believer is largely passive in this process — she is "*made* holy" by the Spirit; and (2) that what is bestowed is sanctity, not dignity — he is "made *holy*" by the Spirit. Admittedly, a saint is called "sanctified," and we sometimes equate "saintliness" either with regularly doing one's duty or with going beyond the limits of duty.[19] But in this case the "duties" in question are duties of justice — honesty, fair dealing, promise keeping, and the like — while the distinctly religious connotation to "saintliness" refers to performing the duties of love — forgiveness, compassion, self-sacrifice, and the like. On the whole, it seems better not to conflate holiness with moral merit, at least not the merit associated with doing justice. Holiness and moral merit are distinct, given that the former is a gifted grace beyond the calculation of worth or attribution of cardinal virtue, while the latter implies a positive appraisal of worth or celebration of cardinal virtue.

The holy is "consecrated" or "set apart,"[20] an upshot of one or more of the theological virtues (faith, hope, love); the morally meritorious is useful or admirable, an upshot of one or more of the cardinal virtues (prudence, temperance, courage, justice).[21] In addition, holiness is sometimes ascribed to

---

17. Compare also Matt. 4:24: "and they brought to [Jesus] all the sick, those who were afflicted with various diseases and pains, demoniacs, epileptics, and paralytics, and he cured them." This verse could just as easily end with "and he loved them." Love is curative precisely in looking not at worth but at need, not at dignity but at sanctity.

18. *The Oxford English Dictionary* (Oxford: Oxford University Press, 1933/1978), 9:80.

19. See J. O. Urmson, "Saints and Heroes," in *Moral Concepts*, ed. Joel Feinberg (Oxford: Oxford University Press, 1969), pp. 61-62.

20. *The Oxford English Dictionary*, 5:345.

21. How active/passive the human being is in acquiring/exercising the theological virtues is much debated in Christian theology, with Catholics sometimes allowing more synergy between divine grace and human freedom than Protestants. I myself am an Anglican Arminian, holding that faith, hope, and love are supernatural gifts offered by God to all. We can do nothing on our own to achieve them, so we are "passive" in that sense; but we can freely accept or reject them, so the relevant grace is not irresistible. The cardinal virtues, on the other hand, are much more subject to human will. Again, to achieve a cardinal virtue is, thus far, to become dignified; to receive a theological virtue is, thus far, to be sanctified.

those who especially need to receive or have the potential to give the fruits of theological virtue, as well as to those who currently possess such virtue. Think of the need for loving care of children or deaf-mutes — we may call them "sacred" or "angelic" — and think of the manifestation in Christian saints of such care. Similarly, moral merit is sometimes ascribed to those who especially need to be treated with or have the potential to show cardinal virtue, as well as to those who actively exercise it. Think of the need for justice of assault victims or slaves — we may call them "deserving" or "righteous" — and think of the manifestation in nineteenth-century abolitionists of such justice.

If keeping one's own counsels, as well as one's promises to and contracts with others, is the quintessence of doing justice today, then blessing the young, the weak, the needy, and the guilty is the quintessence of incarnating love. Kantian dignity would ignore or overcome bodily requirements and emotional inclinations, while Christian sanctity is partially composed of such requirements and inclinations. Kant offers a categorical imperative to persons capable of self-control ("act only in accordance with that maxim through which you can at the same time will that it become a universal law"), while Christ offers concrete beatitudes to "nonpersons" out of control ("Blessed are you who are poor . . . you who are hungry . . . you who weep . . . when they exclude you, revile you, and defame you").[22] It is far from my intention to ridicule Kant's account of personal dignity; it is one of the most insightfully conceived and powerfully written visions of (part of) the moral life we have. Kant preserves the distinction between the personal and the narcissistic,[23] and defending sanctity does not entail vilifying dignity. My aim, rather, is to highlight the distinctive differences between dignity and sanctity, then to show their interdependence. A proper understanding of both is necessary for a full understanding of God's image.

B. Dignity and Sanctity Related

For all their contrasts of meaning, there is an internal relation between dignity and sanctity. The recognition of sanctity is a precondition of the achievement of dignity, so one cannot seek to respect the latter without also honoring

22. See Kant, *Groundwork,* 4:421, p. 73; and Luke 6:20-21.

23. For a discussion of this distinction, though without reference to Kant, see Robert Pinsky, *Democracy, Culture, and the Voice of Poetry* (Princeton: Princeton University Press, 2002), pp. 64-73.

the former. If the young, the weak, the needy, and the guilty are not cared for, they will never grow (back) into persons capable of giving or receiving justice. Even though rationality and autonomy are very great goods, sanctity is the prior value: a function, in fine, of the body and its passions. The needs and potentials that make us human are located first, chronologically and causally, in the nonrational flesh. Moreover, the animated body — the unfolding unity that is uniquely oneself — is bequeathed sexually. (Whether or not original sin is transmitted sexually, à la Augustine, original sanctity clearly is.) Through the unitive and procreative goods of sex, we acknowledge basic needs and vulnerabilities, as well as express deep affections and engender new lives. By and large, male needs female, and female needs male, not simply to perpetuate the species but also to find romantic complementarity.[24] (A schooled *eros* can be the vehicle of *agape*, a.k.a. unconditional care.) The needs and vulnerabilities are not to be lamented, for they make the affections and the lives possible.

Sanctity and dignity are not mutually exclusive, I want to emphasize, nor are they essentially antagonistic. One does not grow out of sanctity once one becomes a self-conscious agent, and truly self-conscious agents appreciate their ongoing physical limits and passional aspirations. When sanctity is defined in terms of impersonal needs and potentials, it is prior to dignity, to repeat, but even dignified persons remain needy and characterized by unfulfilled promise. Even rational individuals making "autonomous" choices are not without profound dependencies on one another and on God.[25] And no finite person is pure act, with an identity that is so fully realized that there is no room for growth, no potential for improvement. Changes and challenges still come, often in unplanned and unexpected ways.

Putting the point more forcefully, dignity and sanctity need each other. Attending to each provides an important check on both.

24. What about cloning as a means of reproduction and homosexuality as a denial of male/female complementarity? Human cloning is now neither medically safe nor morally defensible; until much greater technical mastery and psychological wisdom are had, it is irresponsible to risk the harm likely to be done to the subjects involved. Homosexuals still often speak of "masculine" and "feminine" partners, though these gender roles are no longer so directly tied to sexual difference. The deep need for romantic cooperation by two parties endures.

25. Related points are often made by secular feminists; see, for instance, Eva Feder Kittay, *Love's Labor: Essays on Women, Equality, and Dependency* (New York and London: Routledge, 1999), and Martha A. Fineman, *The Autonomy Myth: A Theory of Dependency* (New York and London: New Press, 2004).

C. Dignity Becomes Self-Defeating

When dignity becomes prideful, it neglects or even despises the exigencies of the flesh — the need for food and drink, the drive for sex, vulnerability to pain and injury, the fear of death — since these remind us of the narrow confines of our personal freedom. Only so much of our lives is under our rational control. A prideful dignity also tends to neglect or despise those human beings who live mostly in the body and its passions: fetuses, babies, the disabled, and the senile. These classes of individuals are literally "nonpersons," inasmuch as they are not self-aware agents capable of independent thought and action. If only rational agents ("autonomous persons") have a right to life, then there will be no substantive moral objection to abortion, infanticide, and involuntary active euthanasia for the irrational or nonrational.[26] Moreover, it has not been too large a leap in the past for an ethic of pure dignity to treat the poor, the illiterate, the criminal, the crazy, the gay, and the female as also outside the bounds of the moral community. These groups also live uncomfortably emotional, even animal, existences, according to some zealots of "reason" or "will" (*vide* Aristotle and Nietzsche on slaves and women, social Darwinists and old-line Stalinists on weaklings and peasants).

Neglect of human sanctity leads to the loss of personal dignity itself. Dignity withers not merely because without care for the young and needy there can be no future generations, but also because persons who do not honor their own neediness and finitude will tend to lapse into either a comic self-importance or a paralyzing despair. A foolish egotism or a degrading pessimism readily besets both groups and individuals who worship exclusively at the shrine of *Dignitas*. At the first extreme, a culture that embraces scientism and technical reason to the denial of humane values will believe it can pollute the environment, practice eugenics, and build nuclear weapons with impunity. Similarly, a man who embraces self-assertion and self-sufficiency to the denial of embodied limits will believe he can mortify the flesh, dominate women and children, and reject civil society with impunity. At the second extreme, a civilization that dwells on past glories compared to present impotencies will believe it has nothing more to lose in indulging resentment, dogmatism, and the terrorist's disregard for innocent human life. Similarly, a woman who holds

26. Peter Singer has argued for exactly this premise and conclusion; see his *Practical Ethics* (Cambridge: Cambridge University Press, 1993); *Rethinking Life and Death* (Oxford: Oxford University Press, 1994); and *Unsanctifying Human Life,* ed. Helga Kuhse (Malden, Mass.: Blackwell, 2002).

that raw power is all and that human sanctity, her own and others', is but a myth will have no grounds to protest abortion for sex selection, the hegemony of dominant males, and the gendered inequalities of unbridled capitalism.

Any ethical system that cannot recognize and preserve the necessary conditions for the emergence and continuance of its own highest good is, on its face, inconsistent. Kant argued that a noumenal agent ought not to take his own life — suicide is literally self-contradictory[27] — but the crucial issue is not whether to respect dignity once it is achieved but how and why to bring it about in the first place. An ethic of pure dignity that values only extant autonomy, cedes rights only to the already autonomous, and constrains the autonomous solely with appeals to rational self-interest, is building castles in the air. Respecting only achieved dignity cannot be willed as a universal law, for the two reasons adumbrated above: (1) without unearned care being given to the "merely" sacred (those who are not yet autonomous agents), no dignified persons ever emerge, and (2) any dignity that already exists is itself eroded when the agent believes, narcissistically, that there is no other value than her freedom or when the society believes, equally narcissistically, that there is no reason to choose one course over another other than that it is collectively chosen. It may be that only dignity, one's own and others', ought to be respected, but respect is not the only necessary moral attitude, even politically; reverence for sanctity is the antecedent virtue by which we continue to live, one that informs and constrains individual and corporate liberty.

I call the opinion that rational dignity alone has legal rights the "We have no king but Caesar" view, because it takes the collective good of autonomy and makes it the *solum bonum.* An ethic of pure dignity would read Western history as the saga of Rome without Jerusalem, of works without grace, of justice without love — that is, of Caesar without Christ. But this tack is self-deceptive, especially for democracies and even when it claims to be limited to politics, as I try to demonstrate at more length in section IV below.[28]

---

27. "A human being cannot renounce his personality as long as he is a subject of duty, hence as long as he lives; and it is a contradiction that he should be authorized to withdraw from all obligation, that is, freely to act as if no authorization were needed for this action." See Immanuel Kant, *The Metaphysics of Morals,* in *Immanuel Kant: Practical Philosophy,* 6:422, p. 547.

28. Some liberal apologists would celebrate personal dignity, and its attendant rights, as the singular *political* value, allowing room for sanctity as a private or familial concern but without extending it substantive legal protections. John Rawls approximates this view — see his *Political Liberalism* (New York: Columbia University Press, 1993), discussed in my chapter 4 — as does Ronald Dworkin, discussed below in this chapter and in chapter 5.

II. Selves and Souls

A. Definitions

Like "dignity" and "sanctity," "self" and "soul" are sometimes treated as synonyms, each meaning roughly "an individual" or "a person." In my lexicon, however, "self" and "soul" denote different aspects of a human being. Taken narrowly, the former term ("self") points to the contingent and idiosyncratic dimension of humanity, whereas the latter ("soul") denotes the necessary and universal. The thesis that there is a universal human nature with identifiable lacks and capacities, beneath or behind what is historically attained or self-consciously constructed, is out of fashion in some quarters these days, but it still has its defenders.[29] My own commitment to this thesis can only be judged by the plausibility of my lexicon and the work I attempt to make it do.

By "self" I mean the subject of the constellation of words and deeds, traits and talents, that flows from and then back into our higher cognitive and volitional faculties. We are defined by our personal virtues and vices, our particular turns of mind and efforts of will. The self is conditioned by time and chance, to be sure, but it is most distinctively associated with conscious reflection and free choice. As *The Oxford English Dictionary* observes, combining "self-" with another word often means "expressing reflexive action, automatic or independent action." The self both thinks and acts, both in relation to others and reflexively. With respect to another, a range of questions must be answerable if we are to claim to know his or her self: How smart is she? How loyal is he? What have been his triumphs and transgressions? To what does she give her attention and energy? More specifically, does he like modern art or classical literature? Does she like me? Similarly, the self asks reflexively: Who am I now and who might I become in the future? If I study hard, might I become a lawyer? If I pray hard, might I become a saint? And why did I decline to ask my best friend Helen to marry me, but then turn around and elope with Ursula, whom I just met? The self is also the part of us that answers the latter questions via inward address or outward action. We often don't know our selves until we overhear our own interior monologue or observe our own exterior behavior.

So regarded, the self is both a state and an activity. It is a state inasmuch

---

29. See, e.g., Martha C. Nussbaum, "Non-Relative Virtues: An Aristotelian Approach," in *The Quality of Life,* ed. Martha C. Nussbaum and Amartya Sen (Oxford: Clarendon, 1993); her *Sex and Social Justice* (Oxford: Oxford University Press, 1999); and her *Women and Human Development: The Capabilities Approach* (Cambridge: Cambridge University Press, 2000).

as it is constituted by whatever mental and moral habits have been cultivated in the past. At any given time, one has an identity composed of a myriad of dispositions and demeanors shaped by experiment and experience. But the self is also an activity inasmuch as it is the ongoing process of relating one's past identity to the future via the present. Given who I have been, what can I do now to become who I want to be? This process requires imagination and determination to be done well, but it is performed by every sentient person to a greater or lesser degree. As Søren Kierkegaard's pseudonym Anti-Climacus puts it, rather playfully: "A human being is spirit. But what is spirit? Spirit is the self. But what is the self? The self is a relation that relates itself to itself or is the relation's relating itself to itself in the relation; the self is not the relation but is the relation's relating itself to itself. A human being is a synthesis of the infinite and the finite, of the temporal and the eternal, of freedom and necessity, in short, a synthesis."[30]

By "soul" I mean those shared vulnerabilities and inchoate powers that come along with being human. Unlike what might be called "self-ish" factors — the things that consciously individuate us — "soul-ish" realities are the common phenomena of our finitude: the ability to feel pain and joy, the need to be loved and to love, the potential for bodily and psychic growth, etc. If "dignity" is identified with the achieved merit of mature selves, then "sanctity" refers to a gratuitous legacy owned equally by all souls. Selves are to desert and prudence as souls are to grace and providence. Selves are intentionally made and making, governed from within — as in "self-made man" — but souls are given and taken, gifted from without. All human selves have souls, but not all human souls have selves. Treating "personhood" as synonymous with "selfhood," all human persons (you and I) have souls, but so do prepersons (fetuses and babies), postpersons (the senile and the anile), and nonpersons (the mentally impaired and even, in a sense, future generations).

B. Emotion and the Body

If intellect and will are the primary seats of the self and its dignity, then emotion and the body are the primary seats of the soul and its sanctity. Rather than associating the soul with some rational and immaterial part of the person, I associate it with the passionate and material flesh. "The human body is the

---

30. Søren Kierkegaard (Anti-Climacus), *The Sickness unto Death,* trans. Howard V. Hong and Edna H. Hong (Princeton: Princeton University Press, 1980), p. 13.

best picture of the human soul," as Ludwig Wittgenstein says.[31] With its multiple orifices of sense perception, food consumption, waste elimination, affect expression, and sexual union, the body is sacred. If to be a dignified self is to be hard and angular, to be a sanctified soul is to be permeable. Love and hate, joy and fear, humor and anger, cynicism and piety flow into and out of our bodies as surely as do air and water, bread and wine, blood and semen, urine and feces. Equally certainly, these "soul-ish" exchanges have little to do with our higher cognitive and volitional faculties. They are not merely autonomic, but neither are they autonomous choices. On the contrary, they often work better when we stop thinking and let go. Mental aptitude and willpower are undeniably important, and their loss is normally tragic, even as their misuse is often criminal. But there is a world of noncognitive well-being[32] and emotional engagement with others that does not depend on "reason" or "rational appetite," and that is prior to questions of merit or demerit. One can be ashamed of the nakedness and dependency of the body, for example, entirely independently of any guilt for bodily wrongdoing.

I learned about the limits of reason, and the potency of charity, while working one summer in the locked Alzheimer's ward of a California nursing home and hospital. There I spoke every day with a lovely woman whose words made absolutely no sense, and there I watched every day as a former ballerina giggled like a five-year-old girl as she pirouetted down the hall strapped to her wheelchair. One must never romanticize the affliction that is Alzheimer's disease, but my sadness over the diminishment experienced by these two elderly women was tempered by a sense that they were still present to me and to God, still capable of receiving and even giving love. In the final stages of dementia, all a patient can do is take, but so long as human caring can get through the ears and eyes, nose and mouth, to touch the soul, so long is that soul sacred. A patient who is beyond all care, giving it and receiving it, is already dead and may be removed from "life support," even if vestigial biological processes remain. But a patient still able to receive care remains alive and one of us, even if independent personality has waned.

The body is influenced by individual choices in time and space, of course — one has the physique at forty that one deserves — but the innate potencies and involuntary systems of the body do not vary much across borders or time zones. Here is no Cartesian dualism, I emphasize, since I do not equate the self

---

31. Ludwig Wittgenstein, *Philosophical Investigations,* trans. G. E. M. Anscombe (Oxford: Blackwell, 1958), p. 178e.

32. I take the phrase "noncognitive well-being" from Stephen G. Post, *The Moral Challenge of Alzheimer Disease* (Baltimore: Johns Hopkins University Press, 1995), p. 9.

with a separate metaphysical substance distinct from the soul and the matter in which it inheres. Again, the self and the soul are dimensions of the maturing human being, inseparable in reality if separated all too often in thought. To consider either the self or the soul to be ethereal or ghostly is more Hellenistic/Greek than Hebraic/Christian. Each human life is an evolving yet indivisible unity of mental and physical properties, volitional and emotional attributes, though at the margins (e.g., in the very young and the very old) the mental/volitional may be minimal and the physical/emotional maximal.[33]

The ancient Greek word *psyche* is usually translated "soul" and then contrasted with *soma*, which is usually translated "body." When construed in this way, "soul" is often connected with "mind" *(nous)* and "volition" *(thelema)*, as quite distinct from (even opposed to) "passion" *(thumos)* and "flesh" *(sarx)*.[34] My account departs from this complex and venerable tradition precisely because it aims to be truer to Moses and the prophets than to Plato and the philosophers. In the King James Version of the Bible, Genesis 2:7 describes how "man became a living soul," the word translated as "soul" here being the Hebrew term *nephesh*. *Nephesh* is usually rendered as "a breathing creature," but it can also connote the broader notion of "vitality" as such. A breathing creature or the embodiment of vitality is much closer to what I mean by "soul" than is a detached or immaterial Greek *psyche* as described above. (Interestingly, the Greek word for passion, *thumos*, can literally mean "breathing hard.") When God breathes into Adam, he is animating dust, making it/him "a living soul"; but Adam has not yet had the experiences, has not yet made the intentional choices, that will constitute him a unique person/persona/self. Adam's self emerges only with reflection and decision — only after he is made aware of the tree of knowledge and perhaps, I am tempted to say, only after he has

---

33. Cf. Peter Strawson's account of "persons" in *Individuals: An Essay in Descriptive Metaphysics* (London: Methuen, 1959).

34. Typical of the Western tendency to identify "soul" with "mind," as well as to associate both with the "self," is Owen Flanagan's *Problem of the Soul: Two Visions of Mind and How to Reconcile Them* (New York: Basic Books, 2002). Flanagan's is a complex and important book, but it employs the sort of intellectualist vocabulary that inevitably leads to "the mind/body problem": Is the mind made in "the humanistic image" of philosophy and theology or in "the scientific image" of biology and chemistry? Is the soul/self nothing but the mutable brain, or does it have a permanent and immaterial essence? For my part, I want to reject Flanagan's initial step of equating human identity with the "mental" powers of reflection and free will. This step makes the brain the privileged organ of inquiry and the soul/self nothing but a synonym for rational agency. Our shared humanity is more than rational agency, I have been arguing, and when the soul is seen as seated in the entire body and as possessed of needs and potentials antecedent to self-consciousness, this fact comes into clearer focus.

eaten from it and thus become "self-conscious." Prior to God's prohibition in the garden, if not Adam's violation of that prohibition, Adam is a living human being but only potentially a responsible moral agent. Prior to God's "Thou shalt not," as Kierkegaard reminds us, "[t]he spirit in man is dreaming."[35]

C. Autonomy and Holiness

The ancient Greek word *autos* is usually translated "self," either alone as the reflexive pronoun or in combination with other personal pronouns, as in "himself" *(heautou)* and "yourself" *(seautou)*. In turn, *nomos* is rendered as "law" or "regulation." Thus something or someone is "autonomous" if it/he/she is literally "self-lawed" — meaning self-regulated or self-governing. The Greek idea was originally at home in the context of relations between city-states, with a polis claiming "autonomy" when it deemed itself neither client, colony, dependent, nor slave of another polis — Athens or Sparta, say — but rather an independent political body entitled to pass its own laws and generally capable of self-rule. As Jerome Schneewind, citing R. Pohlmann, has written, "Initially standing for a political conception in Greek thought, the term ['autonomy'] came to be used in religious controversies during the Reformation; but its main use in early modern times was in political discussions. Kant seems to have been the first to assign broader significance to it, using it in his theoretical as well as his practical philosophy."[36] If the Isle of Milos would claim political autonomy from Athens, Kant would claim personal autonomy from God. Kant was no more motivated by a tendency to licentiousness, of course, than Milos by a desire for anarchy. Rather, Kant "invented" the contemporary conception of "morality as self-governance," to borrow Schneewind's terms, because he believed in "the dignity and worth of the individual."[37]

Kant turned a collective political notion into a matter of individual conscience by insisting that "the true vocation of reason must be to produce a will that is good"[38] and that the good will acts neither for private advantage nor for the common good "but from the idea of the *dignity* of a rational being."[39]

35. Søren Kierkegaard (Vigilius Haufniensis), *The Concept of Anxiety,* trans. Reidar Thomte (Princeton: Princeton University Press, 1980), p. 41.

36. J. B. Schneewind, *The Invention of Autonomy* (Cambridge: Cambridge University Press, 1998), p. 3 n. 2.

37. Schneewind, *The Invention of Autonomy,* p. 6.

38. Kant, *Groundwork,* 4:396, p. 52.

39. Kant, *Groundwork,* 4:434, p. 84.

For Kant, "*[a]utonomy* is . . . the ground of the dignity of human nature and of every rational nature," and an autonomous being "obeys no other law than that which he himself at the same time gives."[40] An autonomous will is, literally, "a law to itself."[41] Thus Kantian morality is not a matter of obedience to the commands of the Deity (much less other people) but a matter of the reflexive activity of our inmost selves. We must freely *choose* to act on rational principles that we ourselves authenticate, and the capacity "of doing . . . actions not from inclination but *from duty*"[42] is the ground of our distinctively moral value as noumenal agents.

In contrast to Kant's frequent use of the German word *Autonomie,* the word "autonomy" appears nowhere in the major English translations of the Bible (e.g., the KJV and the NRSV). Instead of "autonomy," we hear much of "holiness" (*qodesh* in Hebrew, *hagiosune* in Greek). Holiness is a function of being inspired by or reflective of God and God's perfection; a holy human being or person is one "[s]pecially belonging to, commissioned by, or devoted to God."[43] In Scripture, to be holy is to possess sanctity, even as, in Kant, to be autonomous is to possess dignity. The difference is that biblical sanctity is seen as a gift from above, something passive, while Kantian dignity is judged an achievement from within, something active. In English, we speak of a person as "exercising autonomy" and as capable of "self-governance," but it would sound odd to say that the person "exercises holiness" and is capable of "soul-governance." In declaring that the only thing that is unqualifiedly good, "good without limitation," is "a good will,"[44] Kant set the stage for invidious contrasts between personal dignity, something rational, and impersonal sanctity, something religious.

Admittedly, Kant did discuss the idea of "a holy will," but such a will was inhuman. "Complete conformity of the will with the moral law is . . . *holiness,* a perfection of which no rational being of the sensible world is capable at any moment of his existence."[45] The best we humans can hope for is "endless progress" toward perfection in a "postulated" afterlife,[46] on Kant's view, while a truly holy will is outside of the bounds of moral obligation and bodily drive

40. Kant, *Groundwork,* 4:436 and 4:434, pp. 85 and 84.

41. Kant, *Groundwork,* 4:440, p. 89.

42. Kant, *Groundwork,* 4:398, p. 53.

43. *The Oxford English Dictionary,* 5:346.

44. Kant, *Groundwork,* 4:393, p. 49.

45. Immanuel Kant, *Critique of Practical Reason,* in *Immanuel Kant: Practical Philosophy,* 5:122, p. 238.

46. Kant, *Critique of Practical Reason,* 5:122, p. 238.

altogether.[47] The two decidedly unchristian presumptions here are: (1) that holiness is located in the will alone, and (2) that holiness and humanity are incompatible. In Christianity, "holy communion" is equated preeminently with a social and very bodily act of eating and drinking — indeed, the elements consumed are body and blood — rather than with any noumenal free choice, however dutiful. Whatever his merits, and they are considerable, in leaving behind embodied sanctity as a part of the good life (the goodness of life), Kant left behind much of the image of God.

Let me now explore the biblical meaning of the image of God, asking how it might be unrationalized and thereby retrieved for theological and political purposes. Discussion of the *imago* will allow me to pull together the foregoing distinctions between dignity and sanctity, selves and souls. To anticipate a possible misreading, let me say that this is no postmodern exercise in misology: to note the limits of reason is not to be irrational. As a corrective to Kant's allowing reason to criticize itself, I try to overhear the critique of reason by God and the flesh. Reason, like autonomy, has its proper place. As above, I offer, not irrationalism, but what might be called a "critique of pure dignity." This will set the stage for a discussion of the place of sanctity and its accompanying rights in a democratic society.

III. The Image of God

A. Definitions

In Genesis 1:26, God resolves to create "humankind" *(adam)* "in our image" *(tselem).* The Hebrew word *tselem* can mean either an illusory shade/phantom or an accurate representation/figure. Given that God is the artisan, one inclines to the latter reading, but one ought not to gloss over the ambiguity here too quickly. The "shady" or "unfinished" nature of humanity is nicely captured by the Hebrew term. In Genesis 1:27, at any rate, we are given a further unpacking

47. "*Morality* is . . . the relation of actions to the autonomy of the will, that is, to a possible giving of universal law through its maxims. . . . A will whose maxims necessarily harmonize with the laws of autonomy is a *holy,* absolutely good will. The dependence upon the principle of autonomy of a will that is not absolutely good (moral necessitation) is *obligation.* This, accordingly, cannot be attributed to a holy being." See Kant, *Groundwork,* 4:439, p. 88. Given its "subjective imperfection" (meaning "pathological" loves and wayward "inclinations"), "the human will" must flee bodily idiosyncrasy and rely on autonomously chosen imperatives, which autonomy is not attributable to "the *divine* will." See 4:414, p. 67, and 4:399, p. 55.

of *tselem*. There the image of God is equated with sexual differentiation and perhaps gender complementarity: "male and female he created them" and "God blessed them, and God said to them, 'Be fruitful and multiply. . . .'"[48] This accent on bodily difference within the first couple makes it unmistakably clear that the *imago Dei* denotes more than individual mind and will. The image of God may be said, loosely, to inhere in each individual, but, properly speaking, Adam and Eve together constitute the *imago*. Their love for and cooperation with each other highlight the fact that, from the outset, the image of God is social and bodily, not inward and abstract. Adam and Eve need each other, and their union — what will later be called their "one flesh" (Gen. 2:24) — has the potential for procreation.

The second creation story (Gen. 2:4b-25) contains, notoriously, a different chronology from that of the first (Gen. 1:1–2:3), with man being made first, then the animals, then woman. Some commentators construe this account as more patriarchal than the initial story in which male and female are created simultaneously and as a couple constitute the image of God. They point out that Eve's being made from Adam's rib reverses the natural order of biological birth, in which man comes out of woman, and apparently gives a priority and authority to Adam that Eve lacks. Other commentators have disputed this construal, noting that Eve is called a "helper" (literally a "partner") fit for Adam. Her being made from his rib connotes equality and relatedness, they maintain, not subordination. Eve alone is bone of Adam's bone and flesh of Adam's flesh, and the order of her appearance actually makes her the culmination of creation rather than an afterthought. Indeed, rather than being brought in as a mere prop to please Adam, Eve is arguably more active and intelligent than her "husband."[49] I favor the more egalitarian reading of Genesis 2:4b-25,

---

48. Karl Barth is the premier Christian theologian of the last century to interpret the image of God, as referred to in Genesis, in terms of sexual dimorphism and relatedness. See his *Church Dogmatics* III/2 and III/4. In III/2, p. 324, Barth concludes that man's humanity is "fellow humanity," that "[b]ecause [God] is not solitary in Himself, and therefore does not will to be so *ad extra*, it is not good for man to be alone, and God created him in His own image, as male and female."

49. See Phyllis Trible, "Eve and Adam: Genesis 2–3 Reread," in *Womanspirit Rising: A Feminist Reader in Religion* (San Francisco: HarperSanFrancisco, 1979), pp. 75 and 79. While I find Trible's defense of an egalitarian reading of the second creation account generally persuasive, I believe she goes too far in construing the pre-Eve Adam as physiologically androgynous (pp. 74, 76, and 78). He is a "man" *(adam)* made of "soil" *(adamah)*, and before Eve is formed out of his rib he is not yet aware of himself as a male, but the latter is an epistemic point about what he realizes, not an ontological point about what he is. It is exactly because Adam is a human male without a human female that he is dissatisfied with both solitude and

especially when it is paired with Genesis 1:1-23, but one need not deny the ambiguity involved to draw several important conclusions about the *imago Dei*.

In terms borrowed from my previous discussion, to be made in the image of God is to embody an impersonal sanctity that ought to be honored and protected. The bearers of God's image normally also have the potential for a personal dignity that ought to be respected and admired, but this is not always the case (as with the mentally impaired or senile). Adam and Eve clearly want and need each other's love, and this interdependence characterizes them before they fall into sin and shame. The need to receive love or the potential to give it I equate with the core of human sanctity, while the actual extension of love to others (and oneself) I equate with the highest human dignity, so high in fact as finally to outstrip dignity as concerned to give and receive only what is due.[50] Both sanctity and dignity stem from the God who is love, however (see 1 John 4:7-12), and for this reason the first parents and all their progeny are said to be in God's image.

The above equations make two points, the first anthropological and the second theological. (1) They highlight the fact that all human lives, male and female, share equally in the divine. (This is an important corrective if rationality and autonomy are thought of as peculiarly masculine ideals.) The young and the old, the masculine and the feminine, the weak and the wicked all need agapic love and can receive it with profit — usually but not exclusively in the context of family life — hence they must be counted as bearers of God's image. We were not created self-sufficient but rather soul-dependent. (2) The equations represent a truer picture of the biblical God's way with the world

---

the animals. To think Adam initially a hermaphrodite renders it impossible to understand why he pines for a partner and why he is so enthusiastic about being given Eve. Eve awakens Adam to conscious masculinity, but only because he is already biologically male and in some sense incomplete without her. (God's incompleteness theorem is offensive to some feminists, but note that it is Adam who is depicted as poignantly needing Eve. Can I help it if the Deity is a traditional romantic?) To emasculate the body of pre-Eve Adam is to suggest that human sexual differentiation was not part of God's original plan for creation, a story line much more Aristophanic and Greek than Mosaic and Hebrew. See also Trible, *God and the Rhetoric of Sexuality* (Philadelphia: Fortress, 1978), pp. 72-143; and Brevard Childs, *Old Testament Theology in a Canonical Context* (Philadelphia: Fortress, 1986), pp. 188-95.

50. If one helps one's wife with the kids, for example, this may be an expression of moral dignity if it is pursuant to a promise or otherwise part of an agreement regarding the division of family labor, or it may be an act of neighbor love if it is more spontaneous and gratuitous. The point is that loving-kindness is a moral excellence that typically rises above calculations of desert, contract, and compensation. I thank Terence Cuneo for moving me to clarify this distinction.

than one that portrays God as looking only to merit and demerit. Whether one refers to God's calling male and female his "good" image, God's declaring his steadfast love *(hesed)* for Israel, or God's incarnating in Jesus Christ, the Deity's covenantal care does not wait on humanity's maturation or achievement. God loves us first (1 John 4:10), that is, while we are yet insensate in the womb (Ps. 139:13-16; Jer. 1:5) and while we are yet sinners in society (Rom. 5:8). A gracious providence does not overturn temporal justice, but it does precede, uphold, and even temper that justice.

B. *The Priority and Durability of Sanctity*

When the image of God is identified with dignified selves, this tends to encourage social elitism, if not genocidal cruelty, toward the "undignified" souls. As Kurt Bayertz writes, "[i]n Ancient times, the concept of dignity usually referred to respect for individuals with a high social status: a Greek king or a Roman senator, for example."[51] The ancient world valorized socioeconomic class, whereas the modern world worships self-conscious autonomy. But invidious contrasts between "us" and "them" are implicit in both moves. The best way to combat such elitism, to repeat, is by conceiving of the *imago* primarily as the bearer of sanctity and only secondarily as the fount of dignity. Indeed, the image of God endures even when dignity is lost or never appears, so long as the sacred need to receive or ability to give *agape* abides. "God is love" is the one unequivocal thing we can say of the Deity (1 John 4:8), and his image must reflect this fact. If Adam and Eve are made in God's image prior to their exercising any autonomous agency (Gen. 1:27), achieved dignity cannot be essential to the *imago;* and if Cain, the first murderer, retains his status as divine image even after his guilty act (Gen. 4:8-16), loss of dignity cannot be destructive of the *imago.*

The priority of sanctity is indicated by the fact that we are touched by innocent children and pity guilty adults regardless of calculations of merit or demerit. Because of their sanctity, we honor other human beings both before and after we respect them. Drawing on various etymological sources, James F. Keenan allows that "[t]he overarching effect of sanctity is veneration and inviolability; the overriding reason for both is its sacral quality, a point found in

51. Kurt Bayertz, "Human Dignity: Philosophical Origin and Scientific Erosion of the Idea," in *Sanctity of Life and Human Dignity,* ed. Kurt Bayertz (Dordrecht, Boston, and London: Kluwer Academic Publishers, 1996), p. 73.

the Scriptures, e.g., in 2 Maccabees 3.12 and 1 Corinthians 3.17."[52] To appreciate sanctity is to adopt a "do no harm" and "help if you can" attitude that often permits dignity itself to emerge or reemerge. We wonder at the freshness of a newborn (at least once she is cleaned up) but also at her frailty, at the complexity of a child but also at her incompleteness; we justly punish a thief or a murderer, but we also sorrow over her criminality (at least once she is caught) and usually seek to reform her.

The Hebrew-Christian Bible is not the only text to gesture toward an egalitarianism that treasures human life; writings of the Stoics also come to mind.[53] The Bible is unique, however, in attempting to base its universalism not on reason and volition but rather on the social and sexual body. A much more stable equal regard can be grounded in instinctual need and inherited potential, the solidarity of the flesh, than in contemplative aptitude and authentic agency, which tend to generate hierarchies of achievement. We are all mortals who must be fed and clothed, and who require affection and encouragement, but we are not all geniuses or paragons. Of course, bodily criteria can also found elitism — we are not all beauty queens or Olympic athletes — but I associate the image of God first with physical need and potential, not with physical charm or prowess. It is the ill and dependent in whom sanctity most shines and to whom charity most reaches out, not the healthy and (supposedly) self-sufficient.

C. *The* Imago *as Finite and Fallen*

Even as medical doctors can learn about physical health by studying disease, so moral theologians can learn about the image of God by examining how it is "stained" or "warped" by sin. One powerful way to look at the original sin is as an attempt to appropriate for personal use, exclusively for oneself, what should be accepted as an impersonal gift for all souls. Christian scholars have sometimes interpreted the biblical story of the fall of Adam and Eve as a *felix culpa,* a fortunate fault, in which the naïve first parents take their initial steps toward informed, responsible adulthood. Indeed, it is sometimes suggested that God wanted, or should have wanted, Adam and Eve to eat of the fruit of the tree of knowledge to complete their moral education and to realize

---

52. James F. Keenan, S.J., "The Concept of Sanctity of Life," in *Sanctity of Life and Human Dignity,* p. 3.

53. See Bayertz, "Human Dignity," p. 73.

themselves as images of God. Without the initiation into moral knowledge, the argument goes, creatures would have remained dull and benighted. This reading is a colossal anachronism, however, and a dangerous misunderstanding of both human nature and the nature of sin.

One basic point must always be kept in mind in reading Genesis 2–3: God does not prohibit Adam and Eve from *looking at* and *learning from* the tree of knowledge of good and evil; rather, he forbids them to *eat* of it. All other trees in the garden are "fair game" as food, so to speak, but there is this one exception: the tree of ethical values. The previous verses of Genesis have depicted God as majestic Creator, capable of declaring creation "good" even before human creatures are made. Right at the beginning, then, humanity is implicitly warned against a *hubris* that would see itself as the measure of all things. After humans appear, God gives them "dominion" over an exceptionally broad range of creatures; the Creator is not stingy. There are limits, however: the ethical values inherent in Eden are to be apprehended with awe rather than seized as one's own. Unlike seeing and appreciating, eating is a form of appropriation that internalizes and destroys the reality at which it is directed. Eating would turn what is external into a part of one's very self, and it is an "all-consuming" pride that thinks it is the sole inventor of values that is forbidden, then punished, in the garden. When Adam and Eve ate the forbidden fruit, they denied their finitude and became the first moral subjectivists. They clutched the apple of God's eye and claimed it as their own product/produce.

It was not their being curious or sexy that cost Adam and Eve Paradise, then, but their making an idol of their own dignity. It is no wonder that their firstborn son, Cain, became a murderer: when parents valorize their own dignity, children violate others' sanctity, if only to assert themselves or get attention.

D. An Objection and a Reply

It may be objected that my account of the image of God is too expansive or permissive. If the *imago Dei* is minimally a function of the need to receive or ability to give agapic love, does this not mean that plants and animals also bear the divine image? Don't cherry trees and chipmunks, sea kelp and fresh water salmon, all profit from forms of charity? And, if so, aren't they all made in the image of God and possessed of sanctity rights? In a phrase, not likely. By "the need to receive or ability to give *agape*," I refer to what is almost surely a distinctly human phenomenon.[54] Plants and animals have independent value and can be both benefited and harmed by human behaviors, but flora and fauna do not strictly need loving intercourse with humans to flourish. They can, in principle, get along without us. Domesticated animals rely on human beings for food and shelter, and many would die without ongoing support from *Homo sapiens.* This is a contingent dependency, however, and is not inherent to the nature of the beasts as such. God might have declined to create Adam without thereby consigning the rest of biological creation to futility and extinction, but God could not have refrained from creating Eve without thereby condemning Adam to misery and death. Human beings congenitally require the company and cultivation of their own kind, love of *neighbor,* and without it we waste away and perish. The self's catchphrase may be *cogito, ergo sum* ("I think, therefore I am"), but the soul's is *amor, ergo sum* ("I am loved, therefore I am").[55]

Consider a parent speaking animatedly to a babe in arms. The adult is not aiming to communicate information to the child, for the latter is too young to comprehend, nor is the adult looking for an immediate behavioral response. Rather, the parent is calling the baby into personhood by engaging its passive potential for language. The parent is loving the baby unconditionally, meeting its impersonal needs and engaging its nascent capacities, in a touching human communion. Without such agapic love — dignity reaching out to sanctity — the baby will literally die, or be so deeply stunted as never to achieve normal cognitive and emotional function. A few animals may be self-aware enough to qualify as "persons," and these few may well have a right to life, but it seems implausible to say that they either essentially need agapic love or love others agapically.[56] They evidently don't need agapic (or any other kind of) love *from us,* as part of their intrinsic natures. Jesus' "Do not give dogs what is sacred" (Matt. 7:6 NIV) can sound rather harsh, but even the

---

54. I speak here of creaturely *agape.* God loves agapically, but I am concerned with the image rather than the original of Love.

55. Perhaps better is *amatus sum, ergo sum* ("I have been loved, therefore I am"), but perhaps best is *amor, ergo amo* ("I am loved, therefore I love").

56. My Emory colleague Frans de Waal has described behaviors among apes that look very much like "altruism" and "empathy"; see his *Good Natured: The Origins of Right and Wrong in Humans and Other Animals* (Cambridge: Harvard University Press, 1996), pp. 19-20, 56-57, and 228. He cautions, nonetheless, against projecting too robust a moral sensibility onto the higher primates. I can only acknowledge that if chimpanzees, say, genuinely love their neighbors, then they too are made in God's image. Better to expand the moral community to include some animals than to contract it to exclude some humans.

occasionally misanthropic Mark Twain grants that heaven "favors" human beings. No matter how devoted a trainer may be to her thoroughbred horses or a botanist to his hybrid orchids, say, there are inevitable constraints on the love that can or should pass between species.[57]

IV. Democracy and Human Rights

A. Types of Rights

Democracy is often identified with the defense of "human rights," but to understand this identification we must unpack both "human" and "rights." I have begun in previous sections to interpret what it means to be "human," maintaining, among other things, that the soul of humanity is intimately tied to the image of Deity. More specifically, I have argued that God's image inheres in embodied need and potential rather than in disembodied intellect and will. (Christ himself needs to love and be loved.) I now turn to the meaning of "rights." The main point here is that the need-based rights of nonpersons must have an equally important place in a good society as the achievement-based rights of persons, perhaps even a more important place.

Rights are standardly divided into two basic types: positive and negative. Positive rights are claims to goods and opportunities that ought to be provided to one by others. One can claim the goods and opportunities (e.g., education or health care) as due one actively from without. Negative rights, on the other hand, are claims to goods and opportunities that ought not to be tampered

---

57. Edward Albee's play *The Goat, or Who Is Sylvia?* is a powerful study of just how wrongheaded and destructive bestiality can be. Albee deftly suggests that Martin's claim to be in love with Sylvia, a female goat, stems from his forgetfulness of who he is, especially in relation to his wife, Stevie. Martin first sees Sylvia while stopping in the country to buy some (forbidden?) fruits and vegetables, and he subsequently represents an Adam who, unlike the original, would pronounce the animals enough. Stevie (whose name is an apparent play on "Second Eve") must finally kill the goat to impress on her husband that she, Stevie, is the partner fit for him — not just sexually, but also morally and spiritually. Martin's "loving" Sylvia radically distorts his needs and potentials, making it impossible for him to love or be loved by Stevie. (Need I mention the injustice the adultery does to Stevie herself?) By "scapegoating" Sylvia, Stevie shows her husband the difference between human beings, who have a right to life, and animals, which typically do not. Only then can Martin recall himself and say he is sorry for the pain and confusion he has caused. For a contrasting perspective, see Peter Singer's "Heavy Petting," Nerve.com, March 2001. Singer does not quite endorse bestiality, but he finds little to object to in it, so long as it is painless to both parties.

with by others. One can insist on various omissions by others, their passive noninterference with one's internal powers (e.g., with life and liberty). The positive/negative distinction is quite plausible, but it leaves undecided the basis for the relevant rights: Are we due provision of or noninterference with the goods and opportunities as a function of past performance (achieved merit), or are the rights in question grounded in our nature as such (shared need or potential)? Are the rights merely "legal" or "pragmatic" and dependent on cultural variables, or are they "natural" or "human" and applicable to everyone everywhere? (Voting at age eighteen is a legal right in the United States, but immunity from enslavement is a universal human right.) In answering these questions, we need to draw yet another contrast. Whether positive or negative, rights that depend on achieved merit I call "dignity rights," while rights that presuppose only shared need or potential for care I call "sanctity rights."

Respecting dignity rights is a matter of justice, of giving selves their due on the basis of their personal actions and intentions. Honoring sanctity rights is a matter of love, of giving souls their due on the basis of their impersonal liabilities and prospects. Dignity rights are earned, a function of reward, whereas sanctity rights are gifted, a function of inviolability. One can lose dignity rights by acting unethically or breaking the law or declining radically in autonomy. A drunk driver may lose the right to operate a motor vehicle, for example, and an end-stage Alzheimer's patient may be institutionalized and restrained. One can never lose sanctity rights so long as one lives, in contrast, since these rights do not turn on achieved merit or demerit. Even fetuses and capital felons, for example, have the right to life, in my judgment.

B. Human Beings and Democratic Values

Many secular critics see Judaism and Christianity as placing individual human beings at the timeless center of the universe — God's special darlings — and thus as being falsified by Copernican and Darwinian revelations of humanity's marginality and contingency. There is no denying that Western religion has at times encouraged an overweening pride in human nature. As I have indicated, however, one of the chief aims of Genesis 1–3 is to *de*center "man." The tree of knowledge is "in the middle of the garden" (Gen. 3:3), not Adam and Eve, and the creation stories and their sequels highlight the fact that humanity is finite and now fallen. There are limits to human intellect and will, limits on dignity-based rights, to put the point in modern terms. The Lord loves human beings, and he creates Adam and Eve purposefully, but they are an *image* of God, not the Deity herself. It was precisely the effort to deny their dependency on God and one another, to insist on boundless dignity rights, that caused Adam and Eve to trouble each other and thus to suffer and even to die.[58] They wanted to be left alone with their own autonomous creativity, and that is just what God gave them east of Eden.

Many religious critics see liberal democracy as similarly placing individual human beings on the timeless throne of the universe, and thus as being falsified by Aristotelian and Thomistic revelations of humanity's social nature and its reliance on historical traditions and divine graces. There is no denying that Western democracy has at times encouraged an atomistic individualism that loses sight of civility and the common good. One of the chief aims of the Declaration of Independence and the U.S. Constitution, however, is to *de*throne "man." Monarchic sovereignty belongs to the Lord God alone. Humanity's knowledge, sympathy, and power are all finite and fallible, and these facts ought to dictate limited government and cooperative practices. Freedom to make major personal choices is important, but individual freedom does not exhaust democratic values. The first "self-evident" truth mentioned in the Declaration of Independence is "that all men are created equal," and the subsequent "unalienable rights" list "liberty" second after "life," though before "the pursuit of happiness." The preamble to the U.S. Constitution refers to "union, justice, tranquility, the common defence, and the general welfare," leaving reference to "liberty" till the last. And even "the blessings of liberty" are to be secured collectively and prospectively: "to ourselves and our posterity." Dedication to "the proposition that all men are created equal" was central to Abraham Lincoln's understanding of America, and even (or rather especially) after a bloody civil war to preserve "government of, by, and for the people," he could speak "with malice toward none, with charity for all."

C. Sanctity Rights and Democratic Politics

If personal intellect and will generate dignity rights (to exercise free speech, to pursue happiness, to have valid contracts kept, to vote, to practice religious faith, etc.), then impersonal needs and potentials produce sanctity rights (to

---

58. Whether human mortality is "natural," a part of God's original plan, or an "unnatural" calamity visited on the species as punishment by God, Genesis at least suggests that the *fear* of death, seeing it as threatening to meaningful life, is the result of human self-centeredness, the folly of grasping at one's life as a possession.

life, to health care, to education, to equal regard, to fraternal consideration, etc.). One does nothing to merit the gift of life and the nurturance necessary to sustain and develop it, and attention to no positive achievement in time will render all human selves equal. Intellectual and moral accomplishments vary dramatically across individuals. It is not our rational and volitional works but rather our bodily vulnerabilities and potentials that most deeply unite us. We are all subject to injury and death, and we all need unconditional care to mature into autonomous agents capable of dignity.

Some contemporary philosophers conceive of democratic politics as concerned solely with the recognition and protection of dignity rights. Ronald Dworkin and Peter Singer, for instance, agree that only the interest-based rights of currently self-aware agents have substantive legal weight. Dworkin grants that some things without self-consciousness possess sanctity (e.g., great works of art and fetal human lives), while Singer doubts that sanctity exists. But both thinkers would restrict the liberal state to upholding the goods and opportunities associated with achieved selfhood. Consciousness has value, according to Singer, but only persons who are *self*-conscious actors across time have the right to life; personal freedom and equality must be supported by judicial and legislative means, according to Dworkin, but the steel of the law should not be used to enforce controversial judgments about what is impersonally valuable. For Dworkin, dignity decisively trumps sanctity in political and legal contexts; democratic respect for freedom of conscience precludes enforcing axiological views about the status of fetuses or the terminally ill, say, since these views are not generally agreed upon by all citizens. For Singer, again, dignity and pain avoidance are the only goods for the utilitarian to attend to; some animals (e.g., mature chimps) have personal dignity and thus should be seen as having the right to life, but some humans (e.g., newborn babies) lack personal dignity and thus should be seen as subject to swift, elective death.[59]

The problems with a political-legal ethic that focuses so exclusively on present dignity are: (1) it inevitably violates sanctity, and (2) it neglects the necessary conditions for the emergence and preservation of dignity itself. Postpersons, such as those with senile dementia, and nonpersons, such as the disabled and future generations, have little or no legal standing when extant

59. See Ronald Dworkin, *Life's Dominion: An Argument about Abortion, Euthanasia, and Individual Freedom* (New York: Knopf, 1993); *Freedom's Law: The Moral Reading of the American Constitution* (Cambridge: Harvard University Press, 1996); and *Sovereign Virtue: The Theory and Practice of Equality* (Cambridge: Harvard University Press, 2000); and Singer, *Practical Ethics; Rethinking Life and Death;* and *Unsanctifying Human Life.*

dignity dominates. As far as the state is concerned, there can be no compelling obligation to preserve or protect their lives. This is worrisome enough, but even more troubling is the fact that prepersons, such as fetuses and infants, have little or no standing either. They are not yet rational selves, so, on this view, they have few if any rights. One may be required not to visit pointless pain on such "impersonal" beings, but they have no right to life and most wrongs associated with their treatment relate to the interests of their family or caretakers. For Singer, a baby less than twenty-eight days old may be killed at its parents' behest, so long as no unnecessary suffering is involved.[60] For Dworkin, a fetus does not have interests and so is not a rights-bearer, at least not until very late in pregnancy — roughly thirty weeks of gestational age. Hence most abortion is not an injustice to the fetus itself, not a violation of its rights, and the law must not restrict abortion beyond the minimal conditions set by *Roe v. Wade*.[61]

If fetuses and infants, not to mention generations as yet unconceived, have few if any rights, then there is little morally relevant distinction between abortion, infanticide, and so denuding the environment that future human life is impossible. Indeed, there is no legal obligation to care very much for things impersonal, beings not yet possessed of dignity, since dignity rights are the only kind with clout. This is clearly self-defeating, however, for both individuals and groups. Any society that attempts to prescind from normative verdicts about the status of impersonal goods — from life's beginning to its end — will undercut any basis on which to promote the necessary conditions for the personal. Just agents were once loved patients, even as majestic oaks were once tiny acorns, and you can't secure the former without cultivating the latter.

Democratic society is defined by a commitment to the liberty and equality of its citizens, but if only autonomous persons count as democratic citizens, then liberty has undercut equality. Democratic equality has, at its best, looked not to personal excellence (what makes us heroic) but to impersonal need and potential (what makes us human); democracy has stood for inclusive regard for the rights of all, that is, especially the weak and marginalized. Among the weakest and most marginal are those who do not possess dignity: the very young, the very old, the very challenged, and the very guilty. These human lives still embody sanctity, however, and a democracy worthy of the name

60. Singer, *Rethinking Life and Death*, p. 217. Singer has had second thoughts about the twenty-eight-day boundary; see his "Dangerous Words," an interview with the *Princeton Alumni Weekly* (January 26, 2000), p. 19.

61. Dworkin, *Life's Dominion*, pp. 18-19, and *Freedom's Law*, pp. 117-29.

must count them as citizens bearing sanctity rights to care and protection. The needs and potentials of infants, for example, should translate into their right to receive love, even as the realized freedom and dignity of adults should translate into their duty to give love. Otherwise, both decency and democracy falter.

Conclusion: A Gesture toward Cultural Prescriptions

According to *The Oxford English Dictionary,* one meaning of the word *imago* is "the final and perfect stage or form of an insect after it has undergone all its metamorphoses."[62] Mark Twain's dog, not us, may get into a heaven because of merit, but it would be a Kafkaesque nightmare to think that the *imago Dei* is a matter of developmental perfection. Let our selves rejoice in whatever rationality and dignity (not to say perfectibility) they can rightly claim, but let them also pay grateful tribute to the sacred souls from which they must spring. No community can live without some conception of, and moral and legal commitment to, its own dependent and vulnerable humanity. As I have said repeatedly, for personal selves to emerge out of impersonal souls requires unearned care, from "private" parties such as family and friends but also from "public" institutions such as hospitals, schools, churches, and governments. God's grace undergirds all these caregivers, need I say, even as God's image is the recipient of care.

A liberal society will not put all power of nurturance and protection into the hands of the nation-state — subsidiarity and federalism are wise practical principles — and not all liberal citizens will talk of the "image of God." If human life possesses sanctity, however, reverence for that sanctity will have legitimate and substantive political effects. In my judgment, the sanctity of life precludes late-term elective abortion, active euthanasia, torture, capital punishment, unbridled capitalism, and nuclear warfare — to name only a few cultural evils. More positively, reverence for sanctity should enjoin better child care, national health insurance, prison reform, greater pro bono legal work, a more equitable tax system, and a discriminate military — to name only a few cultural goods.[63] These prescriptions are controversial and obviously require detailed defenses not possible in this chapter, but clarifying the

62. *The Compact Edition of the Oxford English Dictionary* (Oxford: Oxford University Press, 1971), 1:1377.

63. I endorse much of what Cardinal Joseph Bernardin has called "the seamless garment" of "a consistent ethic of life." See Bernardin, "A Consistent Ethic of Life: An American-Catholic Dialogue," the 1983 Gannon Lecture at Fordham University.

relation between sanctity and dignity has, I trust, helped lay the foundation for such defenses.[64] When we appreciate the inevitable place of need and dependency in the trajectory of a human life, for instance, we are less tempted to see disability and old age as shameful or otherwise undignified. Thus we are less likely to be seduced by a policy of active euthanasia for the handicapped or senile. And when we appreciate the ineradicability, so long as one lives, of the image of God, we are less tempted to see profound guilt as demonic or otherwise inhuman. Thus we are less likely to be seduced by torture or capital punishment even for terrorists.

Whatever the final persuasiveness of my normative judgments, the spirit behind them is at once Christian and democratic. The faith and the politics are not identical — no idolatrous triumphalism here[65] — but, when properly ordered, they can and should be mutually supporting.

---

64. I provide defenses for many of my normative proposals in Timothy P. Jackson, *The Priority of Love: Christian Charity and Social Justice* (Princeton: Princeton University Press, 2003), and "A House Divided, Again," chapter 5 of this volume.

65. "[The soul] looks not to the Capitol but to the heavens," says Tertullian (*Apology* 17), thereby reminding us of the transcendence of God. But, as a perfectly general statement, this is an overstatement. The two love commands suggest that the soul must look *first* to the heavens, but political love of neighbor (and self) can rightly follow, as Lincoln's Second Inaugural Address so eloquently demonstrates.

CHAPTER 3

The Return of the Prodigal?
Liberal Theory and Religious Pluralism

"But while he was still far off, his father saw him and was filled with compassion; he ran and put his arms around him and kissed him. Then the son said to him, 'Father, I have sinned against heaven and before you; I am no longer worthy to be called your son.' But the father said to his slaves, 'Quickly, bring out a robe — the best one — and put it on him; put a ring on his finger and sandals on his feet. And get the fatted calf and kill it, and let us eat and celebrate; for this son of mine was dead and is alive again; he was lost and is found!' And they began to celebrate."

LUKE 15:20-24

Introduction

Like USC and Notre Dame, liberalism and religion are often thought to be inherently adversarial. How you characterize the struggle, however, depends on which side you're on, if not which state you're in. From one sideline, liberalism is seen to uphold diversity and tolerance, the hard-won ethos of a democratic society. Liberal theory must cope with or compensate for religious faith as a threat to individual liberty and a potential disruptor of social harmony. Religions offer mythic metanarratives about the true and the good and the beautiful, the story goes, but the myths are both unverifiable and incommensurable. We are not sure what agreement would mean, and we can never arrive at even the semblance of agreement without coercion. Indeed, religious traditions tend to inspire nonrational, if not irrational, loyalties that liberalism must constantly neutralize in the name of "civility." On this view, then, liberalism is the champion of reasonable pluralism, including (ironically) religious pluralism.

From the other sideline, religious conviction appears to be the last bulwark against the corrosive effects of modernism and postmodernism. Religious faiths refuse to worship technology and autonomy, the idols of the Enlightenment, since these destroy community and identity. Liberals don't know who they are anymore, and they would make us all self-forgetful Californians. Liberalism would conceive of social discourse in nonmoral or minimally moral terms, for instance, but this leads to well-documented evils: individualism, relativism, MTV. Bourgeois capitalism substitutes a self-interested materialism for a sense of social responsibility, and cultural postmodernism can only venerate idiosyncrasy and power. Our heroine is no longer the Mother of Jesus, say, but rather the *real* Madonna, the "material girl" who gets pregnant by an immaterial boy (not the Holy Spirit). As Stanley Hauerwas puts it, "liberalism makes for shitty people." From this vantage point, then, religion is the solitary champion of personal virtues, both in theory and in practice.

Of course, there is *some* warrant for both of these perspectives. On the one hand, the religious wars of the sixteenth and seventeenth centuries still suggest to many that religions must be kept down, down, down. And more recent memories of Jonestown and the Waco Branch Davidians are vivid and troubling to almost all. Religious zeal seems, with disturbing frequency, to go hand in hand with homicide. On the other hand, the Nazi Holocaust was at least partially the product of scientific rationality and democratic governance. Even where it does not cause them, secularity seems incapable of coping with many of today's most distinctive problems. Ethnicity and national identity — realities the Enlightenment sought in principle to synthesize ("one people, one country") — now seem as intractable occasions for bloodshed as religious creeds. Economic class also plays a role; think of the extraordinarily bloody Hutu-Tutsi strife in Burundi and Rwanda.[1] As problematic as theological motives can be, might it be that in the present age only religious faith can check the genocidal tendencies of political conflicts by appealing to comprehensive norms?

There is warrant for the adversarial picture, but I hope to show that it is finally based on caricatures. It is important to question, to unpack and qualify,

1. Benzion Netanyahu has argued that even the Spanish Inquisition was more motivated by race than by religion. See Netanyahu, *The Origins of the Inquisition in Fifteenth Century Spain* (New York: Random House, 1995).

the preceding accounts of both liberalism and religion. It has been tempting of late for religious believers simply to turn the tables on liberalisms and vilify them for the moral decay of Western culture. Given the historical genesis of much of Western democracy in Christian (especially Protestant) piety, however, this is a colossal irony.[2] It amounts to a disowning of a formerly beloved, however currently prodigal, child. Given its supernatural origin and end, the Christian faith must always preserve a critical distance from any temporal institution or social arrangement, but I would defend nonetheless a modest positive thesis: *a form of liberalism, properly understood, is (or at least can be) itself a religious commitment.* Political freedom and equality are not the only values, but they can be the conscientious upshots of love of God and neighbor; in fact, one can *both* honor God *and* promote the common peace by subordinating the latter end to the former. The question of whether a viable liberalism *must* be religiously based, I leave largely open . . . though I have suspicions.

In part I of this chapter, I discuss two idealized types of liberal theory; in part II, I outline two takes on two types of pluralism. These types and takes are presented not as exhaustive but as instructive. In part III, I sketch a third understanding of both liberalism and pluralism that aims to overcome the problems with the previous two. When it misunderstands conscientious forms of pluralism, liberal "theory" concludes that it must be morally empty or basic; but, in fact, the best defense of liberalism is morally perfectionist, I believe. The best defense recognizes and defends those substantive virtues that make democratic equality possible. In contrast to John Rawls's political liberalism, for example, which relies on minimal moral powers for the balancing of diverse ends, perfectionist liberalism focuses on how people are enabled to acquire and sustain ends in the first place. This is a communal affair. Rather than appealing to rationality (Gewirth) or overlapping consensus (Rawls) or fear (Shklar) or irony (Rorty), perfectionist liberalism puts some form of benevolence first and appeals to empathy. We only acquire ends because others have graciously cared for us beyond what consistency or contract theories or personal prudence can require. And we disguise this fact by talking too devoutly of "appraisive reason" and "distributive justice."

Secular versions of perfectionist liberalism are possible, if problematic.

2. For three superb treatments of Christianity's role in producing and sustaining commitments to human rights, see Max Stackhouse, *Creeds, Society, and Human Rights* (Grand Rapids: Eerdmans, 1984); John Witte Jr., "The Essential Rights and Liberties of Religion in the American Constitutional Experiment," *Notre Dame Law Review* 71, no. 3 (1996): 371-445; and John Witte Jr., ed., *Christianity and Democracy in Global Context* (Boulder, Colo.: Westview Press, 1993).

When life and love are seen as gifts from a Higher Power, however, "religious pluralism" comes into its own. Accordingly, I try in part IV to describe a distinctively Christian version of perfectionist liberalism, one that highlights the transcendent source of all goodness yet still embraces conscientious pluralism. The two defining features of Christian pluralism are: (1) its confidence in a fundamental, if elusive, unity amid the diversity of human goods and faculties, and (2) its readier openness to self-sacrifice, including various forms of forgiveness, than most secular philosophies. Christianity does not endorse all forms of self-sacrifice or recommend suffering for its own sake. But it does insist that the self-giving that flows from charity is indispensable and that charity itself is a divine gift that preserves human existence from chaos.

To elaborate further the meaning of charity, I close part IV by briefly contrasting Origen and Aquinas with Rawls on the goodness of incarnate lives. My thesis here is that Rawls's account of justice — especially its inclination to exclude prophetic voices from public debate — is less compatible with the two types of pluralism than many of the two theologians' views. Whereas Rawls presupposes free and equal persons with basic moral powers as part of the self-image of a democratic culture,[3] prophetic Christianity asks the prior question of how such persons are produced, recognized, and sustained. Suffering love, "primal goodness," is its answer. Without major reworking, I conclude, even Rawls's carefully crafted liberalism is an unwitting threat to genuine pluralism, not its champion; with such reworking, religion may be a supplement to reasonable theory, not a dangerous source of irrationality or discord. This is the constructive reversal, the reconciliation of parent and prodigal, that awaits us: "religious theory" that is more than theoretical sustaining a "liberal pluralism" that is more than political.

I. Two Types of Liberalism: Subjectivity and Objectivity

A. *The Politics of Subjectivity, or Liberalism-as-Morally-Empty*

My first type of liberalism begins and ends with the solidarity of a particular group. No appeal to a universally shared human nature or a categorically

---

3. Robert Nozick criticized Rawls's *A Theory of Justice* for treating "the things people produce" as though they were "manna from heaven." See Nozick, *Anarchy, State, and Utopia* (New York: Basic Books, 1974), p. 198. To my mind, Rawls intentionally treats the things that produce people in much the same way.

binding moral imperative is made or can be made. These ideas are judged remnants of a discredited Judeo-Christian theology or an all-but-discredited Enlightenment philosophy. The good life, privately understood, is a matter of imaginative invention; in more corporate contexts, one relies on pragmatic conventions. "This is how we agree to act together, this is what we do, given what we find commonly desirable, and what we find desirable is democratic freedom and equality." This is the postmodern experiment: the quest for Homeric *dike* without the aristocratic hierarchy . . . a world governed by egalitarian *Sittlichkeit* rather than Kantian *Moralität* . . . Nietzsche without the *Übermensch* . . . or, rather, Nietzsche with *all of us* as *Übermenschen,* poetically (re-)creating ourselves. I call this first type of liberalism, then, liberalism-as-morally-empty. We neither have nor need access to objective values or transcendental principles or the revealed will of God; we stay in Plato's cave and content ourselves with shared appearances of artificial objects (and subjects). "This works best *for us* as we forge our distinct identities."

This is *not* a liberal prescription for nihilism, I hasten to add; it is *not* a refusal to value any particular social arrangement over another. It is rather a political valuation that remains within aesthetic categories. Liberalism-as-morally-empty, what I playfully call the "l-a-m-e" version, would be liberalism-as-aesthetically-full: democratic society as a colony of strong poets. A species of social criticism is possible here, but the criticism is highly parochial and instrumentalist. The critic offers, at most, what Michael Walzer calls "prophetic interpretation," the calling of a community back to its typical script, its defining rituals and original self-understandings.[4] There is no higher standard of good and bad than our own voluntary practices, but our de facto practices may be fine-tuned to make them more effective or fetching or consistent on their own terms.

Liberalism-as-morally-empty, to summarize, is an ethos of local bestowal. There are no objective goods to be appraised, only subjective allegiances to be bestowed;[5] there are no moral truths to be discovered "out there," only social practices to be habituated "in here." Thus liberalism-as-morally-empty consciously rejects *theoria* as a means of arriving at knowledge. There are no general theoretical truths, at least not in ethics and politics. Political knowledge is a matter of *kennen* not *wissen, savoir-faire* not *connaitre.*

4. Michael Walzer, *Interpretation and Social Criticism* (Cambridge: Harvard University Press, 1987), passim.
5. The terminology of "appraisal" and "bestowal," I borrow from Irving Singer, *The Nature of Love,* 3 vols. (Chicago: University of Chicago Press, 1966-1987).

The attractiveness of this perspective is its humility, its acknowledgment of finitude and particularity, contingency and history. The fanaticism that can spring from supposedly "certain" knowledge of timeless truth is ruled out of court at the outset. We intentionally hobble our self-image in order not to run over people. "Better not to believe in moral knowledge and truth if these lead to holy wars and final solutions; better not to talk of virtue and vice, guilt and innocence, if these lead to self-hatred and suicide. We can be maximally tolerant by being minimally metaphysical, most safe by being least credulous." So the argument goes, with some power.

Yet the problems with this picture are familiar: it would purchase tolerance at too high a price. Subjectivity, raised to a group level, does not thereby escape narcissism and ennui; it simply becomes corporate. Purely aesthetic or political categories are not enough to capture our actual self-understanding or to motivate our critical practices. Neither irony nor fear nor sheer power is enough to secure the respect for others necessary to sustain liberal society. *Motives matter,* and one cannot be motivated to care equally for others who are not judged equally valuable (either intrinsically or in the sight of God). Strong poets make dubious neighbors. (Think of the lame Lord Byron — "mad, bad, and dangerous to know" — and his craving for "a hero" like Don Juan.) We are born with concrete aptitudes and potentials that must be cultivated rather than assumed, even as we are born with concrete wants and needs that must be attended to rather than created. Human beings do not stand in solidarity with one another the way God dispenses grace: as an utterly unmerited gift. I accent below the ineliminable place of gratuitous care in a good society, but human care builds on finite potentials already in place. Creatures do not create *ex nihilo;* the integrity of others calls for recognition, not mere invention.

Liberalism-as-aesthetically-full would use irony and humor to deflate pretension, but there is no salt in its tears. Its empathy with others' real pain is ultimately an inconsistent laugh. Thinking that one generates human community *de novo* is not finally humility but something very close to the sin of pride. To be open to others as they are in themselves, in contrast, is to unlock the door to nonlocal discoveries. Lame poets must let themselves be touched by realities beyond their control.

The root problem with liberalism-as-morally-empty is that it leaves us without the resources to distinguish the means to virtue (a political community) from virtue itself (love and justice). Love and justice are social virtues, inseparable in their acquisition and practice from a good society, but no particular society is the telos of love or justice as such. These virtues invariably relativize whatever political community they emerge in.

B. *The Politics of Objectivity, or Liberalism-as-Morally-Basic*

A second ideal type of liberalism models itself on the disinterested philosophical spectator rather than the traditional historical interpreter. To avoid the apparent conservatism and conventionalism of liberalism-as-morally-empty, it aims to specify a liberalism that is morally basic. Moral utterances are now judged to be more than group expressions of practical commitments; they are thought to have truth value. Moreover, moral utterances are to abstract *away* from the distinctive identity and historical community of the utterer. Rational judgers will limit themselves to apprehension of things like aggregate benefits or natural rights. One has left the cave of mere appearances to espy the true and the good and the beautiful from an impersonal vantage point beyond prejudice or passion.

If the politics of subjectivity offers local bestowal of value among "us," the politics of objectivity accents the general appraisal of value as though everybody, including oneself, is a "them." Liberalism-as-morally-basic focuses, that is, on justice as *suum cuique,* the unclouded appraisal of what individuals are due, the detached guarantee of basic human rights. Disinterestedness is key; therefore emotions are suspect. Emotions are thought to carry an ineliminably first-person flavor — we speak of having "the very same idea" as someone else more readily than of feeling "the very same emotion" — while moral judgments tend to be in the third person. "*One* ought to do this because it maximizes utility or is dictated by duty or is the will of God, etc." This is "liberal theory" in the technical sense of *theoria:* a general account aimed at truths rationally communicable to all. Utilitarian and deontological theories share an aspiration to such objective rationality.

The allure of this account of liberalism is its evenhandedness, its fine self-transcendence for the sake of clear vision. Being capable of the long view and not making an exception in one's own case does seem a central part of moral wisdom. It is the wisdom of the "l-a-m-b" that surrenders its distinctive identity for the sake of universal truth; it is the sacrifice of egotism on the altar of impartiality and fairness. Liberalism-as-morally-basic would build securely on the foundation of a rational justice, and as such it is a powerfully moralizing influence on any social context.

The rub, however, as many have noted, is that the perfectly disinterested spectator tends to be insufficiently engaged in or committed to his own culture. And the merely *self*-interested contractor is similarly alienated from others. As much as they may differ concerning the priority of the right or the good, both the disinterested spectator and the self-interested contractor make moral education in personal virtues hard to imagine. Both tend to neglect the social recognition of the good and the interpersonal motivation for doing right. Michael Walzer has noted that in Rawls's original position, for instance, "it ceases to matter whether the constructive or legislative work is undertaken by a single person or by many people. . . . one person talking is enough."[6]

An ethic of pure appraisal, unmotivated by richly individual desires and socially generated commitments, is not sustainable. The view from nowhere, to use Tom Nagel's phrase,[7] seeks to overcome the provincialism of liberalism-as-morally-empty, "the view from now-here." But pure objectivity is less than human. It brackets out of consideration many of the very things that make life in community worth living: friendships, family ties, erotic relations, patriotic emotions, etc. There is an odd, almost masochistic impersonalism in the "l-a-m-b" version of liberalism: a too-willing sacrifice of moral affections like gratitude and devotion, pity and forgiveness. The danger is loss of the sense of embodied selfhood. It is essential in working with divisions to find the common denominator, but if the numerators are all zeros, one is left with nothing.

Basic justice is not enough. The "lamb" must be spared, so to speak, immolation of individuality abolished, if community is to take humane form. Justice defined as *suum cuique,* and elaborated in terms of rights and duties, lifts us out of purely aesthetic categories. It is, as such, a necessary condition for a moral polis of free and equal persons. Yet impersonal justice is derivative. *The prior question is how we generate caring people capable of free agency, respectful of rights and duties, to begin with.* This is first of all a matter of benevolent service rather than appraisive rationality. Moral personality is a strangely belated thing, neither self-creating nor self-fulfilling; we are all "*second* persons," in Annette Baier's terms,[8] dependent on others who have come before and who will go after. Benevolence must look to the needs of persons, potential persons as well as actual, before justice can turn to their deserts. And character formation into the way of caring is a primary personal need.

---

6. Walzer, *Interpretation and Social Criticism,* p. 11. In fact, Rawls appears ambivalent about subjectivity and objectivity. At times, he has seemed allied with Richard Rorty and constructivism, advocating a "political" conception of justice that is all but morally empty; at other times, he has spurned a mere *modus vivendi* in favor of substantive (if basic) moral truth claims. The latter now seems closer to his considered view. I discuss Rawls at greater length below; for a still more detailed treatment, see my "To Bedlam and Part Way Back: John Rawls and Christian Justice," *Faith and Philosophy* 8, no. 4 (October 1991): 423-47.

7. Thomas Nagel, *The View from Nowhere* (Oxford: Oxford University Press, 1986).

8. Annette Baier, *Postures of the Mind: Essays on Mind and Morals* (Minneapolis: University of Minnesota Press, 1985), p. 84.

Forming character well, in turn, requires mythic narratives (stories of heroes with whom we actively identify) rather more than abstract principles (general rules to which we impersonally conform).

But let this suffice for a brief look at two highly idealized liberalisms; I turn next to pluralisms.

II. Two Takes on Two Types of Pluralism: Expansion and Reduction

It is important to distinguish at the outset two types of pluralism.[9] The first, which I will call *"epistemic pluralism,"* is the view that there are many different ways of disclosing (or attempting to disclose) truths — whether the truths be empirical, moral, metaphysical, or theological. Each way has, moreover, its own particular logic and criteria. In specifically moral contexts, epistemic pluralism is often associated with the idea that reason, emotion, and will all have a role in the quest for knowledge of the good life, even as do appeals to tradition and culture. The means to ethical knowing, the faculties of moral psychology, are multiple. Thus practical wisdom is a matter of the discriminate balance or synthesis of various sources, or would-be sources, of insight.

The second type of pluralism might be called *"ontological pluralism."* This is the view that the *objects* of knowledge, rather than the means to discovering them, are multiple. There are empirical, moral, metaphysical, and theological realities, the ontological pluralist typically holds, as well as different realities within each of these large disciplinary categories. In moral contexts, for example, ontological pluralism is often associated with the thesis that there are many genuine virtues, many binding rules or commandments, many valuable ends, etc. Hence the second form of pluralism, understood axiologically, is the opposite of any monism that would equate all worth with a single trait of character or principle of action or consequence of acting. Goodness is variegated, on this account.

As I have defined it, epistemic pluralism is distinct from both epistemic skepticism and epistemic despair. The first form of pluralism is distinct, that is,

9. I have been stimulated in what follows by Charles Larmore's "Pluralism and Reasonable Disagreement," in *Cultural Pluralism and Moral Knowledge,* ed. Ellen Frankel Paul, Fred D. Miller Jr., and Jeffrey Paul (Cambridge: Cambridge University Press, 1994). Larmore does not use the terminology I do, preferring to reserve the label "pluralism" exclusively for what I call "ontological pluralism," but he does draw similar distinctions. I differ from Larmore in thinking that ontological pluralism, as well as the expectation of reasonable disagreement, is naturally aligned with the heart of liberalism.

from both the conviction that the (putative) sources of insight are unreliable or prone to error and the conviction that they are deeply conflictual — whether across disciplines or within an individual discipline. To say that there are many ways to know (or to try to know) is not to comment on whether these ways are inclined to mistake or are otherwise illegitimate, nor is it to say that they are at odds. One might be an epistemic pluralist yet also an epistemic foundationalist, for example, taking the deliverances of revelation, reason, will, and emotion, say, to be incorrigible and harmonious when properly understood. Such a position would no doubt be implausible, but it is not conceptually impossible. Short of foundationalism, one might unite epistemic pluralism with epistemic fallibilism and see the many human faculties as individually subject to error but generally reliable as a group.

Analogously, ontological pluralism differs on my definition from both ontological chaos and ontological agony. The second form of pluralism differs, in other words, from both the thesis that the various objects of knowledge claims are incomparable — whether across disciplines or within an individual discipline — and the thesis that they are somehow intrinsically antithetical ("agonistic" in the classical Greek sense of implacably struggling). To say that there are many realities is not to say that these realities are incoherent or surd, nor is it to say that they contradict each other like matter and antimatter. One might be an ontological pluralist yet also an ontological optimist, for instance, taking the diverse things in the world to be finally intelligible and compatible. In metaphysical treatises, ontological optimists write of "the great chain of being," "the plenitude of existence," "the harmony of the spheres," etc.; in moral tracts, key phrases include "the unity of the virtues," "the consistency of practical reason," "the goodness of being with evil as its privation," etc. This position may also seem implausible to many, but most monotheists embrace such an optimism.

Against this backdrop, let me now clarify two possible takes on epistemic and ontological pluralism.

A. Expansive Pluralism

Expansive pluralism radicalizes epistemic pluralism to entail either epistemic skepticism or epistemic despair. It is chiefly prompted by perceived disagreement about fundamental values, beliefs, and practices — both within and across traditions. The expansive accent is on the irreconcilability of diverse faculties and disciplines (reason and emotion, philosophy and poetry) and on the incommensurability of diverse cultures and practices (the Trobriand Islanders and us, our public selves and our private selves). Even in the West, the reality of paradigm shifts means for expansive pluralists that there is no abiding inquiry, much less consensus after inquiry, that can be called "*our* moral tradition." There are only fluctuating historical traditions of quite local character, with no adjudicating basic epistemic disputes between them. In the extreme, expansivists assert that we should stop talking of "discovering truth" altogether.

In the expansive lexicon, phrases like "religious pluralism" or "cultural pluralism" conjure up images of hopelessly conflicting camps that must be reined in rather than happily coexisting communities that may be cross-fertilized. Thus expansive pluralism often emerges as a *modus vivendi,* a tolerance of what is alien for the sake of getting on. At best, it represents a benign neglect of social patterns that one does not endorse and probably cannot understand; at worst, it amounts to a grudging truce between permanently warring factions. We whoop for our side as they whoop for theirs, but we refrain from throwing stones.

Expansive pluralism also radicalizes ontological pluralism to entail either ontological chaos or ontological agony. The types of realities (or supposed realities) are so complex and discontinuous that we live, quite literally, in many fragmented, even incompatible, worlds. In ethics, this often translates into the affirmation of moral dilemmas. Define a moral dilemma as a situation in which, through no antecedent fault of your own, you cannot but transgress against some sacred value or binding rule, and you cannot but become guilty. I refer not to inescapable *feelings* of guilt but to actual culpability, a scenario involving two equally binding but mutually exclusive ethical requirements. Neither do I have in mind moral ambiguity or weakness of will. No additional information or resolve will help when confronted by a genuine dilemma: you are literally damned if you do and damned if you don't. "It is the case that you ought to be or do *x,* and it is not the case that you ought to be or do *x.*" Expansive pluralism often internalizes the fact of disagreement to the point of affirming such a contradictory scenario. One ought to be "liberal" enough about goods to "dirty one's hands," to do evil that good might come, some expansive pluralists maintain.[10]

10. For a collection of contemporary philosophical essays on dilemmas, together with some historical background pieces, see Christopher W. Gowans, ed., *Moral Dilemmas* (Oxford: Oxford University Press, 1987). For an intelligent rejection of moral dilemmas, see Edmund Santurri, *Perplexity in the Moral Life: Philosophical and Theological Considerations* (Charlottesville: University Press of Virginia, 1987). For an influential defense of the same,

I will have much more to say about expansive pluralism below, but I can anticipate by noting that some commentators find it overly pessimistic about communication across cultural boundaries as well as about the possible coherence of personal loyalties. Conflict and change are taken too much to heart by expansive pluralists, critics assert, and, rather than respecting differences, expansive pluralists leave us with blind tolerance on the cultural level and desperate sadness on the personal level. Hermetically sealed traditions and tragically dilemmatic choices are needlessly affirmed.

B. Reductive Antipluralism

Reductive antipluralism rejects both epistemic and ontological pluralism, at least within ethics. It is an *intra*mural affair, beginning with the fact of agreement, *within a metatradition,* on a single moral value (e.g., happiness) apprehended by a single highest faculty (e.g., reason). Everything revolves around these centers. Reductionism may admit the diversity of human goods and powers, but it would grasp these in a coherent vision by privileging one *moral* datum and one means to *moral* knowledge. This is often done by looking for the common denominator in seemingly incompatible traditions and rituals. The good will or rational consistency or maximal pleasure, for instance, is isolated as the motive force behind all historical praxis. De facto traditions are then understood as variations on the same basic theme, as intelligible dialects of the same mother tongue. We can be pluralistic about mores, if you will, because we are monistic about morals. There is but one *font et origio* of distinctively moral goodness, and when seen from the impersonal point of view, all enlightened cultures flow from it and aspire to it. Wisdom is simply a matter of being able to see through the contingent forms to the abiding content, to rise above peripheral disputes to tap the core consensus. In spite of ethnographic complexity, the epistemological and ontological centers hold.

The objections to reductive antipluralism are the familiar ones to foundationalism. Critics doubt that any Ur-tradition can encompass the vast array of human goods (and ills) — aesthetic, economic, political, moral, religious — within a single coherent picture. More specifically, they object to the essentialism necessary to get everyone talking the same moral language. There

---

see Martha C. Nussbaum, *The Fragility of Goodness* (Cambridge: Cambridge University Press, 1986), esp. chap. 11 and interlude 2, and *Love's Knowledge: Essays on Philosophy and Literature* (Oxford: Oxford University Press, 1990), esp. chaps. 2 and 4.

is no single moral good on the basis of which to explain cultural diversity, the objection runs, no one touchstone for civil discourse. And neither is there a highest or most characteristic moral faculty. Ethical Esperanto based on the definitiveness of reason, say, is, at best, a pipe dream and, at worst, an invitation to tyranny. The fear is of yet another dogmatic Messiah slouching toward Bethlehem to be born.

You see where I am going. Liberalism-as-morally-empty moves hand in glove with expansive pluralism, while liberalism-as-morally-basic is built for or on reductive antipluralism. Liberalism-as-morally-empty is impressed by the fact of broad cultural disagreement and is inclined to talk of "many worlds," "untranslatable paradigms," "us against them," etc.; liberalism-as-morally-basic, on the other hand, opts for semantic ascent and a unified system that looks down on diversity from nowhere in particular and with no one person in mind. This (non)perspective is defined as "the moral point of view," whether elaborated in terms of total hedons or the categorical imperative. In short, the "l-a-m-e" version of liberalism expands "pluralism" to the breaking point by disallowing intrinsic worth altogether, even as the "l-a-m-b" version contracts "pluralism" to a vanishing point by treating all moral goods as one, or at least as measurable in terms of one thing apprehended by one means.

Is there any way to get beyond this twofold either/or? I want now to combine the previous two parts of my discussion and imagine a third kind of liberalism together with a third understanding of pluralism. I think of this exercise in roughly Hegelian terms: striving for an *Aufhebung* of the two contrary liberalisms based on a synthesis of the two contrary views of pluralism.

III. Two Third Alternatives: Conscience and the Care of Persons

A. Conscientious Pluralism

Conscientious pluralism, my third take, aims to do justice to both the reality of cultural disagreement (epistemic concerns) and the plurality of legitimate goods (ontological commitments). It seeks to move beyond the brute diversity of traditions, associated with expansive pluralism, and the too-sanguine unity of an Ur-tradition, associated with reductive antipluralism. The central thesis of conscientious pluralism is that both human faculties and human goods are happily multiple. Most characteristically, conscientious pluralism is a joyful affirmation of the plenitude of the world and the self; diversity and multiplicity are celebrated, not simply tolerated. When such pluralism takes a religious form, we have not the gallimaufry of conflicting faiths but grateful attention to the great chain of being. This chain leads back to a Creator to whom all are responsible, but responsibility involves respect for the consciences of others made in the Creator's image.

Conscientious pluralism rejects all axiological reductionisms. Such views easily degenerate into a *global* monism, in which *all* worth (not just moral worth) is equated with one particular person or thing, and *all* truth (not just moral truth) is grasped by one particular faculty or sense. Human life then becomes a cliff dive into a tidal inlet: one stops one's ears and holds one's breath and plunges to the bottom to retrieve "the pearl of great price" . . . only to drown in an undertow. Thus does an impoverished ontology drive one to an impoverished epistemology, and vice versa. In its hyper-Kantian form, reductive objectivity avers that the only truly good thing is the good will, which acts out of rational respect for duty; in its hyperutilitarian form, pleasure or happiness becomes the sole good, as this is maximized by an impersonal spectator. For conscientious pluralists, however, values and the means to appreciate them are irreducibly multiform. Passion and volition, for instance, are as important sources of moral and religious insight as reason.

Conscientious pluralism is similar to the expansive variety in acknowledging distinct and possibly conflicting goods; one may have to sacrifice physical safety to secure social justice, for example. Yet conscientious pluralism differs in holding that the distinctions and conflicts are still intelligible within a unified system. Aesthetic, moral, and religious diversity stops short of chaos and dilemma. There are many values and many sources of insight into them, but this does not rule out a true vision or a lexical ordering. We must recognize the breadth of life, but we must not overlook its depth. There is that much wisdom in reductive visions. The question is how complete the tension between various goods and faculties can be within a conscientious perspective. Again, both conscientious and expansive pluralists grant that there can be conflicts and trade-offs between the moral and the nonmoral. But many expansive pluralists also argue that moral goods themselves are so fragmented, the agreed sources of ethical insight so at odds, that deep dilemma is sometimes unavoidable. Utility tells us one thing, say, and deontology something incompatible but equally compelling. The challenge to conscientious pluralism is to rebut the expansive case for moral dilemmas without denying tragedy altogether, as reductivists do.

For the conscientious pluralist, seeing moral realities as chaotic is bad enough, but seeing them as utterly agonistic is the death of *any* tradition claiming ethical knowledge. Because a self-contradiction is necessarily false, to affirm a moral dilemma appears to conscience not as pluralism but as schizophrenia. Moral knowledge self-destructs here, even intramurally, for the expansive pluralist. Hence the expansive pluralist's drive toward a liberalism that is highly aesthetic, based on solidarity to a group practice rather than the propositional truth of a moral vision. Moral truth claims run aground on practical paradox. In the face of a Walzerian "supreme emergency," say, our politics is unabashedly fatalistic, if not immoral. When faced with a severe and imminent threat to the nation, we must be willing to murder innocents in other countries to preserve our own. We can give no consistent moral argument, however, for why we should be willing to do so. The agony of ontological "necessity" simply compels us to violate our most basic moral principles and values in order to avoid political calamity.[11]

Expansive pluralists tend to emphasize the fragmentation of goods and powers (even unto admitting moral dilemmas), while reductive antipluralists deny the possibility of any real tragedy in the moral life (even unto going monistic). Conscientious pluralists find both alternatives implausible: the voice of the expansivist is Machiavellian, while that of the reductivist is Pollyannaish. But how does one argue for conscientious pluralism? The best I can do is to try to draw a compelling picture of one version of it. The version I have in mind maintains that literal dilemmas don't exist because aesthetic, moral, and religious goods are ordered by a metavalue. That metavalue is love. In the next section, I will try to spell out what is distinctive about Christian love *(agape)*, but for now I want to keep the discussion general enough to cover what the Stoics called *humanitas* and *misericordia,* Hutcheson and Smith dubbed "benevolence," and contemporary secular philosophers often refer to as "the care of persons" or "personal care."

Care, understood interpersonally, is characterized by two features: (1) practical commitment (emotional and intellectual) to the good of the other and (2) equal regard (local and universal) for the worth of the other. The expansive pluralist is, at most, a *weak* philanthropist who rates care as the first among a host of equals that may be directly at odds: health, happiness, political enfranchisement, personal courage, etc. More than likely, though, she is a *non*-philanthropist who sees universal love of neighbor as unfair to those in special relation to oneself and impossible in any case: empathy should not and, in any

---

11. See Michael Walzer, "Political Action: The Problem of Dirty Hands," *Philosophy and Public Affairs* 2, no. 2 (Winter 1973): 160-80; *Just and Unjust Wars* (New York: Basic Books, 1977), chap. 16; and "Emergency Ethics," Joseph A. Reich Sr. Distinguished Lecture, no. 1 (Colorado Springs: United States Air Force Academy, 1988).

event, cannot extend to everybody (Nietzsche and Freud). As I define him, the conscientious pluralist is, in contrast, a *strong* philanthropist. He sees personal care as that singular good without which we have no substantive access to other values. There *are* other genuine values — here is no love monism — but without love these values are but "glittering vices." Loving care is not simply to be numbered with courage, temperance, prudence, and justice as one more significant virtue. Care is, in Charles Taylor's parlance, *the* hypergood.[12]

To repeat, the reductivist may concede many goods and powers, but the distinctively *moral* candidates reduce to one. Thus, for the reductivist there can be no conflict between moral value*s* or facul*ties*. For the agonized expansivist, there can be an irremediable conflict between *any* two values or faculties: love may sometimes have to sacrifice justice, for instance, and thus dirty its hands. For the conscientious pluralist, the variety of goods and powers does not preclude putting benevolence first. No way of life can attain all goods, so there are multiple and even incompatible ways of flourishing as a person. But all moral lives can, in principle, realize the metagood of care of persons. This is not to say that they will actually do so, only that, when they do not, "the fault is not in our stars, but in ourselves." It is never appropriate to surrender loving care for some other good, moreover, for without care the other good is unredeemable. Personal care always trumps other principles or sources of knowledge, but it does not deny or destroy them as such.[13]

B. *The Politics of Care, or Liberalism-as-Morally-Perfectionist*

We are at last in a position to imagine a third kind of liberalism in some detail. Liberalism-as-morally-perfectionist, as I call it (borrowing from William Galston),[14] aims to transcend a simple dichotomy between subjectivity and

12. Charles Taylor, *Sources of the Self: The Making of the Modern Identity* (Cambridge: Harvard University Press, 1989), pp. 63ff.

13. On the possible competition between love and other goods, Saint Paul perhaps has the last conscientious word: "If I speak in the tongues of men and of angels, but have not love, I am a noisy gong or a clanging cymbal. And if I have prophetic powers, and understand all mysteries and all knowledge, and if I have all faith, so as to remove mountains, but have not love, I am nothing. If I give away all I have, and if I deliver my body to be burned, but have not love, I gain nothing" (1 Cor. 13:1-3 RSV).

14. Galston is picking up on a reference in Rawls. See William A. Galston, *Liberal Purposes: Goods, Virtues, and Diversity in the Liberal State* (Cambridge: Cambridge University Press, 1991), p. 79.

objectivity, on the one hand, and expansion and reduction, on the other. The "l-a-m-p" version of liberalism begins with the proposition that there are distinctively liberal virtues that pivot around a robust fellow-feeling rather than a neutral justice. The question that divides secular and theological lamps, of course, is whether these virtues are natural or supernatural in origin. Do we need the love of God (either subjective or objective genitive) for love of neighbor? A secular theorist might argue on sociological grounds that benevolence is a universal human potential, a latent capacity as common to the species as its genius for hatred. A Christian theist will maintain, in contrast, that a properly ordered charity is a gift of grace and outstrips any requirements articulable by right reason, or even right emotion. Neither secular humanist nor Christian need think that actual persons ever become perfect to speak of "perfectionist *ideals*," however.

Benevolent care is more than the way of discovery; it is constructive. Care does not merely provide theoretical knowledge of another's condition; it carries with it, intrinsically, a practical impetus to action based on emotional identification. Care involves both appraisal and bestowal of value: it appreciates in vivid detail what another is going through but also moves to remedy what is bad and augment what is good. We would not call "caring" someone who had but an abstract understanding of another's pain, however complex that understanding might be. The point here is not merely that care must entail emotional empathy as well as intellectual judgment, for a sadist is emotionally sensitive to another's suffering yet disinclined to diminish it. The point is that care consistently wills and acts on the good for another (and oneself).

Many contemporary liberals are rightly impressed with the fallibility of human minds and the multiplicity of human ends, but in attending to these epistemological and ontological factors, they often fail to appreciate how persons come to be ends in themselves, capable of having and sustaining ends to begin with. John Rawls, for his part, combines a rather skeptical epistemology with a somewhat agonistic ontology. "The fact of reasonable pluralism" means, for him, ongoing and finally intractable disagreement about fundamental questions of meaning and value.[15] Being struck by the reality that reasonable people tend to differ, even after extensive dialogue, in their moral-cultural commitments is not itself skeptical. On the contrary, it is central to a liberal sensibility that would avoid coercing conscience whenever

15. See John Rawls, *Political Liberalism* (New York: Columbia University Press, 1993), p. 4.

possible.[16] What *is* skeptical, however, is Rawls's epistemic prescription in the face of such disagreement.

Rawls would have us reflect on social justice in terms of a hypothetical appeal to political rationality: the veil of ignorance in the original position. As part of this appeal, Rawls is committed to an "ideal of public reason" in which citizens justify their constitutional commitments only in terms that are publicly accessible to all, independently of controversial appeals to religious faith or philosophical theory. A political conception of justice must be "freestanding," in the sense that "we leave aside how people's comprehensive doctrines connect with the content of the political conception of justice and regard that content as arising from the various fundamental ideas drawn from the political culture of a democratic society."[17] A comprehensive doctrine is any worldview that outstrips a basic sense of justice and a thin conception of the good, the sort of worldview that is denied one from behind Rawls's veil of ignorance. Only by relying on an "overlapping consensus" that is compatible with, but does not explicitly rely on, comprehensive moral and metaphysical views can one avoid offending against "the duty of civility," according to Rawls.[18]

But why try to specify a priori what vocabularies can be deployed in the service of important social ends? Why not let a thousand languages bloom, comprehensive or otherwise, constrained only by prohibitions on force and fraud? This is not an abandonment of the general commitment to respect one's political interlocutors; it is rather an acknowledgment that bracketing one's comprehensive doctrines may simply make one incomprehensible to others, as well as to oneself. Sensitivity to rhetorical context is a virtue, but first of all and most of the time we owe others (and ourselves) our best explanation of what we believe and why we believe it, as well as our best motive for acting on this belief. It is an oddly skeptical epistemology that rules robust religious and philosophical visions out of court *ab initio*. Perfectionist liberals hold, *pace* Rawls, that ideals like equal dignity and liberty of conscience can win out in a fair epistemic fight. Or if such ideals can't at least "go the distance," they are not worthy of defense by conscientious persons.

It is an irony of civility that at times more sincere respect is shown to others by confronting them with revolutionary possibilities and transformative vocabularies than by assuming the status quo. Perfectionist liberals do not

---

16. As Larmore points out in "Pluralism and Reasonable Disagreement," pp. 74 and 77-79.

17. Rawls, *Political Liberalism*, p. 25 n. 27.

18. See *Political Liberalism*, esp. lectures 4 and 6, pp. 131-72 and 212-54.

give up the ideal of mutually accept*able* justifications of political judgments, but they do let go of the idea that justifications and their idioms must be mutually accept*ed* prior to discourse. An early criticism of Rawls's *Theory of Justice* was that it characterized justice too decidedly in terms of end-state principles that prejudice the outcome of free public exchange.[19] One need not be libertarian to worry that his *Political Liberalism* depicts public reason too emphatically in terms of nation-state duties that prejudice the outcome of free public dialogue. In both cases, one suspects an effort to evade embodied finitude by foreordaining the result of historical interaction. Rawls vetoes the use of controversial ways of knowing for key political purposes, thus imposing a peculiar (if passive) epistemic abstinence on citizens.

The questionable epistemology is coupled, in turn, with a questionable ontology. On the one hand, Rawls declines to consider how people become (or fail to become) free and equal; on the other hand, he interprets freedom and equality in a fashion weighted toward agony. His contractors are not actively antithetical to one another, but for deliberative purposes they are thought of as "rational and mutually disinterested," as "not taking an interest in one another's interests."[20] Rawlsian deliberators are not meant to model actual moral agents, but their sense of justice and thin conception of the good nevertheless represent an emotionally detached, even implicitly adversarial, anthropology. Such an anthropology may be defensible, but to presume it as part of "political reason" is to beg a host of material questions. The reflection of Rawlsian contractors about how justly to balance ends systematically precludes weighing the fact that persons require more or less gratuitous care, public and private, to grow into rationality and to sustain moral agency itself.

It is crucial to realize that Rawls's justice as fairness is not egoistic in any crude sense: he does not wish to ban benevolence as part of an individual's "comprehensive" account of a well-lived life or part of a society's "background culture." (Indeed, his difference principle is sometimes likened, in its effects, to a Christian preferential option for the poor.) But Rawls declines to let love of neighbor do any real work (epistemic or ontological) with respect to the political. It should be seen in our personal actions but not heard in our public debates. For Rawls's purposes, the primary sense of public goodness is "rationality."[21] This, by perfectionist lights, is too minimalist, *an impossible*

19. See Nozick, *Anarchy, State, and Utopia,* pp. 198-204.

20. See John Rawls, *A Theory of Justice* (Cambridge: Harvard University Press, 1971), p. 13.

21. See Rawls, *A Theory of Justice,* esp. pp. 147-49 and 476-85; and *Political Liberalism,* esp. pp. 12-13 and 173-78.

separation of the "political" and the "nonpolitical" that subverts proper moral motivation. Rawlsian rationality is moved to egalitarian social principles by a prudent fear of being disadvantaged oneself, for example, rather than by an empathetic concern for the least well-off that knows that it need never join them. One endorses principles of justice that guard against worst-case scenarios (e.g., the difference principle) because, from behind the veil of ignorance, one does not know one's place in society and thus cannot be sure that one will not be among the least well-off. Yet to limit moral motivation in this way is to preclude a perfectionist understanding of political virtue, as Rawls himself makes clear. The martyr who chooses to join the poor and afflicted voluntarily, to compel others' moral attention, is unintelligible. Less extremely yet more importantly, the civic republican who would structure society so as to protect the weak for their own sake is also beyond the pale of Rawlsian political reason.

Perfectionist liberalism does not *replace* justice with loving care or fall *below* giving persons their due; it holds instead that a good society should rise *above* both pure appraisal and pure bestowal to give individuals *more* than their due, narrowly defined. We all require a protection and empathy that we have not earned; we live together by supererogation. This does not mean that liberalism-as-morally-perfectionist simply demands the supererogatory of citizens; that would be a contradiction in terms. Say rather that, by the lamp of perfectionist liberalism, citizens publicly do two things: (1) they redraw the usual bounds between obligation and supererogation, construing some of the actions and attitudes normally judged optional as duties of beneficence (cf. child welfare laws and national health insurance), and (2) they safeguard and encourage genuine supererogation against expansive or reductive liberalisms that would effectively (if inadvertently) stifle charity as "unreasonable" or "merely private."

In sum, the perfectionist liberal foregrounds rather than backgrounds love. For the perfectionist liberal, the solidarity of need, in addition to desire and ability, ought to move us to recognize a range of faculties beyond science and common sense, as well as a plethora of goods beyond the idols of the tribe.[22] Again, neither group solidarity (pure subjectivity) nor impersonal rationality (pure objectivity) is sufficient for a stable society of decent citizens.

---

22. For an adept secular defense of charity as "the enforcement of passive forbearance in the face of the needy person helping himself to resources," see Jeremy Waldron, "Welfare and the Images of Charity," chap. 10 in *Liberal Rights: Collected Papers, 1981-1991* (Cambridge: Cambridge University Press, 1993), p. 246 and passim.

IV. The Distinctiveness of Christian Liberalism/Pluralism

A. *Charity and Self-Sacrifice*

I have suggested that a perfectionist liberalism based on personal care is an attractive synthesis of subjectivity and objectivity. At the end of the day, however, I find secular versions of this synthesis problematic. I cannot defend this impression in any detail here, but secular attempts to justify an ethic of benevolence often seem tainted by either despair or self-seeking. A vigorous love of neighbor frequently appears to them either too demanding or simply as a means to narrow, if not resentful, self-interested ends after all. Even the appeals to "sympathy" of some of the splendid British moralists of the eighteenth century grow flat or idiosyncratic as they float free of religious faith. Benevolence in Hume, for instance, is tied ineliminably to reciprocity.[23] Self-interest and reciprocity have their places, of course, but seldom is a prophet cast up by secular versions of these, for they eschew what George Steiner calls the "wager on transcendence."[24]

Prophetic Christianity is often associated with epistemic foundationalism as well as ontological (specifically, axiological) monism. The Protestant prescription *sola Scriptura* is read as inerrancy and the sole legitimacy of the Bible as a source of truth. And the Bible is thought to teach that God is "all in all," exclusively valuable if not exclusively real. This twofold association is unpersuasive, however. A distinctively Christian pluralism can readily endorse both epistemic and ontological pluralism, even while insisting that charity is the first virtue and God is the Creator of all that is. Let me first make the historical case for a rich Christian epistemology, then turn to the logic of a variegated Christian ontology.

Roman Catholicism commonly points to four avenues to knowledge, including moral and religious knowledge: Scripture, tradition, reason, and culture. As the revealed Word of God, the Bible has pride of place, but it is not the unique source of all insight, if only because the Bible itself must be interpreted

---

23. Hume writes: "All our obligations to do good to society seem to imply something reciprocal. I receive the benefits of society, and therefore ought to promote its interests." See "Of Suicide," in *Essays Moral, Political, and Literary,* ed. Eugene Miller (Indianapolis: Liberty Classics, 1985), pp. 577-89, cited in Tom L. Beauchamp and James F. Childress, *Principles of Biomedical Ethics* (Oxford: Oxford University Press, 1994), p. 269.

24. See George Steiner, *Real Presences* (Chicago: University of Chicago Press, 1989), p. 4. As I hope to show, this willingness to gamble is (paradoxically) the last step in recovering from prodigality. It is often decisive for being "energized into creative responsibility" (p. 15).

according to the best literary-critical and historical lights we can command. In addition, the Bible does not provide explicit or exhaustive guidance on all questions, and even where it does address a given issue, individuals must determine how to apply a biblical teaching to a concrete situation. Thus, other forms of wisdom are required: psychological, sociological, etc. It is simply not possible to be thoroughgoing Campbellites, "silent where the Bible is silent."

Due to its wariness of introducing faddish or sinful elements into the sources of faithful response to God, Protestantism has tended greatly to de-emphasize tradition, reason, and culture, at least in theological contexts. Yet there is no unanimity on the matter of degree. Calvin, for instance, allowed some possibility of "lightning flashes of insight" even to fallen human nature. And Roman Catholics are not alone in their fairly inclusive epistemology. The Methodist quadrilateral refers to Scripture, tradition, experience, and reason. Even Karl Barth, that staunch foe of natural philosophy, cautioned against conflating the Word of God (the Trinitarian Son) with the word of man (the Bible). Quite generally, Christians speak of empirical facts apprehended by the five senses, natural laws grasped by practical reason, and supernatural truths appropriated by faith. Faith itself is now widely acknowledged to have rational, affective, and volitional elements.[25]

With respect to ontology, many Christians continue to take their lead from Genesis in calling a complex creation "good." Such biblical pluralism still holds God to be the *summum bonum,* but this does not imply that God is the *solum bonum.* It is judged an expression of divine omnipotence and omni-benevolence that God creates real and valuable entities over against the Godhead. To distinguish the infinite Creator from finite creation in this way is already to distance both a mysticism that would collapse the world (without remainder) into God and a pantheism that would collapse God (without remainder) into the world. There is a common *source* of all being and worth, on this view, but this is not to assert that there is only one worthwhile being. As the creative font of everything that is, the God who is love provides the touchstone with which to evaluate all subjects, objects, actions, and events. To say that temporal goods are intelligible with reference to God, however, is not to say that they are reducible to or directly measurable in terms of God.[26]

25. For debates about how to relate these elements, see Robert Audi and William J. Wainwright, eds., *Rationality, Religious Belief, and Moral Commitment* (Ithaca, N.Y.: Cornell University Press, 1986), esp. the essays in part 1.

26. In "Pluralism and Reasonable Disagreement," p. 73, Charles Larmore writes that liberalism is distinctive for "its refusal, ever more pronounced, to base the principles of political association upon a vision of God's plan or of an ordered cosmos." This may now be

Christians still justify their conscientious valuation of all creatures by gesturing, in faith, toward a Creator who is off the scale of value altogether. Christian pluralism depends, undeniably, on a singularity. But the eternal singularity of God makes possible, in turn, three crucial temporal realities: creation, incarnation, and redemption. These three are the foundation of Christian democratic equality. In creating a single couple (Adam and Eve) to be the first parents (monogenism), God is held to establish the consanguinity of all humanity. Social solidarity ought not merely be local, for the entire species is made in the image of God and stems from a single common origin. Ultimately, all are family. It is hard to overstate what the loss of this self-understanding — to be sure, never adequately acted on — means to Western culture. Second, the fullness of God's love for humanity is believed by Christians to be manifest in the incarnation. God meets fallen humanity where it is, in all its diversity, sin, and suffering, and the soul feels its worth by imitating the Christ. The eternal God is "pluralistic" enough, so to speak, to identify with temporal beings. Lastly, the divine condescension calls for a creative human response. Out of gratitude for the redemption extended to humanity on the cross, an integrating love is now judged both possible and mandatory for believers. "And above all these put on love, which binds everything together in perfect harmony" (Col. 3:14 RSV).

Let me concentrate on the love Christians call *agape.* The two commandments of Matthew 22:37-40 indicate to Christians that the first form of this love is unconditional obedience to God. The second form, love of the neighbor,

---

descriptively true, but it is not normatively so, I have maintained. Perfectionist liberalism is exactly a refusal of the refusal Larmore refers to. Larmore goes on to contend that "pluralism is a doctrine about the nature of value. It asserts that the forms of moral concern, as well as the forms of self-realization, are in the end not one, but many. It stands, therefore, in opposition to religious and metaphysical conceptions of a single source of value" (p. 74). I disagree. I have repeatedly argued that a Christian liberalism that sees God as the *origin* of all value — God as the "single source," in this sense — need not *equate* all value with God. One can believe the cosmos is ordered and thus avoid ontological chaos and agony, in short, without being a reductionist about value.

I can further elaborate these ideas with reference to one of Larmore's own distinctions. Larmore argues for understanding the variety of moral goods as "comparable" but not "commensurable" (esp. pp. 67-69). We can weigh heterogenous values and evaluate alternate courses of action, he contends, without thinking that these are quantifiable within a single metric based on a unique good. This distinction is useful in explaining how strong agapism can hold to the primacy of love without reducing to love monism. Charity can be compared to other real goods without thinking that those goods are but competing instances of charity. *Agape* is the first virtue for many Christians because it is the most direct participation in the life of the Creator and a necessary condition for the other virtues, but there are other created goods and virtues.

embodies the two aspects of care described above, but it combines them with a third that is more radical: *service open to self-sacrifice for the sake of the other.* I use the phrase "open to self-sacrifice" advisedly. Feminist critiques have made clear the dangers, especially for women, in both an uncritical equation of *agape* and self-sacrifice and an uncritical contrast of *agape* and self-regard.[27] (Valorizing self-denial can lead to masochism; vilifying self-development can lead to sloth.) Even so, readiness to serve others remains an evangelical virtue near the heart of Christian ethics. To bear one another's burdens is to "fulfill the law of Christ" (Gal. 6:2).

Steadfast love is not nonresisting in the face of injustice, nor is it even always nonviolent, I believe.[28] But a forgiving mildness is often the only effective means to break the cycle of hatred and retaliation that results from sin. When this can be done freely and constructively, *agape* does surrender certain rights (e.g., to punishment) to restore mutual relation. However, self-surrender is necessary not merely as a remedy for sin. *Agape* must sometimes forgo genuine goods for another's benefit independently of antecedent injustice. Creative service is needed, that is, not simply to restore justice but to inaugurate justice. Mutuality, the joyful communion between free and equal individuals, remains an ideal for Christians. But the genesis of free and equal persons requires sacrifice on the part of individuals as well as groups. (Think of parents working to provide food for their infant children and nations voting to provide health care for their citizens who cannot pay.) This is the great moral truth that prodigal liberalisms have forgotten. Much liberalism, both the morally empty and the morally basic variety, has been so concerned to protect the exercise of autonomy that, like an ungrateful child, it has forgotten at what cost that autonomy has been acquired.

To be finite is to be in need of unearned assistance from others and to be called to give unearned assistance to others. *Pace* many secular philosophers and some feminist theologians, however, Christian faith wagers that there is no ultimate contradiction between caring for the neighbor and properly loving oneself. Both creation stories in Genesis, for example, suggest that humanity's

---

27. For a summary discussion, see Barbara Hilkert Andolsen, "*Agape* in Feminist Ethics," in *Feminist Theological Ethics,* ed. Lois K. Daly (Louisville: Westminster John Knox, 1994). Andolsen writes: "Frequently for women the problem is too little self-assertion rather than too much. Neither self-sacrifice nor other-regard captures the total meaning of *agape.* The full expression of the Christian ideal is mutuality" (p. 156). See also chapter 8 *infra.*

28. For a defense of the just war tradition as compatible with charity, see my "Christian Love and Political Violence," in *The Love Commandments,* ed. Edmund Santurri and William Werpehowski (Washington, D.C.: Georgetown University Press, 1992).

interdependence is a part of God's initial intention for the world. It is good to need each other. *Agape* often entails genuine self-sacrifice, as I have repeatedly indicated, but it is not just a zero-sum game in which loving the neighbor means wronging oneself. Choices have to be made, priorities set, and these will relativize temporal ends and associations. To those without religious conviction, this may seem like world-hatred or self-loathing, the opposite of pluralism; indeed, Christ himself proclaims: "If any one comes to me and does not hate his own father and mother and wife and children and brothers and sisters, yes, and even his own life, he cannot be my disciple" (Luke 14:26 RSV). Yet Christ's own example makes clear the sense in which one is to "hate" personal ties: they are not to be allowed to interfere with obedience to God or concern for the stranger. Faith does not despise finite existence; it is neither masochistic nor slothful. It simply believes that charity is its own reward, a participation in the holiness of God, even when real values like health and happiness and even public cooperation are freely given up out of fidelity to that love.[29]

A prophet must frequently surrender health, happiness, and civic harmony for the sake of a higher loyalty, but applauding this willingness presupposes axiological pluralism. A martyr is admirable exactly because he has sacrificed something really valuable. Less spectacular than martyrdom, forgiveness is an especially neglected form of self-sacrifice in liberal societies, yet it is essential to the prophetic reconciliation of subjectivity and objectivity. The Christian prophet is a more dynamic voice than that described by Walzer, for she is a strong agapist who criticizes the community's self-understanding, not merely interprets it. But her prophetic criticism links judgment with a call for forgiveness, an insistence on social justice (objectivity) with a sense of our common sinfulness (subjectivity). The prophet enjoins bearing one another's burdens, but she wagers on a divine presence in all creatures that makes mercy's burden light. Her steadfast love (*hesed* in Hebrew) is most distinctive in distancing prudential reason without despair. As participation in the life of God, *agape* is willing to serve where appropriate without human reciprocity. The fidelity *of* God on the cross is sufficient for empowering fidelity *to* God and creatures.

---

29. *Agape* is not a zero-sum game, but for Christians it is a categorical command (in addition to Matt. 22:37-40, see John 13:34 and 1 Cor. 14:1): it may not be surrendered as a motive, no matter how much this might contribute to other genuine values like public peace and cooperation. Furthermore, *agape* is, in most respects, a *nonaggregative good:* it aims to foster virtue in others, but it may not be abandoned by individuals for the sake of net increases in *agape* itself. That would be personal apostasy, a form of "self-sacrifice" to which a Christian is not open.

A much-noted threat to liberal culture is its tendency to degenerate into factionalism: special interests vying for scarce resources with little or no sense of the commonweal. This orientation is particularly destructive when calls for distributive and compensatory justice erode into the politics of resentment: past social wrongs forever alienating race from race, gender from gender, faith from faith, etc. *Agape's* capacity for forgiveness together with its sense of a shared human nature, godlike but fallible, comes into its own here. Zeal for justice alone, independent of *agape,* often becomes mere petulance, if not perpetual vendetta. Forgiveness must not be masochistic or uncritical; it must not acquiesce in tyranny or abet indifference. Blessed is he, however, who leavens judgment with understanding. Without a spirit of love that transcends resentment, including the adversarial resentments between caricatured liberalism and religion, I see little hope for truly liberal nations or universities.[30]

As a variety of perfectionist liberalism, civic agapism rises above political morality as exclusively concerned with justice and injustice, rage and counter-rage, to embrace the indispensability of love. *But now the love is of both God and neighbor.* God's love (subjective genitive) for humanity is the source of humanity's love of itself and of God (objective genitive). The politics of charity that result will emphasize how individuals are empowered to have or regain a range of viable ends rather than how they can be unencumbered for the pursuit of ends already entertained. *But now the empowerment is traced back to a supernatural origin not intrinsic to any finite good or any human faculty as such.* In short, Christianity refers the mystery of human belatedness back to a

30. Listening to the militant chants of many campus groups these days, one cannot help but compare them with the civil rights protesters led by Martin Luther King Jr. in the 1950s and 1960s. King's followers sang "We Shall Overcome" and projected a spirit of justice fundamentally tempered by Christian charity. To bigots of all stripes they declared, in effect: "Though you mistreat us, we will stand up for our rights; though you despise us, we will overcome you with nonviolent love. For we refuse to hate you no matter what you do; we aim at *mutual redemption* and so will not diminish ourselves, or you, by mirroring your inhumanity." In the 1990s, in contrast, the message is frequently one of intimidation: "Hey, hey, ho, ho, Xism has got to go!" The anger at racism, sexism, economic exploitation, cultural imperialism, etc., is understandable, even justifiable; righteous indignation is, frequently, the catalyst of moral revolution. But the troubling subtext of much campus anger is: "If you don't give us what we want, we will roll over you! We as a crowd will fight fire with fire, for we are victims and will become victimizers ourselves rather than remain so!" The tactics of intimidation and resentment are so popular because, in the short run, they "work": they get attention, and administrators are often cowed by them. In the long run, however, "liberal" anger alone is an even less reliable moral compass than "liberal" justice alone. Undiluted rage turns readily to a hatred that wills harm; even the noble idea of "multiculturalism" has become an occasion for ethnic groups to bait and loathe each other. And so we fail to show our students how to say a healing word.

timeless Trinity: we "second persons" must rely on a First, Second, and Third Person who loves us unconditionally. Unlike the Stoic citizen of the universe, the Christian agapist is in the world but not of it; her life is not her own but a gift, and her hoped-for destiny is an eternity that transcends any natural harmony or disharmony.[31]

This is not a denial of fragility, a refusal of humanity, but rather a "wager on transcendence" from within a fidelity to immanence. It is attention to both capacities and limits, the effort to be true to both heaven and earth, that gives Christian liberalism its distinctiveness. Christian faith checks modern and postmodern accents on the "fragmentation" and "agony" of values by insisting on the primacy of love, but that same faith augments Stoic and Enlightenment talk of the "harmony of nature" and the "perfectibility of man" with an emphasis on the supernatural origin and end of the prime virtue. Perfection*ist* liberalism is not to be confused with Pelagian perfection*ism*. At the Fall, humanity freely corrupted itself beyond human undoing; but out of the hand of God human beings were not agonistic, and in the hand of God they may cease to be so. Thus the proper response to present conflict is not to accept it as fated or permanent but to remind ourselves of our original possibilities and ongoing redemption by God. "With this faith" (King), Christianity offers a remedy for the degeneration of much secular "theory" into dilemmas incompatible with charity.[32] The Christian agapist is highly critical, for exam-

31. Whether one requires an afterlife to practice *agape* consistently is debated even in Christian circles; see my "The Disconsolation of Theology: Irony, Cruelty, and Putting Charity First," *Journal of Religious Ethics* 20, no. 1 (Spring 1992): 1-35.

32. Some Christian ethicists endorse moral dilemmas as consistent with, even integral to, religious faith. Among the more skillful recent defenders of hard practical paradoxes is Philip Quinn. Quinn holds that "the possibility of a dilemma arising is built into Christian ethics at its foundations. . . . it seems clear that it is possible for a situation to arise in which the two parts of the Great Commandment [to love God with total devotion and to love the neighbor as oneself] are in conflict." Quinn observes in a footnote that "the greatest and first commandment" is "You shall love the Lord your God with all your heart, and with all your soul, and with all your mind" (Matt. 22:37), with the "second," which is "like it," being "You shall love your neighbor as yourself" (22:38). I am not sure, however, why he then continues to refer to the two commandments together as "*the* Great Commandment." There can be tension between the two commandments, for they are not simply identical, but there are limits to the opposition. Referring to the commands in the singular blurs the fact, which Quinn grants, that they are lexically ordered. In any case, the thrust of the Gospels seems to rule out the commandments' being flatly contradictory: "He who loves his neighbor has fulfilled the law" (Rom. 13:8 RSV). I reply at length to Quinn et al. in my *Love Disconsoled: Meditations on Christian Charity* (Cambridge: Cambridge University Press, 1999). Even for Quinn, "[i]t is . . . a typically audacious Christian hope that even a tragic ethical dilemma need not spell tragedy for

ple, of Seneca's defense of suicide and Walzer's defense of emergency ethics: both suggest a superlative mind and heart running up against the limits of a naturalistic philosophy. The result is an all-too-literal self-contradiction that cannot be squared with love of God and neighbor.

B. Origen, Aquinas, and Rawls on Goodness and Incarnation

I have maintained that agapic love outstrips anything that tribal custom or Greek rationality can render plausible, but that it is, nevertheless, the basis of Christian liberalism. To support this claim, if only anecdotally, let me cite two rich resources, Origen and Thomas Aquinas, and compare them briefly with John Rawls. I do not suggest that Origen and Aquinas are straightforwardly liberal in ways that all perfectionists, secular and religious, would validate. My aim is merely to highlight some surprising affinities between their orthodox faith and democratic scruples.

In *De principiis,* Origen writes: "it is one power which grasps and holds together all the diversity of the world, and leads the different movements towards one work, lest so immense an undertaking as that of the world should be dissolved by the dissensions of souls."[33] This belief in the unity of a diverse world, founded in Origen's case on a monotheistic faith, strikes fear in the hearts of many secular philosophers. It may even strike religious traditionalists as a bit quaint. Who thinks of the universe as a single, purposive "undertaking" anymore? Believers in liberal democracy in particular are taught to be wary of "universalist" claims and sweeping "metanarratives," as are sectarian critics of liberalism. Such claims and narratives are thought to foster tyranny. The theists among us will still affirm the workings of divine providence, but even theists may balk at Origen's optimism that "all things are [eventually] to be restored to their original condition" by God's ineffable wisdom.

It is easy enough to find proto-democratic sentiments in Aquinas's explicitly political writings.[34] I want, however, to lift up Thomas's comments on

---

the whole of one's ethical life. Providence may provide a replacement for shattered goodness." See Quinn, "Tragic Dilemmas, Suffering Love, and Christian Life," *Journal of Religious Ethics* 17 (1989): 171, 179, and 181. See also his "Moral Obligation, Religious Demand, and Practical Conflict," in *Rationality, Religious Belief, and Moral Commitment.*

33. Origen, *De principiis,* in *The Ante-Nicene Fathers,* ed. Alexander Roberts and James Donaldson, trans. Frederick Crombie, vol. 4 (Grand Rapids: Eerdmans, 1979), 2.1, p. 268.

34. "Nature has made all men equal in liberty," Saint Thomas informs us, and "the rule of the sovereign" is to be "for the good of the subjects whose servants the sovereigns may call

the Word made flesh as a neglected liberal resource. In the *Summa Theologiae*, he allows that there may, in principle, be multiple incarnations: "the uncreated cannot be comprehended by any creature. Hence it is plain that, whether we consider the Divine Person in regard to His power, which is the principle of the union, or in regard to His Personality, which is the term of the union, it has to be said that the Divine Person, over and beyond the human nature which He has assumed, can assume another distinct human nature."[35] Unlike the Origen quote, this passage might well be greeted with muted applause by secular liberals. It suggests an admirable openness to Goodness appearing in different times and places. The Truth, it seems, may take a plurality of finite forms. For many religious traditionalists, in contrast, this quote may seem disturbingly relativistic. How could there be another incarnation if Jesus is singular, the fullness of God made manifest, "a full, perfect, and sufficient sacrifice" for humanity's sake, the only begotten Son? Isn't the glory of the Christian faith its trusting in the unique salvific significance of the one historic Jesus? (As one of my students put it, "Wouldn't the Third Person of the Trinity say: 'Been there, done that'?") Or are the Jesu*ses* of history separable from the Christ of a common faith?

The quotes from Origen and Aquinas appear antithetical, but this is prima facie. Both Origen and Aquinas offer cues for Christian liberalism in together helping to reconcile expansive and reductive viewpoints. Origen's insistence on this being one world helps rather than hinders a commitment to cultural diversity and individual liberty. His brand of universalism is a study in the potential of reductive sensibilities to become conscientious. Correlatively, Aquinas's celebration of the incarnation holds a key to revising expansive pluralism. Thomas does not simply endorse the goodness of embodied existence, as important as that is; remarkably, he is open to the possibility of numerous Christs. Each Christ remains a singularity, however, in that each embodies the same God, a God who identifies with humanity but remains opaque to creatures in time.[36]

---

themselves." See *Commentary on the Sentences of Peter the Lombard* 2.44.1.3, reply to obj. 1, trans. Vernon J. Bourke, in *The Pocket Aquinas* (New York: Simon and Schuster, 1960), p. 234. Moreover, "the best form of government is in a state or kingdom, wherein one is given the power to preside over all; while under him are others having governing powers; and yet a government of this kind is shared by all, both because all are eligible to govern, and because the rule[r]s [*sic*] are chosen by all." See *Summa Theologiae* I-II, qu. 105, art. 1, trans. Fathers of the English Dominican Province (Westminster, Md.: Christian Classics, 1981), 2:1092.

35. Aquinas, *Summa Theologiae* III, qu. 3, art. 7; 4:2043.

36. Although Thomas might be called an *eschatological* foundationalist — at the end of

Rather than monotheism licensing tyranny and enforcing sameness, Origen allows that "under the influences of different motives, creatures nevertheless complete the fulness and perfection of one world, and the very variety of minds tends to one end of perfection."[37] If one is tempted to see a proto–Adam Smith here, it must be emphasized that the "invisible hand" at work is God's, and that the motive moving God's hand is what Origen calls God's "primal goodness." This goodness does not necessitate, moreover; it is a respecter of personal liberty. Origen writes: "every spirit, whether soul or rational existence, however called, should not be compelled by force, against the liberty of his own will, to any other course than that to which the motives of his own mind led him (lest by so doing the power of exercising free-will should seem to be taken away, which certainly would produce a change in the nature of the being itself)."[38] Note that the Origenal defense of liberty is tied to a reverence for created individuality, not merely for autonomy as the expression of arbitrary or narrowly prudent choice. Origen is working out the implications of respect for creaturely finitude rather than questing after a limitless or merely self-referential freedom. One does not (normally) coerce, for this changes people's specific natures and thus tampers with God's creation.

God's primal goodness, it seems, is nothing less than a love of the diversity of the world; and even in directing that diversity to a discrete end, providence honors particularity. In short, Origen adumbrates a distinctive brand of liberalism: neither Enlightenment universalism based on foundationalist epistemology and justice-centered politics nor postmodernist pragmatism based on relativist anti-epistemology and bourgeois insouciance. The human end for Origen is Christlike love, which cannot be forced but can be freely, that is, conscientiously, shared by all. It is precisely because Origen believes in God's primal goodness that he can celebrate the apparent chaos of the world. Because he holds to the primacy of love, God's own joy in creation, Origen can see the unity in diversity, the harmony in seeming cacophony, and thus not squelch the complexity.

If Thomas can be pluralist about the God-man in thirteenth-century Italy, we can be catholic about human nature in twenty-first-century America. The task for liberalism-as-morally-perfectionist is twofold: (1) to honor the singularity of historical traditions while avoiding sectarianism, yet simulta-

---

time we will contemplate with certainty the full range and meaning of Truth — his epistemic humility about *this* life has much to teach liberal theorists about how to avoid both dogmatism and nihilism. On earth, creatures' rational knowledge of God is at a distance and *ab effectu*.

37. Origen, *De principiis* 2.1, p. 268.
38. Origen, *De principiis* 2.1, p. 268.

neously (2) to affirm the universality of certain truths about human nature and social nurture without going hegemonic. Thomas on the incarnation provides a clue to how this might be done in a characteristically Christian way. For Thomas, Jesus is a singular universal, eternal Goodness having assumed temporal form. The biblical stories of Jesus' life, death, and resurrection are accessible to all believers yet stamped by the ethnic specificity of first-century Judaism. They are the defining narratives, the mythic histories or historical myths, of the early Christian church as well as of contemporary converts. More to the point, they do not exclude the possibility of ongoing revelation in other quarters.

Obviously, claims about incarnate goodness will strike some contemporary liberals as the quintessence of religious irrationality or arationality. But such claims, "the scandal of particularity," were controversial long before modernity, or even Aquinas. Jesus was put to death as an "insurrectionist," after all. It is crucial to realize, however, that Jesus was condemned not because he advocated armed rebellion against the Roman state or because he sought to overturn the Mosaic Law. Jesus was neither a political zealot nor a religious revolutionary; he was, to mix metaphors, a perfect liberal who refused to hide his lamp under a bushel. His message was disturbing precisely because he offered a vision and a vocabulary that highlighted the *limits* of local politics and traditional ritual. Jesus was *offensive* to Pilate and the Sanhedrin because he was mostly indifferent to their powers and ceremonies. He accepted taxes and went to temple, yet he associated with publicans and sinners; he was no ascetic despiser of the earth, yet he gestured toward an unconditional value he identified with a heavenly gift. His charisma did not pander to human subjectivity, nor did his reverence for life absolutize anything objective in the world. In recommending radical love of God and neighbor, Jesus was not directly seditious or blasphemous, but he was (by entrenched lights) uncivil. He trusted conscientiously in a higher good than temporal authority or common rationality could admit, and for this "pluralism" he was killed.

This makes all the more chilling the fact that in *Political Liberalism* John Rawls normally requires a bracketing of one's religious convictions in public debates about basic matters of justice.[39] It is unclear how Rawlsian public rationality and Christian social prophecy are compatible. Rawls as a rule limits public justification to "common sense . . . and the methods and conclusions

39. Rawls, *Political Liberalism,* esp. pp. 217-36; yet cf. the discussion of "free political speech" and "subversive advocacy," esp. pp. 340-56.

of science when these are not controversial,"[40] while prophecy knows no such epistemic bounds. It is not religious voices alone that seem unduly muzzled by the duty of civility. In *Political Liberalism,* Rawls would banish *all* comprehensive doctrines, both religious-theological and secular-philosophical, from explicit advocacy concerning basic justice and constitutional essentials in a well-ordered society. But this evenhandedness is called into question by, among other things, his controversial footnote on abortion.

> Suppose . . . that we consider the question [of abortion] in terms of these three important political values: the due respect for human life, the ordered reproduction of political society over time, including the family in some form, and finally the equality of women as equal citizens. (There are, of course, other important political values besides these.) Now I believe any reasonable balance of these three values will give a woman a duly qualified right to decide whether or not to end her pregnancy during the first trimester. The reason for this is that at this early stage of pregnancy the political value of the equality of women is overriding, and this right is required to give it substance and force.[41]

Rawls is quick to emphasize that his remarks are not an adequate argument for a moral position on abortion; they are an opinion. The disclaimer notwithstanding, many Christians will find these words insensitive to how the image of God becomes incarnate among us. Human life is a vulnerable gift from God, they hold, and gratitude for one's own nurture ought normally to incline one to protect that life throughout its maturation. Even so, Rawls's opinion is not unreasonable. It is the expected upshot of protecting the autonomy of actual persons over respecting the life of potential persons, of basic liberalism's placing justice ahead of love. The point is that Rawls's words are not metaphysically neutral; he does appear, despite protests, to take a key-things-considered stand.[42] And why not grant this? A "public reason" that would prescind entirely from contested issues surrounding human nature and social

---

40. Rawls, *Political Liberalism,* p. 224.

41. Rawls, *Political Liberalism,* p. 243 n. 32.

42. Philip Quinn has pointed out that one need not disagree with the substance of Rawls's remarks on abortion to insist, nevertheless, that they flow from a debatable view about the meaning of life, love, birth, death, autonomy, equality, etc. See Quinn, "Political Liberalisms and Their Exclusions of the Religious," *Proceedings and Addresses of the American Philosophical Association* 69, no. 2 (November 1995): 35-56.

purposes — call this "natural law by artificial means" — seems either vacuous or a misleading way of privileging a particular (often secular) agenda.[43]

An alternative to Rawlsian "civility" is an epistemic pluralism that allows much more readily for the prophetic. The prophetic moment in political discourse comes when a powerful, often suffering, voice challenges the entrenched assumptions of science or common sense and moves fellow citizens to reevaluate these. Rawls's rather adversarial stance against the prophetic is in the name of democracy, rather than empire or synagogue — Kant, rather than Caesar or Herod — but it remains a recognizable syndrome. It is, I am tempted to say, a preference for the German Immanuel over the Israelite one. Christians should be wary of it as (unintentionally) prejudiced against their flesh, as well as their soul: in the name of publicity, communities of faith must disincarnate themselves and their distinctive voices. For Rawls, it seems, the priority of the right supersedes the primal goodness of faith. Thus would the prodigal son of political liberalism slay its original father.

The passages from Origen and Aquinas quoted earlier suggest that neither agnosticism nor atheism is necessary for a viable pluralism; on the contrary, the quotes convey distinctively religious reasons for liberality and civility. Beyond this, a charitable reading of more recent Christian history implies that Rawls's quest for a metaphysical impartiality that is neither agnostic nor atheistic but somehow comprehensively neutral is at best unnecessary. Annealed in the fire of Catholic-Protestant antagonism, Christianity knows all about respect for individual conscience: out of love for the other as a free creature of God, no one should be compelled to speak or act against his will, normally.[44] Even in a highly liberal society, there must be *some* restraint of

---

43. Robert Audi argues for what he calls "the principle of secular motivation": "one should not advocate or promote any legal or public policy restrictions on human conduct unless one not only has and is willing to offer, but is also *motivated by,* adequate secular reason, where this reason (or set of reasons) is motivationally sufficient for the conduct in question." See Audi, "The Separation of Church and State and the Obligations of Citizenship," *Philosophy and Public Affairs* 18, no. 3 (Summer 1989): 284. One may have any number of religious inspirations for a political stance, according to Audi, but one must *also* have and be moved by secular ones. Yet whence comes Audi's implicit faith that there will always be an "adequate" nonreligious rationale in crucial moral contexts? Can't much of a secular society, of any society for that matter, go morally bankrupt (one inevitably thinks of Nazi Germany)? "Adequacy" cannot be a function of rhetorical effectiveness alone, but then what does constitute "adequate secular reason"?

44. As the American evangelical leader John Leland argued in 1791: "Every man must give an account of himself to God and therefore every man ought to be at liberty to serve God in that way that he can best reconcile it to his conscience. . . . It would be sinful for a man to

civic conversation for the sake of mutual respect and public legitimacy. But such restraint cuts both ways. If perfectionist accounts of benevolence risk becoming tyrannical or obscurantist, purely political accounts of justice may invite quietism or despair. There is no neutral way to adjudicate love/justice and theism/atheism debates, and we must be vigilant against the erosion of moral motive that comes from subscribing to views of reason, justice, and personhood simply because they jibe with the considered opinions of the age, however procedurally democratic.

Conclusion

I have not argued that "America must be Christian,"[45] but rather that Christians must not be *merely* American. (Call this the "uncivilizing" of charity.) Neither have I suggested that federal or state government is always to be the vehicle of benevolence. The principle of subsidiarity, allowing those local groups and institutions closest to a need to address it, is quite compatible with the liberalism I defend. Still, it might seem that, at most, I have suggested why non-perfectionist liberalisms may seem derelict *to Christians*. "You can preach love to the choir all you want," the objection might read, "but secular liberals aim at a wider audience and must appeal to a narrower consensus. For his part, Rawls must address atheists, agnostics, believers (of many faiths), rational decision theorists, romantic poets, retired generals, conscientious objectors, et al. Why criticize him, moreover, for not doing what he does not claim to do? He does not offer a comprehensive account of the good life or the best society, and he does not mean to impugn private charity. Indeed, justice as fairness is intended to be endorsable by all reasonable doctrines, including Christianity."[46]

---

surrender to man which is to be kept sacred for God. A man's mind should be always open to conviction, and an honest man will receive that doctrine which appears the best demonstrated; and what is more common for the best of men to change their minds?" See Leland, *The Rights of Conscience Inalienable,* quoted by Witte, "Essential Rights and Liberties," pp. 390-91.

45. This is the troubling title of a book by H. C. Goerner (Atlanta: Home Mission Board of the Southern Baptist Convention, 1947).

46. Several Christian authors have in fact defended justice as fairness as an expression of, or at least as compatible with, *agape*. See, *inter alia*, Harlan Beckley, "A Christian Affirmation of Rawls's Idea of Justice as Fairness: Parts I and II," *Journal of Religious Ethics* 13, no. 2 (Fall 1985), and 14, no. 2 (Fall 1986); and Paul Weithman "Rawlsian Liberalism and the Privatization of Religion: Three Theological Objections Considered," *Journal of Religious Ethics* 22, no. 1 (Spring 1994): 3-28. For a response to the latter, see my "Love in a Liberal Society," *Journal of Religious Ethics* (Spring 1994): 29-38.

My response is that Rawls and others are themselves "preaching to the choir," instructing them not to sing their hymns out loud. If, as I suspect, some politically relevant truths can only be grasped in religiously sonorous terms, then for the choir to stifle itself in the name of "fairness" would be folly. (The parent must call out publicly to the prodigal in her own recognizable voice.) As a matter of sociological fact, I doubt that evacuating most public speech of perfectionist appeals to benevolence (religious or not) will enhance the prospects of civic harmony, much less of private charity. More likely, it will lead to social callousness and the competitive individualism that alienates us from our neighbors in a too-bourgeois culture. Charity needs all the explicit endorsement it can get, and for this the public example and collective diction of the religious may be vital. The important language of "rights" and "duties" must be augmented by reference to compassion for basic needs shared by all but not specifiable in terms of desert or contract.[47]

Admittedly, the language of "truth, goodness, and beauty" — especially when coupled with "the revealed will of God" — may seem to encourage dogmatism. Christianity has a great burden of historical guilt — sexism, racism (including anti-Semitism), triumphalism — but we must not assume that theology or any other perfectionist idiom is inevitably or uniquely the problematic partner in civil discourse. Minimalist liberal "theories" may themselves be stumbling blocks to a decent society, and we must constantly ask how to evaluate them. Once relativism prevails concerning notions like truth, goodness, and beauty, we cannot even talk about "liberal *theory*" in the classical sense of a general account of how things are, rather than how we want or imagine them to be. Rawls's views are clearly animated by a profound concern for his fellow citizens and the world at large. With no metaphysics of the person, however, it would seem his contractors treat people as free and equal not because they actually think them so but chiefly because doing so is part of the (mutable) political culture of their times. Ultimately, one must ask: Is Rawls's "theory" of justice falsifiable, or does it substitute de facto praxis for theory? Disturbing, if the latter (see my postscript in chapter 4).

What, specifically, might liberal theorists learn from the Origenal and Thomistic hints I have so briefly held up? I am under no illusion about the prospect of mass conversions among postmodern citizens: an effective atheism grips us all most of the time. Yet consider what a cultural self-understanding might look like if it began with the idea that human beings are capable, with grace, of at least an echo of what Origen calls "primal goodness." To wager on

47. Elements of this paragraph are drawn from my "Love in a Liberal Society," p. 35.

such goodness is to affirm that our moral faculties are not useless passions, to trust that the burdens of our care for one another are worth it. The tendency of some forms of liberalism to skepticism and agony might then be avoided by a genuine epistemological and ontological pluralism, one that recognizes that there are many ways to know the truth, though all are fallible, and that there are many good things to be known, though all stem from one source. Rather than beginning with an appeal to political rationality, we might then begin with imaginative empathy with fellow creatures; rather than seeing religious belief as a threat or cause for restraint, we might see it as an occasion for celebration.

Basing political action and reflection on distinctly theological virtues would remain, of course, a free choice of equal citizens. Religious liberalism *is* liberal. If the religion of faith, hope, and love were embraced, however, this would be primarily because it is believed to be true, not because it is commonly agreeable or practically expedient. Asking what is reasonably agreeable to all for the sake of public cooperation is an important liberal tactic. But when consensus (even democratic consensus) becomes the sole, or even the central, foundation of liberal respect itself, then political virtue in addition to religious faith is undermined. Political morality cannot wait on the *vox populi,* if only because agreement about public reasonableness itself is virtually as elusive as unanimity on God. This is not to say that religious liberalism is blind to the social origins and consequences of belief. On the contrary, a civic faith could be celebrated (secondarily) because it allows us to transcend cripplingly dilemmatic worldviews without denying the variety and vulnerability of embodied virtue. Taking Aquinas at his word, the faithful might even look for a new incarnation of God's Word in distant persons (male or female) and places (pagan or Christian).

Were liberal "theory" to admit the possibility of such a rebirth, it would cease to be prodigal; prophetic Christianity and liberal democracy would cross-fertilize.

PART II

Replies to Contemporary Liberals and Antiliberals

CHAPTER 4

To Bedlam and Partway Back:
John Rawls and Christian Justice

Justice (fairness) originates among those who are approximately
equally powerful, as Thucydides . . . comprehended correctly. . . .
justice is repayment and exchange on the assumption of an approximately equal power position. . . . Justice naturally derives
from prudent concern with self-preservation; that means, from the
egoism of the consideration: "Why should I harm myself uselessly
and perhaps not attain my goal anyway?"

FRIEDRICH NIETZSCHE[1]

The Gospel makes no distinction between the love of our neighbor and justice. . . . The supernatural virtue of justice consists of
behaving exactly as though there were equality when one is the
stronger in an unequal relationship.

SIMONE WEIL[2]

Owe no one anything, except to love one another; for he who loves
his neighbor has fulfilled the law.

SAINT PAUL, ROMANS 13:8 RSV

1. Friedrich Nietzsche, *Human, All-Too-Human*, p. 92, in *Basic Writings of Nietzsche*,
trans. Walter Kaufmann (New York: Modern Library, 1968), p. 148.
2. Simone Weil, *Waiting for God*, trans. Emma Craufurd (New York: Harper and Row,
1973), pp. 139, 143.

Introduction

The modern secular philosopher most often thought to be congenial to a Christian conception of justice is John Rawls. In this examination of Rawls's work, however, I shall contend that a Christian affirmation of his "justice as fairness" is impossible. My overall thesis will be fairly simple: to appropriate Rawlsian motifs for the elaboration of Christian justice is to be, in Anne Sexton's phrase, "torn down from glory daily." I choose Rawls — need I say? — not because he is ready fodder for Christian social ethics but because he was a most articulate champion of liberal political thought. Indeed, to trace the trajectory of his writing is to plot the instructive course of the greatest American political philosopher of the twentieth century — a course "to Bedlam and part way back," to quote another title from Sexton.[3]

Sexton's title is, for my purposes, more than just a euphonic conceit. "Bedlam" was a medieval name for the town of Bethlehem in Judea, according to *The Oxford English Dictionary,* as well as a name applied to the Hospital of St. Mary of Bethlehem in London. The latter was "founded as a priory in 1247, with the special duty of receiving and entertaining the bishop of St. Mary of Bethlehem [et al.] . . . as often as they might come to England." As early as 1330, however, the original priory was described as "an hospital"; upon the Dissolution of the Monasteries, it was granted to the mayor and citizens of London; by 1402 it was characterized as a hospital for lunatics; and by 1547 it was incorporated as "a royal foundation for the reception of lunatics."[4] The evolution of a Christian priory, designed to receive a bishop, into a secular foundation, designed to receive lunatics, is emblematic of the complex relation between Christianity and contemporary political praxis. Similarly, the translation of a name referring to the birthplace of Jesus into a name synonymous with insane confusion is suggestive for current political theory, including Rawls's.

Rawls, like other liberal theorists, attempts to take a commitment to justice, freedom, and equality originally at home in a religious community (the Judeo-Christian) and either incorporate it into or read it out of a secular framework free of any substantive conception of the self and its virtues. Seeing that this is impossible — for are not the people in his "original position" close to lunatics? — Rawls then retreats to endorse a vision of the person that is thought to command wide agreement (an "overlapping consensus"). It is in

---

3. "Torn Down from Glory Daily" is a poem in Sexton's *To Bedlam and Part Way Back* (Boston: Houghton Mifflin, 1960), p. 6.

4. *The Oxford English Dictionary* (Oxford: Oxford University Press, 1971), 1:189.

this sense that his intellectual course is "to Bedlam and partway back." I say "partway" because what Rawls calls "the fact of pluralism" still keeps him from straightforwardly defending a particular teleological anthropology as true, whether commonly held or not. Having eschewed a dominant end, however, his defense of liberal social arrangements is on the basis of personal and political goods that are anything but neutral. In the end, consensus alone does not give him the requisite critical purchase for a moral theory.

I. To Bedlam: Justice as Fairness, 1971-1985

Although already minimalist, John Rawls's *A Theory of Justice* (1971) still supports its conception of justice as fairness with a morally significant ontology. Its Kantian commitment to the freedom and equality of persons in the original position is at least partially founded on a perception of attributes intrinsic to human nature. Rawls explicitly endorses seeing the people behind the veil of ignorance as akin to Kantian noumenal selves, capable of choice and possessing a sense of justice as well as a "thin" conception of the good for human beings as such.[5] They are ignorant of their particular beliefs and specific places in society, but their social contract is premised on general truth claims and is thus not morally empty. The "basis of equality" is the "natural attributes" of "moral persons" (the capacity for a rational life-plan and for a regulative desire to act upon principles of right); and, as Rawls emphasizes: "Equality is supported by the general facts of nature and not merely by a procedural rule without substantive force."[6] The rules of the justice game are decided voluntaristically (on the basis of rationally self-interested choices), if you will, but membership among the players is decided ontologically (on the basis of who people are prior to choosing).

It is debatable whether Rawls succeeds, in the 1971 volume, in justifying a unique set of principles of justice via such a minimalist scenario.[7] In later work, however, he takes an increasingly pragmatic turn that renders earlier controversies along this line beside the point. In his Dewey Lectures (1980), for example, Rawls accents the senses in which his principles of justice are

5. John Rawls, *A Theory of Justice* (Cambridge: Harvard University Press, 1971), pp. 255-56.

6. Rawls, *A Theory of Justice*, pp. 505-7, 510.

7. See, *inter alia*, Robert Nozick, *Anarchy, State, and Utopia* (New York: Basic Books, 1974), and Michael Sandel, *Liberalism and the Limits of Justice* (Cambridge: Cambridge University Press, 1982).

"constructed" and thus do not follow from antecedent moral rules nor correspond to external moral facts. One begins to wonder, at Rawls's own invitation, whether his project has anything at all to do with moral or epistemic justification. Still, even in the 1980 essays, he conceives of model persons as "free and equal," and it is because of this "part of the truth" that they are "worthy" to participate in the social contract.[8] So at least in places Rawls remains "open" here to truth claims at the level of human nature and has not denied the relevance of objective (moral) truths to a theory of justice.[9] He has not yet merely collapsed theory into practice.

Rawls's 1981 Tanner Lectures begin on a promising note for anyone troubled by the constructivist (occasionally Hobbesian) diction of the Dewey Lectures. In the first paragraph, Rawls contends that "the basic liberties and their priority rest on a conception of the person that would be recognized as liberal and not . . . on considerations of rational interests alone."[10] He goes on to construe the "two moral powers" of a sense of right and justice and the capacity for a conception of the good as "the necessary and sufficient condition for being counted a full and equal member of society in questions of political justice."[11] So far, so good. Yet, toward the end of the lectures we are told that "[t]he essential point here is that the conception of citizens as free and equal persons is not required in a well-ordered society as a personal or associational or moral ideal. . . . Rather it is a political conception affirmed for the sake of establishing an effective public conception of justice."[12] The ultimate reason for endorsing the freedom and equality of persons seems troublingly expedient: to facilitate public cooperation.

The assumption of freedom and equality cannot be called a noble lie, since at this juncture Rawls appears unwilling to commit to either its truth or its falsity, but it is something like an instrumental hypothesis the justification for which is not its plausibility but its practicality. Willing cooperation is not sensible because people are in fact free and equal; rather, people are considered free and equal in order to secure such cooperation.

Whatever the ambiguities of his Dewey and Tanner offerings, by the time

8. John Rawls, "Kantian Constructivism in Moral Theory," *Journal of Philosophy* 77, no. 9 (September 1980): 542-46.

9. Rawls, "Kantian Constructivism," pp. 565-66.

10. John Rawls, "The Basic Liberties and Their Priority," in *Liberty, Equality, and Law: Selected Tanner Lectures on Moral Philosophy*, ed. S. M. McMurrin (Salt Lake City: University of Utah Press, 1987), p. 4.

11. Rawls, "The Basic Liberties," p. 16.

12. Rawls, "The Basic Liberties," p. 83.

of "Justice as Fairness: Political Not Metaphysical" (1985), the theoretical jig is up for Rawls. He assures us early on in this work that "a political conception of justice is, of course, a moral conception";[13] but he goes on to claim that his work "presents itself not as a conception of justice that is true, but one that can serve as a basis of informed and willing political agreement between citizens viewed as free and equal persons."[14] The problem is that, for theoretical purposes, Rawls rules out citizens' agreeing to just political arrangements because they actually believe one another to be free and equal; thus, in fact, he evacuates justice as fairness of any recognizably moral motivation. Reliance on social contract theory supported by a "thin" conception of the good, already vague and arguably unworkable in 1971, now gives way (despite protests) to something very like "Hobbesian" conventionalism. Hence Rawls completes in this piece the shift to postmodernism, the migration from what I would call liberalism-as-morally-basic to liberalism-as-morally-empty. It is a transition from looking for fundamental moral truths about which rational people might agree (a version of what used to be called "natural justice") to giving up on moral truth claims altogether in favor of a radical pragmatism, at least in the political sphere. To be sure, Rawls nowhere argues that religious or moral truth claims are false or unimportant as such — quite the contrary — but in this article he does systematically exclude them as (at best) unnecessary to his theory of justice.

Evidently, there is considerable distance not only between Athens and Jerusalem but also between Athens and Cambridge. May we even speak of a "conflict" between premodern theological accounts of justice and postmodern philosophical ones, or has our era merely changed the subject, as Richard Rorty maintains?[15] Response to these questions depends largely upon which of two strands of the Enlightenment one takes as more persuasive and (perhaps) which of two strands of Christianity one takes as more faithful. The first Enlightenment strand ("liberalism-as-morally-basic") founds the case for democratic equality and cultural pluralism on fundamental truths about human nature and moral obligation, that is, on a substantive conception of the good. Liberal conceptions of justice must here be validated by a standard higher than majority opinion or corporate self-interest, even if lower than the fully articulated worldview of any one moral-cultural tradition. The second

13. John Rawls, "Justice as Fairness: Political Not Metaphysical," *Ethics and Public Policy* 14, no. 3 (Summer 1985): 224.

14. Rawls, "Justice as Fairness," p. 230.

15. Richard Rorty, "Postmodernist Bourgeois Liberalism," *Journal of Philosophy* 80, no. 10 (October 1983): 583-89.

Enlightenment strand ("liberalism-as-morally-empty"), fearing the theoretical or practical implications of the first option, goes radically minimalist and seeks at most to be neutral on the question of the good, relying instead on such nonmoral notions as self-interest and social contract. The argument runs thus: if we start talking about "eternal truths," "the will of God," "the good of man," or even "prudence" (in Saint Thomas's versus Thomas Hobbes's sense), we will end up bashing each other's head in; so we must embrace historicism and speak of "justice" in terms only of consensus and convention.[16]

To the extent that liberalism-as-morally-basic offers a substantive conception of the good entailing the equal worth of persons, it is the secularization of a theme recognizable in both major strands of Western Christian theology (the Thomistic and the Reformed). To the extent that liberalism-as-morally-empty seeks to be neutral concerning conceptions of the good, it becomes, I believe, an impossible theory. It seeks to ground social ethics on the amoral, which is dubious enough; but, more concretely, its minimalism makes it incapable of the neutral specification of the structures of justice it aspires to. In the case of Rawls, as I hope to show, any number of conflicting and even tyrannical positions are compatible with justice as fairness; and in the end his political minimalism becomes morally unsupportable.[17]

The unsuitability, for Christian purposes, of a purely political justice as fairness can be adumbrated by contrasting the Bible's account of the creation and fall of Adam and Eve with John Rawls's depiction of the original position and veil of ignorance. Whether or not the biblical passages may be taken as historically informative, Rawls's scenario is clearly a thought experiment only. But even so, both the ancient and the postmodern accounts can be evaluated as akin to myths of origin. They are meant, like all etiologies, to clarify our self-understanding by telling a (quasi-causal) story of how we might have gotten to where we are. For its part, the book of Genesis begins with an act of divine *kenosis* in which humanity's being created in God's image makes covenant relations between people both possible and mandatory. Out of the hand of God, human beings are disposed to mutual trust and understanding: cooperation comes before reflection. The subsequent refusal or disordering

16. The first Enlightenment alternative is generally represented by Rousseau, Kant, and recently, Ronald Dworkin. The second is approximated by Hobbes, Pufendorf, and at times the later Rawls.

17. See James Fishkin, *Tyranny and Legitimacy* (Baltimore: Johns Hopkins University Press, 1979); "Can There Be a Neutral Theory of Justice?" *Ethics* 93 (January 1983): 348-56; and "The Complexity of Simple Justice," *Ethics* 98 (April 1988): 464-71. See also Michael Perry, *Morality, Politics, and Law* (Oxford: Oxford University Press, 1988), chaps. 3 and 4.

of personal relations is incompatible with humanity as created and is characterized morally as a fall that leads to the loss of original community. The 1985 Rawls's picture is by design, of course, almost exactly the reverse. Rather than beginning with ontological commitments to the finite dignity of men and women, as well as to their interrelatedness — the tie that binds at least some Thomist and Reformed Christians — the individuals in Rawls's original position are stripped of any potentially true (much less thick) conception of their own worth or of the good life together. And rather than moral revelation encouraging personal solidarity, the veil of ignorance must be used to induce them to agree to abstract social principles. Political cooperation is artificial in this sense, the result of human *kenosis.*

We are not to think of the original position as containing literal people trying to decide whether to concern themselves with the interests of others. Again, Rawls is engaged in a thought experiment, and, in any case, the motivation operative in the original position is not meant to model in any rigorous way the real motivation of individuals in liberal democracies. Still, the key question remains: Why should either we or the Rawlsian original posits/parents agree to take the veil, even *in mente?* The veil of ignorance is a vehicle to get (hypothetical) people to agree on specific principles of justice, when in fact only an antecedent and highly developed appreciation of virtue would move them to go behind the veil in the first place. In the Tanner Lectures, Rawls specifies that a sense of justice undergirds individuals' ability to honor fair terms of social cooperation and that this sense (what he calls "the reasonable") is expressed in the restrictions on agreement in the original position. What he calls "the rational," on the other hand, refers to each person's rational advantage, to whatever concrete good the person is trying to advance in society. Crucially, Rawls thinks that the sense of justice is shared, at least among liberals, but that conceptions of rational advantage generally differ and may even be incommensurable.[18]

My point, however, is that one cannot make sense of the reasonable as embodied in a common sense of justice independently of the rational as a determinate conception of the source and nature of human goodness. Acceptance of the fair terms of social cooperation, if it is to be moral, itself depends on a conception of the good life for humanity. Our rules of fair conduct are not separable from who we think we are and vice versa, as is suggested by our treatment of plants, animals, and even fetuses.[19]

18. Rawls, "The Basic Liberties," pp. 14, 17, 19-20.
19. Will Kymlicka has pointed out that "when we affirm equality, it is not because we

Rawls's optimism about universal acceptance of fair terms for public interaction, and thus of the constraints on the original position, is tied to his conviction that "[s]ocial cooperation is always for mutual benefit."[20] But it makes all the difference how this idea is interpreted. If mutual benefit motivates any given individual to accept the constraints on self-interest of the original position, then the question becomes: Why should he or she agree to let all others in as well? Why not contract only with those whose cooperation will further key desires? Even though mutual benefit implies for Rawls something more than crude self-interest, what are we to make of those (such as Saint Paul) whose determinate conception of the good rules out (or at least greatly subordinates) mutual benefit as a basis for community or motive for action?

The fact that, in the absence of prior community, inclusiveness cannot survive even one generation is a biblical lesson lost to the political Rawls. Without a thick appreciation of his good, Cain cannot suffer even his brother Abel (much less an enemy) to live. The question "Am I my brother's keeper?" is, for Rawls, an invitation to liberal political philosophy; but for Christian theology, the question itself is a mark of sin. Any Christian perspective on justice that would be credible, not to mention prophetic, must begin and end with this realization. Thus any philosophical perspective that renders the realization impossible cannot be affirmed.

II. Which Bedlam? Two Sympathetic Readings Rebutted

In a two-part essay, Harlan Beckley argues that "the distinctively Christian moral ideal of love obligates those who adhere to it to embrace the beliefs which undergird John Rawls's idea of justice as fairness. They are thereby obligated to accept something like Rawls's original position as a perspective for justifying principles of justice."[21] He hastens to add that this strong affirmation

---

care more about the right than about the good, but because we think each person's good matters equally." See "Rawls on Teleology and Deontology," *Philosophy and Public Affairs* 17, no. 3 (Summer 1988): 190. I would only add that the thesis that each person's good matters equally cannot be elaborated independently of an understanding of all persons' nature and interests. Again, Kymlicka: "Rawls does not favor the distribution of primary goods out of a concern for the right rather than the good. He simply has a different account [from utilitarians and perfectionists] of what our good is" (p. 187).

20. Rawls, "The Basic Liberties," p. 14.

21. Harlan Beckley, "A Christian Affirmation of Rawls's Idea of Justice as Fairness: Part I," *Journal of Religious Ethics* 13, no. 2 (Fall 1985): 212. Part II appears in *Journal of Religious*

holds only for the issue of distributive justice and not necessarily for the whole of social ethics; but within these confines Beckley believes that Rawls's contract theory "founds the justification for a conception of justice upon general moral beliefs which can be shared by those who hold partially conflicting particular beliefs and moralities."[22]

Beckley is convinced that Rawls can answer the criticism that justice as fairness is unable to provide the contractors with credible reasons for entering the original position. On Beckley's view, Rawls does not simply charge with irrationalism those who reject the veil of ignorance, nor does he propose to impose the original position on those who have divergent personal beliefs. Instead, Rawls's case for the restrictions of the original position depends upon its plausibility to diverse thinkers in reflective equilibrium, "upon continuity between the restrictions and the beliefs persons actually hold after due reflection."[23] In short, Rawls recognizes that for his theory to be credible it must move individuals (including Christians) to bracket their distinctive moral and religious beliefs (including their fully articulated accounts of justice) in a way consonant with at least most of those beliefs themselves. And, according to Beckley, this is exactly what Rawls succeeds in doing.

I want to argue, to the contrary, that a commitment to Christian love positively rules out acceptance of Rawls's theory, at least as elaborated through 1985. Beckley's essay was written prior to the publication of "Justice as Fairness: Political Not Metaphysical," so criticism of his failure to appreciate the radicality of Rawls's "middle" period must be somewhat muted; but, as I have indicated, the pragmatic themes that make a Christian affirmation impossible were already evident in his 1980 article, "Kantian Constructivism in Moral Theory." And if one allows the 1985 piece to govern retroactively the reading of Rawls's prior corpus, as he seems to wish, then even *A Theory of Justice* is beyond Christian ecumenics. In any event, my chief point is that a sympathetic reading of Rawls requires that Christians discount a substantial portion of his authorship. It is only by misconstruing the political Rawls's claims to impartiality that justice as fairness can seem a candidate for Christian endorsement.

Let me proceed by summarizing once more, and as positively as possible, the general contours of justice as fairness as traced in Rawls's late middle period (1980-1985). For this Rawls, reasonableness underdetermines morality.

Ethics 14, no. 2 (Fall 1986): 229-46. See also L. Gregory Jones's "Should Christians Affirm Rawls' Justice as Fairness? A Response to Professor Beckley," *Journal of Religious Ethics* 16, no. 2 (Fall 1988): 251-71.

22. Beckley, "A Christian Affirmation: Part I," p. 212.
23. Beckley, "A Christian Affirmation: Part I," p. 220.

He explicitly grants that there is much more to the good life than prudence narrowly defined as self-interest, and nothing about the original position is intended to endorse egoism or to deny altruism. Conversely, however, in Rawls's estimation the concrete moral traditions that attempt to define the good life in detail overdetermine principles of distributive justice. To dictate social arrangements on the basis of a single metaphysical school would be to impose on others more than reason can justify. Because reasonable people can disagree on the nature of morality (i.e., on what more than self-interest is required for living well), it would be tyrannical to compel everyone to accept a particular moral theory. Hence Rawls attempts to generate acceptable principles of justice by putting external constraints on the contractors in his original position, such as the veil of ignorance. He attempts to rule out egoism and tyranny without having to appeal to controversial moral doctrines, and this necessitates relying on (1) a common but largely premoral interest in public peace and (2) a reasonable but largely undefended picture of persons as free and equal.[24]

There is an odd circularity in this scheme, however. On the one hand, entrance into the original position and acceptance of the restrictions it entails must be agreed to by individuals fully aware of their moral beliefs and particular interests, or else they have no persuasive reason to take the veil and are merely compelled to endorse justice as fairness. On the other hand, if individuals can agree on the relevant restrictions from their fully moral perspectives, it makes little sense to think that an external constraint like ignorance is subsequently required for choices to be fair. Of course, such shifting back and forth between thick and thin conceptions of morality in order to arrive at a stable view of justice is part of what Rawls means by reflective equilibrium.[25] But the issue is whether this idea can be profitably (or even intelligibly) fleshed out; and what is its justificatory, or even explanatory, power?

The problem is that if one's thick conception of the good can move one on reflection to take the veil, then there is in fact little reason to take it. Or, to grasp the other horn of the dilemma, if our actual values and ends must move us to bracket these same aspects of ourselves in the name of fairness, then our set of moral beliefs is in fact contradictory. We must surrender in the name of fairness the very sensibilities that allow us to judge fairness in the first place. If, in the face of this dilemma, one interprets Rawls as relying solely on a thin conception of the good (e.g., mutual benefit) to warrant acceptance of the

---

24. Compare *A Theory of Justice*, p. 13, where "parties in the initial situation" are thought of as "rational and mutually disinterested," as "not taking an interest in one another's interests."

25. Rawls, *A Theory of Justice*, p. 48.

restrictions of the original position, then our actual beliefs and values come off looking like mere prejudices or superstitions. They play no positive part in the decision to take the veil, and in all likelihood stand as stumbling blocks to fairness. In this latter case, de facto moral traditions do not simply overdetermine principles of justice; they undermine them. Thus the challenge of a liberal theory of justice is to disabuse people of any thick moral belief system that outstrips self-interest and cooperation for mutual benefit. This is a far cry from the moral neutrality that Rawls sometimes claims for his theory, but his work in the early to mid-1980s reflects this pragmatic spirit.

In this period, justice as fairness is dubbed "political not metaphysical," as I have noted; but in light of such terminology it becomes all but impossible (*pace* protests) to construe Rawlsian justice as anything other than amoral self-interest (prudence in the narrow sense), however restricted by the exigencies of preserving civic harmony. The decisive move comes in denying, for purposes of political theory, any truth value to normative anthropology. Rather than simply acknowledging multiple rational construals of the implications of such anthropology, Rawls goes conventionalist. He premises his theory of justice on the assumption that persons are free and equal, not because this assumption is believed (much less shown) to be correct but because it is culturally dominant and practically desirable. The seemingly innocuous thesis that "the fair terms of social cooperation are conceived as agreed to by those engaged in it"[26] is anything but. For agreement premised on regnant models of the person — models that can be justified on no other basis than that they are regnant — has by 1985 become constitutive, rather than symptomatic, of fairness. With this, Rawls can no longer claim to be articulating a common moral vision, if only the lowest common denominator across a range of equally rational positions. Even the lowest common denominator view (what I earlier called liberalism-as-morally-basic) requires an epistemic justification from within various traditions to be plausible as a moral theory. To be sure, Rawls nowhere repudiates the belief that persons are free and equal, but he can neither defend nor even endorse it and remain faithful to his putatively neutral method.[27] What the purely political Rawls calls "overlapping consensus"[28] is not enough.

That at this point in his career Rawls has moved from fallibilism about

---

26. Rawls, "Justice as Fairness," p. 235.

27. See Perry, *Morality, Politics, and Law*, pp. 60, 62.

28. Rawls, "Justice as Fairness," p. 247. Rawls attempts here, unsuccessfully I think, to distance this phrase from Hobbesianism.

the good life, and the pluralism it inspires, to political conventionalism is indicated by more than the absence of an epistemic justification for his theory of justice. In 1985, Rawls sees justice as fairness to rule out any such justification even in principle. (If internal justification were possible, it would not be necessary to bracket thick moral beliefs.) In other words, he does not merely refrain from asserting moral truths; his "theory" categorically rules this out with respect to distributive justice. This is more than an acknowledgment of political fallibility; it is not merely an application of the principle of tolerance to philosophy itself, as Rawls suggests in his "Justice as Fairness: Political Not Metaphysical" piece;[29] it is, rather, the death of *theoria,* construed as one distinctive means of arriving at truth. It is not that reality is too rich and variegated to be captured by discursive reasoning (alone), requiring instead (or in addition) something like religious faith. Such a position would represent the kind of transcendence of theory arguably ascribable to biblical Christianity. Rawls here intentionally falls below the demands of classical theory.

Harlan Beckley reminds us that the original position portrays only a partial conception of the moral life (including selfhood), but even this incomplete picture depicts the truth of substantive moralities as irrelevant to justice and thus is not metaphysically neutral. Beckley contends that "the only reason we would 'give up' our particular conception of the good for the purpose of formulating principles of justice is because the restrictions of the original position seem reasonable and assist us, after reflection, in correcting or affirming the judgments we already hold."[30] But then why not rather say that we are working out the implications of our particular beliefs and values rather than bracketing or annulling them with hypothetical ignorance? If our particular conceptions of the good lead us to agree to the restrictions of the original position, and the original position leads us in turn to agree to Rawls's two principles of justice, then in fact the principles are based on a particular conception of the good, if only at one remove.[31] There may be some adjustment, to be sure, but if agreeing to the original position actually requires us to see the truth or falsity of our thick moral beliefs as irrelevant to the issue of social justice, then moral realists at any rate face something more like logical inconsistency than reflective equilibrium.

Rawls's political minimalism is motivated by respect for diversity of

---

29. Rawls, "Justice as Fairness," p. 231.

30. Beckley, "A Christian Affirmation: Part I," p. 232.

31. L. Gregory Jones has also noted that the emphasis on overlapping consensus seems to render the original position unnecessary. See "Should Christians Affirm?" p. 257.

opinion and by the unwillingness to endorse a dogmatic or monolithic conception of the good life, but such respect is given no coherent basis. It is, in fact, undermined by the later refusal to base justice as fairness on moral truth claims, however admittedly fallible. Rawls writes: "One of the deepest distinctions between political conceptions of justice is between those that allow for a plurality of opposing and even incommensurable conceptions of the good and those that hold that there is but one conception of the good which is to be recognized by all persons so far as they are fully rational."[32] He goes on to claim that Plato and Aristotle, as well as Augustine and Aquinas, "fall on the side of the one rational good,"[33] but this is potentially misleading.

It is quite consistent both to think that there is a primary moral telos to human nature and to endorse a tolerant social arrangement. The tolerance may stem from one or more of three sources: (1) an ontological nuance that sees, with Elizabeth Anscombe, that moral reality is a range, with various traditions grasping various parts better than others, (2) an epistemic humility that acknowledges, with John Stuart Mill, that we cannot be certain we are correct even in our limited account of the good life, and (3) a substantive truth claim about the good life itself and the importance of everyone's arriving at practical conclusions via uncoerced conscience. (For most liberals, in fact, the third source is dominant: it is enough to warrant tolerance that a thick conception of the good life be felt or believed to be wrong.) In short, the rational cannot be subordinated to (much less divorced from) the reasonable, since fair terms of cooperation become morally compelling only in light of a more or less fully worked-out moral worldview. Christian agapists, for example, believe that God is just and loving — indeed, that God is justice — and for this very reason respect the consciences of all his creatures.

Rawls's thought experiment through 1985 can be seen as suspect, even as a heuristic device, when we realize the following. No one in the original position would be moved by its restrictions to see (much less treat) others as free, rational, and equal; self-interest and the desire to cooperate do not require such universalism, as the sovereign in Hobbes's social contract illustrates. And even if *(per impossibile)* seeing people in this way did always serve our pragmatic aims, to be motivated by this fact would clearly be antithetical to Christian ethics rather than morally neutral. If, what is truer to the texts, the liberal assumptions about others (what Rawls calls a "sense of justice") are imported into the original position and seen even to motivate its acceptance, then the

32. Rawls, "Justice as Fairness," p. 248.
33. Rawls, "Justice as Fairness," p. 248.

original position itself loses much of its point. Beyond this, however, the whole scheme collapses for Christian purposes when (especially in the middle essays) it requires us to embrace the assumption of freedom, rationality, and equality not because it is believed true but because it is the prevalent "model" in our society and because embracing such a model serves our practical purposes.[34] Such "liberal" relativism is Christianity's last temptation. And, to quote T. S. Eliot, "The last temptation is the greatest treason: to do the right deed for the wrong reason."[35]

To be sure, there are formal affinities between Rawls's principle of structuring inequalities so as to be of the greatest benefit to the least well-off, on the one hand, and what some (usually Catholic) moral theologians call "a preferential option for the poor," on the other. But the biblical theme of God's solidarity with the disenfranchised and the correlative injunction to minister to them cannot be separated from motive. Despite his telling critique of utilitarian social theory, Rawls's contractarianism systematically subverts ethical motivation. Deontology, one must say, is not enough even politically; aretology, or the understanding of personal virtue, is a sine qua non.

If one would support the thesis that Christian love dictates a commitment to freedom and equality, as surely it does in some form, then moral argument involving metaphysical and anthropological truth claims is indispensable. One will naturally want to couch these claims in terms commanding the widest possible agreement, but the fact that Christians would agree not to force (or even to obligate) others to act on Christian principles does not mean that Christians themselves must act from unchristian principles. The critical distinction is between what is morally basic and shared by many traditions and what is so morally thin as actually to rule out appeal to any moral tradi-

---

34. Compare Rawls's 1985 a-alethiology with his comment in *A Theory of Justice*, p. 547, that "our problem is how society should be arranged if it is to conform to principles that rational persons with true general beliefs would acknowledge in the original position."

35. T. S. Eliot, *Murder in the Cathedral*, in *The Complete Poems and Plays: 1909-1950* (New York: Harcourt, Brace, and World, 1971), p. 196. On right action wrongly motivated, see the discussion of egoism in Rawls, *A Theory of Justice*, p. 568. Rawls claims there: "I am not trying to show that in a well-ordered society an egoist would act from a sense of justice, nor even that he would act justly because so acting would best advance his ends. . . . Rather, we are concerned with the goodness of the settled desire to take up the standpoint of justice. I assume that the members of a well-ordered society already have this desire." My point is that the desire to take up the standpoint of justice can only be plausibly "settled" by truth claims about what constitutes moral personality, which claims are cut off in the subsequent essays. If, as Rawls says in *Theory*, "acting justly is something we want to do as free and equal rational beings" (p. 572), then the force of justice cannot be separated from who we really are.

tions at all. No credible theory of justice can call for us to saw off the branch on which we are sitting.

Finally, in spite of Beckley's protests, Christians could not accept Rawls's 1985 views even if they were presented as truth claims, because Christians believe they are bound to promote their neighbors' interests further than any consent to principles of justice flowing from social contract or mutual benefit. It is not the hypothesis of contract but the reality of the kingdom that grounds the treatment of believer and nonbeliever alike. Reasonable self-interest does not merely underdetermine Christian ethics; if given motivational priority, it is antithetical to Christianity's radical universal demand for self-sacrificial love.

In contrast to the objection just lodged, Beckley argues that "Rawls requires bracketing our conception of the good only for purposes of agreeing to a conception of justice. In all other moral matters, Christians are 'free' to be 'bound' by their distinctive commitments. . . . Refusing to make these revisions for purposes of arriving at a common conception of justice is to claim that Christians are not free to accept principles of justice that respect the freedom to hold other than Christian beliefs."[36] But this misses the key point about intention: a commitment to justice that is not motivated by love (or at least something considerably thicker than self-interest or public cooperation) is arguably not a moral commitment at all for Christians. It simply is not the case, as Beckley claims, that Rawls's contract theory resolves "the dilemma of Christians attempting to arrive at a conception of justice which respects the liberty of nonbelievers without being unfaithful to Christian beliefs."[37] Christians would surely want to extol principles of justice that respect others' freedom of conscience; but if this is not motivated by a love of neighbor (and of God), then it is almost certainly idolatrous. Christians will want to respect nonagapists, for example, but precisely because they love them agapically. If Rawls requires that "respect" spring from something other than love, that "tolerance" grow out of the "reasonable" quest for mutual benefit or a mere "model" of persons as free and equal, then these can be but glittering vices to Christians.

I grant that the exegesis of Rawls is difficult on this point, but this is because he (and Beckley) want it both ways, as will become still more apparent in my section III. They indicate at times that Christians may "reason within" their tradition in accepting the views on freedom, reason, and equality evident in the original position, but they also enjoin Christians to "abstract from" their

---

36. Beckley, "A Christian Affirmation: Part II," p. 237.
37. Beckley, "A Christian Affirmation: Part II," p. 240.

concrete moral notions (including *agape*) in order to be suitably thin and publicly persuasive. Is this a prescription for equilibrium or for schizophrenia? Beckley simultaneously claims, for example, that (1) "[t]he strongest ground for a Christian affirmation of justice as fairness is the direct support love as equal regard provides for Rawls's belief in the equality of persons," and (2) "for purposes of formulating principles of justice, agapists will accept restrictions which prohibit them from basing principles upon their distinctive beliefs, including love."[38] His considered opinion seems to be that "[l]ove affirms but does not replace Rawls's idea of justice as fairness";[39] but, again, if Christians allow contract theory to be their justifying and motivating factor, then they have been unfaithful to their religious beliefs. Caesar has been rendered more than is rightfully his, and on his own terms — the terms of secular Bedlam.

A second "sympathetic reading" of Rawls is provided by Richard Rorty, particularly in an essay entitled "The Priority of Democracy to Philosophy." Rorty's reading is distinctive because it extrapolates and extols the very elements in Rawls that make Beckley's affirmation of him problematic. For Rorty, Rawls's "Justice as Fairness: Political Not Metaphysical" article does not represent the theory of justice gone to smash but its coming to increasing pragmatic self-consciousness. If previously it seemed that Rawls was vacillating between several polar opposites — metaphysics/politics, natural justice/practical convention, self-interested individualism/cooperative communitarianism, theoretical neutrality/historicist anti-universalism, in short, Kant/Hegel — by 1985 the ambiguity was resolved in favor of Hegel, or at least along "quasi-Hegelian" Deweyan lines.[40] These lines represent a break not just with Christian theology but also with Enlightenment philosophy. Rorty argues that "Rawls, following up on Dewey, shows us how liberal democracy can get along without philosophical presuppositions."[41] Rawls should be thought of as saying that "[f]or purposes of social theory, we can put aside such topics as an ahistorical human nature, the nature of selfhood, the motive of moral behavior, and the meaning of human life. We treat these as irrelevant to politics as Jefferson thought questions about the Trinity and about Transubstantiation."[42] Rawls helps us see that we need only rely on "the tradition of a particular community, the consensus

38. Beckley, "A Christian Affirmation: Part II," pp. 237 and 239.

39. Beckley, "A Christian Affirmation: Part II," p. 240.

40. Richard Rorty, "The Priority of Democracy to Philosophy," in *The Virginia Statute for Religious Freedom*, ed. M. Peterson and R. Vaughn (Cambridge: Cambridge University Press, 1988), pp. 259 and 264-65.

41. Rorty, "The Priority of Democracy," p. 261.

42. Rorty, "The Priority of Democracy," pp. 261-62.

of a particular culture,"[43] rather than on truth claims about an independent metaphysical and moral order, let alone God. As Rorty puts it, "[t]ruth about the existence or nature of that order drops out [for Rawls]."[44]

The first thing to be noted about the pragmatic program Rorty ascribes to Rawls, as well as to Dewey — "putting politics first and tailoring a philosophy to suit"[45] — is that, if this is what the "priority" of the right to the good amounts to, it is neither deontological nor teleological in any recognizable sense. Traditional talk of "rights" and "duties" no longer makes sense when severed from claims about human nature and rational motivation. But neither can Rorty's Rawls be construed as reversing the usual priority and putting the good first, if this is thought to provide epistemic warrant for moral truth claims. Since Rorty thinks that any extrapolitical justification of de facto social practices is self-deceptive, one cannot speak of "the good" as though this refers to something intrinsically valuable that we are obliged to maximize, including social cooperation. We may wish to put politics (in our case, democratic freedoms) first, but there is nothing to be right or wrong about here; there are only our more or less entrenched customs and those persons with whom we do or do not choose to identify.[46]

It is instructive to compare Rorty's account of the political Rawls with his account of the "pragmatic side" of Thomas Jefferson. "This side," Rorty writes with typical aplomb, "says that when the individual finds in her conscience beliefs which are relevant to public policy but incapable of defense on the basis of beliefs common to her fellow-citizens she must sacrifice her conscience on the altar of public expediency."[47] Rorty leaves no doubt that he thinks that Rawls's mature opinions would lead him to endorse a similar conclusion. The only difference is that whereas Jefferson could mitigate the shock of such a conclusion by appealing to the Enlightenment idea of "reason" and its guarantee that truth will ultimately be justifiable to humanity at large, Rawls does not and could not make such an appeal. The understanding of reason as discloser of universal moral truths is no longer tenable, according to

43. Rorty, "The Priority of Democracy," p. 259.

44. Rorty, "The Priority of Democracy," p. 264.

45. Rorty, "The Priority of Democracy," p. 260.

46. Both Michael Perry and Greg Jones wonder whether the later, more pragmatic Rawls isn't offering a "good-prior-to-the-right" theory of justice. See Perry, *Morality, Politics, and Law*, pp. 61-62, 71-72, and 84-90, and Jones, "Should Christians Affirm?" pp. 253-56. See also the "Erratum" in *Journal of Religious Ethics* (Spring 1989): 190-95. But if Rorty is right about Rawls, the priority issue is nugatory: Rawls offers no theory of justice whatsoever.

47. Rorty, "The Priority of Democracy," p. 258.

Rorty, so there can be no assurance that private truth will coincide with public justifiability. In other words, Rawls can find no solace in the Enlightenment's foundationalist epistemology.

Observe, however, that the "sacrifice" Rorty refers to is also mitigated in Rawls's case. Jefferson could accept the hypothetical proposition, "If privately held truths cannot be justified publicly, then personal conscience must be submerged for the public good," because he was confident that the protasis would never in fact be satisfied. Rorty's Rawls, on the other hand, can embrace the same proposition because he does not see the apodosis as entailing any real loss. Since conscience is not thought of as the revealer of metaphysical truths — much less as the core of the self and the locus of its rights and dignity — to "sacrifice" it is no big deal. There is no violation of personal integrity because there is no such integrity to be violated. "Where there is no honour there is no grief."[48]

Rawls takes Jefferson's "avoidance" of theology a step further, in Rorty's estimation, by sidestepping to boot standard philosophical concerns (e.g., with the dictates of conscience). But if we attribute to Rawls the full measure of Rortian pragmatism, he is even more radically minimalist than the word "avoidance" might suggest. Rorty writes that "presumably, [Rawls] wants questions about the point of human existence, or the meaning of human life, to be reserved for private life."[49] In fact, however, a Rortian does not merely bracket anthropological and ethical theses for purposes of political discourse but rather dismisses them as unintelligible (or at least irrelevant) as such. What is not publicly intelligible is not privately intelligible either. Any and all metaphysical truth claims are dispensable, across the board, because truth, goodness, humanity, etc., are opaque ideas we are better off without. The unexamined life is worth living. Or, better, the examined life is not worth examining, neither for individuals nor for groups, at least not in philosophical terms. This means that, for Rorty and for Rawls (if made in Rorty's image), any entrenched political arrangement — Nazism, communism, plutocracy, in addition to democracy — is "prior" to philosophy. Just as any habitual private behavior — sadism, masochism, fetishism, in addition to kindness — is untouchable by ethics. Psychotherapeutic categories may be applicable, but the question of justifiability simply drops out, on both levels.

The obvious response to a Rortian is to resist the reductionism with re-

---

48. This is one of the *Jacula Prudentum* (1651) collected in *The Works of George Herbert* (New York: Crowell and Co., n.d.), p. 444.

49. Rorty, "The Priority of Democracy," p. 263.

gard to truth, justification, and anthropology and to accept only a very limited version of the public/private distinction. One need not conflate treating particular metaphysical questions as marginal to politics, given the latter's limited means and ends, and treating all such questions as unanswerable or unintelligible. (The former is compatible with liberalism-as-morally-basic, while the latter implies liberalism-as-morally-empty.) More to the point, although many theological and philosophical debates are not directly related to the everyday business of governing society — if only because we must take some things for granted — the acceptance as true of certain basic propositions about human nature and community appears to be essential to a healthy democracy. Without them, it seems impossible not to divinize (our) society and thereby lose whatever critical purchase we may now have on ourselves and our social practices. Attention to others' real wants, needs, hopes, and fears is surely at the heart of moral motivation, even in the public domain.

The danger of divinizing society even while claiming to disenchant the world is latent in Rorty's claim that, "if we want to flesh out our self-image," then "communitarians like [Charles] Taylor are right in saying that a conception of the self which makes the community constitutive of the self does comport well with liberal democracy."[50] It makes all the difference how one unpacks the word "constitutive," but Rorty's extreme minimalism leaves him with precious few resources to qualify the priority of community so as to allow criticism of its constitution. Any normative account of shared human nature is out, it seems; but, more importantly, Rorty is unwilling or unable to draw a sharp distinction between the causal and epistemological priority of community, on the one hand, and its axiological and alethiological primacy, on the other. There is no denying that each of us is deeply conditioned by being born into a web of interpersonal relations and cultural institutions not of our own making. The community precedes the individual not just chronologically, and individual dependency is part of what it means to be finite. Yet what is the larger import of these facts?

Christian anthropology seems wedded to two basic theses: (1) that the social etiology of personal identity should not be confused with the ethical priority of groups over individuals, and (2) that the dependence of our epistemic skills on culturally mediated artifacts (especially language) does not dictate letting go of truth, much less equating it with our conventions. With respect to (1), Rorty's radicalization of Hegel makes it nearly impossible for him to preserve what is common to both Christianity and Kantianism, namely, respect

50. Rorty, "The Priority of Democracy," p. 261.

for the individual. Rorty's central political thesis is that democracy cannot have, but in any event does not need, metaphysical underpinnings. Neither principled love of all neighbors as made in the image of God nor respect for all persons as ends-in-themselves grounds social solidarity. But is solidarity without any reason *moral* solidarity; and even if it is, is it likely to remain solidarity with all individuals, as opposed to with our particular tribe? We can thank Hegel for helping bring to consciousness the contingencies of human existence, but how do we repudiate his idolatrous attitude toward the state as the closest thing to (divine) necessity in our lives? Can Rorty (or Rawls) sustain such a repudiation, intellectually? Does he even want to? With respect to (2), Rorty's notorious identification of truth with "what our peers will, ceteris paribus, let us get away with saying" was eventually displaced by a desire more or less to drop the idea of truth altogether.[51] But isn't either move deadly for self-criticism and thus for an acceptable theory of justice?

At their best, liberals like Rawls and Rorty speak in a pastoral voice: undogmatic, taking us where we are, believing in us, and helping us to grope as a society toward self-understanding. This is an impressive achievement. My worry remains, however, that their technique is entirely too minimalist, too nondirective. The analogy of original-position-as-asylum helps us see that Rorty's Rawls, at any rate, offers the political philosopher's equivalent of Rogerian psychotherapy. His appeal to reflective equilibrium and overlapping consensus is a strategy of echo and adjustment in which normative questions cannot even be asked. Free association in the political sense looks very like free association in the Freudian sense. It is tempting to think of Rorty and Rawls as playing, respectively, the "rich aesthete" and "therapist" roles that Alasdair MacIntyre finds (along with "the manager") so dominant in liberal society; but that would be unfair to their better aspirations. I have already noted that Rawls considers his political conception of justice a moral conception, and I shall return to this point below. For his part, Rorty contends that "we should not assume that the aesthetic is always the enemy of the moral" and that the "light-mindedness" he recommends serves "moral purposes" by helping make people more tolerant and playful.[52] I have rejected Rawls's and Rorty's judgments not because I hold the therapeutic or the aesthetic always to be at odds with ethics, but because I do not believe that they can substitute for ethics.

51. See Richard Rorty, *Philosophy and the Mirror of Nature* (Princeton: Princeton University Press, 1979), p. 176, and *Consequences of Pragmatism* (Minneapolis: University of Minnesota Press, 1982), pp. xxviii-xxx.
52. Rorty, "The Priority of Democracy," p. 272.

Instead of a reduction or elimination of ethics for political purposes, what is wanted is an expansion and refinement: a broad moral and metaphysical context in which to locate liberalism as a limited theory of statecraft, a context that Rortian pragmatism cannot provide.[53]

Although Rorty, unlike Beckley, sees the radical historicism entailed by many of Rawls's articles published after *A Theory of Justice,* what Rorty celebrates in this political Rawls, I lament as incompatible with Christian faith as well as civic virtue. If Rawlsian justice were to make impossible the relativization of de facto political and economic conventions, as Rorty's most extensive interpretation seems to imply, then MacIntyre's "Dark Ages" would be upon us, whether they took the form of state socialism or democratic capitalism or something remote from either. The last thing to be said about Rorty's "Priority" comments on Rawls, however, is that they cannot be the final word. Rawls has not returned to the priory, but neither has he remained camped in postmodern Bedlam. He has continued to write, and his coordinates have continued to shift.

III. Partway Back: Justice as Both Political and Metaphysical?

In two still later essays, Rawls attempts to respond to the charge of moral vacuity and related criticisms. "The Idea of an Overlapping Consensus" (1987) and "The Priority of Right and Ideas of the Good" (1988) defend the same thesis: justice as fairness is a moral conception affirmed on moral grounds, not a mere convergence of self-interests or group interests.[54] An overlapping consensus about the basic structures of society is not a *modus vivendi,* Rawls contends in both places; and he goes on in the 1987 work to offer the following reassuring (and un-Rortian) comments on truth:

> [j]ustification in matters of political justice is addressed to others who disagree with us, and therefore it proceeds from some consensus: from premises that we and others recognize as true or as reasonable for the

53. In *Contingency, Irony, and Solidarity* (Cambridge: Cambridge University Press, 1989), Rorty seems to blink before the vision of postmodern Bedlam. Having praised detachment and traced the (apparent) ubiquity of convention, he then suggests that we do not invent others' pain and should not be ironic about cruelty (pp. 94, 85).

54. John Rawls, "The Idea of an Overlapping Consensus," *Oxford Journal of Legal Studies* 7, no. 1 (Spring 1987): 1-25; and "The Priority of Right and Ideas of the Good," *Philosophy and Public Affairs* 17, no. 4 (Fall 1988): 251-76.

purpose of reaching a working agreement on the fundamentals of political justice.[55]

[I]t would be fatal to the point of a political conception [of justice] to see it as skeptical about, or indifferent to, truth, much less as in conflict with it. Such skepticism or indifference would put political philosophy in conflict with numerous comprehensive doctrines [of the good], and thus defeat from the outset its aim of achieving an overlapping consensus. In following the method of avoidance, as we may call it, we try, so far as we can, neither to assert nor deny any religious, philosophical or moral views, or their associated philosophical accounts of truth and the status of values.[56]

It is hard not to read these remarks as a recantation of the constructivism of "Justice as Fairness: Political Not Metaphysical." Rawls is not yet the strong pragmatist (a.k.a. "strong poet") Rorty makes him out to be. He sounds especially metaphysical in the 1988 essay, referring to the "essential nature" of citizens, to political society as an "intrinsic good," and to seeking "common ground" between various religious, philosophical, and moral doctrines.[57] In emphasizing that it is comprehensive doctrines that he is ruling out in the original position, he acknowledges that what might be called elemental views do in fact play a part. What we are given in the two later pieces is still somewhat ambivalent as between the "l-a-m-b" and the "l-a-m-e" versions of liberalism, however. Rawls grants that "the right and the good are complementary"[58] but nowhere draws the obvious inference that his conception of justice is both political and metaphysical, and with good reason. Such an inference would reintroduce the most problematic questions of truth previously sidestepped and radically deflate the implications of what Rawls calls "the fact of pluralism."

Rawls continues to insist that our inability to arrive at agreement on a thick conception of the good life requires treating the right (i.e., his political conception of justice) as having "priority." But there can be no priority if principles of justice are grounded on claims, however basic, about human nature and political virtue. Indeed, if elemental anthropological and axiological truths are included as ingredients in reflective equilibrium, then the very idea of a (purely) political conception of justice becomes highly suspect. Rawls claims

55. Rawls, "Idea of an Overlapping Consensus," p. 6.
56. Rawls, "Idea of an Overlapping Consensus," pp. 12-13.
57. Rawls, "Priority of Right," pp. 270, 273, and 262.
58. Rawls, "Priority of Right," pp. 252, 253, and 273.

that political liberalism "consists in a conception of politics, not of the whole of life,"[59] but this is either a truism or false. Of course, a pluralistic Catholic will not want to interject all the vagaries of soteriology, Christology, Mariology, etc., into public discourse about who gets to vote. But such obvious cases aside, politics and the good life will be so inextricably linked for such an individual that suggesting an either/or between them is absurd. Rawls himself writes that "a political conception must draw upon various ideas of the good," adding that "[t]he question is: subject to what restriction."[60] But the point is that if the restriction must itself be motivated by (or at least be compatible with) comprehensive moral commitments, then talk of "priority" is misplaced and talk of "neutrality" is highly misleading.

If, in contrast, the restriction stems from a narrowly political concern (social cooperation divorced from all metaphysical truth claims), then my earlier objections remain undiminished. If, for instance, people are "regarded"[61] (i.e., merely regarded) as free, equal, and possessed of moral powers because this facilitates our overriding interest in getting along, then we are back with Hobbes. In this case, practice trumps rather than completes theory, and justice is indeed political only. Rather than "each comprehensive doctrine, from within its own view, [being] led to accept the public reasons of justice specified by justice as fairness," as claimed by Rawls in 1985,[62] a comprehensive doctrine such as Christianity would have to reject Rawls.

From the "constructivist" notion that justice as fairness is not embraced on the basis of any substantive truth claim about the way the world is, two things would follow. Both are at odds with Rawls's cherished ideals, but unavoidable given his 1985 premises. First, there is no way, in principle, to guard against the exigency that social cooperation may someday be advanced by treating certain people as unfree and unequal — it may even be that they welcome their inferior status and would rebel against equal regard (as, perhaps, would the lower castes in India). Second, no morally realistic religion or philosophy can embrace Rawlsian justice and remain internally consistent. For moral realists, "truth" and "falsity" are as inseparable from public moral discourse as "right" and "wrong," "good" and "evil." This holds even if truth, rightness, and goodness are deemed too complex to be captured within the bounds of traditional *theoria*.

59. Rawls, "Priority of Right," p. 253.
60. Rawls, "Priority of Right," p. 253.
61. Cf. Rawls, "Idea of an Overlapping Consensus," p. 7, and "Priority of Right," p. 270.
62. Rawls, "Justice as Fairness," p. 247.

Hence the question of this section reduces to how to interpret Rawls's later essays (post-1985) and whether they are normative. In the opening paragraph of "The Idea of an Overlapping Consensus," he observes that "[w]hat is needed is a regulative political conception of justice that can articulate and order in a principled way the political ideals and values of a democratic regime."[63] I can sum up my misgivings by saying that I do not think that Rawls's characterization of justice as a "regulative" ideal succeeds any better than Kant's similar characterization of God, and for parallel reasons.

Kant wanted to "deny [dogmatic] knowledge in order to make room for faith," while Rawls wants to deny comprehensive faith in order to make room for fairness. Both men offer breathtakingly subtle architectonics but end up bifurcating theoretical and practical reason. Rawlsian political "truths" (the freedom and equality of persons) are as ambiguous as Kantian practical "postulates" (God, freedom, and immortality). To put it yet another way, Rawls stands in roughly the same (unintentionally deconstructive) relation to classical liberalism as Kant did to classical theism: justice within the limits of Rawlsian politics alone is no more recognizable to a traditional democrat than religion within the limits of Kantian reason alone was recognizable to a traditional believer. And even as nineteenth-century critics of theism found ample ammunition in Kant for pronouncing God dead, so twenty-first-century foes of liberalism will find resources in Rawls for declaring democracy decadent. Neither God nor a finite person can survive as a mere *focus imaginarius*.

Conclusion

When Christians attempt to speak about justice to a pluralistic, increasingly secular culture — such as twenty-first-century America — they may experience alienation at not being understood, much less heeded. In the face of this, it is tempting to search for a lingua franca with which to address the age. It is tempting to try to translate Christian accounts of justice (e.g., Jesus' parables or Saint Paul's discussion of *dikaiosune*) into "neutral" terms, to transform the *Vorstellungen* of faith into a *Begriff* of secular philosophy. Rawls's "theory" of justice is often thought to be congenial to such purposes. In light of the problems discussed above, however, I do not believe that Christian ethicists ought to baptize his account of "justice as fairness."

63. Rawls, "Idea of an Overlapping Consensus," p. 1.

Rawls's reliance on overlapping consensus concerning the freedom and equality of persons is problematic for three reasons. First, if personal freedom and equality are construed as "models" without truth value and for which no justification can or need be given in our society, then they are no longer conclusions of dialectical argument but rather are premises of descriptive sociology. This is the side of Rawls that Richard Rorty applauds, but it cuts against viewing *A Theory of Justice* and other works as exercises in moral reasoning and renders a Christian "affirmation" (like that of Beckley) out of the question. Second, if "freedom and equality" are defined substantively, then Rawls's view of persons is not in fact widely shared in contemporary American society. This is the point made by Michael Sandel, Michael Perry, and others. Yet, thirdly, if freedom and equality are defined broadly enough to be uncontroversial, they can do little work in political theory and are not even candidates for affirmation or denial.[64]

This does not mean that Christians should give up on liberal society in favor of theocracy, any more than they should give up on justified (or otherwise entitled) true belief in favor of mere prejudice. As Yoder and Hauerwas have reminded us, Christianity is not a handmaiden to any political philosophy; and as Plantinga and Wolterstorff have shown, the rejection of foundationalist epistemology need not leave us without rational beliefs and truthful traditions.[65] If we want democratic, egalitarian institutions to succeed (as I do), we must first commit our characters to something higher than self-interest, or even social cooperation. And before we can speak about justice to the world, we must embody it as the truth of our life in God. The later Rawls at times finds any anthropological claim deemed true too controversial to be included in the justifying reasons for liberalism. In contrast, moral realists like me believe the basic liberal truths, undergirded by the best of religious and secular thought, to be universally available precisely because they are true.

Without appeal to moral truth and recognition of the codependence of the good and the right, Rawlsian maximization of freedom and equality has a highly ambiguous status — paradoxically seeming like, in Harvey Mansfield's

---

64. One thinks of Kierkegaard's parable of the escaped lunatic who, in order not to be found out and returned to the asylum, repeats at intervals that the earth is round. The extreme generality and insensitivity to context of this statement (a too obvious appeal to "overlapping consensus") betray the very disintegration it is meant to disguise: the escapee goes back to his Bedlam.

65. See, e.g., Stanley Hauerwas, "Should Christians Talk So Much About Justice?" *Books and Religion Reviews*, May/June 1986, pp. 14-16, and Nicholas Wolterstorff, "Evidence, Entitled Belief, and the Gospels," *Faith and Philosophy* 6, no. 4 (October 1989): 429-59.

words, "the criterion of democrats who want no criterion."[66] Moreover, without commitment to moral truth (as opposed to social cooperation) as primary motive, it is unlikely even that just action will be possible. And lastly, without commitment to moral truth — however fallibly worked out and narratively, rather than deductively, formulated — it is impossible to do justice to Christian emphases on the person of Christ as the Truth Incarnate. If Rawls's script requires Christians to surrender love as the touchstone of political decision-making, then he is not extending to them the kind of respect that he seeks to exact from them. In a word, he is being tyrannical.

Christians need not demand that others accept a particular political arrangement out of love, but they themselves must do so or they have violated their own integrity. The issue is one of ethics, not merely psychology: while it may sometimes be permissible to submit to a cognitive impoverishment and act on the basis of less information than one could in fact command, it is never right to submit to a moral impoverishment and act with less virtue. It is never proper to surrender love, even if it were possible to do this out of love itself — an axiom that might be called "the priority of *agape* to political philosophy." It is impossible, therefore, for Christians to found distributive justice on personal prudence, social cooperation, or the thin sense of the good allowed by the political Rawls in the original position. These are blueprints for the secular Bedlam, even if motivated by the noble desire to secure public peace.

In referring to Rawls's course as "to Bedlam and partway back," I do not mean to suggest that he is insane. He does sometimes speak, nevertheless, as though he is in charge of a ward of madmen who have forgotten they are in hospital, much less in an erstwhile priory. He uses veils rather than straitjackets to constrain their more self-absorbed tendencies, but he does not question the bedlam that makes the veils necessary or of which the veils themselves are indicators. On the contrary, he suggests that those disinclined to take the secular veil are the mad ones. Commenting on Loyola's belief "that the dominant end is serving God, and by this means saving our soul" and Aquinas's belief "that the vision of God is the last end of all human knowledge and endeavor," Rawls writes: "Although to subordinate all our aims to one end does not strictly speaking violate the principle of rational choice . . . it still strikes us as irrational, or more likely as mad."[67] For Christians, coming all the way back from Bedlam (as madhouse) would mean returning to Bedlam (as Bethlehem):

---

66. Harvey Mansfield, "Democracy and the Great Books," *New Republic,* April 4, 1988, p. 35.

67. Rawls, *A Theory of Justice,* pp. 553-54.

acknowledging the situatedness of ourselves and our communities before the God who became incarnate in Christ. This would by no means require imposing religious convictions or theocratic institutions on others, but it would mean admitting the inseparability of metaphysical claims about who we think we are and political claims about how we ought to live together.

The best we can hope for in a Western society is a doctrinal convergence supported by distinctive pictures of the good. Granting this apparently harsh reality is preferable to pursuing the impossibly neutral ideal of the political Rawls's "theory" of justice. Yet, again, the best alternative to a morally empty liberalism is not religious totalitarianism, any more than the best alternative to nondirective counseling is shock therapy or brainwashing. A tolerant, pluralistic society is itself a substantive good — not something to be accepted as the result of moral breakdown but worthy of promotion for its own sake. The plenitude of the world is bound to call up diverse forms of life, some equally virtuous; and assisting individuals and groups to pursue virtue freely is part of what it means to treat them as neighbors.[68] The trick is to be rabbinic enough to be transformative without being cruel, ironic enough to admit fallibility without becoming nihilistic or sectarian. But for Christians to suspend scriptural truth claims for the sake of a universalizable "theory" of justice would be (in Paul Ramsey's words) to exchange their birthright for a "pot of message."[69] It would be to migrate from Judea's Bethlehem to London's Bedlam: not a pilgrimage but a defection.

Postscript: Rawls and Religious Reasons

In the original hardback edition of *Political Liberalism* (1993), John Rawls rejected a fully "exclusive view" in which religious reasons are always illicit in the public sphere when basic or constitutional matters are at stake. Moved by the examples of nineteenth-century abolitionists and of Martin Luther King Jr., Rawls conceded that his "inclusive view" properly "allow[s] citizens, in certain [disordered] situations, to present what they regard as the basis of political values rooted in their comprehensive doctrine, provided they do this in ways that strengthen the ideal of public reason itself."[70] This concession could be

---

68. Cf. Perry, *Morality, Politics, and Law,* pp. 90-92; see also Jeffrey Stout, *Ethics after Babel* (Boston: Beacon Press, 1988), chaps. 9; 10; 12.

69. Paul Ramsey, *Speak Up for Just War or Pacifism* (University Park: Pennsylvania State University Press, 1988), p. 36.

70. John Rawls, *Political Liberalism* (New York: Columbia University Press, 1996), p. 247; yet cf. p. 94.

interpreted in a number of ways, but its most natural reading had two problems: (1) it granted voice to religious sensibility as such only in a disordered society, and (2) it required that sensibility to be too motivated by concern for political consensus.

The consequence of both (1) and (2) was, for Christians, to make fidelity to God subordinate to political harmony. When civic disharmony reigns, Rawls suggested, one may appeal to comprehensive doctrine to urge the society in the direction of well-orderedness. In a well-ordered society, however, that appeal is unreasonable since it does not rely only on the existing overlapping consensus. In this way, obedience to God and love of neighbor lost their "regulative primacy," to borrow Rawls's phrase;[71] they were instrumental goods for political purposes, rather than fundamental values perpetually binding. With regard to (2), Paul Weithman argued that Rawls's inclusive standard could imply a serious misdescription of religious activists' aims. It would be highly misleading to characterize Martin Luther King Jr., for example, as invoking a comprehensive religious doctrine for the sake of political values and ideals. The motivation was obedience to God and love of the neighbor as fellow creature of God. Obviously, King had political goals, legislative agendas, etc.; but these were inspired by his antecedent religious faith, not the other way round.[72]

Rawls passed away in 2002, refining his views to the end. In later works, he relaxes still further the rigors of "civility." I cannot respond to all the changes in Rawls's highly nuanced position; I limit myself to three related observations, three connected questions, and a final speculation. *First observation:* in 1996, Rawls subscribes to what he calls "the wide view of public reason" in which "reasonable [comprehensive] doctrines may be introduced in public reason at any time, provided that in due course public reasons, given by a reasonable political conception, are presented sufficient to support whatever the comprehensive doctrines are introduced to support."[73] This is a significant advance on the past, I believe, one allowing a more conspicuous place for "witnessing" to one's comprehensive doctrine in protest of a social policy or practice.[74] Yet it remains an implication of the wide view that, if there are not sufficient public

71. Rawls, *Political Liberalism*, p. 257.

72. See Paul Weithman, "Taking Rites Seriously," *Pacific Philosophical Quarterly* 75 (1994), esp. pp. 281-85.

73. John Rawls, "Introduction to the Paperback Edition" of *Political Liberalism* (New York: Columbia University Press, 1996), pp. li-lii; see also his "The Idea of Public Reason: Further Considerations," *University of Chicago Law Review*, typescript, pp. 11-17.

74. Rawls, "Idea of Public Reason," pp. 15-16.

reasons to be adduced in addition to the comprehensive ones offered, then the latter are illegitimate.

This brings me to my *first question:* Why disqualify freestanding comprehensive doctrines? Simply to assume that this is required by a democratic polis is to beg the question about the indispensability of perfectionist sentiments, but to argue for it is to appeal to some comprehensive doctrine about the point of politics and thus to outrun the Rawlsian duty of civility. Public reasons are not sufficient for Rawls's political conception of justice itself. He grants that many reasonable people are not persuaded that justice as fairness is the *only* reasonable conception,[75] so presumably he ought not to advocate his specific "theory" in basic or constitutional contexts. And given that some reasonably doubt that there is even a reasonable *family* of political conceptions, it appears Rawls should refrain from advocating the ideal of public reason entirely, especially if he ever becomes an elected official or Supreme Court justice. He may be willing to live with this conclusion,[76] but it seems to approach a *reductio* of his ongoing labors.

Second observation: In "The Idea of Public Reason: Further Considerations," Rawls sides explicitly with those who maintain that judges cannot "put aside as irrelevant" or otherwise cease to rely on their comprehensive religious, philosophical, or moral doctrines when judging. That would be an impossible "bracketing" of their deepest identities. Indeed, Rawls imagines a nominee for the Supreme Court properly testifying that "my religion leads me to endorse a political conception of justice that supports the full range of constitutional values and the main political institutions of our society."[77] These essential themes have been struck by Rawls before, but I still find them hard to square with the notion that public reason is "freestanding" or "self-standing."[78]

Hence my *second question:* How are we to understand the logical relation between comprehensive doctrines and public reasons? There are, presumably, seven possibilities here: (a) the reasons are merely compatible with the doctrines, (b) the reasons are rendered inductively probable by the doctrines, (c) the reasons are deductively entailed by the doctrines, (d) the reasons are rendered inductively improbable by the doctrines, (e) the reasons are deductively contradicted by the doctrines, (f) the reasons are incommensurable with the doctrines, or (g) the reasons are utterly incomparable with the doctrines. It would

---

75. Rawls, "Introduction to the Paperback Edition," pp. xlix and lii-liii.
76. Cf. Rawls, "Idea of Public Reason," pp. 17-18.
77. Rawls, "Idea of Public Reason," p. 3.
78. Rawls, "Idea of Public Reason," p. 20, and *Political Liberalism,* pp. 10 and 12.

seem that if (e) is the case, then either the doctrines or the reasons or perhaps both may be deemed unreasonable: they cannot both be true, though both may be false. Yet when unreasonableness is an issue, Rawls talks almost exclusively about "unreasonable comprehensive doctrines" rather than "unreasonable public reasons." The burden of proof seems unfairly on the comprehensive side: doctrines, not public reasons, must be purged of "distorting tendencies."[79]

Third observation: Rawls insists that political liberalism "is not attempting to say why a Christian, or a Kantian, or anyone else, should arrive at the political conception [of justice]."[80] This is fair enough as a self-imposed limitation on scope, but it must be possible for the Christian, the Kantian, et al. to tell herself why. In *Political Liberalism,* Rawls writes that "citizens themselves, within the exercise of their liberty of thought and conscience, and looking to their comprehensive doctrines, view the political conception [of justice] as derived from, or congruent with, or at least not in conflict with, their other values."[81] He echoes these thoughts in "The Idea of Public Reason," noting that each comprehensive doctrine in an overlapping consensus "relies on its leading premises to support, or to arrive at, or to derive, or to approximate, as the case may be, the ideals and principles of the political conception of justice."[82] But note how broad the range of options is here: logical compatibility seems a sufficient condition for reasonableness.

Therefore, my *third question:* How does one reconcile such minimalism with the imaginative testimony I quoted above about being "led" from comprehensive doctrine to political conception? Mere compatibility does not lead in any direction. If one's comprehensive doctrine tends to support public reasons, then "taking the veil" of ignorance seems close to pointless; but if the doctrine does not so tend, then being "civil" seems artificial, if not dishonest. In some instances, even compatibility is surrendered by Rawls. He holds that political and nonpolitical values "may not always line up in a concordant way," and he states explicitly that "[t]here can be a discrepancy in particular cases between the true [comprehensive] doctrine and a reasonable conception of justice."[83] If and when this discrepancy emerges, it is evidently public reason that trumps "the whole truth" for Rawls, the ties of civility that have priority over individual conscience. This is a "troubling" prospect indeed.[84] If I read it

79. Rawls, "Idea of Public Reason," p. 20.
80. Rawls, "Idea of Public Reason," p. 23A.
81. Rawls, *Political Liberalism,* p. 11.
82. Rawls, "Idea of Public Reason," p. 5.
83. Rawls, "Idea of Public Reason," p. 26.
84. See Rawls, "Idea of Public Reason," p. 27.

correctly, it suggests the possibility of a "noble deception" at the core of public reason, a possibility that links ancient Greece's greatest political philosopher with present-day America's. Both Plato and Rawls, unlike most classical Christian theologians, allow for a fundamental slippage between true theory and just practice.

Final speculation: Perhaps Rawls's claim that judges are "under an obligation not to invoke certain kinds of reasons in making their decisions"[85] connotes only that judges must use a certain vocabulary or set of principles in handing down official opinions. His second (appropriate) sense of "bracketing" comprehensive reasons might thus be a matter not of content but of form, rather like an interpreter at the United Nations agreeing to speak, while on the job, only in German. On this analogy, however, either the judge is literally translating into "public reasonese" what her comprehensive doctrine prescribes about some fundamental question — shades of liberalism-as-morally-basic's quest for an ethical Esperanto — or else she is extemporizing in a foreign language without a script (or at least without a translation manual) from her mother tongue. In the former instance, the relation between comprehensive doctrine and public reasons seems far too close for Rawls: something like a deductive relation would have to obtain for reasonableness. In the latter instance, the relation seems far too distant for both Rawls and conscientious liberals: something like incommensurability (or even incomparability) would be enough for reasonableness. In short, I still find in Rawls no answer to the problem of self-referential inconsistency. His contrast between two ways of "bracketing" comprehensive beliefs seems a distinction without a difference.

85. Rawls, "Idea of Public Reason," p. 3.

CHAPTER 5

A House Divided, Again:
Dworkin and Singer on Sanctity and Dignity

A house divided against itself cannot stand.

ABRAHAM LINCOLN,[1] ECHOING MARK 3:25

Introduction

The philosophy of liberal democracy ascendant in the West since the eighteenth century — accent on civil equality, individual liberty, and the rule of law — has arguably been the most effective political defender of the dignity of persons ever devised. The breakdown of class divisions, the protection of freedom of conscience, the enumeration of universal human rights, the abolition of slavery, the progressive liberation of women — all stand among the truly remarkable ethical achievements of the last three centuries. Much remains to be done even within the narrow confines of politics, of course; prejudices based on race, class, gender, ethnicity, and sexual orientation continue to divide us into intolerant and sometimes warring camps. But any account of our situation that denies the advances of the last three hundred years forgets who most of us are or aspire to be. That said, my central thesis in this chapter is that the emphasis on "personal dignity" that is one of the chief Western glories now threatens to subvert our moral lives.

For some time now, our most perceptive social critics have been warning us that "freedom" is becoming an excuse for selfishness toward those who are

---

1. Abraham Lincoln, "'House Divided' Speech at Springfield, Illinois," in *Abraham Lincoln: Speeches and Writings, 1832-1858* (New York: Library of America, 1989), p. 426.

unfree and "reason" is becoming an occasion for cruelty toward those judged irrational or nonrational.[2] We are often so concerned to respect the choices of autonomous agents that we not only become blind to other treasures but also neglect the context and necessary conditions for agency itself. There are many possible explanations for this degradation: misguided neutrality claimed by the state sometimes caused by religious dogmatism, or would-be tolerance of divergent viewpoints leading to impoverishing separations of "religion" from "politics." But it is increasingly clear at the start of the twenty-first century that the "enlightened" safeguarding of existing persons threatens the genesis of personhood itself. Valorization of "the personal" (especially rational individuality) menaces a range of impersonal yet indispensable values (from the environment to future generations).

As I noted in chapter 2, Latin *dignitas* means "a being worthy, worth, worthiness, merit, desert," while *sanctitas* means "inviolability, sacredness, sanctity."[3] *Dignitas* initially referred to the grandeur and authority of a particular office or station, while *sanctitas* originally referred to moral purity or holiness,[4] especially when seen as divine gifts. Here, *in nuce,* is the tension that will occupy this chapter: at their roots, "dignity" suggests achieved merit while "sanctity" suggests gifted inviolability.[5] As I make clear below, the two concepts

2. I have in mind the work of Robert Bellah, Stanley Hauerwas, Eva Feder Kittay, Christopher Lasch, Alasdair MacIntyre, Nel Noddings, Paul Ramsey, Michael Sandel, Steven Tipton, Iris Marion Young, et al. Lasch makes it clear how the "autonomous personality emancipated from custom, prejudice, and patriarchal constraints" has found it hard to see beyond a calculating utilitarianism. See his *The Minimal Self* (New York: Norton, 1984), pp. 205-6.

3. See Charlton T. Lewis and Charles Short, *A Latin Dictionary* (New York: Oxford University Press, 1987), pp. 577 and 1626. For similar points, see the entries for "dignity" and "sanctity" in *The Compact Edition of the Oxford English Dictionary* (Oxford: Oxford University Press, 1971), vols. 1 and 2, pp. 726 and 2633.

4. Lewis and Short, *A Latin Dictionary,* pp. 578 and 1626.

5. Kurt Bayertz writes that "[i]n Ancient times, the concept of dignity usually referred to respect for individuals with a high social status: a Greek king or a Roman senator, for example. It was the Stoics who first developed the idea of a dignity attributable to the human being *per se,* i.e. independently of individual characteristics. In Cicero's writings, we find both interpretations side by side." See his "Human Dignity: Philosophical Origin and Scientific Erosion of an Idea," in *Sanctity of Life and Human Dignity,* ed. Kurt Bayertz (Dordrecht, Boston, and London: Kluwer Academic Publishers, 1996), p. 73. Drawing on various etymological sources, James F. Keenan, S.J., allows that "[t]he overriding effect of sanctity is veneration and inviolability; the overriding reason for both is its sacral quality, a point found in the Scriptures, e.g., in 2 *Maccabees* 3.12 and 1 *Corinthians* 3.17." See his "The Concept of Sanctity of Life," also in *Sanctity of Life and Human Dignity,* p. 3. Interestingly, Glanville Williams's comparatively early work, *The Sanctity of Life and the Criminal Law* (New York: Knopf, 1957), talks very little about "sanctity" as such.

have often been paired, and I do not wish to imply a permanent and irremediable antagonism between them. *As commonly defined today, however, dignity has become increasingly forgetful of its origin in sanctity, respect for worthy persons unmindful of the fact that persons only emerge out of impersonal needs and potentials that are addressed by grace, whether human or divine.* Secular thinkers may speak of the gratuitous care of parents for children, while theists refer to the providence of God sustaining the world, but these are frequently thought to be "private" rather than "public" concerns. In turn, the rational calculation of justice (what persons are due by right based on self-conscious interest) has been largely alienated from both the loving creation and the emotional appreciation of value (what is inherently good though often unself-conscious).

Thus I contrast in this chapter what I call "a political ethic of dignity" with a moral and legal vision that attends to both dignity and sanctity. The politics of dignity entails an exclusive, or at least a trumping, emphasis on self-conscious autonomy. The office of rational agent has overwhelming grandeur and authority, if you will. A defender of this view need not discount the value of all other goods, but, for legal and Constitutional purposes, the ability to form rational intentions and execute independent decisions over time is the criterion for valuable (personal) identity. Such an emphasis tends to exalt reason and volition, then, to the exclusion of such "embodied" faculties as passion, hunger, laughter, forgiveness, and growth. A more holistic and historical ethic, on the other hand, will also take sanctity centrally into account. As I define the term, "sanctity" refers to the impersonal (i.e., humanly shared) needs and potentials that are antecedent to any calculable merit or achievement. In opposition to the cognitivism and voluntarism of an accent on dignity, sanctity encompasses such elements of "noncognitive well-being"[6] as the capacity to feel joy, the need to receive care, and the potential to love and/or be loved. Such holiness precedes and grounds all worthiness.

The word "sanctity" still has religious resonances today, but it need not be understood in explicitly theistic terms, for example, as a creation of the biblical God. (Even some atheists believe in the "sanctity" of human life.) My own views are Christian, but I mean the above definition to leave open the question of the source of our shared needs and potentials; a benevolent Deity, an orderly nature, or a purely contingent evolution might be pointed to — though perhaps not with equal plausibility. Insofar as it points to goods that are not intentionally constructed or individually earned by human beings, at any

---

6. I take the phrase "noncognitive well-being" from Steven G. Post, *The Moral Challenge of Alzheimer Disease* (Baltimore and London: Johns Hopkins University Press, 1995), p. 9.

rate, "sanctity" connotes a gracious giftedness. It gestures toward those forces larger than ourselves, found rather than made, by which we live. If dignity calls forth respect or admiration for some personal exploit, then, sanctity evokes a more amorphous awe and wonder.[7]

One might base observations about the political "triumph" of dignity on any number of ethical literatures, but I want to focus on aspects of the recent debates around induced death: abortion and euthanasia. In a 1997 piece entitled "Assisted Suicide: The Philosophers' Brief,"[8] several prominent American philosophers weighed in favoring a right to die, including a right to practitioner-assisted suicide (PAS). The signers *(amici curiae)* were the following: Ronald Dworkin, Thomas Nagel, Robert Nozick, John Rawls, Thomas Scanlon, and Judith Jarvis Thomson. In his 1994 book *Rethinking Life and Death,* the Australian utilitarian Peter Singer also endorsed forms of euthanasia, again including PAS. The subtitle of Singer's book was *The Collapse of Our Traditional Ethics* — "traditional ethics" meaning a commitment to the sanctity of all human life. If one couples "The Philosophers' Brief" and *Rethinking Life and Death* with the 1994 edition of Thomas Beauchamp and James Childress's influential *Principles of Biomedical Ethics,* a surprising convergence of philosophical opinion appears. For Beauchamp and Childress now defend active euthanasia under certain circumstances as well.[9]

Indeed, concerning euthanasia, a sea change seemed to come upon America in the 1980s and 1990s comparable to abortion-related developments in the late 1960s and early 1970s. The covert practice of active euthanasia,[10]

7. How precisely to characterize the reverence owed human life — especially whether such an attitude is a recognition of intrinsic value, of something that outstrips all "value" language, or of relation to God — continues to be debated. For important discussions of dignity and sanctity, discussions that sometimes conflate the two, see the essays by Barth, Gustafson, Stith, and Lebacqz in chapter 4 of *On Moral Medicine,* 2nd ed., ed. Stephen E. Lammers and Allen Verhey (Grand Rapids: Eerdmans, 1998).

8. "Assisted Suicide: The Philosophers' Brief," *New York Review,* March 27, 1997.

9. As I make clear below, this is not to say that all, or even most, deontologists and utilitarians agree on the precise meaning of dignity, but rather that an interesting cross-section now focuses on this idea to the neglect of sanctity.

10. I define "active euthanasia" as the direct taking of an innocent human life construed as an act of mercy. This form of euthanasia is to be contrasted with "passive euthanasia," in which an individual is allowed to die by withholding or withdrawing futile or inordinately burdensome treatment. In the active form of euthanasia, the death of the person is intentionally aimed at and either causally brought about or directly facilitated by another; here the party dies because of what is done to her, perhaps by the party herself but with another's help. In the "passive" form of euthanasia, the death is neither willed as an end nor used as a means to some other end, but rather accepted as the upshot of a dying process no longer to

including PAS, has been under way for some time,[11] even as forms of abortion were available long before *Roe v. Wade* (1973). But public opinion and legal policy are now shifting explicitly to permit what was once officially prohibited. The 1997 Oregon referendum upholding that state's "Death with Dignity Act" may well provide the sort of historic marker around the end of life that *Roe v. Wade* now provides around the beginning of life. Still, the reasons for the emerging policy consensus remain complicated, if not contradictory;[12] as with abortion, euthanasia rationales vary, and it is unclear what *types* of reasons can legitimately be introduced into civic speech. In spite of the appearance of an increasingly united front, deep divisions remain. On matters of life and death, the American house is deeply divided, with some views not merely opposed but ruled out of court by "liberal" positions.

Specifically, I aim to do four things here: (1) to set abortion and euthanasia discussions against the general background of the relation between human sanctity and personal dignity; (2) to note, more specifically, how both Dworkin and Singer tend to exclude sanctity (often called "religious") considerations from public debate a priori; (3) to draw out what is, nevertheless, a significant difference between them; and (4) to gesture toward an alternative to both positions that defends, morally and legally, the sanctity of human life. The alternative is

---

be resisted; here the party dies because of an underlying injury or disease, not as the result of self- or other-inflicted assault.

As noted below, even when these broad definitions are agreed upon, the moral significance of the acts they describe often is not. One cannot settle the moral debate via terminological fiat, but the above distinctions are important in understanding what is at stake.

11. As long as it remains illegal in most states, the actual incidence of (active) medical euthanasia in the United States will be difficult to determine. The *New York Times* reported, however, that "the first national survey to examine how frequently doctors help people kill themselves finds that while patients often ask for help, they rarely get it." "[A] little more than 3 percent" of doctors who care for the seriously ill and dying said that they had written prescriptions for lethal drugs when asked for by their patients; "and just under 5 percent said they had administered lethal injections to patients on their deathbeds," a figure that includes lethality due to "double effect" as well as direct killing. (See "Assisted Suicides Are Rare, Survey of Doctors Finds," *New York Times,* April 23, 1998, p. A1.)

12. The *New York Times* quotes a salient observation from Dr. Diane E. Meier, an associate professor of geriatrics at the Mount Sinai School of Medicine and the lead author of the survey referred to in note 11 above: "It is odd that there is such strong public support for legalization of assisted suicide, and we find there is so little of this actually occurring." Also noteworthy is how professional practice and conscience might follow law: "When the doctors were asked if they would write lethal prescriptions, defined as assisted suicide, if it were legal, 36 percent said they would. And 24 percent said they would administer lethal injections, defined as euthanasia, if the law permitted it." (See *New York Times,* April 23, 1998, p. A1.)

indebted to Simone Weil and is, in my case, Christian in inspiration; but it is not the only possible Christian position, nor is its basic content necessarily religious.

My thesis is that neither deontological theories of justice nor utilitarian accounts of value have a presumptive claim on a democratic polis. The sanctity of human life is as publicly defensible by a prophetic liberalism as the dignity of persons is by any secular liberalism. More emphatically, neither the *separation* of value from legally enforceable interest-based rights (Dworkin) nor the *identification* of value preeminently, if not exclusively, with self-conscious bearers of interests (Singer) provides a viable basis for a just society. In neglecting to support human life in its most vulnerable stages, germinal and geriatric, neither school can nurture and sustain the very persons they would protect. One need not think that all human lives will be aborted before birth or that all adult children will euthanize their infirm parents to believe that future generations are endangered by the loss of moral standing by the very young and very old. A perilous line has been crossed when the continuation of the human community becomes a matter of contingent choice by the few rather than a presumed obligation of all.

Christian convictions about sanctity will quite possibly lose out in the twenty-first-century debates concerning life and death, but they ought not to be excluded from public discourse as such. Indeed, if theological beliefs about sanctity are judged illegitimate by the new "liberal" culture, so must all substantive accounts (religious or secular) of human needs and potentials. Excluding such accounts produces an artificial policy convergence that masks two profound distinctions, however: that between sanctity and dignity in the moral life and that between deontology and utility in moral philosophy. If the social divisions that grow up around these distinctions are not acknowledged and democratically adjudicated, civil war is one possible result. If, to echo Lincoln, a house divided against itself (half slave and half free) cannot continue to stand, then one so divided as to preclude recognition of what it is (religious and secular, impersonal and personal) may have already fallen.

I. Dignity and Sanctity

On one common reading, "dignity" refers to a basic faculty; it denotes the bare capacity for intelligent free choice[13] possessed by all nondamaged persons.

---

13. I say "*intelligent* free choice" to make clear the self-conscious dimension of dignity. "Lower" animals like fish and fowl are capable of "voluntary" actions, in some sense, but they

One's rational freedom may be misused, but the simple possession of it is the ground of respect. Kant, for instance, held that all persons are to be treated as ends, and not as means only, because they are capable of acting autonomously — that is, according to imperatives they willingly give to themselves out of respect for the moral law.[14] On another reading, in contrast, "dignity" is explicitly a term of achievement; it requires that actual choices be meritorious or at least responsible. Here respect awaits some historical performance that claims our special acknowledgment; only a limited number of individuals (e.g., the noble) possess personal dignity and the rights that go along with it. An ethic emphasizing dignity as something common to rational agents will tend, naturally, to equality (among persons); one in which dignity is something achieved, to hierarchy (even between persons).

Both of these senses of "dignity" are at work in liberal political contexts, and it is important to appreciate the differences between them. For present purposes, however, a fundamental similarity is most germane. On both readings, dignity is a function of the freedom of self-conscious agents, their ability to choose intentionally or their having chosen rightly or virtuously. Indeed, even if dignity is taken to stem from simple rational agency, rather than actual excellent choices, it still requires that a threshold of cognitive maturation be

---

are not significantly self-aware actors across time. They are not capable of moral agency, that is, as far as we know. "Higher" animals like human beings and perhaps chimpanzees and other nonhuman primates, on the other hand, are. For careful discussions of what is and is not distinctive about human nature, see Alasdair MacIntyre's *Dependent Rational Animals: Why Human Beings Need the Virtues* (Chicago and La Salle: Open Court, 1999), and Frans de Waal's *Good Natured: The Origins of Right and Wrong in Humans and Other Animals* (Cambridge and London: Harvard University Press, 1996).

14. Immanuel Kant, *The Critique of Practical Reason,* trans. Lewis White Beck (Indianapolis and New York: Bobbs-Merrill, 1956), pp. 89-90; and *Foundations of the Metaphysics of Morals,* trans. Lewis White Beck (Indianapolis and New York: Bobbs-Merrill, 1959), pp. 46-51. Practical reason is motivated by "the idea of the dignity of a rational being who obeys no law except that which he himself also gives," according to Kant, and "morality and humanity, so far as it is capable of morality, alone have dignity" (*Foundations,* p. 53). Aesthetic judgments of the beautiful and sublime have their place, but Kant's *ethic* is one of pure dignity based on personal autonomy. For him, only persons, that is, those capable of autonomous agency, possess moral worth. "Respect always applies to persons only, never to things" (*Practical Reason,* p. 79). This means, more specifically, that only persons can be the subject or the object of moral obligations. We may be morally required not to be cruel to animals, but this is finally a function of our duties to persons, not to the animals themselves. "The *autonomy* of the will is the sole principle of all moral laws and of the duties conforming to them" (*Practical Reason,* p. 33; and see also *Foundations,* p. 59), Kant says, and when we act out of a regard for duty, we have "respect for ourselves in the consciousness of our freedom" (*Practical Reason,* p. 165).

reached. Even the first sense of "dignity" demands, after all, a kind of achievement — namely, that one has passed one's spiritual nonage and acquired a fairly robust self-awareness. Only subjects who are aware of themselves as abiding rational agents are "persons," properly so-called, on this view.[15]

A liberal society may champion dignity, therefore, both by clearing space de jure for all persons to act freely and by adjudicating the interest claims that arise from de facto free actions across time. But immediately three human groups become "problematized" by this approach: (1) human lives that are prepersonal (the very young), (2) human lives that are postpersonal (the senile), and (3) human lives that are never-personal (the mentally handicapped). Very little that is politically substantive can be said in defense of these groups if dignity is the overriding concern of liberal reflection. Both clearing space for personal freedom (e.g., protection of the individual from sacrifice to general utility) and adjudicating personal claims (e.g., enforcement of valid contracts) are indispensable matters of justice. A problem arises, however, when justice, defined as giving extant persons what their rational dignity demands, is taken to be the overriding (if not the only) political virtue. Such an elevation of justice ignores two crucial facts: (1) there are other values than personhood, even within the political sphere, and (2) personhood itself does not just happen but must be cultivated historically. Various aesthetic and ecological goods, as well as fetal, senile, and demented human beings, are nonpersonal yet politically and religiously salient. And the dignity associated with autonomous agency — whether defined as a basic capacity or a contingent performance — depends on a sanctity given loving attention rather than mere procedural justice.[16]

"Sanctity" is sometimes used as if synonymous with "dignity," to be sure; some authors, especially those writing within the Judeo-Christian tradition, use the terms virtually interchangeably to affirm the veneration and

15. Bayertz argues that "[t]here are three central elements constituting human dignity within Modern philosophy": (1) consciousness and ability to think, (2) freedom of the will, and (3) the capacity to create values and norms. See Bayertz, "Human Dignity," pp. 74-77. While I would accent more strongly *self*-consciousness, all these ingredients can be understood to fall under the rubric "rational agency" or "personal autonomy."

16. Not all who talk of "persons" and "dignity" exclude fetuses, infants, the mentally handicapped, and the senile. For purposes of this chapter, however, I accept the definition of "personhood" as requiring autonomous agency. This is done to highlight the fact that, even on this definition, not all moral wrongs and legal harms affect persons. "Nonpersons" have needs and potentials that make them subject to help and harm too. For an analysis of "fundamental or noninstrumental need" as "a normative concept," and of "harm" as not tied to (conscious) "desires," see Garrett Thomson, *Needs* (London and New York: Routledge and Kegan Paul, 1987).

protection owed all human beings.[17] But, as suggested by their etymologies, the two terms are best seen as distinct. They are intimately related, I shall maintain, but unless we appreciate their individual meanings, we will not recognize the danger of overstressing one or the other. Especially but not exclusively in secular literature, "sanctity" (correlated with reverence for humanity) and "dignity" (correlated with respect for liberty) are now in danger of floating free of one another — to the detriment of both, but particularly of sanctity.[18] As noted, dignity is now frequently associated with the present faculty of autonomy and/or the expressed desires of autonomous persons; sanctity, on the other hand, is traditionally a matter of the essential potentials and vital needs of all human lives. The meaning of sanctity is notoriously hard to capture in words, but the Christian tradition has often associated the sanctity of human life with its "being made in the image of God" (cf. Gen. 1:26-27). This notion may be conceived ontologically (as an intrinsic feature of human beings as such) or relationally (as a function of being valued or sustained by God).[19] Given 1 John 4:16's affirmation that "God is love, and those who abide in love abide in God, and God abides in them," I find it edifying to associate the image of God with the ability to give or the need to receive loving care *(agape).* Conceived in this way, sanctity has an inviolable claim on us; moreover, it is both pre- and postpersonal, something coexten-

17. See, for instance, Glenn Tinder, *The Fabric of Hope: An Essay* (Grand Rapids: Eerdmans, 2001), p. 45; cf. also Pope John Paul II, *The Splendor of Truth ("Veritatis Splendor")* (Washington, D.C.: United States Catholic Conference, 1993), pp. 78-84 and 103, and *The Gospel of Life ("Evangelium Vitae")* (Washington, D.C.: United States Catholic Conference, 1995), passim. In the latter work, the pope frequently refers to the "sacred value" or "sacredness" of human life as well as to "the dignity of the person" — sometimes on the same page (e.g., pp. 5 and 145).

18. See, for instance, the essays in *Sanctity of Life and Human Dignity,* some of which link dignity and sanctity, others of which aim to separate them, and still others try to do without one or the other of them. In the introduction to that volume, Kurt Bayertz argues that, although both "sanctity of life" and "human dignity" have undergone "secularisation," "[t]he term 'sanctity of life' has not been party to a comparable legal institutionalisation — at least not in these words" (p. xiv). Protection of (human) life remains "one of the highest priorities of a modern State," in Bayertz's view; but he notes, nevertheless, that both the charter of the United Nations and the Universal Declaration of Human Rights of 1948 refer to the "inherent dignity" of the human being, but not to "sanctity" (p. xiv). In the context of abortion, he also observes, the two principles of sanctity (of life) and dignity (of self-determining agents) come into direct conflict. One of the concerns of my present chapter is to ask if dignity is not, in fact, unfairly winning this fight.

19. See the essay by Karl Barth entitled "Respect for Life," in *On Moral Medicine,* cited above.

sive with humanity itself.[20] Because it makes sense to talk of nonvoluntary development and noncognitive well-being, fetuses, babes in arms, the frail elderly, as well as the permanently demented may all be said to benefit from loving care. Although they are not "rational persons," in the technical sense described above, these human beings have needs and capabilities that can be addressed constructively by others or by God. They can be served as fellow creatures, and this service redounds to both their and others' good. They possess a given sanctity to be revered, in short, even if not an achieved dignity to be respected.

If justice looks to the temporal claims of self-aware actors, and thus is centrally *appreciative* of worth and agency, love attends to the enduring liabilities and prospects of embodied souls and thus is chiefly *productive* of worth and agency.[21] Sanctity precedes dignity, in that we are all vulnerable and dependent human lives before (and possibly after) we are reflective and autonomous persons; and love precedes justice, in that if impersonal human lives are not cared for, there will be no earthly persons with rational wills to be respected. Sanctity and dignity are not simply opposed, any more than love and justice, but you cannot have the latter of either pair without the former.[22] An ethic of dignity in which autonomy has a preemptive claim on us will see little or no reason to flinch from infanticide (as well as elective abortion) or from nonvoluntary euthanasia (as well as assisted suicide); therefore such an ethic must call into question its own long-term viability. When an appreciation of "love's labor" is eclipsed by an ethic of autonomy, who will care for the caregivers? When nurturance of the weak loses social sanction and support and becomes at best a private option, how will we keep those who care for the dependent (still mostly women) from being themselves marginalized and exploited?[23]

---

20. Some have argued that a few human lives, for example, those in a persistently vegetative state, are beyond both giving and receiving care and thus beyond the category of love based on sanctity. I am persuaded by the argument that someone who is permanently vegetative — having irremediably lost not merely reason but also emotion, sensation, social relation, and the potential for these things — has no meaningful well-being and thus is outside the ambit of human caring. She is, in effect, already dead. The psychosomatic unity that once undergirded sanctity has forever dissolved (at least in this world). Thus one may remove all "life support," because "life support" is a misnomer.

21. Cf. Irving Singer, *The Nature of Love*, vol. 1 (Chicago: University of Chicago Press, 1966).

22. See my *The Priority of Love: Christian Charity and Social Justice* (Princeton: Princeton University Press, 2003), esp. chaps. 1 and 5.

23. These are among the major concerns of Eva Feder Kittay in *Love's Labor: Essays on Women, Equality, and Dependency* (New York and London: Routledge, 1999).

The fact that respecting personal entitlement cannot be separated from honoring human value is made evident by the problems presented by Ronald Dworkin and Peter Singer, and I turn now to their illustrative work.

II. Dworkin and Singer: Striking Similarities

The first similarity to note between Dworkin and Singer is an emphasis on personal liberty and control: for them, individual freedom means, primarily, freedom from constraint by others (negative freedom). In his introduction to "The Philosophers' Brief," Dworkin appeals to "a very general moral and constitutional principle — that every competent person has the right to make momentous personal decisions which invoke fundamental religious or philosophical convictions about life's value for himself."[24] The brief itself argues that "respect for fundamental principles of liberty and justice, as well as for the American Constitutional tradition, requires that the decisions of the Courts of Appeals [allowing the right to assisted suicide] be affirmed."[25]

For his part, Singer notes that "[t]he desire among citizens of modern democracies for control over how they die is growing," and the desire for such control "marks a sharp turning away from the sanctity of life ethic."[26] This turning, he notes, "will not be satisfied by the concessions to patient autonomy within the framework of that [the sanctity of life] ethic — a right to refuse 'extraordinary means' of medical treatment, or to employ drugs like morphine that are 'intended' to relieve pain, but have the 'unintended but foreseen side-effect' of shortening life."[27]

The second similarity between Dworkin and Singer is a rejection of both the active/passive euthanasia distinction and the principle of double effect. For Singer, it is easy to see how the rejection follows from his consequentialism. If the valuable end is release from personal suffering, then it does not matter how it is brought about, actively or passively; correlatively, double effect is otiose, on Singer's utilitarian view, since the net effect is the same, regardless of motive or means: a dead patient.

It is somewhat harder to see why leading deontologists might reject the distinction and principle in question, until one realizes that Dworkin, for

24. Ronald Dworkin, introduction to "Assisted Suicide: The Philosophers' Brief," p. 41.
25. "Assisted Suicide: The Philosophers' Brief," p. 43.
26. Peter Singer, *Rethinking Life and Death: The Collapse of Our Traditional Ethics* (Oxford: Oxford University Press, 1994), p. 147.
27. Peter Singer, *Rethinking Life and Death*, p. 147.

instance, defines (legal) justice in terms of the adjudication of individual interests. He argues that neither the courts nor the Constitution should pronounce on questions of value, including the value and meaning of human life. Instead, they should be concerned only with the upholding of the rights of extant persons, especially the right to control their own lives without governmental coercion. As "The Philosophers' Brief" puts it, in discussing the Washington and New York cases then before the United States Supreme Court:

> These cases do not invite or require the Court to make moral, ethical, or religious judgments about how people should approach or control their death or about when it is ethically appropriate to hasten one's own death or to ask others for help in doing so. On the contrary, they ask the Court to recognize that individuals have a constitutionally protected interest in making those grave judgments for themselves, free from the imposition of any religious or philosophical orthodoxy by court or legislature. . . .
>
> Denying [the] opportunity [for physician-assisted suicide] to terminally ill patients who are in agonizing pain or otherwise doomed to an existence they regard as intolerable could only be justified on the basis of a religious or ethical conviction about the value or meaning of life itself. Our Constitution forbids government to impose such convictions on its citizens.[28]

In short, Dworkin et al. draw a sharp contrast between questions of value/ the good (such as the sanctity of life) and questions of justice/the right (such as the fair adjudication of the liberty interests of persons). They then go on to argue that legal sanctions should only be applied in the latter context. The active/passive euthanasia distinction and the principle of double effect simply do not get off the ground when a competent person wishes to die, for instance, because these notions depend on a substantive conception of the value or meaning of human agency that is overridden by an expression of agency itself. Dignity always trumps in politics, on this analysis.

A third similarity between Dworkin and Singer is that they define personhood in terms of the ability to be self-aware across time, to form plans and intentions, to make autonomous choices, etc. Dworkin describes a "person," at least for Constitutional purposes, as "a human being with interests of its own that should be protected by rights,"[29] with interests in turn depending

---

28. "Assisted Suicide: The Philosophers' Brief," p. 43.

29. Ronald Dworkin, *Life's Dominion: An Argument about Abortion, Euthanasia, and Individual Freedom* (New York: Knopf, 1993), p. 112.

on possession of "a mental life";[30] while Singer endorses a definition of "person" in which the term refers to "a being with certain characteristics such as rationality and self-awareness."[31] This convergence is the most profound, in that it tends to move both men (sometimes in spite of themselves) to glorify mind and will to the demotion of other human qualities. Self-awareness and self-control are the sine qua non; without these, one is not a person with full moral and legal standing.[32]

This picture is complicated in Dworkin's case, I hasten to add, by his inconsistent use of the terms "dignity" and "sanctity." On the one hand, he sometimes defines "dignity" in terms of autonomy: "The right of procreative autonomy has an important place not only in the structure of the American Constitution but in Western political culture more generally. The most important feature of that culture is a belief in individual human dignity: that people have the moral right — and the moral responsibility — to confront the most fundamental questions about the meaning and value of their own lives for themselves, answering to their own consciences and convictions."[33] On this reading, we ought to be (politically and legally) tolerant of others' views on abortion and euthanasia, even when we strongly disagree with them, out of "our love of liberty and dignity,"[34] our unwillingness to force persons to act on beliefs they do not consciously endorse. At other times, however, "dignity" is defined so as to conflate it with respect for the intrinsic value of life as such, that is, with reverence for what Dworkin himself calls "sanctity": "Dignity — which means respecting the inherent value of our own lives — is at the heart of both arguments [on abortion and euthanasia]. We care intensely what other people do about abortion and euthanasia, and with good reason, because those decisions express a view about the intrinsic value of all life and therefore bear on our own dignity as well."[35] This understanding of dignity comes just a couple of paragraphs after Dworkin writes, eloquently, that "we disagree so deeply [on abortion] because we all take so seriously a value that unites us as human beings — the sanctity or inviolability of every stage of every human

30. Dworkin, *Life's Dominion*, p. 20.

31. Peter Singer, *Rethinking Life and Death*, p. 180. See also Dworkin, *Life's Dominion*, pp. 15-19 and 109-14; and Singer, pp. 180-83 and 218-19.

32. For more on the significance of "standing" in contemporary philosophy, see Mary Anne Warren, *Moral Status: Obligations to Persons and Other Living Things* (Oxford: Oxford University Press, 1997).

33. Dworkin, *Life's Dominion*, p. 166.

34. Dworkin, *Life's Dominion*, p. 167.

35. Dworkin, *Life's Dominion*, pp. 238-39.

life."[36] The key point here, as Dworkin well knows, is that if dignity is a function of making autonomous choices, it is not a characteristic "of every stage of every human life." First of all and most of the time, in fact, Dworkin seems to favor the dignity-as-personal-autonomy view, rather than the dignity-as-human-sanctity view — as when he says that "[b]ecause we cherish dignity, we insist on freedom, and we place the right of conscience at its center."[37] But the picture is rather unclear.[38] In any event, the struggle to allow a place for both dignity and sanctity (in *some* fashion) represents a significant difference between Dworkin and Singer.

III. A Key Difference

Despite the similarities outlined above, an important contrast endures. In *Life's Dominion,* Dworkin acknowledges the intrinsic worth of various *non*personal goods, including the sanctity of human life, even when that life is fetal.[39] There is an important place for a wide range of judgments of intrinsic value in a well-

36. Dworkin, *Life's Dominion,* p. 238.

37. Dworkin, *Life's Dominion,* p. 239.

38. "A person's right to be treated with dignity," Dworkin maintains, "is the right that others acknowledge his genuine critical interests: that they acknowledge that he is the kind of creature, and has the moral standing, such that it is intrinsically, objectively important how his life goes" (*Life's Dominion,* p. 236). I do not see, however, how this is compatible with his further thesis that a seriously demented individual "remains a person" with a "right to dignity" (p. 237). Does not having "critical interests" require being self-aware and intentional, on Dworkin's own account (e.g., pp. 15-16)? Dworkin explains that "a person who becomes demented retains his critical interests because what happens to him then affects the value or success of his life as a whole" (p. 237). But then why not say that fetuses and other unborn generations also have "critical interests" in the meaning of their lives? Those who are not-yet-but-are-potentially-self-aware seem no more removed from "dignity" than those no-longer-and-never-again-to-be-self-aware. If "sanctity" alone applies to one group, it would seem to apply alone to the other.

39. Dworkin contends that a fetus does not have interests, and thus is not a rights-bearer, at least not until very late in pregnancy — roughly thirty weeks of gestational age. Hence most abortion is not an *injustice* to the fetus itself, not a violation of its rights. Abortion may be wrong on other grounds, such as the violence it does to the intrinsic value or sanctity of the terminated human life. But the key point is that having intrinsic value does not require or entail having interests, and interests alone are legally protectable in a just society. According to Dworkin, once more, one must not conflate values and interests in arguing about abortion or euthanasia (see *Life's Dominion,* esp. p. 18). I argue that, on the contrary, the law must attend to both the good and the right, both values and interests, if society is to be either just or loving.

lived life (e.g., aesthetic evaluations of works of art and religious veneration of creatures of God), according to Dworkin, but he nonetheless insists that "the jackboots of the criminal law"[40] ought not to be called in to settle disputes. The steel of the law must remain neutral in this regard, or else we have tyranny. Dworkin believes in human sanctity, then, but this is not the law's business when there is disagreement among autonomous persons on how to construe this basic value. To repeat, the law adjudicates the interest-based rights of existing persons only, remaining agnostic about controversial axiological issues, however morally important.

Singer, in contrast, more explicitly allows both medicine and law to make quality of life judgments.[41] More to the point, he leaves far less room for intrinsic value outside of or beyond personal value — that is, outside of or beyond the worth of persons able to form rational intentions — than does Dworkin. Singer does grant some moral significance to consciousness, in addition to self-consciousness, in the sense that he holds that sentient beings with the ability to feel pleasure and the desire to avoid pain ought not to be tormented.[42] But only autonomous persons have an inherent right to life, on his view. According to Singer, not all human life has a claim on us, whether one calls this "sanctity" or "dignity"; some human life is of insufficient quality or desirability to be worthy of respect and protection. Those who are in a persistently vegetative state, for example, are alive but effectively worthless. Singer goes so far as to remark that "life without consciousness is of no worth at all."[43] In addition, it follows from Singer's cognitivist criteria that "newborn infants, especially if unwanted, are not yet full members of the moral community."[44]

Indeed, both fetuses and not-quite-one-month-old babies may be directly and legally killed as nonpersons, according to Singer, subject to the autonomous choices of their parents. As Singer puts it, "in the case of infanticide, it is our culture that has something to learn from others, especially now that we, like them, are in a situation where we must limit family size"; thus "a period of twenty-eight days after birth might be allowed before an infant is accepted as having the same right to life as others."[45] Because fetuses and newborns

---

40. Dworkin, *Life's Dominion*, p. 15.

41. See Peter Singer, *Rethinking Life and Death*, e.g., pp. 86 and 93.

42. Peter Singer, *Rethinking Life and Death*, p. 219.

43. Peter Singer, *Rethinking Life and Death*, p. 190.

44. Peter Singer, *Rethinking Life and Death*, pp. 130-31.

45. Peter Singer, *Rethinking Life and Death*, p. 217. Singer has had second thoughts about the twenty-eight-day boundary; see his comments in "Dangerous Words," an interview with the *Princeton Alumni Weekly*, January 26, 2000, p. 19. The problem, however, is not that

have no awareness of themselves as existing over time, they are nonpersons, with at most a tenuous claim to life that can be legally trumped by the desires of adults. This goes for *all* fetuses and newborns, not merely disabled ones, since Singer denies real standing to any being without intentionality and self-awareness. As he puts it, "only a person has a right to life."[46] Like "lower" animals, unself-conscious human infants are interchangeable and can be killed at adult discretion so long as this is done mercifully, without causing suffering.[47] Dolphins, chimpanzees, and other "higher" mammals, on the other hand, are persons in Singer's sense, and thus may not be killed or injured upon human demand. To think otherwise is speciesist, in his estimation.

In sum, Dworkin accepts the importance of traditional claims that human life has "sacred value,"[48] but he nevertheless wishes to deny these claims political and legal cogency in the name of the dignity of persons, that is, persons' rights to make up their own minds about value. Singer, on the other hand, rejects the very heart of the sanctity of life position. For him, not all human lives are inviolable, whether the context is moral, medical, political, or legal. Thus, according to Singer, "the traditional doctrine of the sanctity of human life is today in deep trouble."[49]

IV. A Christian Response

How might a Christian ethicist respond to Dworkin and Singer?

A. First, Dworkin

There are three related steps in Dworkin's argument, each of which is implausible by orthodox Christian lights: (1) the separation of intrinsic value from social justice, (2) the equation of social justice exclusively with the protection of rights, and (3) the reduction of rights to matters of self-conscious personal interest. With regard to step 1, Dworkin fails to see that some values are so foundational to justice itself that they may be given legal defense. Human

---

infanticide is morally wrong in any substantive sense, but rather that the twenty-eight-day cutoff is "too arbitrary" and thus won't "work" as public policy.

46. Peter Singer, *Rethinking Life and Death,* p. 198; see also p. 218.
47. Peter Singer, *Rethinking Life and Death,* pp. 208-18.
48. Dworkin, *Life's Dominion,* p. 25.
49. Peter Singer, *Rethinking Life and Death,* p. 188.

life, even in its nascent stages, is one of these values. If both social and natural environments are not protected sufficiently to make future generations possible, then no form of justice as the balancing of personal interests will be possible. With regard to step 2, having intrinsic value does not directly *entail* having rights that must be justly balanced; as Dworkin points out, we think of a beautiful painting or sculpture as valuable (perhaps even sacred), without ascribing rights to it. But part of the intrinsic worth of early human lives is the fact that they will naturally grow into beings with interests and therefore rights, even as those rights will develop across time according to the degree of maturation. Dworkin ignores the fact that human fetuses, unlike material artifacts, have the essential potential for interests,[50] and that respecting fetal value may stem from anticipating the interests/rights that will grow out of that potential. We honor early human life, in other words, as a sacred good here and now but also as a *future* interest-based rights-bearer. Hence social justice is a matter of defending both rights and the necessary conditions for rights. The intrinsic value of fetuses is a necessary (but not a sufficient) condition for interest-based human rights, and we defend that value as a matter of charity and prudence in part precisely to make rights-based justice possible.

Even more importantly, *pace* Dworkin's step 3, not all rights are based on the interests of extant persons. In the Judeo-Christian tradition in particular, some rights are *need*-based, inhering in both persons and nonpersons. Indeed, it is often the neediness of "nonpersons" that has special claim on us: the lives of the young, the weak, the marginalized, and the diminished take priority as such. We lobby for national health insurance and various social security programs, say, not because they are "deserved" in some merit-based sense, nor even because they are self-consciously wanted, but because they are humanly *needed*. Moreover, we legislate against child abuse and infanticide not simply because these practices diminish social utility but because they harm vulnerable human beings, beings due reverence as such.

If the foregoing is accurate, the killing of fetuses or incompetent adults may still be unjust even if they are not considered rights-bearers. Again *pace* Dworkin, it is not the case that political justice and injustice are exclusively functions of respect for, or violation of, rights — much less existing *personal*

---

50. Essential potentials are distinct from mere contingent possibilities. The fulfillment of the former is a matter of growth, the unfolding of intrinsic powers and proclivities, while the realization of the latter requires external manipulation or at least arbitrary luck. Because undamaged human fetuses, with proper care, are disposed to develop self-consciousness, they may be said to have the essential potential for personhood; any given sperm or egg, on the other hand, has only the contingent possibility of contributing to the identity of a person.

rights. Justice is a matter of giving individuals their due, but only a narrow liberalism defines what is due exclusively in terms of what others have a present interest-based right to. Wouldn't we call "unjust" a person who secretly used up resources essential to future generations or even who needlessly chopped down a majestic redwood or gratuitously slaughtered the last snail darter? That person would have harmed lives other than his own, would have failed to show them due reverence, even if we decline to say that he has violated any interest-based rights of actual persons. (Though bald eagles are no longer on the endangered species list, we still arrest people who kill them.) Many theists think it *unjust to God* willfully to destroy a creature (whether in a rain forest or in a human uterus), but atheists as well as theists may think it *unjust to the creature itself* to take its life, because that life has intrinsic worth or sanctity that ought to be protected . . . and protected legally.

It is by no means a logical or moral necessity even for a liberal democratic society to tie legal protectability entirely to rights, and rights entirely to personal interests. Again, many need-based rights and impersonal values are protected in contemporary American law, as in the case of newborns and those with Alzheimer's disease. Think also of future generations and what they are owed; it is often unjust to thwart future persons, and the law properly limits pollution, fishing and mining rights, etc., to ensure that as-yet-unconceived persons are left enough to live on, if not as good as we now have (cf. Locke). If the ability to feel pain is what gives one interests, moreover, rather than the more robust ability to make plans, have hopes, etc., then arguably twelve-week-old fetuses have interests and should be legally protected. For twelve-week-old fetuses have measurable brain function and the ability to interact discriminately with the uterine environment.[51]

Dworkin will argue that Christians and others are free to make the value judgments they choose in these connections, just not to enforce them legally. As indicated, Dworkin claims that there are two separate questions here: one about inherent value, which is controversial and not to be settled at law in a liberal society, and one about justice and the procedural adjudication of competing interests of persons.[52] This is a false dichotomy, however. Wherever one comes down on abortion, infanticide, intergenerational duties, endangered species legislation, and the like, it is not the case that "grave" questions of the

---

51. William P. Smotherman and Scott R. Robinson, "The Uterus as Environment: The Ecology of Fetal Behavior," in *Handbook of Behavioral Neurobiology,* ed. E. M. Blass, vol. 9 (New York and London: Plenum Press, 1988), pp. 168 and 188.

52. As he puts it, "The crucial question is whether a state can impose the majority's conception of the sacred on everyone" (Dworkin, *Life's Dominion,* p. 109). His answer is no.

good can be left to individual conscience, while coercion at law can be on "neutral" or purely "reasonable" grounds. *To claim that only the interests of extant persons are legally protectable is already to make a controversial value judgment.* The judgment may be defensible, but it is not a question of justice free of debatable axiological assumptions, much less a "simple matter of logic," as Dworkin claims. It is not possible to separate judgments of rightness from judgments of goodness; we cannot determine what is just without also determining the goods to be justly produced, preserved, as well as distributed.[53] We only understand justice when we have clarified the value of justice itself (e.g., its relation to charity, dependency, and faith). In fact, questions of value precede questions of justice as more basic.

A community's judicial and legislative systems cannot escape acting on some rough social consensus concerning fundamental values and meanings, not excluding the value and meaning of human life. And part of democratic governance involves making room for the volatile educational and conversational processes whereby key axiological issues are publicly debated and acted on. Unanimity will not be had, but there is no escaping the need to hear multiple social voices discussing momentous moral values. Compromise and majority vote, reined in by Constitutional checks and balances, will often be the best a democracy can hope for. But the constructive tension that moves a society to ponder the meaning of its shared (and vulnerable) humanity is far preferable to a bogus "pluralism" or "fairness" that claims to prescind from controversial value judgments about life and death. As Gilbert Meilaender has written, "Especially when we are deliberating the fate of those whom some would regard as the weakest and least powerful *members* of our community, whose selfhood might easily be excluded and taken less seriously, the give and take of political argument is far preferable to the deliberations of a panel that supposes itself to be free of any religious or philosophical perspective."[54] These words, aimed at President Clinton's Human Embryo Research Panel and its recommendations on abortion and embryo experimentation, are equally relevant to Dworkin et al. and their advice to the Supreme Court on euthanasia and assisted suicide. The fact that most (but not all) candidates for active euthanasia or assisted suicide are competent (though ill) adults does not negate the reality that they are often weak and vulnerable and that the

53. The limits of an ahistorical focus on distributive justice is much commented on today; see, for instance, Iris Marion Young's *Justice and the Politics of Difference* (Princeton: Princeton University Press, 1990), esp. chap. 1.

54. Gilbert Meilaender, *Body, Soul, and Bioethics* (Notre Dame: University of Notre Dame Press, 1995), pp. 98-99.

meaning of their deaths is not a merely "private" matter. (Is the suicide of a *healthy,* competent adult an autonomous affair beyond all legal regulation?) Even if a gravely ill person has reached an assisted death decision in concord with family, friends, and physician, the public effects still go well beyond this circle. When doctors and nurses are asked directly and legally to aim at death, via technical means, the meaning of basic caring professions is at stake. There can be no neutral doctors or nurses here, any more than there can be neutral legislators and judges/justices.

Electoral processes may, after free and open discussion, bring a practice like assisted suicide under legal protection. (This has happened in Oregon but been rejected elsewhere, most notably in Michigan.) But, in that event, the facade of neutrality has been stripped away; those who would dissent have at least had their say and can choose to resist the practice with protests that have been put in religious or philosophical perspective. When, in contrast, appeals to "neutrality" or "tolerance" succeed in foreclosing public debate on a moral issue, civil war may threaten precisely because no real social compromise is possible. In the name of political liberality, the requisite argument and negotiation have been preempted. Substantive opinions cannot be aired as such, so political discussion itself comes to be labeled "fanaticism" or "incivility." In such a context, competing viewpoints can *only* degenerate into factions that bait and loathe one another, all the while "respecting" one another's "rights." Without a sense of common destiny worked out in open dialogue, we get not the Hobbesian war of all against all but the postmodern peace of none for none.

No doubt, one of the more telling examples of political preemption is Harry Blackmun's majority opinion in *Roe v. Wade.* Claiming that "[w]e need not resolve the difficult question of when life begins," Justice Blackmun went on effectively to write fetuses off the rolls of humanity, at least during the first six months of their lives.[55] As many have noted, it is not just the substance of the *Roe* decision, but the manner in which it was or was not justified, that has made elective abortion such an abiding and volatile issue. The point, again, is that to define protectable humanity in terms of the ability to have self-conscious interests is a metaphysically freighted decision — a political ethic approaching "pure dignity" — and once it is made, that decision has profound implications for society as a whole. It is instructive that Peter Singer (like Ronald Dworkin) embraces the interest criterion for personhood, but Singer

---

55. See "Roe v. Wade: The 1973 Supreme Court Decision on State Abortion Laws," in *The Ethics of Abortion,* ed. Robert Baird and Stuart Rosenbaum (Buffalo: Prometheus Books, 1989), pp. 18ff.

then judges even four-week-old babies not to have a right to life. Because such babies are not (yet) self-aware, they are effectively the disposable property of their parents. So much for the neutrality and privacy of basic judgments about life and death.

Perhaps the most poignant upshot of their liberal "neutrality" is that Dworkin and his fellow *amici* are unable legally to protect the necessary conditions for interests and thus for justice itself. There is a strangely self-defeating quality to Dworkin's writings on both elective abortion and assisted suicide, in that he seems to forget that persons only get to be persons and only continue to be persons because they have been extended a care that outstrips strictly adjudicative or meritarian justice. If nascent human beings are to come to have self-conscious interests, and if diminished human beings are to maintain whatever welfare they can, their lives must be revered and protected by society at large. Thus, the survival of justice itself dictates that legal rights cannot be based on extant interests or autonomous choices alone. *Needs count, including the need to be cared for by others* — at both the beginning and the ending of embodied life. So any *amicus curiae* should also be an *amicus humani generis*. Even if the species survives (biologically) without the vulnerable being given legal protections, community does not survive (politically), since community presupposes some principled commitment to the common good. If talk of "the common good" is judged "religious" and thus to be excluded from "liberal" political debate, then the American experiment has been tainted from beginning to end.

At the two edges of our existence, sanctity is not a matter of making independent decisions but of receiving and giving unearned care, a care that allows us to "go on." All of us begin dependent and in need of suffering love, and all of us (if we live so long) will end dependent and in need of suffering love. There is nothing shameful in this human trajectory; it is the indispensable context of our virtue. The nurturance given infant children by their parents, the attention given the frail and elderly by the young and strong, the patient service of the mentally impaired by the morally caring, the forethought given future generations by present persons, etc. — all these make little or no sense in an ethic of personal dignity uncoupled from human sanctity. Political dignity alone cannot explain, to repeat, why we continue to hold individuals criminally liable for abuse of their dependent children and neglect of their incapacitated parents. We are still, even today, our brothers' and sisters' keepers.[56]

56. Compare Norman Daniels's *Am I My Parents' Keeper?* (New York and Oxford: Oxford University Press, 1988).

We need not sentimentalize human weakness and vulnerability, but we can courageously accept them; we ought not elevate biological animation to the status of *summum bonum,* but we can refuse to neglect or lay violent hands on human life simply because it is not autonomous. (If mere physical life were the highest good, then even passive euthanasia would be wrong.) The point is that liberal justice alone is not enough for a viable, not to mention a good, society. The first virtue, publicly as well as privately, is something very like what Judaism has called *hesed,* Christianity *agape,* Buddhism "the way of compassion," and secular humanism "sympathy." Without embedding justice in a higher virtue like charity, wherein the strong care for the weak, justice itself withers and dies.

In a democratic society many elements of care can be left to generous individuals or philanthropic organizations. Nothing I have written dictates statist solutions to social ills; everything above is compatible with the Catholic doctrine of subsidiarity in which human needs are best addressed by those social bodies (churches, synagogues, clubs, businesses, hospitals) closest to them. Sometimes the coordinating and coercing power of government will be called for, though this power is prudently limited. The fact remains, nonetheless, that basic standing within the moral community and basic furtherance of communal ends cannot be left to "private conscience" or "personal choice" alone, or else the very existence of society is threatened. To repeat, a legal and political commitment to certain shared goods, personal and impersonal, is the necessary condition for justice itself.

B. Now Singer

Singer endorses the view that infanticide is "the natural and humane solution to the problem posed by sick and deformed babies." He recommends "very strict conditions on permissible infanticide," but these conditions stem almost entirely from concern for the "terrible loss" suffered by adults who happen to "love and cherish the child" and have nothing to do with any inherent wrongness of the act or any intrinsic value of the baby.[57] There is no such wrongness or value, in his opinion. When those closest to a small child do not want it to live, its life is effectively forfeit, since real moral standing requires the capacity for rational desires and self-conscious interests.[58] Neither fetuses

57. Peter Singer, *Practical Ethics* (Cambridge: Cambridge University Press, 1993), p. 173.
58. Peter Singer, *Practical Ethics,* p. 182.

nor newborn babies are rational or self-conscious, Singer repeatedly reminds us, so they have no right to life.[59] They are sentient, of course, and Singer admits that conscious pleasures and pains are goods and ills in some sense. But existing personhood trumps so decisively that the only limitation on killing an unwanted, four-week-old child is that it be done without causing suffering — rather like "mercifully" slaughtering a chicken. One is left to wonder why parents or anyone else would want to *love* a human babe in arms. The only motivation that seems "rationally" intelligible is the parents' stake in their own present personal gratification or future economic support, but this is not love *for the baby herself.*

At least for legal purposes, Singer and other hypercognitivists value only *present* consciousness and self-consciousness, thus they can find no real reason to object to either abortion or infanticide, even when these are done for reasons of parental convenience or social utility.[60] This is tragically forgetful, however, of the temporal trajectory of a human life. One of Singer's central concerns in *Rethinking Life and Death* is to probe the ways in which death may be a process, the phases of which lack clear lines of demarcation. (Higher brain death, permanent loss of the cerebral cortex and limbic system, can come before whole brain death, permanent loss of brain stem function, as well. So when do we declare a patient "deceased"?)[61] But he seems oddly oblivious to the ways in which life is a process, requiring different types of care at different times. The oddity is explained when we realize that self-consciousness, here and now, is what matters to Singer, not how we define either death or life. What he is fundamentally "rethinking" is not the definitional criteria for life and death but the moral worth and meaning of certain lives and deaths. Even if a human is "living," in some sense, if he lacks self-awareness, he has little or no significance for Singer — at either end of his historical span, fetal or senile.

Singer's atemporality notwithstanding, it is always salubrious to remember our beginnings in the past care of others (infancy) and to anticipate our likely ends in the future care of others (old age). Such remembrance and anticipation are part of a humility that sees the sanctity in a dependent life, both one's own and another's, and the vanity in a supposedly independent life. For Jews and Christians, the Bible teaches a bracing lesson in this regard: God called creation "good" even before the appearance of sentient beings, including humans (see Gen. 1:4 and 1:12), and God will remain good even after the

59. Peter Singer, *Practical Ethics*, p. 183.
60. Peter Singer, *Practical Ethics*, pp. 173-74.
61. See Peter Singer, *Rethinking Life and Death*, esp. pp. 20-56.

disappearance of all beings from the face of the earth. Indeed, frequently "what is prized by human beings is an abomination in the sight of God" (Luke 16:15).

Is there any more palpable paradox, any more literal self-contradiction, than Singer's heartfelt concern for persons being coupled with an explicit endorsement of infanticide? One should not think of Singer as ethically monstrous — he is manifestly too thoughtful and kind for that — but one can think of him as tragically myopic. His utilitarianism leaves him with little or no sense of the temporal genesis of autonomous personal agents out of dependent impersonal fetuses/babies. He knows human biology, of course, but he is blind to the humane morality that must sustain that biology from beginning to end. There is no question of attributing malice to Peter Singer; he is simply the rock of a new Gnostic church that would worship self-awareness and self-control. Even a liberal society must strive for a symbiosis between the goods of dignity and sanctity, however, if it is to address such issues as abortion, infanticide, mental disability, and euthanasia without self-destructing.

It is hard to say who represents the greater threat to the liberal house, Dworkin or Singer. I recall reading Singer's *Animal Liberation* in the mid-1970s and being impressed with his earnestness and convinced by his moral argument. I am still persuaded by his case against speciesism. He has gone on to take pure dignity to such cruel extremes, however, that he has virtually *reductio*-ed his own larger position. However cogent his argument for animal rights, since Singer's utilitarianism implies the moral defensibility of human infanticide and nonvoluntary euthanasia, few liberals have been convinced by it (yet). Many liberals *are* taken with Dworkin's segregation of "justice/politics" from "value/religion," however, without fully realizing that it too stems from the valorization of self-consciousness and rational agency. It is tempting, therefore, to see Dworkin as the more subtle eroder of Western principles. Both men are actually Gnostics, in the straightforward sense of elevating rational self-knowledge; but Dworkin appears to play the heretic — a friend of liberal democracy who has lost his way and leads others astray with the best of intentions — to Singer's infidel.[62]

The merit of treating Dworkin and Singer together, in any case, is that they highlight each other's personolatry. If their assumptions are as inadequate as I have argued, both men's visions must be rejected in favor of something rather like agapic love. Whether *agape* requires the theistic convictions of Christian faith is an open question — Buddhism seems the great counterex-

---

62. I wish to thank Jon Gunnemann for illuminating discussion of this point, as well as for its phrasing; I do not mean to imply that he agrees with my diagnosis, however.

ample — but the primacy of the virtue ought not to be disputed. The needs and potentials of human lives, which I have associated with sanctity, must be attended to before the choices and achievements of persons, identified with dignity, can be respected.

Conclusion

Familiar Western struggles for social justice have usually centered on efforts to enfranchise a disadvantaged group into the ranks of full personhood. In America, the emancipation of the slaves and the birth of organized labor in the nineteenth century, as well as the securing of civil rights for blacks, women, and gays/lesbians in the twentieth, were movements that focused on the personal dignity of the parties in question. Much remains to be accomplished on these and related fronts, but by demonstrating their subjects' capacity for rational self-governance, these campaigns could militate for their equal membership in the moral community. By and large, even as God helps those who help themselves, democracies have liberated those shown to be already free persons.

Personhood does not spontaneously generate, however, nor, by Christian lights, is individual personhood an end in itself (certainly not the highest). The rational agency associated with autonomous persons is to be used for the sake of ends outside of and larger than the self: most importantly, love of God and service to the neighbor as fellow creature.[63] The moral keynotes of the last three centuries have been personal liberty and contractual justice precisely because fundamental values like love and creaturely life have been (due to Judaism and Christianity) mostly unquestioned ends. When the liberation of women came to be associated with the right to elective abortion, personal dignity evidently came into conflict with the sanctity of human life. But this is the exception that proves the rule, the transition to something largely new. There is no easy way to balance dignity and sanctity — abortion and euthanasia are real challenges to good conscience — but it is crucial to note the need for *some* genuine balance.

63. As Robert Kraynak points out, for Thomas Aquinas, for instance, "freedom is only a conditional good that is lawful, right, or licit to the extent that it attains or at least seeks to attain reason's proper end." See Kraynak, "'Made in the Image of God': The Christian View of Human Dignity and Political Order" (manuscript), p. 27. I am more confident than Kraynak about the affinity between Christianity and a (prophetic) form of liberal democracy, but he is surely correct that a *Kantian* liberalism based on personal autonomy rights is far from the New Testament and the Church Fathers.

In the twenty-first century, impersonal values will require a much more explicit articulation and defense. Relations that make possible personal freedom and goods that have a claim on that same freedom are suffering eclipse; the modern ethic of personal dignity has succeeded too well, increasingly leaving us without the wherewithal to recognize and protect human sanctity. Thus is our house divided; not just split, as in Lincoln's day, between two geopolitical camps each claiming legitimacy for its way of life, but riven by a cult of personality that denies legal standing to what is impersonal. It is vital, and comparatively easy, to warrant that the South's winning the Civil War would have been a calamity for black, and other, persons; it is less easy, but no less vital, to insist that a similar tragedy is now transpiring for "nonpersons," and thus for all of us who once sojourned as strangers in our mothers' wombs or may yet struggle for memory in hospital wards.[64] When Dworkin et al. maintained in the 1990s that the federal government should be "neutral" on the social status of the very young and the very old, they were mirroring Stephen Douglas's refusal in the 1850s to comment, morally or legally, on the social status of slaves. Douglas wanted to leave the slavery issue to settlement by the individual states, and Dworkin took this "popular sovereignty" argument one step further in wanting abortion and euthanasia questions to be decided by individuals, period. Lincoln eventually saw that such "liberal" civility is inconsistently applied and finally ethically bankrupt . . . and so should we.[65]

For all this, a liberalism that would honor human sanctity as well as respect personal dignity is not without resources, even in this century. Though difficult to categorize, Simone Weil offers valuable instruction. In a 1943 essay entitled "Human Personality," she writes with the rhetorical elegance and moral authority of a biblical prophet:

> There is something sacred in every man, but it is not his person. Nor yet is it the human personality. It is this man; no more and no less. I see a passer-by in the street. He has long arms, blue eyes, and a mind whose thoughts I do not know, but perhaps they are commonplace. It is neither his person, nor the human personality in him, which is sacred to me. It is he. The whole of him. The arms, the eyes, the thoughts, everything. Not

64. Ronald Dworkin (RIP) died on February 14, 2013. On the importance of both remembering and being remembered, morally, see David Keck's *Forgetting Whose We Are: Alzheimer's Disease and the Love of God* (Nashville: Abingdon, 1996).

65. A baby under one month of postnatal age is to Peter Singer what Dred Scott was to Chief Justice Taney: though living for a time in "a free territory," it is still a piece of property to be controlled by its owner(s).

without infinite scruple would I touch anything of this. . . . So far from its being his person, what is sacred in a human being is the impersonal in him. Everything which is impersonal in man is sacred, and nothing else.[66]

The other-regarding implication of this view of sanctity is that we should love and nurture others just as we find them; the self-regarding implication, in turn, Weil takes to be an emphatic ego-negation. "I do not in the least wish that this created world should fade from my view, but that it should no longer be to me personally that it shows itself."[67] Reminiscent of those mystics who favor metaphors of personal extinction over transubstantiation, she makes a virtue of ardent self-effacement. At times she goes too far in this direction and becomes rather masochistic, I fear,[68] but her great merit is to offer a potent remedy for the individualism and rationalism that many associate with Western culture since the eighteenth century. Her own ambivalence about the body makes her acutely sensitive to the fragility of the flesh, as well as of the soul, but she does not despise this. As Weil remarks: "The vulnerability of precious things is beautiful because vulnerability is a mark of existence."[69]

Weil's highlighting of the impersonal dimensions of existence shared by us all can provide clues to a better handling of moral issues ranging from elective abortion to senile dementia. Weilan impersonalism can remind us that fetuses and babies have needs and potentials to be engaged before the dawn of personal consciousness, and that Alzheimer's patients are capable of a noncognitive well-being to be cared for even after the dusk of rational self-control. Those suffering from end-stage Alzheimer's disease may no longer have either the reality of or the essential potential for autonomous agency, but they manifestly have needs and are still capable of giving or receiving love, or both. They have souls, if you will, even if their idiosyncratic selves have withered.[70] As Weil notes, it is the entirety of someone capable of undergoing

66. Simone Weil, "Human Personality," in *The Simone Weil Reader*, ed. George A. Panichas (Mt. Kisco, N.Y.: Moyer Bell, 1977), p. 314. I discuss this and related Weilan passages at more length in my *Love Disconsoled: Meditations on Christian Charity* (Cambridge: Cambridge University Press, 1999), pp. 72-79.

67. Simone Weil, *Gravity and Grace*, trans. Emma Craufurd (London and New York: Ark Paperbacks, 1987), p. 37.

68. See, for example, her so-called terrible prayer, quoted by Robert Coles in *Simone Weil: A Modern Pilgrimage* (Reading, Mass.: Addison-Wesley, 1987), pp. 131-32.

69. Weil, *Gravity and Grace*, p. 98.

70. Ted Smith has suggested in conversation that my references to the ability to give or receive loving care — an ability shared by the very young and the very old, the undeveloped and the severely demented — is my better definition of sanctity than references to even the

good and evil, help and harm, that is sacred and commands our attention.[71] And this attention must be social, "rooted" in a moral and legal ethos that acknowledges the situatedness of human beings: "A human being has roots by virtue of his real, active and natural participation in the life of a community which preserves in living shape certain particular treasures of the past and certain particular expectations for the future. This participation is a natural one, in the sense that it is automatically brought about by place, conditions of birth, profession and social surroundings."[72]

A human being's embeddedness in and dependence upon time, chance, and society is not shameful; indeed, human needs and potentials are what make agapic love possible, as well as necessary. That personal autonomy emerges out of impersonal neediness and eventually returns to it is no more scandalous than that an oak tree grows out of an acorn and finally itself falls to the ground. (Falling naturally is not the same as being violently grubbed.) One need only augment Weil's attention to the impersonal with the recognition that we have every reason to preserve both the personal and the impersonal, to treasure both dignity and sanctity. A nation that denies sanctity is divided against itself, to reiterate, politically uprooted by its own hand.

---

potential for autonomy. All human lives have some inherent potential for growth or responsiveness, I believe, but Smith is certainly correct that (1) not all have the potential for rational personhood, as I have defined it, yet (2) they are no less sacred for that. We may love fetuses partially anticipating the selves they will become, even as we may love Alzheimer's patients partially remembering the selves they once were. But both sets of human lives are, here and now, souls whose needs and potentials have a claim on us.

71. Weil, "Human Personality," p. 315.

72. See Simone Weil, *The Need for Roots: Prelude to a Declaration of Duties towards Mankind* (London and New York: Ark Paperbacks, 1987), p. 41.

CHAPTER 6

The Theory and Practice of Discomfort: Richard Rorty and Liberal Patriotism

Introduction

Richard Rorty (1931-2007) was one of the most consistently incisive critics of traditional Anglo-American philosophy in the twentieth and early twenty-first centuries. Few contemporary writers could match the vigor, breadth, and intelligence of his books and articles, even as few readers could accept the radicality of the views they expressed. Rorty disturbed and astonished like spring weather. His pages mounted like cumulus clouds in our intellectual sky, saturated by the past and promising (ambiguously) either to irrigate or to inundate the present fields of our culture. Almost everybody complained about him, but could anything be done? This chapter is an attempt to come to grips with at least part of Rorty's multifaceted and troubling corpus. His diagnosis of the root problems of epistemology and their larger significance (or insignificance) for Western intellectual life is often brilliant, but I shall argue that his prescription for the future is unattractive. His uncompromising war on dogmatism is based on a rejection of conventional notions of objective truth and metaphysical comfort and is presented in the name of human freedom. It represents, however, a potentially disastrous kind of pragmatism that can be criticized on both theoretical and practical grounds. Of the two, the practical considerations may perhaps be the more telling.

I. The Problems of Reading Rorty

In *Philosophy and the Mirror of Nature,* Rorty evaluates modern philosophy's common self-understanding.[1] One assumed occupation of the discipline, on his view, is the discovery of the "foundations" of knowledge and thus the validation or invalidation of specific claims to know made in such various fields as science, ethics, art, and religion. Philosophy can claim to take the measure of these other areas of intellectual life because it claims to understand the nature of the mind and its capacity for accurate representation of reality. Philosophy can claim to be foundational with respect to the rest of culture because it claims to *encompass* the rest of culture, because it claims to know better than science and religion, for instance, what communion with reality they can and cannot attain to. Or so many philosophers would (perhaps only implicitly) believe.

Rorty suggests that this conception of philosophy stems largely from intellectual developments beginning in the seventeenth century, and in this vein he isolates three key contributions: (1) Descartes's idea of the mind as a separate substance, the "inner" workings of which are uniquely knowable to itself; (2) Locke's idea that a "theory of knowledge" is both necessary and possible on the basis of an understanding of the mind and how it works; and (3) Kant's idea that philosophy both can and should provide other fields with overarching canons of reason by dissecting a priori the structure of reason itself. These three contributions to modern philosophy's self-image are inter-related but nonetheless distinguishable. Each played its own crucial part in suggesting a foundation for that discipline, philosophy, which claimed to be foundational for all others.

Over against this common picture of philosophy and its proper labors stand Rorty's "heroes": Wittgenstein, Heidegger, and Dewey. These three men agree, in Rorty's estimation, that the picture (common to Descartes, Locke, and Kant) of knowledge as needing certain foundations and of the mind as locus of privileged epistemic processes needs to be abandoned. They agree that both epistemology and metaphysics can and should be "set aside as possible disciplines" in the name of a therapeutic form of life and a postmodernist self-image.[2] It is the deconstructive, therapeutic line that Rorty wishes to champion. Philosophy should no longer conceive of itself as underwriting

1. Richard Rorty, *Philosophy and the Mirror of Nature* (Princeton: Princeton University Press, 1979).

2. Rorty, *Philosophy and the Mirror,* p. 6.

links between the human mind and the "objective" world; we have no access to the objective world as it is in itself; so most of traditional epistemology is misguided.

Rorty characterizes his efforts as more akin to moral suasion than to rigorous argument, claiming that the epistemological positions to which he takes exception are immune to such argument but objectionable (or at least optional) even so.[3] It is not unusual, for example, to find him remarking that major philosophers on the Continent (like Derrida) no longer take epistemology — much less skepticism — seriously, the implication being that others should do the same. But this presents a problem. One should always be interested in what intelligent people have to say about important matters, and it would be narrow-minded simply to dismiss Rorty's comments as instances of fallacy, but one is still left to wonder why the fashion on the Continent (or elsewhere) should be of concern per se. It is clear which philosophical positions Rorty does not like, yet how are we to construe the force of his recurrent recommendations to "set aside" such positions? Indeed, do they have any real force, other than the personal?

One strategy might be to prop up these recommendations, recasting them in the form of traditional philosophical arguments. Such a strategy could take one of two turns, or perhaps both intermittently: (a) it could mold Rorty into something like an old-style dogmatist, whose opposition to some particular doctrine (such as realism) is to be understood as an endorsement of one of that doctrine's contraries (such as idealism); or (b) it could mold him into something like an old-style skeptic, whose opposition to a particular doctrine is to be seen as an endorsement of that doctrine's contradiction. In reality, however, both (a) and (b) trade on the perceived legitimacy of skeptical questions, differing only on whether (or perhaps how) they can be answered. And Rorty protests not to seek to address skeptical questions, but rather no longer to take them seriously. A key step in this therapeutic approach is to deny the need for a theory of knowledge, or, more specifically, to deny the "objectivity" of those truths the knowability of which the skeptic claims to doubt. The attempt to explicate "objectivity" in terms of neutral apprehension of realities as they are in themselves, for instance, is seen as self-deceptive, even though it has defined traditional Western philosophy and even though some such attempts have claimed to be successful. All apprehension involves interpretation, and interpretation entails the use of criteria and faculties conditioned by time, place, and various human purposes. If we cease to worry whether "objective"

---

3. Rorty, *Philosophy and the Mirror*, pp. 364-65.

truths exist, beyond such conditions, then there is nothing for a traditional theory of knowledge to explain.

The bad faith of epistemology stems in part from the fact that historically conditioned metaphors for knowing (e.g., ocular metaphors as the mind as "mirror of nature") are treated as necessary and timeless. When one realizes, however, that modern philosophy has been shaped by three such questionable influences as Descartes, Locke, and Kant, one sees that the traditional conception can be abandoned in favor of pragmatism. When warrant and justification are a matter of social convention,[4] philosophical skepticism (and, therefore, much of modern philosophy) withers away. "Skepticism and the principal genre of modern philosophy have a symbiotic relationship. They live one another's death, and die one another's life. One should see philosophy neither as achieving success by 'answering the skeptic,' nor as rendered nugatory by realizing that there is no skeptical case to be answered. The story is more complicated than that."[5]

If Rorty's way with skepticism is correct, it suggests, of course, that a third interpretive-critical strategy is open to his reader. Rather than casting him in the role of dogmatist or skeptic and attacking or defending him as such, one might adopt Rorty's own technique and point out that his "Wittgensteinian" line is also time-bound and hence optional. In the absence of more substantive criticisms of the tradition, the question becomes that of specifying more or less personal reasons for choosing one "philosophical" option over another: therapy over skepticism, or, better, therapy x over therapy y. And if the issue is the vitality or utility of particular metaphors rather than the representational accuracy of particular statements, a defender of the correspondence theory of truth might simply claim that the traditional metaphors for knowing are optimally vital or utilitarian. Apart from suffering from self-contradiction, however, this attempted peritrope would distort Wittgenstein himself. To point out that an idea has a history and that to hold it has consequences is not thereby to say that it is either mistaken or dispensable, regardless of utility.

Rorty does not adopt just one polemical strategy; so he must be read in a number of ways. As we shall see, despite protests to the contrary, he does

4. Richard Rorty, "Intuition," in *The Encyclopedia of Philosophy*, vol. 4 (New York: Macmillan and Free Press, 1972), p. 211.

5. Rorty, *Philosophy and the Mirror*, p. 114. Contrasting perspectives on the significance of skepticism and its relation to modern philosophy are presented by M. F. Burnyeat, "The Sceptic in His Place and Time," in *Philosophy in History*, ed. Richard Rorty, J. B. Schneewind, and Quentin Skinner (Cambridge: Cambridge University Press, 1984), and Barry Stroud, *The Significance of Philosophical Scepticism* (London: Oxford University Press, 1984).

employ skeptical arguments against a realist understanding of truth; he does endorse at times an idealist metaphysics; and he does argue (via Sellars and Quine) that a foundational theory of knowledge is impossible, not just uninteresting or wearisome.[6] This is not to say that the claim to advocate, as opposed to argue for, a radically new intellectual vision is disingenuous, or even completely false. But one of the effects of this claim is to suggest, spuriously, a queer sort of neutrality or unexceptionability for Rorty's work. If Rorty simply "chose" an idiosyncratic vision and beckoned others to follow, he would be quite uninteresting. There *are* junctures at which major aspects of his view of philosophy are (and must be) merely contrasted with their alternatives, but it is a *virtue* of his work that important facets of the Cartesian-Lockean-Kantian legacy are grappled with on their own terms. Without some such dialectical overlap, Rorty's concerns would be, by definition, totally discontinuous with those of his "interlocutors." Genuine conversation would not be possible.

Rorty, like Jean-François Lyotard, distrusts dogmatic metanarratives that appeal to some superhuman reality to explain or justify our situation. No prediction concerning the noumenal self or Absolute Spirit or the proletariat can deliver us from our contingency.[7] Rorty too offers a kind of metanarrative, however. Apparent denial of this is neither plausible nor necessary.[8] Short of lobotomy, one cannot live without some metanarrative about how our theoretical and practical lives hang together. Rorty has written many books and articles arguing the metacase that there is no justification for our beliefs and practices beyond themselves, no intrinsic values or a priori principles. So the truth is that he prefers a metanarrative of a particular (hyper-romantic) sort, not no metanarrative at all. Any other suggestion would be disingenuous.

What makes Rorty's corpus interesting is its de facto departure from its own paradigm of good philosophy. If epistemology is to have no successor subject, as he contends, and the postmodern philosopher is to concern himself or herself only with sociohistorical patterns of agreement among persons,[9] then there is no room to write such a revolutionary, critical volume as *Philosophy and the Mirror of Nature*. If truth and justification are both completely socially determined,[10] then the good philosopher need only document the shifting tides of social practices; but, as Ian Hacking allows, "to talk of practices is

---

6. Rorty, *Philosophy and the Mirror,* esp. pp. 165-88.

7. Richard Rorty, "Postmodernist Bourgeois Liberalism," *Journal of Philosophy* 80, no. 10 (October 1983): 585.

8. Rorty, "Postmodernist Bourgeois Liberalism," p. 589.

9. Cf. Richard Rorty, "Realism and Reference," *Monist* 59, no. 3 (1976): 336.

10. Cf. Rorty, *Philosophy and the Mirror,* p. 196.

not even to begin to ask a question."[11] Unquestionably and happily, Richard Rorty asks questions — *malagré lui.* The real question is whether his answers can be correct without also being self-refuting, either in theory or in practice. Can his view of language and thought as nonrepresentational, in the classical sense, leave room either for historiographical contentions or for historical continuity and progress?

II. Questions, Theoretical and Speculative

It is commonplace that the classical Greek gods were not really supernatural. They were products of and partially subject to natural forces, including error and violent emotion, and not the transcendent or impassive creators of all that is. Men, women, and gods were all subject to the Fates, the three daughters of black-winged night — children of Chaos. If we think of reference to the gods as a primitive attempt to justify beliefs or actions, the seniority of the Fates should not be overlooked. It represents the conviction (however mythically or symbolically expressed) that brute causality is intellectual rock bottom. The Greek gods were, ultimately, fallible middlemen; the Fates, on the other hand, could not make a mistake; so skepticism could gain no foothold with them. A human being could have doubts about them, but they could not have doubts about themselves; and if ever a moral were able to see the world *sub specie Parcae,* this would guarantee both knowledge and power. Some version of the latter has always been the foundationalist ideal in epistemology, and it has not been abandoned in the present day — however demythologized.

The problem of unraveling the connection between knowledge and causality has seemed quite acute to several of the best philosophical minds of this century. Some moderns (e.g., Kripke and Swain) have turned to causal theories of meaning and reference in an effort to "naturalize" epistemology, in an effort to eliminate intentional relations between words and the world and thus to guarantee mechanically that certain terms refer, certain propositions describe, etc. If language is to hook up with nonverbal reality, they reason, something like ostensive definition must provide the meaning connection between individual words and individual things. In this way, the philosophical interpretation of a sentence is able to cut out the fallible middleman, so to speak — to bypass the particular language user's desires and beliefs to appeal

11. Ian Hacking, "Is the End in Sight for Epistemology?" *Journal of Philosophy* 77, no. 10 (October 1980): 587.

to some sure, "neutral" convention for picturing reality. If a speaker's linguistic behavior stands in the right causal relation to an object, then he has named it, whether he realizes it or not. The problem with this scenario, however, as Richard Rorty points out, is that nonintentional relations are as theory-relative as intentional ones.[12] There is simply no theory-independent, "mechanical" way to determine the meaning (or truth) of a piece of language; the meaning of an appeal to causes will itself always be a function of our best current understanding of such relations, one that is mutable and fallible. Thus modern philosophy of language cannot give us what lesser Greek heroes longed for and what traditional foundationalist epistemologies have failed to provide.

Rorty is unsurpassed in exposing the pretensions of contemporary linguistic analysts to have done the impossible, but he makes too much of a good thing. He so presses his denunciation of epistemic *hubris* that even the humblest of annunciations seems impossible. Having granted that the attack on foundationalism is brilliant and devastating, the reflective individual is still left to wonder, How am I to separate the wheat from the chaff in my own culture? It is not just the philosopher (in some pejorative sense) who asks, more mundanely, How am I to justify important personal judgments on everything from whether to vote for a pro-life politician to whether there is a God? One does not have to be a self-deceived foundationalist to ask and answer such questions intelligently, and neither does being an antifoundationalist deliver one from the responsibility of such asking and answering. It is because Rorty fails (at least in places) to appreciate this, that his admirable critique of dogmatism tends to lapse into a too easy subjectivism. Although he commends the model of "skillful conversation" over that of "quest for certainty," he is still mostly silent about the positive role of philosophy in the future. (Ian Hacking, in public conversation, has gibed that Rorty appeals to "conversation" where he has nothing to say.)

A distinctive charm and largeness of mind shine through Rorty's pages, together with a deep love of intellectual freedom and concern to preserve pluralistic social institutions. These qualities and preferences seem oddly detached from good reasons, however. They are not grounded in views about the intrinsic nature of human beings or the inherent value of certain human societies. As Rorty puts it,

> [O]nce we say that what human beings are *in themselves* suits them to be described in terms which are less apt for prediction and control . . . , we

12. Rorty, *Philosophy and the Mirror,* p. 299.

are off down the same garden path as when we say that what atoms are *in themselves* suits them to be described in terms which *are* apt for prediction and control. . . . Why not just say that there are lots of things you can do with people — for instance, dwelling with them, loving them, and using them — and that you should employ different vocabularies depending upon what you want?[13]

The upshot seems to be an almost schizophrenic divorce between theory and practice: the avuncular professor as nihilist. The Greek ideal of unity between life and thought seems almost totally absent. In contrast to Rorty's postmodernism, the classical mind at its best seeks to meet the challenge of discerning and describing reasons for acting and willing in a particular way, even while displaying Aristotelian scruples about not expecting more certainty in an area than the subject matter allows. It insists that the demise of foundationalism give neither carte blanche for arbitrariness nor reason for despair. Such an insistence turns on the belief that traditional foundationalism and postmodern nihilism do not represent an inevitable either/or: there is a defensible middle ground.[14]

A critical, "skeptical" realism seeks to preserve some relation between subject and object as the nature of truth while acknowledging both the absence of incorrigible beliefs and the presence of many different kinds of objects in the world. Though difficult to argue for without begging major questions, this Peircean perspective seems to me intuitively compelling. It suggests that Rorty's mistake stems from two related, and more or less self-conscious, conflations: that of alethiology (theory of the nature of truth) with epistemology (theory of the test for truth), and that of epistemology with ontology (theory of what there is). With respect to the first pair, he is quite right to argue that correspondence to reality cannot be appealed to *in epistemology* as a criterion against which to measure knowledge claims. We cannot hold up candidates for belief opposite unmediated reality and see if they correspond, for if we already grasp reality there is no need to test beliefs. In fact,

13. Richard Rorty, "A Reply to Dreyfus and Taylor," *Review of Metaphysics* 34 (September 1980): 44.

14. Compare Richard Bernstein's argument in *Beyond Objectivism and Relativism* (Philadelphia: University of Pennsylvania Press, 1983). His critique of modern philosophical trends is lively and informed but somewhat marred by a failure to distinguish adequately between foundationalism and realism (pp. 8-9). As I argue below, one can and should let go of the former while preserving the latter. See also Hilary Kornblith, "Beyond Foundationalism and the Coherence Theory," *Journal of Philosophy* 77, no. 10 (October 1980): 597-612.

the correspondence theory is an alethiological theory only and thus does not enter into the justification of claims to know. The "given" in epistemology is a foundationalist myth, as Sellars has shown. Rorty sometimes goes beyond this observation, however, to indicate that the demise of foundationalist epistemology implies the end of realist alethiology as well. He goes out of his way to license the inference from "not incorrigible" to "merely conversational"; thus truth either disappears altogether (a-alethiology) or in fact becomes synonymous with "intersubjective agreement," "what our peers will, *ceteris paribus,* let us get away with saying," and the like.[15] These latter phrases all conflate epistemology and alethiology; they all conflate tests of truth with the nature of truth. Rorty's excess is to suggest, at least in places, that the absence of the indubitable and timeless test for knowledge demanded by Descartes leaves us without anything objective to test for here and now — a kind of philosophical thanatopsis.

When talk of "truth" is de-emphasized in favor of "warranted assertability," the skeptic's worry that even our best justified beliefs might be mistaken is less pressing. But when Rorty explicitly *identifies* desirable or warranted belief with truth,[16] he is contradicting his own best insights and drifting into nihilism. He opens himself to the standard rebuttal that many assertions that were once justified have since been discovered to be false. Elsewhere, Rorty acknowledges that there are semantic differences between truth and assertability.[17] Warranted assertability (as opposed to "justified *true belief*") is all that *epistemology proper* can be about, but this leaves open the possibility of realism in *alethiology.*

The move from antifoundationalism to emphasis on conversation is the outgrowth, Rorty implies, of ceasing to think of the mind as a mirror of nature. But his critique of mirror imagery can be misleading. It may seem to suggest that some other relationship between subject and object besides seeing is characteristic of knowledge, when, for Rorty, no *relationship* at all seems appropriate.[18] Ocular metaphors are out; but neither smelling, hearing, nor making love to an object is an appropriate model either. In rejecting a realistic alethiology, Rorty radicalizes the standard critique of representational epis-

---

15. See Richard Rorty, "Solidarity or Objectivity?" in *Post-Analytic Philosophy,* ed. John Rajchman and Cornel West (New York: Columbia University Press, 1985), p. 6; "Science as Solidarity" (draft of a paper discussed at a legal theory workshop at Yale University, November 1984), p. 4; and *Philosophy and the Mirror,* p. 176.

16. Rorty, *Philosophy and the Mirror,* pp. 10, 176, 308.

17. Rorty, *Philosophy and the Mirror,* p. 301 n.

18. Rorty, *Philosophy and the Mirror,* pp. 156-57.

temology by denying the subject/object distinction lying behind it. A denial of the subject/object distinction undoes dogmatic foundationalist theories of language and knowledge, meaning and justification; but it also undoes alethiological realism in favor of what must be for most an implausible idealism or an even less plausible nihilism.

Rorty claims not to be an idealist, but it is hard to know how to read this.[19] His postmodernism seems distinctive precisely in pushing the second conflation (of epistemology and ontology) for idealist effect. His remarks on the "ubiquity of language" and the impossibility of a theory of knowledge are too extensive to be dismissed as pithy overstatements; and they do imply that sense-independent objects have dropped out of his meta-metaphysics.[20] Rorty does not want to say that philosophy has "proved" that language cannot refer beyond itself and rejects what he calls "weak textualism," because both of these moves suggest one more old-style ontology.[21] But just as a rejection of demonology as senseless implies (by default) a denial of the existence of demons, so a rejection of ontology as senseless denies the existence of its subject matter, being(s) in the world. There is little difference, finally, between denying the intelligibility of objective facts and values (as Rorty does) and just denying their existence. If, *faute de mieux,* conversation can only be about other bits of conversation, then words as epistemic signs have been conflated with words as things signified. Hence in the end, as in the beginning, is the word — but now the word is *with us* and *is us.*

Rorty's "strong textualism" defines intellectual success as the adoption of whatever vocabulary allows us to get what we want, and this is to happen without "something [being] discovered to be the case" and "without argument."[22] But then, what does motivate it? Must I not at least have discovered by a method thought reliable that, as a matter of fact, my old vocabulary did not get me what I wanted? Rorty can only sidestep this epistemological question by, in turn, deconstructing ontology — by denying that there are facts and that people, objects, and desires have natures. It is this move that presses a form of idealism, if somewhat paradoxically: words or ideas are the only candidate for reality left, even as they inform us that nothing is the case. But it is one thing to say with the romantics that no vocabulary (e.g., natural science) is primary or capable of seeing reality unmediated; it is quite another to say with the

19. Richard Rorty, *Consequences of Pragmatism* (Minneapolis: University of Minnesota Press, 1982), p. xxxix.

20. Rorty, *Consequences of Pragmatism,* pp. xxxix-xl.

21. Rorty, *Consequences of Pragmatism,* pp. 153-55.

22. Rorty, *Consequences of Pragmatism,* pp. 141-42, 155.

idealists that none represents nonverbal reality or with the nihilists that none represents anything at all.[23]

If I am right, Rorty does not simply follow in the tradition of philosophers who criticize the monolithic conception of language as only referring. His is not the pluralistic point that words can convey meaning in a wider variety of ways than a "picture theory" can communicate; his is not the humanistic point that speakers have more important things to do with their time than describing the world. Since the world as it is in itself is "well lost," the attempt to apprehend it is vanity. Thus Rorty stands in approximately the same relation to Ryle and Austin as an anarchist stands to a suffragette, as Emma Goldman stands to Susan B. Anthony.[24] He encourages individuals to treat their own art, religion, science, and politics as they would treat ancient or distant variations never personally embraced, that is, as forms of life and shards of culture rather than as true or false, good or bad. One continues to want certain things and defend certain views — his pragmatism is peculiarly American in its "healthy-mindedness" — but in the absence of reasons other than convenience this seems not so much *phronesis* as alienation.

III. Questions, Practical and Political

The theoretical merits of Richard Rorty's work are worth debating. As is apparent, however, such debates tend to run up against conflicting basic conceptions of truth, knowledge, and being. The really fascinating questions then turn out to be practical, the theoretical issues being perhaps forever moot. Assume that Rorty's (sometime) nihilism is accepted: How are we to think and feel about ourselves without realist appeal to truth, goodness, and the like? And how does such thought and feeling bear on how individuals and groups behave across

23. Cf. Rorty, *Consequences of Pragmatism*, p. 142. The elusiveness of Rorty's position is highlighted in a footnote to his introduction to *Consequences of Pragmatism*. In otherwise praising Nelson Goodman's *Ways of Worldmaking*, he writes: "I think that Goodman's trope of 'many words' is misleading and that we need not go beyond the more straightforward 'many descriptions of the same world' (provided one does not ask, 'And what world is *that*?')" (p. xlvii). It would seem that talk of "many worlds" is misleading only if there is just one world, but in eschewing ontology Rorty is in no position to comment on this issue. And what do "descriptions" amount to for a pragmatist anyway? Quite a lot of metaphysical cake is being simultaneously had and eaten here.

24. I am grateful to Cornel West for the Goldman/Anthony analogy, though I do not think he would apply it to Rorty.

time? Which personal virtues and cultural legacies can be preserved, which must be let go — and why? These are questions not primarily of logic but of human nature and human history.

To begin, consider the three "theological" virtues of faith, hope, and love. If Enlightenment philosophy left religious language with a problematical status vis-à-vis empirical science, it might seem that Rorty's postmodernism promises to restore some of religion's lost prestige. Pragmatism does seem a great leveler. By its lights, no discipline can claim a monopoly on "truth" or "rationality" for the simple reason that there is no interesting sense to be assigned to either term. The success of empirical science does not stem from its corresponding to the way the world really is or from its speaking "nature's own language."[25] Science is useful because it allows us to predict and control our environment, but other vocabularies may be just as utilitarian for other equally important purposes. Might not theology be legitimated in a postmodernist culture, together with physics and poetry? I think not.[26]

As I indicated in section II, pragmatism is not ontologically neutral. The conflation of alethiology, epistemology, and ontology — the loss of realism generally — means the loss of any and all realities independent of or transcendent to inquiry. In this respect, God must suffer the same fate as any other transcendent subject or object. Because faith makes sense only when accompanied by the possibility of doubt, Rorty's distancing of skepticism means a concomitant distancing of belief in "things unseen." He, unlike Kant, denies both knowledge and faith; but for what, if anything, is this supposed to make room? Faith may perhaps be given a purely dispositional reading, being seen as a tendency to act in a certain way, but any propositional content will be completely lost. The pull toward religious faith is at best a residue of metaphysical realism and of the craving for metaphysical comfort. The taste for the transcendent usually associated with a religious personality will find little place in a Rortian world. Similarly, hope and love, if thought to have a supernatural object or source, lose their point. The deconstruction of God must leave the pious individual feeling like F. Scott Fitzgerald after his crackup:

25. Rorty, *Consequences of Pragmatism*, pp. 191-92.

26. In *The Nature of Doctrine* (Philadelphia: Westminster, 1984), George Lindbeck offers an innovative account of theology "in a postliberal age" that seeks to skirt the realism-pragmatism debate, remaining neutral on major questions of truth and justification. For an argument against this possibility, see my review, "Against Grammar," *Religious Studies Review* 11, no. 3 (July 1985): 240-45. Rorty himself characterizes pragmatism as "a thorough-going abandonment of the notion of *discovering the truth* which is common to theology and science" (*Consequences of Pragmatism*, pp. 150-51).

"a feeling that I was standing at twilight on a deserted range, with an empty rifle in my hands and the targets down."[27] The deconstructed heart is ever restless, yet the theological virtues stand only as perpetual temptations to rest in inauthenticity. We live in a world without inherent telos; so there simply is no rest as Christianity has traditionally conceived of it.

What of the possibility of naturalizing or humanizing faith, hope, and love, so that genuine (though secular) virtue is possible? The taste for the Wholly Other is clearly passé, for Rorty, but might not the taste for the *human* other be preserved, even cultivated? This is the central issue for an intelligent critique of Rorty's larger cultural program. It is not obvious, at least to his admirers, that Rorty's views are antithetical to the best of humanism; indeed, his attack on "objectivity" as the West's central intellectual virtue goes hand in hand with advocacy of "solidarity" as a preferable and viable alternative. Culture is to be construed as public conversation involving many diverse voices, rather than as the quest for indubitable knowledge pursued by an elite few. This strikes some as proposing a very happy marriage between epistemological pragmatism and political liberalism: an effort to preserve democratic institutions while, in Rorty's words, "abandoning the traditional Kantian backup."[28] Rorty, the grandson of Walter Rauschenbusch, carries Protestantism to its natural conclusion: a world without hierarchies and priestcraft, but full of voluntary associations; a world without dogmas and regulations, but full of neighborly talk. Just as Protestantism sought to recapture religious spontaneity by breaking down pharisaical fixations on the Law, so Rorty seeks to recapture philosophical spontaneity by breaking down Cartesian fixations on the world. With this, the many goods of human society effectively replace the one God of divine science, and the divorce between free commitment and abstract reason is complete.

The two main problems with such a postmodernist philosophy parallel those with post-Reformation theology: antinomianism and irrationalism. Those very beings with whom one is to have solidarity and hold conversation, for example, appear no longer to command moral respect. This is evident from Rorty's view of the social sciences. According to Rorty, "the demise of logical empiricism means that there is no interesting split between the *Natur-* and the *Geisteswissenschaften*."[29] Because neither the natural nor the human sciences

27. F. Scott Fitzgerald, *The Crack Up*, ed. Edmund Wilson (Boston: Beacon Press, 1964), pp. 77-78.

28. Rorty, "Postmodernist Bourgeois Liberalism," p. 584.

29. Rorty, "Reply to Dreyfus and Taylor," p. 39. For a critical appraisal of Rorty's relation to Gadamer on this point, see Georgia Warnke, "Hermeneutics and the Social Sciences: A Gadamerian Critique of Rorty," *Inquiry* 28, no. 3 (September 1985): 339-57.

can be seen to describe reality as it is in itself, it is impossible to found a sharp contrast between them in terms of the "essence" of their respective subject matters. It is not the case that differing subject matters dictate differing methods and conclusions. The utility and relative precision of the empirical sciences are not due to their depicting physical objects "in their own terms," any more than the social sciences, in leaving room for freedom, are recognizing something about human beings "in themselves."[30] The vocabulary and grammar of any science are human constructs formulated for human purposes within human language. The upshot is a radicalization of fideist conceptions of commitment, with respect for persons, not something due them because of who they are but an unpredictable and unmerited favor, like the grace of God. It is not that Rorty thinks people are actually *un*worthy of respect, but rather that the question inherent in worthiness or unworthiness does not even arise for him. How then *does* one justify loving others rather than using them? Not even "faith alone" will suffice, it seems. For the individual conscience ("what you want") is now entirely unfettered by external authority, either human or divine.

I do not think, on balance, that the political center can hold with such voluntarism at its core. Liberal ideology has traditionally appealed to objective truths as the basis of rational social philosophy. When Hobbes, Locke, Rousseau, and Kant revolutionized political discourse by replacing appeals to revelation with appeals to reason and reference to the kingdom of God with reference to the social contract, they ushered in a new self-image for Western society. Two centuries of religious strife seemed to demonstrate the need for a new vocabulary and syntax with which to address pressing public concerns, from the legitimacy of a particular government to the morality of a particular economy. Explicit talk of God and a confessing community tended to lead to sectarianism and holy wars. Yet, however much this new language may have represented the beginning of a shift from a theistic to a secular and (to a lesser degree) from a communitarian to an individualistic paradigm, it did not eschew general truth claims about reality as the basis of social ethics. God tended to recede into the background of the Enlightenment picture in favor of natural law or the common good, but (with the possible exception of Hume) human choice was seldom in and of itself considered constitutive of *all* binding norms and moral truths. The character of justice and of the social contract was determined by the nature of the world and the people in it, so that some imperatives were universal and categorical. Many protested in the seventeenth and eighteenth centuries (and some still protest today) that forgoing divine

30. Rorty, "Reply to Dreyfus and Taylor," p. 44.

sanctions for public policy must lead to anarchy, however democratically validated, and Rorty suggests that these and his own critics are similarly alarmist and narrow-minded. He claims to have glimpsed the possibility of a "better way," even as did Locke and Rousseau. In effectively embracing nihilism, however, Rorty is offering a vision discontinuous with the entire Western realist tradition of which the bulk of the Enlightenment is still recognizably a part.[31] It is not therefore mistaken, necessarily, but we must appreciate its radicality.

Rorty declares that both the emperor and the democrat have no clothes. Nothing and no one is the ground of authority, save insofar as we choose to recognize them as such; thus political legitimations (like epistemic justifications) are more than tentative and dialogical; they are relativist. The question, to repeat, is whether a liberal society, thus convinced of the bankruptcy of those realist traditions by which it has been supported, can continue to function. Rorty asks for one more turn of the screw, but can Western civilization stand the strain? I doubt it, though the historical evidence is not clearly decisive.

There are few exceptionless generalizations about the connection between philosophical theory and political practice. The permutations are multiple. Mussolini was a student of James's pragmatism, and Heidegger was, at least

---

31. Figures such as Hobbes and Pufendorf complicate the Enlightenment picture. I would maintain, even so, that despite the voluntarist elements in their work, their understanding of reason and natural law saves them from a nihilistic social philosophy. Thomas Hobbes, at any rate, though seeking generally to found morality on prudence, never doubted that self-preservation was a universal duty. The *lex naturalis* preceded and governed the social contract, not vice versa. More recently, John Rawls has claimed Locke and Kant as his precursors, but it is less clear whether his theory of justice is a departure from *their* moral realism. See *A Theory of Justice* (Cambridge: Harvard University Press, 1971) and "Kantian Constructivism in Moral Theory," *Journal of Philosophy* 77, no. 9 (September 1980): 515-72. Several commentators have argued that the ontological theses about reason and human nature grounding the contract theories of both Locke and Kant are (or must be) jettisoned by Rawls, leaving him with a rather bare voluntarism implied by the "original position" and the "veil of ignorance." See Michael J. Sandel, *Liberalism and the Limits of Justice* (Cambridge: Cambridge University Press, 1982), pp. 115-22, and George Parkin Grant, *English-Speaking Justice* (Notre Dame: University of Notre Dame Press, 1985), pp. 13-46. If this is so, then for Rawls, as for Rorty, philosophy can make no connection between general truths about reality and how we ought to live together. I believe, however, that Rawls should (or at least can) be read as a *limited* moral constructivist. He views justice as "constructed" but also as premised on truth claims about who and what a "moral person" is ("Kantian Constructivism," p. 520). The principles of justice agreed to from behind the veil of ignorance are "pure procedural" and thus do not themselves follow from antecedent moral rules or correspond to external moral facts. But they depend on a form of moral realism inasmuch as "moral personality itself" is counted as "a source of claims" (p. 544).

for a time, pro-Nazi; but the nexus between antirealism and totalitarianism is not consistent.[32] John Dewey is a recent and great counterexample. Neither is the link secure between realism and respect for human rights or for political pluralism: many Marxist-Leninists insist they are "scientific realists," however repugnant their social policies. Nonetheless, the case can be made that *alethiological realism coupled with epistemological fallibilism* is a necessary (if not sufficient) condition for a viable (codification of) political and economic democracy. Max Stackhouse has argued persuasively that acknowledgment of universal human rights has historically depended upon a marriage between creedal commitments to intrinsic human value and philosophical commitments to finite but shared human reason.[33] Such a happy union emerged in the seventeenth and eighteenth centuries between Puritanism and the liberal Enlightenment, and is reflected in the franchise (though not always the practice) of the United States. It remains the bulwark of whatever pluralism and tolerance now exist in the West and is a missing ingredient in such nonliberal societies as North Korea and India.

Dogmatism and intolerance of whatever kind are enemies of an open society, but these are endemic to foundationalism, not to realism per se. One may reject foundationalism, moreover, without endorsing nihilism; one may acknowledge the perpetual uncertainty and fallibility of any human judgment without letting go of a realist theory of truth. In fact, fallibilism *assumes* an objective world of physical and moral fact about which one may be mistaken. Conversely, letting go of realism will in all probability leave a society without the wherewithal to found or sustain a commitment to liberty, equality, or fraternity — much less sorority. Such a society may live for a time on past cultural capital embodied in liberal institutions and traditions, but a purely conventional virtue will not last long. The issue is one of motivation and consistency.

Rorty's emphasis on innovation and his distaste for all forms of hegemony (intellectual and practical) unite him with the libertarian strand of Anglo-American political thought, but in pure form this strand must lead to chaos. The loss of moral realism radicalizes libertarianism beyond even the appeal to self-interest. One must act, presumably, but now both self-interest and interest in others fail as *reasons* for action. It is hard to see how one can truly value what is not thought to be objectively valuable or be loyal to what

32. Georg Lukács, *The Destruction of Reason,* trans. Peter Palmer (Atlantic Highlands, N.J.: Humanities Press, 1981), attempts to link various "irrationalists" with modern German fascism. Others note, in turn, that for Karl Popper it is the political left that is irrational.

33. Max L. Stackhouse, *Creeds, Society, and Human Rights* (Grand Rapids: Eerdmans, 1984).

is not thought to be worthy *in itself.*[34] Why respect oneself or the rights of minorities and women if there is nothing of intrinsic value in people that demands it, independent of mere power? With no appreciation of innate human dignity on which to build, how does a nation or a people fashion consensus on justice and the nature of political community? To Rorty, these may seem two questions too many, but they are pressed on us by the very grammar of liberal ideology itself. A *purely* "constructivist" view that what cannot be discovered may yet be created seems not the fulfillment, but the death, of that ideology; for it implies that in the absence of their being granted, no one has substantive rights or freedoms to be denied.[35]

Individual liberty and political pluralism lie at the heart of Western civilization. One can distinguish, however, between a merely tactical *tolerance* and an in-principle *respect* for such values. Tolerance — being a limiting of the means to disagreement rather than an agreement on ends — is liable to change with changing circumstances. Respect is less mutable because more heartfelt. To respect personal freedom and social pluralism is to agree on the virtue of *dis*agreement itself, a show of confidence in human nature paired (ironically) with a kind of epistemic humility. Human beings, especially human groups, are subject to error, but the promotion of competing ideas by free inquirers is thought to offer the surest method for arriving at truth. Power and the means to power are not to be concentrated in any one group or any one ideology, for this leads inevitably to either tyranny or stagnation or both. In a Rortian world, however, despite his explicit wishes, respect for persons would be hard to come by: even tolerance might well be in short supply.

Consider this notorious passage from the introduction to Rorty's *Consequences of Pragmatism:*

> Suppose that Socrates was wrong, that we have *not* once seen the Truth, and so will not, intuitively, recognize it when we see it again. This means that when the secret police come, when the torturers violate the innocent, there is nothing to be said to them of the form "There is something within

34. Cf. Rorty, "Science as Solidarity," p. 10.

35. Sandel, *Liberalism and the Limits of Justice,* elaborates a radically constructivist brand of "liberalism," but goes on to criticize it as incomplete and false to experience. As William Galston has argued, entirely formal or consensual accounts of liberalism are untenable: they inevitably appeal to substantive conceptions of the good and must be justified on that basis. See Galston, "Defending Liberalism," *American Political Science Review* 76, no. 3 (September 1982): 621-29. When defenders of liberalism begin with the premise that it is morally empty, they simply play (unnecessarily) into the hands of its critics.

you which you are betraying. Though you embody the practices of a totalitarian society which will endure forever, there is something beyond those practices which condemns you." This thought is hard to live with.[36]

Rorty does more here than deny the Socratic doctrine of recollection: he denies objective knowledge as such. Rorty does more than deny the Socratic thesis that justice ultimately pays: he denies justice (and, simultaneously, *injustice*) as such. Thus one reads the quoted passage with a sense more of uncanniness than of disagreement. The insouciance about lack of moral truth, in particular, seems altogether too sublime. The pragmatist's claim to live within comfort sounds as incredible as the fakir's claim to live on air. Hard to live with is the thought that you may be a coward or that your wife is dying of cancer or that the Nazis killed millions of innocents before the Allied governments protested. It no more seems "hard" to live without real values, however, than it is "hard" to live without food and drink. The neo-pragmatist, unlike the more traditional nihilist, wills value; but just as willing that hunger be satisfied does not always make it so, so willing that aims and associations be respectable does not always make them so. We are not *that* free. To think otherwise is to believe ourselves capable of creating all good *ex nihilo*.

Rorty anticipates a great deal of this as possible criticism, yet he tends to shrug it off as an acceptable consequence of his preferred intellectual vision. Much of his polemical impact depends, in fact, on an avant-garde willingness simply to place many standard philosophical concerns under the rubric "Don't care" or "No need." This approach is not without power — a kind of dying to the world — but it remains unsatisfying. Rorty presents a personality of immense grace and geniality, thus challenging his critics to integrate ideology with biography, to explain where he gets his virtue and why he isn't telling. He embraces liberal sentiments but can give few reasons why, other than upbringing or taste. And what of those not similarly reared?

In any event, the turn from discovering objective truth to prescribing subjective therapy, from emphasis on theory to emphasis on praxis, does not itself guarantee absence of dogmatism. The long history of intolerance bears this out. Even Stoicism and Epicureanism, which originally emerged as pragmatic philosophies of life, tended toward dogmatism and in turn called up skeptical reactions. Similarly, Rorty's modern accent on solidarity over objectivity by no means ensures freedom, tolerance, or pluralism. One can just as easily be tyrannical and dogmatic in one's views of social status and the good

---

36. Rorty, *Consequences of Pragmatism*, p. xlii.

life as in one's views of epistemology and (meta)physics. In fact, there is often *more* of a tendency to hegemony and closed-mindedness here since claims about inclusiveness and purpose generally elicit more of a personal stake than empirical or logical claims. More common than intellectual arrogance is the *will* to power, and illiberal use of power is not ruled out (even in theory) by democratic procedures or institutions alone.

Conclusion

There is much to appreciate about Richard Rorty. He was most at home and most impressive in the role of iconoclast, less so, however, in that of prophet. He wished to rescue Western philosophy's good fruits from its bad epistemology via a moral critique of the foundationalism and reductionism to which it gives rise. And insofar as belief in incorrigible intuitions or immutable dogmas leaves tolerance with little point — "error has no rights" — he was correct to resist such schools in the name of human freedom. Even the general appeal to natural law can, at times, lead to the squelching of diversity. But nihilism as a therapy is at least as problematic as dogmatism as a disease. It tends as readily to oppression, inasmuch as disbelief in objective values or impersonal norms leaves respect with no subject. Pragmatic tolerance has a distinctly solipsistic character and can mount no theoretical objection to deference being given to convention or power or nothing at all; *vide* Nietzsche's instructions to look to the likes of Cesare Borgia for his prototype. With no consistent conception of truth or epistemic justification, modern pragmatists such as Rorty, I fear, are incapable of supporting the liberal values on which genuine respect for individual rights and the common good is founded. They represent a critical menace to the very roots out of which many of their ideas have grown. The Rortian turn from accent on discovery to accent on choice may not necessitate oppression or wantonness, but it tends to undercut the virtue that supports the alternatives. Intellectual and moral virtue (even prophecy itself) makes no sense if no room is left for fallibility or peccability.

Here the proper mode of response is counterprophecy; thus I have suggested that the political and cultural tradition characteristic of the modern West is incompatible with a Rortian future. If we believe that we must invent right and wrong, that "there is nothing deep down inside us except what we have put there ourselves,"[37] then that tradition has simply died. No society —

37. Rorty, *Consequences of Pragmatism*, p. xlii.

especially a liberal, and increasingly secular, one — is likely long to survive without some common sense of virtue and the good life founded not on power or preference but on principle. Solidarity and objectivity do not represent an either/or, as Rorty implies;[38] for solidarity as a personal virtue is only possible in a community that fosters objective self-scrutiny and attention to others as they are in themselves. *To advocate solidarity is to assume a view of human nature, not just of language.*[39] Our cultural memory is very short and precarious as it is, and without some fundamental convictions about the true, the right, and the real informing community life, we are likely to decline into the very war of all against all that Rorty sometimes ridicules. Whether tragic or comic or merely absurd, such a fate is all too predictable given human proclivities.

In his 1979 presidential address to the American Philosophical Association, entitled "Pragmatism, Relativism, and Irrationalism," Rorty, too, worried about the practical question, "about whether we can be pragmatists without betraying Socrates, without falling into irrationalism."[40] But he ended his piece quite inconclusively:

> Nothing that I have said . . . is an argument in favor of pragmatism. At best, I have merely answered various superficial criticisms which have been made of it. Nor have I dealt with the central issue about irrationalism. I have not answered the deep criticism of pragmatism . . . : the criticism that the Socratic virtues cannot, as a practical matter, be defended save by Platonic means, that without some sort of metaphysical comfort nobody will be able *not* to sin against Socrates.[41]

38. As with the title (and contents) of his essay "Solidarity or Objectivity?"

39. Rorty elaborated a "mechanistic" account of the self in a piece entitled "Freud and Moral Reflection," appearing in *Pragmatism's Freud: The Moral Disposition of Psychoanalysis,* ed. Joseph K. Smith and William Kerrigan (Baltimore: Johns Hopkins University Press, 1986). This creative defense of "*Macht durch* Freud" (Chambers) tends to reinforce my basic point about Rorty and anthropology. Odd though characteristic is the work's preoccupation with "vocabularies" and its often wonderfully insightful depiction of human nature (including its multiplicity) coupled with a denial that such can be had or is needed. It may be that an individual has no one "true self" (p. 9), but presumably one attends to *this* truth by honoring a pluralistic version of Delphi: "Know thyselves." (Not all views of who we are need be ahistorical or reductionist.) And only Richard Rorty could write the following sentence and make it sound even remotely plausible: "The availability of a richer vocabulary of moral deliberation is what one chiefly has in mind when one says that we are, morally speaking, more sensitive and sophisticated than our ancestors or than our younger selves" (p. 12).

40. Rorty, *Consequences of Pragmatism,* p. 169.

41. Rorty, *Consequences of Pragmatism,* p. 174.

I have noted that the historical evidence on these matters is not decisive, but such pure ambivalence is not very persuasive either. In any case, prophecy cannot wait for certainty. It is just possible that Rorty foresaw our intellectual future in a way that will allow him, under the new dispensation, to be an early and effective voice for political liberalism and personal decency. I have no knockdown argument to the contrary (could there be one?), but I am skeptical. He too often downplayed the fact that human arrogance and pride are seldom checked without reference to a reality or realities larger than themselves.

In *Achieving Our Country,* published in the last decade of his life, Rorty tried to reanimate the "national pride" of the American Left and to direct it away from endless debates about "cultural theory" and toward practical legal and political reforms. His embracing of patriotism was anything but an un-critical celebration of U.S. history; he was well aware that "too much national pride can produce bellicosity and imperialism."[42] It was, instead, a moving attempt to replace both American triumphalism and anti-American cynicism, almost equally common after the end of the Cold War, with a utopian vision of the future. Like Dewey and Whitman, Rorty "hoped that America would be the place where a religion of love would finally replace a religion of fear"; like them, he "wanted to put hope for a casteless and classless America in the place traditionally occupied by knowledge of the will of God."[43] This effort to replace God with the ideal nation is Rorty's best book, full of the moral zeal and frank critique of selfishness that make him worth reading. It is also the acid test of whether a political vision can be sustained when "there is no standard, not even a divine one, against which the decisions of a free people can be measured."[44] In many respects, I see Rorty as one of "Lincoln's heirs,"[45] and I applaud his goal of "substituting social justice for individual freedom,"[46] though I think he is too sanguine about the power of "government" in this re-gard. What I do *not* find plausible, however, is the notion that Lincoln's virtues can be achieved or sustained on a pragmatic basis in which "nothing is sacred" and there are no objective values, no shared human nature, and no God.[47]

It seems a psychological, if not a theological, truth that in the absence

42. Richard Rorty, *Achieving Our Country* (Cambridge: Harvard University Press, 1998), p. 3.

43. Rorty, *Achieving Our Country,* pp. 17-18.

44. Rorty, *Achieving Our Country,* p. 16.

45. Cf. Rorty, *Achieving Our Country,* p. 47.

46. Rorty, *Achieving Our Country,* p. 101.

47. Richard Rorty, *An Ethics for Today: Finding Common Ground between Philosophy and Religion* (New York: Columbia University Press, 2008), p. 12; see also p. 24.

of standards and interests "not just our own," we tend to be incapable of any standards at all, even of prudence. This fact mainline Protestantism never lost sight of. Our conceptions of individual and civic virtue cannot have (and do not need) incorrigible foundations, but they do need (and, I believe, have) rational justifications. These justifications rely on provisional but reasoned opinions about the world and the nature of the individuals in it; and such practical wisdom and moral nihilism are incompatible. At its overly cautious worst, skepticism can lapse into the "avoidance of love" (Cavell); but the skeptic can at least still hope to know and be known — the nihilist lacks any such virtue. Mainline Protestantism denied the authority of Rome and the possibility of justification by works, but it preserved an objective correlative to faith. It insisted on the reality of a transcendent Deity whose will was normative for, and whose grace was redemptive of, human nature. An omniscient and righteous God continued to provide a goal for human theory and practice beyond any temporal convention, just as he continued to be capable of self-revelation as "the very Spirit of Truth." On this basis, Reformed epistemology (unlike Rortian pragmatism) can even today respond to the charges of antinomianism and irrationalism, without going foundationalist.[48]

If the willingness to believe that objective reality may fail to be as we think lies at the heart of both skepticism and faith, the *refusal* to believe that it may *be* as we think lies at the heart of nihilism. The willingness is essential for self-criticism; the refusal leads logically to radical pragmatism, merely "internal" realism, historicism, etc. At its best, the willingness gives one a hard-won (but not necessarily "comforting") respect for the "otherness" of other minds, other places, other things; the refusal is, I believe, an acoustic illusion tending at its best to complacency and at its worst to cynicism. To be sure, reference to practical consequences, unsupported by further considerations, counts very little against the *truth* of Rorty's nihilistic version of pragmatism. Even a lot of knowledge can be a dangerous thing, but it is no less knowledge for that; so if nihilism can be shown to be cogent, my comments have the force — but only the force — of a lament. To deny this, one would have to incline, a priori, to the principle that some things (e.g., the nonobjectivity of values) are too bad

48. Alvin Plantinga and Nicholas Wolterstorff are two examples. See Plantinga, "How to Be an Anti-realist," *Proceedings and Addresses of the American Philosophical Association* 56, no. 1 (September 1982): 47-70, and "Reason and Belief in God," in *Faith and Rationality*, ed. Alvin Plantinga and Nicholas Wolterstorff (Notre Dame: University of Notre Dame Press, 1983); and Wolterstorff, "Can Belief in God Be Rational If It Has No Foundations?" in the same volume. For a general treatment of the relation between Protestantism and modern epistemology, see W. W. Bartley's *The Retreat to Commitment* (La Salle, Ill., and London: Open Court, 1984).

to be true. Religious faith may entail this, but in the absence of a compelling theory of the goodness of God or the order of the universe, this amounts to a *petitio.* Nothing may be too bad to be true. Something may be too true to be bad, however. If nihilism is true (a contradiction?), then in fact nothing *at all* is morally bad (or good). And even if theoretical considerations are a draw, which is debatable, the implications of this last fact must be significant, especially for an erstwhile pragmatist.

So what can be done? Ludwig Wittgenstein informed us that the philosopher is like a fly caught in a fly bottle; Richard Rorty has the philosopher (the epistemologist) apparently trapped in a house of mirrors. The critical realist can finally only beg the question and contend that, in either case, the task is the tedious one of determining which passages and doorways are actual outlets. Whatever faculties or criteria are used will be finite and partial, but that need not preclude them from apprehending reality. For a die-hard realist, this affirmation is simply what it means to trust in reason while acknowledging its limits. One does not believe in the truth because one thinks one's best ideas correspond to reality, but rather the other way around. (The theological equivalent to this is Descartes's conviction that "God is no deceiver.") A degree of faith will be implicit in any empirical, moral, or theological truth claim; but it is arguably more plausible and more prudent to believe ourselves capable of thinking valid thoughts and our societies capable of respecting real values than to see both language and communities as having no outside. (Should we doubt, for instance, that pain — as opposed to "pain" — is real and not to be visited upon innocents?) *Rejection of realism is both unnecessary and ineffective as a means of combating intolerance.* Therefore, in Coleridge's words, "Let us beware of that proud philosophy which affects to inculcate philanthropy while it denounces every home-born feeling by which it is produced and nurtured."[49] With a grace and sympathy no less than his own, Rorty's peers must not let him "get away" unanswered. We may never know anything with absolute certainty, but it will not do to settle in a bottle or to be content with a reflection: that would be to live in a cramped or inverted world. Such a world would be uncomfortable indeed.[50]

---

49. From *The Political Thought of Samuel Taylor Coleridge,* as quoted by Michael D. Clark, *Coherent Variety: The Idea of Diversity in British and American Conservative Thought* (Westport, Conn.: Greenwood Press, 1983), p. 78.

50. I would like to thank Richard Hays, Gene Outka, David Smith, Rulon Wells, and Cornel West for helpful comments on an earlier draft of this chapter. I have also profited from the discussion of Rorty's work in a legal theory workshop held at Yale, especially from the comments of Michael Williams. Finally, special gratitude is owed to Jeffrey Stout, whose extended correspondence saved me from substantive errors.

CHAPTER 7

Defending Democracy without Traducing Tradition: Jeffrey Stout's "Pragmatic Vision"

> Democracy is for the stout of heart who know that there are things
> worth fighting for in a world of paradox, ambiguity, and irony.
>
> JEAN BETHKE ELSHTAIN[1]

A Personal Introduction

I first met Jeffrey Stout when I was an undergraduate at Princeton majoring in philosophy and he was a graduate student there in religion. We shared several teachers at the time, but my first personal contact with Jeff came with *him* in the position of superior power and authority. He was the preceptor in a class I was taking on "religious conceptions of the self," and I will never forget the written response Jeff gave to my first course paper. It was a two-page, single-spaced missive outlining in detail the strengths and weaknesses of my sophomoric critique of Kierkegaard's *The Sickness unto Death*. The care Jeff had shown was made all the more impressive by three facts: (1) this was the mid-1970s and thus the precomputer age — he had actually to type his notes without benefit of cut, paste, delete, and restore buttons; (2) he had made it clear that he was not a Christian, but here he was defending Kierkegaard's conception of faith; and (3) he had responded, I later found out, at equal length to all the other students in the precept. Three stout sentences in particular remain emblazoned in my memory. About my prose style, Jeff observed, and I quote more or less verbatim: "You tend to write in long and complex sentences. This works *in German,* but not really in English. Be *kind* to your reader, and aim next time for more focus and simplicity."

---

1. Jean Bethke Elshtain, *Democracy on Trial* (New York: Basic Books, 1995), p. 89.

237

How benevolently, but firmly, I had been schooled: "This works in German, but not really in English." I could fancy myself an abstruse Nordic thinker who has to tone it down for the masses: Kant acquiring the common touch. Yet there was also more than a hint of moral reprimand in the last line: "Be kind to your reader," Jeff wrote, which was bracing enough, but I understood the subsequent calls for "focus" and "simplicity" to imply: "Be *harder* on *yourself.*" In Jeff's preceptorial performance, forty years ago, were already evident the character and commitments — the intellectual and moral virtues — of the author of *Democracy and Tradition:*[2] (1) the determination to give a charitable reading of others, including the young and self-satisfied, but without pulling punches; (2) equal respect for all, especially those subject to power and authority; and (3) an appreciation of diversity between, but also originality within, various perspectives, including perspectives he does not share. To this day, Jeff-the-non-Christian encourages me, like an older brother, to wrestle with my own Christian tradition. This requires remarkable patience and empathy.

I divide the chapter into two basic parts: first, I offer some diagnostic, and appreciative, reflections on Professor Stout's analysis of democracy; second, I critically address some epistemological and alethiological issues that he and I have gone around on for several years. On the latter head, we have grown closer over the decades, it now seems, though he still has not *quite* seen the light.

I. An Appreciation of Stout on Democratic Culture

In *Democracy and Tradition (DT),* Jeffrey Stout attempts to defend democracy against both its neo-traditional detractors and its neutralist-liberal champions. Chief among "the new traditionalists" are Alasdair MacIntyre, Stanley Hauerwas, and John Milbank, all of whom are Christians; chief among the "neutral liberals" are John Rawls and Richard Rorty, both of whom may be seen, for political purposes at least, as pragmatists. Stout himself embraces a version of pragmatism (about which more later), even as he affirms what many would call "liberalism." But his pragmatism and liberalism look to Whitman, Emerson, and Dewey to reconstruct a vision very different from what we find in Rawls and Rorty. Stout is after a conception of democratic citizenship that implies substantive moral virtues and concrete social practices. Before we

2. Jeffrey Stout, *Democracy and Tradition* (Princeton: Princeton University Press, 2004). All parenthetical page references in the text are to this work, unless otherwise noted.

turn to Stout more directly, we will briefly summarize the two broad camps he wishes to oppose.

The Christians Stout focuses on tend to see democracy as a morally corrosive social arrangement, emphasizing three values commonly associated with the Enlightenment: personal autonomy, universal reason, and the primacy of the nation-state. Accent on personal autonomy contributes to an inordinate individualism, the Christians judge, where claims and counterclaims, rights and the promotion of self-interest, become the dominant ethical ethos. This makes a truly cooperative community impossible. Accent on universal reason, in turn, contributes to a bogus sense of disembodiedness, as though anyone and everyone has unmediated access to timeless speculative and practical principles. This blinds us to the historical practices and traditional stories that actually shape our hearts and minds — our characters — and it may tempt us to be dogmatic and overbearing toward others who do not acknowledge the one shared *ratio*. Finally, accent on the nation-state and its sovereignty contributes to a reliance on secular norms and institutions that are often idolatrous. The nation-state teaches us, indeed, to turn to violence and deception to sustain domestic security and international order.

Hauerwas is representative of the neo-traditionalist Christian camp in insisting that, though modern pagans crave self-sufficiency and self-control, and modern nation-states rely on war and mendacity, Christians are called by God to live as servants who are "out of control" and who embody the locally narrated "truth" of a nonresistant Christ. Thus the church must stand apart from secular society as a "counterpolis" with a "counterstory."[3]

The liberals Stout concentrates on tend to see democracy as a politically compelling social arrangement, but its force stems for them precisely from its prescinding from robust moral or metaphysical claims. Western societies are typically so pluralistic, with so many factions and special interest groups and so much disagreement on what constitutes the true and the good and the beautiful, that religion *and philosophy* must be privatized or otherwise muzzled in or evacuated from a democratic culture. Discourse in the political sphere is to be limited to the lowest common denominator or to the lingua franca of a "neutral" or "constructed" public reason. To allow the full-throated expression of controversial metaphysical views, especially when these are then backed up with the steel of the law, would be at best uncivil and would at worst lead to a war of all against all. A "liberal" respect for individual conscience, as well as

3. See Stanley Hauerwas's works *The Peaceable Kingdom; Against the Nations; Resident Aliens; Dispatches from the Front;* etc.

a prudent regard for civic peace, should move us, for legislative and judicial purposes, to let go of traditions or tenets that cannot command a very particular kind of general consensus.

Here a Rawlsian contract theory that construes justice-as-fairness purely procedurally, relying on a "thin" conception of the good and a "basic" sense of justice, is the order of the day. Real people will have complex motivations and may embody thick virtues like charity and self-sacrifice, but for *political* purposes they are to be conceived of as "self-interested rational agents who take no interest in the interests of others," to use Rawls's language from *A Theory of Justice*. Tyranny and intolerance are the great social evils to be avoided, and both Rawls and Rorty frequently allude to the sixteenth- and seventeenth-century wars of religion as grist for their antidogmatic mills. What Rorty once called "postmodernist bourgeois liberalism" counsels such an extreme form of epistemic humility, indeed, that one seemingly can make no truth claims at all in public, and perhaps even in private.

Early on in *DT*, Stout begins to lay out his alternative take on democracy, affirming that it is itself "a tradition" and that it is "anything but [morally] empty" (p. 3). Put negatively, "the notion of state neutrality and the reason-tradition dichotomy should not be seen as [democracy's] defining marks"; put more positively, central democratic "ideals" include, for Stout, "equal voice and equal consideration for all citizens" (p. 3). This allegiance to equality requires, moreover, a range of personal skills and public practices. The first frontispiece quotation in *DT* is John Dewey's observation that "democracy is a form of government only because it is a form of moral and spiritual association." And Stout fleshes this out with:

> Central to democratic thought as I understand it is the idea of a body of citizens who reason with one another about the ethical issues that divide them, especially when deliberating on the justice or decency of political arrangements. It follows that one thing a democratic people had better have in common is a form of ethical discourse, a way of exchanging reasons about ethical and political topics. The democratic practice of giving and asking for ethical reasons, I argue, is where the life of democracy principally resides. (p. 6)

Where traditional Christians talk of "church" (if not "sect") and bourgeois liberals speak of "contract" (if not "laissez-faire competition"), Stout praises the "citizen." "The point of view of a citizen is that of someone who accepts some measure of responsibility for the condition of society and, in particular, for the political arrangements it makes for itself. To adopt this point of view is to participate in the living moral tradition of one's people, understood as a civic nation" (p. 6).

Now, how is a Christian believer who also appreciates the need for responsible civic engagement — that is, someone like myself — to respond to Stout's analysis? There will always be tension between Christian faith and temporal governments; indeed, the calls to civil disobedience will likely be multiple for those with ears to hear. Stout helps one see, nevertheless, that Christians ought to think of political governance and the state in much the same way they think of ecclesial governance and the church: as a finite and fallen attempt to embody the holiness of God, to live kingdom values into being for the sake of the Lord and one's neighbor.

Everything turns on the concrete form the state takes. How ought Christians to think of *democracy's* distinctive forms of political, economic, and cultural governance? No nation-state or no church polity is the kingdom come, but democracy and the attendant language of "rights" remain the most defensible political arrangement yet devised by the faithful or the faithless. I cannot be satisfied with purely secular accounts of democracy, however, including Stout's own. He wisely allows that "the problems come from asking rights-talk to do too much" (p. 206), but one wants to hear more about what other norms and dictions are required.

I myself defend a *prophetic* version of liberal democracy, animated by an unapologetic form of political *agape*. This entails an ongoing commitment — executive, legislative, and jurisprudential, but also theological, moral, and aesthetic — to the dignity *and sanctity*, the equality *and interdependence,* of all human beings. Stout is committed to the dignity and equality of citizens, but his repeated emphasis on "exchanging reasons and requests for reasons" (p. 209) makes me worry about those who are *unable* to give and receive such reasons. Is there a creeping rationalism, even elitism, at work here after all, too much emphasis on intellectual virtues of conversation and achieved dignity rather than on human needs and potentials and vulnerable sanctity? What about fetuses, infants, the mentally handicapped, and the senile-demented — all those who cannot participate in democratic dialogue? How do we generate and sustain Brandom's "I-Thou" sociality (p. 281) with these needy and marginal ones, some of whom are *not* now counted as citizens? Do they not fall under what Whitman calls the "principle of individuality" (p. 282)? One need not want to recommend theocracy to wonder how Stout's vision of democracy can recognize "the least of these."

Now, Jeff and his wife Sally have raised three children and sent two of them to Emory, so I am referring here to slippage between his personal practice and the theory that makes its way into *DT.*

I join Stout in saying to the neo-traditionalists and the neutralist liberals, in effect, "a pox on both your houses." Yet I remain a Christian theologian. I in no way retreat from seeing the biblical account of Christ's life and death, teaching and example, as the master moral narrative for my own existence. I have written two books on how Christlike love, open to self-sacrifice and empowered by the Holy Spirit, takes priority over but also clarifies and sustains all other human goods, including physical safety and social justice. Yet I find extremely moving these words — they might even be called a prophetic warning — from Jeffrey Stout: "We should . . . recognize . . . how disastrous it would be — in an era of global capitalism, corporate corruption, identity politics, religious resentment against secular society, and theocratic terrorism — if most citizens stopped identifying with the people as a whole and gave up on our democratic practices of accountability altogether" (p. 7).

II. A Reply to Stout on Modest Pragmatism, Justification, and Truth

For all my deep and abiding admiration for Stout's ability to defend democracy without traducing tradition, I still fear that the political values we share will not be sustainable if coupled with his pragmatic understanding of justification and truth. The "ironist sky" (p. 257) that seemed foreboding over Richard Rorty has perhaps *too* fully cleared over Jeffrey Stout. The danger now is not from an irony or narcissism that directly *corrupts* moral practice, but rather from a theoretical minimalism that cannot *account* for our (and his) practical love of neighbor. The hazard is not, so to speak, from swelling storm clouds that threaten to inundate and drown us, but instead from a protracted drought that will leave us culturally parched. But here, admittedly, there is a fine line between a bracing disconsolation and a debilitating despair, a line that may ultimately be traced according to psychic and aesthetic imponderables: Jeff likes Perugino's *Vergine Adorante* . . . I like Botticelli's *Madonna e Bambino.* . . . I want to see what/who the Virgin is adoring . . . Stout is content with the face of adoration alone.

I continue to find plausible a version of critical realism — a.k.a. meta-skeptical realism — a position that combines a fallibilist epistemology with a realist alethiology and a pluralist ontology. Stout once equated this stand with "the obsessions of a half-successful cure," comparing me to "someone who wants to be his own father and then has the nature of that desire brought to light in therapy."[4] I have never before so graciously been called a "motherf---er," but I will not let these remarks be a conversation stopper. In the spirit of democratic dialogue, I will briefly describe and defend my views in opposition to Stout's "pragmatism."

As I conceive it, "realism" is not to be confused with "foundationalism." Foundationalism is the view that knowledge claims can and must be justified with reference to indubitable or incorrigible apprehensions. According to foundationalists, some human faculty (e.g., reason or intuition) or some superhuman agency (e.g., God or the angels) gives us unmediated and infallible access to reality — whether empirical, moral, or theological. We cannot be mistaken about the first principles of practical reason, say, or about the commandments of the Creator, because we have direct awareness or self-validating revelation of these things. Some assertions may be mere preference or opinion, but there is a bedrock of absolute certainty on which genuine *knowledge* can and must be built.[5]

Realism, in contrast, is a claim about the nature of truth claims, rather than about their certainty. Ever since Plato, knowledge has generally been defined as "justified true belief about *x*,"[6] but there remain a number of possible ways to construe truth, justification, and this *x*. In turn, there are three disciplines focusing on these three features of knowledge. As I dub them, alethiology is concerned with the *nature* of truth; epistemology with the *justification* of truth *claims;* and ontology with the *being* or *constituent parts* of *x*.

More specifically, alethiological realism is the view that truth is a matter of correspondence or adequation between something subjective (e.g., words or ideas) and something objective (e.g., heaven or earth). As such, alethiological realism stands opposed to coherentist alternatives that let go of the objective pole of truth and see it merely as agreement of words with other words or ideas with other ideas. Coherentism is just another form of nihilism, in the sense that it does not grant a nonlinguistic referent even for our "true" sentences.

Epistemological fallibilism is the view that lets go of absolute certainty and sees justification as probabilistic all the way down. Such fallibilism rejects foundationalist alternatives that insist that we can stop the regress of justification in indubitable or incorrigible apprehensions. For the epistemic fallibilist,

4. Jeffrey Stout, *Ethics after Babel* (Boston: Beacon Press, 1988), pp. 254-55.

5. To be sure, one might be a foundationalist in one field of inquiry (e.g., empirical science) and not in another (e.g., ethics). But to embrace foundationalism in any discipline is to affirm the sort of "given" incorrigibility I have described.

6. I ignore so-called "Gettier counterexamples" as interesting but irrelevant for my purposes; see Edmund Gettier, "Is Justified True Belief Knowledge?" *Analysis* 23 (1963).

we have no sure tests for knowledge based on immediate cognitions or intuitions; to think otherwise is a prideful denial of our finitude. Fallibilism does not imply universal or dogmatic skepticism, I hasten to add, but rather what might be called "metaskepticism": we can never know with utter assurance that we know anything, but first-order beliefs can be justified, and we can trust that most of them track reality.[7] Importantly, such fallibilism is quite compatible with — in fact, it presupposes — conceiving of truth as correspondence to reality. To admit fallibility is to admit changeable standards and thus to be self-critical over time, a key democratic and Stoutian virtue.

Once one sees an error in judgment, one ought to correct it, and one can come to see that one's "traditional" standards of judgment themselves are mistaken and in need of reform . . . in the name of "truth." Stout refers to this as "the cautionary use of 'true'" (p. 257), and we both do endorse it, especially as a means of resisting "a tendency to attribute indefeasible authority to the ethical opinions of the citizenry taken as a whole or on average" (p. 281). But avoiding the authoritarianism of the *vox populi* is not the *meaning* of "truth," even if such avoidance is part of the pragmatic *effect* of "truth"-talk. I concede that Stout does not wish to reduce the meaning of "truth" to the practical consequences of referring to it, but I just don't see, more positively, what he does take even the "commonsense" meaning of the term to be.

Ontological pluralism, finally, is the view that there are many different sorts of entities in the world (e.g., persons, places, values, numbers, and God). Such pluralism contrasts with various forms of ontological monism, in which all reality is equated with or reduced to a single substance (e.g., fire, air, mind, or spirit). To be sure, my kind of moral philosopher and theologian holds that reality, as created by God, forms a coherent and at least partially intelligible "universe," but she does not collapse perceived complexity into an abstract uniformity.

I can unify my comments so far by noting that my ideal ethicist assumes that human sensation and thought point, fallibly, beyond themselves and toward a common world. This world is made up of a number of types of beings encounterable, in principle, by all undamaged persons with suitable training. In technical terms, my ethicist is an *alethiological realist,* an *epistemological fallibilist,* and an *ontological pluralist.* More to the point, he finds the case for moral realism more compelling than that for empirical realism. Rocks, trees,

7. See my "The Possibilities of Scepticisms," *Metaphilosophy* 21, no. 4 (October 1990): 303-21. In the past, I evidently led Stout to believe, erroneously, that I endorsed Pyrrhonian or perfectly general skepticism.

and tables may not care how they are represented — nature may have no pre-ferred language, as Richard Rorty suggests — but human beings, even very early on, have an inwardness that makes them objects of *ethical* knowledge. Persons have a historical reality — aptitudes, needs, and potentials — to which psychologists, philosophers, and theologians must be true. In this sense, ethics is on a surer "realistic" footing than physics, as Plato understood.

There is such a thing as what it's like to be in pain, for example, regardless of whether other people recognize this.[8] One's experience of either suffering or joy is (partly) constitutive of its ontological reality, and all normal persons are capable of such experience. (Even neo-pragmatic Rorty, actually one of the most compassionate men I know, grants that "pain is nonlinguistic.")[9] Furthermore, this experience is morally salient; other things being equal, we are missing something important if we do not recognize and act to increase joy and decrease suffering for all. As Stout helps us see, at the very heart of democratic culture is a tradition of taking everybody's pain seriously, which means giving everyone a chance to voice that pain — physical, psychological, and moral — in public.

An individual's thoughts, words, and deeds are obviously influenced by interaction with diverse persons and things across time, but a lived identity is not simply invented by majority opinion or personal preference. Bestowing care on others with the need and potential to benefit from it involves seeing the social world aright, an attention to truth that is central to a well-lived life and a just social order. Yet this felt-depth of human existence, together with the claim it has on other agents, makes ethics more a matter of discovering and nurturing goods than of creating them *ex nihilo*.

Pace J. L. Mackie[10] and other subjectivists, the lack of agreement on moral matters may be a function of their complexity and our limited imagi-nation and empathy, and the peculiarity of objective values is no more pro-

---

8. Cf. Thomas Nagel's famous essay, "What Is It Like to Be a Bat?" in *Mortal Questions* (Cambridge: Cambridge University Press, 1979).

9. Richard Rorty, *Contingency, Irony, Solidarity* (Cambridge: Cambridge University Press, 1989), p. 94.

10. Mackie maintains that realism in ethics is undermined by what he calls "the argu-ment from relativity" and "the argument from queerness." Because there is so little consensus on moral questions and because real values would have to be such odd things, we have reason to believe that moral terms do not refer as such, that objective goods do not exist. We can discover what we want or how we talk, but there are no realities beyond our historical tradi-tions that have a normative claim on us. See his *Ethics: Inventing Right and Wrong* (London: Penguin Books, 1977).

nounced or problematic than that of quarks and tachyons. In fact, it is arguably less, since we are aware of the goods of sanctity and dignity from the inside, so to speak — we *embody* and *ensoul* them. To doubt the reality of these goods, however fragile and hard to recognize and achieve, is to doubt our own identities as well as those of others. This, as much as terrorism, is the real threat to democracy.

Conclusion

Jeffrey Stout is no subjectivist; on the contrary, he is the most unnarcissistic of men. *Democracy and Tradition* is a beautifully written and tightly argued plea for us to expand our sympathies beyond our immediate tribe or favorite tale, religious or secular. Neither sectarian resentment nor liberal constructivism is true virtue. Clearly, Stout's "modest" or "minimalist" pragmatism would affirm much of what I have maintained above — indeed, I *learned* large parts of it from him — but then I simply don't see why he refuses to call his own position a version of "fallibilism" about justification, "realism" about truth, and "pluralism" about beings. ("Realism" and "antirealism" continue to seem an exhaustive either/or to me, especially in relation to human beings, in spite of Stout's protests on page 257.) After all, I am not asking this "righteous Gentile" to convert (explicitly) to Christianity! The main point is that both Christian love and Stoutian democracy affirm that the neighbor has a claim on us that is not merely a matter of convention. Richard Rorty notwithstanding, there *is* something beyond our traditional practices that measures and judges them.

For the political agapist, liberal patriotism is as suspect as traditional ecclesiocentrism. Neither nation nor church (nor town hall) can substitute for the holy will of God and the sanctity of human life. Stout's pragmatic liberalism differs from the prophetic variety in letting go of the divine will, of course. He believes it possible fully to love the neighbor without loving God. Whether or not that is possible, I am convinced it is *impossible* fully to love the neighbor without *being loved by* God. This is the chief sense in which *agape* is a supernatural virtue.

CHAPTER 8

The Cross and Democratic Politics:
Agape, Self-Sacrifice, and Human Rights

Introduction

Is the cross an obsolete symbol of supreme love, too masochistic to promote liberation of the oppressed, too esoteric to speak to a democratic culture? In part I of this chapter, I consider two Christian feminists — Barbara Hilkert Andolsen and Ada Maria Isasi-Diaz — who are extremely wary of traditional definitions of *agape* that equate it with self-sacrifice or altruism. They look away from the cross for other emblems of social virtue. In part II, I turn to a Christian philosopher — Nicholas Wolterstorff — who has recently rejected "classical *agape*" as antithetical to justice and human rights. I find his case deeply flawed. In part III, I consider Stanley Hauerwas's theological critique of "justice," "rights," and "democracy." Inevitably, the issue of violence and nonviolence arises here. Finally, in part IV I look in some detail at Dietrich Bonhoeffer's migration from nonresistance to evil, to nonviolent resistance, to violent resistance. My cumulative argument is that Christ's cross is not the only valid image of prophetic love but that it remains an indispensable one for Christians in both ecclesial and political settings. In spite of assaults, the cross continues to be an inspiring source of both religious piety and democratic liberty and equality. Julia Ward Howe's famous line, "As He died to make men holy, let us die to make men free,"[1] is relevant to both state and church.

---

1. Julia Ward Howe, "The Battle Hymn of the Republic."

I. Two Christian Critics of Traditional *Agape* (Andolsen and Isasi-Diaz)

Barbara Hilkert Andolsen

Traditional accounts of *agape* typically suffer from several liabilities, according to Andolsen.[2] First, they tend to valorize self-sacrifice and to deny the legitimacy and importance of self-love, thus depriving believers of a crucial source of psychological health and moral integrity. Second, they often treat all sin as fundamentally self-assertion and desire for personal gain (pride/self-ishness), thus failing to recognize and respect women's experience of love and sin, especially sin as excessive self-*less*-ness and lack of personal development (timidity/sloth). Third, they too radically divide the public sphere from the private sphere, frequently relegating women to the latter. Fourth, they remain within masculine Christian metaphors for the divine, thus alienating women from God. Fifth, and quite generally, they almost inevitably become vehicles used by men to victimize and subordinate women.

Andolsen draws on a number of authors — D'Arcy, Goldstein, Cady Stanton, Shaw, Farley, Harrison, Daly, et al. — to provide an alternative to the above. Mining their countervailing insights and accents, she adumbrates several key proposals. First, we should recognize that love is typically gendered in our society, with women still the primary familial caregivers, often called upon for inordinate self-giving. Second, we ought also to recognize that sin is typically gendered in our society, with women as "tempted" by autonomy. Third, we should de-emphasize self-sacrifice (especially for women) in favor of "honesty, courage, and self-assertion" (Anna Howard Shaw).[3] Fourth, we ought to strive to reintegrate public and private life, insisting that both men and women are called to practice *agape* in all spheres of existence. Fifth, we must generate feminine images and metaphors for the divine, focusing on the mutuality and friendship implied by the Trinity rather than on the suffering and sacrifice of the Atonement.

I find many of these points quite compelling. Undeniably, as Andolsen notes, "idealization of sacrifice has played a role in the victimization of women" (p. 156). Paraphrasing Margaret Farley, Andolsen plausibly argues

---

2. Barbara Hilkert Andolsen, "Agape in Feminist Ethics," in *Feminist Theological Ethics: A Reader*, ed. Lois K. Daly (Louisville: Westminster John Knox, 1994).

3. Andolsen, "Agape in Feminist Ethics," p. 153. Page numbers to this article have been placed in the following text.

that "women have too often found in practice that Christian self-sacrifice means the sacrifice of women for the sake of men" (p. 152). It is important to appreciate, however, that neither Andolsen nor Farley is rejecting suffering and sacrifice as such. "Mary Daly repudiates self-sacrifice," Andolsen observes (p. 153), but Andolsen herself and most of her feminist colleagues are objecting to an overemphasis on or overstatement of it. Suffering and sacrifice are sometimes necessary and justified for the sake of a larger good (e.g., human dignity), but recommending them for their own sakes or as unqualifiedly right is masochistic and unjust (pp. 151-55). Largely inspired by the feminist critique, I have elsewhere argued that, to be moral, self-sacrifice must be charitably motivated, consensual in form, and constructive in effect.[4] Self-hating, coerced, or profligate self-surrender is no Christian virtue. Continuing to reflect on these matters, I now believe that a fourth criterion is required: not only must self-sacrifice be voluntarily enacted by the giver, but it must also be freely welcomed by the receiver.[5] This stipulation is necessary lest agapic service to others be manipulative or patronizing.

Although I concur with the major feminist objections to *agape* as essentially or uncritically self-sacrifice, I nevertheless worry about the language of "mutuality" or "friendship" or "solidarity" that is sometimes offered as an alternative. Professor Farley "defines *agape* as a full mutuality marked by equality between the sexes," Andolsen writes (p. 154), but what are we to do if such reciprocity is not present or forthcoming? Is mutuality as reciprocal affirmation or egalitarian fellowship a necessary condition for *agape*, such that no such fellowship means no agapic love? Again, the cross is not the only valid symbol of Christlike love, but is it always indicative of a disordered situation and thus a corrective or rare expedient, as Andolsen implies?[6] In short, can or should *philia* supplant *agape* as the first Christian virtue, either theologically or politically? To better answer these questions, let me turn to the work of Ada Maria Isasi-Diaz.

Ada Maria Isasi-Diaz

Isasi-Diaz is a formidable champion of a "*Mujerista* theology [that] brings together elements of feminist theology, Latin American liberation theology and

---

4. Timothy P. Jackson, *The Priority of Love* (Princeton: Princeton University Press, 2003).

5. Nicolette Paso made this point to me in conversation.

6. Andolsen, "Agape in Feminist Ethics," p. 155.

cultural theology, three perspectives which critique and challenge each other, giving birth to new elements, a new reality, a new whole."[7] In "Solidarity: Love of Neighbor in the 1980s," she writes: "Our mission is to challenge oppressive structures which refuse to allow us to be full members of society while preserving our distinctiveness as Hispanic women."[8] Her positive ideal is justice and self-determination for all, a solidarity she defines as "the union of fellowship arising from the common responsibilities and interests, as between classes, peoples, or groups; community of interests, feelings, purposes, or action; social cohesion" (p. 79).[9] Two main elements of solidarity for her are "mutuality and praxis" (p. 81). Strikingly, Isasi-Diaz believes that "charity" falsifies the true meaning of solidarity, which "moves away from the false notion of disinterest, of doing for others in an altruistic fashion" (p. 79).

It is the language of "common responsibilities and interests" that gives me pause, especially when Isasi-Diaz goes on to call common interests "the heart of solidarity" (p. 81). I admire her equation of "salvation" with "the love between God and individual human beings and among human beings" (p. 79). Her analysis of "alienation" as the chief obstacle to salvation is equally persuasive. Her attempt to ground love in "common interests," however, can appear to insist on sameness as a precondition for attending to the neighbor, which is problematic. I fully appreciate her point that *agape* should not be a condescending "charity" that accents the privilege of the giver and the dependence of the receiver. That sort of patronizing hierarchy is as destructive as she says it is. I also applaud her call to expand our identification with the marginalized and oppressed. In that spirit, indeed, the "common interests" that she puts at the core of solidarity might be read simply as "our shared finitude and mortality" or "our common human nature." ("Mankind was my business," as Jacob Marley says.) The rub is that such universalism is not the usual meaning of "interests." Isasi-Diaz seems aware of the ambiguity of her own terminology. She avers that "solidarity is *not* a matter of agreeing with, of being supportive of, of liking, or of being inspired by, the cause of a group or people" (p. 78). But then why refer to "common interests"?

I have emphasized that *agape* is a passionate and active willing of the good for the other, neither abstract well-wishing nor supererogation. *Agape* wants intimate personal relationships, including the active giving and receiv-

7. Ada Maria Isasi-Diaz, "Mujeristas: A Name of Our Own!!" *Christian Century,* May 1989.

8. Ada Maria Isasi-Diaz, "Solidarity: Love of Neighbor in the 1980s," in *Feminist Theological Ethics,* p. 77. Page numbers to this article have been placed in the following text.

9. She is quoting *The Random House Dictionary.*

ing of care, and love of the other is a moral duty rather than a mere admirable option. My key point, nevertheless, is that *agape* does not insist on reciprocity or mutuality as a precondition or necessary condition. Sympathy cannot and need not always be translated into empathy. I do not have to be a widow or an orphan to care about and for widows and orphans. Furthermore, if I must share and be motivated by the concrete interests of those I assist, have I not replaced love of neighbor with prudence? Has not self-interest supplanted other-regard? (Cf. John Rawls on rejecting discriminatory principles because one fears one may fall victim to them, rather than because they demean others among whom one will never be numbered.) Isasi-Diaz explicitly denies that altruism (i.e., disinterested sacrifice for the other) is possible, or at least that it is desirable (p. 79). But the unintended upshot is Greek eudaimonism, rather than Judaic *hesed* or Christian *agape*.

In Christian Scripture, the Good Samaritan aids the man beaten, robbed, and stripped — presumably a Jew — in spite of the absence of common interests. The person in distress is loved *qua* fellow creature of God rather than as a comember of some ethnic or economic faction. In fact, Samaritans and Jews were traditional enemies. Enemies are precisely those for whom I feel little or no solidarity, but I am to love them nonetheless as bearing the image of God. When a volunteer rocks a crack baby at Grady Hospital in Atlanta, for instance, he no doubt receives personal gratifications of various sorts. But it is hardly plausible to say that he experiences reciprocity with an equal or that he is moved by common responsibilities and interests. Isasi-Diaz associates "the praxis of mutuality" with "friendship" (p. 81), and friendship may be the paradigmatic relation in heaven, but here below *philia* remains a preferential and exclusive love that cannot take the place of *agape*'s indiscriminate bestowal of worth on the needy and vulnerable. To suggest otherwise is to preach a different gospel.

Prophetic liberalism takes these truths to heart and seeks to translate them into political and economic policy. It affirms a genuine pluralism of interests yet a commonality of nature: all of us bear the image of God, thus all of us are due charity, regardless of our specific beliefs, actions, memberships, and concerns. For the prophetic liberal, the cross is not always emblematic of an injustice in need of remedy. We sometimes accept suffering and self-sacrifice — as in parenting young children, assisting victims of natural calamity, and conserving the planet for future generations — not because of a moral wrong but because of the human condition. In chapter 9, for example, I argue that a civic refusal of the death penalty ought to be an expression of a long-suffering love that rises above strict justice. Such clemency is in spite of guilt; it is not a plan to eliminate guilt. It is not a corrective to evil or a defense of human dignity; it is a manifestation of good and an appreciation of human sanctity. Sometimes the political cross acts to overcome sin (atonement), sometimes in spite of sin (mercy), sometimes independently of sin altogether (as in tragedy).

II. "Classical Modern *Agape*" and Justice/Rights (Wolterstorff)

Nicholas Wolterstorff's *Justice in Love (JIL)* (2011) is the companion volume to his *Justice: Rights and Wrongs (JRW)* (2008), which is a deft and balanced treatment of the language of "rights" and "duties" and of the proper relation of that language to Christian ethics. In *JRW*, Wolterstorff drives the final nail in the coffin of the view that talk of "rights" and "mutual respect" is merely a product of the Enlightenment or a form of Christian apostasy. Wolterstorff demonstrates, on the contrary, that rights and reciprocal justice have been crucial to the Christian tradition and are essential to any viable Christian morality. That being the case, readers of his first book on justice would be entirely justified in expecting a similarly fair and insightful treatment of agapic love in the second. But, alas, in one key respect they would be disappointed.

For reasons that still elude me, in *JIL* Wolterstorff spins "the classical version of modern day agapism" into a gossamer man by equating it with the overheated views of Anders Nygren. Nygren's *Agape and Eros* (1930-1936) notoriously set agapic love at odds with both erotic desire and justice, and Wolterstorff is correct in criticizing this position.[10] The problem is that he tries to tar all "modern day" agapists — from Søren Kierkegaard to Karl Barth to Paul Ramsey — with the same brush. He argues that their accounts of agapic love, like Nygren's, must lead them not merely to be neglectful of justice but also actively to perpetrate injustice. This is a misreading. Wolterstorff's critique hits home in some places, but Kierkegaard, Barth, and Ramsey differ significantly among themselves, and Wolterstorff often blurs this fact. Worse, he lumps them together with Nygren's assault on *eros* and *justitia* and thus treats them unfairly.

Professor Wolterstorff marshals telling criticisms of "love monism" — the view that *agape* is the only virtue — and his elaborations of the claims of justice are often innovative and credible. In many ways, *Justice in Love* is a su-

---

10. Wolterstorff also defends Nygren after a fashion, appreciating the "influence" and "systematic rigor" (*Justice in Love* [Grand Rapids: Eerdmans, 2011], pp. 21-22) of his claims, even while disagreeing with them. Page numbers to *Justice in Love* have been placed in the immediately following text.

perb text. Nevertheless, it is marred by a fundamental misapprehension. There is no such thing as "classical modern day agapism," as Wolterstorff describes it.

Some Representative Passages

Here are some representative passages from *Justice in Love:*

> [A]ll the modern day agapists agreed that if one loves someone agapically, one does not treat him as one does because justice requires it, and conversely, if one treats someone as one does because justice requires it, one is not loving him agapically. Loving someone agapically and treating him as one does because justice requires it are conceptually incompatible. Agapic love casts out all thought of justice and injustice. Agapic love is blind and deaf to justice and injustice. (p. 42)

> Agapic love is blind to all requirements coming from the side of the recipient. It is in that way spontaneous. But when I seek to treat you justly, I treat you as I do because your worth requires it. (p. 43)

> [T]here is another aspect of the nature of forgiveness that Nygren and the other agapists ignore. Notice that one cannot dispense forgiveness indiscriminately hither and yon. I can forgive you only if you have wronged someone, and only *for* the wrong you did them. (p. 54)

> [N]ot only can one not *understand* oneself as forgiving someone without employing the concepts of rights and wrongs, justice and injustice. One cannot even *perform the act* of forgiving someone without employing those concepts. (p. 55)

> Agapic love perpetrates injustice. (p. 57)

> The position of the agapist implies that I am sometimes permitted to do what I ought not to do [perpetrate injustice]; sometimes it is even the case that I *should* do what I ought not to do. (p. 61)

What can one say in response to these provocative lines? Let me mount a defense of *some modern forms of agapism* by drawing several important distinctions.

Agapic Love as Sometimes Rising Above Justice but Never Falling Below It

Compare Wolterstorff's words above with those of Paul Ramsey:

> [S]ometimes love does what justice requires and assumes its rules as norms, sometimes love does more than justice requires but never less, and sometimes love acts in a quite different way from what justice alone can enable us to discern to be right. When one's own interests alone are at stake, the Christian governs himself by love and resists not one who is evil. When his neighbor's need and the just order of society are at stake, the Christian still governs himself by love and suffers no injustice to be done nor the order necessary to earthly life to be injured.[11]

Wolterstorff fails to register that *not being limited to* justice is not the same as *being blind and deaf to* justice or to *violating* justice. If modern justice is plausibly defined in terms of rewarding merit, punishing demerit, or keeping contracts, it is quite possible to go beyond these practices without either ignoring them or offending against them. Wolterstorff himself makes the point that, in Jesus' parable of the vineyard (Matt. 20:1-16), the owner commits no injustice: he pays to the early-comers the amount agreed upon, even though he also generously gives the latecomers an equal sum. This important point is devastating against Nygren, but not against Ramsey.

Wolterstorff marks the crucial contrast between *acting in accordance with* justice and *being motivated by* justice,[12] and he argues persuasively that an agapist as such may do the former without doing the latter. The main question, nonetheless, is not whether an agapist *must* be motivated by justice in *all* circumstances but whether she *may* be so motivated in *some* circumstances. One might maintain that, by definition, an agapist who is motivated by justice is, to that extent, not an agapist. But that begs the question of whether agapic love and justice are compatible or even cooperative. For his part, to repeat, Wolterstorff thinks that classical modern agapists must be unconcerned with justice and even actively violate it. Paul Ramsey disagrees, as do many (if not most) contemporary agapists. I myself have contended that concern for distributive, retributive, and procedural justice goes hand in hand with *agape* but

---

11. Paul Ramsey, *War and the Christian Conscience* (Durham, N.C.: Duke University Press, 1961), p. 178.

12. Wolterstorff, *Justice in Love*, p. 45.

that *agape* has priority over them and often goes beyond them.[13] Hans Urs von Balthasar explicitly ties love to awareness of guilt and thus injustice: "the spirit of love cannot teach man the meaning of the Cross, without laying bare the guilt of the world."[14] He is convinced that "love alone can fulfill the law," but, rather than ignoring or contravening justice, he *relates* it to love: "the Church's proclamation of the principles of social justice, and any efforts she may make to realize them, must be steeped in the love of the New Testament."[15] Was Balthasar not a classical modern-day agapist?

Wolterstorff rightly returns contemporary Christian ethics to the teachings of Jesus and Saint Paul. But modern-day agapists have not been as forgetful of how those teachings intimately connect love and justice as Wolterstorff claims. Building on Scripture and Paul Ramsey, I have argued for many years that justice is an indispensable ally of love.[16] Martin Luther King Jr. comes to mind as explicitly and actively tying love to the combating of *in*justice: "Love, *agape,* is the only cement that can hold this broken community together. When I am commanded to love, I am commanded to restore community, to resist injustice, and to meet the needs of my brothers."[17] Was King not a classical modern-day agapist?

Wolterstorff's own version of agapism ultimately "incorporates" *justitia* into *agape:* "doing justice is *an example* of love."[18] Biblical teachings do not simply identify love and justice, however. Jesus himself praises agapic love foremost — his final love command is "love [*agapao*] one another as I have loved you" (John 15:12) — but he also sanctions the demands of justice, honesty, humility, and piety. The parable of the vineyard reconciles contractual justice and "generosity" (Matt. 20:1-16), as Wolterstorff recognizes, but it also distinguishes them. Jesus was no love monist who imprudently reduced ethics to fairness-blind benevolence: think of his indictment of the scribes and Pharisees as "hypocrites" for neglecting "the weightier matters of the law: justice

13. See Jackson, *The Priority of Love.*

14. Hans Urs von Balthasar, *Love Alone: The Way of Revelation* (London: Sheed and Ward, 1968), p. 76.

15. Balthasar, *Love Alone,* p. 105. The title, *Love Alone,* can make Balthasar sound like a love monist, but the quote cited illustrates that he endorses both love and justice.

16. "Love without justice or a love that lapses into injustice is less than loving, but a justice without love or that does not aspire to love becomes less than just"; see *The Priority of Love,* p. 38.

17. Martin Luther King Jr., *Stride toward Freedom* (New York: Harper and Row, 1958), p. 106.

18. Wolterstorff, *Justice in Love,* pp. 72 and 84.

and mercy and faith" (Matt. 23:23). (Note that "justice" [*krisis*] and "mercy" [*eleos*] are mentioned serially; they are not conflated.)

The Case of Reinhold Niebuhr

Interestingly, Wolterstorff considers Reinhold Niebuhr a "nonclassical" agapist. "Classical modern day agapists" hold that one must love one's neighbor agapically "under all conditions," Wolterstorff writes, but Niebuhr allows that "there are conditions under which one should treat one's neighbor as justice requires rather than loving him agapically."[19] Although he notes some of the complexities of Niebuhr's position, here again Wolterstorff overstates the case. He accents Niebuhr's conceding the impossibility of Christian love, at least on the group level, and construes him as saying that we must simply leave *agape* behind as a political ideal, favoring justice instead. Otherwise, *agape* will "perpetrate injustice or invite victimization."[20] Yet this reading misses Niebuhr's exquisite, sometimes tortured ambivalence. Admittedly, Niebuhr is not always consistent. In *Moral Man and Immoral Society,* for example, he writes: "A rational ethic aims at justice, and a religious ethic makes love the ideal. A rational ethic seeks to bring the needs of others into equal consideration with those of the self. The religious ethic . . . insists that the needs of the neighbor shall be met, without a careful computation of relative needs."[21] Given his frequent claims that *agape* is nonresisting while politics is built on the balance of power, it is tempting indeed to ascribe to Niebuhr a sharp (almost cynical) discontinuity between love and justice, Christianity and politics; but this too easily resolves the central paradox of prophetic morality. The kingdom is "both here and not yet."

Reminiscent of Kierkegaard's pseudonyms, Niebuhr's characteristic trope is to resist all reductive gambits and to depict Christianity paradoxically. The law of love, for example, is both a cogent norm and an impractical ideal; it is neither simply possible nor simply impossible, but rather an "impossible possibility."[22] A philosophical turn of mind will immediately pounce on this as contradictory, and so it is on one level. Niebuhr's point, however, is that prophetic religion avails itself of myths and mysteries that transcend philo-

---

19. Wolterstorff, *Justice in Love,* p. 25.
20. Wolterstorff, *Justice in Love,* p. 63.
21. Reinhold Niebuhr, *Moral Man and Immoral Society* (New York: Scribner, 1960), p. 57.
22. Niebuhr, *Moral Man,* p. 37.

sophical reason. Any rationalistic attempt to dismiss the love command as impractical and therefore irrelevant, and any romantic attempt to preach it as fully realizable and therefore straightforwardly binding, evacuates Christian piety of its distinctive tension, according to Niebuhr. "Prophetic Christianity . . . demands the impossible," Niebuhr writes, and yet "the prophetic tradition in Christianity must insist on the relevance of the ideal of love to the moral experience of mankind *of every conceivable level.*"[23] To see in Niebuhr, as does Wolterstorff, a simple or complete disconnect between agapic love and social justice, is to lose Niebuhr's nuance.[24]

Agapic Love as a Duty to the Individual

Wolterstorff contends that *agape* is unmotivated by the being or doing of the other and is thus a form of "benevolence" or "gratuitous generosity."[25] He recognizes that such love "seeks to promote the good of [the] person as an end in itself,"[26] but he is oddly insensitive to the fact that *agape* earnestly attends to the needs and potentials of the neighbor in all their concreteness. Even if unintentionally, Wolterstorff gives the impression that agapic love, as interpreted by moderns, is a form of optional philanthropy that wells up in the giver utterly arbitrarily and independently of "the recipient." Otherwise, to use his phrase, "the serpent of requirement would have wriggled its way into the garden of pure agape."[27] Wolterstorff surely knows, however, that this is not how many modern agapists understand the virtue. For Kierkegaard, *agape* is "spontaneous" and "unconditional" in not being premised on "worth," defined as achieved merit or demerit, and in not demanding reciprocity. Yet he spends numerous pages in *Works of Love* (1848) elaborating "our *duty* to love *the people we see.*"[28] Balthasar echoes the sentiment in claiming that "absolute love" is a *"duty"* that "transcends individual 'inclination.'"[29] For both men, *agape affirms obligations that are grounded in the reality of God and the neighbor,*

23. Niebuhr, *Moral Man,* pp. 62, 63, emphasis added.

24. These paragraphs on Niebuhr are taken largely from my *The Priority of Love,* pp. 101-3.

25. Wolterstorff, *Justice in Love,* p. 42.

26. Wolterstorff, *Justice in Love,* p. 22.

27. Wolterstorff, *Justice in Love,* p. 45.

28. Søren Kierkegaard, *Works of Love,* trans. Howard V. Hong and Edna H. Hong (Princeton: Princeton University Press, 1995), pp. 154-74, emphasis added.

29. Balthasar, *Love Alone,* p. 97, emphasis added.

especially his need for love. Otherwise, it is mere abstract well-wishing, if not self-indulgence — a kind of moral masturbation.

For many present-day agapists, the "requirements" of charity have a different basis from those of justice; in my estimation, charity looks to sanctity, the image of God born by all, whereas justice looks to achieved dignity.[30] But charity, including forgiveness of sins, is not simply supererogatory. Justice cannot demand forgiveness as something actively deserved, as Wolterstorff seems to concede, but this does not mean that forgiveness is not obligatory and directed toward the other. This realization is very near the heart of Christian ethics: out of gratitude to God and concern for both self and others, forgiveness is required of the victim but cannot be insisted upon by the victimizer. This is precisely why it is a duty of charity and not of justice. If *agape* and forgiveness were merely supererogatory, Jesus could not have commanded them, Kierkegaard and Balthasar should not have considered them duties, and Ramsey would not have focused on the "Thou shalt's" of Matthew 22.

Agapic Love as Equal Regard Rather Than Identical Treatment

Wolterstorff seems to think that having equal regard for the neighbor must entail treating everyone the same or as close to the same as possible, however unjust this might be.[31] This is not so. Most agapists from Kierkegaard to Ramsey to Gene Outka have recognized that love must respond to the individual in her particularity — feeding the hungry, clothing the naked, giving solace to the grieving, forgiving the guilty, and so on. If one tries to feed the satiated, clothe the well-dressed, comfort the joyful, or forgive the innocent, this will be folly, not charity. Outka has been especially careful to highlight the equal consideration versus identical treatment distinction,[32] but Wolterstorff mentions his work only in passing. Moreover, Outka takes great pains not to oppose charity and justice, even affirming that "justice may have a limiting effect on

---

30. See chap. 2 of this volume; see also Jackson, *The Priority of Love,* esp. p. 211.

31. See his imaginative discussion of the judges of the Gilmore Award (Wolterstorff, *Justice in Love,* p. 57): "as convinced agapists of the classical modern day sort, they treat the good of these two [competitors] with equal regard. So they give the honor and money to the loser in the competition. . . . this comes as close to treating them with equal regard as is possible in the situation. But the winner would then be wronged."

32. See Gene Outka, *Agape: An Ethical Analysis* (New Haven: Yale University Press, 1972), p. 20.

agape qua radical other-regard."[33] For him, nothing about *agape* requires or even permits one to behave unjustly, including giving the prize to the loser in a competition.[34] Is Outka not a classical modern-day agapist?

Agapic Love as Not Unqualified Self-Sacrifice

Like Barbara Hilkert Andolsen, Wolterstorff finds fault with any account of *agape* that is uncritically self-sacrificial or that vilifies self-love. Unqualified calls for self-sacrifice would inevitably make agapists complicit in tyranny and thus be a threat to justice, as Wolterstorff perceives it, even as the failure to respect one's own worth is a kind of moral "malformation."[35] But who, other than Nygren, disagrees with this? Jesus Christ endorses self-love at least eight times in the Gospels, and he prudently escapes the violent crowd when his time had not yet come.[36] He is *open* to surrendering himself and his legitimate interests, but only under the proper circumstances. Jesus is premodern, but many modern feminists — for example, Andolsen and Isasi-Diaz — have made similar points about the limits of self-sacrifice. As noted above, I myself have argued that moral self-immolation must be properly motivated (kindness rather than masochism), properly structured (voluntary rather than coerced, on both ends), and properly effective (productive rather than profligate).[37] I have also contended that "agapic love is antithetical to neither erotic desire nor reasoned justice for oneself or one's friends."[38] Am I not a classical modern-day agapist (at least in theory)?

More on Søren Kierkegaard on Love and Justice

Before concluding this part of the chapter, let me say more about Søren Kierkegaard and Wolterstorff's appraisal of him. Wolterstorff notes that, unlike Nygren, Kierkegaard admitted the legitimacy of self-love,[39] but Wolterstorff

---

33. Outka, *Agape*, p. 301.

34. Cf. Wolterstorff, *Justice in Love*, p. 57.

35. Wolterstorff, *Justice in Love*, p. 95.

36. I discuss Jesus and self-love at some length in *Love Disconsoled: Meditations on Christian Charity* (Cambridge: Cambridge University Press, 1999), esp. chaps. 1 and 3.

37. Jackson, *The Priority of Love*, pp. 21-27.

38. Jackson, *Love Disconsoled*, p. 55.

39. Wolterstorff, *Justice in Love*, p. 25.

leaves us with the impression that Kierkegaard shared Nygren's blanket rejection of *eros* and justice. To be sure, Kierkegaard was very wary of preferential affinities, such as *eros* and *philia,* and he does refer to *agape* as "true love." But he repeatedly makes it clear that romantic love and friendship are not inherently evil or somehow antithetical to *agape.* They are unstable and tend to overweening pride, thus they must be "dethroned," but they have their proper place. As he puts it in *Works of Love,*[40]

> [L]ove the beloved faithfully and tenderly, but let love for the neighbor be the sanctifying element in your union's covenant with God. Love your friend honestly and devotedly, but let love for the neighbor be what you learn from each other in your friendship's confidential relationship with God! (p. 62)

> The Christian may very well marry, may very well love his wife, especially in the way he ought to love her, may very well have a friend and love his native land; but yet in all this there must be a basic understanding between himself and God in the essentially Christian, and this is Christianity. (p. 145)

"Christianity through marriage has made erotic love [*Elskov*] a matter of conscience" (p. 139), Kierkegaard maintains, and clearly he allows a more positive role for preferential desire than does Nygren.

And what about justice? Wolterstorff rightly observes that Kierkegaard recommends transcending the adversarial calculations of justice. According to Kierkegaard, "justice pleads the cause of its own, divides and assigns, determines what each can lawfully call his own, judges and punishes if anyone refuses to make any distinction between *mine* and *yours*" (p. 265). In contrast, "take away entirely the distinction 'mine' from the distinction '*mine* and *yours.*' What, then, do we have? Then we have the self-sacrificing, the self-denying-in-all-things, the true love" (pp. 267-68). Justice does "shudder" before the revolution of love (p. 266). It is worth underscoring, nonetheless, that it is the "mine" that is removed from the equation, not the "yours." The Kierkegaardian agapist ignores justice *for himself,* but this might be compatible with championing justice for others. There is more room for this reading than Wolterstorff seems to think, but there is no escaping that the author of *Works of Love* does not leave it at that.

40. References in the following text are to this work.

Kierkegaard goes so far as to aver that "Christianity does not want to make changes in externals; neither does it want to abolish drives or inclination — it wants only to make infinity's change in the inner being." This sentiment does indeed make social justice impossible, and I wish he hadn't said it. It is not Kierkegaard at his best. This familiar Lutheran dualism is actually a betrayal of his account of "spirit" and "the self" given in *The Sickness unto Death*. In that work, any existence that accents one pole of selfhood to the neglect of the other — soul over body, freedom over necessity, infinitude over finitude — is a form of "despair" (i.e., sin). Yet the contrast between "internals" and "externals" in the quote from *Works of Love* reflects precisely this kind of "disrelationship." To think that one can change "the inner being" and leave "externals" alone is to treat the person as if she were an angel: disembodied and atemporal. It is to fail to synthesize infinity with finitude. Genuine social justice is inconceivable on such a dualistic basis.

To the extent that Kierkegaard obscures the rights and wrongs of justice, Wolterstorff has a valid case against him. Toward the end of his brief life, however, Kierkegaard himself appears to have seen the light: hence his "Attack on Christendom" (1854-1855). Reportedly, he would sit out in front of a church on Sunday and encourage people *not* to go in. This is not quite Jesus driving out the money changers, but even Kierkegaard could not finally leave externals alone. Even the man Wolterstorff considers the father of modern agapism eventually wanted public reformation, as well as private faith, hope, and love.

There is no denying Nicholas Wolterstorff's dialectical skill and historical sophistication. He is a consummate philosopher, deeply versed in and creatively contributing to Christian theory and practice. This makes it all the more surprising that he conjures the bugbear of "classical modern-day agapism." One can only speculate on why he takes this tack. The most charitable answer I can offer is that he is so concerned to vindicate justice, as well as to vanquish inappropriate paternalism, that he overcompensates. Professor Wolterstorff's depiction of justice is often compelling, but his characterization of "modern agapism" slips into parody. Some moderns who extol charity virtually equate it with justice (Simone Weil and Joseph Fletcher); at least one puts it directly at odds with justice (Anders Nygren); at least one sees it as entirely unrelated to justice (Søren Kierkegaard); and still others view it as distinct from but symbiotic with justice (Karl Barth, Hans Urs von Balthasar, Martin Luther King Jr., Paul Ramsey, and Gene Outka). So who are the true "modern agapists"?

Of course, one can *stipulate* that "modern agapism" is ignorant of or antithetical to justice. But this is far too rarefied a description. It is, as I say, to construct a gossamer man. If a "straw man" is less morally substantive than one's actual interlocutors, a "gossamer man" is painted as hypermoral, absurdly oblivious to the real world and its rights and wrongs. Christlike love, in contrast, gives all neighbors their just due, but it also goes "the extra mile" freely to bestow goodness on those who can benefit from it. *Pace* Nygren, there should be no conflating Christ's life and teaching with a blithe self-destructiveness or an angelic irresponsibility that is inconsiderate of other virtues, including justice. *Pace* Wolterstorff, this truth has not been lost on all (or even most) modern-day agapists.

III. More on *Agape* and Justice/Rights (Hauerwas)

If Nicholas Wolterstorff is currently the leading Christian defender of the liberal language of "justice" and "rights," Alasdair MacIntyre and Stanley Hauerwas are the chief Christian critics. MacIntyre's famous dismissal of human rights — "there are no such rights, and belief in them is one with belief in witches and in unicorns"[41] — still rustles academic dovecotes. But no Christian theologian today has been harder on "rights" talk than Hauerwas, so I will concentrate on him. In chapter 2 of *After Christendom?*, entitled "The Politics of Justice," he contends "that the current emphasis on justice and rights as the primary norms guiding the social witness of Christians is in fact a mistake."[42] A political agapist might very well resonate with this demotion of justice, noting the significance of the word "primary." The problem, however, is that the subtitle of Hauerwas's essay is: "Why Justice Is a Bad Idea for Christians." Not being a primary norm is not the same as being a bad idea. The gloves are even more off when Hauerwas writes, with a nod to Will Campbell, "that appeals to justice are often attempts to subvert our faith in Jesus by confusing Christianity with some variety of humanism."[43] (One now sees Wolterstorff smiling in the wings and saying, "I told you so!") More nuanced is Hauerwas's discussion of "the right to life" in an essay entitled "Memory, Community, and the Reasons for Living: Reflections on Suicide and Euthanasia" (1976). There he allows:

> The right-to-life language has understandably been prominent among Christians today in relation to the abortion problem, but it is important

41. Alasdair MacIntyre, *After Virtue* (Notre Dame: University of Notre Dame Press, 1981), p. 67.

42. Stanley Hauerwas, *After Christendom?* (Nashville: Abingdon, 1991), p. 46.

43. Stanley Hauerwas and Romand Coles, *Christianity, Democracy, and the Radical Ordinary* (Eugene, Ore.: Cascade Books, 2008), p. 88.

to recognize that it is not the language offered by our primary convictions. If Christians use this language, they must keep in mind that they do so only as a political device since only such language offers them a way into the political discourse on this issue. We should nonetheless recognize that right-to-life talk is a foreign language for us, and that the seeming necessity of our using it is a sign of the tension we are now in with our surrounding culture.

. . . [R]ights language suggests we should be able to determine our lives, when our life will end, and what we shall do with it. But it is fundamental to the Christian manner that our lives are formed in terms not of what we will do with them, but of what God will do with our lives, both in our living and in our dying.[44]

Four broadly Hauerwasian theses are:

(1) that "rights" talk is an alien language to Christian faith and tradition
(2) that "rights" talk valorizes autonomy, whereas Christianity extols theonomy
(3) that "rights" talk is intrinsically adversarial, whereas Christianity emphasizes forgiveness and cooperation
(4) that "rights" talk is inherently individualistic, whereas Christianity is communitarian (i.e., ecclesial) in focus

These claims have some prima facie force, but in the end they are too simple, historically and theologically. Regarding (1), Brian Tierney's work has shown that the language of "rights" was not simply a secular, Enlightenment invention but rather grew out of a long tradition of canon law.[45] Regarding (2), "rights" talk has often emerged from a religious desire to protect freedom of conscience from state intrusion or church coercion — that is, such talk affirmed forms of political and ecclesial autonomy *in the name of theonomy and obedience to God.* Regarding (3), Samuel Pufendorf and others plausibly argue that it is precisely due to humanity's intrinsic sociality that rights and the social contract get off the ground. Regarding (4), to the extent that rights typically entail corresponding duties, they imply social obligations beyond mere personal interest.

---

44. *The Hauerwas Reader,* ed. John Berkman and Michael Cartwright (Durham, N.C.: Duke University Press, 2001), p. 587.
45. Brian Tierney, *The Idea of Natural Rights* (Atlanta: Scholars Press, 1997).

To be sure, *some* versions of rights theory are non-Christian or anti-Christian — for example, Thomas Hobbes's — but the mistake is to think that the entire mode of discourse is religious apostasy or mere political expediency. It is, in many cases, an effort to translate Christian convictions into practical actions for the sake of the neighbor. The language of "virtue" that Hauerwas favors can also have its place, but it is wrong to assume that "virtue" talk and "rights" talk are necessarily in tension. Think of Martin Luther King Jr., who was able to speak both the liberal democratic language of "rights/justice" and the prophetic biblical language of "faith, hope, and love." Would that we were all so bilingual! "I just want to do God's will," King often declared,[46] making it clear that his identity as civil rights activist or Vietnam War protestor was second to his "commitment to the ministry of Jesus Christ."[47] Even so, he refused all sectarian divisions between the two.[48]

Hauerwas makes crystal clear his admiration for King:

> King believed that Christians should be socially active. So do I. The crucial question is "how?" King, as far as I am concerned, is a model of such activism for Christians, since he refused to hide his Christian convictions in the name of "pluralism." He fought for his people's "rights," he fought for freedom and equality, but he never failed to remind those for whom he fought, as well as those against whom he fought, that the fight was finally about sin and salvation. That is why King is not just the hero of the American civil religion, he is a saint of the church.[49]

One wonders why Hauerwas puts "rights" in scare quotes, since it suggests that King fought for an illusion, but more exasperating still is Hauerwas's characteristic overstatement on King's liberalism. Again, this time in back-to-back sentences, Hauerwas goes from seeing an idea as not primary to seeing it as wrong or unreal: "King's 'liberalism' was always subservient to his embeddedness in the black Church and the memory of his people that that church embodies. King could confidently appeal to liberal sentiments because he was a black

---

46. See, for instance, Martin Luther King Jr., "I See the Promised Land" (1968), in *I Have a Dream,* ed. James Melvin Washington (New York: HarperCollins, 1992), p. 203.

47. Martin Luther King Jr., "A Time to Break Silence" (1967), in *I Have a Dream,* p. 139.

48. See my "Martin Luther King, Jr., on Justice, Law, and Human Nature," in *The Teachings of Modern Christianity on Law, Politics, and Human Nature,* vol. 1, ed. John Witte and Frank Alexander (New York: Columbia University Press, 2005); the conclusion to this volume.

49. Stanley Hauerwas, *Wilderness Wanderings* (Boulder, Colo.: Westview Press, 1997), p. 232.

Baptist preacher who would never be a liberal."[50] Note once more the use of scare quotes. Because *he* cannot fathom how a prophetic Christian might also be a sincere liberal democrat, Hauerwas implies that King was either a trimmer or downright dishonest in his public speeches. King, in contrast, strove to be true to both "the sacred heritage of our nation and the eternal will of God."[51] Even Friedrich Nietzsche, the supreme critic of Christianity, recognized: "The poison of the doctrine of 'equal rights for all' — it was Christianity that spread it most fundamentally."[52]

Christianity and Democracy

In *Christianity, Democracy, and the Radical Ordinary,* Romand Coles (together with Jean Vanier, Ella Baker, Bob Moses, and others) would do for Stanley Hauerwas what Regina Olsen did for Søren Kierkegaard and what the people of Louisville did for Thomas Merton: teach him "a second immediacy" in which he "gets back" the messy ordinary world, transfigured and transfiguring. (If I may say, Richard Rorty [RIP], together with Jeffrey Stout, helped do the same for me.)[53] Kierkegaard learned the lesson too late to marry, but he eventually acknowledged that "had I had faith, I should have stayed with Regina." Merton remained a monk, but in him a youthful moment of self-congratulatory judgment was consummated and transcended in an instant of ecstatic solidarity with the common clay of the bluegrass.

Let me be less cryptic. As a young man, Thomas Merton found consolation in turning his back, judgmentally, on the ugliness and excess of the modern world and in entering the Abbey of Gethsemani in central Kentucky to live in cloistered community with the Trappists. In middle age, in contrast, he experienced his famous epiphany in downtown Louisville — near, as it happens, where my father owned a restaurant for many years. Walking along the busy city streets in 1958, Merton saw that the shoppers, rushing around with their packages and earthly preoccupations, bore the indelible image of

50. Hauerwas, *Wilderness Wanderings,* p. 229. When I debated Christopher Hitchens on the thesis of his book, *God Is Not Great,* he made the reverse claim: that King was really a liberal democrat and that his "Christianity" was but a popular cover.

51. Martin Luther King Jr., "Letter from a Birmingham Jail," in *I Have a Dream,* p. 98.

52. Friedrich Nietzsche, "The AntiChrist," in *The Portable Nietzsche,* ed. and trans. Walter Kauffman (New York: Viking Penguin, 1982), #43, p. 619.

53. I am neither married nor a monastic, but I finally saw my way clear to dedicate my first book to *both* Paul Ramsey *and* Richard Rorty. I ceased, that is, to try to slay either father.

God. In Merton's words, "In Louisville, at the corner of Fourth and Walnut, in the center of the shopping district, I was suddenly overwhelmed with the realization that I loved all those people, that they were mine and I theirs, that we could not be alien to one another even though we were total strangers. It was like waking from a dream of separateness, of spurious self-isolation in a special world, the world of renunciation and supposed holiness."[54] The pedestrian *demos* too were Merton's neighbors, sinful yet potentially redeemed like himself. Here was the defining moment of Merton's later life, his "identifying with the people as a whole," his refusal to see his own story or community as hermetically sealed. Merton's remarkable patience and empathy led to *Conjectures of a Guilty Bystander* and eventually to *The Asian Journal,* thus it included not just his fellow Americans but finally the whole world. That is true *Christian* universalism, not Enlightenment hyper-rationalism or some other liberal apostasy. It is this sort of epiphany that ought to move all Christians to see that they "have a stake" in democracy,[55] as well as in other religious faiths. (Louisville's Fourth and Walnut is now Fourth and Muhammad Ali, by the way, and my father's former restaurant is an office building: progress and regress?) It is this sort of epiphany that Coles et al. are offering to Hauerwas, and to us. This is a rare gift.

In *Christianity, Democracy, and the Radical Ordinary,* Stanley Hauerwas (together with Martin Luther King Jr., John Howard Yoder, Rowan Williams, and others) would do for Romand Coles what George Herbert did for Simone Weil and what Sufism did for John Coltrane: teach him how to wait for and worship God while not waiting for or worshiping humanity or history. Reading Herbert's poem "Love," Weil felt that Christ himself came down and took possession of her, and she subsequently gave up her Marxist convictions and practices. She did not cease to be an activist for the marginal and afflicted — in fact, she worked for the Free French during World War II and ended up starving herself to death in 1943 in solidarity with the victims of Nazism — but she became a Stoic Christian rather than a postmodern trickster. Coltrane, for his part, was raised in the AME Zion Church, but his 1957 "spiritual awakening" was prompted by his attention being drawn, through Islam, to the divine source of all things. He then gave up heroin[56] and started composing his best music, first to honor God but also "to make others happy through music," as

---

54. Thomas Merton, *Conjectures of a Guilty Bystander* (New York: Doubleday, 1965), p. 156.

55. Cf. Hauerwas and Coles, *Christianity, Democracy, and the Radical Ordinary,* p. 11.

56. I am not implying that Coles is hooked on dope, but I do think that, for all his eloquence, his prose labors at times under the narcotic spell of Derridian diction.

he put it — producing seven years later his undisputed masterpiece, "A Love Supreme." To direct his friend Romand, and us, to the supreme Love behind all inferior ones is Hauerwas's considerable benefaction.

Let me get more specific.

The Ordinary World

Perhaps unexpectedly, Coles makes his point about democratic solidarity with the radical ordinary most forcefully in his discussion of Rowan Williams on Jesus Christ. Coles writes:

> Williams renders each of the Gospels in a way that brings to life how Christ's trial, or *experimentum cruces,* undoes or erodes our confidence in, sense of, and most especially our yearning for an inside (of self, of church, of tradition, of group) that would transcend edge-dwelling; an inside where things are assured, unquestionable, pure, where the distinctions between one's "own" and others are unequivocal, where there is assurance of being right, true, good — in contrast to *them.*[57]

The linking of the cross of Christ with an inclusive solidarity that *distances* church and *relativizes* tradition is a key reason, I believe, why Hauerwas feels "haunted" by Coles and his fellow democrats . . . *and Hauerwas himself appreciates this.* (I am not saying anything that Hauerwas does not already know on some level.) In one of his best lines in the book, Hauerwas acknowledges: "I am haunted by Vanier because my strident polemics on behalf of the church seem so hollow when juxtaposed against the confident, joyful work L'Arche represents."[58] How rare is the ethicist, Christian or otherwise, who can make that kind of admission! And what sort of essays might Hauerwas write if he were *consistently* to think of the whole world, including both biblical traditionalists and liberal individualists, as "mentally handicapped" persons living together in an ark buoyed by God? Let me be still more specific.

Hauerwas is rightly recognized as the most prophetic voice speaking to (if not admittedly in) America today. The fidelity to God and tireless scholarly labor of the man are nothing short of amazing, and I and many others owe him an immense debt. But the familiar Hauerwasian corpus also highlights

---

57. Hauerwas and Coles, *Christianity, Democracy, and the Radical Ordinary,* p. 177.
58. Hauerwas and Coles, *Christianity, Democracy, and the Radical Ordinary,* p. 105.

the *limits* of the prophetic when it is "methodist." The main lesson I draw from *Christianity, Democracy, and the Radical Ordinary,* in fact, is that both the prophetic and the democratic must be fulfilled in the messianic. The advent candles of hope, joy, peace, and love are crucial, but the Christ candle of the Word made flesh *in and for* the world unites and culminates all four of the other lights (including nonviolence). Reading Hauerwas B.C. (before Coles), I frequently felt like I was being inundated by John the Baptist's message of repentant asceticism escaping the sinful world, rather than being blessed by Jesus' good news from God and for the needy neighbor. (The Messiah allowed himself to be baptized, even as he permitted his feet to be washed, but the Spirit that descended upon him made him leave John behind.) Hauerwas talks more positively about "democracy" and "justice" in the present text than in any other I know, but previously his favorite tropes included sharp contrasts between "the world" and "the church," and "our (Christian) story" and "their (pagan) story." Dare I say, echoing Nietzsche, that Hauerwas B.C. at times replaced the faith *of* Jesus that *challenged* the early church with a faith *in* Jesus that *valorized* the traditional church? After his listening to Coles and Vanier, in contrast, we get a kinder, "gentler" Hauerwas, in spite of himself. Or, rather, the deeper and more Christlike voice that was there all along can now be heard, because Coles and Vanier mute the ecclesial static.

In a remarkable self-critique, Hauerwas writes, "I do not want to learn to be gentle. I want to be a warrior on behalf of Vanier, doing battle against the politics that threaten to destroy his gentle communities,"[59] such as L'Arche. But then Hauerwas A.D. (after democracy) emerges, putatively *malgré lui.* Quoting Vanier, he affirms: "What we must realize is that 'this wound [of our loneliness] is inherent in the human condition and that what we have to do is walk with it instead of fleeing from it. We cannot accept it until we discover that we are loved by God just as we are, and that the Holy Spirit, in a mysterious way, is living at the center of the wound.'"[60] In previous volumes, Hauerwas often spoke of the fear of death and anxiety over our finitude as though they were *their* (i.e., the pagans') problems and stood opposed to *our* (i.e., the Christians') joy. But Coles points out, as does Vanier in effect, that the relevant fear and anxiety do not come simply from "outside" the church — from liberalism or Constantinianism or the external world — they are part of the universal human condition. (Cf. Mother Teresa in *Come Be My Light.*) *Mirabile dictu,* Coles and Vanier have managed to democratize the Holy Spirit for Hauerwas, or,

59. Hauerwas and Coles, *Christianity, Democracy, and the Radical Ordinary,* p. 197.
60. Hauerwas and Coles, *Christianity, Democracy, and the Radical Ordinary,* p. 197.

rather, the Holy Spirit has revealed himself in and through the ordinary things of this world, including Coles and Vanier and their good works.

So where does this leave Christians? A Christian is to be in the world but not of it, and the ruling primacy of faith, hope, and love over such traditional "democratic" values as liberty and equality is critical for believers. Yet a Christian must be *in* the world, must love God and the neighbor in and through (and sometimes around) some particular social context. So there is no escaping the burden of articulating and defending those political and economic arrangements deemed most expressive of, or at least compatible with, the holy will of God. There neither can be nor should be a segregation of theological virtues from "worldly" political judgments, any more than there can be or should be a separation of theologians from the unchurched polis. Indeed, the incarnation itself is for the interstices. As Coles observes, following Williams, "the edge between the church and nonbelievers has an essentially ambiguous character," and "the flesh of Jesus extends beyond the committed and is *realized* rather than *corrupted* in so doing."[61]

Nonviolence

Hauerwas shares King's commitment to nonviolence, but this principle too can use some unpacking. Paul Ramsey often challenged Hauerwas to explain why, in light of Matthew 5:39's "Do not resist an evildoer," he did not embrace pure nonresistance, rather than nonviolent resistance, to injustice. Hauerwas's clearest (and least sectarian) response came in his epilogue to Ramsey's *Speak Up for Just War or Pacifism,* entitled "On Being a Church Capable of Addressing a World at War." There Hauerwas writes:

> I find Ramsey's insistence that I make clear my understanding of the relation of nonviolent or passive resistance to nonresistance less than urgent. I do so first because I do not believe that Ramsey's characterization of Jesus' teaching and life as one of absolute "nonresistance" is correct. Jesus' cross was a confrontation with powers that was meant to defeat those forces that hold us to the presuppositions of the old age. He did not restrain from fighting them — and that includes their embodiment in Rome — but rather refused to fight them on their own terms.[62]

61. Hauerwas and Coles, *Christianity, Democracy, and the Radical Ordinary,* p. 190.
62. Paul Ramsey, *Speak Up for Just War or Pacifism* (University Park and London:

This is a palpable refusal to reduce nonviolence to nonresistance to evil, and it makes clear that, for Hauerwas, Christian faith is not oblivious to social (in-)justice and the historical consequences of action and inaction. Admittedly, he declares elsewhere that Christians are "no longer driven by the assumption that we must be in control of history, that it is up to us to make things come out right."[63] This sentiment can seem to flirt with nonresistance and is hard to reconcile with the passage quoted above it. But I believe it is charitably read as a Pauline nod toward a realized eschatology in Christ, who has already decisively redeemed history (see Rom. 8:35-38 and Col. 2:15; see also 1 Pet. 3:17-22). Jesus Christ has eternally vanquished the principalities and powers, but, paradoxically, mopping up exercises are still needed in time. As Hauerwas says, "how" to resist evil is still the issue.[64]

A Christian pacifist who is more consistently skeptical of "outcomes," of "making history turn out right," is Robert W. Brimlow. In *What about Hitler?* he writes: "It is not clear to me that God has laid responsibility on us for the course that history will take."[65] But if not us, who? Jesus? Jesus alone? Am I not called to be perfect as God is perfect (Matt. 5:48), to imitate Jesus, and to take "responsibility" with him for the neighbor? The historical Jesus is not the sole historical actor. To think otherwise is to replace, completely, the faith *of* Christ with faith *in* Christ.[66] This leaves us with a moral dandyism that lets the world go to hell.

Thanks to King, Hauerwas, and John Howard Yoder, every third day I feel that the Christian "how" of resistance should be eucharistic pacifism. The other two days, however, I believe that faith, hope, and love themselves move some of us to take up the sword to defend the innocent from unjust attack.[67] Wars of conquest or conversion are manifestly incompatible with the cross of Christ, but even King depended on police forces to ensure the safety of demonstrators and the rule of law. Nonviolence and just war thinking are

---

Pennsylvania State University Press, 1988), p. 177. This epilogue is included in *The Hauerwas Reader* as chapter 21.

63. Stanley Hauerwas, *The Peaceable Kingdom* (Notre Dame: University of Notre Dame Press, 1983), p. 87.

64. Later in *The Peaceable Kingdom,* Hauerwas writes: "Those who are violent, who are also our neighbors, must be resisted, but resisted on our own terms, because not to resist is to abandon them to sin and injustice" (p. 106).

65. Robert W. Brimlow, *What about Hitler? Wrestling with Jesus's Call to Nonviolence in an Evil World* (Grand Rapids: Brazos, 2006), p. 124.

66. See Nietzsche, "The AntiChrist," esp. #39-#42, pp. 612-18.

67. See *The Priority of Love,* chap. 3.

both defensible forms of Christian conscience, I believe, and to illustrate a conscientious wrestling with both, let me turn now to Dietrich Bonhoeffer. Bonhoeffer is also a "truthful witness" for Hauerwas,[68] and Bonhoeffer never became a standard just war theorist. He judged his eventual decision to participate in the plot to assassinate Hitler to be sinful yet necessary, but he did make a leap from nonlethal to lethal forms of resistance to evil. In the midst of the Nazi Holocaust, cruciform obedience to God became selectively violent.

IV. The Case of Dietrich Bonhoeffer

Bonhoeffer's life and works are a case study in how to overcome both acquiescence in secularity and flight into sectarianism. In a notorious piece from 1933 entitled "The Church and the Jewish Question," he cleaves to a Lutheran "two kingdoms" view of the church and the state. Adolf Hitler has been named chancellor, and the Nazis' violent anti-Semitism is already manifest; still Bonhoeffer writes:

> Without doubt one of the historical problems that must be dealt with by our state is the Jewish question, and without doubt the state is entitled to strike new paths in doing so. . . . But the true church of Christ, which lives by the gospel alone and knows the nature of state actions, will never interfere in the functioning of the state in this way, by criticizing its history-making actions from the standpoint of any sort of, say, humanitarian ideal. The church knows about the essential necessity for the use of force in this world, and it knows about the "moral" injustice that is necessarily involved in the use of force in certain concrete state actions. The church cannot primarily take direct political action, since it does not presume to know how things should go historically. Even on the Jewish question today, the church cannot contradict the state directly and demand that it take any particular different course of action.[69]

Bonhoeffer acknowledges that the church might question the state and that an individual Christian might resist a secular government if it profoundly violates

68. See especially Stanley Hauerwas, *Performing the Faith: Bonhoeffer and the Practice of Nonviolence* (Grand Rapids: Brazos, 2004).

69. Dietrich Bonhoeffer, "The Church and the Jewish Question," in *Dietrich Bonhoeffer Works,* vol. 12, ed. Larry L. Rasmussen, trans. Isabel Best and David Higgins (Minneapolis: Fortress, 2009), p. 363.

its God-given mandate to preserve law and order, but he grants (1) that there is "a Jewish problem" and (2) that the Nazi state can handle it any way it sees fit, without objection from the church as such. In retrospect, such concessions are chilling. Four years later, however, Bonhoeffer changes his tune.

In the wake of the 1935 Nuremburg Laws stripping Jews of citizenship rights, yet prior to 1938's *Kristallnacht,* Bonhoeffer composes the lectures to his seminary students at Finkenwalde that are published as *The Cost of Discipleship* (1937). Here the language of acceptance and accommodation is replaced by that of distancing and escape:

> Like God himself, the Holy One, the people of his sanctuary are also sep-
> arated from all things profane and from sin. For God has made them the
> people of his covenant, choosing them for himself, making atonement for
> them and purifying them in his sanctuary. Now the sanctuary is the tem-
> ple, and the temple is the Body of Christ. . . . that Body has been separated
> from the world and from sin, and made the peculiar possession of God
> and his sanctuary in the world. God dwells in it with the Holy Spirit.[70]

As one of the courageous founders of the Confessing Church in Germany and an architect of its early opposition to Nazism, Bonhoeffer understandably now characterizes the body of Christ as pure and separate, the world as sinful and engulfing. Threatened by escalating fascist tyranny and its totalizing idolatry, he only naturally equates sanctification with "the Christian's separation from the world until the second coming of Christ."[71] He even goes so far as to aver that "like a sealed train traveling through foreign territory, the Church goes on its way through the world."[72] But this sublime attitude could not survive the trials of history and the grace of God in Christ.

In 1940, the Confessing seminary at Finkenwalde (a kind of "Protestant monastery") was shut down by the Gestapo, Bonhoeffer was forbidden to speak in public or to publish, he met Colonel Oster of the *Abwehr,* and he began more actively to plot against Hitler. Only then did Bonhoeffer move to overcome his Christian separatism; only then did he finally put behind him the *Weltschmerz* and hint of *ressentiment* evident in his earlier writings. (Christ's body *on the cross* is anything but a sanctuary from the profane, so how can his

---

70. Dietrich Bonhoeffer, *The Cost of Discipleship* (New York: Simon and Schuster, 1995), p. 273.

71. Bonhoeffer, *The Cost of Discipleship,* p. 278.

72. Bonhoeffer, *The Cost of Discipleship,* p. 278.

body the church be safe and apart?) With *Ethics* (composed 1940-1943) and *Letters and Papers from Prison* (composed 1943-1945), Bonhoeffer abandoned his tendency to limit the Holy Spirit to the church and began to formulate his "religionless Christianity." Such Christianity rejects the claim of moral purity and the quest for institutional aloofness in favor of contrite service to all others in the messy here and now.

In "After Ten Years" (1943) in *Letters and Papers*, Bonhoeffer reflects on a decade of Nazism and his own delusion: "Worse still [than the failure of rationalism] is the total collapse of moral fanaticism. The fanatic imagines that his moral purity will prove a match for the power of evil, but like a bull he goes for the red rag instead of the man who carries it, grows weary and succumbs. He becomes entangled with non-essentials and falls into the trap set by the superior ingenuity of his adversary."[73] Later in *Letters and Papers*, we read:

> [Religionless Christians are] those who are called forth, not regarding ourselves from a religious point of view as specially favored, but rather as belonging wholly to the world.[74]

> The church is the church only when it exists for others. . . . The church must share in the secular problems of ordinary human life, not dominating but helping and serving. It must tell men of every calling what it means to live in Christ, to exist for others.[75]

> May God give [faith] to us daily. And I do not mean the faith which flees the world, but the one that endures the world and which loves and remains true to the world in spite of all the suffering which it contains for us. . . . I fear that Christians who stand with only one leg upon earth also stand with only one leg in heaven (12 August 1943).[76]

In a similar vein, Bonhoeffer declares in *Ethics*: "While we are distinguishing the pious from the ungodly, the good from the wicked, the noble from the mean, God makes no distinction at all in His love for the real man. He does

73. Dietrich Bonhoeffer, *Letters and Papers from Prison*, ed. Eberhard Bethge, trans. Reginald H. Fuller (New York: Macmillan, 1953), p. 17.

74. Bonhoeffer, *Letters and Papers from Prison*, ed. Eberhard Bethge, enlarged ed. (New York: Macmillan, 1971), pp. 280-81. This may be an artifact of translation, but I would flag the subtle difference between being "called *forth*" and being "called *out*."

75. Bonhoeffer, *Letters and Papers*, enlarged ed., pp. 382-83.

76. Bonhoeffer, *Letters and Papers*, enlarged ed., p. 415.

not permit us to classify men and the world according to our own standards and to set ourselves up as judges over them."[77]

With his determination to kill Hitler, Bonhoeffer comes full circle from nonresistance, to nonviolent resistance, to a willingness to use lethal force. Far from a triumphalist, however, he now offers a striking "Confession of Guilt" for the Protestant churches and defines the Christian church itself as "the place where [the] recognition of guilt becomes real."[78] He explicitly rejects as unfaithful to Christ *both* a "radicalism" that sees only "the ultimate" and hates time *and* a "compromise" that sees only "the penultimate" and hates eternity.[79] Any opposing of two "spheres," the sacred and the profane, as though they are static and independent, is a denial of the reality of the Son. "There are . . . not two spheres, but only the one sphere of the realization of Christ, in which the reality of God and the reality of the world are united."[80] Rather than a full break with *Discipleship,* one sees in these later passages a maturation of Bonhoeffer's views, a deepening empathy with "the world" and a more realistic take on "the church." Still, it is not too much to say that Bonhoeffer reconceived his idea of sanctification. It continued to mean Christian growth in holiness, but now it became an engaged leavening of the world rather than a proud escape from it — an open book (a.k.a. the gospel) rather than a sealed train. For the later Bonhoeffer, the point is not to set the natural against the supernatural, the secular against the ecclesial, or to equate one with the other, but instead to witness to their being reconciled in Christ. Christian witness eschews ideological principles cut off from life in God, and it takes special care not to reduce agapic love to an "abstract concept."[81] Such witness is also decisively universal: "all men are taken up, enclosed and borne within the body of Christ," and the church "is concerned . . . with the eternal salvation of the whole world."[82] Saint Augustine and much of the Christian

---

77. Dietrich Bonhoeffer, *Ethics* (New York: Simon and Schuster, 1955), p. 73.

78. Bonhoeffer, *Ethics,* p. 111.

79. Bonhoeffer, *Ethics,* pp. 126-32.

80. Bonhoeffer, *Ethics,* p. 195.

81. Bonhoeffer, *Ethics,* p. 54; and see p. 227.

82. Bonhoeffer, *Ethics,* pp. 203 and 208. More recently, John Howard Yoder has employed the "church/world" distinction to bracing effect, but he strikes the proper cautionary note:

> Frequently the faithfulness of the church has been put to the test the moment believers were asked to follow the path of costly conscientious objection in the face of the world's opposition. Yet *we should not overdramatize the normal expression of our mission in and through society.* The church's calling is to be the conscience and the servant within

tradition notwithstanding, Bonhoeffer tolerates no appeal to two fixed classes of persons, the elect and the damned, for "Jesus Christ became man and died on the cross for the sins of all men."[83]

---

human society. The church must be sufficiently experienced to be able to discern when and where and how God is using the Powers, whether this be thanks to the faithful testimony of the church or in spite of its infidelity. Either way, *we are called to contribute to the creation of structures more worthy of human society.* But the church will also need to be sufficiently familiar with the manifest ways in which God has acted to reconcile and call together a people for himself, so as not to fall prey to the Sadducean or "German Christian" temptation to read off the surface of history a simple declaration of God's will. *God is working in the world and it is the task of the church to know how he is working.*

See Yoder, *The Politics of Jesus,* 2nd ed. (Grand Rapids and Cambridge: Eerdmans, 1994), pp. 154-55, emphases added. The phrases "in and through society" and "in the world" help mitigate any worrisome dualism, even as the call "to contribute to the creation of structures more worthy of human society" guards against sectarian withdrawal. As Yoder observes, the church "is itself a structure and a power in society" (p. 158); moreover, "the saving work of Christ . . . reaches even beyond the realm of the church" (p. 195).

83. Bonhoeffer, *Ethics,* p. 309. Augustine's distinction between "vessels of wrath" and "vessels of mercy" presupposes that Christ's atonement is forever limited to the latter.

PART III

Love, Law, and Modern Moral Issues

CHAPTER 9

Euthanasia and Capital Punishment: Christianity and the Right to Death

I. Euthanasia

In the spring of 2007, I participated in a public discussion entitled "The Morality of Euthanasia" with Margaret Pabst Battin, professor of philosophy at the University of Utah. The discussion was part of a conference at Emory entitled "Changing the Way We Die," and it had originally been planned as a formal debate. I knew Peggy Battin from a conference years before in Athens, Greece, however, and we both agreed that the topic would be better served by relaxed conversation than by impersonal polemics — something more like Socratic dialogue than legal briefs. We knew we disagreed on the permissibility of active euthanasia and physician-assisted suicide (PAS), so we decided to present a "give-and-take" around five sets of related propositions, which I reproduce below.

I began my remarks by telling a story from when I chaired the Ethics Committee of the Northern California Presbyterian Homes (NCPH), a geriatric graduated-care facility based in San Francisco. Early in 1991, it came to the attention of NCPH personnel that many of the residents had joined the Hemlock Society, a group that supports the positive "right to die" and advocates legalizing PAS. Several administrators, physicians, nurses, and staff members were alarmed by this development, so they asked the Ethics Committee to investigate. The committee decided, in turn, to distribute a questionnaire, asking the residents to relate their primary concerns around the end of life. Not surprisingly, three main fears emerged:

(1) the fear of pointless and protracted pain, of being hooked up to a machine and not being able to get off

   (2) the fear of being an undue burden, of bankrupting one's family, both financially and emotionally

   (3) the fear of loss of mobility and control, of losing that elusive yet crucial good called "dignity"

It was clear that these very understandable worries were behind the interest in the Hemlock Society, but it also seemed likely that many residents assumed that the only way to address the worries was active euthanasia, including PAS. The board and CEO of NCPH instructed the Ethics Committee, which included the corporate lawyer, to formulate a policy in response to our findings and to communicate it to all members of the NCPH family. After much discussion, the committee agreed on three major principles:

   (a) that a futile or inordinately burdensome treatment is never medically indicated and thus can be withdrawn or withheld at any time

   (b) that passive euthanasia — allowing to die — is mandated whenever a process of death is invincible, but that actively taking a resident's life is never warranted

   (c) that physicians, nurses, and staff will never abandon a resident, even when curing is not possible

I was quite impressed by the committee's work, especially since a corollary to (a) was that if nutrition and hydration were judged to be futile or inordinately burdensome, they could be discontinued. This was a very controversial stand at the time and one that I had only recently come round to, based on my experiences at NCPH. The norm was also at odds with the law of the land. Our corporate lawyer nonetheless signed off on it, I believe, because he realized that the law was under extreme pressure and was likely to be changed. But it still took courage and a commitment to the best interest of our residents to consent to the new idea.

     The committee's next step was to hold public forums at all six of the Bay Area homes affiliated with NCPH. At these forums, we explained to the residents that we had heard and affirmed the legitimacy of their fears, and that we had taken care to formulate corporate policy in light of them. We described our three main principles, emphasizing that active euthanasia was not the only or the best way to address their fears. More specifically, we stressed that active euthanasia, including PAS, is *not needed* on the basis of mercy and is *not justified* on the basis of self-determination (a.k.a. respect for autonomy). This hands-on approach seemed to strike a chord with all concerned. Although some residents continued to belong to the Hemlock Society, I was not aware of a single formal request for active killing by medical, nursing, or chaplaincy professionals during my time at NCPH (1991-1994).

For her part, Professor Battin started by pointing out that, with the progress of modern medicine, it is now often possible to keep a person alive across the lengthy course of an illness, an illness that previously would have been rapidly fatal. This course, in turn, may involve a slow downhill path bringing great mental and physical pain and suffering. In effect, in decreasing short-term mortality, we have increased long-term morbidity. I countered by repeating that no one is obliged to undertake a futile or inordinately burdensome treatment: a request to withhold or withdraw a particular "therapy" because it would be too painful or merely protract death is perfectly permissible within a policy of passive euthanasia.

Battin and I concurred that improving the way we die must not blind us to improving the way we live. My Emory colleague Corey Keyes has argued that, because the absence of illness is not constitutive of true health, any approach to health care that focuses exclusively on disease and its elimination will be inadequate. According to Keyes, and he is not alone, we ought to accent full human flourishing. More specifically, we need to combine a *pathogenic* approach that seeks to prevent or remedy disability, disease, and premature death with a *salutogenic* approach that seeks to promote "positive states of human capacities and functioning in thinking, feeling, and behavior."[1] (Keyes and others call this "the complete state" model of health.) The analogous point is that, in addition to seeking to prevent painful and protracted *death,* we ought to seek to promote meaningful and adaptive *life.* Indeed, a holistic approach to health care that supports such positive attributes as resilience, courage, patience, compassion, and hope — not to mention faith — can make some forms of disease and suffering much more bearable.

This brought us to one of the deeper issues surrounding euthanasia: the dependency of dependency. How we understand both the loss of autonomy and the presence of pain — whether we judge them ugly, shameful, too costly, unbearable, etc. — depends in large measure upon the wider social context and the availability of sympathetic care and support. I noted that if we embrace active euthanasia, we may erode or neglect our resources for fostering hope. To put it technically, active euthanasia is a pathogenic approach that cuts against salutogenic approaches like hospice. Relatedly, it is not so much that I fear that

---

1. Corey Keyes, "Promoting and Protecting Mental Health as Flourishing," *American Psychologist* 62, no. 2 (February-March 2007): 96.

legalizing PAS will lead to "abuse," as currently understood, but rather that what is recognized as abuse will change, be perverted, over time. How one *defines* "abuse" is at stake, as is whether even competent patients may make immoral or imprudent requests that are binding on health-care professionals. In Holland, for example, the original requirement that a patient be terminal as well as experiencing significant physical suffering has been dropped. Now it is sufficient that the person be in mental distress, whether or not the person is dying or even physically impaired. Presymptomatic AIDS patients and nonterminal anorexia patients have been actively euthanized. This is the problem of premature closure or the social validation of despair: not just fear of nonvoluntary and involuntary euthanasia, but of a subverting of what is judged *worthy* of voluntary choice, or at least of acceptance.

Battin appealed to self-determination and mercy as basic moral principles[2] — what I would call "personal dignity" and "other-regarding charity" — and she argued vigorously that these trump slippery slope and other consequentialist arguments against active euthanasia. I responded that even self-determination is not a self-evident and unchanging good: the value and meaning of self-determination are partially socially determined and upheld. In my judgment, there are human (and professional) values that can override or temper self-determination: the sanctity of life and the "Do no harm" rule. Battin admitted the possibility of competing principles, but she herself weighed "control" over life and death as higher than various duties of acceptance, and she suggested that not all forms of suffering are edifying. As she has said in print, "there are circumstances where the patient's right [to self-determination and mercy] overrides these scruples [a physician's scruples against active euthanasia and PAS]."[3]

This quickly brought us to the issue of the intrinsic rightness or wrongness of active euthanasia and the much larger question of the meaning of life. Battin was fully aware that, according to Christians, our lives are not our own, to be surrendered as we see fit, but a gift of God with special joys and obligations. Her point was that, in a democratic society, those who have a different view should not be compelled to surrender autonomy. For her, a legal policy of passive euthanasia was not enough, for two central reasons. First, even though it may achieve mercy, it does not respect autonomy/self-determination. Second, what actually goes on in hospitals and nursing homes

---

2. See Margaret Pabst Battin, *Ending Life: Ethics and the Way We Die* (Oxford: Oxford University Press, 2005), pp. 89 and 97.

3. Battin, *Ending Life*, p. 100.

often goes beyond allowing to die to a de facto practice of direct killing or assisted suicide.[4] What we need, she maintained, is a positive right to die. For my part, I wondered: Why insist on mercy if self-determination is so important? Is autonomy really sufficient here? And so we proceeded, trying very hard to hear one another.

For clarity and convenience, we organized our two-step into "rounds," fully aware of the pugilistic overtones of the word but determined to invoke the musical meaning instead.

ROUND ONE

BATTIN: People should be recognized as entitled to (try to) control their own lives (consistent with the Do No Harm Principle), and this includes the very ends of their lives.

JACKSON: Autonomy and informed consent are undeniably very important, yet dependency is not inhuman or shameful; moreover, the doctor or nurse or chaplain is not merely a hired gun of the patient but rather a practitioner of a craft that has internal goods that may override competent wishes.

ROUND TWO

JACKSON: Most pain is manageable with good palliative care, but, most importantly, we must not think that the only alternatives are curing or abandoning: doctors, nurses, and chaplains (all of us) must learn to care even when we can't cure. This is the credo of hospice and ought to be that of hospitals.

BATTIN: Do doctors ever have an *obligation* to help patients end their lives? Usually not, but sometimes yes, and when they do they often bring this obligation on themselves. (Plus a note about why doctors can't understand this problem.)

ROUND THREE

JACKSON: There is a great potential for a conflict of interest among medical experts, who may be tempted to get rid of their "failures" with "killing compassion," especially with managed care's inducements to reduce expenditures.

BATTIN: There's no evidence of abuse of vulnerable people where eutha-

4. Battin, *Ending Life*, pp. 101-2. See also Margaret Pabst Battin, *The Least Worst Death* (Oxford: Oxford University Press, 1994), pp. 93-94.

nasia or physician-assisted suicide is legal and well studied, namely, the Netherlands and Oregon.

ROUND FOUR

BATTIN: "Suicide isn't what God wants" — why this claim doesn't work.

JACKSON: A right to die does not equal a right to be killed by another, especially a health-care professional. (Pointless suffering is indeed an evil, but we must not lose hope over the possibility of learning from and in affliction; the neglected danger here is of premature closure, of despairing too soon over life/love, and thus of subverting the common good.)

ROUND FIVE

JACKSON: End results are not the only morally significant factors: motives and dispositions matter — not just for doctors/nurses/chaplains but also for patients — and one cannot directly intend the death of an innocent without brutalizing one's character (cf. double effect).

BATTIN: Helping someone die can be an act of highest moral character. This is clear in terminal illness, but what about the claim that assistance in suicide should be available for people in extreme old age, not just for people who are terminally ill? — why this is the next issue on the horizon.

Throughout it all, I enjoyed the lively exchanges with Peggy. Neither one of us convinced the other that day, but over drinks afterward we both judged that the audience had been given a nuanced account of the issue.

Fast-forward six months. In the fall of 2008, my eighty-seven-year-old father's health began to decline: "cascading systemic failures," as the doctors called it. After a month and a half in hospital, undergoing several more-or-less-painful treatments, Dad wanted no more attempted cures, so we transferred him to hospice care. Toward the end, he was in such pain, struggling to breathe, that the hospice physician agreed to give him increasing doses of morphine every few hours. Seeing Dad slowly expire was like watching a man drowning. It took the morphine some ten hours to do its job, and it was clear to my brother and I that the procedure pressed double effect to the breaking point. The nurse continued to inject the drug long after Dad was deeply unconscious and no longer suffering, ever more repressing his cardiopulmonary function. On December 13, 2008, we intentionally ushered my father into death, and I was very grateful for the ability to do so.

These events led me the next day to e-mail Peggy Battin, with whom I had not spoken since the Emory conference in 2007. I related the details of my father's passing and noted that, although I had not fully migrated to her position on euthanasia, I had a new appreciation of its essential humaneness. I was still unprepared to make active euthanasia legal, but I certainly had a greater appreciation for the murky moral and medical boundaries of "indirect killing" and "double effect." Astonishingly, Peggy wrote back commenting on "an awful twist of fate." Just a month earlier, on November 14, 2008, her husband, Brooke Hopkins, had been in a bicycle accident, had broken his neck, and was now a quadriplegic. Peggy then echoed my remarks, saying that though she had not fully embraced my position, she had a new understanding of "the sanctity of human life." She continued to uphold the right to die, but she was more personally aware of the dangers of pressuring the disabled to end their lives. We had been moving toward each other from opposite ends of the ethical spectrum, and we were both grateful for the candor and aware of the irony. Before the fragility of life and the mystery of death, we were largely speechless. There is a Holy Spirit that allows us to face these realities with faith, hope, and love, I reminded myself, but we should never deny our perplexity and grief. Even Jesus wept over the death of Lazarus.

To their immense credit, Peggy Battin and Brooke Hopkins eventually decided to share their family saga with the public. In an extensive *New York Times* article entitled "A Life-or-Death Situation," Robin Marantz Henig recounted the tale: part tragedy, mostly love story. The moral bottom line: "Suffering, suicide, euthanasia, a dignified death — these were subjects [Margaret Battin] had thought and written about for years, and now, suddenly, they turned unbearably personal. Alongside her physically ravaged husband, she would watch lofty ideas be trumped by reality — and would discover just how messy, raw and muddled the end of life can be."[5] Add *"agape"* and "sanctity" to that opening line, and the passage could describe me by my father's deathbed. On July 27, 2013, Brooke Hopkins concluded that he had had enough, and two days later he requested that his ventilator, diaphragmatic pacer, external oxygen, cardiac pacemaker, and feeding tube be turned off or removed, and that he be referred to hospice care. He died on July 31 in Peggy's arms.

---

5. Robin Marantz Henig, "A Life-or-Death Situation," *New York Times*, July 17, 2013.

II. Capital Punishment

A Brief against the Death Penalty

Euthanasia, as discussed above, is the question of when we might ask for our own death. Capital punishment, like just war theory, asks when we might ask for the death of another. I find the following proposition to be undeniably true: a competent adult who is guilty of first-degree murder, and found so via due process, deserves in justice to die. Not everyone who affirms retributive justice affirms the death penalty, but many do (including Thomas Aquinas and Immanuel Kant). I base my own judgment in part on my witnessing two capital murder trials in my hometown of Louisville, Kentucky. In both cases, the family of the victim wanted the murderer to be executed, yet these were not bloodthirsty or vengeful people. Their chief concerns were (1) that the value and meaning of their loved one's life be recognized and honored, and (2) that the wrongdoer be held accountable and properly punished. I find both of these concerns morally compelling. As is often pointed out, there is a difference between vengeance, which is driven by hatred and tends to be limitless, and retribution, which is driven by a sense of justice and seeks to make the punishment fit the crime. Indeed, I believe just retribution to be the necessary and sufficient condition for punishment. In any penal action by a legitimate authority, one hopes for rehabilitation of the actual criminal, for deterrence of possible criminals, and for restitution of the *status quo ante*. These are desiderata, however. They may or may not ensue. (For murder, of course, there can be no restoring of the lost life.) What is crucial is that the individual in question be guilty and thus deserving of punishment. If not, the old and powerful argument goes, why not incarcerate or execute an innocent person, if this would help rehabilitate others, deter crime, or otherwise multiply social utility?

Now, a critic will quickly note that American jurisprudence is riddled with racial, class, and gender bias. If you are white, rich, and female, you are far less likely to be put to death for murder than if you are black, poor, and male — even if you have actually killed someone. Moreover, even at its moral best, the adversarial system is fallible, and there is no way to rectify a mistake in the case of the death penalty. I readily acknowledge that the U.S. legal system has many deep flaws, and that these flaws make the de facto practice of capital punishment unjust. But let's imagine that the system could be perfected, such that all and only those genuinely guilty of a crime (including first-degree murder) are arrested, tried, and sentenced. What should our attitude to capital punishment be in this (very hypothetical) case? Again, I would argue that an adult who is *compos mentis* and premeditatedly murders another human being deserves in justice to die. Such a murderer has autonomously surrendered his dignity — his achieved moral worth, if not his rational agency altogether — and is owed retribution. As Kant would maintain, punishing him is part of respecting him as an autonomous person, responding fittingly to his "inner wickedness."[6]

I am aware that some theorists who give political priority to justice over love (e.g., John Rawls) or legal priority to dignity over sanctity (e.g., Ronald Dworkin) are opposed to the death penalty. But their arguments are usually based on imperfections in the system — for example, its culpable bias and its innocent fallibility — rather than on the ideal requirements of justice or dignity as such. Interestingly, although Dworkin is against capital punishment, he thinks the case that it violates human rights or is irreconcilable with human dignity is "at best inconclusive."[7] I myself would take the stronger, more Kantian line and argue that, if justice and dignity are the main criteria, it is hard to see how the death penalty is *not* required for a capital felon.

All that said, I am nevertheless against the death penalty. I am against it because justice and dignity are not the only values or criteria at stake here. Killing a first-degree murderer is just, in my estimation, but it is too unloving to be countenanced, politically or otherwise. Execution tends to brutalize the society that practices it,[8] but, more importantly, it is oblivious to the good that remains in the criminal. Although the capital felon has surrendered his dignity, he still bears the image of God and thus has sanctity. The state's honoring that sanctity means admitting its inviolability, not directly assaulting the life once it has been rendered socially harmless.[9]

6. See Immanuel Kant, *The Metaphysics of Morals*, in *Immanuel Kant: Practical Philosophy*, trans. Mary J. Gregor (Cambridge: Cambridge University Press, 1996), 6:333, p. 474.

7. Ronald Dworkin, *Is Democracy Possible Here?* (Princeton: Princeton University Press, 2006), pp. 39-40.

8. Much depends on how one defines "brutalization." William J. Bowers and Glenn L. Pierce define it as tending to increase homicides; see their "Deterrence or Brutalization: What Is the Effect of Executions?" *Crime and Delinquency* 26, no. 4 (October 1980): 453-84. Joanna M. Shepherd defines it more generally as "creating a climate of brutal violence"; see her "Deterrence versus Brutalization: Capital Punishment's Differing Impacts among States," *Michigan Law Review* 104 (November 2005): 203-56. For my part, I accent the corruption of character more than the fomenting of bad consequences.

9. Thomas Aquinas suggests that executing a murderer can be a "praiseworthy" act aimed at defending the common good, even as Saint Augustine sees it as a potentially "benevolent severity" toward the criminal himself. See, for example, Aquinas, *Summa Theologiae*

I applaud Cesare Beccaria's desire to make punishment humane, but I cannot agree with his utilitarian approach to law, captured in his claim that "if a punishment is to be just, it must be pitched at just that level of intensity which suffices to deter men from crime."[10] This focuses far too much on crime prevention, over against condign retribution. Beccaria famously writes, "It seems absurd to me that the laws, which are the expression of the public will, and which hate and punish murder, should themselves commit one, and that to deter citizens from murder, they should decree a public murder."[11] This is an abuse of words. Murder is, by definition, the unjust taking of a relevantly *innocent* human life.[12] When a state executes a person, it is *ex hypothesi* because that person is heinously *guilty*. (Recall that we are presuming a perfected judicial system.) Capital punishment, properly applied, is not murder, but it is still morally wrong, I believe. It does not violate duties of justice, which are based on merit, demerit, and contract; rather, it violates duties of charity, which are bound to honor the sanctity of human life. We can debate when human life begins — I favor conception and thus consider elective abortion to be unjustifiable homicide — but a competent adult surely qualifies as a human life.

Am I claiming, then, that in the context of the death penalty justice and love are at odds? Does justice demand that the murderer be executed, while love requires that he be spared? No. As Paul Ramsey emphasized, love sometimes rises majestically above justice, giving more than is strictly due, but love never falls below justice, giving less.[13] A capital felon deserves in justice to die, meaning that her guilt, considered alone, would warrant the imposition of death (the *lex talionis*). But here love rises above what justice alone permits

---

II-II, qu. 64, art. 2; and Augustine, *Letters* 138.9-15, collected in *The Political Writings of St. Augustine,* ed. Henry Paolucci (South Bend: Regnery/Gateway, 1962), p. 178. Even so, their defenses of killing an aggressor are usually in the context of war, rather than capital punishment. The fact that a capital felon has been disarmed makes killing him far less necessary and far less compatible with charity.

10. Cesare Beccaria, *On Crimes and Punishments and Other Writings,* trans. Richard Davies, ed. Richard Bellamy (Cambridge: Cambridge University Press, 1995), p. 68.

11. Beccaria, *On Crimes and Punishments,* p. 70.

12. No one is *entirely* innocent of crime or vice, but we must draw some morally relevant distinctions. The fact that my wife lies to me about her age does not mean that I can rightly execute her. Justly to execute someone requires that I have proper authority, that the person be profoundly guilty in very specific ways, etc. In turn, to murder someone does not require that the person be without sin altogether, only that the person does not deserve death from a fellow human being.

13. Paul Ramsey, *War and the Christian Conscience* (Durham, N.C.: Duke University Press, 1961), p. 178.

and stays the executioner's hand, or ought to. Retributive justice must still be satisfied, and I take this to mean a sentence of life imprisonment without the possibility of parole. The capital criminal should be permanently deprived of freedom. Nothing short of this honors the sanctity of the victim's life, which was permanently cut short, and nothing short of this holds the victimizer adequately accountable. This I learned in the Louisville courtrooms, watching the moral and emotional agony of the survivors of homicide of a loved one. The fact that perpetual incarceration helps solve the recidivism problem is utilitarian gravy. Conversely, even if the death penalty would deter some others from murder, that is, save innocent lives,[14] that would be an extrinsic effect that is secondary to what the sanctity of the life requires of us. Punishing *the innocent* for the sake of deterrence would be doing evil that good might come, but punishing *the guilty* for the sake of deterrence *alone* is also misguided — a doing of the wrong good that evil might go, so to speak.

A capital criminal has surrendered "dignity" as achieved merit, if not rational agency altogether, but he retains "sanctity." He must still be loved and forgiven, politically.[15] When the offender is either incarcerated or executed, his abuse of autonomy has rightly meant defalcation or loss of autonomy. (Sanctity, in contrast, cannot be abused or reduced so long as one lives.) What makes war so vexing is that it demands a *balancing of sanctities* in which defending innocents, and upholding justice itself, requires killing aggressors. The killing may be "an alien work of love," in Martin Luther's phrase, but it is not necessarily a *violation* of sanctity, since it is compatible with willing the good for the unjust and honoring their (and others') fellow humanity. I defend just war in theory, but pacifism nonetheless remains a *permissible* form of conscience, because war is in reality very hard to prosecute within just and

---

14. The debate over whether capital punishment deters violent crime continues, but the traditional "consensus" that it does not has been challenged of late. Some studies have maintained that, when swiftly and consistently administered, the death penalty actually does save lives. See, for instance, Hashem Dezhbakhsh, Paul H. Rubin, and Joanna M. Shepherd, "Does Capital Punishment Have a Deterrent Effect? New Evidence from Postmoratorium Panel Data," *American Law and Economics Review* 5, no. 2 (2003): 344-76; and Joanna M. Shepherd, "Murders of Passion, Execution Delays, and the Deterrence of Capital Punishment," *Journal of Legal Studies* 33, no. 2 (2004): 283-321. Other scholars have disputed these findings. See, for example, John J. Donohue and Justin Wolfers, "Uses and Abuses of Empirical Evidence in the Death Penalty Debate," *Stanford Law Review* 58, no. 3 (December 2005): 791-846. Happily, my main point is independent of the deterrence question. Human sanctity, I have argued, should not be held hostage to social utility.

15. See Timothy P. Jackson, *The Priority of Love* (Princeton: Princeton University Press, 2003), chap. 4. I make the case there for the compatibility of forgiveness and retribution.

loving bounds. Love of neighbor is not a warm fuzzy feeling for the other, but it requires affirming the sanctity of her life, even when she is violently unjust. Whether this is possible in particular cases of conflict and for specific individuals is a judgment call.

On the Killing of Osama bin Laden

Thus far, I have written of capital punishment as a domestic legal sanction imposed by the judicial branch of government. Let me conclude by discussing briefly that form of the death penalty known as international assassination, specifically the case of Osama bin Laden. Shortly after bin Laden was killed by American SEALs in Pakistan, Jonathan Haidt published an opinion in the *New York Times* entitled "Why We Celebrate a Killing."[16] Professor Haidt noted there that, although most Americans agreed that bin Laden's demise was "a good thing," many were disturbed by the public "revelry" that followed. Wasn't the spectacle "a celebration of death and vengeance, not justice"? he asked. Didn't it "lower us to 'their' level?" "No," he answered.

Haidt's chief argument for his conclusion was taken from evolutionary psychology: morality at "the individual level" is not to be confused with what can and should obtain within "groups and nations." When individuals compete, natural selection rewards "selfishness," Haidt informed us, but when collectives compete, that same selection favors groups that can engender internal "unity" and "cooperation." Bees are adept at this, and human beings are also "able to become, briefly, hive creatures." Appealing to Émile Durkheim, Haidt maintained that "collective emotions" can "dissolve the petty, small-minded self" and "make people feel that they are part of something larger and more important than themselves." Such "collective effervescence" (Durkheim's phrase) was what was going on after bin Laden was killed, according to Haidt, and it was "good and healthy."

Haidt was well aware that some consider such solidarity an ugly and menacing form of tribalism. He explicitly asked, "When celebrants chanted 'U.S.A.! U.S.A.!' and sang 'God Bless America,' were they not displaying a hateful 'us versus them' mindset?" His emphatic answer: "Once again, no." We must draw another distinction, he told us. "Nationalism" correlates with racism and hostility to other countries, but "patriotism" reflects a proper "love of one's own country." Nationalism fosters a quest to be "dominant" over others,

16. Jonathan Haidt, "Why We Celebrate a Killing," *New York Times*, May 7, 2011.

while patriotism can be an "altruistic" bondedness with one's fellow citizens. Once one recognizes this difference, one can appreciate the "communal joy" that followed, at least temporarily, America's "bravely and decisively" achieving its goal of terminating a murderous threat. Thus far, Haidt.

In the balance of this chapter, I explain why I consider Professor Haidt's thought-provoking piece gravely misleading. As I have suggested, Haidt makes much of the Durkheimian notion that the human species is *Homo duplex,* "two-level man." Individuals need to forge personally satisfying relationships with other individuals, but they also need to be bound to larger and more anonymous moral communities. With religion increasingly waning across Europe, Durkheim looked to "collective emotions" for the natural glue requisite to meet the second challenge. If one looks to Simone Weil's analysis of "force" and human nature, in contrast, one is led to a very different position. Weil emphasizes that our species is, by inclination, *Homo duplicitas,* "mendacious man." We do not merely manage our instincts at two levels; left to our own devices, we are inclined to dishonesty and manipulation in all dimensions of life. We are often self-deceived and other-duping, denying common vulnerabilities and afflicting others by turning them into objects to be exploited for our own egotistical or corporate purposes. Rather than extolling group sentiments as the solution to social fragmentation, Weil typically associates them with the mass proclivity to peck the weak to death. For her, "the collective is the object of all idolatry," and she calls it "the Great Beast."[17]

For Weil, no natural inclination is sufficient to overcome the human cycle of domination and destruction, which she associates with "gravity." We are in need of a "supernatural justice"[18] in which the strong treat the weak as equals, which she associates with "grace." Such grace is not explicable on evolutionary or any other temporal grounds. As she avers, "the (balanced) division of power between the strong and the weak is only possible through the intervention of a supernatural factor."[19]

Like Haidt, Weil recognizes the importance of shared history and communal cohesion, what she calls "the need for roots."[20] Her list of "the needs of the soul" includes "collective property" and "disciplined participation in a

17. Simone Weil, *Gravity and Grace* (London and New York: Ark Paperbacks, 1987), p. 144.

18. Simone Weil, *Waiting for God,* trans. Emma Craufurd (New York: HarperCollins, 1973), p. 87.

19. Weil, *Gravity and Grace,* p. 152.

20. Simone Weil, *The Need for Roots: Prelude to a Declaration of Duties towards Mankind,* trans. A. F. Wills (London and New York: Ark Paperbacks, 1987).

common task."[21] Weil also appreciates the occasional necessity of using violent force to protect innocent life and preserve essential values. Yet Weil is far less sanguine than Haidt that one can draw a sharp contrast between patriotism and nationalism, or between just and limited war (including assassination) and unjust and self-perpetuating force (including mob frenzy). She realizes that we all wish to lose ourselves in a large, impersonal reality, but when this reality is a temporal institution or assembly, it inevitably becomes idolatrous. For Weil, nothing finite — neither our own passions nor the nation-state — can satisfy the human desire for transcendence. "At the centre of the human heart, is the longing for an absolute good, a longing which is always there and is never appeased by any object in this world."[22] "Man would like to be an egoist and cannot."[23] To repeat, Weil grants the importance of temporal traditions and social loyalties, but these must be constantly scrutinized and balanced. Above all, they are not to be absolutized. As Jane Doering has observed, "[Weil] lamented that because of the contemporary loss of traditional contexts for one's obedience — the family, the workplace, and the local culture — unconditional allegiance gravitated by default to the state, which in the long run diminished individual freedom."[24]

There is no need to deny a *theoretical* difference between individuals and groups or between patriotism and nationalism, but these distinctions are blurred *in reality*. Human thought and action are often, if not always, practically ambiguous. As Weil constantly reminds us, we are personally and politically moved by both love and force. No doubt, some of the revelers after bin Ladin's killing were motivated largely by patriotism and a sense of justice; equally indubitably, however, some were fully glorying in death and vengeance. The majority — and I would include myself in this — oscillated somewhere in between. Such is the ambivalence of the human heart: it is pulled simultaneously toward civility and cruelty, compassion and *Schadenfreude*. When we are not honest about and on guard against this, abomination happens. For example, some of those fighting for Nazi Germany in WWII were animated by love of country and a sense of duty, while others were committed anti-Semites who affirmed the ongoing genocide. But the majority of Germans were too oblivious to their own half-hearted complicity in hatred to

21. Simone Weil, "Draft for a Statement of Human Obligations," in *Two Moral Essays by Simone Weil*, ed. Ronald Hathaway (Lebanon, Pa.: Pendle Hill Publications, 1981), pp. 11-12.

22. Weil, "Draft for a Statement," p. 5.

23. Weil, *Gravity and Grace*, p. 53.

24. E. Jane Doering, *Simone Weil and the Specter of Self-Perpetuating Force* (Notre Dame: University of Notre Dame Press, 2010), p. 93.

check the slaughter.[25] If Weil is right, this double-mindedness is a universal human disposition.

This is not to say that Haidt is obtuse or has fascist sympathies. He is an impressive scholar and a civilized man, but he is not a civilizing influence. He is too unwary of mass humanity to be a wise, much less a prophetic, voice. He does not take seriously enough the tendency of violence to contaminate even those who are seeking justice, nor does he sufficiently sympathize with the (possibly unintended) victims of violence. I do not contest the need to "go after Osama"; condign punishment and deterrence of future terrorism have their place. Weil would insist, however, that, at best, bin Laden's death was a necessary means to the combating of brutality, rather than a good end to be celebrated. There is a fine line indeed between retributive justice and vengeful will to power. (This is especially true in the era of Abu Ghraib and Guantanamo, where suspected terrorists are humiliated and denied basic human rights.) But Haidt blurs this line. Moreover, he does not even mention the fact that, in addition to bin Laden, the American soldiers killed bin Laden's courier, the brother of the courier, the brother's wife, and bin Laden's son. The courier evidently fired at the SEALs, but he was the only one of the five people killed who had a weapon.[26] One can debate whether the unarmed bin Laden should have been shot on sight or captured and brought to trial — I would have favored the latter, as does traditional just war theory — but the killing of the brother, wife, and son (arguably noncombatants) is a different matter. If intentional, the killing of noncombatants is always to be forbidden; if unintentional, it is always to be lamented. We have no right, individual or collective, to effect the death of innocents, even to bring a notorious terrorist to book. When we Americans figuratively danced on Osama's watery grave, we inured ourselves to the "collateral deaths." And even bin Laden himself, profoundly guilty and dangerous though he was, still bore the image of God. To deny or overlook this fact risks pandering to injustice.

Again, I do not consider Professor Haidt to be personally unjust, but, to use Weil's term, he "(mis-)reads" our moral situation in a way that encourages others to be inattentive to evil. By Weil's lights, he is too optimistic about naturalism and too pessimistic about supernaturalism. Evolution-as-natural-selection is his explanatory bottom line, and this rules out any reference to the divine. Competitive advantage, for individuals and groups, is the engine

25. See Daniel Goldhagen, *Hitler's Willing Executioners: Ordinary Germans and the Holocaust* (New York: Knopf, 1996).

26. "The Death of Osama bin Laden," *New York Times*, May 9, 2011.

that drives history and limits moral ideals. Thus Haidt is insouciant about the inclination of groups to annihilate outsiders and anesthetize insiders, even as he seems skeptical of a self-sacrificial love for all human beings. In short, Haidt overestimates what Weil calls "gravity" and underestimates what she calls "grace." He seems blind to both the Great Beast and God.

This is not to say that only a theist, much less only an explicit Christian, can be a just social critic. But any cultural commentator who encourages us to celebrate a killing based on natural selection and group solidarity owes it to his readers to explain how and where he draws the limits of proper force. It is a great merit of Doering's volume that she helps us see the hazards of a fascination with force and a denial of transcendence. Via a careful reading of both published and posthumous essays, Doering highlights Weil's wariness of the temptation to dehumanize others. Haidt, on the other hand, allows us to lower our guard. He is silent where he should speak up, and he endorses raucous display where we should be silent.

As the sole remaining superpower, America stands in roughly the same relation to the world as Rome did after it had vanquished Carthage. If America is to conduct a just war against terror, if it is to have a post–Cold War conscience that prevents another imperial fall, Darwin and Durkheim are not enough. We need Simone Weil. Weil does not despair over humanity's fallibility but turns our attention to God's perfection, while Jonathan Haidt can only encourage us to buzz with the hive. The latter is imprudent, even dangerous, but above all it reflects an inadequate view of reality. Or so we Weilans believe.

CHAPTER 10

Both Shylock and Oedipus: Why Many Accounts of Christian Complicity in the Holocaust Are Only Half Right

In the name of the old
high magic
he commands
families to be burned alive
and children mutilated

. . .

the old atrocity,
the old obsolete atrocity.

LEONARD COHEN[1]

Introduction: Moses and Jesus

The question is grave and familiar: How could members of a faith whose Messiah is a Jew and that endorses Judaic conceptions of love and justice countenance and even support the Nazi Holocaust of European Jewry? In struggling to answer, many have focused on the differences, real or imagined, between "Moses and Jesus." Many have written on how the early Christian church and later Christian theologians — from Saint Paul to Martin Luther to Emanuel Hirsch — draw sharper and sharper contrasts between Judaism and its founder and Christianity and its founder.[2] Such contrasts often include the following six:

---

1. Leonard Cohen, from "Too Old," in *Book of Longing* (New York: HarperCollins, 2006), p. 79.

2. Eric W. Gritsch contrasts Saint Paul's take on Moses and Jesus with that of Martin Lu-

(1) Jewish works righteousness versus Christian justification by faith
(2) Jewish tribalism versus Christian universalism
(3) Jewish retribution versus Christian mercy
(4) Jewish bondage to guilt versus Christian freedom of conscience
(5) Jewish militarism/violence versus Christian pacifism/nonviolence
(6) Jewish materialism and this-worldliness versus Christian spiritualism and otherworldliness

At the core of these dubious dichotomies is that between law and gospel. Moses insists on external obedience to rules, while Jesus preaches a message of spontaneous and inner love. Moses imposes burden and judgment; Jesus brings the good news of salvation and forgiveness. Or so the story goes.

To be sure, most who focus on this traditional story are at pains to refute its contents. They argue, with considerable plausibility, that the supposed contrasts are either nonexistent or radically overdrawn. The Jews were *falsely* accused of being inhuman, "the malevolent other," and this charge helped precipitate violent anti-Semitism. Once we see the actual affinities between Judaism and Christianity, we will recognize how criminally mistaken was Christian participation in "the Final Solution." Once we Christians recognize that the Jews are really "like us," all conflict should and will cease.

No one has articulated this appeal to common humanity more eloquently than Shakespeare's Shylock:

"I am a Jew. Hath not a Jew eyes? Hath not a Jew hands, organs, dimensions, senses, affections, passions; fed with the same food, hurt with the

---

ther. For Paul, both biblical figures preach divine commands and are indispensable instruments of God's grace, thus Jews and Christians "are kin in a never-ending covenant." For Luther, Moses is to be affirmed only insofar as he anticipates and points to Christ, and many Jews get lost in Mosaic legalism and wrongly refuse to convert. "The Jewish denial of this point of view is the theological premise of Luther's anti-Semitism," even as anti-Semitism would have been unthinkable for Paul. See Eric W. Gritsch, *Martin Luther's Anti-Semitism: Against His Better Judgment* (Grand Rapids: Eerdmans, 2012), pp. 41 and 47. Four hundred years after Luther, Emanuel Hirsch takes the final step of construing Moses' message as completely antithetical to that of Jesus and thus concludes that, in the words of Robert Ericksen, "the Old Testament and Jewish religion can only represent evil reliance upon law and religiosity, against which the pure truth of the gospel must constantly be directed." See Robert P. Ericksen, "Assessing the Heritage: German Protestant Theologians, Nazis, and the 'Jewish Question,'" in *Betrayal: German Churches and the Holocaust,* ed. Robert P. Ericksen and Susannah Heschel (Minneapolis: Fortress, 1999), p. 30.

same weapons, subject to the same diseases, heal'd by the same means, warm'd and cool'd by the same winter and summer, as a Christian is? If you prick us, do we not bleed? If you tickle us, do we not laugh? If you poison us, do we not die? And if you wrong us, do we not revenge? If we are like you in the rest, we will resemble you in that."[3]

The Shylockian sensibility depicts anti-Semitism as stemming from a basic factual error and a fundamental failure of empathy. Better biblical exegesis and historiography, better psychology and even biology, will confirm that we are brothers and sisters under the skin and in the sanctuary. And this will make for harmony, the counterstory goes.

I. Shylock and Oedipus

Now, what is wrong with such "liberal" reasoning? When one begins with the issue of *difference,* the main question is whether the supposed contrasts are genuine. When one demonstrates that they are *not* genuine, the rationale for opposition is easily thought to disappear. Alas, however, the worm at the heart of human nature goes deeper than this. This line forgets that *similarity* can also occasion fear, competition, and resentment. It fails to explain, moreover, why a faith that flows from and closely resembles another should vilify that close relative to begin with. The presumption that common lineage or status will provide a tie that binds is challenged by the phenomenon of slaying the father. Over against Shylock and his brief for a shared human nature stands Oedipus and his embodiment of patricide.[4] (I might also mention the sibling rivalry of Cain and Abel, but I want to concentrate on the father-child analogy.) Christianity and Islam grant that they are children of Abraham, yet they still often hate each other and assail their mutual paternity. Like Oedipus, Christianity and Islam would deny (if not kill) their vetust Father and venerate (if not marry) their virgin Mother.[5] (Moses, if not Abraham, is constantly pilloried, but even Protestants seldom ridicule Mary.) Truly discontinuous religions, like Christianity

---

3. William Shakespeare, *The Merchant of Venice,* act 3, scene 1, lines 58-68.

4. In what follows, I draw primarily on Sophocles' *Oedipus the King, Oedipus at Colonus,* and *Antigone,* but I also make use of the more ancient epic *Thebaid.*

5. The Koran asserts the virgin birth of Jesus by Mary, but Mary's *perpetual* virginity is not clearly affirmed.

and Hinduism, on the other hand, typically evince far less animosity and ambivalence. But why?

Why should familiarity and even consanguinity breed contempt? Why do we invent bogus dissimilarities and gainsay genuine affinities? Harold Bloom's discussion of "the anxiety of influence" offers some help in this regard.[6] Bloom maintains, with much evidence, that strong poets seek to deny their temporal origins. If one has been influenced by precursors — and who has not? — one must prove one's power and uniqueness by obscuring this fact. You write as though you are without precedent; you may even write, paradoxically, as though your forerunners have been shaped *by you.* The anxiety of influence is evident even in the Christian Scriptures. The Gospel writers try, awkwardly, to disguise the fact that Jesus was initially a disciple of John the Baptist. Similarly, the early church sought to deny its Judaic roots, a denial that would reach absurd proportions when the *Deutsche Christen* made Jesus over as an Aryan. One seeks to slay the father as a step toward individuation.[7]

The key point, anticipated by Søren Kierkegaard, is that anxiety frequently leads to a desire to negate others, or one's own situated self. Anxiety does not necessitate aggression or antipathy, according to Kierkegaard, but it is the occasion for such. The influence of anxiety, so to speak, is despair (a.k.a. sin). We swoon before our own limited freedom and try to take others down with us.[8] Bloom concentrates on original authors, but Kierkegaard carries us back to the original sin that besets us all. Something deep in human nature seeks to elevate self by denigrating "the other." "The other" may be marked by conspicuous difference, but it may equally well be uncomfortably similar to oneself. One may scapegoat someone who is highly eccentric, but one may

---

6. See Harold Bloom, *The Anxiety of Influence* (Oxford: Oxford University Press, 1973).

7. In *Approaches to Auschwitz: The Holocaust and Its Legacy* (Louisville: Westminster John Knox, 2003), pp. 44-45, John Roth and Richard Rubenstein argue that Christian hostility toward "the Jews" resulted from the early church's need to disparage Judaism in order to reduce cognitive dissonance and achieve separation. Emerging Christian question: How could the Jews not recognize their own Messiah, and how could the Romans have destroyed the temple in 70 A.D.? Emerging Christian answer: Those who put us out of the fold are willfully benighted about their own faith, and God is punishing them, so we can and should disown them. (I thank Robert Ericksen for this reference, via e-mail.)

8. See Søren Kierkegaard (Vigilius Haufniensis), *The Concept of Anxiety,* trans. Reidar Thomte (Princeton: Princeton University Press, 1980). See also, Kierkegaard (Anti-Climacus), *The Sickness unto Death,* trans. Howard V. Hong and Edna H. Hong (Princeton: Princeton University Press, 1980).

also make "the other" artificial by disavowing real identities. The motive in both cases, I think, stems from human finitude.

Personal vulnerability and mortality, even our unavoidable dependency on each other, generate such anxiety that we will go to virtually any lengths to escape it. More specifically, in order (momentarily) to forget our own vulnerability, we exploit or celebrate that of others. It may or may not be significant that the Germans have a special word for this, *Schadenfreude,* but we all experience it. If you deny that you have ever enjoyed another's misfortune, you are either a saint or a liar. (I suspect the latter.) Even a central symbol of Christianity, the crucifix, invites ambivalent reactions. Most of its power derives from compassion and gratitude for Jesus' suffering for our sakes, but some of its effect is no doubt attributable to a sense of relief: "Thank God, it's him and not me up there!" At the extreme, displaced sadism can be at work, or displaced masochism.

The Nazi leadership included some extreme sadists, but we are *all* disposed to that vice. Even more importantly, sadism does not require external threats or alien interlopers to be triggered. Being able cogently to set "us" against "them" may be a sufficient condition for injustice, but it is not a necessary one. We may actually plague more those who are most like us, those on whom we are most dependent, and those we most admire and want to resemble. In the context of post–World War I Germany, this means that, even as *fear* of the Jews was fueling anti-Semitism, so too was *envy.* My hunch is that, in the midst of rampant inflation and violent social unrest, the solidarity of the Jews, if not their (supposed) economic prosperity, occasioned in many non-Jewish Germans the desire to be like them. This is not to say that your average Nazi was tempted to convert to the faith of Abraham, but rather that he or she resented not being able to emulate Jewish assets and attributes. This, in turn, contributed to the demonization of the Jews as "scheming against us," "anti-Christian," "enemies of the *Volk,*" etc. The Jews *did* (and do) have a traditional culture with a number of distinctive rituals and doctrines, but my thesis is that this was not the only, or even the main, cause of their victimization. Rather than being oppressed and killed primarily because they were different, they were often *made* to seem all the more "different" *in order to* allow them to be oppressed and killed.

Take the issue of usury. For centuries and to this day, the Jews have been accused of being moneygrubbing and profiteering, lending cash at confiscatory rates of interest, thus betraying their cupidinous nature. As is often pointed out, in reality medieval Christian Europe forced Jews into relying on liquid assets by denying them the right to own property and to participate in regular commerce and the professions.[9] For millennia, usury has been but one aspect of a basic Jewish Catch-22:[10] either assimilate, intermarry, and enter the trades, and then be charged with seeking to dilute or destroy the wider Christian culture; or don't assimilate, intermarry, and enter the trades, and then be indicted for being stiff-necked and self-righteous. "You know what he'll do when he comes back?" Philip Marlowe asks in *The Big Sleep*. His answer: "Beat my teeth out, then kick me in the stomach for mumbling." That is the Jewish plight *in nuce*. For many Christians, anticipating the second coming of Christ has meant faulting the Jews for being who and what we have made them in the meantime. This no-win situation reveals the standard illogic behind virtually all discrimination. One justifies enslaving blacks because they are so needy and, well, enslaved; one justifies not educating women because they are so ignorant and, well, uneducated; one justifies denying the marriage sacrament to gays and lesbians because they are so promiscuous and, well, unmarried; and so on.[11] Why can't we awaken from this slumber?

The desire to annul and dehumanize, in short, runs deeper than any ethnic identity or divergence. It is part of human nature and human history, original sin. This does not mean that genocide is inevitable or irresistible, but it does mean that a "world culture" in which creedal and sociological singularities are blurred will not put an end to mass murder. Where there is no substantive variation, it will likely be invented. ("Assume a vice if they have it not," to reverse Hamlet.) If Jesus can be turned into an Aryan who denies Yahweh and hates the Jews, then we should not wonder that the Menendez brothers can invent molestation and turn shotguns on their parents. Literature, as well as life, is full of such volatile irrationality. As a nation, we are still in shock over Adam Lanza's murderous spree at Sandy Hook Elementary School in

---

9. Even Martin Luther accepted this extenuating explanation, at least in 1523, and called for patience and tolerance in addressing Jews; see his "That Jesus Was Born a Jew." By 1543, Luther's rage over the Jews' nonconversion had exploded, and he called for the burning of Jewish synagogues and schools, the razing of Jewish homes, the confiscation of Jewish holy books, and the enslavement of Jews on farms; see his *On the Jews and Their Lies*.

10. It can't be accidental that the phrase "Catch-22" entered the English language via Joseph Heller, an American Jew whose parents were Russian émigrés.

11. Some, even many, gay men might not want to surrender promiscuity and be married, but (a) many straight men don't want to let go of promiscuity either, and (b) how can we fault promiscuous gay men if there is no sacramental option available to them that might provide an alternative discipline? See my "Keeping Marriage Sacred," chap. 11 of this volume.

Newtown, Connecticut, a massacre of twenty children and six adults that began with his slaying his own mother with one of her own guns. Former world chess champion Bobby Fischer was never actually homicidal, as far as I know, but he took Oedipal tendencies to the extreme, verbally. Though himself an American Jew,[12] his final years were spent looking for a suitable homeland and religious faith, mentally unstable and spewing the most nasty anti-American and anti-Semitic rhetoric imaginable. (He celebrated the terrorist attacks of 9/11, denied the Holocaust ever happened, etc.) Dread projected outward onto the sources of the self thus becomes self-consuming.

II. Fulfilling and Reversing Stereotypes

As noted, in the midst of cultural difference, Shylock pleads human similarity; in the midst of biological similarity, Oedipus creates lethal difference. Less often highlighted is that both tragic figures end up losing their children. Embittered by physical and verbal abuse and that his only daughter, Jessica, married a Gentile and converted to Christianity, Shylock demands his "pound of flesh." He is thereby further alienated from the wider society and his own family. There is no question that Shakespeare availed himself of traditional anti-Semitic stereotypes in drawing Shylock's character, but the debate rages on as to whether the Bard was endorsing or subverting these stereotypes.[13] In my judgment, Shakespeare was drawing on his experience as a Roman Catholic growing up marginalized, if not persecuted, in Protestant England to show us how a stereotype can become self-fulfilling.[14] Spat upon and discrim-

---

12. Fischer's mother, Regina, was Jewish, and some speculate that his biological father was the Hungarian mathematician and physicist, Paul Nemenyi, who was also Jewish.

13. Harold Bloom declares, "One would have to be blind, deaf, and dumb not to recognize that Shakespeare's grand, equivocal comedy *The Merchant of Venice* is nevertheless a profoundly anti-Semitic work." See Bloom, *Shakespeare: The Invention of the Human* (New York: Riverhead Books, 1998), p. 171. Kenneth Myrick, among others, is not so categorical. He grants that "Shakespeare has many times connected Shylock's worst qualities with the Hebrew religion," but he also notes that "it is hard to believe that Shakespeare approved Antonio's way of publicly denouncing the usurer [Shylock]. The words he gives Shylock seem designed to show us how it feels to be an outcast in a Christian society." See Myrick's introduction to *The Merchant of Venice* in *The Complete Signet Classic Shakespeare* (New York: Harcourt Brace Jovanovich, 1972), pp. 602 and 601. Bloom reads Shylock as a comic villain, while Myrick sees him as at least partially sympathetic.

14. Shakespeare was baptized just six years after "Bloody Mary's" reestablishment of Roman Catholicism in Britain was reversed, after her death in 1558, by her younger half sister

inated against as a violent and greedy Jew, Shylock is a victim who becomes a victimizer. He is indeed vicious, but who has made him so? ("I and the public know / what all schoolchildren learn, / those to whom evil is done / do evil in return.")[15] Shylock is the equivalent for Shakespeare of "Nigger Jim" for Mark Twain or, more extremely, of Nat Turner for William Styron: an "other" who remains illegal and even dangerous but is nonetheless being humanized for readers. The final unchristian treatment of Shylock by medieval Venice was to compel him to convert to Christianity. The final unchristian treatment of the Jew by Nazi Germany was to convert him to ashes.[16]

For his part, Oedipus judges his sons and half brothers, Polynices and Eteocles, to be disrespectful and curses them to die by each other's hands as they struggle over the throne of Thebes. And so they do. Oedipus's two daughters and half sisters, Antigone and Ismene, also wind up dead without issue. Antigone disobeys King Creon and buries her brother, Polynices. Caught, she hangs herself, rather than be starved to death. The more obedient Ismene is eventually murdered by Tydeus. Oedipus's line perishes in conflict, even as he had violently ended his own father's life. If Shylock is a self-fulfilling caricature of Jewishness, Oedipus is a self-consuming image of rashness.[17] He not only kills his father and marries his mother, he also dooms his own lineage. Admittedly, Oedipus did not know he was taking the life of his father, Laius, but neither did Saint Paul think he was delegitimating Judaism, and neither did Martin Luther originally aim to break with Roman Catholicism. Distinction often becomes denigration, even as reformation often becomes revolution, with unforeseen and unintended consequences — at least on the conscious level.

The Oedipal parallel goes deeper. What is the Christian doctrine of the perpetual virginity of Mary but an attempt to marry the mother? (I ask this as an Anglo-Catholic.) Oedipus was innocent of intentional incest, but, in

---

and successor, Elizabeth I. The young William lived under Protestant tyranny and must have heard about recent Catholic tyranny, so it seems reasonable to speculate that he was sensitive to both. Like Myrick, I see such sensitivity in his depiction of Shylock, at least in key places.

15. W. H. Auden, "September 1, 1939," in *Selected Poems*, ed. Edward Mendelson (New York: Vintage Books, 1979), p. 86.

16. Cf. Job 30:19: "He has cast me into the mire, / and I have become like dust and ashes." Even more chilling is Job's cry at 42:6: "therefore I despise myself, / and repent in dust and ashes." Are we to assume that affliction, whether human or divine in origin, rightly turns a sufferer to self-loathing and soot?

17. I borrow this language from Stanley Fish's *Self-Consuming Artifacts: The Experience of Seventeenth-Century Literature* (Berkeley: University of California Press, 1972). Fish does not discuss Shylock or Oedipus in this text, however.

light of Delphic prophecy, he acted precipitously in wedding and bedding Jocasta, a woman whose bloodline he did not know. The truth revealed, Jocasta committed suicide. Hitler's *hamartia* was strangely similar to Oedipus's: brash fascination with the taboo. Hitler's first love was a Jewish girl named Stefanie Isak, according to August Kubizek,[18] and *der Führer* remained captivated by Jewish women for the rest of his life, even as he tried to wipe out Jewish men. (Hitler's second romantic infatuation was with Geli Raubal, his half niece, who felt suffocated by her half uncle and committed suicide with his pistol at age twenty-three.)

Jewish women were victims of the Holocaust, of course, but I can't recall a single image from Nazi propaganda that pillories a Jewess. "Germania" is often depicted as an Amazon, and German mothers are treated sympathetically, but of the hundreds of Nazi posters and photographs I have seen, not one explicitly disparages a female, Jewish or non-Jewish. Jewish women and girls were terrorized and raped, shot and gassed, by the Nazis during World War II, and a few German military photos show Jewish women and girls in need or at work. Oddly, however, they were not degraded visually in Nazi propaganda. Nor do the Wehrmacht films of the mass executions by *Einsatzgruppen* ever show women or girls being killed. Manifestly, Nazi ideology encouraged violent assault on female bodies and souls, but, evidently, the myth of Nazi machismo forbade overt desecration of the *image* of "the weaker sex," regardless of race or ethnicity. I would not be surprised if Hitler himself ordered that women and girls not be the subjects of demeaning propaganda. He knew how furious even symbolic molestation would have made Allied soldiers and the whole civilized world. Perversely, he might even have considered such public display unchivalrous.[19]

Did the Nazis hate Jewish women the way they hated Jewish men, or did they torment and kill the women chiefly in order to hurt the men and to make them more pliant? If Hitler despised Jewish men in part because he feared he might have a Jewish grandfather,[20] was the Shoah actually an expression of self-loathing? Did Hitler try to slay the unknown "father" on a global scale? John Toland observes that Hitler was a depressive man, anxious enough over

18. August Kubizek, *The Young Hitler I Knew* (London: Greenhill Books, 2006), pp. 66-75.

19. For the *lack* of National Socialist vilification of women, see *State of Deception: The Power of Nazi Propaganda* (Washington, D.C.: United States Holocaust Memorial Museum/W. W. Norton and Co., 2009).

20. John Toland, *Adolf Hitler: The Definitive Biography* (New York: Anchor Books, 1992), p. 4.

his pedigree that he had the Nazi law defining Jewishness written to exclude Jesus and himself.[21] One need not be a strict Freudian to find all this blurring of alterity and kinship very suggestive, if highly speculative.

Few subjects are more delicate than how the innocent can be distorted by radical injustice. Especially in the context of the Holocaust, we are rightly wary of "blaming the victim," and our main focus is properly on the Nazi murderers and their being held accountable. Part of the lesson of Shylock, nevertheless, is that someone of profound human sympathy can be rendered brutal, even complicit in crime, by diabolical cruelty. (One thinks of the horrible dilemmas forced on the *Judenräte* by the SS.) An analogous moral of Oedipus's story is that both fathers and sons, both mothers and daughters, both leaders and followers are put in grave jeopardy by *hubris*. Is Shylock eerily evil or warped by Christian mistreatment? Both. Is Oedipus a pawn of fate or a flawed hothead? Both.

How, then, do we combat cruelty and pride? How do we reverse the stereotypes on which they feed? One way is to be honest about one's own racist past. Race slavery was accepted by the founders of the American republic and permitted by the U.S. Constitution, even as the majority of Christians in the Third Reich endorsed or at least tolerated violent anti-Semitism.[22] Victoria Barnett and others have properly pointed out that even the Barmen Declaration (1934), often touted as the Confessing Church's bold resistance to Hitlerite tyranny, was a prudent defense of church self-governance rather than a moral protest against Nazi mistreatment of the Jews.[23] Just as many Unionists during the American Civil War fought to preserve the integrity of the federal government without giving a damn about blacks and slavery, so many Confessing

21. Toland, *Adolf Hitler*, p. 507.

22. See *Betrayal*, especially the essays by Doris L. Bergen, Susannah Heschel, Shelley Baranowski, and Michael B. Lukens; see also Victoria J. Barnett, *Bystanders: Conscience and Complicity during the Holocaust* (Westport, Conn.: Praeger, 1999).

23. Victoria J. Barnett, "Barmen, the Ecumenical Movement, and the Jews: The Missing Thesis," *Ecumenical Review* 61, no. 1 (March 2009): 17-23. Karl Barth penned the Barmen Declaration in the spring of 1934, in an effort to preserve the independence of the Christian church, but by the summer of 1935 he realized that its muteness on the criminality of the Nazis and the fate of the Jews was indefensible. In "The Confessing Church in National Socialist Germany," he wrote: "She [the Church of Jesus Christ] has fought hard to a certain extent for the freedom and purity of her proclamation, but she has, for instance, remained silent on the action against the Jews, on the amazing treatment of political opponents, on the suppression of the freedom of the press in the new Germany and on so much else against which the Old Testament prophets would certainly have spoken out." See Karl Barth, *The German Church Conflict* (Cambridge: Lutterworth, 1965), p. 60.

Christians fought to preserve the integrity of the sovereign church without caring a whit about the (unconverted) Jews. This "unconcern" ran the gamut from an active racism that was disdainful of blacks, in the American case, and of Jews, in the German case, to a truly blasé attitude that just did not notice or feel for the different.

More positively, *identity with difference* is the order of this day and every day if we are to get beyond feuding stereotypes. Here Shakespeare and Sophocles again come to our aid. Portia's "the quality of mercy is not strain'd, it droppeth as the gentle rain from heaven,"[24] and Antigone's loyalty to her brother, Polynices, in disobedience to Creon, are our icons of political *agape*. Charity, humility, and recognition of the limits of all collectives are essential. Only a love that *both* affirms our shared vulnerability and mortality *and* celebrates personal, racial, and theological idiosyncrasies can begin to bring us peace. In addition, we must be forever wary of concentrated power and groupthink. Losing oneself in mass humanity — either the secular state or the sectarian church — is a perpetually perilous way of trying to escape our finitude. Individuals are never entirely free of the temptation to demonize others; and complete and stable peace awaits eternity. But we can do better than we have been by attending to both Shylock and Oedipus.

III. Covenant and Election

Another way to do better is critically to reexamine the ideas of covenant and election through the lens of the Holocaust. A traditional Christian tale, popular for centuries, has four main phases: (1) the Jews are chosen by God for special covenant and to be the recipients of the Messiah; (2) the Jews fail to recognize and actively reject the Messiah (the crucifixion of Jesus); (3) as a result, the covenant is extended to Gentiles and withdrawn from the Jews; and (4) God elects some Gentiles for salvation and reprobates or ignores others unto damnation.

There are two major problems with this putatively biblical scenario. First, it makes God's coming into covenantal relationship with (some) Gentiles turn

24. Shakespeare, *The Merchant of Venice,* act 4, scene 1, lines 183-184. Is Portia herself virtuous? Is she guilty of anti-Semitism? Bloom thinks Portia talks a good game, but he considers her "at worst [*sic*] a happy hypocrite, far too intelligent not to see that she is not exactly dispensing Christian mercy." In the end, she and her friends are "all about money." See Bloom, *Shakespeare,* pp. 178-79. Again, I think Bloom is too harsh, but his point is telling enough for me to concede that my focus is more on Portia's famous words than on her ambiguous deeds.

on a mistake, if not the profoundest of sins. It is only because the Jews "reject" Jesus Christ that God becomes robustly gracious to non-Jews. This implies that God's love is not initially of all people; God would have been happy to remain in uniquely redemptive relation to the twelve tribes, had they affirmed the Messiah. God would always be the Creator of all life, but had the Jews accepted Jesus, they would have remained "the one true people." Second, once the Gentile half of sacred history is under way, the election of some to be "the church" reintroduces the idea of a limited covenant. Again, God is less than universally caring: the true *ecclesia* is his special and legitimate family. Even if one grants that everyone has sinned and thus that the reprobate are not such because of idiosyncratic fault, they are still beyond the pale, not "one of us, the beloved of the Deity." Jesus did not come potentially to save all, on this reading, but rather to deliver only the elect few from hellfire (limited atonement). Even Thomas Aquinas endorses theological *Schadenfreude,* averring that "in order that the happiness of the saints may be more delightful to them and that they may render more copious thanks to God for it, they are allowed to see perfectly the sufferings of the damned. . . . The everlasting punishment[s] of the wicked will not be altogether useless. . . . they are useful, because the elect rejoice therein, when they see God's justice in them, and realize that they have escaped them."[25]

What would political theology, and human history, look like if we refused this tale and the distinctions on which it turns? Such a refusal is not merely permitted by theological reflection and biblical exegesis; it is required by them, I believe. The task involves considerable pruning of the tradition, however. To begin, the language of "the one true people" is so reminiscent of Nazi ideology and its contrast between *das wahre Volk* (Aryans) and *das Scheinvolk* (the Jews) that the very words should set off alarms. It does not matter who is doing it, to claim to be the "real" or "exclusive" or "true" people is repugnant and inevitably an invitation to murder. Supersessionist narratives, in which Christianity supplants or annuls Judaism, display this same dynamic. We must give up such false consolations. How tragic an irony that religious believers should fight over the Prince of Peace and make him the occasion for setting "ins" against "outs"!

Jesus' most striking attribute was his sense of the intimate and loving presence of God, and this made him both inclusive and iconoclastic. He had table fellowship with publicans and sinners, the ritually unclean and the po-

25. Thomas Aquinas, *Summa Theologiae,* trans. Fathers of the English Dominican Province (Westminster, Md.: Christian Classics, 1981), vol. 5, supplemental qu. 94, art. 1, p. 2960; and supplemental qu. 99, art. 1, ad 4, p. 2997.

litical pariah, precisely to demonstrate the ubiquity and graciousness of the Father's care. When Jesus himself is made the rationale for brutal ostracism of the weak or nonconforming, then his name is truly taken in vain.

Does this mean that one must stop calling Jesus the Messiah? Does this imply that he is not, in some sense, the fulfillment of the Hebrew witness? No, Jesus was born a Jew, ethnically, and he was a born Jew, theologically, but precisely as such he was the Anointed One who broke down social and cultural barriers between Jew and Gentile, slave and free, and male and female (cf. Gal. 3:28). To put it another way, *Christ is too sacred to be left to the Christians.* He and his teachings are the common property of anyone with ears to hear and the will to act accordingly. Like Leonard Cohen, the faithful should be willing and able to move with ease and without apology between "Jewish" and "Christian" values and metaphors, not to mention between the koans of Zen Buddhism and the poems of the Sufi Rumi. Cohen is a Jew, is happy to be a Jew, and blesses those who read and hear him by making them honorary Jews.[26] He is also a Buddhist monk, yet he knows that all religions are halting efforts to eff an ineffable goodness, to name the nameless. God is the real and infinite source of all life and love — we don't invent the Deity — but S/He remains transcendent. Even Jesus, the Immanuel, says "Why do you call me good? No one is good but God alone" (Mark 10:18). Hence, who can claim finality? If Jesus teaches us anything, it is that the pretense to rhetorical finality should give way to the practice of temporal charity. That is "eternal life," a participation in God's own holiness.[27]

And what of "chosenness"? This idea is closely tied to being "the singular people," but it may be separable from that cancerous notion. Israel was chosen to be "a light to the nations" (Isa. 42:6), but this was always an expression of God's antecedent will that all men and women should be saved. As is often pointed out, the special divine covenant with the Jews is more of a burden than a privilege, and it is a means to the ideal end of universal salvation rather than recognition of merit on Israel's part or an end in itself.

Undeniably, some passages in the Hebrew Bible sound rather self-satisfied. Deuteronomy 7:6-10, for instance, reads:

> You are a people holy to the LORD your God; the LORD your God has chosen you out of all the peoples on earth to be his people, his treasured

26. He does this by letting you suffer with him, and, in so doing, one's burden is made a little lighter.
27. I thank Bradley Burroughs for moving me to revise this paragraph.

possession. It was not because you were more numerous than any other people that the LORD set his heart on you and chose you — for you were the fewest of all peoples. It was because the LORD loved you and kept the oath that he swore to your ancestors, that the LORD has brought you out with a mighty hand, and redeemed you from the house of slavery, from the hand of Pharaoh king of Egypt. Know therefore that the LORD your God is God, the faithful God who maintains covenant loyalty with those who love him and keep his commandments, to a thousand generations, and who repays in their own person those who reject him.

Nonetheless, throughout the Scriptures God takes the initiative in establishing a special bond with Israel, rather than Israel antecedently earning this. And God sustains the relation, in spite of Israel's repeated sin. God takes peculiar delight in Israel, even as a mother rejoices over her firstborn, but divine love is not a limited resource. It remains the case that all humans bear the image of God, and all humans stand in intimate relation to the heavenly Father. Human beings are free to accept or reject God's grace, but that grace is offered to all. This is what it means to call Abraham "the father of many nations" (Rom. 4:16-18). Or so we Arminians believe.

On this counter-reading, Judaic chosenness is a technique of divine irony and indirect authorship. It is aimed by God at a higher purpose than its face value, bringing the Gentiles up to speed by giving them something and someone to emulate. If this reading of God's providence is correct, then self-congratulatory contrasts between Jews and Gentiles, on either end, should be rejected as venal, if not inchoately genocidal. All subsequent dichotomies between "the Old and the New Testaments" (Marcion), "the two cities" (Augustine), "the two kingdoms" (Luther), "the church and the world" (Hauerwas) — indeed, the time-honored language of "the elect and the damned" — should also be transcended as incitements to smugness, or worse. Yet once that is done, we will still have to resist goring our own ox, slaying our own father. We will still have to accept being human, together.

IV. Nazi Conscience and the Sociopathic Society

Was Nazi Germany a sociopathic society, and, if so, did the sociopathy of individual Nazis entail that they did not know the difference between right and wrong? *The Oxford English Dictionary* defines a "sociopath" as "a person with a personality disorder manifesting itself in extreme antisocial attitudes and behavior and a lack of conscience."[28] But how are we to construe "lack of conscience," and did the Nazis manifest this lack? The most straightforward construal of want of conscience is precisely "not knowing the difference between right and wrong," but this phrase admits of at least two contrasting readings. It may mean (1) the perfectly general incapacity to make moral judgments of any kind or (2) the failure to make a moral judgment in a particular case. If (1), the perfectly general incapacity, were characteristic of Nazi minds, then our moral outrage over the Holocaust would be misplaced. If the Nazis did not know that some things were wrong, then they were morally blind rather than malevolent. Similarly, if (2) were the Nazis' reality, such that they did not realize that genocide of the Jews in particular was an ethical matter, then they were morally myopic rather than evil. The morally blind or myopic are diseased and dangerous, but one pities and sequesters them, rather than condemning and punishing them. In reality, however, *the Nazis did have consciences.* They were neither blind nor myopic, morally; they did (1) distinguish in principle between right and wrong and (2) judge the mass killing of the Jews to be a moral issue.

This brings us to a third and a fourth possibility concerning Nazi consciences. Though not strictly speaking "*lack* of conscience," we sometimes indict a "sociopath" for (3) a radically mistaken moral judgment or action in a specific case or (4) a perverse endorsement or enactment of what she knows to be concretely wrong. Category 3 might be a function of culpable ignorance or weakness of will and thus be condemnable, but it remains within what might be called "ordinary sinfulness." Category 4, on the other hand, is truly demonic, the self-conscious choice of what is recognized as evil. ("Evil be thou my good," says Milton's Satan.) Nazi anti-Semitism falls ambiguously and self-deceptively within these third and fourth categories, in my estimation. It is frequently argued that the Holocaust is so troubling, in part, because the perpetrators thought that what they were doing was right. They were horribly misguided, but at least they were sincere. This would be a case of (3), and it may be true of some committed Nazis. Indeed, the more convinced a Nazi was that genocide of the Jews was the proper and natural course, the more intelligible he and his evil might seem. I suspect, nevertheless, that the more typical Nazi phenomenon was genuine perversity of will.

A fundamental egotism is at work in all sociopathy, putting the person at odds with society and its norms. In my lexicon, however, the most extreme "sociopath" is the sadistic serial killer, someone who murders with little or no provocation and little or no external point. There is simply personal pleasure in

---

28. *Oxford English Dictionary,* s.v. "sociopath."

the act of dominance and destruction itself, including pleasure in the knowledge that what one is doing is the ultimate moral violation. *One relishes the transgressive act and the fact that it is transgressive.* This is true abomination, evil raised to the second power, so to speak.[29] Having seen or heard hundreds of postwar interviews with Nazis, military and civilian, I suspect that the cavalier and unrepentant attitudes of many were actually a smoke screen. They knew that what they were doing was grossly unethical, but they loved it and there was safety in numbers. Only after the fact did they seek to hide behind moral sincerity. Even the apparent "banality" of Adolf Eichmann was deceptive. His "I was only following orders" defense was akin to Uriah Heep's claim in *David Copperfield* to be "so very umble,"[30] merely a modest clerk doing his modest duty. If one says this often enough, one might almost come to believe it oneself — *almost!* In any event, whether Nazi perpetrators own up to their crimes is now less important than that we all concede that we are capable of perversity. There is no denying the depth of Nazi depravity and guilt — never before or since has human evil reached the murderous proportions of the Holocaust — but the demonic potential is a human universal. One need only recall the Spanish Inquisition, American slavery, and the 800,000 (mostly Tutsis) slain in Rwanda in 1994.

Though the frame of reference is typically an individual, the term "sociopathic" can also be applied to a group, even to an entire society. Nazi Germany was such a society, a society in which anxiety had reached such a fever pitch that the fundamental scruple against genocide was repressed. The more anxiety, individually and collectively, the more release was sought in *Schadenfreude*. As a sociopathic society whose "huge imago made a psychopathic god,"[31] the Third Reich fed off of the degradation and death of others. The Aryan *Volk* had to have a counterpeople, just as Ted Bundy had to have innocent prey. Even as Bundy was suave and highly intelligent, yet his fragile sense of self required objectifying women, so the National Socialist state was cultured and technologically proficient, yet its very being demanded Jewish slaves and corpses.

The Nazis really were Christ killers, as symbolized by Hitler becoming the antithesis of the Jewish Messiah embraced by Christians. If Jesus sought to "redeem" the Jewish nation, it was in a spiritual sense, rather than by violently overthrowing Israel's Roman occupiers and reestablishing a Davidic kingship.

---

29. See my *Love Disconsoled: Meditations of Christian Charity* (Princeton: Princeton University Press, 1999), chap. 4.

30. Charles Dickens, *David Copperfield,* chap. 17.

31. Auden, "September 1, 1939," p. 86.

His message was indeed "political," but precisely in relativizing all temporal powers and institutions and bringing them under the judgment and mercy of God. *Pace* the Zealots, Christ's kingdom was "not from this world" (John 18:36). Most importantly, Jesus' call to revolutionary love of God and neighbor was grounded in *his own* suffering and sacrifice. Hitler, in contrast, sought to "redeem" the German nation in a decidedly material and bloody fashion by making *others* (especially the Jews) suffer and sacrifice. If Jesus ultimately aimed to bring peace to the entire world, Hitler eventually aimed to make war on the entire world. Many thought of Hitler as "the Savior of Germany," but a *biblical* Messiah must be for the world as such, or he is an idol. It is possible for one man to be the "father" of a country (e.g., George Washington of America or Giuseppe Garibaldi of Italy); one leader may be the "preserver" of a nation (e.g., Abraham Lincoln of America or Winston Churchill of England); but to be *the Savior* of a particular state, exclusively, is a pagan notion. It is the ancient principle of Baal, "the old atrocity," that for one to live another must die.

That said, the purpose served by the Nazi Holocaust was not the usual, limited political objective. The rhetoric about getting even for the betrayal of World War I, protecting German blood and honor, putting the exploitative Hebrews to work, etc., was *ex post facto* rationalization — deception and self-deception. In 1933, less than 1 percent of Germans were Jewish,[32] thus they could not be a serious threat to the German nation; and the vast majority of the 6,000,000 Jews murdered between 1939 and 1945 (roughly, 5,100,000) were in *non-Germanic* territories *invaded* by the Nazis (especially France, Hungary, Holland, Italy, Poland, Slovakia, and the Soviet Union).[33] The desire for *Lebensraum* no doubt helped motivate going to war, and plunder of property, especially Jewish property, was a widespread practice by 1938 and an expanding goal once war was declared.[34] But geographical and material cupidity was finally secondary to genocidal pride, what Toland called "[Hitler's] dream of cleansing Europe of Jews."[35]

One must distinguish three factors in the run-up to World War II: (1) desire for the realization of "Greater Germany" *(Grossdeutschland),* (2) genocidal

32. Robert P. Ericksen, *Complicity in the Holocaust: Churches and Universities in Nazi Germany* (Cambridge: Cambridge University Press, 2012), p. 9.

33. See Raul Hilberg, *The Destruction of the European Jews* (New York: Harper and Row, 1961), p. 767.

34. On the "expropriation" of Jewish money and possessions, including the "forced Aryanization" of businesses, the "Reich Flight Tax," and the "Jewish Atonement Payment," see Hilberg, *Destruction,* pp. 54-105.

35. Toland, *Adolf Hitler,* p. xiv.

hatred of the Jews, and (3) ambition for a Nazi empire. Greater Germany was one of Hitler's aspirations from before World War I and involved the unification of Germanic-speaking regions (minimally, Germany; Austria, his own country of birth; the Sudetenland; Bohemia-Moravia).[36] Deep-seated prejudice against the Jews was part of the air that Hitler breathed from childhood, but his genocidal hatred toward them appears to have emerged only after Germany's defeat in World War I and the punitive Treaty of Versailles in 1919. It was during the formative years of 1919-1922, when Hitler was refashioning the fledgling German Workers' Party, and then after the Beer Hall Putsch (1923) as he wrote *Mein Kampf* (published 1925-1926), that Hitler's virulent anti-Semitism becomes self-conscious and articulate. Referring to the inflated and at times murderous rhetoric of *Mein Kampf,* Toland reports that "[Hitler's] comrades at the front [in World War I] never heard him talk like this; he appeared to be no more anti-Semitic than they were."[37] Again, he evidently came to judge Jewish financial and political plotting and lack of patriotism to be responsible for Germany's 1918 "collapse of morale,"[38] so he, in turn, premised the resurrection of national morale on race vilification and purification.

I say "evidently" because it is possible to wonder to what degree Hitler actually believed his own anti-Semitic rhetoric. His sincere detestation of Jewish habits and convictions seems indubitable, but pandering to others' racism as a means to galvanize the German public and prepare them for war is another matter, a further step. (Did Hitler actually think, as he often charged, that the Jews were so diabolical as to be orchestrating *both world capitalism and world communism,* to be pulling the strings *in Britain, America, and the Soviet Union,* to embody both the proletariat and the bourgeoisie?[39] Did he give credence to *The Protocols of the Elders of Zion,* or did he merely tout that fraudulent document for political purposes?)[40] In any case, the second factor (genocidal hatred)

36. The more ambitious view of Greater Germany had it including Denmark, Norway, Sweden, and lowland France. The point remains that, had Hitler stopped with the fulfillment of even a robust form of pan-Germanism, the Holocaust would not have happened and World War II would not have been the general conflagration it became.

37. Toland, *Adolf Hitler,* p. 66.

38. Toland, *Adolf Hitler,* p. 66.

39. See *State of Deception,* pp. 44, 102-3, 124, 136-37.

40. With stunning illogic, Hitler writes: "How much the whole existence of this people [the Jews] is based on a permanent falsehood is proved in a unique way by 'The Protocols of the Elders of Zion,' which are so violently repudiated by the Jews. With groans and moans, the *Frankfurter Zeitung* repeats again and again that these are forgeries. This alone is evidence in favour of their authenticity." See Adolf Hitler, *Mein Kampf,* trans. Ralph Manheim (Boring, Ore.: CPA Books, 1942), p. 174. Toland writes: "Hitler's hatred of Jews had come primarily

was initially distinct from hope for Greater Germany, and it provided a segue to the third factor (empire). Above all, we must appreciate that a Nazi empire was more than a consolidation of Germanic-speaking lands; it entailed the aggressive conquest of nations with little or no Germanic cultural or linguistic heritage.

My unoriginal observation is that only after World War I did Hitler seek to synthesize (1) and (2) above, combining the growing of the German state with the persecution and finally the extermination of the Jews.[41] Indeed, Hitler came to realize that a kind of *Aufhebung* of his theory and practice was needed, that (3), a Nazi empire, could only exist as a new form of civilization that went beyond pan-Germanism to become an ever-expanding juggernaut based on race slavery and mass murder.[42] (Recall that Greater Germany had already been largely achieved before September 1939, without widespread war.) What is comparatively novel is to recognize in the *Führer*, and eventually the Reich leadership, a shift from seeing war as a means to political ends to seeing war as the end of politics itself. (In place of Kant's ideal of "Perpetual Peace," Hitler would give Germany very real "perpetual war.") And not any old kind of war would do. National *regeneration* through specific acts of violence — a.k.a. corporate revenge for Versailles — differs from the ongoing *generation* of the nation through unbridled genocide — a kind of social vampirism. Genocidal assault on the Jews, that "the Jewish peril" be "stamped out,"[43] became the Nazi telos, and not as the Jews were randomly found but as they were systematically sought out. "The Jews" and "the Reds" were Hitler's two great postwar hates, which he frequently conflated, and since "the Jewish Reds" were a global reality, his hatred had also to be without boundaries.

The Nazi polis did not invade Poland on September 1 of 1939 to protect itself from existing internal or external threats, nor was the extension of national boundaries and the swelling of state coffers as such the main goal. Nazi Germany precipitated World War II chiefly to become, paradoxically, a viable Empire of Death, to sustain its solidarity of hatred by creating the endless perception of "enemies" and then annihilating them. This is the familiar pattern of the sociopath: affirm me by denying you, even to the point of your destruction constituting

---

from his own observation in the last days of the war [WWI] and during the revolutions that followed. What he learned from Rosenberg, the Thule Society, or from Gobineau, Luther and other famous anti-Semites merely buttressed his own conclusions. He borrowed only what he wanted from such sources." See Toland, *Adolf Hitler*, p. 103.

41. Toland makes this basic point in *Adolf Hitler*, pp. 226-32.

42. Cf. William Styron, "Hell Reconsidered," in *This Quiet Dust and Other Writings* (New York: Vintage Books, 1993).

43. Hitler, *Mein Kampf*, p. 174.

my very identity. It is perhaps even more nefarious, certainly more sociopathic, when the credo is collective: "affirm *us* by denying *them*."[44]

Conclusion: Both Abraham and Christ

The Jews were shot and gassed during the Holocaust for the same reason that Socrates, Jesus, Lincoln, Gandhi, and King were murdered: they denied that might makes right, that predation and survival of the fittest are the ultimate principle of reality, and thus they themselves became the prey of "the mighty." Socrates and Jesus denied the omnipotence of empire and were executed as seditious; Lincoln, Gandhi, and King denied the omnipotence of ethnicity and were assassinated as traitorous or uppity. But the dynamic in all five cases was basically the same: appeals to a transcendent goodness were met with a very mundane evil. In the case of the Jews, their embodiment of monotheism and neighbor love heaped burning coals on everyone else. As Eugene Borowitz has put it, "Because the Jews are a witness to God and testify that the world remains unredeemed, the nations hate them."[45] When Nazi Germany combined empire and ethnicity, Rome and race, the hatred of the Jews became genocidal.

Throughout history, when someone names and challenges the human proclivity to elevate self by denigrating others — a.k.a. original sin — that someone is dispatched. Speaking anachronistically, the Jews rejected Darwinian natural selection as morally normative, and as a result they suffered the horrific backlash of social Darwinism. Rather than setting "us-the-excellent-and-powerful" against "them-the-decadent-and-weak," the Hebrew prophets expand our care to include the stranger, the widow, and the orphan. For them, the needy and vulnerable "other" has a special claim on us. This is a violation of the biological imperative of kin selection and in-group dominance, and for this the prophets must die.

On what basis did the biblical prophets propound their "unnatural" vision? The remembering of the Supernatural. Jewish theology (like Christian) is not univocal, and some "rabbis" have preached a hate-filled and excluding Deity, but both the prophets and the law consistently teach a love of God and

44. I thank my Emory colleagues Jon Gunnemann and Steve Tipton for helping me to articulate this portion of my essay, especially the points in these last three paragraphs. Whether or not they agree with my analysis, they have forced me to clarify my thesis. My doctoral student, Zach Eyster, also provided constructive criticism that improved the final product.

45. Eugene B. Borowitz, *Choices in Modern Jewish Thought* (Springfield, N.J.: Behrman House, 1995), p. 207.

neighbor that is strikingly inclusive. Jeremiah 7:5-7 insists to Judah that "if you truly act justly one with another, if you do not oppress the alien, the orphan, and the widow, or shed innocent blood in this place, and if you do not go after other gods to your own hurt, then I will dwell with you in this place, in the land that I gave of old to your ancestors for ever and ever." Leviticus 19:33-34 reads: "When an alien resides with you in your land, you shall not oppress the alien. The alien who resides with you shall be to you as the citizen among you; you shall love the alien as yourself, for you were aliens in the land of Egypt: I am the LORD your God." And in Psalm 146, we find:

> Do not put your trust in princes,
> in mortals, in whom there is no help.
> When their breath departs, they return to the earth;
> on that very day their plans perish.
>
> Happy are those whose help is the God of Jacob,
> whose hope is in the LORD their God,
> who made heaven and earth,
> the sea, and all that is in them;
> who keeps faith forever;
> who executes justice for the oppressed;
> who gives food to the hungry.
>
> The LORD sets the prisoners free;
> the LORD opens the eyes of the blind.
> The LORD lifts up those who are bowed down;
> the LORD loves the righteous.
> The LORD watches over the strangers;
> he upholds the orphan and the widow,
> but the way of the wicked he brings to ruin.

We are all radically indebted to a gracious Creator, and we are all fallen before that Holy Presence; thus we must be grateful for all life and humbly repent of our sins. In the face of such an anti-Hitlerite message, the world typically prefers its aggrandized princes and tribal gods and will kill to preserve them.

To remember both Shylock and Oedipus is to recognize that we are the world. All can be on either end of sociopathology. All can be both victims and victimizers, both as different and as the same, both as individuals and as groups. The Nazi combination of aggressive war and the gospel of hate is a constant human temptation. Indeed, Nazi anti-Semitism was finally nothing but stunted misanthropy. It was a striking projection onto a peculiar minority, by a despairing majority, of the universal human dread of difference and mortality. We want to be rid of the strangeness of life — the foreignness of other people (their recalcitrance and unassimilability) and of ourselves (our own faults and limitations) — so we murder the most conspicuous strangers we can find or invent. Thus we deny or disguise, for a brief time, the real object of our anxiety: ourselves and our vulnerable nature. When victimizers forget our shared fallenness, their prayer becomes puke; when victims confront it, their puke becomes prayer. When historians and ethicists are perplexed by the ability of so many Germans to be so cruel and callous toward the Jews, they forget that Jewish suffering and death were the direct source of Nazi joy and solidarity, not some unhappy burden that had to be tolerated for the sake of other aims. As I have argued, the Second World War itself was in the service of the racial hatred, not the other way around.

This is not a prescription for hopelessness, but rather a plea for humility. The Jew is the mirror of the world; the Holocaust, the mirror cracked; the means to recovery, to set aside the narcissism that makes us want a mirror in the first place. When we look in the mirror, we inevitably don't like what we see and are moved to violence. (We are always hardest on the crimes by which we are the most tempted, and we always try to shore up our self-respect by demeaning others; original sin = *Schadenfreude*.) Not narcissism, nor counternarcissism, but divine grace accepted overcomes fallenness — however incompletely — in this life.

The positive counters to the largely negative lessons of Shylock and Oedipus, in sum, are Abraham and Christ. Abraham is the reverse of Oedipus — a father who declines to slay his son;[46] Christ is, in one key respect, the opposite of Shylock — a Jew who, though oppressed, forgives rather than demanding his "pound of flesh" from another. Indeed, Christ *gives* his own flesh *for* others. Together, Abraham and Christ disclose the breadth and depth of divine love, respectively. If Shylock and Oedipus help us to be as wise as serpents, Abraham and Christ teach us to be as innocent as doves (see Matt. 10:16). Given human freedom and the contingency of history, not even God's own holiness can guarantee that another Holocaust will not happen. But if it does, we are, as always, without excuse . . .

46. The meaning of the Akedah in Gen. 22 is endlessly disputed, but I favor seeing it as God's engineering the overcoming of early Israelite child sacrifice. See *Love Disconsoled*, chap. 6.

CHAPTER 11

Keeping Marriage Sacred:
The Christian Case for Gay and Lesbian Wedlock

Introduction

We usually think of the Christian churches, with their commitment to Scripture and tradition, as more likely to be against same-sex marriage than the secular state. I argue in this chapter, however, that, if anything, the situation is the reverse: Christians have good theological and historical reasons to offer gay and lesbian marriage, but the secular citizens of a liberal state may have a harder time discerning these or related reasons. If such citizens are primarily concerned to oversee the natural goods of marriage, especially procreation, then they may well have grounds to decline to legitimize marital unions between persons of the same gender, though this is debatable. Christians, in contrast, ought to give primacy to the supernatural good of marriage, the sacramental bond between the partners before God. This bond governs and fulfills the natural goods of marriage — both children and erotic desire — and access to it should be extended to all who are able voluntarily to benefit from it. Whatever the secular state does, the church must keep its own theological counsels, even if this means overriding old ecclesial councils with new. In this way, the church will be a witness to the state, which is itself partly composed of Christians concerned to foster love of neighbor wherever they can.

When "liberal" defenders of same-sex marriage emphasize the importance of erotic love and the need of gays and lesbians to have their romantic commitments publicly and legally recognized, they are highlighting something of profound significance. When "conservative" opponents of same-sex marriage focus on children and their place in traditional marriages, they too are pointing to something of great human moment. But to the extent that defenders and opponents dwell on *eros* or offspring, they are both limiting themselves to the natural goods of marriage. For Christians, this is like haggling over which is the more important element in the Lord's Supper, the bread or the wine, when the salient point is that they are both transubstantiated by grace into the body and blood of Christ. This is a chief reason why the public debate over same-sex marriage is so often volatile and fruitless: both sides tend to be blind to or silent about the supernatural good of marriage, but without that good the others cannot be properly understood or ordered.

If there is a conflict between affirming the sexual desires of some adults and protecting the best interests of children, then surely the children should be given priority. But, *inter alia,* I make two points herein. First, such a conflict is not inevitable. Second, a Christian must look beyond *both* adults' erotic desires *and* children's conception and care for the central meaning of marriage. That meaning is agapic love, and only when this is appreciated can the church think clearly about who should be allowed to participate in the marital sacrament.

I. The Supernatural Good of Marriage

For Saint Augustine (354-430), the three goods of marriage (i.e., monogamous sexuality) are "offspring, fidelity, [and] the sacramental bond."[1] The sacramental bond is, by implication, primary, since Augustine makes it very clear that neither infertility nor absence (failure to quiet concupiscence) dissolves a marriage.[2] Some eight and a half centuries later, Thomas Aquinas (1225-1274) elaborated these themes, contending that the "supernatural" good or end of marriage is the sacramental bond between the two parties before God, with the four "natural" goods being: (1) procreation, (2) care and education of children, (3) honoring of the woman, and (4) honoring of the husband or father.[3] Augustine and Aquinas are usually associated with a conservative appraisal of matters sexual and connubial, but I want to build on their general picture to defend the Christian propriety of gay and lesbian wedlock. In a straightforward sense, my defense is "liberal," in proposing something new; in another sense, however, it too is "conservative," in seeking to preserve the distinctive sanctity of Christian matrimony.

1. See Augustine, *On Marriage and Concupiscence,* in *The Nicene and Post-Nicene Fathers,* vol. 5, ed. Philip Schaff (Grand Rapids: Eerdmans, 1971), 1.19, p. 271; see also *The City of God,* trans. Henry Bettenson (New York: Penguin, 1972), 14.22, pp. 584-85.

2. Augustine, *On Marriage and Concupiscence* 1.11, p. 268.

3. Thomas Aquinas, *Summa Theologiae,* trans. Fathers of the English Dominican Province (Westminster, Md.: Christian Classics, 1981), vol. 4; II-II, qu. 151-156; pp. 1796-1828.

Secular critiques of same-sex marriage generally point to an inherent "pathology" in same-sex erotic relationships, while defenses appeal to the "right" of gays and lesbians to choose an important social institution. Distinctively Christian critiques often focus on God's ordaining marriage to be between a man and a woman (Gen. 2:18, 21-24) or on the precepts of natural law. In the latter case, critics argue that a homosexual union subverts or violates some or all of the natural goods specified by Saint Thomas, especially (1). People of the same sex cannot conceive children, nor, the argument goes, can they adequately raise children. Christian defenses of gay marriage, in turn, frequently point to the ways in which homosexuals might fulfill the four natural goods in metaphorical or analogical fashion. For example, a lesbian couple might foster or adopt or they might contribute "procreatively" to their wider community by way of art or politics.

The four natural goods of marriage (in some form) are highly significant, and I can even see the point of claiming (as did the Roman Catholic Church prior to Vatican II) that procreation is "primary" among the four natural ends. But critics and defenders (both Christian and non-Christian) often displace our attention away from the *supernatural* end — the sacramental bond — which both Augustine and Aquinas considered the primary good of marriage full stop. Indeed, it is the sacramental bond that "sanctifies" the other goods of marriage all the way down, by founding them on the love of God. By "the love of God," I mean both the subjective and the objective genitive — that is, both God's love for the couple and the couple's love for God — but the former has priority, in temporal and causal senses.

Like many heterosexuals born in the 1950s and 1960s, I was raised to see homosexuality as "disordered" or "unnatural," but this is a worldly judgment based almost entirely on biology and aesthetics. Surely Christians of all people should want to interpret and govern "nature" based on the transcendental holiness of God. If grace "heals" and "perfects" nature, as Thomas believed and I too affirm, then we should actively want gay and lesbian relations to be brought under the auspices of *agape*.[4] (This is the goal for straight relations too, of course.) This requires, I believe, offering the sacrament of marriage — with all its joys and sorrows, benefits and burdens — to one and all, regardless of sexual orientation. This argument is not based on the right of homosexuals

---

4. Augustine and Aquinas both employ the word *caritas* for the theological virtue of love. This word is sometimes said to be the Latin equivalent of the New Testament Greek term *agape*, but I am not persuaded. (See my *Love Disconsoled: Meditations on Christian Charity* [Cambridge: Cambridge University Press, 1999], chap. 1.) For my part, I prefer the biblical terminology of *agape*, as in Matt. 22:38-40; John 13:34-35; and John 15:12, 17.

to participate in a social good but rather on the eucharistic meaning of the Christian sacrament.

Emphasizing the eucharistic character of marriage should make Christians "countercultural on both ends," so to speak.[5] Against traditionalists who want heterosexuals to retain a monopoly on matrimony, Christians must insist that the sacrament is not primarily about conceiving offspring and, more importantly, that God is constantly renewing all of creation through the blessing and discipline of love.[6] Against queer theorists who reject marriage as a bourgeois or oppressive ideal, Christians should note that a refusal to sacramentalize one's erotic relations is a Gnostic rejection of both embodied creation and the transcendent Creator.

Inevitably, someone will ask at this juncture: How "pluralistic" can marriage be? Can children wed one another? Can a man marry a mare or a machine? My answer is: Whoever can give informed consent to the marriage vows, whoever is competent to love and be loved agapically, is a fit conjugal subject. This criterion is precisely what rules out children, animals, and inanimate objects and what rules in gays and lesbians. Can a human being wed an angel, then? I suppose so, though I would not recommend it . . . for the angel's sake.

The fundamental point is that Christians, either *qua* members of a biblical faith or *qua* members of a liberal democracy, must subordinate the temporal to the eternal. This means construing positive law of both church and state in light of eternal law, as well as interpreting natural law in light of the revelation of Christ. This does not mean establishing a theocracy, requiring faith tests for voting rights and the like. But it does entail, for Christians, asking conscientiously what the will of God requires in any particular setting. Let me turn now to explaining why I think affirming gay wedlock is Christlike.

II. Christ's Ministry as Inclusive and Iconoclastic

Jesus the Christ was strikingly *inclusive and iconoclastic,* two attributes that are related but not synonymous. His inclusivity was reflected in his having table fellowship with both those judged guilty of sin and those considered

5. I thank my colleague Luke Johnson for helping me, in conversation, to clarify this point.

6. On God's making a new creation, see Luke Johnson, "Scripture and Experience," part of "Homosexuality and the Church: Two Views," in *Commonweal* 134, no. 12 (June 15, 2007).

unclean or otherwise marginal by traditional society. In addition to associating with adulterers and tax collectors, for instance, Jesus also kept company with women and the physically ill, refusing to shun even the woman "suffering from hemorrhages for twelve years" (Mark 5:25).[7] We moderns are inclined to see the first category, sinfulness, as ethical and the latter, uncleanness, as aesthetic or liturgical, but ancient Israelite religion did not draw such a sharp contrast.[8] Its more holistic vision of the universe linked the immoral/vicious with the outré/anomalous as equally out of step with God's providential governance of the world. Having fellowship with sinners did not mean that Jesus endorsed their behavior, but it did illustrate that he did not write them off the rolls of humanity. Similarly, Jesus did not deny that the diseased or indisposed were diminished in some sense, but he continued to recognize their needs and potentials. Even though Jesus said to the guilty "do not sin again" (John 8:11), and even though he sought to cure the afflicted and comfort the disenfranchised, he did not cease to love them as neighbors and fellow children of God. Moreover, he explicitly rejected the principle that all physical anomaly (e.g., blindness) must be due to sin (see John 9:1-3).[9] Must we not say the same about psychic anomaly?

As impressive as was Jesus' inclusivity, his iconoclasm was even more so. He went beyond sustaining relationships with the evil and alien; *he changed our understanding of what constitutes sin and uncleanness themselves.* Importantly, his changes were not always in a relaxed or libertarian direction; indeed, they were often just the opposite. He showed that healing on the Sabbath and

---

7. Whether the blood flow was due to menometrorrhagia, heavy and irregular periods, or some other medical condition, the woman was ritually unclean and probably infertile. This rendered her social status even more tenuous than that of the average woman in first-century Palestine, likely destined to be a wife and mother. The fact that she touches Jesus technically makes him unclean as well, but he does not berate or reject her. Instead, as L. Lewis Wall observes, he "deliberately violat[es] a ritual restriction in order to perform an act of compassion." He says to her, "Daughter, your faith has made you well; go in peace, and be healed of your disease" (Mark 5:34). See Wall, "Jesus and the Unclean Woman," *Christianity Today* (posted 1/13/2010). In contrast to the tenor of his times, Jesus seems to have been remarkably free of male chauvinism. He clearly had female followers — Mary Magdalene, Joanna, Susanna, Mary of Bethany, and Mary and Martha, the sisters of Lazarus — and he typically considered women to be fully capable of faith, as Mark 5 illustrates. Are gays and lesbians our era's "unclean woman"?

8. As Richard Hays puts it, "The Old Testament . . . makes no systematic distinction between ritual law and moral law." See Hays, *The Moral Vision of the New Testament* (New York: HarperCollins, 1996), p. 382.

9. I thank Zach Eyster for reminding me of this passage.

eating outside of kosher might be righteous; but, more radically, he insisted that what might technically be lawful action — for example, laying a gift at the altar and not committing adultery — can actually be sinful if done with the wrong attitude or motivation. Hatred and lust in the heart make one guilty before the Father, regardless of external performance (see Matt. 5:23-28). Clearly, Jesus' key measure of propriety, moral and religious, was the summary of the law and prophets recorded at Matthew 22. The love of God and of neighbor, both of which are sustained by God's self-giving grace, was the touchstone. Jesus forgave the guilty, and he accepted the ostracized, but he brought both under the firm discipline of charity.

Whether or not one thinks that Christ miraculously cured the sick in a physical sense, I have emphasized that his healing ministry involved a shockingly close relation to sinners, the unclean, the outcast, and other marginalized folk.[10] Often the most painful and debilitating dimension of bodily illness, behavioral anomaly, or ethnic otherness was that it led to social exclusion. In being ostracized, a difficult condition was made much more burdensome. In contrast, by offering restored community to those with "dis-ease" of some kind, including the woman with hemorrhages, Christ made it possible to cope with or even thrive amidst personal trial. Although we tend to segregate the ethical and the aesthetic more completely than did ancient Palestinians, even in modern America we sometimes conflate and confine sickness and sin — think of the stigma still associated with AIDS.

If one does consider homosexuality a "disorder," the key question is how best to heal or redeem it; if one judges homosexuality to be merely an unusual habit or a different disposition, the issue of how responsibly to govern it abides. In either case, the basic good is to remain ensconced in a social, political, and ecclesial context that both affirms one's humanity and holds one accountable before God for the use of one's sexuality. The debate goes on as to whether or in what sense homosexuality is a pathology, but the preponderating evidence suggests to me (and to many) that the orientation is usually so much a function of neurophysiology and early childhood imprinting that it is not normally a matter of voluntary choice.[11] Not being subject to volition, it is hard to see the

10. See, for instance, John Dominic Crossan, *The Birth of Christianity* (New York: HarperCollins, 1998), pp. 291-304.

11. In the early 1970s, the diagnostic manual of the American Psychiatric Association (APA) classified homosexuality as such as an illness, "a sociopathic personality disturbance." Due to the work of Dr. Robert L. Spitzer and others, the Association dropped this characterization in 1973 and referred to "sexual orientation disturbance" only when a person's sexual affinity, heterosexual or homosexual, was the source of distress. In short, the Association no longer

condition as such as culpable. One might maintain that homosexual *acts* are morally wrong, even if homosexual orientation is not. But can one sustain this thesis if the acts in question are between consenting adults who are expressing their love for one another in a socially responsible way? (Pederasty, rape, compulsive sadomasochism, and other forms of sexual abuse are to be vigorously condemned, but this principle applies to straight as well as to gay and lesbian relations.) Even on "the worst-case scenario" of some sort of unnaturalness in homosexual acts, one might still be in favor of legalizing and sanctifying gay and lesbian unions as a form of civil and ecclesial amelioration.

Where, concretely, does this leave gays and lesbians and their ability or inability to marry? My hunch is that for many Christians, at least the straight ones, homosexuality seems both sinful and unclean: homosexual acts are guilty, and homosexual orientation is unnatural. Even if one does not consider gays and lesbians to be culpable as such, one might still think of same-sex desire and behavior as infravetatory, humanly inferior but not morally wrong. I myself may go to my grave feeling, on some level, that homosexual orientation is impoverished, not a full participation in the good gift of sexuality, but I am perpetually challenged by the inclusive and iconoclastic example of Jesus.

More generally, I am struck by how elastic the meaning of the word "natural" can be. Elsewhere, I have identified ten senses of the term: (1) the

---

considered homosexuality a "mental disorder." The issue remained (and remains) whether treatment of various kinds can "reorient" or "convert" someone's sexual urges and behaviors, and Spitzer himself authored a study in 2003 reporting that "the majority of [200] participants gave reports of change from a predominantly or exclusively homosexual orientation before therapy to a predominantly or exclusively heterosexual orientation in the past year." Spitzer did not interpret his data to mean that being gay or lesbian was simply a reversible choice, but many in the wider culture understood them in this way — as underwriting a "cure" for homosexuals who are strongly motivated to reform. After initially defending his paper, Spitzer admitted in 2012 that it was seriously flawed in relying on self-reports rather than on objective measures of real change. He offered a public "apology" to the gay community. See Benedict Carey, "Psychiatry Giant Sorry for Backing Gay 'Cure,'" *New York Times,* May 18, 2012.

In a related development, Alan Chambers, the president of Exodus International, recently challenged some of his own organization's key tenets. Exodus International is a Christian ministry group that for thirty-seven years has argued that prayer and psychotherapy can "cure" individuals of unwanted same-sex attractions. As reported in the *New York Times,* however, Chambers now says that "Exodus [can] no longer condone reparative therapy, which blames homosexuality on emotional scars in childhood and claims to reshape the psyche." In addition, in the words of the reporter, Chambers believes "that those who persist in homosexual behavior [can] still be saved by Christ and go to heaven." Chambers's opinions are strongly criticized by others in the "ex-gay" movement, of course. See Erik Eckholm, "Rift Forms in Movement as Belief in Gay 'Cure' Is Renounced," *New York Times,* July 6, 2012.

physical or biological and thus what is contrasted with the immaterial or spiritual, (2) the common or universal and thus what is contrasted with the idiosyncratic or singular, (3) the un-man-made or spontaneous and thus what is contrasted with the artificial or forced, (4) the simple or orderly and thus what is contrasted with the complex or chaotic, (5) the real or objective and thus what is contrasted with the illusory or merely subjective, (6) the abstract or timeless and thus what is contrasted with the traditional or historical, (7) the traditional or historical and thus what is contrasted with the abstract or timeless, (8) the cosmic or holistic and thus what is contrasted with the material or what is characteristic of any other subset of beings smaller than the (created) universe as a whole (cf. Spinoza's *"deus sive natura"*), (9) the commonsensical or indubitable and thus what is contrasted with the dubious or unknowable, and (10) the pristine or noble and thus what is contrasted with the sullied or base.[12] Manifestly, these ten senses have ontological, epistemological, and ethical implications. They bear on *what* is known, *how* it is known, and *whether* we ought to approve it.

Since "natural" does not always mean morally normative, the key question for my purposes is: How far does Christlike love go in the case of the "unnatural" (a.k.a. queer) neighbor, from tolerance all the way to affirmation? Does the example and teaching of Jesus suggest the need to reevaluate homosexuality as unusual but neither intrinsically immoral nor socially dishonorable? Homosexual orientation and behavior may be "natural" for some, and, in any case, the issue is how to appraise and respond to them.

III. The Four Dimensions of the Christian Moral Life

If, as I have argued, the Christian moral life has four dimensions, we can continue our moral appraisal of homosexual relations, including potential marriage, by examining these four gradients.

(1) *Aretology:* Need the motive for same-sex relations be inherently selfish, malevolent, or otherwise vicious? A traditional worry is that there is "insufficient otherness" between persons of the same gender for love between them to be anything other than narcissistic. Erotic love should be for the different, "the opposite sex" that calls one out of oneself to attend to "the other"; this is how the argument goes, and with some real force. Admittedly,

---

12. Jackson, "Naturalism, Formalism, and Supernaturalism: Moral Epistemology and Comparative Ethics," *Journal of Religious Ethics* 27, no. 3 (Fall 1999): 477-506.

virtually all human relations are tainted by egotism, but I can't see this as a distinctly homosexual problem. (Think of "trophy wives," "cougars," *Sex in the City*, and so on.) Narcissism is notoriously hard to quantify and surprisingly easy to disguise, but the studies with which I am familiar suggest that gays and lesbians are, as a group, no more and no less self-absorbed or vice-ridden than straights. For its part, the American Psychiatric Association affirms that "homosexuality per se implies no impairment in judgment, stability, reliability, or general social or vocational capabilities."[13] Same-sex couples have the same general body types, of course, but even so there is massive variation in specific physiologies. More importantly, differing personal histories and mental and emotional makeups guarantee that there will be real psychological diversity between homosexual partners. The gay or lesbian is not simply making love to a mirror; the opportunities for give and take, for genuine honoring of a complex and elusive other, are surely there. Again, homosexuals can be generous or greedy, creative or involuted, but so can we all. What counts is that a sincere resolve to affirm each other's good before God is an animating possibility.

(2) *Deontology:* Are same-sex relations intrinsically unjust, regardless of the conscious motives or traits of character behind them? Is there a moral duty that is objectively neglected or violated by gays and lesbians who enact their love? Once more, deceit or manipulation is certainly a possible element in homosexual acts, as in heterosexual ones, but I can't see that either mendacity toward or objectification of the other is inevitable. Gay and lesbian sex is not *biologically* procreative, and if one thinks that all erotic activities must be aimed at (or at least open to) this end — if deontology and teleology are tied in this way — then obviously homosexual acts will be deemed warped or incomplete. But must openness to "procreativity" always be interpreted in physicalist terms, and is the absence of physical reproduction always wrong? Manifestly, many heterosexuals indulge sexual desires without any thought about having children, immediately or ever. It would be a lame defense of gay relations, however, if the best one could say is that straights can be irresponsible hedonists too. But what more can be said?

I have indicated that the integrity of Christian marriage, keeping it sa-

13. "Position Statement on Homosexuality," *American Journal of Psychiatry* 150, no. 4 (April 1993); the APA reaffirmed this document in July 2011. Sam Vaknin, the Internet guru of Narcissistic Personality Disorder, writes: "Research [has] failed to find any substantive difference between the psychological make-up of a narcissist who happens to have homosexual preferences — and a heterosexual narcissist. They both are predators, devouring Narcissistic Supply Sources as they go." See Vaknin, *Malignant Self Love: Narcissism Revisited* (Prague and Skopje: Narcissus Publications, 2001), p. 90.

cred, demands that we retrain the unitive and procreative goods but in an ordered hierarchy. I have noted that for Augustine and Aquinas and the sacramental tradition they represent, the highest good of marriage is the supernatural bond between the parties. The Roman Catholic Church continues to hold, of course, that the natural good of procreation must be understood in biological terms. For it, sex without (openness to) biological reproduction is sinful under all circumstances, as is biological reproduction without sex.[14] It is possible, however, to construe the obligation to "be fruitful and multiply" in other terms.[15] Insisting that sex be confined to marriage and that the marital relation be "productive" is a plausible means of elevating *eros* above the mere pursuit of personal satisfaction, but productivity might be understood in ethical, aesthetic, or social terms — as opposed to strictly biochemical ones. Gay and lesbian couples might rightly be expected, for instance, to direct their energies beyond themselves and toward enhancing the common good. The natural good of biological progeny is not an option for them as a couple, but foster care, adoption, and other forms of social service may be available. If the supernatural good of sacramental bonding is indeed paramount, and if the bodily union of the pair is leavened with repair of the republic, then where's the rub? It is not a universal duty to have children, especially for those who are psychosomatically ill-equipped to do so. Otherwise, we would have to condemn celibate priests and infertile spouses. More pointedly, if it were a duty for all to have children, then the fertile spouse in an infertile heterosexual marriage would be *obliged* to divorce and marry a partner with whom the fertile spouse could conceive a child.

14. See, for instance, Pope Paul VI's 1968 encyclical *Humanae Vitae*. In "On Responsible Parenthood" (1966), the Majority Report of the Papal Birth Control Commission concluded that artificial contraception within marriage should be allowed. The final vote was sixty-five in favor to seven opposed. Nevertheless, Pope Paul sided with the seven dissenters to craft *Humanae Vitae*. A papal encyclical is not dogma or even doctrine, and not everything a pope says/writes is done *ex cathedra*, but the magisterium also promulgates the position I describe. The *Catechism of the Catholic Church* includes the following: "the Church, which is 'on the side of life,' teaches that 'it is necessary that each and every marriage act remain ordered *per se* to the procreation of human life.'" See *Catechism* (New York: Doubleday, 2003), paragraph 2366, p. 628. For a critique of the Catholic position as a form of "physicalism or biologism," see Charles E. Curran, "The Contraceptive Revolution and the Human Condition." Both the pope's and Curran's texts are reproduced in Stephen E. Lammers and Allen Verhey, eds., *On Moral Medicine* (Grand Rapids: Eerdmans, 1998), pp. 434-50.

15. A case in point is Margaret Farley's *Just Love: A Framework for Christian Sexual Ethics* (New York: Continuum, 2006); see especially her discussion of "fruitfulness" (pp. 226-31) and how it might apply to a same-sex ethic for Christians (pp. 289-90).

Don't misunderstand me. If I were a priest, asked to marry a healthy heterosexual couple but aware that they never intended to have children, I would decline to do so. A straight and fertile man and woman, wishing to wed but intending perpetually to frustrate biological procreation, would fail to comprehend the meaning of their marriage. They would be violating one of the natural goods of *their* union. But the case of gay and lesbian couples is different. Their very identity rules out the possibility of biological reproduction within the union, so they are not violating a good that is natural *to them*. In short, heterosexuals have a duty to aim at physical reproduction within marriage, but homosexuals do not. Not all heterosexuals need marry, but if they do, their union requires openness to physical procreation. To demand that homosexuals physically procreate, on the other hand, is like insisting that the deaf hear. (I explore this analogy further below, fully aware of how explosive the analogy may be.)

(3) *Teleology:* Beyond the character of agents and the form of their actions, do the *consequences* of homosexuality prove morally unacceptable as such? Would gay and lesbian wedlock be especially disutilitarian? During the millennia over which *Homo sapiens* was struggling for survival, the imperative for everyone to procreate and thus swell the tribe was no doubt selected evolutionarily. The more the viable offspring, conceived and nurtured in stable families, the more likely the clan would be able to compete with others and sustain itself over time. To this day, some fault homosexuals for not doing their part to produce the next generation. But times have changed, and now over-population is usually more of a threat to the common good than is infertility, abstinence, or homosexuality. The greatest happiness for the greatest number no longer requires that everyone procreate genetically. We need not let our genes push us around, so to speak. Any given person's life, especially her old age, may be put at risk by the absence of genetically related children to be parental caregivers, but this is no longer a general phenomenon. We typically leave it to the discretion of the individual whether to marry and have kids, and social security provides a safety net for all, at least in theory. To aver that social utility requires all to conceive is a needless anachronism at best and a tyrannical collectivism at worst.

One might contend that allowing homosexual marriage would undermine heterosexual marriage and thus do significant public harm. William Muehl, for instance, explicitly focuses on "social consequences" and asks, "Can the battered institution of Christian marriage stand the sight of gay unions being solemnized at the altar? What will be the effect upon all sexual relationships of the consecration of what are essentially sterile unions characterized by a very high degree of instability?"[16] Muehl is skeptical of any blanket appeal to good intentions, including love: "One of the most popular errors in the realm of Christian ethics has been the effort to make love an omnipotent spiritual quality which has the power to sanctify anything that is done in its name."[17] Regardless of purity of motive, if gay marriage is approved, then straight marriage is likely to be subverted; and if straight marriage is subverted, the whole of society will suffer, Muehl's argument goes — particularly women and children. But let us unpack these "ifs."

Why should the blessing and discipline of marriage be ruined for straights if marriage is made available to gays and lesbians? The relevant grace is not a limited resource, and treating it as such betrays the logic of *ressentiment:* "If I can't have a good all to myself, then it is meaningless and nobody should have it." Is this really what the disciples of Christ should be saying, or even implying? I share Professor Muehl's conviction that if straight marriage is derided or denied, the wider body politic is in profound trouble, but I would say the same about *gay and lesbian* marriage. In fact, the surest way to support and defend traditional heterosexual marriage is to require that the institution be opened, *mutatis mutandis,* to homosexuals too. David Brooks concludes, still more emphatically, "We shouldn't just allow gay marriage. We should insist on gay marriage."[18]

I also second Muehl's contention that virtuous motive is not enough — neither *agape* nor *eros* is a self-justifying emotion — hence my attending to the other three "dimensions" of the Christian moral life. But the point is that Muehl's predicted social consequences are not backed up by plausible sociological data. He assumes that significantly more people will embrace a gay or lesbian lifestyle if it is approved by the church, but he provides no empirical evidence for this. He appreciates that the nature and genesis of sexual identity remain a "mystery," even granting that "it is altogether possible that much of what seems essentially destructive in the gay life style is really the neurotic consequence of a hostile environment."[19] He earnestly declares that "Christians have a serious moral obligation to support basic civil rights for homosexuals" in employment, housing, and so on.[20] Yet he still worries that

16. William Muehl, "Some Words of Caution," in *Homosexuality and Ethics,* ed. Edward Batchelor Jr. (New York: Pilgrim Press, 1980), p. 75.

17. Muehl, "Some Words of Caution," p. 76.

18. David Brooks, "The Power of Marriage," in *Same-Sex Marriage: Pro and Con, A Reader,* ed. Andrew Sullivan (New York: Vintage Books, 2004), p. 198.

19. Muehl, "Some Words of Caution," pp. 71 and 75.

20. Muehl, "Some Words of Caution," p. 72.

genital homosexuality "may well be a ritual of hatred or aggression" toward the opposite sex, and he recommends "a firm reassertion of the time-honored distinction between toleration on the one hand and approval on the other."[21] Here "caution" has led to paralysis, if not paradox. How can I support basic civil rights for homosexuals if I deny them the good of marriage, and how can I presume to tolerate what is likely hateful and aggressive?

(4) *The Will of God:* The undergirding and overarching dimension of the moral life for Christians is the will of God, particularly eternity entering time in the person of Jesus Christ. What does God-in-Christ want of marriage? This question takes us directly back to the primacy of the sacramental bond between spouses and to the Father's promotion of faith, hope, and love through the person of the Son. Undeniably, some biblical passages condemn homosexual acts, if not homosexual people (e.g., Lev. 18 and Rom. 1), and I will discuss these in more detail in section V below. But for now it is sufficient to register (1) that Scripture is not inerrant, in my estimation, and (2) that God remains free to do new things for humanity, to bring us to an ever-deepening comprehension of divine love. Indeed, if the love of God and neighbor is the primary criterion for Jesus, then straights may no more need to "cure" gays and lesbians than Christians need to "convert" the Jews or men need to "make over" women into ersatz males.[22] To repeat, Christian charity is not an inner disposition alone, nor is it an invitation to libertinism. It must examine critically the full range of aretological, deontological, teleological, and theological factors behind sexual ethics. Nevertheless, sometimes such love balances these factors best by accepting the other rather than seeking to remold him in one's own image.

How does the discernment of God's will relate to developments in modern medicine and psychoanalysis? As a moral theologian, I can add little to the scientific debate about the genesis of homosexuality and its supposed voluntariness or involuntariness, perversity or normality. I have referred to the American Psychiatric Association's uncoupling of homosexuality from personality disorder, and still more general theses might be quoted. In the comprehensive *Textbook of Psychoanalysis,* Karen Gilmore allows that "most

---

21. Muehl, "Some Words of Caution," pp. 72 and 77.

22. The *Gospel of Thomas* has Jesus offering one of the great backhanded compliments of all time: he proclaims "every woman who will make herself male will enter into the Kingdom of Heaven." See Willis Barnstone, ed., *The Other Bible* (New York: HarperCollins, 1984), p. 307. One thing that makes this text Gnostic is its inability to accept embodied personhood in all its diversity. I find the contemporary effort of straights to offer "conversion therapy" to gays and lesbians similarly Gnostic.

psychoanalysts (especially North American analysts) no longer assume an exclusively psychological etiology for homosexuality . . . ; they assume a genetic or biological contribution and recognize healthy homosexual development."[23] This seems to be the majority opinion, but there is no unanimity among experts. What I *can* do is invite my readers, anecdotally, to ask themselves whether they "chose" their own sexual orientation and what it could mean that that orientation is condemned by God. I suspect that in the vast majority of cases, heterosexuality or homosexuality feels like a complex and given identity, rather than a simple and alterable option. In my own experience, sexual preference is such a deep and entrenched aspect of personality — again, a function of nature and nurture largely beyond conscious control — that calling it a "selection" is absurd. Similarly, changing my sexual orientation from heterosexual to homosexual is virtually inconceivable. I can only imagine the neurosis that would ensue if I were repeatedly humiliated for being straight and pressured by others to "convert." What, then, can be the point of claiming that someone's very being, someone's psychosomatic self, is contrary to God's will?

Especially in our post-Holocaust world, we should be alarmed anytime a human being is condemned or belittled simply because of who she is, regardless of the ability to choose or change that identity. This is especially true if the "other" in question is notably weak or politically disenfranchised. Today, in America, the most vulnerable human lives among us are gays, lesbians, and fetuses. (Blacks and Jews are doing better but are still far from home free.) As I have emphasized throughout this book, self-congratulatory dichotomies between "us" and "them" are the bane of the Western tradition, if not all of recorded history. Ancient versions of God's providential will emphasized "the elect" versus "the damned"; classical philosophical anthropologies spoke of "the rational" and "the irrational"; while the modern secular polis refers to "persons" and "nonpersons." But all these are antitheses of Jesus' inclusive and iconoclastic gospel. They are an invitation to despise or despoil our neighbor, sometimes "in the name of God." Christians, of all people, must say a staunch "no" to these invidious vocabularies.

At the very least, I admit that my lingering feeling that homosexuality

23. Karen Gilmore, "Childhood Experiences and the Adult World," in *Textbook of Psychoanalysis,* ed. Glen O. Gabbard, Bonnie E. Litowitz, and Paul Williams, 2nd ed. (Arlington, Va.: American Psychiatric Publishing, 2012), p. 119. Muriel Dimen and Virginia Goldner are more blunt: "sexuality has nothing inherently to do with mental health or mental illness. You may be ill if you are heterosexual or transvestite, and you may be healthy if you are homosexual or bisexual or . . . whatever." See their "Gender and Sexuality," p. 148.

is impoverished is quite possibly a function of limited powers of empathy. *Homosexuality presents a problem if one wants biological children with the opposite sex, but wanting children in this way is typical of heterosexuality, though certainly not definitive of it.* If homosexuality is not intrinsically immoral, nor even "unnatural" for some, then talk of "impoverishment" may well be the last vestige of a lexicon of *hubris*. (Perhaps I just want the luxury of feeling sorry for queer neighbors.) Of course, gays and lesbians too can procreate, even biologically, just not with their same-sex partners. All that said, let me continue in the next section to try to work out the logic of sacramental equality, even with physical "limitation," for those who (like me) are striving to bring private emotions under the sway of political *agape*. If the language of "poverty" or "limit" is misplaced or otherwise mistaken, then the case for gay and lesbian wedlock is that much stronger.

IV. Deaf Citizens and "Illegal Aliens"

Why put homosexual pairings, which some deem disordered, in the same category as heterosexual pairings? Why not distinguish between civic unions or commitment ceremonies for gays and lesbians and traditional marriages for straights? The answer is two-part. First, the Fall taints all human relations: heterosexual couples can be just as faithless, manipulative, and selfishly infertile as homosexual couples, and we need to acknowledge this solidarity in sin and need for grace. (Correlatively, homosexual couples can be just as faithful, generous, and creative as heterosexual ones.) Second, if a "separate but equal" philosophy did not work with respect to race, a "separate but unequal" doctrine will work even less well with respect to sexual orientation. A distinctive category of "union" or "commitment" would lead to second-class citizenship for gays and lesbians, whether in the state or in the church.

Consider two analogies: to being deaf and to being an "illegal." Deafness is undeniably a physical disorder,[24] and not being able to hear car horns and

---

24. I am aware that some deaf individuals claim that insensitivity to sound is not a "disorder" or "disability." Indeed, some deaf parents reportedly want to forgo corrective surgery for their infants' deafness or even to *make* their hearing children deaf. But this is medically and morally indefensible. Clearly, learning sign language or lip reading can help to compensate for an inability to hear. In addition, how much of a liability deafness is does turn, in part, on how the wider society treats the deaf. Finally, having a positive attitude about oneself, in spite of hearing loss, is admirable as well as pragmatic. (No doubt, virtue

ambulance sirens may make it more difficult to drive safely at times. Never-theless, we give driver's licenses to deaf people, so long as they learn to operate a motor vehicle competently. Some states require a deaf person's car to have mirrors on both sides, but this is important for *any* driver and is now standard on all American automobiles. Moreover, some maintain that the deaf are ac-tually *better* drivers, because they are more focused, less distracted. (Which is worse for safety purposes, to be deaf or to be able to hear yet have an in-car stereo blasting at max volume?) The point is that, in the name of equality, we don't issue a qualitatively different license for the deaf.

Think also of "illegal aliens." Few want to defend the initial violation of law and the clandestine crossing of borders, but how are we to handle these "strangers in a strange land" once they are here? It would be just, in some respects, to deport those who are caught, and in 2008, 270 "illegals" were even sent to prison in Iowa in order "to maintain the integrity of the immigration system."[25] But what of those not apprehended? Can a case be made for a general amnesty? Should we keep undocumented individuals on the fringes of society and its public institutions, often fearful and desperate, or should we allow (even encourage) them to become citizens, with all the rights and responsibilities that attend that status? Becoming a citizen means, at least in theory, learning the languages and practices of liberal democracy, including paying taxes, being required (and allowed) to educate one's children, voting and possibly running for office, and so on. All these civic exercises improve the individuals concerned, as well as contribute to the common good. Sim-ilarly, becoming a spouse within a sacramental marriage would mean being schooled in the diction and rituals of Christian faith, hope, and love and the subsequent taming of egotism and idolatry. If one of the things that is problematic about gay male relations in particular is their tendency to be promiscuous, then how better to bring them under moral governance than to subject them to the constancy and fidelity of the nuptial vow? Such virtue requires the grace of God, but surely this is accessible to all God's children, regardless of orientation.

---

often grows out of adversity.) But to deny that deafness is, in a straightforward sense, less than optimal functioning for a human being is either self-deceived or malevolent. The same can be said for blindness. Once again, analogizing homosexuality to deafness or blindness is an argumentative gambit: "Even if there is a disability here, the case for the marriage option is compelling." If homosexuality is in no way disordered, then, a fortiori, gay and lesbian wedlock ought to be quite uncontroversial.

25. See "270 Illegal Immigrants Sent to Prison in Federal Push," *New York Times,* May 24, 2008.

V. Jews and "Gentiles"

A third analogy is still more telling for Christians: that between homosexuals and "Gentiles." To affirm the Old Testament is, in part, to affirm the status of the Jews as God's chosen people. Chosenness is not the mark of virtue or privilege, however. God extends the covenant to Israel independently of Israel's merit, and God sustains the covenant independently of Israel's demerit. In addition, chosenness carries with it a peculiar obligation to be "a light unto the nations" instead of a special right to be a lord over the nations (see Exod. 6:2-9; Deut. 7:7-8; 14:2; Amos 3:2; Isa. 42:6; 55:1-4; etc.). To affirm the New Testament, in turn, is to affirm that Christ broadened the original covenant to include non-Jews. The redemptive love of God, sent in the form of the Son, is no longer limited to the chosen people but is offered even to ethnic outsiders (see Matt. 12:17-21; Luke 22:19-20; John 3:16; Rom. 3:28-31; 15:5-16; etc.). Now, is not offering Christian marriage to gays akin to offering the Hebrew covenant to Gentiles? Does not Christlike love expand the bounds of the kingdom to include those who were previously judged unclean or otherwise beyond the pale? To debate whether or how gays and lesbians need to fulfill the four natural goods of marriage is to risk missing the main point, rather like debating whether Gentiles need to be circumcised to enter the church. The main point is that there is a supernatural grace that both sets free and binds anyone and everyone willing to accept it.

Even as God's steadfast love *(hesed)* called the Jewish people to a particular form of righteousness, one reflecting God's own faithfulness in delivering Israel out of bondage in Egypt, so that same love called Gentiles to turn from sin and to embrace the Son. Jesus' first miracle was at the wedding at Cana (John 2:1-11), and Christ is the bridegroom of a church that includes Jews and Greeks (John 3:29; cf. Rev. 19:6-8), so marriage is undeniably a central symbol of God's redemption of the world. This redemption, like the original covenant itself, was not humanly earned but divinely gifted, however. So how can we deny this gift to our homosexual neighbors? *God,* not humanity, initiated, preserved, and expanded the covenant, and so too does God institute, sustain, and define marriage according to his love.

To be sure, the initial marriage was between a male Adam and a female Eve, just as the original covenant was between a Hebraic God and a Semitic people. But Christ rendered all such arrangements less parochial. Many Christians see gay unions as a violation of the sacrament of marriage, just as many Jews (including pre-Paul Saul) saw extending the religious franchise to Gentiles as an offense to Yahweh. But how do we determine what is a corruption and what is an elaboration of God's will? I begin with the premise that *divine wisdom makes room in the ark.* God means to save us all, poor sinners that we are, and his covenant fidelity is constantly pushing us beyond limited sympathies and fractious contrasts between "us" and "them." God's mercy never fails, and our own love is measured by our willingness to attend to the despised and vulnerable. Jeremiah does declare at one point that God abrogates the covenant because of Israel's sin, but Jeremiah goes on to assure that God will write a new law and covenant "on their hearts" (Jer. 31:31-34). Celebrating same-sex marriage would be a fruit of that same ongoing, heartfelt process.

There is no question but that this picture of marriage would represent a paradigm shift within Christendom, even as Jesus' preaching an inclusive kingdom was revolutionary within first-century Judaism. In a sense, heterosexual Christians' being called to give up their monopoly on marriage is a "cross to bear," a kind of redemptive suffering for (and sufferance of) "the other." But the legal and theological innovations that eventually rejected slavery, endorsed the equality of women, closed the door to child sacrifice, and opened the door to miscegenation were similarly painful and iconoclastic. (There was a time when blacks marrying whites seemed as abominable to many Christians as same-sex unions do today.)[26] Yet there is another sense in which permitting gay and lesbian marriages would be in palpable continuity with Saint Paul's famous declaration that "there is no longer Jew or Greek, there is no longer slave or free, there is no longer male and female; for all of you are one in Christ Jesus" (Gal. 3:28). We still struggle today to announce that "there is no longer gay or straight in Christ," even as we can't yet find it in our hearts to say that "there is no longer fetus or adult." I look forward to the day, nonetheless, when Christians universally see heterosexism and abortion as opaque sins of our benighted past, even as we now see racism and sexism.

VI. A Reply to Richard Hays on Tradition and Volition

Richard Hays has argued that "the few biblical texts that . . . address the topic of homosexual behavior . . . are unambiguously and unremittingly negative in their judgment."[27] He goes on to maintain that "from Genesis 1 onward, Scripture affirms repeatedly that God has made man and woman for one another

26. It was only with *Loving v. Virginia* (1967) that the United States Supreme Court (unanimously) invalidated antimiscegenation laws as unconstitutional.
27. Hays, *The Moral Vision*, p. 381.

and that our sexual desires rightly find their fulfillment within heterosexual marriage."[28] I do not dispute either of these exegetical claims, but I doubt that they settle our ethical question. I applaud Hays for demonstrating, contra John Boswell and others, that Leviticus 18 and Romans 1 are condemnations of homosexual acts,[29] but honesty about these texts is only the beginning of the normative story for us. Hays considers it "prudent and necessary" to allow Scripture and tradition to "order the life of the church" on these matters and thus to preclude same-sex marriage.[30] With fear and trembling, I must disagree.

The Bible as a whole is inspired; tradition is the repository of the insights of the church; and the church itself is the indispensable community for the teaching of theological virtue. So these resources are not to be belittled or lightly dismissed. As important as are personal prayer and private devotion, no one can learn or live the truth about God in isolation. But for all the epistemic import of the church and the practical value of its texts and traditions, they remain fallible and are not to be divinized. Doctors and councils and even scriptures can be mistaken — as can I, of course — and anything finite must sometimes be overcome *in the name of God.* This does not leave us with relativism or despair, precisely because God is real and reliable. It does compel us to trust in Christ and the Holy Spirit, however, rather than in historic certainties or collective conventions, whether political or ecclesial.

Revelation can and should be ongoing, and the church's complicity in ignorance and injustice must be constantly struggled against. I have no doubt that Saint Paul considered all persons to be "naturally" heterosexual, for example; thus he saw homosexual acts as perverse and selfish refusals of God's law for homosexuals' lives. But we now plausibly judge some people to be "naturally" homosexual, and we have good sociological evidence of committed and loving gay and lesbian relationships. Hays contends that causal etiology

---

28. Hays, *The Moral Vision*, p. 390.

29. See especially Hays's analysis of Saint Paul's use in Rom. 1 of the phrase *para physin,* usually translated as "against nature" (KJV) or "unnatural" (RSV), to characterize homosexual practices. John Boswell reads Paul's words as purely descriptive, as commenting on homosexual acts as "unexpected" or "unusual," rather than "immoral." See John Boswell, *Christianity, Social Tolerance, and Homosexuality* (Chicago and London: University of Chicago Press, 1980), p. 112. Hays makes a compelling case, nonetheless, that Paul's words are fundamentally normative. For Paul, to quote Hays, "those who indulge in sexual practices *para physin* are defying the Creator and demonstrating their alienation from him." Hays, *The Moral Vision*, p. 387; and see also Hays, "Relations Natural and Unnatural: A Response to John Boswell's Exegesis of Romans 1," *Journal of Religious Ethics* 14, no. 1 (1986): 184-215.

30. Hays, *The Moral Vision*, pp. 399-400.

does not matter to the normative evaluation of homosexual orientation. Even if it is not subject to voluntary choice, it might still be judged pathological, and acting on it might still be deemed sinful. Saint Paul for one does not flinch from labeling as sinful things that are now beyond our control, Hays observes, and, in this connection, he invites us to consider homosexuality as analogous to alcoholism.[31] Liability to alcoholism might well be a matter of genetic inheritance or early psychological conditioning, and thus be beyond one's conscious selection or rejection, but it remains nonetheless a disease to be resisted. Moreover, to indulge an alcoholic constitution and willfully drink hard liquor is to be guilty of wrongdoing. Similarly, homosexuality is an "afflicted" condition, according to Hays,[32] the predisposition to which may be outside one's choosing, but it is nevertheless contrary to God's will and not to be acquiesced in or acted on, much less baptized or celebrated.

Hays sincerely wishes to offer "loving support"[33] to homosexuals — to love the sinner but hate the sin — and I appreciate his humaneness in approaching the morality of this complex issue. The fundamental problem with his analogy, however, is that alcoholism (unlike homosexuality) is manifestly harmful to its subject, regardless of social circumstance. To be habitually "under the influence" is to be thwarted in one's capacity to love others, God, and oneself. I simply cannot say the same thing of homosexuality. Given that gay and lesbian couples share the same basic physiology (sex), if not psychology (gender), it *might* as a rule be somewhat harder for them to overcome self-absorption, what used to be called "love of the second self," compared to straight pairs. But, as I noted above, all of us are in the clutches of narcissism, and there is so much variability within groups and across individuals that the "insufficient otherness" argument carries little real weight. Straight individuals in a conventional union can be just as prideful and oblivious to the needs and wishes of their partners as queer folk. The challenge in any loving relation is to align oneself with the will of God and the good of the other, but this is precisely what opening oneself to the sacrament of marriage empowers one to do. It is to avail oneself of a grace larger than one's own will power or emotional affinity, but, again, this is an option for any adult creature who bears the image of God.

If Christians see all of nature, including human nature, as fallen, then it is always dicey for them to look to the natural world for ethical or religious

31. Hays, *The Moral Vision*, pp. 390 and 398.
32. Hays, *The Moral Vision*, p. 398.
33. Hays, *The Moral Vision*, p. 398.

norms.[34] Furthermore, even though the "natural" evolutionary purpose of sexual dimorphism seems to have been for more variegated reproductive power, the original biological genesis of something does not necessarily dictate its present moral use. It is generally granted, for example, that sex can be used for mutual pleasure and emotional bonding, as well as for procreation, even as our large brains can be employed for the sake of artistic beauty and political harmony, as well as for victory in combat. (Evolutionary biologists call this "functional shift," though the question remains how complete the shift from one purpose to the other can or should be.) My main point, once more, is that the natural must be brought under the sway of the supernatural — in particular, all human *eros* (gay and straight) must be subordinated to and elevated by divine *agape*. Not all of us need be parents, but the one ideal or end that is applicable to everyone is the beatitude of loving and being loved by God and neighbor; this is what we are all made for.

If I thought, as does Hays, that homosexual orientation or action, or both, are prohibited by divine command, I would have to concede that the various aretological, deontological, and teleological arguments I have deployed are irrelevant. Pondering the life and teaching of Jesus and the latest findings of psychology and sociology, however, I cannot think this. Hays has convinced me that *the author of Leviticus and Saint Paul condemn homosexuality, at least in action (see n. 28 above), but they are not God.* I'm not God either, need I say, so I may be mistaken, but in any case the Trinity is not to be confused with or limited to tradition or Scripture. Unlike God, the latter are fallible.

VII. A Sympathetic Objection from "Justice"

Some who concur with my conclusion about gay wedlock might object, nonetheless, that the case is better couched in terms of "social *justice*" than "Christian *love.*" All this talk of "expanding covenants" and "bearing crosses" makes us forget, they may contend, that gays and lesbians *deserve* the marital option as a *right* grounded in their human dignity. To suggest otherwise is to patronize homosexuals and to make a matter of benevolence and philanthropy what ought to be a matter of fairness and desert.[35] The problem with this objection,

---

34. No doubt, I am simply announcing my Protestant sensibilities here, but for a defense of this view, see my "Naturalism, Formalism, and Supernaturalism."

35. Nick Wolterstorff often worries that agapic love neglects or falsifies the demands of justice, but I don't know if he shares my take on same-sex marriage.

however, is that it fails to see that affirming same-sex marriage means changing the basic definition of the institution. What is at issue is a reformulation of the ecclesial (if not the social) contract, so to speak, rather than its honest application. As predominant as the supernatural good of marriage has traditionally been, theologically, the conception of the sacrament has always included reference to a man and a woman. Heterosexual couples, properly situated, might plausibly claim a dignity right to be married, therefore, but not homosexual couples up until now. Our conception of sanctity and the sacred must transform our conception of dignity and what the church owes to gays and lesbians.

Is it my position, then, that endorsing same-sex marriage is supererogatory on the part of the church, a kind of favor that it might do homosexuals but not a moral requirement? (Again, I distinguish between moral and legal requirements.) No, for I consider the extension of the sacrament to be a *duty of charity*, rather than an optional philanthropy. It would be wrong for Christians not to do this. A distinctive feature of many duties of charity is that they have no correlative rights attached to them. A paradigm case is forgiveness: a Christian is required to forgive a wrongdoer unconditionally (Matt. 18:21-35), but the wrongdoer has no right to insist on forgiveness from the wronged.[36] It must be freely given by the agent, and the patient has no just claim on it. Did the Gentiles have a "right" to the Abrahamic covenant? Did the first-century synagogues have a "duty" to open their doors to the Pauline Christians? My point concerning Christian marriage is that the obligation to open it to gays and lesbians is a function of attending to their needs and potentials, rather than of keeping former promises or respecting current choices.

Some thinkers object to the very idea of a duty without a correlative right, or of a right without a correlative duty,[37] but there are counterexamples to both couplings. Christian peacemaking provides the example of forgiveness as a duty without a right, as noted, and just war–fighting provides an obverse example. It is commonly granted, for instance, that a prisoner of war has the right to try to escape but that a captor has no duty to allow him to do so.[38] If one wants to speak of "a right to sacramental marriage" for gays and lesbians, the least one must recognize is that it is an abiding-need-based right rather

36. See Timothy P. Jackson, *The Priority of Love: Christian Charity and Social Justice* (Princeton: Princeton University Press, 2003), chap. 4.

37. For example, Marcus Singer, "The Basis of Rights and Duties," *Philosophical Studies* 23 (1972): 48-57; Joel Feinberg, *Social Philosophy* (Englewood Cliffs, N.J.: Prentice-Hall, 1973), p. 62; and James Fieser, "The Correlativity of Duties and Rights," *International Journal of Applied Philosophy* 7 (1992): 1-8.

38. See Michael Walzer, *Just and Unjust Wars* (New York: Basic Books, 1977), pp. 46-47.

than a historical-interest-based right. If homosexuals have a right to Christian wedlock, it is a matter of their participation in God's holiness (sanctity), rather than of their or others' self-conscious intentions (dignity). The insistence that, if there is a right here at all, it is of a very special kind, stems from untying covenantal marriage from modern notions of merit, demerit, and contract.

In endorsing gay and lesbian nuptials, the Christian church would be making a *new* promise to the world, reconfiguring future justice along better lines, rather than fulfilling just commitments from the past. Transmuting the meaning of justice in this way is sometimes a requirement of love, but it obviously cannot be a duty of the antecedent justice itself. (Compare passing an amendment to the U.S. Constitution. No constitution can require that a specific mandate be immediately amended in a particular way, for then the "amendment" would already be a part of the founding text, but a constitution can permit future amendments that follow a general protocol.) God's offering the covenant to Gentiles might have been purely gratuitous, even as was the original act of creation, but once we Christians are the beneficiaries of these gifts and commanded to love as Christ loves, we can no longer innocently withhold comparable goods from others. Such uncharitability would not be "unjust" — in modern procedural, distributive, or retributive senses — but it would be "unrighteous," in the biblical sense.[39]

If the church is, in some respects, "redefining" marriage, rather than simply correcting an injustice it has committed in the past, does that make the church an arbitrary agent of change? What is central is that our understanding of Christlike love should illuminate and qualify how we think about justice, including justice in marriage. To return to the earlier analogy, was it unjust for God not initially to extend the covenant to the Gentiles? Could the Gentiles have cried "foul," so to speak, for not being included? On the other hand, did the early Christian church merely "redefine" the people of God, or did it come to a more profound appreciation of the universality of God's love all along? My thesis, again, is that no argument from natural justice will get you to the new order, but that does not mean that the church is simply "inventing" (or "reinventing") the covenant on its own authority.

I am wary of claiming that (fallen) nature can specify any ontological "laws" that will elevate us to the supernatural love of God. This reflects my ongoing skepticism about *eros*/just appraisal in relation to *agape*/kenotic bestowal. This may seem to be the residual Protestant in me, but Thomas Aquinas

---

39. For more on the distinction between biblical love and modern justice, see Jackson, *The Priority of Love*, esp. chap 1.

himself emphasizes that neither natural law nor human law is freestanding. They cannot be properly interpreted without reference to eternal law and divine law. Indeed, grace must redeem and perfect nature; that is, God must stoop to meet us where we are. In short, the incarnate Christ is the key, the kerygma, that is prior to any other value, virtue, or institution — including the church. Christ is the authority; the church is a minister of that authority.

It may appear, then, that either Christ is substantially (even arbitrarily) redefining the sacrament of marriage or the church has been a faulty minister of the Lord and incorrect in its understanding of who can marry. But I am struggling to articulate a third alternative, or at least to nuance this stark either/or, based on an interpretation of Jesus' life and teaching. Consider abortion and infanticide. I have no doubt that Jesus' words and deeds preclude elective abortion and infanticide as sins. But this judgment is not a mere application of his teaching, since he did not explicitly talk about either practice. Moreover, there was a time when abortion and infanticide were thought to be perfectly "natural," even pious, within Judaism.[40] The moral revolution that overcame this view required love's correcting justice, *agape*'s transforming paternal power into something much more kenotic and egalitarian. Was Abraham "incorrect" in thinking that God wanted Isaac to be sacrificed? In a sense, yes. But I'm inclined to say that Abraham's mind-set was too impoverished to be "mistaken" in the usual sense. *He had to undergo a paradigm shift, based on a fuller understanding of God's love, rather than simply correct a verdict of the old system of justice.* He had, that is, to recognize a duty of charity.

Thomas Kuhn argues that a scientific revolution involves an unstructured "transition," a "switch of gestalt," that is not compelled or even directly justified by the normal science of the day.[41] I am suggesting that the same goes for a religious revolution in relation to the normal ethics of the day. Consider the eventual ordination of women in many Christian denominations. Of course, we might say retrospectively that the church should have been ordaining women all along, but for the early church a priest was, by definition, a male minister of Christ on the order of the twelve disciples. By that definition, women were not unfairly excluded, because the office, by common consent, was reserved for males.

The analogy is clear: marriage was once defined exclusively in terms of heterosexual men and women, even as the priesthood was once defined

---

40. See "Is Isaac Our Neighbor?," chapter 6 in my *Love Disconsoled.*
41. Thomas S. Kuhn, *The Structure of Scientific Revolutions,* 2nd ed., enlarged (Chicago: University of Chicago Press, 1970), pp. 84-85.

exclusively in terms of (celibate?) men. I favor the ordination of women, not because women have changed, or even because the early church was mistaken, but rather because a mature understanding of Christlike love has moved us to rethink ordination, to make it more inclusive. Again, one might say, "This has been God's will all along," but that statement seems rather Whiggish. This is not to say that the church is never mistaken or unjust, of course; examples of ecclesial evil abound — for example, the complicity of the *Deutsche Christen* in the Nazi Holocaust and the ongoing pederasty scandal in the Roman Catholic Church. Moreover, a monumental action or event must certainly be behind such a profound paradigm shift as endorsing gay and lesbian wedlock. For agapic Christians, this is the life and death of the Messiah.[42]

VIII. Divine Love and the Limits of Positive Law

I have written in previous contexts of a fetus's "right to life,"[43] and in chapter 12 of this volume I defend an orphaned or abandoned child's "right to be adopted." The state has a duty of charity to protect both of these rights, I argue, even though the concerned parties have not "earned" the relevant good by some action or agreement. Why, then, am I reluctant to say that adults have the right to be forgiven and that gays and lesbians have the right to be married? Here an interesting moral intuition comes into play. Human lives that *have not* yet reached full rational agency (a.k.a. moral maturity) have sanctity rights that are correlative to duties of charity, whereas humans that *have* become fully autonomous agents do not have such rights. It is as though being a rational agent disqualifies one from correlative charity rights. This must be explained at more length.

As noted in my opening paragraph, Saint Augustine held that one of the goods of monogamous sexuality (for heterosexuals) is "the promotion of fidelity by the quieting of concupiscence," and I see no reason why it could not function in a similarly pragmatic fashion for homosexual couples. More importantly, however, giving gays and lesbians access to the sacramental bond, with all its benefits and burdens, would keep marriage "sacred." It would preserve the distinctively supernatural core of marriage, its reliance on the holiness of God, rather than reducing it to biological stereotypes or sociological utilities. If after decades of solemnized gay and lesbian weddings, the wider

42. I wish to thank Katie Pimentel Toste for moving me to clarify my position in this section of the chapter.

43. See "Abortion and an Ethic of Care," chapter 5 in *The Priority of Love*.

society or the participants themselves came to see that same-sex unions are in-trinsically stunted or ungovernable by charity, then the church would need to listen to this testimony. But, given the contemporary incidence of adultery and the fact that nearly 50 percent of heterosexual marriages in the United States currently end in divorce, I suspect that straights will have little justification to point fingers. Sexual desire is a capricious and recalcitrant thing, straight or gay. In any event, the Christian community can only find out the relevant truth by trying the practical experiment in sanctification offered to all believers.

Is recommending this experiment antithetical to respect for religious history or conciliar forms of church decision making?[44] As indicated above, I am wary of any understanding of Christianity that supplants christocentric love with ecclesio-centric tradition. I am equally skeptical about elevating the legal precedents of secular society to oracular status. We do better to try to discern the kerygma of Christ's life and teaching and to subordinate all else to that kenotic pattern. We certainly ought to avoid drawing invidious distinc-tions between persons who are essentially equal before God and who can strive to love and profit from grace.

When Jesus turned the gallons of ordinary water into first-rate wine at Cana, he was suggesting the quantity and quality of the gifts he has to offer.[45] He was also foreshadowing how the purity rituals for Jews involving washing would be fulfilled by the drinking of his own blood by all. Jesus makes his bodily self-sacrifice explicit at John 6:53 — "Very truly, I tell you, unless you eat the flesh of the Son of Man and drink his blood, you have no life in you" — thus, in effect, linking the hospitable wedding at Cana to the Last Supper before Calvary. Wedding wine purifies, and bloody death expiates, with a com-memorative meal in between. All the wedding guests at Cana were served the best wine (Christ himself), even as "those who eat [Christ's] flesh and drink [his] blood have eternal life" (John 6:54). How, then, can we fence the tables against homosexuals in either holy matrimony or Holy Communion? I cannot see such exclusion as compatible with Christian faith, hope, or love.

Does this mean that I would support a federal or state law that *requires* religious congregations (Christian or non-Christian) to marry gays and les-bians? No, and for the same reasons I would not support a law that *forbids* these same congregations from doing so. I have two related reasons for this.

44. Paul Valliere has pressed this important question on me; on related matters, see his "Called Together: A Conciliarist Solution for the Anglican Communion" (unpublished manuscript).
45. See Gail O'Day, "The Gospel of John: Introduction, Commentary, and Reflection," in vol. 9 of *The New Interpreter's Bible*, ed. Leander E. Keck et al. (Nashville: Abingdon, 1995).

First, I am enough of a fan of the free-exercise clause of the U.S. Constitution to want the state to stay out of this aspect of church polity. This is a function of the standard liberal fear of big government. Second, I am enough of a fan of freedom of conscience not to want to coerce individuals to violate their basic beliefs, however flawed those beliefs may be, unless necessary to protect life and limb. This is a function of the Christian endorsement of conscientious objection to temporal power.

Prophetic democracy would not be statist, so it respects the principle of subsidiarity and honors a host of private associations — including families, clubs, cliques, churches, synagogues, and mosques — as schools of virtue and bastions of liberty. As distasteful as it may be, I favor permitting most non-governmental groups to discriminate against persons based on race, gender, creed, and sexual orientation — short of bodily harm or public defamation of character. I support, that is, the right of a country club to be all white, a private college to be all black, a sports team to be all female, a Boy Scout troupe to be all heterosexual, and yes a denomination to be all Christian. Such discriminatory policies may be immoral, depending on context, motive, and so on, but tolerating them legally is the price one pays for a free society, as well as a safeguard against political tyranny. (Nothing prohibits one from vigorous social protest: marching, writing editorials, boycotting racist schools, keeping one's sons out of the Boy Scouts, and the like.) State institutions together with public accommodations and businesses, on the other hand, including collectives that receive significant public funds, may not so discriminate unless they pass constitutional "strict scrutiny" tests. It may be defensible to draft only men for combat, for example, based on physiological and psychological differences between the sexes (as groups) and for the sake of the common defense. But there can be no jurisprudential rationale for simple governmental prejudice or exploitation — for example, Jim Crow laws, denying women the vote, keeping homosexuals out of the military, etc.

Churches, then, should be at legal liberty either to offer or to withhold marriage to homosexuals. How sad would it be, however, if the secular state is more open and compassionate than the Christian church?

IX. The Meaning of Marriage:
The Poverty of "Rights" and the Priority of Love

In the House debate on the Defense of Marriage Act (1996), John Lewis eloquently criticized the act as "a slap in the face of the Declaration of Independence" and as denying "gay men and women the right to liberty and the pursuit of happiness."[46] I have immense respect for Congressman Lewis and for the quintessentially American rights he defends, but the latter are not nearly enough to settle the same-sex marriage issue, at least not for Christians. Personal freedom is never absolute, and the unqualified appeal to marital "liberty" in theory opens the door to polygamy, incest, bestiality, etc. What do we do, moreover, when one person's pursuit of happiness impinges on another's? To what do we appeal when a majority of straight people believe that gay and lesbian nuptials would erode the institution of marriage and thus impede social tranquility (at least for heterosexuals)? Most crucially, what guides our judgment if and when the pursuit of erotic fulfillment by adults destroys the lives of children in their care?

The language of "rights" alone is insufficient to answer these questions, and when this poverty is recognized, the debate over same-sex marriage inevitably turns to the question of what marriage is "for" or how it is "defined." A conservative stance often focuses on a stable context for procreation and child rearing as the key concern, while a liberal position tends to emphasize love (i.e., *eros*) and personal commitment. Conservatives note that marriage has traditionally been a compact between a man and a woman, and that only a man and a woman together can be biologically procreative.[47] Liberals point out, in turn, that sterile or intentionally childless heterosexual marriages are permitted by tradition and that allowing gay men and lesbians also to wed is a matter of equal protection before the law. All these considerations are important, and they are not mutually exclusive, but I have argued that neither the good of procreation, nor the exigency of erotic love, nor the precedent of positive law should provide the main touchstone for Christian attitudes toward same-sex marriage.

Children are a gift of God, and attention to their well-being is a fundamental obligation for all adults, not merely their parents. Similarly, sexual self-expression and bodily communion are essential to the well-being of virtually everyone, and these ends are typically (though not exclusively) realized for adults through genital intercourse.[48] Finally, no state or church can survive

46. See the (partial) transcript of Lewis's remarks in *Same-Sex Marriage: Pro and Con*, p. 230.

47. The possibilities of parthenogenesis and cloning complicate this claim, of course, but as of 2015, these are not realistic, much less moral, options for human procreation.

48. The possibilities of celibacy and eremitism complicate this claim, of course, but even those who have taken vows of chastity usually live in community, and even a hermit can voluntarily choose asexual solitude only after an infancy and youth characterized by some measure of nurturant (though nonerotic) touching.

without written statutes and an accompanying jurisprudence detailing their meaning and proper enactment. Yet the issue of same-sex marriage is, for Christians, not primarily about who can conceive offspring, who can have committed sex, or who can form legal partnerships. It is not first about *bios* or *eros* or *nomos,* that is, but rather about *agape.*

What does love of neighbor require of us, and how are we to inculcate such love in ourselves and others? That is the prime theological question, in both marital and nonmarital contexts, and Christians must find their answer to it where they find all their answers: in the self-giving righteousness of God, as revealed in Jesus Christ. I have maintained that the *imitatio Christi* should lead the faithful, heterosexuals and homosexuals alike, to endorse the marital option for gay men and lesbians. If such an option threatened the care of children or made heterosexual marriage untenable, then no presumptive appeal to "liberty" or "the pursuit of happiness" could justify it. Nobody has the right directly to harm the innocent — in the womb or out of it — or to subvert the common good, no matter how otherwise beneficial or enjoyable the behavior may be to some. But the majority of the sociological evidence I have seen indicates that committed lesbian and gay couples can raise sound, well-adjusted children, even as can single parents.

Some data suggest that the *optimal* family structure is two monogamous parents of the opposite sex, especially when these parties are the biological father and mother.[49] Why this should be is debatable, however. As an evolutionary rule, an individual will tend to care more for her biological progeny than for others genetically unrelated, but the reality of profoundly loving adoptive and foster parents is undeniable. We are not slaves to the sociobiological criterion of reproductive success; indeed, altruism and empathy are admirable precisely to the extent that they break free of nepotism and tribalism. I am traditional enough to wonder if the gender complementarity of a father and a mother

49. See, for example, Wade F. Horn, David Blankenhorn, and Mitchell B. Pearlstein, eds., *The Fatherhood Movement: A Call to Action* (Lanham, Md.: Lexington Books, 1999), and David Blankenhorn, *The Future of Marriage* (New York: Encounter Books, 2007). Blankenhorn remains an articulate champion of fatherhood and traditional marriage, but he now finds the denial of the wedding option to gays and lesbians to be indefensible. He writes: "I don't believe that opposite-sex and same-sex relationships are the same, but I do believe, with growing numbers of Americans, that the time for denigrating or stigmatizing same-sex relationships is over. Whatever one's definition of marriage, legally recognizing gay and lesbian couples and their children is a victory for basic fairness. Another good thing is comity. Surely we must live together with some degree of mutual acceptance, even if doing so involves compromise." See his "How My View on Gay Marriage Changed," *New York Times,* June 22, 2012.

doesn't make for the richest environment for bringing up children of both sexes, but the empirical findings on this are controversial, as is how to interpret them.[50] In any case, even if a "traditional" family is marginally superior, other things being equal, we need not make the ideal the enemy of the good. Especially with so many needy children in the world, there is room for acceptable diversity here, so long as the basic interests of the children are served.

Maggie Gallagher, a passionate and literate defender of the traditional family and critic of same-sex marriage, asks, "Do children need mothers and fathers, or will any sort of family do?"[51] She raises all the right questions when she goes on to write: "If marriage is just a way of publicly celebrating private love, then there is no need to encourage couples to stick it out for the sake of the children. If family structure does not matter, why have marriage laws at all? Do adults, or do they not, have a basic obligation to control their desires so that children can have mothers and fathers?" (pp. 268-69). Gallagher powerfully gives the lie to what might be called "the legend of Romulus": a child reared by a she-wolf to become the founder of a civilization. Gallagher is correct to insist that family makeup and dynamics *do* matter, and that without their proper forms, civility and culture are impossible. Not just any parent or parents will do for the next generation, and marriage is not merely about erotic fulfillment for the spouses. Children have "dignity" — her term (p. 268) — and I agree that they should take priority *over the other natural goods of marriage,* including "the quieting of concupiscence." Nobody can reasonably believe, for instance, that an adulterous father or a drug-addicted mother or a violently quarrelsome pair of any gender can provide a stable, loving home that produces healthy, responsible children.

Nonetheless, Gallagher misconstrues the matter of same-sex marriage in two interrelated ways: (1) she neglects the supernatural good of sacramental bonding between the spouses, as though the only values in question were *eros* and *proles,* and (2) she wrongly assumes that same-sex marriage would inevitably privilege "the sexual desires of adults," that is, homosexual adults, over "the interests of children" (pp. 264-65). Many gay and lesbian couples, like many straight couples, want to marry precisely to escape sexual egotism and to share their love with children. To assume, as Gallagher does, that a same-sex couple *by definition* cannot adequately care for the young is to beg the question.

50. It is especially difficult to unravel the impacts of gender and class. See, for example, Yvette Taylor, *Lesbian and Gay Parenting: Securing Social and Educational Capital* (Houndmills: Palgrave Macmillan, 2009).

51. Maggie Gallagher, "What Marriage Is For," in *Same-Sex Marriage: Pro and Con,* p. 264. Page references to this article have been placed in the text.

Gallagher thinks that "acceptance of family diversity" is "elitist," since it implies that children without parents of both sexes — especially children without dads — are of lesser worth than children of traditional heterosexual unions (p. 268). For her, to permit a child to be born into or raised by a homosexual family is to deny that child its basic right to a father and a mother — in fact, she indirectly likens it to treating that child as a "throwaway" (pp. 267-68). If true, this would be a decisive argument against same-sex marriage, but I judge the elitist slipper to be on the other *pied*. Gallagher avers that "democratic principles" require us "to hold up a single ideal for all parents," namely, "a married mom and dad" (p. 268). Yet this is to confuse equal regard with identical treatment. All children have equal dignity *and inviolable sanctity*, in my view, but this does not mean that there is only one way to respect that dignity and honor that sanctity. Indeed, democratic pluralism favors finding multiple paths to essential social goals, lest a totalitarian sameness be imposed on citizens from above. For purposes of argument, I can grant that heterosexual marriage may be *the best* context for raising kids, but were it *the solely acceptable* context, we would have to spirit away the children of widows and widowers, as well as forbid single-parent adoption. In the absence of supporting evidence — indeed, in the presence of significant counterevidence — to think that only married straights are capable of amorous commitment and intergenerational nurturance is, well, elitist. It is also highly implausible, as modern culture (from Gertrude Stein to Donald Trump to Ellen DeGeneres to Paris Hilton) illustrates.

Again, the sociological data are complex and still emerging, but Abbie E. Goldberg's *Lesbian and Gay Parents and Their Children* is a thorough review of the relevant studies and their findings. She concludes that "the research has been consistent in suggesting that [lesbians and gay men] are no less equipped to raise children than their heterosexual counterparts. They appear to possess the skills necessary to be good parents, and they describe positive relationships with their children. . . . Notably, the research has suggested that children and adolescents with sexual minority parents, despite their vulnerability to heterosexism, are developing normally."[52] A number of other scholars agree. Suzanne M. Johnson and Elizabeth O'Connor write:

> the evidence from our study and the many other studies that have been done on gay- and lesbian-headed families shows that gay men and lesbians make very effective parents. Our study, and the other studies we have re-

---

52. Abbie E. Goldberg, *Lesbian and Gay Parents and Their Children: Research on the Family Life Cycle* (Washington, D.C.: American Psychological Association, 2010), pp. 178-79.

viewed, found that gay and lesbian parents show strengths in the security of attachment to their children; in their parenting styles, including how they discipline their children; in the quality of their own couple relationships; and in how they share the work associated with raising children and running a household.[53]

Robert A. Bernstein affirms that "research studies have consistently shown that children raised by gay and lesbian parents do just as well on all conventional measures of child development, such as academic achievement, psychological well-being and social abilities, as children raised by heterosexual parents."[54]

Not all experts are of one mind, of course. Trayce Hansen, for instance, writes:

> Same-sex marriage may be in the best interest of adult homosexuals who yearn for social and legal recognition of their unions, but it's not in the best interest of children. . . . It's clear that children benefit from having both a male and female parent. Recent medical research confirms genetically determined differences between men and women and those fundamental differences help explain why mothers and fathers bring unique characteristics to parenting that can't be replicated by the other sex. Mothers and fathers simply aren't interchangeable. Two women can both be good mothers, but neither can be a good father. One-sex parenting, whether by a single parent or a homosexual couple, deprives children of the full range of parenting offered by dual-sex couples.[55]

But does this imply that single or homosexual parents should have their children taken from them or that single-parent or homosexual adoption should be illegal? Once more, this strikes me as making the (possibly) ideal the enemy of the (actually) good. Robert Bernstein points out that "between 1 million and 9 million children are being raised by gay, lesbian, and bisexual parents in the United States today."[56] This is important because, whatever one may think

53. Suzanne M. Johnson and Elizabeth O'Connor, *The Gay Baby Boom: The Psychology of Gay Parenthood* (New York and London: New York University Press, 2002), p. 171.

54. Robert A. Bernstein, *Families of Value: Personal Profiles of Lesbian and Gay Parents* (New York: Marlowe and Co., 2005), p. 255.

55. Trayce Hansen, "Same-Sex Marriage: Not in the Best Interest of Children," *Therapist*, May/June 2009, p. 1; the *Therapist* is a publication of the California Association of Marriage and Family Therapists (CAMFT).

56. Bernstein, *Families of Value*, p. 247.

normatively about same-sex marriage, the reality *descriptively* is that many children are already being reared by homosexuals. Can we plausibly imagine that these children are better off by our denying to their parents the good of a stable sacramental union? At the end of the day, there is no escaping making a prudent judgment about what the empirical evidence suggests concerning the well-being of children in various family contexts. I am persuaded by Bernstein, who allows that "many of us grew up believing that everyone needs a mother and a father, regardless of whether we ourselves happened to have two parents, or two *good* parents. But as families have grown more diverse in recent decades, and researchers have studied how these different family relationships affect children, it has become clear that the *quality* of a family's relationship is more important than the particular *structure* of families that exist today."[57] I also find it telling that, as Bernstein notes, the following organizations support same-sex parenting:

> American Academy of Pediatrics
> American Academy of Family Physicians
> Child Welfare League of America
> National Association of Social Workers
> North American Council on Adoptable Children
> American Bar Association
> American Psychological Association
> American Psychiatric Association
> American Psychoanalytic Association[58]

Appealing to august professional bodies is not dispositive for the ethical or theological debate, to be sure. It is possible that all these groups are ignoring, misreading, or even falsifying the data. But I doubt it. To say the least, the emerging consensus reflected above is significant for anyone who holds that our moral and religious convictions must be informed by the best of modern science. We do indeed know some things about human biology, psychology, and society that Moses and Saint Paul did not.

Three relevant points are worth emphasizing, then. First, there is much variability in the membership and practices of so-called heterosexual families, with a lifelong and exclusive partnership between biological parents raising only their own offspring being increasingly rare. Often contemporary families

57. Bernstein, *Families of Value*, p. 255.
58. Bernstein, *Families of Value*, p. 254.

are composed of remarried couples, with children from previous unions being raised by one biological parent, one stepparent or adoptive parent, and perhaps a grandparent or two. This may be regrettable, and it is certainly a departure from the historical ideal, but it is still accepted as a viable setup so long as there is an abiding commitment to responsible care by all the adults involved.

Second, what is paramount in any caregiver or set of caregivers is the love, dedication, and simple practical wisdom directed to the well-being of the young in their charge. Due to constraints on time, emotional energy, and financial resources, two nurturers are *generally* better than one, so I am troubled by singles who intentionally conceive outside of a stable relationship and have no intention of marrying. But a single, caring parent who adopts an orphaned or displaced child is certainly virtuous, even as is a widow or widower who carries on as sole child-rearer after a spouse has died. (This is addressing a need that already exists, rather than creating it.) To the critical question of whether two same-sexed parents are "as good" as two opposite-sexed parents, I can only say that any minute discrepancy across groups here should make no moral difference to social policy. Variation within groups is enormous, so one must look at particulars. Manifestly, some lesbian and gay couples make better parents than some heterosexuals, and, again, our measure ought to be whether the specific caregivers are committed and knowledgeable. If a same-sex couple is grossly incompetent, neglectful, or abusive, then they ought to be denied parental rights, even as a straight couple should be denied adoptive children or have their own biological children taken from them if they are similarly derelict or deficient.

Third, to repeat, even though children's well-being rightly takes priority over the erotic desires of adults, to dwell *exclusively* on this fact is to be blind to the sacramental dimension of marriage. This supernatural dimension must be the first concern of Christians, and it is that on which all natural goods depend. More specifically, the sacramental bond of matrimony is a gift of God that can surely both benefit and discipline both homosexuals and heterosexuals. Any children present will certainly be served by that dual blessing.

X. A Caveat

Even with the above three points in hand, I feel compelled to offer a caveat before concluding. To gesture as I have toward straightness as "the ideal" for individuals and their marriages is to risk betraying the gospel of Christ. Consider some historical parallels. Is Christianity the "ideal" religion, over against

Judaism, and is maleness the "ideal" gender, over against femaleness? Many have thought so, and thereby caused no end of misery.[59] Surely Jesus' life and teachings should make us wary of all such hierarchies, in spite of millennia of social and psychological reinforcement.

The depiction of Jews has been as traditionally mixed in Western culture as that of women. Sometimes they have been seen as downright evil; sometimes as fascinating but unclean; sometimes as innocent but nevertheless inferior; sometimes as markedly superior; and so on. (This is not surprising given that much of Western culture has been dominated by Christians and men.) Aristotle, Saint Augustine, and Martin Luther notwithstanding, Jews and women are now generally regarded in the West as morally equal to their counterparts in rights and duties, aptitude and value, dignity and sanctity. The decline of anti-Semitism and misogyny is far from complete, and we forget how labored the process has been, but my main point is that the story of gays and lesbians may yet trace a trajectory similar to that of Jews and women. From ontologically evil to essentially similar would be Good News indeed. It is a sign of the maturity of Christians that they feel no need to convert Jews — "Judaism was good enough for Jesus, and it's good enough for me" — and straights will probably eventually overcome the inclination to "flip" gays and lesbians. The perfect is not to be made the enemy of the good, but who can claim perfection?

Conclusion

One of the strongest arguments I know for keeping marriage heterosexual is the duet "La ci darem la mano" from Mozart's *Don Giovanni*.[60] Giovanni's declaration to Zerlina, "there we will join hands, there you will say 'yes,'" is so powerful precisely because it can be heard both as a promise to wed and as a prediction of sexual conquest. The audience knows the Don to be a roué, of course, and the scene from his point of view to be one of seduction. But Zerlina, already engaged to Masetto, is simultaneously skeptical about and hopeful

59. On Christian claims to supersede or correct Judaism as contributing to the Holocaust, see my "Both Shylock and Oedipus," chapter 10 of this volume. For a discussion of femaleness, especially female inferiority, in a broad swath of Western philosophical thought, see Sister Prudence Allen, R.S.M., *The Concept of Woman: The Aristotelian Revolution, 750 B.C.–A.D. 1250* (Grand Rapids: Eerdmans, 1997).

60. I especially like the performance by Gilles Cachemaille and Juliane Banse at the 1995 Glyndebourne Festival.

for something more spiritual and permanent from Giovanni. She wants to have him but also to reform him. The singular erotic energy between them, sung and dramatized, is unsurpassed in opera and one of our most enduring icons of the complementarity of the sexes. Mozart's male and female go together so beautifully — physically, emotionally, and musically — that it is hard for me to imagine two men or two women matching this contrapuntal agony and ecstasy. Yet this is an *aesthetic* judgment and, no doubt, an expression of my own heterosexuality.

When I try to reflect *morally* on the matter, I find myself asking: Why not let it be a competition in virtue? Why not allow gay men and lesbians to demonstrate that they can create a nuptial reality as wondrous, vexing, lyrical, fragile, and just as anything in history? They may fail, but so do many straights. When I take a still higher view and think *religiously,* I have to move from what natural goals human beings can achieve to the supernatural good given by God. In the name of heaven, don't homosexuals deserve the chance to be faithful, hopeful, and loving in and through marriage (cf. 1 Cor. 13)? Don't they deserve to sing their duets to one another, but also before the Lord? Without the divine Commendatore, there is no way for them to consign the callow and promiscuous Don Giovanni to the flames.

I am convinced, in any case, that when Christians speak up in defense of same-sex marriage, we do not threaten the care of children, but rather enhance it; we do not subvert *eros,* but rather govern it; and we do not ignore law, but rather transform it. Most importantly, because marriage is a sacrament and thus a grace-filled school of compassion and caring, in allowing same-sex marriage Christians both express charity and help to foster it. Indeed, to shift from praising Mozart to paraphrasing Lincoln, "In *giving* marriage to the *gay,* we *assure* marriage for the *straight* — honorable alike in what we give, and what we preserve."[61]

61. See Abraham Lincoln, "Annual Message to Congress" (December 1, 1862), in *Abraham Lincoln: Speeches and Writings, 1859-1865* (New York: Library of America, 1989), p. 415.

CHAPTER 12

Suffering the Suffering Children:
Christianity and the Rights and Wrongs of Adoption

Suffer the little children to come unto me, and forbid them not:
for of such is the kingdom of God.

MARK 10:14 KJV

Through much of recorded history . . . adoption by nonrelatives
has been utilized more to meet the needs of adults than to help
children.

ADAM PERTMAN[1]

We are fighting abortion with adoption.

MOTHER TERESA[2]

---

1. Adam Pertman, *Adoption Nation: How the Adoption Revolution Is Transforming America* (New York: Basic Books, 2000), p. 20.

2. Quoted in *Mother Teresa: A Film by Ann and Jeanette Petrie* (Petrie Productions, distributed by Dorason Corporation, 1986).

I wish to thank three groups for their helpful discussion of an earlier draft of this chapter: the participants in the Adoption Roundtable at Emory Conference Center on March 30, 2003; members of Emory University's Center for the Interdisciplinary Study of Religion, Project on the Child, especially Don Browning, Martin Marty, and John Witte Jr.; and those present at the Candler Faculty Research Lunch on February 16, 2004, especially the convener, Luther Smith, and my respondent, Jon Gunnemann.

Introduction

Christians have compelling reasons to pay close attention to adoption practices. These reasons may occasion both pride and embarrassment. On the one hand, Christian charity has traditionally called on the faithful to care for the needy and vulnerable, especially children, and this virtue has made the church a supporter and facilitator of many admirable adoptions. Christianity itself grew out of God's "adoption" of the Gentiles, the gracious extension of a covenant to those not originally God's people. On some accounts, Jesus himself was "adopted" either by Joseph or by God. Therefore, a positive attitude toward adoption is tied to the very identity of Christian belief and believers.

On the other hand, various Christian ideals have served to condemn certain adoptions as unnatural or vicious, thus making life miserable for all those involved in the adoptive relation. For example, conceptions of a divine separation of the races have led some Christians to reject interracial adoption as against God's will, even as conceptions of a divine endorsement of heterosexual monogamy have led other Christians to oppose single-parent and gay or lesbian adoption.

The issue is not simply whether Christian churches or individuals endorse or reject particular adoption practices; rather, it is *how* these practices are approached that makes a crucial difference. Even where adoption is championed, the method may be cruel or counterproductive. Shaming unwilling or vulnerable young mothers into surrendering their offspring, for instance, is itself a shameful practice, whether supposedly motivated by Christian *agape* or not. Facilitating a willing transfer of parental oversight for the sake of a better life for a child is, in contrast, to aid a Christlike self-sacrifice.

This chapter aims to clarify Christianity's historical judgments of, and contributions to, adoption theory and practice — admittedly, a mixed picture. The essay has five sections. Section I examines how the Bible defines adoption, noting how a fundamental complexity here bears on Christian attitudes toward the practice. Section II looks at the rights that ground the moral and legal permissibility of adoption and how they relate to the Christian notion of sanctity. Section III investigates the ethics of single-parent and gay adoption as particularly pressing issues. Section IV looks briefly at the right of adoptees to know their biological identities and those of their birth parents. Finally, in section V, I return to explicitly biblical themes and ask how views on Christology affect basic perceptions of adoption.

My enduring assumption is unremarkable but worth stating: no mother or father should be intimidated, shamed, or coerced into surrendering her or his child for adoption, unless the parent is demonstrably negligent or abusive, but voluntary adoption is sometimes the most loving act *for* the child and *by* the birth parent. My specific theses are more substantive and controversial: (a) adoption is not merely the bestowal of a new (legally created) identity but also the acknowledgment of a preexisting (divinely created) humanity; (b) the primary adoption right is that of orphaned, unwanted, destitute, or abused children to be adopted; (c) it is the sanctity of these children's lives, rather than their dignity, that gives them the positive right to be cared for by conscientious adults;[3] and (d) attention to the sanctity rights of adoptive children should move us to permit both single adults and same-sex couples to adopt.

Traditional conceptions of Joseph and Mary, Jesus and God, can both aid and hinder a proper appreciation of the morality of adoption, so Christian theologians ought to make it abundantly clear why adoption is (or should be) an act of love rather than a shameful secret. As with artificial contraception and assisted reproductive technology, this will require reevaluating the ancient Alexandrian principle that having sex without getting children and getting children without having personal sex are inherently illicit. The principle should be amended, I argue, but not merely set aside.

I. Biblical Definitions and a Key Complexity

There is no endorsement, or even explicit mention, of adoption as an ongoing practice in Old Testament law. There are, in effect, three references to *acts* of adoption — of Moses (Exod. 2:10), of Genubath (1 Kings 11:20), and of Esther (Esther 2:7, 15) — but, as is often noted, these all take place outside of Palestine and thus in contexts foreign to Jewish rule and custom.[4] Torah tradition as such simply does not admit that someone who is not one's biological child can be rendered one's son or daughter by legal fiction. It was Saint Paul who first introduced the notion of adoption into Judeo-Christian theology.

The New Testament Greek word translated by the NRSV as "adoption" is *huiothesia*, from *huios* (meaning "son") and *tithemi* (meaning "to put or place"). The term appears five times in Paul's epistles (Rom. 8:15, 23; 9:4; Gal.

---

3. A negative right is a claim not to be interfered with, not to have something taken from one, while a positive right is a claim to be actively assisted, to have something provided for one independently of personal effort or merit.

4. My colleague Hendrik Boers has pointed out to me that, although these adoption *locations* were outside of Jewish rule, the *stories* are not simply records of the incidents and do partly reflect Jewish custom.

4:5; and Eph. 1:5), but not once in the Gospels. Construed literally, *huiothesia* is gendered and connotes a placing or taking in of someone as a male heir. *The International Standard Bible Encyclopedia (ISBE)* defines the word, generally, as "the legal process by which a man might bring into his family, and endow with the status and privileges of a son, one who was not by nature his son or of his kindred."[5] One can readily see why Paul — that liminal figure at the dividing line between the historical Jesus and the Holy Spirit, Judaism and Christianity, Rome and barbarism — would have been attracted to adoption metaphors. In many ways, he knew himself to have been an outsider graciously allowed in: a man who never met Jesus called nevertheless to be an apostle, a persecutor of the early Christian church converted into its greatest champion, as well as a Pharisaic Jew enabled to be a Roman citizen. It was definitive of Paul's genius that he saw in his personal experiences a model of God's way with the wider world and was able to translate this into a powerful message of gifted salvation: "He [God] destined us for adoption as his children through Jesus Christ, according to the good pleasure of his will, to the praise of his glorious grace that he freely bestowed on us in the Beloved" (Eph. 1:5-6).

The *ISBE*'s general definition of adoption captures Paul's central theological usage, but it also hides an important complexity. In the Greco-Roman culture against whose background Paul wrote, the "placing" associated with *huiothesia*[6] evidently involved either (1) the production of a new (legal) identity for someone who was not a natural son or (2) the affirmation of a preexisting (legal) identity of someone who was in fact a natural son.[7] "Adoption" entailed, that is, either the generation of an entirely novel filial status or the recognition and formal celebration of a filial status that was already real though perhaps denied, occluded, or only partially realized. When a Roman boy came of legal age, for instance, he might be said to be "taken in" or "adopted" by his father as his heir. Or when a prodigal son mended his ways and returned to his home and biological family, his father might welcome him and "place" him back into the domestic fold as again a son. The first case is a rite of passage

---

5. T. Rees, "Entry for 'Adoption,'" in *The International Standard Bible Encyclopedia,* ed. James Orr; http://www.searchgodsword.org/enc/isb/view.cgl?number=T221, pp. 1-2. This view is shared by *Easton's Bible Dictionary,* which defines "adoption" as "the giving to any one the name and place and privileges of a son who is not a son by birth." See http://bibletools.org//index.cfm/fuseaction/Def.show/RTD/Easton/Topic/Adoption, p. 1.

6. The Latin equivalent is *adoptio* or *arrogatio (adrogatio),* depending on whether the son is or is not still under his birth father's legal authority *(patria potestas).*

7. See "Adoption," in Merrill F. Unger and William White Jr., *Vine's Complete Expository Dictionary of Old and New Testament Words* (Nashville: Nelson, 1996), pp. 13-14.

in which a present identity is fulfilled, while the second case is a painful trial in which a proper identity is rediscovered. But both are very different from a transformation in which an altogether alien identity is conferred. Even if a biological son has, in some sense, publicly to grow into himself, this "adoptive" process is one of maturation in which intrinsic attributes are unfolded, rather than a whole-cloth change imported or imposed from without.

The pressing question asks itself: Is the "adoption" referred to by Paul in Ephesians, Romans, and elsewhere the production of a new identity or the affirmation of an old one? Does the adoptive operation have an "ontological" basis in human nature, or is it an "artificial" contrivance engineered by God alone? Putting the query yet a third way, are even elect human beings not naturally God's sons, such that Christ's agency changes their very essence, or does the Messiah's life, death, and resurrection reveal a filial relation with God the Father that is already (part of) humanity's birthright?

I can only sum up the studied ambivalence of the Christian tradition by answering "both/and." Many orthodox theologians have held that being made "in the image of God" (Gen. 1:27) is an empirical fact about humanity, and that this created identity constitutes a "resemblance to" or "consanguinity with" God, in some analogical sense.[8] We are by nature God's "children," rather than God's accidents, playthings, or victims, and even the fall into sin has not totally destroyed this "genetic" legacy. Even so, the infinite qualitative difference between creature and Creator remains. Only Christ, the second person of the Trinity, is of one substance with the Father; only Christ, the eternal Son, is begotten, not made. Moreover, after the dawn of sin, Christ's redemptive act on the cross is an indispensable means of restoring right relation with God. The believer's adoption as son or daughter, his or her being filled with the Holy Spirit so as to address the Deity with "Abba" (Rom. 8:15-17), is not simply a recognition of a preexisting reality but a "new creation" (2 Cor. 5:17). The new creation must have some continuity with the old — how else can I say that it is *I* who am saved? — but it is not enough to be reminded that we are images of God. We must be ransomed, as a freeman might purchase a slave out of captivity (cf. Rom. 7:14), not merely edified. All are in bondage to the law and to sin (Rom. 3:9), and no amount of repentant introspection or just external action can liberate us. Still, God does not just annihilate the old order, she redeems it.

8. Some theologians — for example, Karl Barth, Helmut Thielicke, and Karen Lebacqz — prefer to see the *imago,* or what is sometimes referred to as the "dignity" of human life, as a relational phenomenon, a matter of God's grace rather than anything inherent in human beings. As understandable as this is as a safeguard against both pride and despair, however, it threatens the biblical doctrine of the goodness of creation.

Indeed, Christ wins for the faithful even more than Adam lost in the Fall. The elect are eventually sealed in permanent and loving communion with God beyond anything experienced by the innocent first parents in the garden. The adoption made possible by the Redeemer builds on incarnate human nature, so to speak, but it is, most dramatically, an in-breaking of eternity into time. As such, it is itself incomplete, both here and not yet. Through the practice of faith, hope, and love, human beings can have a foretaste of the new creation in history ("the first fruits of the Spirit"), but full adoption ("the redemption of our bodies") comes only in heaven and must be awaited with patience (Rom. 8:18-25).

In short, the distinction between sonship-created and sonship-recognized is not always clear-cut, in either Roman society or biblical theology.[9] Rather than lamenting this complexity, however, we can and should appreciate its implications for contemporary adoption. Even as the "sacred" adoption of individuals through Christ is partly God's re-creation of them in his Son's image and partly God's affirmation of them as already made in his image, so the "secular" adoption of individuals through the courts should be seen as having two sides or moments. On the one hand, secular adoption as currently practiced is the bestowing of a new legal identity on someone, male or female, who is not one's biological progeny. It is a matter of *invention* in the sense that filial rights and responsibilities now obtain by judicial fiat, where formerly there had been none. On the other hand, secular adoption is also the recognition of the shared humanity of the one adopted, his or her needs and potentials. In spite of loose talk about "adopting" a highway or a tree, the adoption that inaugurates a novel civic identity and familial relation is not purely arbitrary. Positive law does not generate human beings, or even legal heirs, *ex nihilo*. There are reasons why someone is or ought to be adopted, reasons stemming from our *discovery* of the person's indelible sanctity. Or so I will argue.

Let me now elaborate the meaning of sanctity by first contrasting it with dignity and then relating both notions to the idea of rights.

---

9. Even the possible senses in which Jesus was adopted, either by God or by Joseph, have been much debated by Christians. When, for example, God says of Jesus, "You are my Son, the Beloved; with you I am well pleased" (Mark 1:11, at Jesus' baptism) or "This is my Son, the Beloved; listen to him!" (Mark 9:7, at Jesus' transfiguration), is this a statement that describes reality, a performative that alters it, or perhaps both? The question becomes particularly complicated when one compares parallel passages, such as Matt. 3:17 and 17:5. I will return to the question of Jesus' nature in section V, but here I focus on humanity's "adoption as sons" (Gal. 4:5 RSV) and how it bears on civil adoption.

II. Dignity, Sanctity, and Their Correlative Rights

"Dignity," as I have repeatedly defined it (see chap. 2), is a contingent achievement: a function of either the meritorious exercise of personal agency or, minimally, the bare possession of such agency. In either case, dignity inheres only in individuals sufficiently mature to be aware of themselves and their intentional plans across time. Dignity requires, that is, a robust sense of self. (The Latin term *dignitas* means "a being worthy" and originally applied to those few persons or political offices filled with grandeur and authority.)[10] Entailing an admirable or powerful display of self-governance, dignity, in turn, inspires respect in others. The dignity of persons, their rational autonomy, moves Immanuel Kant, for instance, to insist that they be treated as ends and not as means only.[11] Free agents are intrinsically valuable and not merely instruments to the maximization of others' utility.

Only persons, defined as autonomous subjects, have dignity. Insofar as fetuses and infants are not yet self-conscious agents, they lack dignity in the technical sense and thus are not the subjects of respect. They are prepersons. Insofar as the profoundly mentally impaired are not and never will be morally self-aware, they too are without dignity. They are nonpersons. And insofar as the permanently comatose and demented are no longer autonomous, they are nondignified postpersons.[12] So the etymology dictates.

If "dignity" refers to contingent personal achievement, "sanctity," in contrast, refers to essential human nature. As I understand it, it is a function of universal human needs and potentials that do not presuppose self-awareness, self-control, or any other temporal attainment. (The Latin word *sanctitas* denotes "inviolability, sacredness," and was originally at home in a religious context.)[13] The relevant qualities include the need for food, shelter, clothing, and companionship, and/or the potential for growth, awareness, emotion, and inspiration. If dignity calls forth respect, sanctity calls forth reverence; if dignity moves others not to thwart one's noumenal self, then sanctity calls on others

---

10. See Charlton T. Lewis and Charles Short, *A Latin Dictionary* (New York: Oxford University Press, 1987), pp. 577-78.

11. Immanuel Kant, *The Critique of Practical Reason*, 5:87, in *The Cambridge Edition of the Works of Immanuel Kant: Practical Philosophy*, trans. Mary J. Gregor (Cambridge: Cambridge University Press, 1996), p. 210.

12. I do not mean to imply that Kant would conclude that fetuses, infants, the mentally handicapped, the comatose, and the demented may properly be treated as mere means to an end, but I do maintain that he gives us little or no basis on which to resist this conclusion.

13. Lewis and Short, *A Latin Dictionary*, p. 1626.

to cultivate one's vulnerable soul. Shared human needs and potentials are not so much intrinsically valuable as the necessary conditions for value itself. On my reading of the Christian tradition, the most basic form of sanctity is the need or ability to give or receive agapic love. To give or receive such love is to know eternal life, to be a child of God.

And who, specifically, is a child of God? Even though fetuses, early infants, the mentally impaired, and those with dementia are not dignified "persons" (i.e., not rational agents), they are nevertheless sacred human beings. If, to repeat, the measure of sanctity is the need or ability to give or receive agapic love, then the very young, the very old, and the very diminished "count." They all share our human needs and can profitably *receive* love, even if they cannot self-consciously give it.[14]

The sanctity of human lives has a claim on us that is utterly unearned and entirely inalienable. I call this claim a "sanctity right," and it stems from human need or potential; it has nothing to do with past merit or demerit, present contract or breach of contract, or future status or lack of status. Moreover, the claim is not merely to inviolability, as in the case of dignity, but also to active assistance. Regardless of whether orphaned or unwanted children have been culpably injured by others, for example, it is the duty of those responsible for the common good (both church and state) to see to it that the children find a loving home. Tragic accident or natural calamity may be responsible for the fate of these children, but their "sanctity rights" to nurturance obtain in any case. They have, I maintain, a right to be adopted that precedes the interests and contingent choices of would-be parents.[15] Those in authority have a duty

---

14. Some ten years ago, many observers were troubled by the case of Terri Schiavo, a brain-damaged patient from whom food and water were withheld. Though her condition meant that she was no longer an autonomous actor, the issue was whether she was beyond benefiting from the attention of others. I noted at the time that, if she was in fact so deeply comatose as to be incapable of receiving care, then she was effectively already dead. Given the complexity and uncertainty, however, including doubts about Ms. Schiavo's previous wishes, I believed that the state should assume and protect the sanctity of her life.

15. There is precedent for the right I am defending. Section 28 of the South African Constitution, for example, specifies that "Every child has the right — . . . (b) to family or parental care, or to appropriate alternative care when removed from the family environment; . . . [and] (d) to be protected from maltreatment, neglect, abuse or degradation." Quoted by Barbara Bennett Woodhouse in "The Constitutionalization of Children's Rights: Incorporating Emerging Human Rights into Constitutional Doctrine," *University of Pennsylvania Journal of Constitutional Law* 2, no. 1 (December 1999). The South African document is marred, I believe, by its attempt to ground children's rights in "dignity" rather than "sanctity," but the overall thrust of its case is clear and cogent. See also the United Nations' "Declaration of the Rights

of charity to enlist and empower adoptive parents to care for needy children, rather than wait for such parents to present themselves or for such children to seem appealing.[16]

In our late capitalist culture, it is hard not to assume that all things are either dignified persons or fungible property. It is hard, that is, to find the cultural space to recognize the sanctity of human life. If children are products with only use-value for their parents and the larger society, rather than human beings with sanctity in and of themselves, then the rights of would-be parents are consumer rights or property rights. If dignity rights are the only kind that are legally enforceable, as some have argued,[17] then being without dignity makes young children into mere commodities, at least for purposes of the law. How they are treated — indeed, whether they are suffered to live — is thus a matter of personal choice for others instead of human decency for themselves. If, in contrast, even prelinguistic children have a sanctity that is morally and legally significant, then the language of "free choice" and "consumer options" for adoptive (and biological) parents must give way to that of "human rights" and "loving care" for adopted children.[18]

I will eventually note the limits of the language of "rights" with respect to adoption, but the foregoing suggests an important clarification of that language. When talk of "rights" is used in adoption contexts, it is usually with reference to *the negative rights of would-be parents to adopt,* their right not to be legally restricted because of race, creed, gender, age, national origin, income level, marital status, or sexual orientation. This is a reflection of the fact that rights are normally attributed to autonomous adults, self-conscious agents who have "personal dignity."[19] Personal dignity rights are important, but they are not the only or even the most important variety of moral claim in adoption

---

of the Child" (1959) and "Convention on the Rights of the Child" (1989), especially articles 20 and 21 of the latter.

16. Thomas Aquinas is at best misleading when he writes that "man does not make him worthy whom he adopts; but rather in adopting him he chooses one who is already worthy" (*Summa Theologiae* IIIa, qu. 23, art. 1). Like all sanctity rights, the right to be adopted does not depend on *achieved* worthiness but on intrinsic nature.

17. See, for instance, Ronald Dworkin, *Life's Dominion: An Argument about Abortion, Euthanasia, and Individual Freedom* (New York: Knopf, 1993), and Peter Singer, *Rethinking Life and Death: The Collapse of Our Traditional Ethics* (Oxford: Oxford University Press, 1995).

18. On the perverting influence of consumerist language on our understanding of adoption, see Rickie Solinger, *Beggars and Choosers: How the Politics of Choice Shapes Adoption, Abortion, and Welfare in the United States* (New York: Hill and Wang, 2001).

19. See my *The Priority of Love: Christian Charity and Social Justice* (Princeton: Princeton University Press, 2003), esp. chap. 5.

contexts. In fact, the impersonal interests of needy children are increasingly being placed center stage in adoption debates. *The positive sanctity rights of children to be adopted* matter decisively.

Once the difference between dignity rights and sanctity rights is recognized, we can appreciate the possible conflict between personal claims by parents or society, on the one hand, and impersonal claims for adoptees, on the other. Does a woman who does not wish to carry a pregnancy to term have the right to kill the fetus or only to be free of the burden of its (late) gestation and (later) care?[20] How do we balance her dignity with the sanctity of the life she is carrying, a life that may eventually be put up for adoption? Does an intermittently dysfunctional pair of birth parents have the right to retrieve their children from foster care over and over again, thus submitting the children to repeated traumas of dislocation? How do we weigh the claims of blood against the well-being of the brood? In cases of transracial or transnational adoption, do the adoptive parents have the right to choose the culture and religion in which their children will be raised, or should they feel obliged to learn about the race and native creed of their adoptive offspring and teach them about the same? How, in such cases, do we promote what much of the Christian tradition has taught should be a central concern of well-ordered sexuality: the care and education of children?[21] Do heterosexual couples have the exclusive right to adopt, when single parents or gay couples might provide a more caring home for the children? How do we substantiate or gainsay the traditional judgment that gay and lesbian relations are intrinsically disordered, "abominations" or "degrading passions" that are "unnatural" and "contrary to right reason"?[22]

We can only begin to adjudicate the "rights" and "wrongs" of adoption by placing primacy on the sanctity rights of needy children. What suffering children need most is a secure and loving environment, and the best interests of these children dictate that they be placed in whatever situation best promises such ongoing support. Keeping biologically related families intact remains an important goal, but it does not trump all other factors. Rather than

---

20. Early on in pregnancy, the only way to escape the burden of gestation is an abortion that kills the embryo or fetus, but after about the twenty-third week, a C-section can often lead to "live birth" and thus to the possibility of adoption. Moreover, technology is pushing the survival date for "premies" further and further back. This strikes me as a Gnostic nightmare, but we may eventually see MEG (mechanical external gestation) remove pregnancy from the female body altogether.

21. See, for example, Aquinas, *Summa Theologiae*, Supplement, qu. 49.

22. See, for example, Lev. 18:22; Rom. 1:26-27; and Aquinas, *Summa Theologiae* IIaIIae, qu. 154, arts. 11 and 12.

social service offices always struggling to return foster care infants to their birth parents, which often means shuttling the infants back and forth between volatile homes and multiple caretakers, the governing ideal is rightly stability and permanence.[23] The rights of the biological parents may be forfeited if they are repeatedly drug dependent, abusive, neglectful, or otherwise unwilling or unable to care consistently for their children. Conversely, some single, gay, disabled, and older parents are equally capable of attending to the needs and potentials of adoptive children as some married, heterosexual, healthy, and younger couples. In other words, *agape* can and does govern many "nontraditional" relations and households, even as it governs many traditional ones.

Once we acknowledge that "natural" family bonds can be severed from within, and that this severance licenses the state to intervene, then we must affirm a "political" right to be adopted or else we are simply whistling in the dark. If there is no right to be adopted, then it may actually be hurtful to hold up stability and permanence as child-care desiderata, since these will seem cruel illusions to many in distress. To insist on a needy child's right to be adopted is not, need I say, to imply that each individual in society has a personal duty to adopt. Quite specific circumstances may *occasionally* translate into a perfect duty to adopt, at least for a Christian, as when one's sibling and spouse both die, leaving one's niece or nephew orphaned. But these cases are rare. I am maintaining, rather, that society as a whole has an imperfect duty to provide adequate adoption possibilities for its members. In addition to the direct claim that sanctity has on us, the motive for this duty of beneficence may be found, in part, in a collective sense of gratitude for the unearned care that we ourselves have received — starting, if we are lucky, with our parents but including essential social services to which we have not antecedently contributed. The primary motive for Christians, however, is not intrahuman indebtedness or reciprocity; it stems from that fact that we are loved first by God and are called on, in turn, to incarnate a holy will toward our neighbors (1 John 4:10-21). Human needs and potentials are attended to by the God who is agapic love, in spite of human powerlessness and sin (Rom. 5:6-8), and finite agents are commanded to do likewise.

In baptism, the whole congregation promises to help raise the child, so there is a theological model of the kind of communal responsibility I have in mind. Adoption services need not always be handled governmentally, through the state, moreover. Churches and other nonprofit organizations and communities can take on the responsibilities involved, with the state applauding and

---

23. Cf. Pertman, *Adoption Nation*, p. 215.

licensing, but not directly running, a host of faith-based or social-justice-based initiatives.[24] Such initiatives have the virtue of keeping family creation close to the parties most immediately involved, in accordance with the principle of subsidiarity.[25] Some worry that "independent" adoptions that work outside of governmental agencies are readily corrupted by financial incentives, and the so-called gray market in adoptable children does at times approximate baby selling. So even an exponent of subsidiarity, such as myself, must affirm the state's proper (if limited) place in regulating adoption procedures.

To flesh out and back up these claims, let me examine in more detail two forms of adoption called by some "abominable" and by others "liberating": single and homosexual adoption. These forms of adoption clearly challenge traditional conceptions of sex, marriage, and the family. But how should we understand them, morally, when the focus is on the sanctity of the children involved, rather than on the dignity of the would-be adoptive parents or the utility of the general society?

III. Abomination, Liberation, and Two Controversial Forms of Adoption

Nontraditional adoption crosses time-honored boundaries (e.g., of race and ethnicity) and calls into question the meaning of gender in marriage (e.g., gay and lesbian unions). Sometimes the undermining of social divisions or the blurring of familial boundaries is deeply troubling and harmful. Most of us would agree, for instance, that the Bible rightly calls incest, child sacrifice, and bestiality "abominations" (Lev. 18:6-30). The devastating effects of these practices are well documented. At other times, however, past distinctions between groups or types of people are themselves destructive and in need of subversion. Few of us would now applaud the idea that it is an "abomination" for the Egyptians to eat with the Hebrews (Gen. 43:32) or an incitement to "prostitution" for ethnic groups to intermarry (Exod. 34:16).[26]

Is nontraditional adoption necessarily abominable, or might it actually be liberating for all concerned? The basic meaning of the word "abominable" is indicated by its etymology, which *The Oxford English Dictionary* notes is either

24. I wish to thank Brent Waters, Mary Stewart Van Leeuwen, Stephen Presser, and John Witte for helping me to clarify the points made in this paragraph.

25. Cf. Lisa Cahill in my *The Morality of Adoption* (Grand Rapids: Eerdmans, 2005).

26. Old prejudices die hard, of course; Anwar Sadat was assassinated, in part, precisely for being civil to Menachem Begin.

absit + *omen* or *ab* + *homine.*[27] The former possibility, which I will call "the theological reading," is the older of the two and construes the abominable as what is without good omen or God's blessing, what offends the Fates or incurs God's wrath. The latter, "anthropological" reading entered the English language through John Wycliffe's 1382 translation of the Bible — he and his associates followed the French medievals in spelling "abhominable" with an *h* — and sees the abominable as what departs from or destroys the essentially human.[28]

As with "abomination," two general readings of "liberation" are possible. The Latin root of the word "liberate" *(liber)* means "free";[29] but there are at least two possible elaborations of this freedom, elaborations as old as Augustine: mere freedom of choice *(liberum arbitrium)* or the more holistic notion of good disposition, candor, and personal integrity *(libertas)*. Bare freedom of choice (liberty of indifference) refers exclusively to the will and says nothing about the ends to which free choice is put, while *libertas* is a more normative notion in which the whole person (rather than just the will) flourishes. Liberation in the sense associated with *libertas* entails more than having an external encumbrance removed. We do speak of "liberating" a town, say, when we mean delivering it from foreign occupation; but the most robust sense of "liberation" involves internal empowerment, a revolution in the soul rather than in its circumstances, an immense heightening of crucial capacities.

If love is from God and God himself is love (1 John 4:7-8), and if the fundamental human need and capacity are to come into loving relation with God and other human beings (Matt. 22:36-40), then we have a basic definition of both "abomination" and "liberation." The abominable is what fundamentally thwarts or destroys the potential to love or be loved, while the liberating is what fundamentally expands or generates this potential. To be capable of loving care is to be capable of knowing and pleasing God and of furthering human beings themselves as of intrinsic worth, while to be in need of loving care is to need valuing by God and others. To care for human beings as such is to value their status as (real or potential) valuers, and to need care from other human beings is to require their valuation in order to acquire moral ends of one's own. Personal care is, in other words, self-conscious and other-regarding. Yet, more importantly, developing personhood, becoming ourselves, requires that others

27. *The Compact Edition of the Oxford English Dictionary* (Oxford: Oxford University Press, 1971), 1:26.

28. This paragraph and the ones that immediately follow borrow extensively from my *Love Disconsoled: Meditations on Christian Charity* (Cambridge: Cambridge University Press, 1999), chap. 4.

29. *Compact Edition of the Oxford English Dictionary,* 1:239.

extend to us gratuitous attention before we are self-conscious agents. Because of their need and potential to give and receive love — what I have called their "sanctity" — the prepersonal lives of children have profound worth. Not until full personhood is actualized do our lives self-consciously matter to us: only then do we value ourselves as valuers. But the need and potential for agapic love, even in fetuses, are at the root of the possibility of an abominable thwarting or a liberating expansion of humanity.

Loving care is the great gift given in adoption, a favor that is usually returned once the adoptee is capable of personal response. The chief aim of adoption is to foster human beings who are themselves caring and cared for, in a context where attentive care is otherwise missing. However stunted institutionalized children may be, and however different they may be from their prospective adoptive parents, the need and capacity for loving care is a universal human trait, as ubiquitous as language competence among undamaged individuals. If it is not cultivated by other caring human beings, it atrophies and is never actualized. In denying the importance of and opportunity for loving care, we not only deprive others of care here and now but also render them (and us) unable to care or to be cared for in the future. The loss is ultimately of the potential for dignity, as well as of the reality of sanctity.

Just as abominations contract humanity's capacity to care or be cared for, thus making for bondage to bondage, so liberations expand that capacity, thus making for "freedom to be free" (in Arturo Paoli's phrase, echoing Gal. 5:1). To be liberated is not first of all to change our circumstances but to be changed ourselves. Unlike abominations, however, liberations undermine our prevailing social categories in highly beneficial ways — ways that allow for new and exponentially better forms of being and acting. Liberations make for a broader expanse of humanity both individually and collectively as well as, for believers, a deeper communion with divinity. Blood ties between parents and children are among the most powerful human connections, but adoption transcends these to a large degree — even if adoptees and birth parents remain in contact — by placing custodial responsibility for raising children in the hands of persons who are not those children's biological parents. This empowerment augments the moral identity of the adoptive parents, making them more giving, but it most centrally augments the moral development of the adoptees, making them more stable, secure, and fulfilled. Adoption allows us to integrate as many loving individuals as completely into the moral community as possible. Thus "liberation leads to liberation."

Do single-parent and gay or lesbian adoptions affect prevailing ideas of sex, marriage, and family in negative or positive ways? Are they "unnatural" in the sense of being abominably destructive of the goodness of nature, "unnatural" in the sense of liberatingly broadening that goodness, or perhaps neither? There are different kinds of single parents — never married, adoptive, divorced, and widowed — and the households of each will tend to vary. But concerns over single parenting typically focus on three issues: (1) the economic stability of the household, (2) the psychological development of the children, and (3) the moral impact on the wider society. These worries are perhaps inevitable for a culture historically founded on heterosexual marriage. Looking at the relevant sociological data, however, I am increasingly convinced that a committed single person can give the type and amount of care that liberates all parties to an adoption to be better human beings.[30] Even if one maintains that single parenting is not ideal (see below), it ought not to be stigmatized as such, independently of context, motive, concrete actions taken, and social consequences achieved.[31] One's personal dignity does not depend on having a spouse, nor does one's ability to give love to a child. The possibility of good single parenting is implicitly recognized by the state when it does not automatically remove even minor children from the home of a widow or widower.

Similar things might be said about gays, lesbians, the elderly, and the physically impaired. The dignity of such individuals, so often denied a priori, is a function of their willingness and ability to embody love and justice, in parental contexts and elsewhere, even as any indignity stems from the opposite. Some queer, old, and handicapped folks behave abominably, but so do some who are straight, young, and able-bodied. There is no escaping the need to look at specifics rather than "types."

That said, as important as it is to recognize the dignity rights of a range of adults, adoption debates are best served, I believe, by looking carefully at the sanctity rights of needy children. Rather than focusing on the rights of marginalized would-be parents, we should accent the rights of suffering children to be adopted by the marginalized. This is dictated by the charitable principle of attending first to the most vulnerable — an idea as old as Jesus' identification with "the least of these" (Matt. 25:45) and as new as liberation theology's "preferential option for the poor." What is abominable — that is, what is against God's will or stifling of humanity — is to deny a suffering child a loving home that the child might otherwise have. Many singles and homosexuals could

30. For a review of the literature, see Nancy E. Dowd, *In Defense of Single-Parent Families* (New York: New York University Press, 1997).

31. As Dowd herself notes, "Removing the stigma against single-parent families should not, *must* not, keep us from recognizing the problems they confront. At the same time, recognition of the value of single-parent families is also crucial." Dowd, *In Defense*, p. xviii.

provide such a home to the hundreds of "unadoptables" trapped in foster care or warehoused in large institutions. It is not being raised in a nontraditional family that causes needless human suffering, but rather being uncared for, in utero or out. A child without a consistent adult caregiver often becomes all but incapable of love and trust himself; thus the spiral of abuse and neglect perpetuates itself into the next generation.

Consider the legal implications of shifting focus from the right to adopt to the right to be adopted. There is no explicit constitutional right to adopt, so challenges to a state's ban on gay adoption, for example, must rely on general appeals to "due process and equal protection" (for both gay males and lesbians), as enunciated in the Fourteenth Amendment.[32] The problem, however, is that cases that do not involve explicitly protected classes or fundamental rights shift the burden of proof to plaintiffs — for instance, homosexual persons who wish to adopt. All the state need do is show a "rational basis" for precluding nontraditional adoption, such as its authority to regulate family law in accordance with local standards. A more plausible case can be made for the constitutional right to *be* adopted by available and willing parents. Amendment 14, section 1, of the United States Constitution reads: "All persons born or naturalized in the United States, and subject to the jurisdiction thereof, are citizens of the United States and of the state wherein they reside. No state shall make or enforce any law which shall abridge the privileges or immunities of citizens of the United States; nor shall any state deprive any person of life, liberty, or property, without due process of law; nor deny to any person within its jurisdiction the equal protection of the laws." To be denied adoptive parents that one might otherwise have — for example, a single person or a gay or lesbian couple — is close to being deprived of "life, liberty, or property" in basic ways, as well as to being denied "the equal protection of the laws." An adult's life, liberty, and property are not fundamentally at risk if the adult does not adopt a child, but a needy child's life, liberty, and property may be so at risk if the child is not adopted. The Fourteenth Amendment safeguards citizens from the unwarranted deprivation of life, liberty, and property, and this is traditionally interpreted as a negative right not to be interfered with. I have contended, however, that human sanctity entails some positive rights to be assisted. In this regard, the right to be adopted is analogous to the right to basic health care or to social security.

Children always do better with reliable, ongoing parental oversight. In

---

32. See, for example, Laurie Cunningham, "Florida's Gay-Adoption Ban Goes to 11th Circuit," *Daily Report*, March 5, 2003, pp. 1 and 6.

addition, singles and homosexual couples often will embrace "special needs" children — the older, the impaired, the biracial, the ethnically alien — either because the would-be parents identify with these neglected and marginalized souls or because these children are the only candidates that the system will consider handing over to a nontraditional household. All persons who are willing and able to provide a caring home should be allowed to adopt any available children, but, given present institutional realities, to deny a special needs child the possibility of a single father or mother or of homosexual parents may be to deny that child/citizen her only real chance at being loved.

Some worry that endorsing single-parent adoption will encourage women to get pregnant out of wedlock, and perhaps men to impregnate them. If an unmarried adult, male or female, can properly raise a child, male or female, why should society continue to hold out a marital union of husband and wife as the most proper context for procreation? Won't countenancing single adoptive parents mean more "illegitimate" children, since the stigma of single parenthood will have been removed, including from the very young? This is a reasonable concern about unintended social consequences. It is important to distinguish, however, between adopting a child who already exists without supportive parents and purposely conceiving a child out of wedlock. For a father or mother intentionally to conceive a child out of wedlock does a disservice to the child. In spite of the increasing emotional, economic, and political independence of women from men, denying a child the benefit of two parents committed to each other increases the likelihood of juvenile and long-term difficulties for that child. The debate rages on concerning the extent to which family form, such as single parenthood, *causes* problems of poverty and other disadvantages for children and the extent to which it merely *correlates* with them.[33] But, as Wade Horn has written,

> The empirical literature is quite clear . . . that children do, indeed, do best when they grow up in an intact, two-parent, married household. Even after controlling for differences in income, children who live with their married parents are two times less likely to fail at school, two to three times less likely to suffer an emotional or behavioral problem requiring psychiatric treatment, perhaps as much as 20 times less likely to suffer child abuse,

33. See Dowd, *In Defense,* esp. pp. 26-27. In sometimes suggesting that a family's form has little or nothing to do with how well its members fare, Dowd overstates her case, I believe. But, in accenting the centrality of poverty, gender stereotyping, racial discrimination, and other variables not directly equatable with family structure, she nonetheless provides a helpful corrective to a narrow traditionalism that would vilify all single parents.

and as adolescents they are less likely to get into trouble with the law, use illicit drugs, smoke cigarettes, abuse alcohol, or engage in early and promiscuous sexual activity. One is hard pressed to find a single indicator of child well-being which is not adversely impacted by divorce or being born out-of-wedlock.[34]

One may grant the goodness of single-parent adoptions as (partial) remedies for the plight of homeless children — we must not make the perfect the enemy of the good — and one may also acknowledge the right of single birth-parents to keep their offspring if they can provide for them. (Emphasis is typically on single birth-*mothers,* thus the dignity and rights of single birth-*fathers* are frequently overlooked.) Yet one may still affirm, as I do, that stable marriage is the ideal setting for raising children. The ideal abides not simply because two parents can be more efficient than one but also because two can more fully model, in their interpersonal relations, the give-and-take of love.

An extended family of grandparents, aunts, uncles, cousins, et al. can of course provide a wide range of affection and support for the children of a single parent, as well as for the parent himself. (The same can be said for an extended church of ministers, deacons, elders, lay leaders, et al.) And I in no way mean to imply that single-parent households, per se, are faulty or undesirable.[35] In spite of a 50 percent divorce rate in the United States, however, the conjugal love of two people still promises dynamics of care and commitment — touching God, one another, and any children — that simply cannot be had in any other way. Indeed, it is for just this reason that I favor legalizing same-sex marriage. For gays and lesbians who wish to adopt, no less than for heterosexuals, stable marriage should be the primary familial context. That

34. See Wade Horn, "Take a Vow to Promote Benefits of Marriage," *Washington Times,* November 2, 1999. The disadvantages of single-parent households are not due exclusively to the impact of divorce or illegitimacy, moreover. See, for example, Arthur J. Norton and Paul C. Glick, "One Parent Families: A Social and Economic Profile," *Family Relations* 35 (1986): 9-17. For more on the benefits of the "committed, intact, equal-regard, public-private family," see the essay by Don Browning in my *The Morality of Adoption.* Browning and Nancy Dowd can be usefully read together. Despite their different accents and agendas, they both would affirm, I believe, Dowd's thesis that "Powerful incentives remain — and should remain — for raising children in two-parent families. Supporting single-parent families need not translate into destabilizing two- or multiple-parent families." See Dowd, *In Defense,* p. xix.

35. A man contemplating becoming a single adoptive father can take encouragement from Barbara J. Risman's judgment, shared by an increasing number of experts, that " 'mothering' is not an exclusively female skill." See Risman, "Can Men 'Mother'? Life as a Single Father," *Family Relations* 35 (1986): 95.

context stands the best chance to benefit, maximally, all three elements of the adoption triad: the child, the biological parents, and the adoptive parents.

In spite of the three issues identified above, single fathers and mothers, biological and adoptive, are ever more socially acceptable these days. But two major objections to homosexual adoptive parents are less easily overcome: (a) the fear that the same-sex couple will intentionally or unintentionally drive an adopted child into a gay or lesbian "lifestyle," and (b) the fear that one or both members of the couple will molest the child in their care, especially a child who is of the same sex as the couple. On the first score, states like Florida (and Utah and Mississippi) commonly maintain that adoptees need hetero-sexual role models to develop "normal" sexual identification.[36] A same-sex household frustrates healthy child development, the argument runs, so even if the best interests of the child translate into the right to be adopted, the pool of potential parents should be limited to the heterosexual. On the second score, the ready association of homosexuality with pederasty still persists in our culture.[37] The recent scandal of numerous Catholic priests abusing children in their care, across decades and seemingly with impunity, has bolstered the tendency both to equate gayness with child molestation and to take public steps to stop the predation.

It is tempting to address the first fear, of same-sex couples pushing ad-opted children into homosexuality, by "biologizing" the issue. Some are com-forted by the thought that sexual orientation seems largely a matter of genetic predisposition, as though having little or no choice in a mode of being is sufficient ground to affirm it (or at least to tolerate it).[38] Virtually all gays and lesbians come from traditional heterosexual families, which indeed suggests that their orientations are more a matter of nature than of nurture. Moreover, the sociological evidence does not appear to support the thesis that gay and lesbian parents are more likely to raise gay and lesbian children.[39] But to think

36. Cunningham, "Florida's Gay-Adoption Ban," p. 6.

37. Take, for example, the statement by the Ramsey Colloquium on "The Homosexual Movement," in *First Things* 41 (March 1994): 15-21. Though thoughtful and nuanced in many ways, the statement rather uncritically maintains that "public anxiety about homosexuality is preeminently [and legitimately] a concern about the vulnerabilities of the young," especially their vulnerability to "seduction and solicitation."

38. For a detailed review of the literature on possible physiological bases of homosexu-ality, see Qazi Rahman and Glenn D. Wilson, "Born Gay? The Psychobiology of Human Sexual Orientation," *Personality and Individual Differences* 34, no. 8 (June 2003): 1335-1559. For the cau-tious suggestion that this study gives us ethical grounds on which to settle gay rights disputes, see Nicholas D. Kristof, "Gay at Birth?" editorial in the *New York Times*, October 25, 2003.

39. See Ann Sullivan, ed., *Issues in Gay and Lesbian Adoption* (Annapolis Junction, Md.:

that these data settle the *moral* question is to be guilty of the genetic fallacy. The issue is not whether sexual identity is biologically determined, individually chosen, or socially conditioned — it may well be a function of all three factors — but whether homosexual parents can be just and loving to their children. If they cannot, then the causal reasons why they are same-sex oriented matter very little: they should not be allowed to adopt. If, in contrast, they can be good parents, they should be permitted (even encouraged) to adopt. To have no freedom of choice with respect to an action or disposition may well be ex-culpating, but pathologies are to be checked regardless of whether they involve personal guilt. Even if alcoholism is understood as a disease, for instance, we still arrest people for DWI and eventually take away their driver's licenses.

The second fear, of homosexual child-molestation, can be guarded against in the same fashion as heterosexual child-molestation: with careful public oversight and strong legal sanctions. If a couple, gay or straight, has a history of child abuse, they are obviously not fit candidates for adoptive parent-ing. And if a couple, gay or straight, is convicted of child abuse, they should be severely punished with fines and imprisonment, as well as the loss of parental rights. Just as a loving straight father would be offended by the suggestion that he is sexually interested in his daughter, just as a loving straight mother would be offended by the suggestion that she is sexually interested in her son, so a gay or lesbian parent who loves his or her child will take umbrage at the innuendo of incest. Incest is indeed an abomination with devastating effects on young psyches,[40] but gay parents are just as capable of honoring the sanctity of their children's lives as are straight parents. (If this is not so, one wonders why even Florida permits homosexuals to be foster parents, even to care for the same foster child for a period of years.) The virtue and criterion that ought to govern all relations between adopters and adoptees is a charity that actively promotes the good of all parties, including the good of untroubled psychic individuation

---

Child Welfare League of America, 1995); Stephen Hicks and Janet McDermott, eds., *Lesbian and Gay Fostering and Adoption: Extraordinary Yet Ordinary* (London: Jessica Kingsley, 1998); and Frederick W. Bozett and Marvin B. Sussman, eds., *Homosexuality and Family Relations* (New York: Haworth Press, 1990).

40. On the destructive psychological and social effects of incest, heterosexual and ho-mosexual, see Jean Renvoize, *Incest: A Family Pattern* (New York: Routledge and Kegan Paul, 1983); Robin Fox, *The Red Lamp of Incest: An Enquiry into the Origins of Mind and Society* (Notre Dame: University of Notre Dame Press, 1983); Diana E. H. Russell and Rebecca M. Bolen, *The Epidemic of Rape and Child Sexual Abuse in the United States* (Thousand Oaks, Calif.: Sage, 2000); and Susan Forward and Craig Buck, *Betrayal of Innocence: Incest and Its Devastation* (New York: Penguin Books, 1988).

for children. Putting the key point cautiously, most studies with which I am familiar find no detrimental impact on children of parental homosexuality.[41]

A final word is in order about the linkage, for juveniles, between abomination and liberation. It is precisely the "unfinished" quality of children, their innocence and dependency, that makes them so readily both the victims of abomination and the beneficiaries of liberation. If children were not so undeveloped and unself-aware, they could engineer their own care and not be so subject to adult cruelty or kindness. As it is, they can be radically stunted or enriched by their elders. We do not know why some adults are moved to solicitous wonder by the "mystery" of a child, to use Martin Marty's term,[42] while others are induced by that same "mystery" to take advantage of that same child. But to dismiss, prey upon, or otherwise despise the young and vulnerable is virtually definitive of inhuman and impious behavior.[43] To check such abomination, liberating adoption policy will put the best interests of the child ahead of adult rights. That done, new rights and old wrongs are brought to light for both children and adults.

IV. Identity, Dignity, and the Right to Know

Even as needy children, especially when younger, have a sanctity right to be adopted, including by single or homosexual parents, so adopted children, especially when older, have a dignity right[44] to know their biological identities, including who their birth parents and siblings are, if this knowledge is available.[45] Knowing one's genetic history can be indispensable to wise or

41. See Julie Schwartz Gottman, "Children of Gay and Lesbian Parents," *Marriage and Family Review* 14, no. 34 (1989), cited in Dowd, *In Defense,* p. 51.

42. See Martin Marty, "Mapping the Frontiers of the Study of Religion and Children: In Theology and Ethics" (unpublished manuscript), pp. 16-18.

43. I follow an ancient exegetical tradition in holding, for instance, that Abraham is "father of the faith" not because he is willing to sacrifice Isaac but because he is willing to overturn the ritual burnt offering of the firstborn son in favor of a more egalitarian and charitable view of father-child relations. See "Is Isaac Our Neighbor?" chap. 6 of my *Love Disconsoled.*

44. As noted, a central motive for adopting individuals, early and late, is reverence for their sanctity, but parents taking in older persons (e.g., troubled teenagers) may also look to the latter's dignity and what it takes to respect it. Need I say, all human lives possess sanctity, while some (the personal) have both sanctity and dignity.

45. In some instances, information on birth parents and siblings is unlikely to be available. For many Chinese adoptees, for example, there simply are no records with actual names. I thank Cindy Meyer for helping me to clarify this point.

timely health decisions, as in choosing between types of cancer treatment or searching for donor organs for transplant. Beyond this biomedical benefit, however, there is a profound psychosocial good at stake. Knowing personal origins, genetic and cultural, is often crucial for forming a healthy sense of self. (Dignity itself I have defined as requiring self-awareness or self-control over time.) We are historical beings, and to appreciate one's relation to other people in the present, one must understand one's own genesis in the past. Here secrecy and shame are abominable, stunting of mature development, while openness and pride are liberating. As Rickie Solinger notes,

> In many ways, the idea of adoptees searching for their biological roots and claiming rights to information about themselves was, itself, shaped by liberation movements emerging in the 1960s. In the 1970s, through ALMA [Adoptees' Liberty Movement Association] and other organizations, adoptees claimed the right to own the truth about their origins. Among the pioneers of "identity politics," adoptees fused liberation, the search for self-hood, and special group identity to define and assert a political cause.[46]

An adopted child may decline to exercise her right to know her birth parents and any siblings, but having the option to know or not know is itself empowering, a recognition of her dignity as a free agent. A birth mother who relinquished her child to adoption may decline to interact with that child in later life, but to conceive and deliver a child carries with it the obligation to allow that child to know who she is, her full selfhood in relation to others. The same goes, *mutatis mutandis,* for a birth father. Due to legal constraints or medical disabilities, birth parents may not always be free to fulfill the duty of disclosure I describe. But nondisclosure should be the exception rather than the rule. This becomes especially clear when one reads what Solinger calls "adoptees' heart-wrenching expressions of their need to find themselves by finding their lost parents."[47] This need seldom has anything to do with how kind or unkind adoptive parents have been. The desire to uncover the truth is usually a function of neither dissatisfaction with stepfamilies nor morbid curiosity; it appears to be an innate and healthy drive toward self-awareness for many adoptees.[48] Jesus himself, history's most famous adopted

46. Solinger, *Beggars and Choosers,* p. 81.
47. Solinger, *Beggars and Choosers,* p. 84.
48. Solinger, *Beggars and Choosers,* pp. 83-84.

child,[49] seems to have been driven by a passionate desire to know his lineage, even as Matthew and John take particular interest in his genealogy — Matthew biologically and John metaphysically.

V. Jesus Christ as Adopted Son

Was Jesus Christ adopted, and if so by whom and for what purpose? Nestorians and other adoptionists separate the human and divine natures of Christ, maintaining that he represents a dual sonship. "Christ as God is indeed the Son of God by generation and nature, but Christ as man is Son of God only by adoption and grace."[50] Jesus the historical figure, that is, is not coeternal with the heavenly Father but rather "adopted" by God at a particular moment in time (at his baptism, transfiguration, or resurrection). On this view, Mary is not *Theotokos* (Mother of God) but rather the birth mother of a human child. In turn, Jesus' unity with the divine will is a moral union, not a hypostatic one. For Nestorians, Jesus is not the divine Logos but the Son of God by way of transspecies adoption of the lower by the higher. God took in Jesus, so to speak, to foster a redemptive providential plan, but Jesus is not an eternal Person of the Blessed Trinity.

Adoptionists typically hold that their position is required if the true humanity of Jesus is to be preserved and if normal human beings are to have any hope of following Jesus into heavenly salvation, as fellow adoptees of the Father.[51] Broadly adoptionist views have genuine appeal precisely because they seem to allow a greater connection between actual people and the exemplary life and teaching of Jesus. The Bible nowhere calls Jesus the adopted Son of God, but Jesus himself calls people to become sons and daughters of God. "Love your enemies and pray for those who persecute you, so that you may be children of your Father in heaven," he declares in Matthew 5:44-45, ending with the injunction: "Be perfect, therefore, as your heavenly Father is perfect" (Matt. 5:48). Becoming "children of the Most High" (Luke 6:35) is open to all who love their enemies, do good, and lend without expecting return. And this process sounds very much like being adopted by a righteous and powerful Fa-

49. Moses finishes a close second, I suppose, or is it a dead heat?

50. "Adoptionism," in *New Advent Catholic Encyclopedia*, http://www.newadvent.org/cathen/01150a.htm, p. 1.

51. See the discussion of Elipandus of Toledo and Felix of Urgel, both writing in the eighth century, in "Adoptionism in Spain," in *The Westminster Dictionary of Church History*, ed. Jerald C. Brauer (Philadelphia: Westminster, 1971), pp. 8-9.

ther. In fact, it resonates well with my emphasis on the right of needy children to be adopted by responsible adults.

In addition, to aver that Mary is the Virgin Mother of God and that Jesus of Nazareth is of one substance with the Father *(homoousion)* may suggest that ordinary sexual reproduction is dirty or shameful and that Jesus Christ is something like a clone of God miraculously placed inside of Mary's womb. Such a picture makes it difficult to take seriously imperatives to embody Christlike love in this life. If Jesus Christ is superhuman and utterly sui generis, how can we take to heart his final commandment to love as he loves? An impossible model is arguably no model at all.

For all its power, however, the adoptionist scenario presents a number of moral and theological problems. First, it makes adoption by God depend on one's personal merit or achievement, when, as I have argued, it is the sanctity of human life that inspires the strong to take in the weak. Surely the point of Jesus' comments on becoming "children of God" is the existential one that we must become who and what we already are: made in God's image and called to holiness. According to Genesis, we are already God's sons and daughters, so our "adoption" is, at least in part, a recognition of an ongoing identity. Second, adoptionism negates the powerful doctrine that the incarnation is God's kenotic act of self-humbling that *allows us to adopt him*. God takes on human form to show us both the need and the potential of a sacred child — and all children are sacred — and Joseph (and Mary?) rise to the occasion as "adoptive" parents. Joseph is frequently the forgotten man in traditional accounts of the nativity, but the generosity of his not putting away a pregnant Mary and of raising a son not his own is entirely lost on adoptionists. Third, adoptionism fails to take sin seriously as a blight on humanity in need of redemption. We cannot overcome sin, and thus love as we ought to love, without divine assistance. The fact that this assistance comes through acceptance of vulnerability, first in the manger and then on the cross, should not surprise us. This is God's characteristic way with the world. As 1 John observes, "In this is love, not that we loved God but that he loved us and sent his Son to be the atoning sacrifice for our sins" (1 John 4:10). Once more, God's adoption also rescues us from a bondage that we ourselves cannot break.

There are good reasons, then, why the various brands of adoptionism have been labeled problematic, indeed heretical, by the overwhelming majority of Christian denominations. Most Catholics and many Protestants insist that Mary is the Virgin Mother of God and that Jesus as man is the "natural" (i.e., supernatural) Son of God, not merely his adoptive son. Mary's virginity and Jesus' Sonship are affirmations of the sanctity of human life, not denials of its earthiness, since both doctrines highlight the redemptive presence of God with us in the flesh. If Jesus were merely the biological son of Mary and Joseph, his life, death, and resurrection would make holiness an impossible ideal; even as, if Jesus were but the adopted Son of God, this would make filiation with God depend on our own contingent achievement. There are moral justifications, in short, for declaring that Mary is *Theotokos,* and that in Jesus Christ there is but one nature, one person, fully divine and fully human. "Christ, Son of God, by His eternal generation, remains Son of God, even after the Word has assumed and substantially united to Himself the sacred Humanity; Incarnation detracts no more from the eternal sonship than it does from the eternal personality of the Word."[52] Jesus is adopted by Joseph, to repeat, but in insisting on knowing and living out his divine Sonship, the Christ himself affirms the right of all adoptees to discover their full identity.

If Jesus was adopted by Joseph, and if Jesus nevertheless insisted on affirming his true identity, his supernatural "Sonship," then we should not forbid suffering children from being adopted by those radically different from themselves or, where possible, from knowing their actual ancestry. On the contrary, adoptive children in "nontraditional families" have an especially privileged role in the *imitatio Christi.*

There is, of course, a more radical form of "adoptionism" that leaves God entirely out of the picture and sees Jesus as the bastard son of Mary and an anonymous human father, perhaps a Roman soldier who impregnated Mary while she was betrothed to Joseph. On this account, Mary is either an adulteress or a rape victim, and the cuckolded Joseph is supremely admirable for either forgiving her sin or overlooking her violation. For Joseph to consent to wed Mary and to raise Jesus as his own child makes him, not Jesus, the second Adam who undoes the poisonous male myth of Eve's transgression in the garden. And it is Jesus' awareness that he is illegitimate that makes him intensely concerned with his own identity and gives him his deep empathy with those who are socially outcast.[53] This naturalistic view can teach us much about the courage of adoptive fathers and the right of birth mothers *not* to surrender their children to strangers; it can also help us reject the contempt for illegitimate children that has plagued Hebrew-Christian culture at least since Ishmael.[54] But with this secular story, we have left the fold of Christian faith altogether.

52. "Adoptionism," p. 3.

53. For a defense of this early Ebionite view, see Stephen Mitchell, *The Gospel according to Jesus* (New York: HarperCollins, 1991), esp. pp. 21-28 and 95-97.

54. On these subjects, see John Witte's essay, "Ishmael's Bane: The Sin and Crime of Illegitimacy Reconsidered," in *The Morality of Adoption;* also Witte, *The Sins of the Fathers: The Law and Theology of Illegitimacy Reconsidered* (Cambridge: Cambridge University Press, 2009).

Conclusion: The Image of God and the (Un)Naturalness of Sex

If God is agapic love (1 John 4:16), then to be made in God's image must be to possess a love-related feature. We tend to think here of the *capacity to give love*, but divine blessing exists perhaps even more profoundly in the *need to receive love*. The need for love is itself a sublime part of love. Thus I equate the image of God with the essential need *or* ability to give *or* receive *agape*, a condition that includes fetuses (wanted and unwanted), children (legitimate and illegitimate), the handicapped, the senile, and, need I add, the single and the married, the gay and the straight. In God, goodness and power merge, but we must always remember that that power is made perfect in weakness (2 Cor. 12:9). Indeed, in children we see that we are fundamentally "mirror images" of God, not because children are demonic but because they need so palpably to receive love that they thereby reverse our typical understanding of God as pure might and sovereign independence. The mystery of both Yahweh and youth is gifted yearning. God started out self-sufficient yet chose to create the world, an imponderable willingness to cease to be all-in-all. God then became incarnate in this world, in part to redeem creatures but also to receive their love in return. We, in contrast, start out entirely dependent on others and grow to, at most, a partial autonomy in which we can freely give of ourselves. To adopt a needy child is to participate in this holy dialectic of giving and receiving.

This account of the *imago Dei* might seem to settle things, but the issue of adoption cannot be separated from the backdrop of increasingly divergent religious and secular criteria for proper sexual and familial relations. Adoption practices both shape and are shaped by those criteria. At its best, adoption is motivated by the desire to care for and educate children, but it might seem to be a problematic case of acquiring offspring without benefit of personal sex. If the Roman Catholic Church forbids artificial means of conception, why does it permit adoption? Similarly, if traditional postnatal adoption is admirable, why not think of artificial insemination by donor as very early prenatal adoption? Why should parent-child consanguinity be essential to "reproduction" here? In spite of its historical commitments to forms of "natural law," Christianity ought to be wary of too readily identifying the "natural" with the normative. What is natural, as opposed to artificial, is often hard to specify. And Protestants, at any rate, are generally reluctant to take fallen human proclivities, much less nonhuman nature, as definitive of virtue. "Nature is red in tooth and claw," as Tennyson observed, and many instinctive human impulses are cruel or thoughtless. At the heart of Christianity, and thus of Christian views on adoption, stand two *super*natural acts:

the incarnation and the passion of Christ. These, not instinct or habit, provide the moral cues for how to live, as any sophisticated version of natural law theory recognizes.

Getting children without personal sex or having sex without getting children is not the issue; the issue is whether the sex is loving and the children are loved. Christian sex (and adoption) is not finally defined by what is "natural" or "unnatural," but by what is Christlike and thus perfecting of nature. Marriage and the fruit of children may have initially been confined to a procreative Adam and Eve in the Garden of Nature, but we now live east of Eden and, even without the Fall, Christ represents a *donum superadditum* who wins for us (gay and straight) forms of community not "naturally" possible. If, by the grace of the incarnate Word, we are to love those who are strangers or enemies to us and to let them teach us virtue, then surely we can permit inspired singles and homosexuals to be parents. Better still, surely we can support them and even see in them part of the meaning of (God's) parenthood and family.

Jesus Christ was an iconoclast, associating with the poor and marginalized and putting the immediate needs of vulnerable human beings ahead of social conventions and religious traditions. His iconoclasm was liberating in the extreme. If Jesus was single, as the Gospels suggest, then Christians cannot idolize the married state; if children are among the most vulnerable, as surely they are, then Jesus' own example ought to move us to provide for them; and if Jesus was inspired by a quest to determine his true ancestry, as Peter appreciated, then we cannot deny contemporary adoptees the chance to discover who they are. If Jesus Christ is the supernatural and sinless Son of God whom the Father allows Joseph (and us) to adopt, in sum, then Christians have the best motive imaginable to endorse the rights of suffering children to be given loving homes and genetic histories. The language of "rights" and "duties," even "sanctity rights" and "duties of charity," may ultimately cede pride of place to talk of "faith, hope, and love." (Exclusive reference to "rights" and "duties" may imply an overly adversarial set of relations.) But both God and Joseph express their love across bloodlines and social divisions, and both are faithful to children gotten without benefit of "natural" sex. We as a society can only hope to do the same. Not only does adoption revere the sanctity of a human life, but to the extent that we nurture "the least of these," we also care for Christ himself (cf. Matt. 25:45).

My overarching conclusion is straightforward: supporting the positive right of helpless or abused children to be adopted ought to be a fundamental Christian, and national, commitment. This is especially true if one holds, as I do, that elective abortions are immoral and should be illegal after the first trimester.[55] One cannot be pro-parent, advocating the negative rights of would-be adopters not to be interfered with, without first being pro-child, advocating the positive rights of adoptees to be cared for. And one cannot be anti-abortion, recognizing in fetuses the right-to-life, without also being pro-adoption, recognizing in infants the right-to-life-in-a-family. Being pro-adoption does not mean humiliating unwed or indigent birth parents, or denying them the right to care for their children if they are able and responsibly choose to do so, but it does mean putting the best interests of the children first. The interests of the adoptees should also be the primary factor in determining the extent of contact that birth parents might later have with their relinquished children.

My thesis that needy children have the right to be adopted invites the question of how, practically, to offer a remedy to these children. To stop excluding single people and same-sex couples from adopting is one concrete step, but even more important is the cultivation of a sense of corporate accountability for the problem. This is a matter not so much of legal policy as of lived charity. We must stop flushing and freezing embryos, even as we must cease doing the equivalent to children already born.

---

55. See *The Priority of Love,* chap. 5. Pertman notes that, sadly, there is still often more stigma associated with putting one's child up for adoption than with having an abortion. See *Adoption Nation,* p. 12. Does any other social attitude better crystallize the conflict between the culture of death and the culture of life?

Prophetic Conclusion: Martin Luther King Jr.

Any person . . . who shall be guilty of printing, publishing, or circulating printed, typewritten or written matter urging or presenting for public acceptance or general information, arguments or suggestions in favor of social equality or of intermarriage between whites and negroes, shall be guilty of a misdemeanor and subject to fine of [*sic*] not exceeding five hundred (500.00) dollars or imprisonment not exceeding six (6) months or both.

MISSISSIPPI "JIM CROW" LAW[1]

It seemed as though I could hear the quiet assurance of an inner voice, saying, "Stand up for righteousness, stand up for truth. God will be at your side forever."

MARTIN LUTHER KING JR.[2]

1. "Jim Crow Laws," Martin Luther King Jr. Center for Nonviolent Social Change Web site, http://www.nps.gov/malu/documents/jim_crow_laws.htm. Accessed November 15, 2000.
2. Martin Luther King Jr., *Strength to Love* (Philadelphia: Fortress, 1963), p. 113.

I wrote portions of this chapter while a visiting fellow at the Center for the Study of Religion at Princeton University. I would like to thank Robert Wuthnow and Marie Griffith, the director and associate director of the Center, for their support. For their helpful discussion of this material, I am also grateful to Leora Batnitzky, Eddie Glaude, Eric Gregory, John Kelsay, Albert Raboteau, Jerry Schneewind, Jeffrey Stout, Cornel West, and the other participants in the "Lounge Seminar" at Princeton's Department of Religion. Finally, I owe a deep debt to John Witte Jr., Frank Alexander, and the other members of the "Law and Human Nature Project," hosted by Emory University's Law and Religion Program, for their constructive criticism and encouragement.

Introduction

Martin Luther King Jr. was neither an influential legal theorist nor a major systematic theologian. Rather, he was something much more necessary to his time, and arguably all times: a person of righteousness and faith who stood up for his convictions in obedience to God and in service to his neighbors. He was schooled in sociology and divinity, as well as skilled in practical jurisprudence, and he wrote very insightfully of his creed and causes. Yet King is remembered because he brought about constructive social change, by both legal and extralegal means, and because he inspired others to do the same. He embodied, above all, the "uses" of the law and theology, rather than their innovation or scholarly analysis. In short, he was a prophet rather than a pedant.

King courageously cross-fertilized Christian doctrines and democratic principles in a way that is rare today. In an age in which preeminent theorists of both the Christian church and the liberal state often seem to lose their way — by retreating into a narrow sectarianism on one hand or an empty proceduralism on the other — King's example still has much to teach us about justice, law, and human nature. He refused to divorce the sacred (the God worshiped by Jews and Christians) and the secular (the legal realities of American democracy). As a Baptist clergyman, King considered it not merely permissible but actually obligatory to engage publicly controversial political and economic issues. He offered neither dogmatic self-congratulation to believers nor neutral self-interest to nonbelievers, and in the process, he lived out the meaning of the First Amendment. Indeed, it was precisely because he believed that the call to and capacity for justice are built into the nature of "all of God's children"[3] that King was the foremost American public intellectual of the second half of the twentieth century.

King's legacy turns, in large measure, on a concrete moral commitment and a more elusive personal talent: his lived dedication to the poor and oppressed, together with his capacity for holism and synthesis. In his life, work, and death we have a model of service to the marginalized and vulnerable — the scriptural "widow and orphan" — as well as a guide to balancing a range of human goods, public and private. We have, more specifically, a picture of how to relate American law and the Christian gospel. This prophet eventually

---

3. Martin Luther King Jr., "I Have a Dream" (1963), in *I Have a Dream: Writings and Speeches That Changed the World,* ed. James M. Washington (San Francisco: HarperSanFrancisco, 1992), p. 105.

averred that "we as a nation must undergo a radical revolution of values,"[4] and the dialectic he suggested between politics and Scripture is necessarily incomplete. Indeed, he gave decisive priority to the gospel. But King knew that "all life is interrelated" and that "life at its best is a creative synthesis of opposites in fruitful harmony."[5] He knew that a good society could no more separate social justice from personal charity, for instance, than it could segregate its white and black citizens.[6] King's life and thought were not without flaws, of course,[7] and one may question, as I do, aspects of his optimism and personalism. His ongoing influence for the good is testified to, however, by the fact that both lawyers and theologians still read and discuss him in trying to comprehend civic virtue.

There is often a backlash today when Martin King is held up as a moral hero. The understandable fear is that King, since his assassination, has become the darling of white conservatives, that invoking King's name will call up images of patient suffering and a "color-blind" community that take the edge off radical calls for black pride, black self-defense, and black separatism. What of the countervailing messages of W. E. B. Du Bois and Marcus Garvey, of Elijah Muhammad and Malcolm X, of Huey P. Newton and Stokely Carmichael, of Louis Farrakhan and Elaine Brown? In focusing so much on King, the thesis runs, the impression may be given that resistant African American identity is monolithic; it might even seem that the struggle for civil rights and racial justice is a thing of the past. I hope to illustrate in this chapter, in contrast, the depth of King's critique of American law and culture, together with the height of his faith in the biblical God. His critique and the faith are still relevant today; in fact, in King's case (if not our own), the latter is indispensable to the former.

---

4. Martin Luther King Jr., *The Trumpet of Conscience* (San Francisco: Harper and Row, 1967), p. 32.

5. King, *The Trumpet of Conscience*, p. 69; King, *Strength to Love*, p. 9.

6. Compare the appraisals of King by Stanley Hauerwas in *Wilderness Wanderings: Probing Twentieth-Century Theology and Philosophy* (Boulder, Colo.: Westview Press, 1997), pp. 225-37, and by John Rawls in *Political Liberalism* (New York: Columbia University Press, 1993), pp. 247 n and 250.

7. With respect to the charges of plagiarism and marital infidelity, I can only say that, in Dr. King, "we have this treasure in earthen vessels" (2 Cor. 4:7 KJV). For more, see the work of Clayborne Carson, senior editor of the King Papers Project and professor of history at Stanford University, including the introductions to *The Papers of Martin Luther King, Jr.*, 4 vols. (Berkeley: University of California Press, 1992-2000). See also Scott McCormack, "Carson: King Borrowed Ideas for Famous Speech," *Stanford Daily*, March 6, 1991, p. 2.

I. Biography

In dealing with a prophet, an exemplary public voice, there can be little understanding without some biography. In the case of Martin Luther King Jr., law and human nature are writ large in the story of a particular life, leaving us to comprehend and respond.

Martin Luther King Jr. was born on January 15, 1929, into an upper-middle-class home on Auburn Avenue in Atlanta, Georgia. His father, a Baptist preacher, was active in the NAACP, while his mother was a homemaker and church organist. Young Martin, called "M.L.," was shaped by three basic factors: his family's emphasis on spiritual and cultural values, such as biblical literacy and piety, secular education, and social service; his family's social and financial standing in a comparatively prosperous (though largely segregated) black neighborhood; and the racism of the South, including the Jim Crow laws that enforced white supremacy and racial separatism. Growing up on "Sweet Auburn," just a few hundred yards up the road from Ebenezer Baptist Church, where his father was pastor, allowed King to see three worlds at once: a vibrant black church, a thriving black community, and an unjust wider society. This vantage point clearly influenced how he would eventually understand justice, law, and human nature. He was given a moral education and sense of self that allowed him both to perceive social problems and to address them without despair, to see the importance and power of human laws and to appreciate their limit and fallibility.

This education took time. "In his preschool years," Stephen B. Oates informs us, "M.L.'s closest playmate was a white boy whose father owned a store across the street from the King home."[8] When the two boys eventually entered separate schools, his friend's parents declared that Martin could no longer play with their son. This was King's first real experience of the race problem. "I was determined to hate every white person," King later wrote,[9] and his ire was further aggravated when, as a high school student, he and a teacher were forced to give up their seats to whites on a crowded bus. "It was the angriest I have ever been in my life," he subsequently observed.[10]

8. Stephen B. Oates, *Let the Trumpet Sound: The Life of Martin Luther King, Jr.* (New York: New American Library, 1982), p. 10. I am dependent on Oates for a good deal of the biographical material that follows. I have also relied on the chronology provided in King, *I Have a Dream*, pp. xxiii-xxx; and on David J. Garrow, *Bearing the Cross: Martin Luther King, Jr., and the Southern Christian Leadership Conference* (New York: Vintage Books, 1988).

9. Oates, *Let the Trumpet Sound*, p. 10.

10. Oates, *Let the Trumpet Sound*, p. 16.

How did King avoid growing into a bitter and lawless young man? The maturing prophet did not initially endorse Christianity. Though his father was a Protestant minister, the younger King grew up doubting that religion could ever be "emotionally satisfying" or "intellectually respectable." Fundamentalist belief in particular seemed to have little relevance to the modern world, Oates informs us, including interracial relations.[11]

When King entered Morehouse College at age fifteen, however, several teachers began to revolutionize his worldview. George D. Kelsey helped him to see that Daddy King's fundamentalism was not the only form of Christianity, and thus Martin started to rethink his religious opinions. Benjamin Mays, the college president, also deeply affected King with his attack on "socially irrelevant patterns of escape" for the black church and his accent on liberation through knowledge and social engagement.[12] By 1946, the once-skeptical King felt called to the ministry, and in 1947 he was licensed to preach and became assistant to his father at Ebenezer Baptist Church. On February 25, 1948, King was ordained to the Baptist clergy. While still at Morehouse, he read Thoreau's "Civil Disobedience" and for the first time was exposed to the idea of nonviolent resistance: the power "of refusing to cooperate with an evil system."[13] In June 1948, King graduated from Morehouse College with a B.A. in sociology, and in September he entered Crozer Theological Seminary in Chester, Pennsylvania.

At Crozer, King became a disciple of Walter Rauschenbusch and the Christian activism of the Social Gospel movement. In Rauschenbusch, King found what Oates calls "a theological foundation for the social concerns he'd had since he was a boy," "a socially relevant faith" that could "deal with the whole man — his body and soul, his material and spiritual well-being."[14] King also read Marx and Lenin at this time, but he came to have three major objections to their thought. As he later recalled in *Stride toward Freedom*, "First I rejected their materialistic interpretation of history. . . . Second, I strongly disagreed with communism's ethical relativism. . . . Third, I opposed communism's political totalitarianism."[15] King concluded that both communism and capitalism were partial truths, and he forever after insisted that no just

11. Oates, *Let the Trumpet Sound*, p. 14; the phrases in quotations in this paragraph are King's, as quoted by Oates.

12. Oates, *Let the Trumpet Sound,* p. 19; the phrase in quotations in this sentence is Mays's, as quoted by Oates.

13. Martin Luther King Jr., *Stride toward Freedom* (New York: Harper and Row, 1958), p. 91.

14. Oates, *Let the Trumpet Sound,* p. 26.

15. King, *Stride toward Freedom,* p. 92.

reform movement could separate means from ends.[16] We are so embedded in our actions, he recognized, that to do evil that good might come is to pervert ourselves as well as our societies.[17]

About this time, King heard a lecture by Mordecai W. Johnson, president of Howard University, on the life and teachings of Mahatma Gandhi. Johnson argued that the moral power of nonviolence *(ahimsa)* could improve race relations in the United States. King was impressed by the fact that Gandhi was not out to harm or humiliate the British but to redeem them through love.[18] After reading Marx and Nietzsche, King had "about despaired of the power of love in solving social problems."[19] But Gandhi's notion of *Satyagraha* (literally "truth-power") reconciled love and force and convinced King that it was the only moral and practical means for an oppressed people to struggle against social injustice. As King later noted:

> Prior to reading Gandhi, I had about concluded that the ethics of Jesus were only effective in individual relationship. The "turn the other cheek" philosophy and the "love your enemies" philosophy were only valid, I felt, when individuals were in conflict with other individuals; when racial groups and nations were in conflict a more realistic approach seemed necessary. But after reading Gandhi, I saw how utterly mistaken I was.
>
> Gandhi was probably the first person in history to lift the love ethic of Jesus above mere interaction between individuals to a powerful and effective social force on a large scale. Love for Gandhi was a potent instrument for social and collective transformation. It was in this Gandhian emphasis on love and non-violence that I discovered the method for social reform that I had been seeking for so many months.[20]

King always insisted that Christ provided the "spirit and motivation," and Gandhi the practical "method," of the civil rights movement.[21]

16. King, *Stride toward Freedom*, pp. 94-95.
17. See, for example, King, *Strength to Love*, p. 98.
18. See Oates, *Let the Trumpet Sound*, p. 32.
19. King, *Stride toward Freedom*, p. 95.
20. King, *Stride toward Freedom*, pp. 96-97.
21. King, *Stride toward Freedom*, p. 85. For an engaging study of "the prior basis for Gandhi's appeal in the African-American community," one that explores the "pre-1950s traditions upon which King and others built," see Sudarshan Kapur, *Raising Up a Prophet: The African-American Encounter with Gandhi* (Boston: Beacon Press, 1992); quoted phrases from Kapur are on pp. 3-4.

In June 1951, King graduated from Crozer with a bachelor of divinity degree; in June 1953, he married Coretta Scott in Marion, Alabama; and in June 1955, he received his doctorate in systematic theology from Boston University. Shortly after he embraced Gandhi at Crozer, King had to come to grips with Reinhold Niebuhr and his critique of Protestant liberalism's optimism about human nature and tendency toward a vapid pacifism. This King did at Boston University. For all of Niebuhr's insight, King concluded,

> Many of his statements revealed that he interpreted pacifism as a sort of passive nonresistance to evil expressing naïve trust in the power of love. But this was a serious distortion. My study of Gandhi convinced me that true pacifism is not nonresistance to evil, but nonviolent resistance to evil.
>
> I came to see that Niebuhr had overemphasized the corruption of human nature. His pessimism concerning human nature was not balanced by an optimism concerning divine nature. He was so involved in diagnosing man's sickness of sin that he overlooked the cure of grace.[22]

Part of what contributed to King's own optimism was his study at Boston University of personalist philosophy with Edgar S. Brightman and L. Harold DeWolf. "Personalism's insistence that only personality — finite and infinite — is ultimately real strengthened me in two convictions: it gave me metaphysical and philosophical grounding for the idea of a personal God, and it gave me a metaphysical basis for the dignity and worth of all human personality."[23]

In January 1954, King received an offer from Dexter Avenue Baptist Church in Montgomery, Alabama, to give a trial sermon. He preached a sermon entitled "The Three Dimensions of a Complete Life" — about love of self, love of neighbor, and love of God — was offered the post, and began his full-time pastorate on September 1, 1954.[24] The Kings' first child, Yolanda Denise, was born in Montgomery on November 17, 1955. On December 1, Rosa Parks, a forty-two-year-old Montgomery seamstress, refused to relinquish her bus seat to a white man and was arrested. On December 5, local organizers (mostly black churchmen and churchwomen) began a boycott of city buses to coincide with the trial of Mrs. Parks. At a meeting of movement leaders that same day, King was unanimously elected president of what had come to be

22. King, *Stride toward Freedom*, pp. 98, 100.
23. King, *Stride toward Freedom*, p. 100.
24. King, *Stride toward Freedom*, pp. 16-23; see also *The Words of Martin Luther King, Jr.*, ed. Coretta Scott King (New York: Newmarket Press, 1983), p. 64.

called the Montgomery Improvement Association (MIA). On December 10, the Montgomery Bus Company suspended service in black neighborhoods.

At biweekly meetings of the MIA, King related his philosophy of nonviolent love and redemptive suffering. Yet his call for Negro self-respect and his appreciation of the vagaries of law and violence were also evident from the beginning. In an early essay entitled "Our Struggle," written in 1956, King summarized several of his basic beliefs and objectives:

> The extreme tension in race relations in the South today is explained in part by the revolutionary change in the Negro's evaluation of himself and of his destiny and by his determination to struggle for justice. *We Negroes have replaced self-pity with self-respect and self-depreciation with dignity.*[25]

> Although law is an important factor in bringing about social change, there are certain conditions in which the very effort to adhere to new legal decisions creates tension and provokes violence. We had hoped to see demonstrated a method that would enable us to continue our struggle while coping with the violence it aroused. Now we see the answer: face violence if necessary, but refuse to return violence. If we respect those who oppose us, they may achieve a new understanding of the human relations involved.[26]

> We do not wish to triumph over the white community. That would only result in transferring those now on the bottom to the top. But, if we can live up to nonviolence in thought and deed, there will emerge an interracial society based on freedom for all.[27]

The vision of an interracial society governed by the "liberal" values of freedom and equality continued, in part, to define the balance of King's career.

Even as King and others attempted to put a just vision into practice in Montgomery, hate mail and crank calls flowed in. On January 26, 1956, King was arrested on speeding charges — going 30 in a 25 mile per hour zone — and feared for his life when he was taken out of town to the jailhouse. In the face of death threats and legal obstructionism, anxiety and frustration grew among members of the MIA and in King's own soul. The day after his short stay in jail, as King later recalled, things came to a head:

25. Martin Luther King Jr., "Our Struggle" (1956), in *I Have a Dream*, p. 5.
26. King, "Our Struggle," p. 7.
27. King, "Our Struggle," p. 13.

After a particularly strenuous day, I settled in bed at a late hour. My wife had already fallen asleep and I was about to doze off when the telephone rang. An angry voice said, "Listen, nigger, we've taken all we want from you. Before next week you'll be sorry you ever came to Montgomery." I hung up, but I could not sleep. It seemed that all of my fears had come on me at once. I had reached the saturation point.

I got out of bed and began to walk the floor. Finally, I went to the kitchen and heated a pot of coffee. I was ready to give up. I tried to think of a way to move out of the picture without appearing to be a coward. In this state of exhaustion, when my courage had almost gone, I determined to take my problem to God. My head in my hands, I bowed over the kitchen table and prayed aloud. The words I spoke to God that midnight are still vivid in my memory. "I am here taking a stand for what I believe is right. But now I am afraid. The people are looking to me for leadership, and if I stand before them without strength and courage, they too will falter. I am at the end of my powers. I have nothing left. I've come to the point where I can't face it alone."

At that moment I experienced the presence of the Divine as I had never before experienced him. It seemed as though I could hear the quiet assurance of an inner voice, saying, "Stand up for righteousness, stand up for truth. God will be at your side forever." Almost at once my fears began to pass from me. My uncertainty disappeared. I was ready to face anything. The outer situation remained the same, but God had given me inner calm.[28]

Thus unfolded the most memorable moment of King's life, one resonant with the legendary pronouncement of his sixteenth-century namesake[29] and one to which King returned again and again for inspiration.[30] Three nights later, an unknown assailant threw a bomb onto the porch of King's Montgomery home. Though Coretta, Yolanda, and a family friend were in the house, no

28. King, *Strength to Love*, p. 113.

29. Martin Luther is often quoted as concluding his remarks before the Imperial Diet of Worms with "Here I stand, I can do no other. God help me. Amen." This may be an early redacted press report, however. Many scholars believe he actually said, "I cannot and I will not recant anything, for to go against conscience is neither right nor safe. God help me. Amen." (See "Luther at the Imperial Diet of Worms (1521)," http://www.luther.de/en/worms.html. Accessed December 19, 2003.)

30. For more on the historical context and aftermath of this night, see Garrow, *Bearing the Cross*, pp. 56-60.

one was injured. Three days after that, on February 2, a suit was filed in federal district court asking that Montgomery's travel segregation laws be declared unconstitutional. On June 4, the federal district court ruled that racial segregation on city bus lines was unconstitutional. On November 13, the Supreme Court affirmed the lower court, thus voiding Alabama's state and local segregation laws. And on December 21, 1956, a year and twenty days after Rosa Parks's protest, the Montgomery buses were integrated.

King's leadership of the MIA inaugurated a dozen years of crusading for social justice via neighbor love. Elected to the leadership of the Southern Christian Leadership Conference (SCLC) in Atlanta on January 10-11, 1957, he was assassinated on a balcony of the Lorraine Motel in Memphis on April 4, 1968. King and his associates were strikingly effective in bringing about legal reforms in America and often used federal courts to challenge state practices and regulations. But King also suffered many setbacks. It is notable that, in his 1956 "kitchen table epiphany," he was not promised legal successes or even personal safety. (He was murdered before reaching the age of forty, after all.) Instead, he was given a mandate to champion those things that undergird positive law — righteousness and truth — together with an assurance of the presence of God. The distinction between political efficacy and moral principles, between temporal goods and an eternal God, shaped much of King's subsequent thought and action.

II. Law and Justice in Love

Two of King's favorite biblical passages were "Be not conformed to this world: but be ye transformed by the renewing of your mind" (Rom. 12:2 KJV) and "Let judgment [justice] roll down as waters, and righteousness as a mighty stream" (Amos 5:24 KJV).[31] The ability to hold these two quotations together in a lived unity, faithful to both heaven and earth, defined King's genius. More concretely, he recognized and acted on both the limits to and the potency of human laws. On the side of law's limits, King was no moral constructivist or legal positivist, refusing to appeal to a higher authority than regnant social conventions.[32] In his famous "Letter from a Birmingham Jail" (1963), for

31. He quoted both of these lines often; see, e.g., King, *Strength to Love,* chaps. 2 and 10.
32. How precisely to define "legal positivism" is much disputed, as is its cogency as a theory of law. At one extreme, some construe positivism as making only the descriptive, conceptual claim that, given a certain historical pedigree, something may be both a law and immoral. Having the status of law says little or nothing about whether the law should be

example, he insisted that there are "two types of laws": just and unjust. With Augustine, he held that "an unjust law is no law at all," and with Thomas Aquinas, he affirmed that "an unjust law is a human law that is not rooted in eternal and natural law."[33] More politically, "an unjust law is a code inflicted upon a minority which that minority had no part in enacting or creating because they did not have the unhampered right to vote."[34] These distinctions permitted King to explain how he could advocate the breaking of certain legal statutes in the name of civil rights; civil disobedience is permitted, even required, in order to resist codified social wrongs, because there is "a higher moral law" with a prior claim on us.[35]

The logic of King's lawbreaking is notable. One might expect him to hold that, since an unjust law is not really a law, one might violate it at will and with impunity. There will be *practical* consequences, of course — one will likely be arrested and imprisoned, or worse — but *morally* one is unconstrained. One might even expect King to conclude that, in the face of a system of predominantly unjust laws, the entire system is null and void. These were not King's judgments, however. He argued that, rightly understood, civil disobedience must be properly motivated and should not be allowed to slip into anarchic disregard for law in general. As King wrote: "One who breaks an unjust law must do it *openly, lovingly* . . . and with a willingness to accept the penalty. I submit that an individual who breaks a law that conscience tells him is unjust, and willingly accepts the penalty by staying in jail to arouse the conscience of the community over its injustice, is in reality expressing the very highest respect for law."[36]

Why accept a penalty for violating an immoral (non)law? One reason, of course, is pragmatic; in undergoing punishment without retaliation, one is more likely to engage the scruples of the wider society and thus to encourage legal reform. But political utility is not the whole story. Requiring that civil

---

obeyed, on this account. At the other extreme, some see positivism as defending the normative thesis that something's being a law is, in and of itself, a compelling (perhaps even the only) ground for obeying it. My use above of the phrase "legal positivist" presumes the latter, stronger definition. For careful discussions of positivism, especially its relation to competing views (such as natural law theory), see Robert P. George, ed., *The Autonomy of Law: Essays on Legal Positivism* (Oxford: Oxford University Press, 1996).

33. Martin Luther King Jr., "Letter from a Birmingham Jail" (1963), in *I Have a Dream*, p. 89.

34. King, "Letter from a Birmingham Jail," p. 90.

35. King, "Letter from a Birmingham Jail," p. 90. As King puts it in *Stride toward Freedom*, p. 212: "Noncooperation with evil is as much a moral obligation as is cooperation with good."

36. King, "Letter from a Birmingham Jail," p. 90.

disobedience be practiced in a particular way and that a penalty be accepted was King's way, I believe, of granting that even an unjust law remains a "law" in some sense. It is a fundamental Protestant conviction that, after the Fall, all human efforts and institutions are tainted by sin and that even an unjust law is the fruit of temporal powers ordained by God to restrain evil. For King, this means that, especially within a society that aspires to be democratic, the social processes by which laws are passed, as well as the political actors who interpret and enforce these laws, are due a measure of respect. This is the case even when the processes are in fact undemocratic, the actors personally corrupt, and the laws themselves horribly unfair. In spite of statements suggesting the contrary, even unjust laws retained some moral force for King. What he objected to was these laws' being given *undue* force or authority, their "lawness" alone being taken as a compelling reason for obedience.[37]

Especially troubling to King in the 1950s and 1960s was the appeal by "the white moderate" to "law and order," well-meaning but paternalistic advice to the American Negro to be "patient" and to "wait" for a more opportune moment for social protest. King saw this advice as "more devoted to 'order' than to justice," and he insisted that "law and order exist for the purpose of establishing justice, and . . . when they fail to do this they become dangerously structured dams that block the flow of social progress."[38] As *Why We Can't Wait* makes clear, it was precisely because King had a sense of the patience of a personal God that he could be "impatient" with human injustice without becoming either cynical or despairing.[39] In learning over a cup of coffee how to wait for the righteous Lord, he also learned how *not* to wait for an unjust or indifferent humanity.

On the side of law's potency, King recognized the power of constitutional ideals and jurisprudential traditions. In "Letter from a Birmingham Jail," he

37. Kent Greenawalt has offered an interesting critique of the view that an unjust law is not truly a law, as well as a sympathetic reading of chastened forms of legal positivism; see his "Too Thin and Too Rich: Distinguishing Features of Legal Positivism," in *The Autonomy of Law*, pp. 1-29. For Greenawalt, positivism involves both descriptive and normative theses. Nonetheless, its descriptive emphasis on the social origins of law makes it more plausible to an "outsider-observer" of the legal system than to an "insider-participant," who looks more tellingly to law's content and moral validity (p. 20). King, for his part, often straddled these two perspectives. In giving more weight to moral validity, however, his accent is on the participant who must decide whether to obey an unjust law or to go to jail. King's personalism dictates that, in cases of conflict, individual conscience and decision must supersede group structures and traditions.

38. King, "Letter from a Birmingham Jail," p. 91.

39. Martin Luther King Jr., *Why We Can't Wait* (New York: Mentor Books, 1963).

called the nation back to "those great wells of democracy which were dug deep by the Founding Fathers in the formulation of the Constitution and the Declaration of Independence."[40] And in his "I Have a Dream" speech, he again makes a point of referring to "the architects of *our* republic" and "the promise that all men, yes, black men as well as white men, would be guaranteed the unalienable rights of life, liberty, and the pursuit of happiness."[41] He was well aware that the Constitution itself had left slavery intact — even as had the Bible. But he typically countered American history with more American history, in citing the Emancipation Proclamation and the Thirteenth, Fourteenth, and Fifteenth Amendments, for example.[42] That said, King was not a historicist; he had no interest in merely codifying the practices of a distant past. Rather, he availed himself of both natural law arguments and a version of what Ronald Dworkin has called "the moral reading of the Constitution."[43] In interpreting and appealing to the Constitution, that is, King sought to honor American ideals and principles, not simply to follow American practices and precedents.[44]

In 1957, King had vigorously condemned the Supreme Court's 1896 *Plessy v. Ferguson* decision, which endorsed a "separate but equal" understanding of race relations. "Through this decision," he wrote, "segregation gained legal and moral sanction. The end result of the Plessy doctrine was that it led to a strict enforcement of the 'separate,' with hardly the slightest attempt to abide by the 'equal.' So the Plessy doctrine ended up making for tragic inequalities and ungodly exploitation."[45] On the hundredth anniversary of the Emancipation Proclamation, which was issued in 1863, King lamented how little progress had been made in the true liberation of African Americans over the past century.[46] But his critique of *Plessy* and his refusal to be satisfied with the paper equality promised by *Brown v. Board of Education* (1954) avoided the snare of looking *only* to legal remedies from Washington. Law was important, but so was education. As King, presumably thinking of the debates between Booker T.

40. King, "Letter from a Birmingham Jail," p. 100.

41. King, "I Have a Dream," p. 102, emphasis added.

42. King, *Why We Can't Wait*, p. 25.

43. Ronald Dworkin, *Freedom's Law: The Moral Reading of the American Constitution* (Cambridge: Harvard University Press, 1996).

44. James E. Fleming discussed the distinction between "aspirational principles" and "historical practices" in constitutional interpretation in "Are We All Originalists Now? I Hope Not!" (The Alpheus T. Mason Lecture given at Princeton University, September 19, 2002).

45. Martin Luther King Jr., "Facing the Challenge of a New Age" (1957), in *I Have a Dream*, p. 17.

46. King, *Why We Can't Wait*, pp. 23-25.

Washington and W. E. B. Du Bois over a generation earlier, put it, "We must continue to struggle through legalism and legislation. There are those who contend that integration can come only through education, for no other reason than that morals cannot be legislated. I choose, however, to be dialectical at this point. It is neither education nor legislation; it is both legislation and education. . . . The law cannot make a man love — religion and education must do that — but it can control his efforts to lynch."[47] In addition to pushing for legal redress and reform (for example, a voting rights act), then, King's discontent with the status quo took the form of petitions to individual conscience (in the Negro and in the nation at large) as well as calls for community resistance (direct but nonviolent protest). King's strength was always to wed theory and praxis, but he was emphatic that "nonviolence is no longer an option for intellectual analysis, it is an imperative for action."[48]

King knew how important state legislatures, Congress, federal courts, the Supreme Court, and finally the public could be in ensuring civil rights for African Americans. He knew the power of laws and lawmakers to resist or reform other laws and lawmakers. He also knew the power of the executive branch to rein in or augment the other two branches of government, especially at the local level. King had a sound understanding of American political theory — majority rule subject to judicial review, constitutional checks and balances, and so forth. And he explicitly acknowledged that in demonstrating for the rights to adequate housing, adequate income, and adequate education, "we have left the realm of constitutional rights and we are entering the area of human rights."[49] But his signal contribution was to galvanize all these legal, political, and cultural mechanisms into proper practice, at least for a time and to some significant degree. Put most briefly, King helped induce the American system (morally and materially) to recognize and act on its highest principles, even as he inspired individuals (black and white) to be their best selves. His success was not complete, of course, but it was remarkable even so.

Again, King was not merely interested in conserving past historical practices or even in realizing stated yet unattained legal and ethical goals. King's Christian faith in an eternal and righteous God allowed him to relativize *all*

47. King, "Facing the Challenge," p. 25.

48. King, *The Trumpet of Conscience*, p. 64. For a detailed examination of how King combined the "theoretical and experiential deconstruction/reconstruction" of law and society, see Anthony E. Cook, "Beyond Critical Legal Studies: The Reconstructive Theology of Dr. Martin Luther King, Jr.," *Harvard Law Review* 103, no. 5 (March 1990): 985-1044.

49. Martin Luther King Jr., "Nonviolence: The Only Road to Freedom" (1966), in *I Have a Dream*, p. 131.

temporal human systems and to question *each* temptable human heart. Like Socrates having glimpsed the Good above Athenian "democracy," King was able to challenge even the (erstwhile) highest principles of his country and the (putative) best selves of his interlocutors. Especially in the mid- to late 1960s, King vigorously denounced "the giant triplets of racism, materialism, and militarism."[50] He proclaimed the need for "a radical restructuring of the architecture of American society" and asserted that "a new set of values must be born."[51] He brought capitalism under particularly sharp criticism and called for an economy that is "more person-centered than property- and profit-centered."[52] This meant, among other things, "a guaranteed income," "a revitalized labor movement," and "a broader distribution of wealth."[53] King's prophetic gift to the American state was to challenge it to become what it was not and perhaps never wanted to be: a democracy without "compromise."[54] Similarly, King's prophetic gift to the American church was to call it to become much more than it had ever been: "the true Body of Christ."[55] Neither the democratic state nor the integrated church, as such, is the realized kingdom of heaven,[56] but both can plausibly aspire to be part of what King, following Josiah Royce, called "the beloved community."[57]

Always the Baptist minister, King focused on spiritual ends as well as political means, and he was far from alone in his efforts.[58] Andrew Young and a cadre of lawyers were often King's point people in court, and King himself emphasized his dispensability in the context of the mass movement for racial justice; as David Garrow has observed, as early as Montgomery, King and other leaders came to realize that "the people, and not simply their lawyers, could win

50. Martin Luther King Jr., "A Time to Break Silence" (1967), in *I Have a Dream*, p. 148.

51. Martin Luther King Jr., *Where Do We Go from Here: Chaos or Community?* (Boston: Beacon Press, 1968), p. 133.

52. King, *Where Do We Go?* p. 133.

53. King, *Where Do We Go?* pp. 162, 142, and Martin Luther King Jr., "Where Do We Go from Here?" (1967), in *I Have a Dream*, p. 176.

54. King, *Why We Can't Wait*, p. 131.

55. King, *Strength to Love*, p. 141.

56. King warned against this mistaken identification in *Stride toward Freedom*, p. 91.

57. King, *Stride toward Freedom*, p. 220.

58. For a compelling narration of the larger context of King's activism, including his dependence on and disagreements with other civil rights leaders (Ralph Abernathy, Septima Clark, W. E. B. Du Bois, Medgar Evers, Robert Graetz, Fannie Lou Hamer, Vernon Johns, Martin Luther King Sr., E. D. Nixon, Rosa Parks, A. Philip Randolph, Bayard Rustin, Fred Shuttlesworth, Roy Wilkins, Andrew Young, et al.), see Taylor Branch, *Parting the Waters: America in the King Years, 1954-1963* (New York: Simon and Schuster, 1988).

their own freedom."[59] Yet the record, starting with the MIA bus boycott, is impressive. King and the SCLC had a significant hand in President Eisenhower's establishing the Civil Rights Commission and sending in the National Guard to integrate Arkansas public schools; in President Kennedy's federalizing the Alabama National Guard to integrate that state's schools and then delivering a televised speech to the nation in which he spoke out against segregation and racism; in Congress's passing and President Johnson's signing the Civil Rights Act of 1964, "to enforce the constitutional right to vote" and "to provide injunctive relief against discrimination in public accommodations"[60] and more.

King did not hesitate to use the language of "freedom and equality" and "citizenship rights," so dear to liberal democrats — indeed, he boldly declared that "the goal of America is freedom."[61] But neither did he flinch from a trumping emphasis on spiritual values such as faith, nonviolence, "soul force," and "the glory of the Lord."[62] To those who were tempted to accommodate Christianity too completely to temporal politics, King insisted that "the calling to be a son of the living God" is "beyond the calling of race or nation or creed."[63] "I just want to do God's will," he often declared.[64] Even his identity as a civil rights activist or Vietnam War protester was second to his "commitment to the ministry of Jesus Christ."[65] To those who were tempted to withdraw from political and economic struggles because they were too messy or worldly, in contrast, he emphasized that faith without works is sterile. He advocated "nonviolent direct action" and "a practical pacifism" as obligations in the quest for social justice. Only in this way could one be true to both "the sacred heritage of our nation and the eternal will of God."[66]

III. Law and Gospel

In both Martin Luther and John Calvin, as well as in Thomas Aquinas, the word "law" can denote one or more of four things: (1) eternal law, which is

59. Garrow, *Bearing the Cross*, p. 86.

60. *Civil Rights Act of 1964, U.S. Code*, vol. 42, title VII, beginning at section 2000e.

61. King, "Letter from a Birmingham Jail," p. 98.

62. See King, "I Have a Dream," pp. 102-5.

63. King, "Time to Break Silence," p. 140.

64. See, for instance, Martin Luther King Jr., "I See the Promised Land" (1968), in *I Have a Dream*, p. 203.

65. King, "Time to Break Silence," p. 139.

66. King, "Letter from a Birmingham Jail," p. 98.

the very Being of God, God's heart/mind as it is in itself; (2) divine law, which is the special revelation of God's requirements for humanity, as recorded, for example, in the Old Testament Decalogue; (3) natural law, the principles of moral order built by God into creation itself, including human reason and will; and (4) human law, the civil statutes of a particular political regime aimed at applying the natural law to concrete times, places, actions, and individuals.

Beyond the denotation of "law," there is the question of its connotation, its purpose or meaning.[67] According to Calvin, the three meanings or "uses" of the law are: (1) theological: "by exhibiting the righteousness of God — in other words, the righteousness which alone is acceptable to God — it admonishes every one of his own unrighteousness, certiorates, convicts, and finally condemns him";[68] (2) civil: "by means of its fearful denunciations and the consequent dread of punishment, to curb those who, unless forced, have no regard for rectitude and justice";[69] and (3) didactic: "enabling [believers] daily to learn with greater truth and certainty what that will of the Lord is which they aspire to follow, and to confirm them in this knowledge."[70] For his part, Luther spoke of only two "uses" of the law: (1) the civil use *(usus civilis),* in which political norms and mechanisms both restrain evil behaviors and encourage good ones; and (2) the theological use *(usus theologicus),* in which God employs the law as a hammer or fire to indict the conscience of the sinner.[71] All these senses of the "law" were evident, more or less explicitly, in the life and work of Martin Luther King Jr.

As we have seen, King also distinguished between the positive statutes of a specific political body and the eternal law and natural law that the statutes are ideally to express or apply. He, too, thought that one of the functions of human law is to restrain evil actions, and he, too, held that divine law aims to prick the consciences of persons and thereby goad them to repentance and reform. Foundational to all these points about the law, however, was an additional commitment that he shared with Aquinas, Luther, Calvin, and ultimately Augustine: the priority of the gospel of Jesus Christ. Because King

---

67. See Edward A. Dowey, "Law in Luther and Calvin," *Theology Today* 41, no. 2 (July 1984): 148.

68. John Calvin, *Institutes of the Christian Religion* (1536/1539), trans. Henry Beveridge, 2 vols. (Edinburgh: Calvin Translation Society, 1845), 2.7, 1:304.

69. Calvin, *Institutes,* 1:307.

70. Calvin, *Institutes,* 1:309.

71. Martin Luther, "A Commentary on Saint Paul's Epistle to the Galatians" (1531), in *Martin Luther: Selections from His Writings,* ed. John Dillenberger (Garden City, N.Y.: Anchor Books, 1961), pp. 139-45.

believed that Christ embodies the very person of God, Immanuel here with us, King had confidence that God's mercy and forgiveness are even more basic or powerful than God's condemnation and punishment. In the cross of Christ, God gratuitously restored right relationship to a fallen world by taking its guilt and suffering onto himself. Christ named personal sins and resisted social evils, but he did so without indulging in hatred or violence. Faith in Christ, in turn, allowed King to identify human injustices and to struggle against them, but also to trust in divine providence (not just in human law or power) to carry the day.

IV. Law and Power

Confidence in the gospel (good news) of God's love did not render King naïve about social realities. He saw the importance of power in human relations, including those between the races. He frequently noted that oppressors do not give up their privileges voluntarily but must be forced to do so by "determined legal and nonviolent pressure" from the oppressed.[72] Moreover, he never confused legal statutes alone with real power. "Laws only declare rights," he observed; "they do not deliver them."[73] King never tired of highlighting the "tragic gulf between civil rights laws passed and civil rights laws implemented,"[74] a gulf that required African Americans in the North and South alike to continue to agitate for social equality. If the *goal* of America is freedom, its *history* was that of "the inexpressible cruelties of slavery."[75]

Eventually defining power as "the ability to achieve purpose . . . the strength required to bring about social, political or economic changes,"[76] King emphasized that "power is not only desirable but necessary."[77] Even so, he insisted that law is not merely a matter of power but also of right. It is remarkable that in spite of centuries of slavery, lynchings, and Jim Crow,[78] King did not give up on law as one means of human advancement. It is even more remark-

---

72. King, "Letter from a Birmingham Jail," p. 87.

73. King, *Where Do We Go?* p. 158.

74. King, *Where Do We Go?* p. 82.

75. King, "Letter from a Birmingham Jail," p. 98.

76. King, *Where Do We Go?* p. 37.

77. King, *Where Do We Go?* p. 37.

78. As one enters the display area of the Martin Luther King Jr. Center for Nonviolent Social Change in Atlanta, one is confronted by a range of Jim Crow laws displayed on a large glass wall. The laws date from the 1880s to the 1960s; the following examples, from various

able that he insisted that law is wedded to a "new kind of power" — "power infused with love and justice."[79]

To the end of his life, King continued to believe in the project of mar-

---

states, are taken from "Jim Crow Laws" at the Center's Web page, http://www.nps.gov/malu/documents/jim_crow_laws.htm. Accessed November 15, 2000.

> *Nurses*: No person or corporation shall require any white female nurse to nurse in wards or rooms in hospitals, either public or private, in which negro men are placed. (Alabama)
>
> *Buses*: All passenger stations in this state operated by any motor transportation company shall have separate waiting rooms or space and separate ticket windows for the white and colored races. (Alabama)
>
> *Restaurants*: It shall be unlawful to conduct a restaurant or other place for the serving of food in the city, at which white and colored people are served in the same room, unless such white and colored persons are effectually separated by a solid partition extending from the floor upward to a distance of seven feet or higher, and unless a separate entrance from the street is provided for each compartment. (Alabama)
>
> *Toilet Facilities, Male*: Every employer of white or negro males shall provide for such white or negro males reasonably accessible and separate toilet facilities. (Alabama)
>
> *Intermarriage*: The marriage of a person of Caucasian blood with a Negro, Mongolian, Malay, or Hindu shall be null and void. (Arizona)
>
> *Intermarriage*: All marriages between a white person and a negro, or between a white person and a person of negro descent to the fourth generation inclusive, are hereby forever prohibited. (Florida)
>
> *Education*: The schools for white children and the schools for negro children shall be conducted separately. (Florida)
>
> *Intermarriage*: It shall be unlawful for a white person to marry anyone except a white person. Any marriage in violation of this section shall be void. (Georgia)
>
> *Burial*: The officer in charge shall not bury, or allow to be buried, any colored persons upon ground set apart or used for the burial of white persons. (Georgia)
>
> *Housing*: Any person . . . who shall rent any part of any such building to a negro person or a negro family when such building is already in whole or in part in occupancy by a white person or white family, or vice versa when the building is in occupancy by a negro person or negro family, shall be guilty of a misdemeanor and on conviction thereof shall be punished by a fine of not less than twenty-five ($25.00) nor more than one hundred ($100.00) dollars or be imprisoned not less than 10, or more than 60 days, or both such fine and imprisonment in the discretion of the court. (Louisiana)
>
> *Promotion of Equality*: Any person . . . who shall be guilty of printing, publishing or circulating printed, typewritten or written matter urging or presenting for public acceptance or general information, arguments or suggestions in favor of social equality or of intermarriage between whites and negroes, shall be guilty of a misdemeanor and subject to fine of [sic] not exceeding five hundred (500.00) dollars or imprisonment not exceeding six (6) months or both. (Mississippi)

79. King, *Where Do We Go?* p. 66.

rying American law with biblical morality. Put less pointedly, he steadfastly refused to segregate positive law (acts actually on the books) from natural law (timeless dictates of a good conscience) and eternal law (the will of God). The latter two must ground and judge the first, and without this moral foundation, no one in the struggle for racial justice could hope for true victory. This cognizance of something beyond time and chance, something transcending skin color and factional interest, allowed King to be critical of both whites and blacks. He could indict white racists for their overt hatred and aggression, as well as white moderates for valuing peace and mere (positive) legality over justice. But he could also fault black leaders who were tempted to lapse into a hatred or irresponsibility of their own. King was able to appreciate "the marvelous new militancy"[80] that surged up among young black activists in the 1960s, and he saw a "broad and positive meaning" in black power as "a call to black people to amass the political and economic strength to achieve their legitimate goals."[81] He did not refrain, nevertheless, from also identifying "Black Power" as a slogan fraught with peril. To the extent that it suggested violent intimidation or cynical lawlessness, he believed it to be both counterproductive and wrong. "Power and morality must go together, implementing, fulfilling and ennobling each other."[82]

V. Law and Nonviolent Resistance

Yet why, specifically, should nonviolence have been so key to King's social activism? Once one rejects passivity, complete nonresistance, and accepts the moral obligation to stand athwart injustice, and once one maintains that some positive laws are unjust and thus that civil disobedience may be legitimate, why insist on *nonviolent* resistance? Why not work against evil "by any means necessary," to echo Malcolm X's notorious phrase?[83] King's answer was that actions and intentions matter, as well as consequences.[84]

---

80. King, "I Have a Dream," p. 103.

81. King, *Where Do We Go?* p. 36.

82. King, *Where Do We Go?* p. 59.

83. John Kelsay has noted, in conversation, that in some Islamic texts, the Arabic phrase commonly translated into English as "by any means necessary" is better read as "by the necessary (i.e., appropriate) means." I am not sure whether Malcolm X had this latter sense in mind, but, given his other early views, I doubt it.

84. At one point, Malcolm X considered "an integrationist like King" to be akin to a "house Negro" of the pre–Civil War days, a slave who identified with "the master" and ulti-

In addition to maintaining that some laws are improper ends, King held that violence is an improper means for several reasons. In *Stride toward Freedom,* King's first book, he listed six basic points to help explain and justify the nonviolent resistance under way in Montgomery:

(1) "Nonviolent resistance is not a method for cowards; it does resist."
(2) "Nonviolence . . . does not seek to defeat or humiliate the opponent, but to win his friendship and understanding."
(3) "It is evil that the nonviolent resister seeks to defeat, not the persons victimized by evil."
(4) "Nonviolent resistance is [characterized by] a willingness to accept suffering without retaliation, to accept blows from the opponent without striking back."
(5) "Nonviolent resistance . . . avoids not only external physical violence but also internal violence of spirit. The nonviolent resister not only refuses to shoot his opponent but he also refuses to hate him."
(6) "Nonviolent resistance . . . is based on the conviction that the universe is on the side of justice. Consequently, the believer in nonviolence has deep faith in the future. This faith is another reason why the nonviolent resister can accept suffering without retaliation. For he knows that in his struggle for justice he has cosmic companionship."[85]

Across the years, King's briefs for nonviolence appealed to traits of character, principles of justice, social utility, as well as theological convictions. The moral eclecticism of his views is quite clear in this oft-quoted passage: "[Vio-

---

mately sold out to him. Minister Malcolm clearly had Reverend King in mind when he said in a 1963 interview, "I think that any black man who goes among so-called Negroes today who are being brutalized, spit upon in the worst fashion imaginable, and teaches those Negroes to turn the other cheek, to suffer peacefully, or love their enemy is a traitor to the Negro" (Malcolm X, "The Old Negro and the New Negro," in *The End of White World Supremacy,* ed. Imam Benjamin Karim [New York: Arcade Publishing, 1971], p. 116). Malcolm met King face-to-face only once, in March of 1964; after Malcolm's transforming trip to Mecca in April of 1964, he tempered his remarks on the SCLC and its leadership.

85. King, *Stride toward Freedom,* pp. 102-3, 106. In his "Letter from a Birmingham Jail," written five years after the publication of *Stride,* King responded to various white clergy's deploring of the civil rights "demonstrations" under way in Birmingham by noting that "in any nonviolent campaign there are four basic steps: (1) collection of the facts to determine whether injustices are alive, (2) negotiation, (3) self-purification, and (4) direct action." He went on to assert that "[w]e have gone through all of these steps in Birmingham," and that the protests were thus appropriate (p. 85).

lence] is impractical because it is a descending spiral ending in destruction for all. The old law of an eye for an eye leaves everybody blind [a consequentialist argument]. It is immoral because it seeks to humiliate the opponent rather than win his understanding; it seeks to annihilate rather than to convert [a deontological argument]. Violence is immoral because it thrives on hatred rather than love [an aretological argument]. It destroys community and makes brotherhood impossible."[86] As King summarized in his final book, *Where Do We Go from Here?*: "Beyond the pragmatic invalidity of violence is its inability to appeal to conscience."[87]

VI. Human Nature/Personality and Agapic Love

Having a conscience was, for King, central to being made in the image of God. And being made in God's image was, in turn, foundational to what he intermittently called "the nonviolent affirmation of the sacredness of all human life" and "respect [for] the dignity and worth of human personality."[88] In a powerful Christian universalism, King affirmed that "every man is somebody because he is a child of God. . . . Man is more than a tiny vagary of whirling electrons or a wisp of smoke from a limitless smoldering. Man is a child of God, made in His image, and therefore must be respected as such. . . . We are all one in Christ Jesus. And when we truly believe in the sacredness of human personality, we won't exploit people, we won't trample over people with the iron feet of oppression, we won't kill anybody."[89] The common integrity of the human personality is the lynchpin in much of King's comments on law. Or, rather, the creative kindness of the *divine* Personality is the *anti*lynching pin. "Human worth lies in relatedness to God."[90] If all finite persons are equal before God, how then can they be treated as unequal before the state or the wider society? Because all human persons are loved by God, they have value and are capable of loving themselves and one another. Injustice is quite often due to willful blindness to the image of God in others, a point King could put in either Kantian or biblical terms. "The immorality of segregation," for instance, "is that it treats men as means

86. *The Words of Martin Luther King, Jr.*, p. 73; see also King, *Stride toward Freedom*, p. 213.

87. King, *Where Do We Go?* p. 59.

88. King, *The Trumpet of Conscience*, pp. 72, 77; see also King, *Where Do We Go?* p. 180.

89. King, *The Trumpet of Conscience*, p. 72.

90. King, *Where Do We Go?* p. 97.

rather than ends, and thereby reduces them to things rather than persons."[91] Conversely, "the highest good is love."[92] One of the most sublime lines that King ever wrote, in my estimation, is this: "Since the white man's personality is greatly distorted by segregation, and his soul is greatly scarred, he needs the love of the Negro."[93]

The New Testament Greek name for the love in question is *agape,* "the love of God operating in the human heart."[94] This graced capacity allows individuals to hold in balance justice and power by transcending yet comprehending both. *Agape* transcends justice in that it does not limit itself to economies of exchange, calculations of merit and demerit, or even the natural sympathies of friendship. (Think of the parable of the generous vineyard owner in Matthew 20:1-16.) Rather, *agape* entails "an all-embracing and unconditional love for all men."[95] *Agape* comprehends power in that it is active and bold rather than passive and timid. "Structures of evil do not crumble by passive waiting."[96] As King put it, "When I speak of love I am not speaking of some sentimental and weak response. I am speaking of that force which all of the great religions have seen as the supreme unifying principle of life."[97]

King unabashedly placed agapic love at the core of his political thought and social action and offered four defining theses about such love:

(1) "*Agape* is disinterested love. It is a love in which the individual seeks not his own good, but the good of his neighbor (I Cor. 10:24). *Agape* does not begin by discriminating between worthy and unworthy people, or any qualities people possess. It begins by loving others *for their sakes.*"

(2) "[*Agape*] springs from the *need* of the other person — his need for belonging to the best in the human family. The Samaritan who helped the Jew on the Jericho Road was 'good' because he responded to the human need that he was presented with. God's love is eternal and fails not because man needs his love."

(3) "*Agape* is a willingness to sacrifice in the interest of mutuality. *Agape* is a willingness to go to any length to restore community. . . . The cross is the

91. King, *Where Do We Go?* p. 97.
92. King, *Strength to Love,* p. 145.
93. King, *Stride toward Freedom,* p. 105.
94. King, *Stride toward Freedom,* p. 104.
95. King, "Time to Break Silence," p. 150; see also his *Where Do We Go?* p. 190.
96. King, *Where Do We Go?* p. 128.
97. King, "Time to Break Silence," p. 150.

eternal expression of the length to which God will go in order to restore broken community. The resurrection is a symbol of God's triumph over all the forces that seek to block community."

(4) "*Agape* means a recognition of the fact that all life is interrelated. All humanity is involved in a single process, and all men are brothers. . . . Whether we call it an unconscious process, an impersonal Brahman, or a Personal Being of matchless power and infinite love, there is a creative force in this universe that works to bring the disconnected aspects of reality into a harmonious whole."[98]

If *agape* comprehends yet transcends justice and power, it also embodies both law and gospel. King suggested more than forty-five years ago that, as a matter of *justice,* the United States government owes African Americans reparations for slavery.[99] And he was clear that *agape* never intentionally falls below the just requirements of the law, in all four senses. But King also knew that, in expanding sympathy and inspiring forgiveness, love rises above legalism to the prophetic. It is divine love, King would "re-mind" the world, that transforms and renews us (cf. Rom. 12:2), by breaking us out of grasping self-interest (me versus you) and offensive group elitism (us versus them).

As understandable, historically, as was Marcus Garvey's call for black nationalism; as inspiring, intellectually, as was W. E. B. Du Bois's insistence that "the talented tenth" pursue a liberal education; as indispensable, legally, as was Thurgood Marshall's victory in *Brown v. Board;* as galvanizing, psychologically, as were Malcolm X's and Angela Davis's commitments to black manhood and womanhood; the most effective remedy, both politically and morally, for American racism and Jim Crow laws has been Martin King and Christlike love.

98. King, *Stride toward Freedom,* pp. 104-7. King's lines on Christian love are highly indebted to the writings of Anders Nygren and Paul Ramsey; see Garrow, *Bearing the Cross,* p. 112. Nicholas Wolterstorff has maintained, in discussion, that King's comments on *agape,* its appreciation of mutuality and of the worth and dignity of the individual, are actually more applicable to *eros.* To the extent that *eros* looks to the merit of the other and to what that merit can do for one's own interests, however, I believe that King is correct in distinguishing it from *agape.* As King defines *eros,* it is concerned with justice and giving admirable persons their due rather than with charity and service of needy strangers. *Agape* and *eros* are not necessarily opposed, but they are not identical either.

99. King, *Where Do We Go?* pp. 79, 109; see also King, *Why We Can't Wait,* pp. 134-39.

VII. King's Prophetic Optimism and Personalism

King's realism, what might be called his "holistic pessimism," enabled him to see that "injustice anywhere is a threat to justice everywhere."[100] As the preceding four quotes make clear, however, King's holistic optimism triumphed in his account of the harmonizing power of love. King was well aware that practitioners of *agape* would suffer at the hands of their unjust fellows, but he continued across the years to affirm "the faith that unearned suffering is redemptive."[101] I wish he had said "*may be* redemptive," but he was not indiscriminate or masochistic in his call for suffering, any more than he was Machiavellian or cynical in his call for resistance. As he allowed in "Letter from a Birmingham Jail": "it is wrong to use immoral means to attain moral ends . . . [but] it is just as wrong, or even more so, to use moral means to preserve immoral ends."[102] Yet even when moral means and ends seem to fail, King held that "right defeated is stronger than evil triumphant."[103]

Unquestionably, Jesus Christ was "an extremist for love,"[104] but does love always employ exclusively nonviolent means? I am not as sure as King that *agape* must eschew the use of lethal or injurious force under all circumstances. King consistently affirmed "the reality of evil" and "man's capacity for sin," and, at his best, he avoided both "superficial optimism" and "crippling pessimism."[105] Still, I am not as confident as he that "evil carries the seed of its own destruction."[106] In a fallen world, at any rate, I believe that protecting the innocent may move some Christians, properly, to take up the sword against evil, as in the American Civil War. Regrettably, the law sometimes needs the support of police forces, national guards, and armies, and love itself may enlist in these services under appropriate circumstances.[107] One may doubt the consistency of King's protesting to President Eisenhower that Montgomery blacks were "without protection of law,"[108] when King himself was unwilling to endorse the necessary (moral) means to enforce the law.

100. King, "Letter from a Birmingham Jail," p. 85.
101. King, "I Have a Dream," p. 104; see also *Stride toward Freedom*, p. 103.
102. King, "Letter from a Birmingham Jail," p. 99.
103. King, "Letter from a Birmingham Jail," p. 98.
104. King, "Letter from a Birmingham Jail," p. 94.
105. King, *Strength to Love*, pp. 109, 130, 83.
106. King, *Strength to Love*, p. 82.
107. See my *The Priority of Love: Christian Charity and Social Justice* (Princeton: Princeton University Press, 2003), esp. chap. 3.
108. See Branch, *Parting the Waters*, p. 191.

Unquestionably, American blacks have for centuries been "drained of self-respect and a sense of 'somebodiness.'"[109] But is personality the highest good? I sometimes worry that King neglected the value of the *im*personal: the natural or animal world and those shared human needs and potentials that have nothing to do with freedom or self-conscious dignity.[110] Human nature is more than autonomous personality, as fetuses, babies, the mentally impaired, and the senile demonstrate. Still, it is important to emphasize that, for King, the person is not some disembodied mind or self-sufficient will. King consistently took care to avoid "a completely otherworldly religion which makes a strange, unbiblical distinction between body and soul, between the sacred and the secular."[111] Moreover, for him, "other-preservation is the first law of life . . . precisely because we cannot preserve self without being concerned about preserving other selves."[112]

I have suggested that part of what made Martin Luther King Jr. prophetic was his commitment to the will of God and the full range of human existence: bodies and souls, self and others, thought and action, church and state, the private and the public, means and ends, love and justice, time and eternity.[113] I have also suggested that his upbringing at the intersection of societies in tension — black and white, rich and poor — prepared him for his prophetic vocation of recognizing the marginalized and empathizing with the weak. Indeed, as an embodiment of the theological, civil, and didactic "uses" of the law, King himself indicted our consciences, helped restrain social evils, and educated the church concerning the will of God.

Secular liberals typically fear that admitting the prophet's "Thus saith the Lord" into public discourse will lead to intolerance: Christian optimism and personalism run amok into theocratic dogmatism and oppression.[114] This was a reasonable worry in the West during the sixteenth and seventeenth centuries, even as the dangers of fundamentalism remain a concern in the Near East today. There is still a point to the worry in America today, hence the separation of church and state that prohibits a national religion, creedal

109. King, "Letter from a Birmingham Jail," p. 93.

110. See my *The Priority of Love*, esp. chap. 5.

111. King, *Why We Can't Wait*, p. 90. This phrase from "Letter from a Birmingham Jail" is printed somewhat differently in the version of the letter in *I Have a Dream*, p. 96. I use the quoted version because its employment of the present tense better suits my purposes.

112. King, *Where Do We Go?* p. 180.

113. For more on these themes, see King, *Stride toward Freedom*, pp. 36, 91.

114. Jeffrey Stout has pressed this point, in conversation; see also chapter 11 of Richard Rorty, *Philosophy and Social Hope* (London: Penguin Books, 1999).

tests for voting rights, etc. But our chief domestic threat is currently from social fragmentation and the hegemony of possessive individualism, rather than from religious tyranny and the hegemony of the Protestant church. In King's case, Christian convictions led him to affirm freedom of conscience and the ubiquity of sin and error, as well as to champion racial equality, the right to vote, and so on. His righteous indignation at injustice was paired with a self-limiting humility. Rather than denying liberal values, then, he clarified and disciplined them.

Christian traditionalists often fear, in turn, that prophetic defenses of liberal democracy and human rights will erode true virtue and amount to a sellout of the ancient church to the modern state. They suspect, in Robert Kraynak's words, "that democracy is tyrannical in its ruthless leveling of higher and lower goods and of the hierarchies of the soul that are absolutely necessary for spiritual life."[115] Ever since Constantine, the argument goes, secular laws and loyalties have perverted the Christian gospel. On King's behalf, nevertheless, I must enter a plea of "not guilty." The epiphany at the kitchen table in Montgomery — hearing God over a cup of coffee and in the midst of a bus boycott — provides a graphic image of how the sacred and the profane, Christian faith and democratic politics, converged in King's life. By placing all human existence under the governance of *agape,* he taught Christians to be in the world but not of it. King was under no illusions about the sins of U.S. culture — its history of slavery, its ongoing racial and economic exploitation — but he was still able to trust God and serve his neighbors in situ.

King's legacy partly consists in the civil rights acts he helped to pass into law, and a legal holiday now honors his memory. But perhaps his main contribution was to stir in Christians in America (and around the world) a political conscience. His example may still move us to ask: Even though religious fanaticism is dangerous, did not democracy itself spring, in part, from Christian teachings about God and humanity? Are we to forget the Puritans and the religious rationales behind so many of the state constitutions of the newly liberated colonies? If commitments to freedom, equality, and the rule

115. Robert Kraynak, "Statement of Author Prepared for Background for Discussion [of his *Christian Faith and Modern Democracy*] at American Maritain Association Meeting" (Princeton University, October 2002), p. 2. On Christianity and democracy, see also Stanley M. Hauerwas, *Wilderness Wanderings: Probing Twentieth-Century Theology and Philosophy* (Boulder, Colo.: Westview Press, 1997), and *Against the Nations: War and Survival in a Liberal Society* (Minneapolis: Winston Press, 1985); *In Good Company: The Church as Polis* (Notre Dame and London: University of Notre Dame Press, 1995); and *With the Grain of the Universe: The Church's Witness and Natural Theology* (Grand Rapids: Brazos, 2001).

of law seem to undermine biblical faith, hope, and love, are the latter virtues really being practiced?

There is more than one version of liberal democracy and its relation to law, society, and human nature, just as there is more than one version of Christian faith. Yet Martin Luther King Jr. was a peculiarly American prophet in being able to speak the broad languages of democracy and Christianity, simultaneously, without confusing the two. For all the preceding observations, even so, it is ultimately a mystery what makes someone prophetic.[116] Jurisprudence, religion professors, and the general population can only be grateful, both to God and to the individual, for the prophet's life and work. It is appropriate, therefore, that I give our American Amos the last word:

> Man-made laws assure justice, but a higher law produces love. . . . A vigorous enforcement of civil rights will bring an end to segregated public facilities, but it cannot bring an end to fears, prejudice, pride and irrationality, which are the barriers to a truly integrated society. These dark and demonic responses will be removed only as men are possessed by the invisible inner law which etches on their hearts the conviction that all men are brothers and that love is mankind's most potent weapon for personal and social transformation. True integration will be achieved by men who are willingly obedient to unenforceable obligations.[117]

---

116. King himself observed: "Not every minister can be a prophet, but some must be prepared for the ordeals of this high calling and be willing to suffer courageously for righteousness." King, *Stride toward Freedom*, p. 210.

117. King, *Where Do We Go?* pp. 100-101.

Index of Names

Abel, 162, 297
Abernathy, Ralph, 395n58
Abraham, 74, 297-99, 308, 316, 338, 340, 373n43
Adam, 12-13n28, 13, 99-100, 103-8, 109n57, 110-11, 138, 160, 333, 358, 379
Aelred of Rievaulx, 89n12
Albee, Edward, 109n57
Alexander, Frank, 381
Ali, Muhammad, 266
Allen, Prudence, R.S.M., 351n59
Amos, 77
Anderson, Robert, 83n66
Andolsen, Barbara Hilkert, 139n27, 247-49, 259
Anthony, Susan B., 224
Antigone, 297n4, 302, 305
Aquinas, Thomas, 85, 119, 143-44, 146, 148, 151, 167, 180, 210n63, 286, 287n9, 306, 318-19, 326, 339, 361n16, 391, 396-97
Aristarchus, 3
Aristotle, 31, 53, 94, 167, 351
Auden, W. H., 302, 310
Audi, Robert, 137, 148n43
Augustine, 3, 12-13, 15, 18, 31, 93, 167, 274, 275n83, 287-88n9, 308, 318-19, 326, 341, 351, 365, 391, 397
Austin, J. L., 224

Baal, 311

Baier, Annette, 123
Baker, Ella, 265
Balthasar, Hans Urs von, 255, 257-58, 261
Banse, Juliane, 351n60
Baranowski, Shelley, 304n22
Bar Kokhba, Simon, 5
Barnett, Victoria J., 304
Barth, Karl, 17, 50-52, 84, 86, 103n48, 137, 189n7, 252, 261, 304n23, 357n8
Bartley, W. W., 235n48
Batnitzky, Leora, 381
Battin, Margaret Pabst, 279, 281-85
Bayertz, Kurt, 105, 187n5, 193n15, 194n18
Beauchamp, Tom L., 136n23, 189
Beccaria, Cesare, 288
Beckley, Harlan, 149n46, 162-63, 166, 169-70, 175, 179
Begin, Menachem, 364n26
Bell, Daniel, 39n72
Bellah, Robert, 187n2
Bennett, Lerone, Jr., 62, 65n21, 71
Bergen, Doris L., 304n22
Berlin, Isaiah, 45n84
Bernardin, Joseph (Cardinal), 114n63
Bernstein, Richard, 221n14
Bernstein, Robert A., 348-49
bin Laden, Osama, 290, 293
Birnbaum, Jonathan, 83n66
Blackmun, Harry, 205
Blair, Montgomery, 73

Index of Subjects

abomination/s, the abominable, 3, 50, 209, 292, 310, 362; and adoption, 364-73

abortion, 51, 94, 95, 112n59, 113-14, 147n42, 189-90, 194n18, 195, 197n29, 198, 199n39, 203-12, 262, 288, 334, 340-41, 353, 361nn17-18, 362n20, 379-80

Abu Ghraib, 11, 48, 80, 293

adoption, 2, 46, 326, 347-48, 353-80

afterlife, 101, 142n31

agape: definition and priority, 2-3; as a metavalue, 42n81, 130; strong vs. weak, 44-45, 138n26, 140; three interpersonal features of, 41

aggression, aggressor/s, 51, 288n9, 289, 298, 313, 315, 329, 400

alethiology, 168n34, 173, 221-25, 229, 238, 242-44

altruism, 35, 108n56, 164, 247, 250-51, 291, 345

America, the American, 2, 5-11, 14n29, 19-23, 27, 39-40, 48, 59-83, 85-86, 111-14, 118n2, 145-49, 156, 178-79, 185-86, 189-90, 196-236, 264, 267, 286, 290-94, 300n10, 301, 304-5, 310-12, 322, 330-32, 344-49, 353n1, 382-83, 386n21, 390-408

anger, 74, 98, 141n30

animal/s, the animal, 33, 84, 94, 103-4, 107-9, 112, 161, 191n13, 192n14, 201, 209, 320, 406

anti-Semitism, 14n30, 19, 150, 271, 292, 295-316, 351

anxiety, 65n22, 100n35, 268, 298-99, 310, 316, 371n37, 388

appetite, 31-32, 85, 98, 295

appraisal (of worth), the appraisive, 19, 48, 91, 118, 120-23, 132, 135, 226n29, 259, 318, 324, 339, 383n6

aretology, the aretological, 168, 324, 329, 337, 402

atheism, atheist/s, 85, 148-50, 188, 203

atonement, the Atonement, 19, 25, 81, 248, 252, 272, 275n83, 306, 311n34

autonomy, the autonomous, 3, 6, 8, 13n28, 27-28, 38, 44-45, 48, 54-55, 65, 74, 82, 86-90, 93, 117, 139, 145-47, 187-213, 239, 248, 263, 280-89, 341, 359-61, 378, 391n32, 392n37, 406

beauty, the beautiful, 39-40, 106, 116, 122, 150, 192n14, 202, 212, 239, 246, 337, 352

benevolence, the benevolent, 118, 123, 130-37, 149-50, 188, 238, 255, 257, 287n9, 337

bestowal (of worth), 36, 41, 91, 120, 122, 132, 135, 245, 251, 262, 339, 355-58

Bible, the biblical, 1n1, 1n3, 4, 6n18, 8, 11-12, 16, 26, 43-44, 59-61, 68, 74, 81, 85, 99-106, 136-37, 146, 160-62, 166-68, 188, 208, 211, 242, 255, 264, 267, 296n2, 297, 305-7, 311, 314, 319n4, 320, 329, 334-35, 339, 342n45,